The History Of
THE CRICKET WORLD CUP

Printed in the UK by MPG Books, Bodmin

Published by Sanctuary Publishing Limited, Sanctuary House, 45-53 Sinclair Road, London W14 0NS, United Kingdom

www.sanctuarypublishing.com

Copyright: Mark Baldwin, 2003

Photographs: © and courtesy of Getty Images

Cover photograph: © Getty Images

World Cup statistics 1975-99 © CricInfo Ltd. For further information visit www.cricinfo.com

ISBN: 1-86074-485-0

The History Of
THE CRICKET
WORLD CUP

Mark Baldwin
Foreword by Shaun Pollock

Sanctuary

Acknowledgements

First, I'd like to thank the following: Jack Bailey, Raman Subba Row, Bernard Coleman, Peter Perchard, Ben and Belinda Brocklehurst, Michael de Zoysa, Mark Souster, Iain MacGregor, Laura Brudenell, Colin Bryden, Barry Richards, Imran Khan, David Lloyd, Mark Williams, Derek Pringle and Ihithisham Kamardeen.

In addition, the following books or publications were consulted: *Wisden Cricketers' Almanack*, *The Cricketer* magazine, *The Times*, *Living For Cricket* by Clive Lloyd (Stanley Paul), *Big Bird Flying High* (Arthur Barker), *White Lightning* by Allan Donald (Collins Willow), *Under The Southern Cross* (Harper Sports), *Marshall Arts* (MacDonald Queen Anne Press), Programme Publications.

Finally, thanks are also due to Michele, Jamie and Holly for keeping out of my study and off the computer!

Contents

Foreword

Leading South Africa in the Cricket World Cup in my own country will be an enormous honour and a huge responsibility.

The World Cup captures the imagination of South Africans like nothing else in cricket. The 1992 World Cup in Australia and New Zealand was the first major event in which South Africa competed after the country's return to the international fold.

The excitement as Kepler Wessels' team beat Australia in their first match was phenomenal. I was at university and skipped lectures to watch the games on television. South Africa reached the semi-finals in 1992 and have been strong contenders in subsequent tournaments.

In 1992, I was still trying to secure my place in the Natal provincial team. I didn't realise I would play in the next two World Cups. It has been like playing in the Olympic Games of cricket, with all the leading cricketers of the world coming together in one tournament.

South Africa played magnificent cricket in 1996. We won all our round-robin matches before losing to the West Indies in the quarter-finals in Karachi. We made some errors in the field and Brian Lara batted brilliantly to make a century. We showed some inexperience in our approach to chasing a target of 265 and too many of our batsmen got out playing big shots. The fact that we finished only 20 runs short showed that, if we had been a bit calmer earlier, on we could have won.

In England in 1999 we were settled as a unit and again played well. Many people have said our tied semi-final against Australia was the best one-day match of all time, but there were not many South Africans who could say they enjoyed what happened. It is not much consolation to know that we didn't actually lose. The fact was that we were eliminated.

Again, with hindsight, we had our opportunities – we bowled well but lost wickets at crucial times. Despite that, we were within one run of reaching the final.

Going into the 2003 World Cup, we have a core of experienced players. Allan Donald and Jonty Rhodes will be playing in their fourth World Cup, while Jacques Kallis and I will be turning out for the third time. Many of the other members of our squad played in 1999. We have been in some tough situations and have learned from them.

We realise there are special challenges about playing in our country. There will be many demands on our time, and we can expect to be the centre of attention at airports and hotels as we move around the country. That is part and parcel of playing in a big event at home, and we will feed off that positive energy. It will be great to know the public are right behind us.

Our planning has taken into account the 'home-country factor'. We will not be hiding ourselves out of sight but we will need to be able to put in some serious practice and to have some quality relaxation time.

People want to know whether we can win the World Cup. We believe we can win it, but we're not looking that far ahead at this stage. As I write this, we're playing a series against Pakistan and our focus is on that. We will have a good World Cup if we play to 100 per cent of our abilities, with individuals in form and at the same time performing as a unit.

Businessmen say that if you have a good product it will sell. We intend to make sure that our cricket at this World Cup is a very good product.

Shaun Pollock
South Africa captain

Chapter 1

The Growth Of The World Cup

Cricket's 2003 World Cup in South Africa is expected to generate US$188 million in revenue for the game, and will be watched by a global television audience of 1.2 billion people; estimates for the profit from the scheduled 2007 tournament in the West Indies already stand at $235 million dollars, and rising.

Just 28 years ago, by contrast, when the very first World Cup was staged in England in 1975, overall takings amounted merely to a little over £200,000.

These figures alone provide a stark illustration of how far the World Cup has travelled since its inception, deep in the committee rooms of Lord's in the early 1970s. And don't forget, the profit made by that inaugural tournament was considered an excellent return and was the source of much relief, given that it was such a gamble to stage it in the first place!

Prize money in 1975 totalled £8,000, half of which went to the winners. This year, in South Africa, the pot on offer to the world's best cricketers is a cool US $5 million – in itself five times as much as was put up for the seventh World Cup in 1999.

Ah, but a lot of dirty water has passed under the dark shadows that lie beneath world cricket's bridge since 1999 – the match-fixing crisis, for a start, of course, which is one of the major reasons why the prize fund has been hiked up so dramatically.

The Cricket World Cup, however, has become very big business – in many ways – in a very short time, as a glance through this book so readily shows. Much responsibility now lies with hosts South Africa and the International Cricket Council (ICC) as the eighth World Cup prepares to reveal itself to the watching world.

Globally, cricket has grown far stronger since 1975. Commercially, it has become a multi-limbed, powerful and ravenous beast. Crucially, though, and perhaps in the nick of time, the ICC has at last grown up enough too, so that it is currently a body capable of professionally administering the affairs of a world sport.

The deal struck in 2000 with the Global Cricket Corporation, which netted ICC a minimum income of $550 million over seven years for its selling of the 'bundled up' commercial rights to all major ICC events (including the 2003 and 2007 World Cups), has given world cricket a financial security that it could only have dreamed about ten years ago, let alone back in 1975.

To the modern eye, it's remarkable to look back at how cricket was when its World Cup story began. It was only a generation ago, mind you, but it was a different age.

The ICC itself was, in the early 1970s, merely a forum for discussion rather than, as now, a fully-fledged governing body with an annual operating budget of $8 million. The secretariat of the Marylebone Cricket Club (MCC), a private members' club, acted as the ICC secretariat. It was a cosy little world, a postscript of empire, if you like, and it was all about to change.

Perhaps the first man to try to sell the idea of a Cricket World Cup was Ben Brocklehurst, the owner of *The Cricketer* magazine, and his fascinating story is told in the next chapter. It is a tale which also features many of the leading figures in the game in the late 1960s and early 1970s: Sir Donald Bradman, Sir George (Gubby) Allen and EW (Jim) Swanton to name but one holy triumvirate.

This book will also tell of how the first World Cup of 1975 actually came into being, and how it was England – and emphatically not Australia, though that might surprise modern audiences – which took the lead and performed the role of trailblazers. English cricket setting trends? Yes, strangely but truly, that story can also be told.

'England took the initiative, and deserves the credit,' says Raman Subba Row, a former England batsman and former chairman of the Test and County Cricket Board (TCCB). 'From quite humble beginnings, it has quickly become a magnificent event.'

What it is most important to remember now, however, and indeed to stress to anyone born in the last 30 years, is that one-day international cricket – plus any form of limited-overs senior cricket, for that matter – was in its infancy in 1975.

One-day internationals have been such a boom industry in the last two decades that we have forgotten just how new and daring an idea they were back in the early 1970s.

Why, India played its first limited-overs international only in July 1974, less than a year before the inaugural World Cup. More remarkably, it was not until November 1981 that India staged its first home one-day international. Neither Pakistan (October 1976) nor West Indies (March 1977) hosted a limited-overs international game until well after the first World Cup had taken place.

Now, of course, no self-respecting world-class cricketer can claim to have had a significant one-day international career until he has clocked up 200 or more appearances.

Moreover, such has been the demand for instant cricket that elite modern players like Sachin Tendulkar can expect to go far past the 300-plus mark set by the first three members of that exclusive club – Mohammad Azharuddin, Wasim Akram and Steve Waugh.

Part of the wonder of cricket's World Cup story is that the first tournament happened as early as it did, little more than four and a half years after the birth of one-day international cricket itself.

That birth, too, was premature and unplanned. On 5 January 1971, a hastily arranged exhibition match of 40 eight-ball overs per side was played at the Melbourne Cricket Ground to give local cricket fans something to see following the loss to rain of all five days of the scheduled third Test match of that season's Ashes series between Australia and England.

Even then, once the match had been proposed, meetings were required between Bradman, the chairman of the Australian Board of Control, and Sir Cyril Hawker, president of the MCC, before it could be agreed that the two competing teams would be called Australia and England.

A crowd of more than 46,000 sat entranced as Australia successfully chased England's total of 190 to win by five wickets and with more than five overs to spare. Ian Chappell, with 60, top-scored for the Australians, but the $200 Man Of The Match award went to England's John Edrich for his 119-ball 82.

Australia, however, proved slow on the uptake of one-day international cricket, despite rather fortuitously being in on its beginning. The Australian Board was not untypical of the time in its arch-conservatism, but it was far more concerned with protecting and promoting the five-day and first-class game as the most desirable form of cricket.

In late August 1972, it was England who organised the first one-day series, defeating Australia 2–1 in the three matches tacked onto the end of that summer's Ashes rubber.

New Zealand, too, took up the limited-overs international baton by staging their first match at Lancaster Park, Christchurch, on 11 February 1973. Their opponents, Pakistan, were also appearing in their first one-day international.

West Indies, soon to be crowned the first World Cup champions, did not make their one-day international bow until 5 September 1973, when they lost a thrilling match against England at Headingley, Leeds, by one wicket.

In short, it was a very inexperienced set of international teams that pitched up for the 1975 World Cup, a reality underlined when Indian opener Sunil Gavaskar was so certain that England had posted an impregnable total in the opening match, at Lord's, that he batted out the entire 60 overs of the Indian reply in order to get some batting practice for the games still ahead. Gavaskar faced 174 balls for his 36 not out, hitting a solitary four!

That may be one of the more amazing statistics from the early days of World Cup cricket, but almost everything about that first tournament would look foreign to modern eyes: the tactics, the field placings and the team selections.

It produced some scintillating cricket, though, none more so than in the epic final between the West Indies and Australia, and it was the success of that very first World Cup – hoped for but not expected by the authorities of the day – which accelerated the acceptance of the one-day international game. Here was a version of cricket that could, indeed, stand alone and flourish without the help of its Test-match big brother.

Part of the aim of this book is to chart this development of the one-day international game, specifically in terms of the quadrennial gathering of nations which is about to take place for the eighth time. The seven World Cups, to date, forms a revealing set of windows through which the growth of cricket as a global sport can be viewed.

Commercial, physical and political changes have arrived thick and fast during the past three decades, and the furious pace of modern cricket history is clearly visible during this process of charting the history of the sport's showpiece World Cup.

From Gavaskar's go-slow in June 1975 to the Herculean hitting of Lance Klusener in the seventh World Cup of 1999, the four-yearly dips into the archives of the game which this book provides neatly summarise the many advances that have been made since the tournament was but an idea in the mind of Ben Brocklehurst and others.

The feats of many great cricketers are, of course, part of the story. The one-day stage may not have the scope of Test cricket, but great performers can also be depended upon to catch the attention in even the most crowded of spaces.

At the end of each of the chapters in this book, which act as a detailed record of all seven World Cups to date, I have permitted myself the privilege of picking a select XI from that particular tournament.

Set out together, the seven fantasy teams represent a constellation of many (but by no means all) of the cricket stars who have shone out so brightly in this modern age of World Cup cricket.

And, based on their performances in the event, what about this XI as the best the World Cup years can offer: Graham Gooch (England), Sachin Tendulkar (India), Viv Richards (West Indies), Aravinda de Silva (Sri Lanka), Steve Waugh (Australia), Clive Lloyd (West Indies, captain), Dave Houghton (Zimbabwe, wicket-keeper), Imran Khan (Pakistan), Wasim Akram (Pakistan), Shane Warne (Australia), Joel Garner (West Indies).

We have been fortunate, indeed, these last 30 years, to witness the breadth and depth of entertainment that one-day international cricket has produced. What should not be underestimated, too, is the impact the instant game has had on the hearts and minds of three decades of impressionable youth: the connoisseurs may carp about a seemingly endless diet of limited-overs cricket, but it is the one-day game (allied to television) which has been largely responsible for making cricket – and its stars – more accessible and attractive to the young.

The match-fixing crisis, linked as it was to the surge in the numbers of one-day international matches and series, has nevertheless had the effect of providing a vital check-and-balance debate, at world level, on how future limited-overs games should be scheduled and policed.

Significantly, too, it has become noticeable in the past five years just how much more popular Test cricket has become, in terms of public awareness and attendance. Just as one-day cricket was born in England to be the financial saviour of that country's first-class game, so one-day international cricket has helped to produce a far healthier world market in which Test cricket can restate its own historic and matchlessly wide appeal.

There has been a price to pay, though, and the corruption scandal alone has underscored that. Other criticism of instant cricket is that it has undermined techniques, bullied subtlety into the corners of the game, and put unfairly onerous physical and mental demands upon the leading players.

Regulating the number of one-day internationals played is still a leading issue for the ICC to address, as is the general subject of how much cricket each year the game's biggest names should be allowed to play.

What is undeniable, however, from the huge body of one-day international and World Cup evidence of the past 30 years, is that the very best players remain the very best players, irrespective of the form of the game they're playing.

Batsmen like Tendulkar, Viv Richards and Brian Lara have in many cases become even more dominant in the one-day arena than at Test level – they can certainly win more matches single-handedly in the shortened version than they can over five days.

Bowlers did at first regard run-saving as the prime requirement of one-day cricket, but again the passage of time has shown that, in fact, it is the ability to take wickets which makes just as much difference to the outcome of a limited-overs match as it does in Test matches.

Class spinners, in particular, have emerged in the past decade as significant one-day match-winners and, often, run-savers to boot; it could be argued, in fact, that the disciplines of instant cricket has helped and not stifled the development of the likes of Shane Warne, Mushtaq Ahmed, Saqlain Mushtaq, Anil Kumble and Muttiah Muralitharan as powers within the game.

There has been, of course, the odd emergence of career one-day specialists like Michael Bevan of Australia, England's Nick Knight and the New Zealand pair of Chris Harris and Gavin Larsen, but by and large it is the established Test stars who have the greatest lasting success in the limited-overs amphitheatre.

Even the harshest critics of the one-day game, meanwhile, acknowledge the positive effect it has had on fielding standards around the world. Indeed, smaller countries like Zimbabwe have rightly regarded fielding as the one area of the game where their more modest resources do not prevent them from reaching true world class. Hard work on fielding skills has increased their all-round competitiveness.

A study of the history of the World Cup enables one to take long and lingering glimpses at the many ways in which one-day cricket (and the image of the game itself) has modernised and changed.

Constant tightening up and re-working of the rules has, for instance, been brought about by the increased competitiveness and popularity of one-day international cricket. Restrictive fielding circles took a large step towards becoming compulsory once Mike Brearley, the England captain, had angered Australians in November 1979 by (quite logically) moving all his fielders and wicket-keeper back on the boundary edge to defend a situation in a World Series Cup match against West Indies when four runs had been required off the final ball.

Then, in February 1981, Australian captain Greg Chappell caused an international incident by ordering his brother Trevor to bowl underarm the last ball of a match in Melbourne in order to prevent New Zealand from hitting the six they required to claim a tie. Because of that furore, indeed, the rules were changed within 24 hours!

South Africa's terrible experience in the 1992 World Cup semi-final against England, when a short rain interruption ended up costing them the chance of victory, has resulted in the universally accepted (if not fully understood!) Duckworth-Lewis method for deciding weather-affected one-day matches.

The relatively recent clampdown on what constitutes a limited-overs wide has been another illustration of how the one-day game has been constantly evolving. Indeed, largely thanks to the flexibility of thinking required by limited-overs rule-making, a degree of adaptability with regard to wide-calling has now been officially handed to Test umpires whenever they need to make a judgement on negative bowling outside the batsman's leg stump.

Bowlers, however, have regained the right, in one-day international cricket, to deliver one bouncer per over after it was felt that the balance in power between bat and ball had grown too one-sided.

Evolution, like cricket's World Cup, is by definition an ever-changing story.

Chapter 2

Brocklehurst's Dream

Late one summer afternoon in 1969, staring out of the carriage window as the branch-line train chugged its way from Oxted in Surrey to his little home station of Ashurst, Kent, an idea struck Ben Brocklehurst that could – and perhaps should – have created the first cricket World Cup.

Sir Donald Bradman endorsed it, EW Swanton supported it and Sir Gubby Allen gave it his early blessing, but in the end Brocklehurst's detailed proposal for a groundbreaking first World Cup tournament in 1972 (initially 1971) was allowed to wither on the vine following official consideration by various committees at Lord's.

The then-fledgling Test and County Cricket Board even passed up the opportunity of a huge £50,000 sponsorship, secured by Brocklehurst, and the prospect of overall profits confidently and consistently predicted to be in excess of £60,000. Moreover, when the inaugural World Cup was indeed launched in England, in 1975, its structure looked suspiciously like the one he had proposed six years earlier.

Ironically, estimates for income and public interest that he had included in his 1969 blueprint – outlined later in this chapter – proved to be extremely conservative when set against the actual successes of the 1975 tournament. In 1969 and 1970, however, they had been rejected by cricket's authorities as being unrealistic.

Ben Brocklehurst was 80 last year but is still saddened at the way his original idea was shelved. Somewhat unwillingly, after keeping it to himself for more than 30 years, he has kindly agreed that the contents of what he calls his own World Cup files – previously unseen by the general public – should be included in this book.

This chapter will tell the story of how Brocklehurst, the chairman of *The Cricketer* magazine and a former captain of Somerset, fought valiantly to get his World Cup idea off the ground. One of the rocks he foundered on was the sub-committee at Lord's which was given the task of carrying forward his

World Cup idea. Billy Griffith, the secretary of the TCCB and MCC, signed letters from those whose reasons for not taking Brocklehurst's plan further make for particularly interesting reading.

When they are studied, it is hard to disagree with the view of John Woodcock, a director of *The Cricketer* and the former *Times* cricket correspondent and editor of *Wisden* who, when in the summer of 1983 was shown (in confidence) selected correspondence between Brocklehurst and the TCCB, wrote in reply, 'The letters are an indictment, I am afraid, of a Lord's committee, but as we agreed they were acting protectively and with a caution which I expect they saw as their duty.

'How sad, though, that it is not the *The Cricketer* World Cup, as you deserved to have it be.'

Brocklehurst's working title for his proposals had been 'the *Cricketer* World Cup' because, as a businessman, he saw that the status of his magazine would be greatly advantaged by an association with the event. He repeatedly made it clear to Lord's, however, that the magazine would not benefit in a direct financial fashion from being involved with the organisation and promotion of a World Cup tournament. He simply wanted to make money for the game, and it was this concern for cricket's welfare – and English cricket in particular – that had been at the root of his original idea. What must be remembered today is that the overwhelming reality in 1969 was that English cricket – and world cricket, for that matter – was facing a financial crisis.

This chronic lack of investment in the game had set Brocklehurst thinking during his railway journey home from London. 'I had been reading the London *Evening Standard* on the train, and there was a report in it about how the English counties, between them, had lost £165,000 in the preceding year,' he said. 'That started to get me thinking, and I distinctly remember sitting there in an otherwise deserted carriage when this idea occurred to me. Obviously, the football World Cup in England in 1966 had been a huge success, and I began to think about the possibilities for cricket.

'I had just taken over *The Cricketer* at that time, and one of the things I was keen to do through the magazine was to set up events that would provoke more interest in cricket and bring more money into the game. It was around that time, too, that we began our still-popular National Village Cricket Championship, the Lord's Taverners Cricketer Colts Trophy for schools and the Cricketer Cup for old boys' sides.

'Cricket in those days was really struggling, and the situation was appalling to people who loved the game and had been involved in it. The World Cup idea came in a sort of flash, and I immediately wrote down what I was thinking, which was based on my belief that people would come to watch the most attractive cricketers in the world playing against each other in a series of one-day matches.

'The Gillette Cup had been very successful in England since its launch in 1963, and the John Player Sunday League had just begun in 1969, but English cricket was still in the doldrums and my motivation was solely to try to get something started that would be of benefit to the county clubs and the game here in general.

'I think my idea was viewed with a lot of suspicion. Billy Griffith asked me what I or *The Cricketer* wanted out of it. All I said was that I would like *The Cricketer*'s name linked to the World Cup. I knew Billy well, and I do remember him once saying to me that he wished he was a benevolent dictator and not just a mouthpiece for TCCB committees, whose views he had to express! Billy, actually, was very helpful and encouraging, despite having to sign letters which reflected the negative views of the sub-committee concerned.

'But what frustrated me more than anything was that the Board never allowed me to go and speak to them personally, even though Jim Swanton asked Billy Griffith on my behalf that a meeting should be set up.

'I also met with Don Bradman in Australia, during the England tour of 1970–71, in a meeting at which a TCCB representative was present, and received Sir Don's and the Australian Board's acknowledgement that they would like to take part in a World Cup event during our 1972 season. But it never happened, and I was left to feel that I was dealing with faceless committees at Lord's. I also got the feeling that some people didn't like an outsider suggesting an idea for something that could be a great success.'

Brocklehurst also reveals here that he and Bill Heald – the man who had promised £50,000 of sponsorship money from his company, WD and HO Wills in Bristol – were so frustrated at being continually dead-batted by Lord's that they even considered setting up a World Cup in a private capacity. The £50,000 sponsorship would have made it possible, but these plans were scuppered when Heald was tragically killed in a car crash.

It was on 7 August 1969 that Ben Brocklehurst first formulated his World Cup proposals in a confidential internal memo at *The Cricketer*. Initially, he planned a straight seven-match knock-out event between eight teams (including South Africa and both an England A and B side), played entirely at Lord's. He envisaged it taking place in alternate years from 1971.

On 27 October 1969, following further thought, Brocklehurst was ready to circulate a fleshed-out version of his original proposal to *The Cricketer* board, which included Jim Swanton, cricket correspondent of the *Daily Telegraph* and certainly a man with the ear of those who held power in the world of cricket at that time.

Swanton responded with lengthy, considered views in a letter to Brocklehurst on 12 November, calling the proposal 'a thrilling idea'. He advised on format, team preparation, organisation, likely revenue and expenses. He estimated that £21,000 would be forthcoming from television fees and proposed that player match fees should be £250, rising to £500 with 'result bonuses'.

With Swanton's suggestions taken on board, Brocklehurst finally delivered his confidential plan to Billy Griffith and Gubby Allen, the MCC treasurer, on 20 November 1969. When he asked Griffith if anyone else had come up with a similar idea, the administrator said, 'No'.

The proposed idea was for seven teams (all Test-playing countries bar South Africa, plus either an England second team or a Rest of the World side) to meet every third year, starting in 1972, when the Australians were due to tour, and play a 21-match event over three weeks from early September. Matches were to be staged at Lord's and Headingley only.

Brocklehurst also proposed an organisational structure comprising a management committee (made up of nominees from the MCC, the TCCB, *The Cricketer* and a sponsor), a cricket committee run by the TCCB and a publicity committee. *The Cricketer*, with a sponsor, was planning to fund the rental of Lord's and Headingley and to fly in and cater for the competing teams. An expected profit in excess of £60,000 was shown in carefully researched balance sheets attached to the formal proposal.

Part of that research had been carried out by a youthful Christopher Martin-Jenkins, now the cricket correspondent of *The Times* and a well-known radio commentator but then a 24-year old employee of *The Cricketer*. On 24 November 1969, he wrote an internal memo to Brocklehurst, with a copy sent to Jim Swanton, in which he professed, 'Someone is bound to organise a World Cricket Cup sooner or later. Rothmans have come near to doing so with their "Rest of the World" matches against England and the current touring side at the end of the domestic season.

'Although televised, which cannot have done the sponsors any harm, these matches were not a complete success, failing to attract Test-match-size gates, which one would have thought, logically, the best Test players would attract.

'There could only be one reason for this lack of appeal: the stakes were not high enough. One refers here not necessarily to financial stakes, but to the fact that the competition held no prestige in the public mind. To attract big public interest, we must somehow get over to the public that this IS the first genuine one-day championship of the world, and endeavour to create a patriotic interest in England's own efforts.'

CMJ's further suggestion, for an event in September 1972, was a six-country tournament culminating in a final.

On 22 January 1970, a meeting between Brocklehurst and two other members of *The Cricketer* board, John Haslewood and Philip Zimmerman, decided to make a second approach to Gubby Allen. Following further consultation with Jim Swanton, it was agreed to scale down the proposal to a competition involving four teams: England, Australia, West Indies and a Rest of the World side including players from South Africa, India, Pakistan and New Zealand.

As a result, it seems that both Allen and Griffith were sufficiently interested in the *Cricketer* World Cup proposals to agree to a meeting with Brocklehurst and Haslewood. A day later, on 6 February, Brocklehurst wrote to Griffith thanking him for his and Allen's 'general acceptance' of the scheme.

Swanton, who had also received a copy of the letter, wrote to Brocklehurst on 19 February: 'I am very glad, naturally, that you and John have had a favourable reaction from Gubby and Billy Griffith on our World Cup idea, or rather yours!'

Griffith had made some suggestions about the format and timing of the proposed event and had also raised several queries which he wanted answered, but nevertheless on 21 February he sent Brocklehurst a copy of the TCCB accounts for the 1968 Australia tour of England so that more detailed financial costs could be predicted.

Less than two weeks later, Brocklehurst was ready to circulate a third, and final, draft of his by now highly detailed proposal. It was sent to Griffith on 4 March 1970, and in Brocklehurst's covering letter he wrote: 'As you will see [from the enclosed] it looks as though we could plough back up to £90,000 into cricket with only six matches.'

Taking Griffith and Allen's views on board, Brocklehurst had now limited his idea to a four-team competition between England, Australia, West Indies and the Rest of the World. Each would play the other once in a limited-overs match, making six days' cricket in all. He added that an expanded competition might be thought preferable, in terms of fairness, but said that such detail could be debated 'once the principle of the *Cricketer* World Cup has been accepted'.

Three matches would be at Lord's and three at Headingley, Leeds. The whole event would be of ten days' duration, including reserve days. Brocklehurst, using the 1968 Australia tour accounts as his guide on exhaustively detailed costs such as police (£650), gate and ground attendants (£2,200) and match balls (£50), estimated all expenses would total £40,000 and projected a profit (including a £50,000 sponsorship) of £90,784. Fascinatingly, his calculations – again, guided by Allen's records – reveal that it cost just £600 to stage a day's cricket at Lord's in 1969, and that the BBC paid £90,000 for that summer's Test match coverage.

Brocklehurst's two full pages of predicted accounts also show that he proposed only a sum of less than £9,000 to be paid to *The Cricketer* in the form of its general expenses. This was before the estimated profit figure was reached, and he said in his proposal that he hoped the overall revenue 'would flow back into cricket for the benefit of the county cricket clubs and governing bodies of competing countries'.

Following official TCCB committee examination, Brocklehurst received on 22 July 1970 a reply from Griffith which caused him his first serious doubts about whether his idea was being fairly treated. Griffith wrote, 'Dear Ben, The Test and County Cricket Board Public Relations and Promotion Sub-Committee have now had the chance of examining in some depth the proposals put forward for the *Cricketer* World Cup in 1972. They do not consider themselves to be financial experts, although they do have a great deal of experience in the field of sponsorship and allied subjects.

'Basically, their reactions to the proposals put forward were enthusiastic as to its concept, but they did express several strong reservations about certain points which I feel sure you would like to take into consideration. The doubts expressed were as follows:

'1. The possible public reaction to such a series following on a major Test

Series between England and Australia. Would the public have had a surfeit of the most exciting form of international cricket? Games staged by such as Rothmans in the past have brought in nothing like the returns estimated and the Sub-Committee were doubtful as to whether your own estimates weren't extremely optimistic in this respect.

'2. Allied to this was a considerable doubt over the public interest in (say) a match between the West Indies and Australia played in this country or indeed Australia and the Rest of the World or West Indies and the Rest of the World. You will, no doubt, have noticed initial public response even to a full-scale Test series between England and the Rest of the World.

'3. The structure of cricket could possibly be changed by 1972, but under the present system it would seem that the end of the season well into September, allied with the start of the football season early in August and the possibility of a clash with the Olympic Games, could well work against the viability of your enterprise in 1972.

'4. The Sub-Committee also wondered how far you had got with your efforts to obtain a £50,000 sponsorship for which, in their estimation, you would do well to get.

'5. Your television estimates have undoubtedly been carefully worked out, but our own experience would lead us to believe that the estimated income from this series could well be on the high side and that it would be safer to look at a reduction – always assuming television were interested in the idea – of probably not less than half.

'You may think this is [sic] enough doubts to be going on with, and I am sorry that this letter is not more optimistic or encouraging. Perhaps you would be kind enough to let me have any further reactions in due course. Naturally, the Sub-Committee would want some reassurance on the points mentioned before submitting the idea for approval by the TCCB as a whole. Yours ever, Billy.'

Bloodied, but still determined to press on, Brocklehurst then began to search for a World Cup sponsor – this, of course, at a time when cricket was not exactly awash with people keen to sink their money into a struggling game.

In October, he struck gold. The tobacco company WD and HO Wills, through their public affairs manager, Bill Heald, expressed a willingness to sponsor the venture. Not only that, they were prepared to spend £50,000 for the privilege – a huge sum at the time – and also wanted to secure an option on further World Cups.

Immediately, Brocklehurst sent a copy of Heald's commitment to Griffith, adding in a covering letter his confidence that 'this series will provide a wonderful opportunity to try out new forms of promotion to stimulate interest in the game at large'.

But if he expected the Lord's wheels to crank into rapid motion at last, he was wrong. A short initial reply, on 21 October, was non-committal, with Griffith promising, 'We shall be writing more fully once consideration has been given to the interesting facts you have outlined.'

A fuller letter from the TCCB was duly sent out on 3 November, yet its contents, even when he read them out again more than 22 years later, still left Brocklehurst shaking his head in amazement. Griffith wrote, 'My dear Ben, The Public Relations and Promotion Sub-Committee has now had the opportunity to reflect on the contents of your letter of the 14 October, and I am writing to acquaint you with their views which will be the subject of a report to the TCCB.

'First, may I say that they are extremely appreciative of the work put in at your end. But, though you have allayed some of their original doubts and your own keenness is hard to deny, there are still certain reservations regarding the points made in your letter.

'The Sub-Committee appreciates that your suggestion of a combined committee would aim to resolve these, but I have been asked to say that there are over-riding considerations which, as I think you will see, preclude this possibility – at least for the present.

'These considerations rule out the recommendation of such a competition in 1972, and may be briefly reported as follows:

'1. Any concept of the dimension of a World Cup should be all-embracing in its scope and should have a similar impact on the cricket world to that made by the Jules Rimet Trophy on the soccer scene.

'2. Because of this, they feel that the concept should be organised and run at international level, and they see all sorts of side benefits accruing from such an organisation if it were set up.

'3. While they are not slow to recommend sponsorship in the normal way, they do not at the moment feel that such a prestigious event should be the subject of commercial sponsorship in a direct sense. In the staging of such a competition as this, they feel that cricket should be seen to stand on its own two feet.

'They will be recommending to the Board that the possibilities be examined at international level at the earliest opportunity, and I am therefore obliged to ask you to hold your horses until the TCCB have had an opportunity to consider the matter in December.

'I hope you will not be too dismayed by this letter. The Sub-Committee have given a considerable amount of time to thought and discussion on this matter, and it was only after very careful consideration that they came to the conclusion they did. Yours ever, Billy.'

Though stunned, Brocklehurst immediately fired off another letter to Griffith, on 6 November, in which he wrote, 'I confess I am puzzled by what the TCCB PR & P Sub-Committee have had to say and, with respect, there seems to be a certain inconsistency in their argument.' He then detailed the inconsistencies before adding, 'The point I have tried to make since the idea was first put up a year ago is that the scheme must remain flexible as to scope and timing while discussions take place.

'The original concept outlined to you, you will remember, was to include all Test-playing countries. It was later scaled down after discussions with you and Gubby Allen, so as to make it possible to fit it into the 1972 season and create a minimum interference with the first-class programme.

'Having established the success of the scheme in its modified form, I hoped that the original concept could be adopted in subsequent years. Any participation of the sponsor, and for that matter *The Cricketer*, can obviously only be decided in discussion with the TCCB.

'In this sense, therefore, it can be argued that the TCCB PR & P Sub-Committee have pre-judged the matter without discussion with the authors of the plan.

'In passing, too, I can't help wondering if the counties in their present financial state will want to turn away an offer of such a large sum.'

Then, on 9 November, Brocklehurst met with Griffith to discuss the matter further, although in a letter on 18 November to John Haslewood, who was also an MCC committee member besides being on *The Cricketer*'s board, he outlined his scepticism at the way in which the TCCB was handling the proposal. 'My understanding of Billy's letters to date,' wrote Brocklehurst to Haslewood, 'which were in fact written by Jack Bailey on behalf of his sub-committee, suggest that if they do go ahead with it they will do it without us. They will pick out ideas from our draft and set it up without consultation with us.

'All we asked them to do was to approve or disapprove the principle of the concept so that we could take it a stage further with them. My inclination is to press that by a certain date they should either agree or reject the scheme, and if they reject it we can then have it back and set it up ourselves in the West Indies in the winter of 1972-73. In this case, though, the counties won't benefit and the distribution of the profits will be organised in a different way.'

On 27 November, meanwhile, from Brisbane, where he was reporting on the start of England's winter Ashes tour, Swanton wrote to the TCCB secretary, urging him to allow Brocklehurst to present his plans in person to the Board. 'My dear Billy,' wrote Swanton, 'as I expect you will understand, from our point of view it is rather galling having had the promise of £50,000 to have had no opportunity as yet of putting the proposition and talking things over personally with the TCCB.

'This is Ben's brainchild, not mine, though I am fully behind him in the idea should it prove practicable from all points of view. I feel it would be a bad thing for cricket if a sponsor prepared to put up that sort of money were to be summarily turned down.

'I do feel that Ben should have the chance of putting the thing across personally to the TCCB top people, or some of them. I do hope you will feel that this is a reasonable point of view.'

Ten days later, Brocklehurst received a letter from Bernard Coleman, of the TCCB's PR & P Sub-Committee, informing him that it would not be possible to set up the type of steering committee that the proposals had recommended.

By mid-December, meanwhile, Bill Heald at Wills was growing a trifle impatient at the lack of official reaction to his company's generous offer. On 15 December he wrote to Brocklehurst: 'If they do not make up their minds fairly quickly they may lose out on sponsorship. I think you and I ought to have a word about this some time in the New Year.'

Brocklehurst wrote back to him, apologising but adding that Swanton was to organise a meeting with Bradman in Australia in an effort to bring some international pressure to bear.

Happily, Brocklehurst was in Australia over the Christmas and New Year period, to holiday and to watch part of the 1970-71 Ashes series, and so was present at the Melbourne Cricket Ground on 5 January 1971, when the historic first official one-day international took place. The game, between Australia and England, happened only by chance, of course (as is detailed elsewhere in this book), but its success merely reinforced in Brocklehurst's mind just how right he had been to crusade for a limited-overs World Cup competition.

Back in England, too, *The Sunday Times*' 'Inside Track' column of 12 January reported, 'The success of the one-day international cricket match in Melbourne, which drew some 46,000 fans, gives support to an idea which is kicking around Lord's: a World Cup cricket competition. "The Test and County Cricket Board is considering it," admits a Lord's spokesman, "but it needs discussing. Who would play? When? Where? What form would it take?"'

Moreover, when the meeting with Bradman and several other Australian officials took place, after being organised by the England tour manager David Clark for 2 January, Brocklehurst was heartened by the immediately positive reaction of the Aussies. He wrote to Griffith on 25 January 1971: 'Dear Billy. David Clark kindly arranged a meeting with Sir Donald Bradman, Bob Parish, Ray Steele, Bernard Coleman and I to test the reactions of the Australians to playing in the World Cup during the 1972 tour to England.

'As you will have already heard, they were enthusiastic about the idea, which was in contrast to [your] Sub-Committee's forebodings. At the same time, the Australians made the following points.

'1. The cricket should be run by the TCCB and not by an international committee as recommended by the Public Relations and Promotion Sub-Committee.

'2. They would like to be consulted about players' salaries before they are announced.

'3. They would welcome an outline of the scheme from the TCCB as soon as possible.

'4. In general terms they were not concerned as to when the competition takes place during the season.

'5. They did not mind what the competition is called.

'6. They were particularly interested because a sponsor was covering expenses, as with their own V&G competition.

'I confess the Australians' prompt and positive reaction left me more than ever puzzled by the Sub-Committee's attitude to the scheme in general and to our sponsor's generous offer in particular. Not only have they held things up for over seven months but they do not appear to have provided any constructive alternative.

'In November 1969 we suggested the World Cup concept to the MCC as a package. As part of the package we undertook to find a sponsor to put up £50,000 to cover expenses. Plenty of time remained to tie things up for 1972. Since it was put in the Sub-Committee's hands, however, nothing constructive has happened.

'Whilst in no way wishing to encroach on the TCCB's preserves, we suggested that as part of the package an early meeting should take place with two TCCB members, the sponsor and two *Cricketer* nominees so that a specific proposition could be agreed and relayed to TCCB for their approval.

'Not only was this refused by the Sub-Committee but Wills' offer, the largest ever made to cricket, was ignored to the point of discourtesy.

'On 2 January in Melbourne, during discussions with Sir Donald, Bob Parish and Ray Steele, the Sub-Committee's Bernard Coleman said, "We do not accept *The Cricketer*'s sponsor but we will find another." This led Bob Parish to ask what nefarious business our sponsor was involved in!

'Frankly, I am worried that Cricket Administration will fall into needless disrepute with future sponsors unless Wills' offer quickly receives official acknowledgment, regardless of the final outcome. It is fair to say, however, that if Wills' offer is discarded for another sponsor, some very discordant notes will be struck.

'Rumour now has it that John Player have a contract, renewable in 1972, that precludes another cigarette company from sponsoring a major cricket event. Since Wills and Players are part of Imperial Tobacco Group, I'm sure that this need not necessarily be a problem providing frank discussions take place at once.

'Perhaps there is still just time for the Sub-Committee to release its stranglehold on the project so that it can be set up as planned in 1972!'

The TCCB, however, was not for turning, and on 25 May 1971 Brocklehurst wrote to Swanton to express his dismay at the whole affair. After setting out the history of the case, he added, 'In 1970 the counties, it transpires, lost between them £156,000, yet the TCCB wrote back to us in November last year an astonishing reply in which they "did not feel that such a prestigious event should be subject to commercial sponsorship in the direct sense". At the same time they said that the possibilities would "be examined at international level at the earliest opportunity", which led us to ponder how else one could set up an international competition but at international level. In the event, however, the "earliest opportunity" turned out to be the International Cricket Conference to be held eight months later.

'In the meanwhile, a direct approach was made to leading members of the Australian Board of Control at a meeting in Melbourne at which, after half an hour's discussion, they agreed to come in if the TCCB could fit it in to their 1972 tour. They were unanimous in welcoming the concept, particularly as all expenses were covered by sponsorship.

'On Wednesday, 3 February, I also arranged for Bill Heald, who holds the purse strings at Wills, to meet Billy Griffith so that he could get a firm idea of when the money would be required. Billy explained then that it was now too late to set it up for 1972 and asked him to reserve [the money] for 1973.

'Earlier this month, information of the impending competition was leaked from the TCCB to the press, and even the sponsor was named by *The Guardian*, together with the sum involved.

'A few days later, Billy Griffith was quoted, in *The Daily Express*, as saying, "financial viability would be a number one requirement, and as I see it that would mean an international sponsor prepared to put up £100,000 or more".

'Most of us want to support the establishment but the methods they follow are difficult to follow, and so far *The Cricketer* has been given no acknowledgement for the idea, which was theirs.

'Where do we go from here?'

On 21 July 1971, reporting on the previous day's ICC annual meeting, Swanton used his column in The Daily Telegraph to round on cricket's administrators: 'The World Cup idea had an airing, but as readers of my Commentary last Friday will have gathered I expected no finality even in principle and none has emerged.

'The subject will be talked about again by the ICC next year, but the secretary of the Cricket Council, SC (Billy) Griffith, is quoted as saying that agreement is "doubtful" even then.

'This is the sort of depressing outcome to ICC meetings with which over the years one has become all too familiar. Here is an exciting prospect needing only the intelligence and imagination of an international committee to bring to reality.

'There is a sponsor (WD & HO Wills) ready and waiting to inject £50,000 into a scheme that could not fail to bring money and interest on a large scale. Yet so far as can be gathered, no headway has been made.

'If there were any further evidence required that cricket needs an international government with power to act, then here it is.'

Another leading cricket journalist, Tony Pawson, writing about the ICC meeting in *The Observer* later that week, added, 'The idea of a cricket World Cup competition was shelved indefinitely and no interest was shown in the large sponsorship offer of WD and HO Wills. Seeing that the counties made a loss of £156,000 last season, [this] seems somewhat surprising.

'Even more surprising is the lack of interest in a competition certain to inspire immense enthusiasm. The proposal has been under consideration since 1969, but it is now impossible for anything to happen before 1974.

'What was required to give cricket the shot in the arm it needs was a bold decision to go ahead as soon as possible with a limited-over competition between England, Australia, West Indies and the Rest of the World as a trial run – certain of financial success and popular support.'

Brocklehurst's continued embarrassment towards Bill Heald is revealed by a letter he sent on 21 September 1971 in which he wrote, 'I'm afraid the World Cup idea still stagnates in the Lord's corridors of power. The main problem that remains is not being able to discuss the project with the responsible committee. The result has been, therefore, that although all of them agree with the principle of the scheme, none of them can agree how to set it up.'

And so it was to stagnate, for at least another two years, until the march of time – and the increasing popularity of the one-day international game – forced cricket's administrators to consider, once again, the question of a World Cup.

The story of how it eventually came about, from the official viewpoint, is told in the next chapter. Imagine for a moment, however, how Ben Brocklehurst felt when, in 1975, he sat at Lord's watching the epic first World Cup final between – yes! – the West Indies and Australia.

It was, of course, a glorious occasion and a fitting finale to a transparently successful tournament. At last, although seemingly still experiencing significant opposition from traditionalists, cricket had a world-class event capable of winning new revenues, new audiences and a new profile.

Did cricket's first World Cup, though, take place at least three years later than it should have done?

On 10 July 1975, less than three weeks after he and a capacity Lord's crowd had applauded as Clive Lloyd raised aloft the new World Cup trophy, Brocklehurst wrote to members of *The Cricketer* board (Colin Cowdrey, Buzzer Hadingham, John Haslewood, Gordon Ross and Jim Swanton) to remind them of the five points raised by the TCCB in objection to the magazine's own World Cup proposals of 1970.

Each one (as detailed earlier in this chapter) had been more than answered. Brocklehurst had been vindicated in terms of the profit made, the huge success of an Australia v West Indies final on English soil, the fact that it could be fitted into an English domestic season, the fact that he had indeed raised a sponsor, and the size of the television-rights income. He concluded in his letter, 'It is hard to imagine that the TCCB could have been more wrong. Ah well!'

Chapter 3

A Tournament Is Born

Officially, at least, Ben Brocklehurst's part in the birth of the World Cup has remained unrecognised. Looking back, however, he himself admits that, as a private individual, it was naïve of him to think that he could easily influence the decision-making of the great and the good who ran cricket in the late 1960s and early 1970s.

The establishment of the day, moreover, was indeed suspicious of anyone attempting to muscle in on what, in reality, was a relatively small and cosy little world. There was no ICC, in effect, to run world cricket in the way we recognise as being so important today.

It was the MCC – also acting as the ICC secretariat – which still controlled cricket, even though it had given up part of its power in 1968, when the English professional game was put into the hands of the newly created TCCB.

The MCC, however, had made sure it carefully placed certain individuals into important TCCB positions. Furthermore, Gubby Allen, formally the treasurer of the MCC, was still the main power in the game, with Sir Donald Bradman holding similar authority in Australia. Billy Griffith, as secretary of both the TCCB and the MCC, was technically a servant but also a master of much of what he surveyed from his office at Lord's.

The birth of the TCCB, in 1968, had however led to a certain reorganisation and modernisation of the way in which English cricket ran itself. The MCC had been moved to give up its authority in this area because, as a private club, it knew it would receive no government grants for the benefit of English cricket.

A working party had been set up by the MCC in 1967 to look into how the new TCCB should structured – and, of course, a good number of MCC members and officers were involved in that working party!

It was almost as an afterthought, during this process, that Gubby Allen was asked by MCC committee member Raman Subba Row, a former England batsman now involved in the public relations business, whether the TCCB was to have a marketing arm.

'Gubby did not know what marketing meant!' recalled Subba Row. 'I can vividly remember raising the matter, right at the end of one of the working party's last meetings, and there was a long pause around the table. Then Gubby said, "Raman, what's marketing?" I duly explained it, and why I thought it was important, and then Gubby said, "OK, we will do it." He didn't ask anyone else, and there wasn't a vote! From that moment on, I was chairman of the marketing committee. That is how it happened, and it is difficult today for people to imagine just how much power Gubby Allen wielded in those days.'

Subba Row and a fellow businessman, Bernard Coleman, had been involved in the first marketing and promotions operation set up in English county cricket. At Surrey, they were responsible for the first advertising board ever seen on an English ground, a sign promoting an insurance company, which was put up at the Oval during the England v Australia Test of August 1968. 'We sold the space for a fee of £500, and it went up at the Vauxhall end of the ground,' said Subba Row. 'When Gubby Allen arrived in the Surrey committee room at 10 minutes to 11 on the first morning of the Test, as he always did, the first thing he saw from out of the window was that advertising board on the opposite side of the ground. He said, "What on earth is that?" and Bernard Coleman said to him, "That, Mr Allen, is £500 and we need it because we are flat broke!" I remember we soon received an official letter from Billy Griffith at Lord's asking us if we realised the implications of what we were doing. We certainly did – and now ground advertising is worth millions of pounds every year to the game!'

Subba Row was to remain chairman of the TCCB's Public Relations and Promotion Sub-Committee for seven years. Coleman, later to become a long-serving chairman of the TCCB's marketing committee, was also an early member of the Public Relations and Promotion Sub-Committee. Also on this 12-strong committee in the late 1960s and early 1970s sat the likes of Derrick Robins, a self-made millionaire chairman of Banbury Buildings and Coventry City Football Club; Brian Johnston, then the BBC cricket correspondent; and Fred Rumsey, the former Somerset and England fast bowler.

Jack Bailey, later to become secretary of MCC from 1974 to 1987, acted as the committee's secretary. At the time, Bailey was an assistant secretary of the TCCB, and in an article published during the 1999 World Cup, he wrote, '30 years ago, cricket worldwide was tacking its way out of the doldrums. When the idea of a World Cup for cricket was first suggested, plans for a three-match series of one-day games between England and the visiting Australians of 1972 had already been put in train. The John Player Sunday League was packing them in up and down the country, and if county treasurers were not exactly full of good cheer, the occasional smile was discernible.

'It was against this background of a surge in the one-day game that Derrick Robins suggested that cricket should stage its own World Cup. Robins was one member of a group which acted as the movers and shakers of the day.

'Despite the achievements of the committee during the past couple of years, it is true to say that it was a group which was regarded with some suspicion by the hierarchy of the day. And the idea which we were kicking around then concerned a World Cup of Test matches – five-day cricket with preliminary matches taking place all over the world and culminating in a final at Lord's.

'So it was that, after the idea had been filtered through various TCCB committees at Lord's, a proposal was put to the International Cricket Conference in July 1971. Here it met with scant support.

'The expense involved in such an operation was at the heart of objections, as was the time taken in its accomplishment. So yet another sub-committee was set up by ICC, with Gubby Allen in the chair.

'But it was a TCCB committee, with Cecil Paris at the helm and admirably serviced by Donald Carr, which made all the progress and reported to ICC in 1972. By then, the originally suggested year of 1973 had been ruled out; 1975, when the Australians would be visiting the UK for an Ashes Test series, was ruled in. Potential television and sponsorship revenue was considered as being able to help cover the costs.

'Slowly but surely, the objections were swept aside – but a tournament based on five-day cricket remained the objective.

'By the time the ICC met again in 1973, and again in 1974, the format of the competition put forward for their approval consisted essentially of eight teams – the six Test-playing countries plus two nominated associate members, Sri Lanka and East Africa – taking part in a series of one-day matches in England in 1975. A sponsor now had to be found, and TV and radio rights had to be sold.

'Quixotically, the tournament was supposed originally to be called the "International Competition", but those of us at the sharp end knew that in time it would have to be the "World Cup" – and the sponsor's name would have to be attached if we were to attract the kind of money required to pay the teams, cover the costs of expenses for travelling and maybe make a profit for the benefit of the smaller cricketing countries.

'In the same way, it became obvious that a formula based on the lines of the 1966 World Cup in England would best suit our purposes. The one-day Prudential Cup series between England and Australia in 1972 had pointed the way with an enthusiastic public response and some tense cricket.

'To be on the safe side, we included in the ball park estimates £100,000 for sponsorship, though even in 1974 nothing had been finalised either with a sponsor or with BBC Television. The costs of the enterprise were estimated at £200,000.

'Interest had been received from several companies, but Prudential Assurance, already sponsors of all the one-day internationals that had by then been played in England and tried and trusted friends of the game, not only offered the most money (£155,000) but had the added cachet of being the people who gave the City of London a cold if they so much as sneezed. The Prudential World Cup it was.

'What with sponsorship and TV, all potential costs were more than covered before a ball was bowled. Compared with the sort of money bandied around today, this may not seem a great achievement, but in those days, when ground admission for the early rounds was £1, for the semi-finals £2, and when for the final you got a reserved seat for £4, there were fewer noughts flying around than now. As it was, a clear profit of more than £200,000 was made for cricket worldwide.'

That, then, is the official version of how the first World Cup came to be born, and Bailey's recollection of Robins' original idea for a five-day World Cup held around the globe – climaxing with a single five-day final at Lord's – is particularly fascinating. If nothing else, it was a revolutionary concept some 30 years ahead of the modern-day ICC's eventual initiative to install the current World Test Championship.

Subba Row can also add an amusing anecdote to Bailey's record of how the Prudential sponsorship package was raised. 'My understanding is that, initially, there was only an offer of £50,000 on the table from the Prudential,' he said. 'The Board really wanted Prudential to be the sponsors, but on our sub-committee we were getting twitchy because we really didn't think that £50,000 was a large enough amount for the sort of event that was being planned. We felt the event was being badly undersold.

'So Bernard Coleman and myself took it upon ourselves to make a visit to the Burmah Castrol oil company, who were based in Swindon. Denis Thatcher, husband of the then Conservative MP Margaret Thatcher, was a director of the company and someone we knew from cricketing circles: 'Denis saw us, introduced us to the right people to talk to within the company, and the upshot was that – almost immediately – we had secured a potential sponsorship of £100,000 from them!

'Once this new offer was known to the Board, they went straight back to Prudential, and it was as a result of this that their own final offer was increased to £155,000. But no more than seven days later, Burmah Castrol fell into financial difficulties because of a huge problem with their tanker fleet and had to withdraw their £100,000 sponsorship offer anyway! By then, though, it had already served a fine purpose!'

Bailey, meanwhile, does recall Brocklehurst's early representations to the TCCB, but adds, 'I don't think you can call the World Cup his brainchild. There were a lot of ideas floating about in those days, and if the idea of a cricket World Cup was not talked about before Ben wrote in, then there were similar ideas being presented parallel to it.

'Ben's idea to have a sponsor attached to the competition was a good one, but the idea of the *Cricketer* World Cup was shot down by the sub-committee. They felt that if we were going to have a World Cup here then it should be run by England and not have *The Cricketer*'s name attached to it.

'Derrick Robins' idea, however, was specifically a proposal for a World Cup based on five-day cricket, with qualifying matches played around the world in areas, and then with a grand final at Lord's.'

Bailey stresses that the five-day World Cup option was 'closely examined' by several different committees, but that 'most opinion seemed to be against it because it would disrupt current programme schedules, and the "pattern" would be disturbed irrevocably'.

The one-day option was then studied, simply because it could be more easily fitted in to the established international calendar. 'That's how things worked in those days,' added Bailey, 'and having a one-day event was clearly the only answer to the need to have something which was compatible to existing schedules.'

Bailey also reveals that Australia, despite what Brocklehurst found in his informal Melbourne meeting, 'needed quite a lot of persuading that a World Cup tournament would be a good idea'. He said, 'I clearly remember a meeting in the TCCB offices when the Australian Cricket Board representatives were saying, "Do we really need it?" And, it must be remembered, the Australians did at first look quite unfavourably on the influx of one-day international cricket into tour itineraries. They might deny it now, but it is true!

'Cricket was a very conservative game then, and actually it would also be fair to say that there were reasonable misgivings all round about the decision to hold that first World Cup. No country had anything like a specialist one-day squad in those days – you just fielded your best team as you would for a Test match.

'It was only the playing of the first World Cup tournament itself which provided the impetus for the way one-day international cricket then took off. The likes of India and Pakistan, in particular, took to it after 1975, but at the start it was England who were at the forefront of the development of limited-overs international cricket simply because we were the ones with the experience.

'We also needed it badly in England, in a financial sense. The Gillette Cup had already proved during the 1960s that there was a market for one-day cricket, domestically, and because England was the only country which played cricket at our time of the year, all the other countries were keen to come to us because it did not disrupt their own domestic seasons.

'The World Cup has been a great success, and that first tournament really was the start of something big. Nowadays, however, I believe we have got far too much one-day international cricket being played. It has become ridiculous. Yes, Mars Bars are fine, but there is much better food about. Test-match cricket is real cricket, and although it was good that we produced a World Cup vehicle for one-day international cricket back in the 1970s, the product is perhaps oversold now.'

Chapter 4

1975: First Blood To The Windies

It has always seemed typical of the contrariness of cricket that it should have originated in England – a green and pleasant land, to be sure, but it does also rain a lot. Moreover, just five days before England hosted the first matches of the first Cricket World Cup, it snowed!

On 2 June 1975, at Buxton in Derbyshire, play at a county match was called off because of an inch-thick covering of snow, but on 7 June the launch date on which four matches were being played simultaneously (how's that for the days before television called the shots?), the inaugural Cricket World Cup got under way without even a single raindrop in sight. The show had begun, and it was indeed all right on the night.

As if blessed by the very weather gods that often made cricket in England a lottery, the 15 matches that made up the 1975 tournament were contested in fine and often hot and sunny conditions.

Three days had been allocated for each game by the organisers, so fearful were they of the English elements, but – miraculously, some said – none of the scheduled match dates of 7, 11, 14, 18 and 21 June were interrupted.

There were only 15 matches in all, however, on those five dates, and the good fortune with the weather undoubtedly helped the World Cup concept to get off the ground in terms of popularity. It is revealing to learn that, upon the successful completion of the event, relief that it had all worked was the main emotion of those responsible for staging the first World Cup.

It seems inconceivable now, though, that the organisers should allow all 12 group matches to be played on just three days. Good crowds did turn up to watch at the four venues – on the opening day there was a capacity 21,000 at Headingley for Australia v Pakistan (the ground's first full house for nine years), and almost 20,000 gathered at Lord's to see England v India – but how much more marketable could the 1975 tournament have made itself had all the major games, at least, been given a stage to themselves?

Yes, at the time of writing, less than 28 years have gone by since the inaugural

World Cup, which could be described in historical terms as little more than a single generation, but there are so many aspects of the first tournament that expose it – in terms of cricket's evolution – as being truly from a long-ago era.

No helmets or arm guards were worn, of course, and no fielding restrictions existed, bar the long-accepted ruling that no more than two fielders could be stationed behind square on the leg-side. Wide balls were not so rigorously enforced, and head-high bouncers were allowed. Coloured clothing was still something up Kerry Packer's sleeve, and one-day internationals in these early days were fought on much more traditional lines until the frantic last overs.

Nothing, in fact, sums up the almost prehistoric approach to one-day cricket in 1975 better than the performance of Sunil Gavaskar, then perhaps the most accomplished opening batsman in the world, during India's first World Cup match.

Astonishingly, Gavaskar batted throughout the full 60-over allocation for just 36 not out as India decided not to pursue England's large total but to seek batting practice instead. In reply to 334–4, the Indians finished on 132–3 from their own 60 overs. Gavaskar faced 174 balls and hit only one boundary. Unsurprisingly, both the Indian captain, Srini Venkataraghavan, and the team manager, GS Ramchand, were furious.

India, of course, were banking on winning their remaining two group matches to progress through to the semi-finals, but defeat to New Zealand a week later put paid to those ambitions.

The West Indies were the pre-tournament favourites, with England also strongly tipped because of home advantage and due to the greater experience of their players in domestic limited-overs cricket. Australia, spearheaded by the fast-bowling partnership of Dennis Lillee and Jeff Thomson that had terrorised England's batsmen in the 1974–75 Ashes series of the previous winter, were another strong outfit – as were Pakistan, who boasted powerful batting.

Again, poor planning had left Australia, the West Indies and Pakistan in the same group, which meant that one of them would not make it to the semi-final stage. Only England and Australia had been seeded in the draw for the two groups.

With South Africa excluded from international cricket, the six remaining Test countries were joined by Sri Lanka and East Africa, the two leading associate member countries of the 21 cricketing nations that then made up the ICC.

The first four matches were played at Lord's, Headingley, Old Trafford and Edgbaston and were of 60 overs per side, as in the English Gillette Cup competition.

THE MATCHES
7 June

Lord's: England 334–4 (60 overs) beat India 132–3 (60 overs) by 202 runs

To Dennis Amiss, now the chief executive of Warwickshire, went the honour of scoring the first World Cup 100. Amiss struck his 137 from 147 balls, with 18 boundaries, and was joined in a second wicket stand of 176 by Keith Fletcher, who made 68. A buccaneering, unbroken partnership of 89 between Yorkshire fast bowler Chris Old and Mike Denness, the England captain, set the seal on what was then the highest total in a 60-over match in Britain. Left-hander Old's unbeaten 51 took him just 30 balls, as he struck two sixes and four fours off the dispirited Indian attack. The contest descended from high entertainment to low farce as Sunil Gavaskar and the rest of the Indian top order opted for batting practice rather than an assault on England's bowlers.

Man Of The Match award: Dennis Amiss

Edgbaston: New Zealand 309–5 (60 overs) beat East Africa 128–8 (60 overs) by 181 runs

Glenn Turner, New Zealand's world-class opener and captain, overwhelmed the East Africans with a wonderful 171 not out, full of powerful drives both sides of the wicket. Turner, who two years earlier had performed the rare cricketing feat in England of reaching 1,000 runs before the end of May, hit two sixes and 16 fours.

Man Of The Match award: Glenn Turner

Headingley: Australia 278–7 (60 overs) beat Pakistan 205 (53 overs) by 73 runs

Dennis Lillee, perhaps the game's most charismatic and talented fast bowler at the time, picked up the first five-wicket haul in World Cup history as the Australians pressured the gifted Pakistanis into a headlong collapse from 181–4. Until Lillee, with four wickets to take his figures to 5–34, and Max Walker got among their middle and lower order, Pakistan had made a courageous effort to overhaul an Australian total boosted by a canny unbeaten 80 off 94 balls by the much-underrated Ross Edwards. Majid Khan, opening the Pakistan reply, stroked 11 boundaries in his 76-ball 65, before Asif Iqbal (53) and Wasim Raja (31) put on 77 for the fifth wicket.

Man Of The Match award: Dennis Lillee

Old Trafford: Sri Lanka 86 (37.2 overs) lost to West Indies 87–1 (20.4 overs) by nine wickets

Outclassed by a West Indian pace attack founded on the raw speed of Andy Roberts, and the knowhow of seasoned all-rounders Keith Boyce (3–22) and Bernard Julien (4–20), the Sri Lankans could not prevent the game finishing as early as 3:30pm. Roberts took 2–16 from 12 overs on his one-day international debut, while another young Antiguan was also making his limited-overs international debut in this match. Viv Richards, however, did not bat or bowl as Sri Lanka were routed. Happily, though, both teams then agreed to an additional 20-over-per-side exhibition match in an effort to give the Manchester crowd its money's worth.

Man Of The Match award: Bernard Julien

11 June

Trent Bridge: England 266–6 (60 overs) beat New Zealand 186 (60 overs) by 80 runs

A masterly innings of 131 from 147 balls by Keith Fletcher set up England's comfortable victory. John Morrison's 55 was the Kiwis' only 50 and Tony Greig (4–45) was well supported by tight bowling from both Derek Underwood and Chris Old as the New Zealand reply was squeezed lifeless.

Man Of The Match award: Keith Fletcher

Headingley: East Africa 120 (55.3 overs) lost to India 123–0 (29.5 overs) by 10 wickets

Bishen Bedi, the great Indian left-arm spinner, conceded only six runs from his 12-over allocation – eight of which were maidens – as the East Africans were again no match for Test opposition. Jawahir Shah (37) did manage five boundaries but their total was woefully inadequate. Sunil Gavaskar (65 not out) and Farokh Engineer (54 not out) made the most of some more batting practice.

Man Of The Match award: Farokh Engineer

The Oval: Australia 328–5 (60 overs) beat Sri Lanka 276–4 (60 overs) by 52 runs

The Aussies won the match but the Sri Lankans took all the plaudits for producing brave and often exhilarating strokeplay against the odds. Two batsmen, Sunil Wettimuny and the 22-year-old Duleep Mendis, were taken to hospital for X-rays after being struck by Jeff Thomson's thunderbolts, but Sri Lanka's top six all contributed to a plucky display which, undoubtedly, helped to pave the way for their elevation to Test status six years later. At one stage, although both Wettimuny and Mendis had retired hurt, Sri Lanka were 246–2 as Anura Tennekoon, the stylish captain, and the elegant Michael Tissera reached 48 and 52 respectively. There were 37 fours struck in the Sri Lankan innings, compared to just 22 (and two sixes) in an Australian total built upon a fine 101 from opener Alan Turner.

Man Of The Match award: Alan Turner

Edgbaston: Pakistan 266–7 (60 overs) lost to West Indies 267–9 (59.4 overs) by one wicket

The first real classic match of the World Cup competition, and still one of the most remarkable games in the history of one-day international cricket. The West Indies, in short, never looked like winning until, from the fourth ball of the final over, number 11 batsman Andy Roberts pushed a ball from Wasim Raja, the part-time leg-spinner, towards mid-wicket and scrambled through for the decisive single. Roberts finished 24 not out and had helped Deryck Murray, the piratical-looking Trinidadian wicket-keeper, to add 64 in 14 overs for the tenth wicket. Murray, who made a brilliant and cool 61 not out under severe pressure, had already put on 37 for the ninth wicket with Vanburn Holder when Roberts strolled out at 203-9. The Pakistanis clearly panicked as the last pair crept closer and closer to their target. Sarfraz Nawaz took 4–44 in an heroic bowling effort, while a 17-year-old Javed Miandad, bowling medium pace on his one-day international debut, added the prized wicket of Clive Lloyd for 53 to an invaluable little innings of 24 earlier. Majid Khan, Mushtaq Mohammad and Wasim Raja all hit half-centuries, too, but at the end of an epic contest Pakistan were out of the World Cup and inconsolable.

Man Of The Match award: Sarfraz Nawaz

14 June

Edgbaston: England 290–5 (60 overs) beat East Africa 94 (52.3 overs) by 196 runs

The East Africans fought hard, but their final group match went the way of the previous two: a heavy defeat, and a further reminder to their band of club cricketers that a considerable gulf lay between them and the Test-playing nations. Barry Wood, Dennis Amiss and Frank Hayes all helped themselves to half-centuries before John Snow, with 4–11 in 12 overs, ripped through the East African top order. Last man to fall was number 11 Don Pringle, the father of former England all-rounder Derek and a 43-year-old Lancashire-born medium-pacer who had earlier delivered his 12 overs at a tidy cost of only 41 runs.

Man Of The Match award: John Snow

Old Trafford: India 230 (60 overs) lost to New Zealand 233–6 (58.5 overs) by four wickets

Glenn Turner was the hero again for his New Zealand side, who won what was in effect a quarter-final against India with seven balls to spare. Turner, the opener, remained 114 not out, and although he received solid middle-order support from Brian Hastings, Ken Wadsworth and Richard Hadlee, this victory was all about Turner's magnificently paced effort. India, so disappointing in this inaugural tournament, had earlier rallied from 101–6 largely because of a fighting 70 from Abid Ali.

Man Of The Match award: Glenn Turner

The Oval: Australia 192 (53.4 overs) lost to West Indies 195–3 (46 overs) by seven wickets

A memorable assault on Dennis Lillee's bowling by Alvin Kallicharran, the diminutive and curly-haired left-hander from Guyana, produced the biggest talking point from a match that had been eagerly awaited. In truth, the Australians did not perform, with only nuggety half-centuries from Ross Edwards and Rod Marsh enabling them to post any sort of total after a slide to 61–5. Roy Fredericks often glittered during his 58, but it was Kallicharran who seized centre stage as he plundered 35 runs from 10 successive deliveries from Lillee. Seven fours and a six flew off Kallicharran's flashing blade during this sequence – starting with five boundaries in a row – as thrilling pulls and cuts answered Lillee's increasingly desperate attempts to unsettle the batsman with the short ball. Lillee did get his man in the end, but not before Kallicharran had plundered 78 from 83 balls with, overall, 14 fours, plus the hooked six.

Man Of The Match award: Alvin Kallicharran

Trent Bridge: Pakistan 330–6 (60 overs) beat Sri Lanka 138 (50.1 overs) by 192 runs

A match which meant nothing as far as qualification for the semi-finals was concerned, but at least the talented and, to a large extent, unlucky Pakistan side was able to bow out with the consolation of a convincing win against the gallant Sri Lankans. There was another beautiful innings of 84 from Majid Khan and knocks of 74 and 97 for the Gloucestershire pair of Sadiq Mohammad and Zaheer Abbas.

Man Of The Match award: Zaheer Abbas

SEMI-FINALS
18 June

Headingley: England 93 (36.2 overs) lost to Australia 94–6 (28.4 overs) by four wickets

Gary Gilmour's game, and a match of huge drama that was played on a damp, green pitch and in heavy, overcast conditions. Ian Chappell, the Australian captain, had little hesitation in choosing to bowl first, and Gilmour, making his left-arm fast-medium swing late and also dart around off the seam, took 6–14 from his 12 overs. Nor was the 24-year-old, the youngest member of the Aussie team, finished after picking up the first six England wickets. The greatest day of his cricketing career continued with him walking out to bat with Australia themselves in the mire at 39–6 against the England quick bowlers Chris Old, John Snow and Geoff Arnold. Soon he was 28 not out, from only 28 balls, and also claiming the highest individual innings of a remarkable day. Gilmour and Doug Walters, who ended up 20 not out, put their side into the World Cup final with an unbroken stand of 55.

Man Of The Match award: Gary Gilmour

The Oval: New Zealand 158 (52.2 overs) lost to West Indies 159–5 (40.1 overs) by five wickets

It was a magnificent slip catch by the 39-year old Rohan Kanhai, to send back New Zealand's star batsman Glenn Turner for 36, which swung this second semi-final towards the West Indies. Turner had added 90 for the second wicket with Geoff Howarth (51), but Andy Roberts sent both of them back, and from 98–1 the Kiwis went into freefall. Bernard Julien took 4–27 and Vanburn Holder 3–30, and then the in-form Kallicharran hit 72 from 92 balls to dominate a match-clinching second wicket partnership of 125 with opener Gordon Greenidge (55). In the end, the West Indians eased past the finishing post with almost 20 overs in hand.

Man Of The Match award: Alvin Kallicharran

THE 1975 WORLD CUP FINAL
21 June

Lord's: West Indies 291–8 (60 overs) beat Australia 274 (58.4 overs) by 17 runs

An epic match, and still the best final of them all. If world cricket didn't know before that the sporting gods were smiling benevolently on their new creation, then this magnificent high summer day at Lord's was the ultimate confirmation.

It was a game filled with incident and excitement from morning until near-dusk: it began at 11am and didn't end until 8:42pm. Thankfully, it was also literally the longest day of the year, and the light was still good at just before 9pm, when Clive Lloyd, the West Indies captain, accepted the World Cup trophy from Prince Philip, the Duke of Edinburgh, in front of the Lord's pavilion. Thousands of spectators, many of them West Indian, had swarmed on to the outfield to watch the ceremony and begin a carnival celebration. It was a party that continued on in the streets of north London and throughout the Caribbean.

Lloyd's 102 from only 85 balls remains a World Cup classic, yet it was a display of brilliant fielding from perhaps the least known of the 22 fine cricketers on show that day which ultimately decided the contest. Viv Richards, then 23, ran out three of Australia's top order with superb fielding – two with direct hits – to give the West Indies the inspiration they needed to keep in check a determined Aussie challenge.

Ian Chappell, the Australian captain, had put the West Indies in and, with the total 12, saw Roy Fredericks swivel into his own stumps as he hooked Dennis Lillee thrillingly into the Tavern for what would otherwise have been one of the most memorable sixes in history. As it was, the West Indies slipped to 50–3 and the crowd couldn't take its eyes off the action.

Enter Lloyd. With the veteran Rohan Kanhai supporting him with 55, the gangling Guyanan decided to counter-attack. Helped by several Australian dropped catches, the fourth-wicket pair added 149 in 36 overs and Lloyd – missed at mid-wicket on 26 – struck two sixes and 12 fours. His hooking and driving, even off the back foot, were breathtaking for their power, timing and apparent lack of effort. When he finally became one of Gary Gilmour's five victims, Lloyd loped off to a standing ovation which tingled the senses. Keith Boyce and Bernard Julien then underlined the depth of the West Indies' batting by adding a further 52 in 10 overs for the seventh wicket, and a couple of blows from Deryck Murray also helped to boost the total to intimidating proportions.

Back came the Australians, however, as Alan Turner, the left-handed opener, struck 40 off only 24 balls to give his side a flying start. Turner, though, then became the first of Richards' run-out scalps, and the young Antiguan scored another sensational direct hit from square of the wicket to claim the important wicket of Greg Chappell for just 15.

Ian Chappell fought hard to keep his side in the game, scoring 62 and putting on 47 with Doug Walters before he, too, became a Richards run-out victim. When their ninth wicket fell, Australia were still 59 runs away from victory…but the day's drama was not yet done.

Joining his great fast-bowling partner Jeff Thomson at the crease was Dennis Lillee, and the numbers 10 and 11 proceeded to take up the challenge of winning the game for their country with their bats instead. And so a great match was provided with a great finish as the two bowlers put together a big-hearted stand of 41. At one stage, the umpires, Dickie Bird and Tom Spencer, had to stop the game after Lillee had been caught off a no-ball and the crowd had invaded the playing area, thinking that Australia were all out.

In the end, with the West Indies beginning to fear the worst, Thomson was sent back by Lillee, the non-striker, when trying to sneak a bye to the wicket-keeper. Murray's underarm lob hit the stumps, with Thomson still out of his ground. There were eight balls left unbowled.

Man Of The Match award: Clive Lloyd

THE INTERVIEW
Clive Lloyd

Now 58 and an official ICC match referee, Clive Lloyd is the original giant of the World Cup. The big man from Georgetown, Guyana, captained the West Indies a record 74 times during his 110 Tests, but will anyone again be able to match his other achievement of lifting the World Cup twice?

Lloyd, in fact, almost made it a hat-trick in the 1983 World Cup, before India upset the West Indies in the final to deny him a third triumph to add to the victories of 1975 and 1979.

No other man alive can have the sort of World Cup memories that Lloyd has gained from leading his country to three successive finals and scoring a match-winning 102 from 85 balls in the first of them. Perhaps the unlikeliest experience of them all, however, came in his second World Cup match, when, during the nail-biting one-wicket victory against Pakistan at Edgbaston, Lloyd found himself drinking the best part of 12 bottles of pale ale in under an hour!

On 11 June 1975, the pre-tournament favourites found themselves almost down and out in the group match against a Pakistan team who had earlier totalled 266–7. At 166–8, the West Indies were in need of a miracle, and soon the combination of some tail-end defiance out in the middle and some unscheduled liquid refreshment in the dressing room seemed capable of providing it.

Lloyd's accountant, local Warwickshire member Gordon Andrews, had made a bet that the West Indies would win, and in keen anticipation of collecting his winnings later that day he had appeared in the dressing room with a crate of pale ale. Celebrations seemed the last thing possible when Vanburn Holder, the number 10, went out to join Deryck Murray, but Andrews said he was still confident – and runs did start to come.

Holder's dismissal for 16, however, left the West Indies at 203–9. But last man Andy Roberts also began to play well in support of wicket-keeper Murray, and after huge tension the last wicket pair succeeded in adding the 64 runs required for a famous win.

'I think I drank a bottle of the ale after each over so, by the time Andy and Deryck saw us safely home from the fourth ball of the final over, I was feeling neither pain nor tension,' said Lloyd. 'We looked dead and buried in that game against Pakistan, but after Deryck and Andy had saved the day, we knew – absolutely knew – that we could win the World Cup itself.'

In his book *Living For Cricket*, Lloyd gives an even more detailed account of the pale ale story, and how the emotion of the occasion remained unequalled even in his great career: 'Run by run, the target came closer and closer and we got noisier and noisier in the dressing room, cheering every shot like excited schoolboys.

'The Pakistanis began to panic and, the more they did, it seemed the cooler Deryck and Andy, who are two unflappable customers at the best of times, became. Bottles started to disappear from the crate of ale faster and faster, and when, against all the odds, Andy pushed Wasim Raja into the leg-side for the winning run with two balls remaining, the scenes were incredible.

'West Indians in the crowd mobbed Deryck, and it was some time before he could get inside to join the celebrations and receive his deserved congratulations.

'In all my days of playing cricket, I have never known such elation in a dressing room. Some years later, when we won a similarly close World Series Cricket match in Australia, there was great jubilation, but it wasn't quite as emotional. Men with years of cricket experience were jumping up and down and hugging each other. Several were sobbing uncontrollably. And don't get the idea that I was all calm and dignified through it all. I did a bit of hugging and shouting myself.'

Lloyd makes the point, too, that this miraculous never-say-die victory against Pakistan, coming when it did at both a crucial moment of this first World Cup and at an important stage in the evolution of a side bound for world domination, 'helped to erase the age-old feeling that the West Indies were no good fighting from behind'.

Don't forget that, in 1975, the West Indies – multi-talented though they were – remained some distance away from the mean machine that Lloyd later used to subjugate the rest of the Test-playing countries. In 1975–76, the West Indies were trounced 5–1 in Tests in Australia, and when they came to England the following summer, in 1976, the England captain Tony Greig was still referring to their propensity to fold under pressure when he said (rather rashly, as it turned out!) that he intended to make his opponents grovel.

Lloyd, however, offers the following appreciation of the side he commanded in the field almost 28 years ago: 'You needed a good all-round side that batted most of the way down in one-day cricket back then, and that is still the case today. We were pretty confident going into the competition because we had a powerful batting line-up, some wonderful fielders and several good all-rounders like Keith Boyce and Bernard Julien. Even I bowled some right-arm optimistic.'

Modesty forbids Lloyd from saying that his bowling figures in the final were 12–1–38–1, making him the most economic of the West Indian attack. In the semi-final win against New Zealand, moreover, he produced an analysis of 12–1–37–1, and also took 1–31 from eight overs in that group thriller against Pakistan.

Like many cricketers who enjoy long and successful careers, Lloyd is often remembered in modern times for his image as a veteran player. In his case, it was as the rather dour, statuesque figure who stood emotionless at slip while rotating his fast bowlers mercilessly as a succession of 1980s opponents met with their destruction. What is forgotten is the all-round inspiration he brought to West Indies cricket, both with the ball and, most significantly, with the cat-like patrolling of the covers in his wonderfully athletic youth.

With 7,515 Test runs at an average of 46.67, Lloyd stands the test of time as one of the greatest batsmen to have graced cricket. But this unmistakeable figure is much, much more than that in the greater scheme of things. He held the World Cup aloft twice, almost thrice, and he built an empire of West Indian cricket dominance that lasted for more than a decade.

The World Cup win in 1975 was the start of it all for Lloyd, though, and he adds, 'It's all a long time ago now but the memories are still vivid... I particularly remember the crowd at that first World Cup final. You didn't have a lot of corporate hospitality at grounds back in 1975, so Lord's was packed with what you might call genuine fans. We had a lot of support – I think special buses were laid on from Brixton. It really was a carnival atmosphere and our people partied all day and all night, too, I think.

'I was fortunate enough to enjoy a lot of successful times with the West Indies, but winning the first World Cup stands out as a special achievement. It meant so much for our cricket and our fans. Suddenly we were the world champions and that considerably improved our bargaining power when it came to negotiating tours.'

THE CHAMPIONS

All 11 players in the of the victorious West Indies team in 1975 had gained precious experience of the limited-overs game and English conditions by playing in county cricket. This, no doubt, was a factor in their World Cup success – especially as their final opponents, Australia, had relatively little experience of one-day cricket. The fine weather enjoyed by the inaugural tournament also helped, but it's not just West Indians who feel just that little bit better about life when the sun is on their backs.

No, the West Indies were the first World Cup champions because, for a start, they had the classic blend of youth and experience to add to the sum of their combined talents. They were a team on a mission, too, driven by the fact that success on the cricket field could provide them with the material rewards denied them in so many other areas of Caribbean life. More than that, even, it was cricket that gave the West Indians an identity, and a respect, in the eyes of the world.

Playing county cricket in England, of course, was one of the ways that a West Indies cricketer could earn extra money and learn far more about the game he was seeking to master. Many of the other top international players plied their trades in county cricket during the English summer, too, so it was an invigorating environment in which to develop skills and knowhow.

Viv Richards, Andy Roberts and Gordon Greenidge all made their one-day international debuts during the 1975 World Cup. Rohan Kanhai played his last game for the West Indies in the World Cup final.

In between these extremes, the West Indies also had a hard core of experienced, seasoned professionals, led by Clive Lloyd, the captain. They also, by the end of the competition, had a settled side. Once Greenidge had been brought in for the second game, the monumental one-wicket win against Pakistan, the team remained unchanged for the last four matches.

Roy Fredericks, the flamboyant left-handed opener from Berbice, Guyana, had played county cricket for Glamorgan for three seasons in the early 1970s. His partner, Greenidge, although Barbados-born, grew up from the age of 12 in England and had begun his professional career by playing for Hampshire from 1970.

Rohan Kanhai, Alvin Kallicharran and wicket-keeper Deryck Murray all played for many seasons with Warwickshire, helping the county to the championship title in 1972. Vanburn Holder, the dependable seamer, was an important part of Worcestershire's championship win in 1974, while Roberts made his debut for Hampshire in the 1973 summer in which they were champions.

Richards had played his first season for Somerset in 1974, Lloyd was a fixture at Lancashire and Keith Boyce and Bernard Julien were likewise at Essex and Kent respectively.

Boyce, in particular, was a dynamic all-rounder whose excellence would have brought him far more than 21 Tests if his career had not begun in an era when Sir Garry Sobers was still in his prime. He played for Essex, in fact, from 1966 to 1977 and fully deserved the moment in the sun which his World Cup final performances with bat and ball – 34 off 37 balls and then 4–50 – brought him.

Also in the 1975 West Indies squad was veteran off-spinner Lance Gibbs, who played in the opening World Cup match against Sri Lanka but was then omitted, along with Jamaican batsman and useful off-spinner Maurice Foster and young all-rounder Collis King, who was to experience personal World Cup glory himself in 1979.

Overall, then, it was a balanced team with a respected, unflustered leader and perfectly capable of looking after itself when pitted against any opposition and in any conditions. Roberts provided real pace as the spearhead of a seam attack, containing the skill and deep experience of Boyce, Holder and Julien, while Lloyd's own underrated medium pace provided the fifth bowling option in both the semi-final and final. In the group games, Richards had also bowled usefully.

It was the richness and depth of the batting line-up, however, that gave the West Indies the edge over their rivals in 1975.

Fredericks was almost a prototype of the sort of destructive opener that every side needs in the modern one-day arena. He was, in many ways, an even classier version of Sanath Jayasuriya – if that does not seem a sacrilege. When the mood was with him, Fredericks was as murderous, in fact, as yet another magnificent modern left-hander, Adam Gilchrist.

Kallicharran was in irresistible form during the first World Cup, as his assault on Dennis Lillee in the group matches illustrates. Lloyd was sheer class, too, and there was little future in the faint-hearted to be fielding at mid-off or mid-on when he began to swing his abnormally heavy bat with intent.

Kanhai and Murray were important steadying influences, both on the field and in the dressing room, and they also produced vital runs when the team most needed them.

Add in the high promise of Richards and Greenidge, two true greats in waiting, and the gold-dust in this West Indian mix is clear. This was a great team, about to develop into an even greater team, and the worthy victors of a great cup final.

THE PRIZES

Time's march and inflation make all mention of the prize money on offer in previous eras look faintly ridiculous. This 1975 tournament was also rather a toe in the water of commercialism and not a headlong dive.

Even so, it's remarkable that the World Cup winners received just £4,000 (to be shared between all the players) and the runners-up £2,000. The two losing semi-finalists gained prize money of £1,000 apiece.

Overall gate receipts were more than £200,000, however, from a total attendance of 158,000. Crowds were good, in the main, although only 720 paid to watch India trounce East Africa at Headingley. The Lord's final attendance of 26,000 contributed £66,950, then a record for a one-day match in Britain.

Prudential Assurance, the sponsors, covered the cost of staging the matches and the subsistence claims from all eight teams out of its £155,000 fee.

At its annual general meeting, held at Lord's soon after the competition, the ICC decided to award the 1979 World Cup once again to England, mainly due to the fact that its lengthy hours of daylight during mid-summer was ideal for the staging of 60-overs-per-side matches. India were the only other nation keen on being hosts.

THE QUOTES

'The stroke of a man knocking a thistle top off with a walking stick.' John Arlott, describing to BBC Radio listeners how Clive Lloyd had pulled a ball from Gary Gilmour over mid-wicket for four.

'I couldn't sleep that night, though I was tired. I kept on going through it all in my head – such great players, such a great game. There'll never be one as good as that.' Dickie Bird, one of the umpires, recalling the 1975 World Cup final.

'At the end, one of the West Indian supporters who ran on to the field pinched my white cap. And, do you know, several years later, I saw it being worn by a West Indian bus conductor when I got onto a bus in London!' Bird.

'I was more than a little disappointed at the [West Indies] Board's response – or lack of it – to our success. The team members never received any recognition from the Board, apart from the agreed fee of £350, and this left a somewhat bitter feeling.' Clive Lloyd, West Indies captain.

'A special ceremony, a special match, anything to show that it meant something to the Board would have been appreciated. Instead, it was left to the Guyana government to fly me back home with the trophy for motorcades through the streets of Georgetown and to present every member of the team with a commemorative gold chain. Later, the Caribbean governments agreed to mark the occasion with special stamps. But that was about all.' Lloyd, again.

'It might not be termed first-class cricket, but the game has never produced better entertainment in one day.' Part of the *Wisden* report on the first World Cup final.

TEAM OF THE TOURNAMENT?

Glenn Turner (New Zealand)
Alan Turner (Australia)
Alvin Kallicharran (West Indies)
Majid Khan (Pakistan)
Clive Lloyd (West Indies, captain)
Keith Fletcher (England)
Keith Boyce (West Indies)

Deryck Murray (West Indies, wicket-keeper)
Gary Gilmour (Australia)
Dennis Lillee (Australia)
Andy Roberts (West Indies)

THE ROAD TO 1979...

The West Indies may have been crowned as the first world champions but, in Australia in 1975–76, they found that the Australians were in the mood to show them who was the real boss of global cricket.

Although the series was fairly evenly fought, certainly for the first half, Australia emerged as 5–1 winners, with Dennis Lillee and Jeff Thomson repeating the terror tactics that had so shocked England in the Ashes series of the previous season.

It was, for Clive Lloyd, an experience that made him – and the West Indies team as a whole – determined to fight fire with fire. In that 1975–76 rubber, Lloyd had the young Michael Holding to support Andy Roberts, but Holding was raw and in his debut series. Lloyd felt impotent by the end of it, and so angry was he at the damage that Lillee and Thomson had inflicted on his fine team (with a batting line-up, remember, which included Fredericks, Kallicharran, Richards, Lawrence Rowe and himself) that he decided that the only way to respond was to assemble a fast attack that could outdo even the two Aussie pacemen.

Soon, Wayne Daniel was joining Roberts and Holding in an attack which, in 1976, scattered England, and before long the giant and fearsome pair of Colin Croft and Joel Garner emerged to turn the West Indian attack into a four-engined juggernaut.

Yet, if West Indian cricket lost its innocence against Lillee and Thomson in 1975–76, the whole of the cricket world was soon to be caught up in a crisis caused by its inability to react to the fast-changing reality of commercial growth.

The catalyst was Australian television tycoon Kerry Packer, who realised that the Australian team – in Test terms the best in the world – was full of cricketers who were being rewarded with very little, compared to other sports, in return for their prowess. Packer also wanted to muscle in on the televised-cricket market, which was being monopolised by a long-term deal between the Australian Cricket Board and the traditional Australian Broadcasting Corporation. Putting two and two together, he rationalised that he could buy up the top players, stage high-class matches himself...and televise them himself on his Channel Nine station.

Cricket's establishment, of course, was aghast. At first Packer met with the ICC to see if he could negotiate a deal guaranteeing that his matches would not clash with official Tests or one-day internationals. That soon proved impossible, and when Packer said he intended to go ahead anyway the ICC decided to ban all the cricketers who had signed up to what was being branded 'World Series Cricket'. Packer responded by taking the cricket authorities to court and won his case, which argued that cricketers should not be forced to withstand restraint of trade. The court defeat cost the world cricket establishment £250,000.

The result was, for two seasons from 1977 to early 1979, Packer staged cricket in Australia between an Australian XI, a West Indian XI and a World XI, and later, in the Caribbean, a series between the West Indians and the Australians. It was one of the most controversial events in cricket history, but it shook up the game when, in all honesty, it needed shaking. Night cricket under lights, coloured clothing, fielding circles, the proper treatment of top cricketers and their families, and of course more realistic pay scales – Packer is responsible for it all.

Chapter 5

1979: The Windies Triumphant Again

'It was a victory which meant even more than usual for West Indian cricket – and for me personally.'

– Clive Lloyd

Looking back, it's easy to criticise the 1979 World Cup – again staged by England – as being uninspired in format and production. From this distance it seems merely a pale imitation of the 1975 original, yet it was regarded at the time as another big success.

Politically, it was also an important staging post in the history of the game, coming as it did hard on the heels of a truce being called between the cricket establishment and World Series Cricket. There was a feelgood factor at work in June 1979 and a sense of worldwide relief that the far-flung family of cricket was getting back on speaking terms.

WSC, bankrolled by the Australian television mogul Kerry Packer, had ripped apart the world game since 1977. Now, after two seasons, Packer had agreed a peace deal with the financially embarrassed Australian Cricket Board and, as a direct result, most of the world's best cricketers were back in the official fold.

The only real differences between the World Cup in 1979 and the inaugural tournament four years earlier lay in the fact that England supplanted Australia (weakened by the continued absence of their Packer players) as the nearest challengers to the West Indies' dominance, and that the ICC launched a qualifying tournament (the ICC Trophy) to determine which of the two associate member countries should join the six big Test-playing nations in the event. It also rained a bit.

Sri Lanka and Canada, who beat Denmark and Bermuda respectively in the semi-finals, won through from an ICC Trophy competition involving 15 associates and held on club grounds in the English Midlands in the fortnight directly before the Cup itself began. Sri Lanka won the final at Worcester (a high-scoring affair which produced 588 runs) to earn themselves a place in Group B alongside the West Indies, New Zealand and India. The Canadians joined England, Pakistan and Australia in Group A.

The ICC Trophy, however, was blighted by an abnormally wet two weeks, even by England's standards for late May and early June, and six of the 60-overs-per-side games were abandoned. Nor did the World Cup itself escape the weather's clutches, as it so miraculously did four years earlier, and the fall in attendance figures from 1975 (down 28,000 to 130,000, a significant percentage) reflected the impact of unsettled skies. However, increased admission charges and an increase in the Prudential insurance company's sponsorship to £250,000 meant the total receipts were nearly double those of 1975.

Was this nature's way of showing that the World Cup concept should have been taken on a stride or two from its great inaugural success? Should India's interest in staging the second event have been seized upon gratefully, and imaginatively?

Whatever, the eight competing teams once again contested the Cup over a total of 15 matches, scheduled to be played on just five dates in the two weeks set aside. Unfortunately, rain caused three matches to spill over into a reserve day and also brought the abandonment of the West Indies v Sri Lanka group tie that should have been played some time between 13 and 15 June.

Again, in addition to the prehistoric scheduling in relation to television coverage, with each block of four group games and then both semi-finals all being staged on the same day, only Test grounds were used as venues. This combination denied the wider public a sense of more intimate involvement in the tournament. In contrast, every subsequent World Cup has made it a policy to take games to the 'regions'.

Unlike 1975, there were no seeded teams when the draw for the tournament was made at Lord's in July 1978. One of the highlights of the 1979 event, from an ICC point of view, was that Sri Lanka built upon the good impression they had made in 1975 by gaining their first World Cup victory. This came against India on 18 June and further accelerated their progress towards being granted full Test status. Although the maturing skills of their leading players meant that Sri Lanka were hardly deserving of the sobriquet 'minnows' – more a young, hungry shark swimming in the waters of international cricket – who could have guessed that, less than 17 years later, it would be a captain of Sri Lanka holding up the World Cup itself in triumph?

THE MATCHES
9 June

Edgbaston: India 190 (53.1 overs) lost to West Indies 194–1 (51.3 overs) by nine wickets

Only Gundappa Viswanath, the little Indian batting artist, managed to hold up the awesome champions. The West Indies, powerful enough in 1975 but now armed with a four-pronged fast attack of unprecedented collective power, steamrollered India from the moment that Clive Lloyd decided to bowl first and Andy Roberts dismissed Sunil Gavaskar, the world's best opener, for just eight. Roberts later returned to wrap up the innings and, in between, the fearsomely quick Michael Holding took 4–33 and there was a wicket apiece for Joel Garner, Colin Croft and medium-paced all-rounder Collis King. Viswanath scored a gutsy 75, but then the West Indies top order put everything into perspective: Desmond Haynes (47) and Viv Richards played mere support acts as Gordon Greenidge eased his way to an unbeaten 106.

Man Of The Match award: Gordon Greenidge

Trent Bridge: Sri Lanka 189 (56.5 overs) lost to New Zealand 190–1 (47.4 overs) by nine wickets

Brian McKechnie and Warren Stott, the medium-pacers, were the pick of the New Zealand attack, with three wickets each as Sri Lanka were overwhelmed in Nottingham. Anura Tennekoon, the high-class Sri Lankan number three and captain, scored 59 and hit six boundaries, but the fall of the dangerous Roy Dias for 25, at 107–2, signalled the beginning of the end for the ICC Trophy winners. Glenn Turner, with 83 not out, and Geoff Howarth, with an unbeaten 63, then added 126 for the second wicket to earn their side a comfortable victory after John Wright (34) had been the only Kiwi wicket to fall.

Man Of The Match award: Geoff Howarth

Lord's: Australia 159–9 (60 overs) lost to England 160–4 (47.1 overs) by six wickets

The extent of Australia's problems, with their Packer players still unavailable for official cricket, became all too evident during this thrashing by the old enemy. From 97–1, with Andrew Hilditch and Allan Border set, Australia fell away. There were four run outs and Geoff Boycott, bowling his occasional seamers with his cap turned around the wrong way, took 2–15 in six overs.

Boycott and Derek Randall, however, were out cheaply in reply before a third wicket stand of 108 between Mike Brearley, the captain, and Graham Gooch virtually settled the game in England's favour. Brearley ground out 44 from 147 balls, while Gooch compiled a more fluent 53. When both fell to Trevor Laughlin, the crowd were entertained by a sparkling little unbroken partnership between David Gower and Ian Botham.

Man Of The Match award: Graham Gooch

Headingley: Canada 139–9 (60 overs) lost to Pakistan 140–2 (40.1 overs) by eight wickets

A miserable World Cup debut for the Canadians ended with Sadiq Mohammad anchoring the Pakistan victory canter while Zaheer Abbas and Haroon Rashid played some pleasing strokes at the other end. Left-hander Sadiq finished 57 not out, and earlier the Pakistan captain, Asif Iqbal, had picked up three wickets. As ever, the Pakistanis looked a dangerous outfit, with a good hand of all-rounders and, as a consequence, good depth to their batting.

Man Of The Match award: Sadiq Mohammad

13 June

Headingley: India 182 (55.5 overs) lost to New Zealand 183–2 (57 overs) by eight wickets

The Kiwi seam-bowling battery proved too potent for India at Leeds, with both Lance Cairns and Brian McKechnie picking up three wickets. Only Sunil Gavaskar, with 55, resisted long, and Richard Hadlee then added India's star batsman to the earlier scalping of his opening partner, Anshuman Gaekwad. John Wright and Bruce Edgar, the left-handed New Zealand openers, then added 100, and Edgar (84 not out) stayed to feature in a match-clinching and unbroken stand of 80 for the third wicket with Glenn Turner.

Man Of The Match award: Bruce Edgar

13-14 June

Trent Bridge: Pakistan 286–7 (60 overs) beat Australia 197 (57.1 overs) by 89 runs

Asif Iqbal and Javed Miandad provided the middle-order acceleration as Pakistan swept the Australians aside with considerable ease. Majid Khan's 61 formed the solid base of the innings before Javed's run-a-ball 48 and Asif's cavalier 61 from 57 balls provided a delightful 87-run stand. All Australia could really offer in reply was a workmanlike 72, with just four boundaries, from Andrew Hilditch.

Man Of The Match award: Asif Iqbal

13 (no play)-14 June

Old Trafford: Canada 45 (40.3 overs) lost to England 46–2 (13.5 overs) by eight wickets

Bob Willis and Chris Old enjoyed themselves hugely at the expense of the outclassed Canadians, taking 4–11 and 4–8 respectively as the amateurs tumbled to the lowest score in World Cup history. England were 11–2 themselves before Graham Gooch joined Geoff Boycott to make short work of the target.

Man Of The Match award: Chris Old

13-15 June

The Oval: West Indies v Sri Lanka, match abandoned without a ball bowled (2 points each)

16 June

Trent Bridge: West Indies 244–7 (60 overs) beat New Zealand 212–9 (60 overs) by 32 runs

The favourites were always in control of this match, but the nuggety New Zealanders at least made the West Indians fight hard for the win. Consistent seam bowling nagged away at the powerful West Indies batting line-up, which took responsible innings of 65 by Gordon Greenidge and an unbeaten 73 from Clive Lloyd to keep them ahead on points. In contrast, none of the top order Kiwis could break the shackles of the West Indies pacemen, even though they stood up to them manfully, until Richard Hadlee (42) struck some defiant blows late on.

Man Of The Match award: Clive Lloyd

Edgbaston: Canada 105 (33.2 overs) lost to Australia 106–3 (26 overs) by seven wickets

Alan Hurst took 5–21 to reduce Canada from the comparative riches of 44 without loss to 105 all out. The Australians lost three wickets themselves, but soon completed a straightforward victory.

Man Of The Match award: Alan Hurst

Headingley: England 165–9 (60 overs) beat Pakistan 151 (56 overs) by 14 runs

Mike Hendrick led a brilliant performance in the field by England, who managed to defend a modest total by holding their nerve better than their excitable opponents. Hendrick, the dependable Derbyshire seamer, took 4–15 from his 12 overs, six of which were maidens, as he and Ian Botham initially left the Pakistanis tottering at 34–6. Asif Iqbal, with 51, rallied the lower order, but Bob Willis and Chris Old then removed Asif and Wasim Raja to leave Pakistan at 115–8. Imran Khan, who remained 21 not out, added 30 with Wasim Bari, but Geoff Boycott popped up again with the ball to dismiss both Bari and last man Sikander Bakht in an inspired five-over spell. Majid Khan was the surprise bowling package of the England innings, sending back the prized triumvirate of Boycott, David Gower and Botham to finish with 3–27 from his 12 over stint, but a vital 43 runs were added for the England ninth wicket by Bob Taylor and Willis.

Man Of The Match award: Mike Hendrick

16/18 June

Old Trafford: Sri Lanka 238–5 (60 overs) beat India 191 (54.1 overs) by 47 runs

The first shock result of World Cup competition, with eye-catching half-centuries from Sunil Wettimuny, Roy Dias and Duleep Mendis propelling the Sri Lankans to a challenging total. It all proved too much for India, for whom Dilip Vengsarkar top-scored with 36 and Gundappa Viswanath was wastefully run out. The leg spin of DS de Silva was particularly potent and Tony Opatha, the pace bowler, then returned to polish off the Indian tail with 3–31. It was a triumph for Sri Lanka and their new captain, Bandula Warnapura, and was a result which underlined their claims for full Test status, which arrived in 1981.

Man Of The Match award: Duleep Mendis

SEMI-FINALS
20 June

Old Trafford: England 221–8 (60 overs) beat New Zealand 212–9 (60 overs) by nine runs

A thrilling finish produced a narrow win for England, amid great tension. The England total was built upon a third-wicket stand of 58 between opener Mike Brearley (53) and Graham Gooch, who went on to score 71 from 84 balls. Ian Botham helped Gooch to add 47 for the fifth wicket, after the innings had looked to be wobbling a little at 98–4, and Derek Randall emerged at number seven to play a wonderfully inventive 42 not out from 50 deliveries to guide England to a defendable position. John Wright, with 69, anchored the New Zealand reply, but wickets fell at regular intervals and Bob Willis's removal of Glenn Turner, lbw for 30, was a key moment. Both Wright and Mark Burgess, the New Zealand captain, were run out as England's fielding held up under pressure. Lance Cairns launched a couple of late blows, but the New Zealanders came up just short.

Man Of The Match award: Graham Gooch

The Oval: West Indies 293–6 (60 overs) beat Pakistan 250 (56.2 overs) by 43 runs

A first-wicket stand of 132 between Gordon Greenidge and Desmond Haynes, underlining their emergence as one of the great opening pairs in cricket history, gave West Indies a control of this semi-final that they never relinquished. Greenidge made 73 and Haynes 65 against some testing Pakistan bowling, and solid contributions from Viv Richards, Clive Lloyd and Collis King then made sure of a then West Indian record World Cup total. Majid Khan and Zaheer Abbas, however, gave Pakistan hope with a superb partnership of their own. Majid scored 81 and Zaheer 93, and the two majestic strokemakers put on 166 for the second wicket. Colin Croft, though, followed up dismissing both – Zaheer to a brilliant catch by Deryck Murray behind the wicket – by having Javed Miandad lbw first ball. After that triple blow, Pakistan's challenge faded away.

Man Of The Match award: Gordon Greenidge

THE 1979 WORLD CUP FINAL
23 June

Lord's: West Indies 286–9 (60 overs) beat England 194 (51 overs) by 92 runs

The combined might of three men ruined England's dream of World Cup glory. Viv Richards, Collis King and Joel Garner swept the West Indies to a successful defence of their title in a match in which England's tactics also have to be questioned. West Indies were only in discomfort when, after being put in, they were 99–4 and with most of their powerful top order batting back in the pavilion. But Richards remained, and soon the all-ticket capacity crowd of 25,000 was witnessing some of the finest batting a cup final occasion has produced. It was all-rounder King who played the most murderous shots, hitting ten fours and three sixes in an unconventional but exhilarating 66-ball 86. He dominated a fifth wicket stand of 139 but, on his eventual dismissal, Richards took over. Until then, Richards had concentrated on playing with secure professionalism, but then he began to cut loose. The innings ended with the great Antiguan walking right across his stumps to flick a hip-high full toss from Mike Hendrick into the crowd over square leg for his third six. There were 11 fours besides in an unbeaten 138 from 157 balls.

England were handicapped by the absence of the injured Bob Willis and, fatally, had decided to go into the match with only four front-line bowlers. Geoff Boycott, Graham Gooch and Wayne Larkins needed to share a minimum of 12 overs with their varied assortment of medium pacers, and how King and Richards took advantage! A total of 86 runs were plundered from the part-timers, whereas Richards himself later conceded just 35 runs from his ten overs as fifth bowler.

The other mistake England made was believing that such a large West Indian total could be overhauled by the conventional means of getting a steady start and then accelerating later. Yes, Mike Brearley and Geoff Boycott certainly did succeed in achieving a steady start, but 129 in 38 overs was a partnership that, however worthy, cost England dear. When Brearley, the captain, was caught for 64, off 130 balls, England still required another 158 from 22 overs. Boycott then departed for 57, from 105 balls, and all England could offer thereafter was some initial defiance from Gooch and Derek Randall and then a stream of desperate heaves. Ian Botham was quite brilliantly caught on the run at long-on by Richards, off Colin Croft, but it was the giant Garner who efficiently snuffed out the English challenge with a series of searing yorkers. He finished with 5–38, and four of his victims were clean bowled.

'All five of the wickets came for just four runs from 11 balls,' writes Garner in his autobiography, *Flying High*, 'and I was twice on a hat-trick. The fast bowlers on our side were particularly grateful to the England team for their tactics during their innings. Given 287 to win from 60 overs, Brearley and Boycott started the innings as if they were playing in a five-day Test. Boycott took 17 overs to reach double figures. I remember Colin Croft telling me, sometime during the course of their stay at the crease, that he hoped that neither of them would get out! By the time they were gone, it would have taken a superhuman effort from batsmen even of the calibre of Gooch and Botham to retrieve the situation.'

At one stage during the Brearley-Boycott partnership, West Indies captain

Lloyd provoked a significant amount of comment by dropping a relatively simple catch at mid-on to reprieve Boycott. Lloyd later said, 'There were a lot of people who suggested I put it down purposely just to keep him in. Not true – but it would not have been a bad tactic!'

England's middle-order had been packed with strokemakers, from Randall at three through Gooch, David Gower and Botham to Larkins at number seven. Gooch did hit 32 from 28 balls, but in truth England's approach succeeded only in spiking their own guns. Their last eight wickets fell for 11 runs in the space of just 16 balls. In the glittering captaincy record of Brearley, moreover, this defeat stands out as a day when his leadership and tactical awareness left much to be desired. Should he also have gone for the West Indian jugular after they had stumbled to 99–4 by gambling on ignoring his bit-part bowlers and throwing everything at breaking the crucial Richards-King partnership? To beat this West Indies side, England needed to be more unorthodox and aggressive, and in this match, anyway, Brearley failed the test.

Man Of The Match award: Viv Richards

THE INTERVIEW
Clive Lloyd

Lifting the World Cup for a second time was a personal triumph for Clive Lloyd, but it was only the swift decision of the West Indies Board to reinstate their many World Series Cricket players that cleared the way for Lloyd's team of champions to reassert their dominance on the biggest stage.

Even in the early stages of WSC, the West Indian public had made it very clear that they wanted the best players to be representing the West Indies. Both the Barbados and Jamaica cricket associations called for an agreement between the ICC and WSC. Then, in the middle of the two WSC seasons in Australia, the West Indies Board saw the way in which the wind was blowing in the Caribbean clearly enough to sanction a WSC series of 'Supertests' to be played in the West Indies in the early part of 1979.

There was opposition to the WSC West Indians from certain quarters of the game in the Caribbean which created some unpleasantness, but overall the leading players and administrators were pragmatic in their approach to a venture which Lloyd and his teammates had become involved in, for sound financial reasons.

So, while Australia and, to a much lesser extent, England went into the World Cup with top players still banned from playing official cricket, the West

Indies (and Pakistan) were at full strength.

Lloyd says he still felt a sense of relief, however, when in early 1979 he and the rest of the WSC West Indians received letters from the West Indies Board asking whether they would be available to play in the World Cup. 'As I saw it, we were recalled so hastily by the Board for two main reasons,' he observes in his book *Living For Cricket*. 'The first was the outright condemnation which the Board had received everywhere from the cricketing public, reflected in the resolutions passed by the Barbados and Jamaica associations. The second was financial expediency.

'Without the leading players, the Board had lost heavily and its bank balances had deteriorated from something like £150,000 in the black to a healthy sum in the red. People were simply not going to pay to watch substandard cricket at Test level.

'Our reply to the invitation to be available for the World Cup was a joint one. Following my resignation from the captaincy, the WSC players had acted collectively in withdrawing, and it was only to be expected that we acted similarly in deciding on our return.

'There were still matters to be thrashed out, such as fees and the captaincy, which would be left until we could meet directly with the Board in the Caribbean. As far as the captaincy was concerned, the feeling among the players was that, since we were being reinstated, we should revert to the position prior to my resignation and that I should be reappointed. In principle, however, we all agreed that we would be available to play.'

When Lloyd travelled to Trinidad in March 1979, he met up with Jeffrey Stollmeyer, the president of the West Indies Board and someone he had not met since his resignation from the captaincy a year earlier. He recalls, 'The first thing he said to me as he shook my hand was, "Let's let bygones be bygones. What has passed is all water under the bridge." He was charming and I got the distinct impression that he realised that the Board's initial stand was a mistake. As president of the Board, he was committed to seeing our cricket flourish in every sense of the word. It was obvious it could only do that if all of our best players were available.'

As soon as the WSC Australians had finished their Caribbean tour, in mid-April 1979, the West Indies Board decided that Lloyd should be reinstated as captain at their annual general meeting. The vote was not unanimous, but this was to be expected given the divisions of opinion throughout the cricketing world about the impact of Kerry Packer's millions.

Lloyd was told to play one 'qualifying' Shell Shield game for Guyana before being confirmed in charge of the World Cup squad, which was petty but again perhaps understandable as the West Indies officials tried to maintain at least the show of being back in control of all their players. 'I was happy and, in many ways, relieved to have the job back since I was not certain how the WSC players, who had also been named to form the nucleus of the World Cup squad, would have reacted had I been overlooked as captain,' noted Lloyd.

The reinstated captain was also initially apprehensive about how the presence of official West Indies captain Alvin Kallicharran, and the other non-WSC players in the World Cup party, would affect team spirit. But he was quickly reassured by the immediate sense of togetherness as they set out to retain the World Cup trophy. Kallicharran, despite being back in the ranks, was part of the players' tour committee and Clyde Walcott, the World Cup manager, also played his part in ensuring a common bond.

Walcott had been one of the national selectors responsible for the decisions which led to Lloyd's resignation from the captaincy, and so he could have been bitter about the past. But, said Lloyd, 'the episode which led to the split between myself and the Board was no longer relevant, and both sides treated it as such'. As for the non-WSC players, Lloyd added, 'Kalli was again an integral part of the team, as he always had been, and I was most impressed with Bacchus, Gomes and Marshall, even though they did not play a single game. 'Far from moping and complaining, they were cheerful members of a cheerful team, taking part keenly in team discussions and being very helpful in other respects.

'Having won the first World Cup, I felt even more confident this time. Seven of us who played in that inaugural tournament were still there – Deryck Murray, Greenidge, Kallicharran, Richards, King, Roberts and myself – and we had added to that list three other outstanding fast bowlers in Holding, Croft and Garner. If we lacked the number of all-rounders we had then, with Julien and Boyce, we were certainly stronger in bowling.

'In addition, most of us had played limited-overs cricket as a team consistently during the two seasons of World Series Cricket and had won the WSC International Cup on both occasions.'

As in 1975, the Lord's ground was packed with West Indian supporters intent on celebrating another World Cup triumph. Those celebrations went on into the night.

Yet once again, too, the West Indies Board showed itself to be distinctly underwhelmed at the performance of Lloyd's team. 'The 1979 World Cup victory was one which I felt meant even more than usual for West Indian cricket,' Lloyd remembers. 'We had all gone through a difficult period and this was the perfect way to signal an end to the problems. West Indies cricket was now back on its feet again.

'But again, however, our victory was treated in a very matter-of-fact way by the Board. It was almost as if everyone in the West Indies took it as a foregone conclusion that we would win. We all simply went our different ways when it was all over.'

THE CHAMPIONS

It is a measure of the greatness of the 1979 West Indies side that a certain Malcolm Marshall was included in their World Cup squad that year, although he didn't play in a single game.

Marshall, then 21, went on to become the most complete fast bowler produced by the West Indies in the two decades from 1975, when the Caribbean islands produced a seemingly endless rich seam of world-class pacemen. To the 1979 quartet of Roberts, Holding, Garner and Croft can be added Marshall, Wayne Daniel, Sylvester Clarke, Courtney Walsh, Ian Bishop and Curtly Ambrose. These were the men of power who gave the West Indies world domination.

The awesome foursome of 1979, however, take some beating, even in the West Indian pantheon. Roberts was the leader of the pack, the oldest and most experienced of the four, and an unsmiling, cold assassin. His expressionless face was genuinely chilling to batsmen. Roberts was as quiet on the field as he was off it, but this was not shyness. There was an intensity about the Antiguan, a silent rage. His bouncer was skiddy, quicker and highly dangerous. He hit batsmen more often than others, but he was a fine technician too and, like all truly great bowlers, accurate.

Holding's approach to the wicket was a thing of beauty: light-footed enough that many umpires swore they could not hear him approaching behind them, and athletic in the manner of a man who ran for Jamaica and was of Olympic standard at 400 metres. Charming off the field, and a magnet to female company, he was deadly on it. The fastest of the four, Holding took wickets with sheer speed. However, he too knew how to bowl and, when he put his mind to it, could be as miserly in length and line as the canniest medium-pacer.

Garner would have been many people's choice as the best limited-overs bowler of his generation, while at Test level he undoubtedly suffered from rarely getting the new ball. Nevertheless, his Test record of 259 wickets from 58 matches at an average of 20.97 also reveals just what a class act he was, as stock bowler or strike bowler. At six foot eight inches tall, Garner was a giant among men in every sense. He was also genial and gentle and by far the softer character among the four. 'Joel doesn't really want to bowl fast; it's not in his nature,' said Ian Botham once. To batsmen, however, he was always a nightmare with his steep bounce and shattering yorkers. And when he was really pumped up, which was rare, his usual long lope to the crease became a terrifying charge. He could then be genuinely quick, all right, but even when he settled himself in for longer spells, his accuracy and mastery of his craft made him a tough prospect.

Croft's fiery temperament quickly earned him the reputation of being the nastiest of the quartet, and like Garner he was of well above average height and immensely strong. Croft's action, however, made him even more of a handful. In delivery stride he would lurch to his left and thus angle the ball in awkwardly to the right hander and right across in front of the left-handed batsman. Again, because of this angle of attack, which was far more marked than Walsh's in-slant, for instance, Croft used to hit a lot of players. Fast, lifting deliveries would jam into a right-hander's ribs or force him to fend the ball off from in front of his face and chest. The slip and gully cordon, meanwhile, would really come into play when Croft bowled against a left hander. Winning lbw decisions, of course, was a difficult proposition for him, and Croft's accuracy was never as dependable as his three fellow scalp-hunters, but at his best he was frightening.

The additional collective strength of Roberts, Holding, Garner and Croft, of course, was that each of their individual styles complemented the others'. They all pursued their quarries with different methods, but they were all deadly.

In Test cricket against the West Indies there was no respite from this all-pace assault, especially as the ICC was shamefully lax in the late 1970s and 1980s about plunging over-rates. At least, in limited-overs cricket, opponents knew that the fast men could bowl just four-fifths of the overs due to be delivered to them. According to theory, therefore, the West Indies could be vulnerable to an attack on their fifth bowler.

Like many theories, however, this all too often foundered on reality. In Richards and King, the West Indies in 1979 possessed two top-order batsmen who could be classified as genuine all-rounders in one-day cricket. King bowled 30 overs during the competition, conceding 128 runs and taking two wickets, while Richards delivered 18 overs for 87 runs and three wickets.

The other theory doing the rounds in 1979 was that the West Indies could be vulnerable because of their longish tail: Roberts, coming in at number eight after wicket-keeper Deryck Murray, was considered by some to be two places too high.

Certainly, in the final itself, England almost made it through to the tail early in the innings by reducing the West Indians to 99–4. That was when Richards and King took the game away from them, however, and the truth of the matter was that the West Indies also possessed enough class batsmen for it to be highly unusual that all of them should fail at the same time.

The top five batsmen in the West Indies order were of world class; King was a dangerous hitter, as he proved with the innings of his life in the final, and the veteran Murray could be depended upon to produce runs when his team needed them most. Furthermore, of the four fast bowlers, it was only Croft who was a negligible force with the bat.

The other factor in the West Indies' success of 1979 lay in the political backdrop to the tournament. It was only on the eve of the World Cup that the Australian cricket authorities announced that an agreement had been reached between themselves and Kerry Packer. This promised, in time, to heal the gaping wounds that the Packer Affair had left in world cricket, particularly in Australia itself, and to a certain extent in England and Pakistan too, although the Pakistanis – like the West Indies – did decide to select their World Cup party from both their Packer and official players.

It was the West Indies, however, who proved most adept at letting bygones be bygones. Even when the official West Indian team – then touring India, under Kallicharran's captaincy – issued a statement opposing the policy of welcoming back the World Series Cricket players for World Cup selection, it ended up causing few ripples. The West Indies Board readily welcomed back the rebels and were also keen to allow Clive Lloyd to continue where he had left off as captain.

The World Cup squad of 14 was made up of ten WSC men, plus Kallicharran, Marshall, Faoud Bacchus and Larry Gomes from the official team, and all the evidence from the players concerned point to the immediate harmony attained. Only Kallicharran, in fact, took part in the World Cup matches, but Marshall, Bacchus and Gomes were all to play important roles in the future development of the West Indies as the world's best team.

THE PRIZES

Increased prices meant that the 1979 World Cup produced increased gate receipts of £359,700 (almost double the 1975 figure), despite the comparative fall in attendances.

The West Indies received £10,000 for winning, and England, the runners-up, collected a cheque for £4,000. The two losing semi-finalists were awarded £2,000 per team.

The continuing sponsorship of Prudential (this time worth £250,000) allowed a profit of £350,000 to be made, and at their annual meeting, which immediately followed the tournament, the ICC agreed to keep the World Cup as a four-yearly event and to hold it once more in England in 1983.

THE QUOTES

'The World Series Cricket players had been recalled to the official West Indies side, and although there had been some anxiety about how the players who had represented the West Indies in India while we were playing for WSC would react to us, we found those included in our side to be congenial and understanding.' Joel Garner on West Indies harmony at the 1979 World Cup.

'Our fielding [in the 1979 tournament] was extraordinarily good throughout. Clive Lloyd managed to mould the group into a professional team of the highest standards, with the ex-WSC players forming the nucleus.' Garner again.

TEAM OF THE TOURNAMENT?

Gordon Greenidge (West Indies)
Majid Khan (Pakistan)
Viv Richards (West Indies)
Graham Gooch (England)
Clive Lloyd (West Indies, captain)
Collis King (West Indies)
Deryck Murray (West Indies, wicket-keeper)
Andy Roberts (West Indies)
Joel Garner (West Indies)
Michael Holding (West Indies)
Colin Croft (West Indies)

THE ROAD TO 1983...

In the winter of 1979–80, the West Indies underlined their utter dominance of world cricket by beating a full-strength Australian team 2–0 in a three-match Test series played in Australia. This result was made all the more impressive by the fact that Greg Chappell's side thrashed England 3–0 in a three-match series that ran concurrently.

The Australians, however, were on a downward spiral as their great side of the 1970s began to age together. They managed to win back the Ashes in 1982–83, after failing in England in 1981, but by the time the 1983 World Cup came around they were at the start of one of the most barren periods in their proud history.

This was the golden age of the all-rounder, with Ian Botham, Imran Khan, Kapil Dev and Richard Hadlee all bestriding the world stage. Australia did not have anyone to compare, while the West Indies merely kept churning out the wins in both forms of the game on the back of their magnificent fast bowlers and imperious batsmen.

On 17 February 1982, having been awarded senior status by the ICC the previous year, Sri Lanka played their first Test match. Their elevation was reward for several skilled and spirited showings in World Cup competition and was a considerable boost not just to cricket on that lovely isle but throughout Asia.

Chapter 6

1983: Indian Giant Killers

The West Indies arrived in England for the third World Cup still the lords of all they surveyed and hot favourites to keep their hands on the trophy. What a shock they were in for, as Kapil Dev's unfancied Indians caused one of the sporting upsets of all time in a remarkable final at Lord's.

India, however, quite deserved to win. What is not generally remembered is that they defeated the mighty West Indians twice during the tournament, not just once.

Moreover, it was a result, to be frank, that energised world cricket. The all-conquering West Indies had based their success on the high-octane performances of their four-man fast-bowling battery, and it was all getting a little bit too predictable, even boring. India's triumph struck a chord with romantics, renewing belief around the globe that cricket's traditional ability to embrace the unpredictable was intact, after all. It was such a relief, and a release!

The tournament, too, had eschewed the predictable structure of its predecessor of 1979. That had mirrored the inaugural event of 1975, but this World Cup was almost double the size of its two younger brothers. There were 27 matches instead of 15, with the group stages expanded to allow each team to play the other twice. This was for the dual purpose of reducing the chance of a team being eliminated due to bad weather and enabling a number of matches to be taken around the country and away from the Test grounds that had so far monopolised the event. The new venues added to the World Cup roster were Tunbridge Wells, Swansea, Worcester, Bristol, Southampton, Taunton, Leicester, Derby and Chelmsford.

As it turned out, cricket's limited-overs showpiece again proved to be blessed by the English weather. An unnaturally wet May was followed by a largely dry and sunny June, and only three matches required the use of the reserve day.

The sun came out, *Wisden* records, 'as if by providence', following an early season in which Lord's had lost 14 whole days' play and Gloucestershire, by 3 June, had still to manage a single full day's cricket.

Once more, however, and despite the increased commercial awareness that had followed the Packer schism, television failed to impact on the scheduling. The 27 matches were due to be played on just seven different dates – five for the group matches (again planned to take place in clusters of four matches per day), one for both semi-finals and one for the final. Indeed, despite its increase in size, the tournament lasted for just 17 days.

The matches were again 60-overs-per-side affairs, but the advance of limited-overs expertise around the world led to the authorities making a significant alteration to the playing conditions. Unlike in the previous World Cups, umpires were given dispensation to apply a stricter interpretation of what constituted a wide or a bouncer (in effect, another form of wide).

Sri Lanka, now a fully-fledged Test nation, still won just one match – as they had in 1979 – but Zimbabwe, qualifying by winning the ICC Trophy in 1982, also displayed just what an emerging cricket nation it had become since the country had won independence in 1980. As Rhodesia, it had supplied some fine cricketers to past South African Test sides, and several of the country's current team had gained first-class experience by representing Rhodesia in the Currie Cup. Now they were going it alone and, by beating Australia in memorable fashion at Trent Bridge, they showed they needed to be taken seriously. The Australian attack that day? Lawson, Hogg, Lillee and Thomson.

With hindsight, it's tempting to speculate about how much more Zimbabwean cricket might have developed in the latter half of the 1980s and early 1990s if the country had been given the stimulus of becoming a Test nation on the back of its team's 1983 World Cup performance.

The example of the time it took Sri Lanka to make a real impact at world level is revealing, because the Sri Lankan authorities had the massive advantage of cricket already being the number-one sport among their population. Zimbabwe, with its need (still) to spread the game to a black community which worships football, could certainly have done with being granted Test status far earlier than it finally was, in 1992.

In the Zimbabwean World Cup squad of 1983, too, was a 17-year-old Graeme Hick. Though he did not get a game, his talent was obvious. How much better for his career would it have been if, instead of deciding to spend seven years qualifying for England, he had been given the chance of going straight into Test cricket at the age of 18 or 19? As it was, however, he had turned into something of a flawed genius by 1991, when he at last made his Test debut – under enormous pressure – against the West Indies.

But Hick didn't get the opportunity to play Test and full-time one-day international cricket for the land of his birth for those eight prime years from 1983. Other fine cricketers, like Dave Houghton, Peter Rawson, Kevin Curran, Andy Pycroft and John Traicos, were similarly denied the reward that their efforts of 1983 demanded. Looking back, it is such a waste.

THE MATCHES
9 June
The Oval: England 322–6 (60 overs) beat New Zealand 216 (59 overs) by 106 runs. Man Of The Match award: Allan Lamb

Swansea: Pakistan 338–5 (60 overs) beat Sri Lanka 288–9 (60 overs) by 50 runs. Man Of The Match award: Mohsin Khan

Trent Bridge: Zimbabwe 239–6 (60 overs) beat Australia 226–7 (60 overs) by 13 runs. Man Of The Match award: Duncan Fletcher

9-10 June
Old Trafford: India 262–8 (60 overs) beat West Indies 228 (54.1 overs) by 34 runs. Man Of The Match award: Yashpal Sharma

Three matches in the first round of group games, including Zimbabwe's sensational victory over Australia, were finished on the scheduled first day, but it was the game that spilled over into the reserve day, at Old Trafford, which proved to be the most significant result in terms of the rest of the tournament.

Yashpal Sharma was the inspiration, with 89 from 127 balls, as India upset the odds to beat the West Indies and gain what was only their second Word Cup victory (the previous win was against East Africa in 1975). But what was most interesting was the way their battery of medium-pacers, plus the left-arm spin of Ravi Shastri, also proved more potent than the four-pronged West Indian fast attack, in which only Michael Holding stood out. A blip, or a forerunner of things to come? It was a question soon to be answered.

Zimbabwe's stunning success against the Australians was also a personal triumph for Duncan Fletcher, the captain. To modern eyes, Fletcher is best-known for the coaching expertise which has seen him gain plaudits with Western Province, Glamorgan and now England. In 1983, however, he was a 34-year-old all-rounder coming to the end of a worthy playing career. This was his moment in the sun. Coming in at number six, with his side 86–4 (and soon to be 94–5), Fletcher scored an unbeaten 69 and figured in stands of 70, with Kevin Curran, and an unbroken 75 with Ian Butchart. Then, by taking 4–42 from 11 overs of medium pace, Fletcher reduced Australia to 138–5 and a situation from which not even an unbeaten 50 from Rod Marsh could save them.

Pakistan's victory against Sri Lanka set a then record aggregate of 626 runs for a World Cup match, with Mohsin Khan, Zaheer Abbas, Javed Miandad and Imran Khan all enjoying the West Walian air with attractive half-centuries. Brendon Kuruppu and Guy de Alwis, however, responded with bright innings of 72 and 59 not out respectively to show that the Sri Lankans still had plenty of spirit.

England, meanwhile, launched their own campaign by blitzing the New Zealand bowling attack on a typically true Oval surface. Richard Hadlee's class meant he escaped the carnage with figures of 1–26 from 12 overs, but poor Martin Snedden – now New Zealand Cricket's chief executive – saw his own 12 overs disappear for 105 runs, a limited-overs record! Allan Lamb's brilliant 102 took just 105 balls, and only Martin Crowe (97 from 118 balls) made England's bowlers suffer in anything like the same way.

11 June

Taunton: England 333–9 (60 overs) beat Sri Lanka 286 (58 overs) by 47 runs. Man Of The Match award: David Gower

Leicester: Zimbabwe 155 (51.4 overs) lost to India 157–5 (37.3 overs) by five wickets. Man Of The Match award: Madan Lal

11-12 June

Edgbaston: New Zealand 238–9 (60 overs) beat Pakistan 186 (55.2 overs) by 52 runs. Man Of The Match award: Abdul Qadir

Headingley: West Indies 252–9 (60 overs) beat Australia 151 (30.3 overs) by 101 runs. Man Of The Match award: Winston Davis

Leg-spinner Abdul Qadir won the Man Of The Match award on his one-day international debut for following up his bewitching 4–21 with a defiant unbeaten 41 in a losing cause. The man who made the real match-winning contribution, however, as New Zealand overpowered Pakistan, was Richard Hadlee, who had Mohsin Khan lbw with the third ball of the innings before bowling Zaheer Abbas three balls later. Then, after Lance Cairns had also removed Mudassar Nazar with his second delivery to leave Pakistan 0–3, Hadlee dismissed Imran Khan later in his new ball spell to make the total 22–4. From there, despite some defiance from Javed Miandad, Wasim Bari and Qadir, it was New Zealand's match.

At 32–3, the West Indies were facing another mini-crisis after being sent in by Australia at Headingley. But Larry Gomes and Faoud Bacchus, the two unsung members of the West Indian batting line-up, rescued them with a fifth-wicket stand of 76 after Gomes (78) had initially put on 46 with Clive Lloyd. Eventually, the West Indies built a commanding total and Winston Davis, one of the replacements called in because of injuries to Joel Garner and Malcolm Marshall, soon made it look an insurmountable target by wrecking the Australian batting. Davis, from the Windwards, was a hurricane force and finished with 7–51.

A scintillating 130 from 120 balls by David Gower at Taunton gave the Sri Lankans the same sort of run-mountain to climb as they had faced at Swansea two days earlier. They made a similarly spirited reply, too, with Guy de Alwis, the wicket-keeper, coming in at number nine, once again finishing up with a hard-hit but unbeaten half-century. There was an entertaining 56 from Duleep Mendis, too, but no one could match the majesty of Gower, who struck five sixes and 12 fours and featured in stands of 96 with Allan Lamb (53) and 98 with Ian Gould (35). Somerset's Vic Marks, playing on his home ground, took 5–39 with his off-breaks, but Ian Botham, the centre of attention as he also made his first England appearance on home soil, was run out for a first-ball duck and then took 0–60!

Zimbabwe, meanwhile, were brought back down to earth by India, who continued their fine start to the competition by bowling out the giant-killers for 155 – their seamers once more to the fore – and then easing to a five-wicket victory. Sandeep Patil hit an attractive 50 from 54 balls and added 69 for the third wicket with Mohinder Amarnath.

13 June

Lord's: Pakistan 193–8 (60 overs) lost to England 199–2 (50.4 overs) by eight wickets. Man Of The Match award: Zaheer Abbas

Bristol: Sri Lanka 206 (56.1 overs) lost to New Zealand 209–5 (39.2 overs) by five wickets. Man Of The Match award: Richard Hadlee

Trent Bridge: Australia 320–9 (60 overs) beat India 158 (37.5 overs) by 162 runs. Man Of The Match award: Trevor Chappell

Worcester: Zimbabwe 217–7 (60 overs) lost to West Indies 218–2 (48.3 overs) by eight wickets. Man Of The Match award: Gordon Greenidge

Only an unbeaten 83 off 104 balls from Zaheer Abbas kept Pakistan from a trouncing by England at Lord's. As it was, after a stylish 48 from David Gower, England ran out comfortable winners as a result of an unbroken stand of 106 between Graeme Fowler (78 not out) and Allan Lamb.

Richard Hadlee took 5–25 in three deadly spells to spearhead New Zealand's emphatic victory against Sri Lanka. Only a fourth-wicket partnership of 71 between Duleep Mendis and Ranjan Madugalle (60) held up the Kiwis for long in the field. Glenn Turner and John Wright then replied with a speedy opening stand of 89, and Geoff Howarth's 76 from 79 balls took New Zealand to the brink of their target.

Trevor Chappell claimed his own page in the bulging family cricketing scrapbook by bursting India's bubble with a superb innings of 110 at Trent Bridge. Chappell was joined in a second wicket stand of 144 by his captain, Kim Hughes, who made 52, and although Kapil Dev later picked up 5–43, an unbeaten 66 from 73 balls by Graham Yallop ensured an intimidating Australian total. It proved far too much for the Indians, who slid to 158 despite some typical late fireworks from Kapil (40). Ken MacLeay, the medium-pacer, picked up 6–39 as the Indian innings self-destructed.

Brave innings of 71 not out by Duncan Fletcher and 54 from Dave Houghton enabled Zimbabwe to emerge from their first meeting with the West Indies with their heads held high. A total of 217–7 was never likely to embarrass the West Indians, but Peter Rawson's two strikes with the new ball did leave them at 23–2 before Gordon Greenidge, with an unbeaten 105, and Larry Gomes (75 not out) saw them home.

15 June

Edgbaston: England 234 (55.2 overs) lost to New Zealand 238–8 (59.5 overs) by two wickets. Man Of The Match award: Jeremy Coney

The Oval: West Indies 282–9 (60 overs) beat India 216 (53.1 overs) by 66 runs. Man Of The Match award: Viv Richards

16 June

Headingley: Pakistan 235–7 (60 overs) beat Sri Lanka 224 (58.3 overs) by 11 runs. Man Of The Match award: Abdul Qadir

Southampton: Australia 272–7 (60 overs) beat Zimbabwe 240 (59.5 overs) by 32 runs. Man Of The Match award: Dave Houghton

Another brilliant innings by David Gower was not enough for England against New Zealand, who won with just one ball remaining. Gower struck four sixes and six fours in an unbeaten 92 from 96 balls after Graeme Fowler (69) had provided the early groundwork. But with Richard Hadlee and Lance Cairns taking three wickets apiece, the England middle and late order fell away too quickly. Crucially, 4.4 overs were left unused – a cardinal sin in the one-day arena. Bob Willis knocked over both New Zealand openers with the new ball and also took two more wickets later in a desperate bid to prevent his side from losing, but Jeremy Coney and Hadlee built on Geoff Howarth's earlier 60 by adding a vital 70 together for the seventh wicket. Hadlee fell to Willis for 31, but Coney remained 66 not out at the end. Four runs were required from the final over, bowled by Paul Allott, and the scores were level when John Bracewell struck the fifth ball to the boundary.

Viv Richards was in a rather subdued mood at the Oval, hitting just seven boundaries in his 119, but it was still the best innings of the game as the West Indies made it 1–1 for the tournament with India by beating them convincingly. Richards faced 146 balls, featuring in stands of 101 and 80 for the second and third wickets with Desmond Haynes and Clive Lloyd respectively. Mohinder Amarnath, relishing once again the battle against the Caribbean pacemen, hit a fine 80 in reply, but Dilip Vengsarkar had to retire hurt after being struck in the mouth by a lifting ball from the fit-again Malcolm Marshall.

Sri Lanka twice seemed to be getting the better of Pakistan at Leeds, only for their hopes to be cruelly dashed. First, from 43–5, Pakistan were rallied by their captain, Imran Khan, who scored an unbeaten 102 and found in Shahid Mahboob (77) a resolute sixth wicket partner. They added 144, and Imran then stayed to ensure a defendable total was raised. At 162–2, however, following skilful contributions from Roy Dias and Duleep Mendis, the Sri Lankans looked to be in complete command again. However, they had reckoned without Abdul Qadir, whose magical leg-breaks and googlies now brought him three wickets in eight balls and 5–44 in all. Sri Lanka lost seven wickets for 37 runs before their last pair of De Mel and John spiritedly made 25 of the 37 runs required for victory from the remaining six overs before Sarfraz Nawaz struck the final blow.

Australia avenged their earlier beating at the hands of Zimbabwe with a 32-run success at Northlands Road, but not before the Zimbabwean sixth-wicket pair of Dave Houghton (84) and Kevin Curran (35) gave them a fright by adding 103 in 17 overs. Graeme Wood's 73 had formed the basis of a decent Australian total, but the gameness of the Zimbabwe effort again underlined the quality of the sole non-Test-playing country in the competition.

18 June

Old Trafford: Pakistan 232–8 (60 overs) lost to England 233–3 (57.2 overs) by seven wickets. Man Of The Match award: Graeme Fowler

Derby: New Zealand 181 (58.2 overs) lost to Sri Lanka 184–7 (52.5 overs) by three wickets. Man Of The Match award: Asantha de Mel

Lord's: Australia 273–6 (60 overs) lost to West Indies 276–3 (57.5 overs) by seven wickets. Man Of The Match award: Viv Richards

Tunbridge Wells: India 266–8 (60 overs) beat Zimbabwe 235 (57 overs) by 31 runs. Man Of The Match award: Kapil Dev

A highly professional victory over Pakistan in Manchester earned England qualification for the semi-finals. England bowled and fielded well as a unit, and Ian Botham scored a direct hit to run out Javed Miandad for 67 just when Pakistan's most accomplished batsman was looking to accelerate the scoring. Graeme Fowler (69) and Chris Tavare (58) then set up England's equally efficient display with the bat by putting on 115 for the first wicket.

Sri Lanka's only win of the tournament hit hard New Zealand's hopes of reaching the knockout stage and a place in the last four. Asantha de Mel, the underrated Sri Lankan fast bowler, was the chief destroyer, with 5–32, but New Zealand at least gave themselves a fighting chance when Martin Snedden and Ewen Chatfield cobbled together a last-wicket stand of 65. Sri Lanka, at 129–2, were coasting home, but then Brendon Kuruppu was caught and bowled for 62 and the middle order fell away alarmingly. The classy Roy Dias remained, however, and went on to finish 64 not out as Guy de Alwis provided overdue lasting support.

The West Indies unfurled their true batting power at Lord's to pass, with almost arrogant ease, a challenging Australian total. Kim Hughes, David Hookes and Graham Yallop all hit splendid half-centuries, and Rod Marsh came up with heavy-duty hitting at the end, but Gordon Greenidge (90) and Viv Richards (95 not out) simply cruised along. Lillee and Thomson, now both shadows of their former selves, went wicketless and conceded 116 runs between them from the 23 overs they delivered.

A defining moment, not just of this World Cup but also of cricket history, occurred in the beautiful but unlikely setting of the Nevill Ground, Tunbridge Wells, when Kapil Dev single-handedly turned around the fortunes of his country. After perhaps unwisely choosing to bat first on an initially seaming pitch, Indian captain Kapil found himself walking to the crease with his side at 9–4. Soon, indeed, it was 17–5 as Peter Rawson and Kevin Curran sliced through the top half of the Indian batting order. India's very World Cup future – in terms of qualification for the semi-finals – was hanging by a thread, but what a golden thread it proved to be! Kapil's epic 175 not out contained six sixes and 16 fours and was the highest individual score in the World Cup. The purple rhododendrons that ring the Nevill in June provided an imperious backdrop to the splendour and cleanliness of Kapil's strokeplay, and it is an innings which has rightly passed into legend. A week later, of course, India were world champions and Kapil was standing triumphant on the Lord's pavilion balcony, but here he was reacting to a desperate situation by counter-attacking in glorious fashion while Roger Binny, Madan Lal and finally Syed Kirmani hung on grimly at the other end.

A remarkable match almost had a twist in the tail, too, with Curran blazing away himself to reach 73 as Zimbabwe made a good fist of reaching their target of 267. Indeed, it wasn't until Curran was ninth out at 230, in the 56th over, that India could begin to breathe more easily.

20 June

Headingley: Sri Lanka 136 (50.4 overs) lost to England 137–1 (24.1 overs). Man Of The Match award: Bob Willis

Trent Bridge: Pakistan 261–3 (60 overs) beat New Zealand 250 (59.1) by 11 runs. Man Of The Match award: Imran Khan

Chelmsford: India 247 (55.5 overs) beat Australia 129 (38.2 overs) by 118 runs. Man Of The Match award: Roger Binny

Edgbaston: Zimbabwe 171 (60 overs) lost to West Indies 172–0 (45.1 overs) by ten wickets. Man Of The Match award: Faoud Bacchus

The shortest match of the tournament saw England's bowlers take full advantage of a seaming surface at Leeds to rout the Sri Lankans. Bob Willis, who had won the important toss, took 1–9 from nine overs and Ian Botham picked up 2–12 from his nine. Sri Lanka fought hard to post some sort of total after slipping to 54-6, but Graeme Fowler then hit an unbeaten 81 as England made short work of their target.

Pakistan overcame twin obstacles to earn a place in the semi-finals. Not only did they need to beat close rivals New Zealand, but they had to score enough runs from their 60 overs to make sure that their run rate remained better than the New Zealanders throughout the competition. This latter aim was achieved in some style by Zaheer Abbas (103 not out) and Imran Khan (79 not out), who added an unbroken 147 for the fourth wicket that included the considerable feat of plundering 47 from Richard Hadlee's last five overs. Even though Imran was unable to bowl throughout the tournament because of injury, the Pakistan attack was still potent enough to make New Zealand struggle in reply. That they finally launched a meaningful challenge was due to Jeremy Coney and John Bracewell, who responded to the equation of needing 85 from the final ten overs by smashing a 59-run stand in just five. In the end, 13 were required from the last over, to be bowled by Sarfraz, but by then Bracewell had fallen for 34 and Coney, attempting a second run from the first ball of the over, was run out by Imran's throw. Pakistan were through to the last four, their run rate 4.01 to New Zealand's 3.94.

Australia were humbled at Chelmsford, where they would have qualified for the semi-finals had they beaten India, whose run-rate was lower. Instead, after a sloppy performance, they were thrashed by 118 runs. David Hookes captained Australia in place of the injured Kim Hughes, and Lillee was also absent, but there could be no excuse for the 15 no balls and nine wides that led to extras of 37 being the second highest score during an Indian innings which began slowly but finally prospered thanks to consistent contributions all the way down the order. Australia's batting then foundered embarrassingly upon the gentle medium-paced swing of Roger Binny (4-29) and Madan Lal (4-20).

After being reduced to 42-5 by the pace and bounce of Malcolm Marshall and a fit-again Joel Garner, reaching 171 represented something of a triumph for Zimbabwe, for whom Kevin Curran hit a bold 62. The Zimbabweans then bowled tidily enough themselves, but Desmond Haynes (88 not out) and Faoud Bacchus (80 not out) batted serenely to the target.

SEMI-FINALS
22 June

Old Trafford: England 213 (60 overs) lost to India 217–4 (54.4 overs) by six wickets. Man Of The Match award: Mohinder Amarnath

The Oval: Pakistan 184–8 (60 overs) lost to West Indies 188–2 (48.4 overs) by eight wickets. Man Of The Match award: Viv Richards

A slow, low pitch at Manchester was tailor-made for the Indian seamers and looked like mitigating against England's chances. True enough, after a brisk start against the new ball, the England innings began to misfire against accurate bowling of no real pace, while the Indian batsmen seemed to be able to play far more shots against the extra pace of the England attack. The run outs of both Allan Lamb and Ian Gould did not help the English cause, either, and by the end Yashpal Sharma (61) and Sandeep Patil (51 not out) were able to play some joyous shots as they sped India to a memorable win.

The West Indies managed to get their first-choice but injury-troubled fast-bowling combination into the field for only the second time in the tournament, and the result was a Pakistan struggle to post any kind of target on a good pitch at the Oval. The Pakistanis also badly missed Javed Miandad, who had been struck down with flu, and Mohsin Khan's anchor role of 70 was the only innings of substance. In contrast, Viv Richards (80 not out) and Larry Gomes (50 not out) put on an unbroken 132 to take the West Indies into their third World Cup final out of three.

THE 1983 WORLD CUP FINAL
25 June

Lord's: India 183 (54.4 overs) beat West Indies 140 (52 overs) by 43 runs. Man Of The Match award: Mohinder Amarnath

A punishment for West Indian hubris, or a reward for Indian spirit? Whatever, there was an epic, Olympian feel to this third World Cup final as the overwhelming favourites toppled to defeat in a low-scoring but highly dramatic and absorbing contest.

First, after the early fall of Sunil Gavaskar, there were heroic innings from Kris Srikkanth and Mohinder Amarnath as the awesome foursome of Roberts, Garner, Marshall and Holding strove to sweep all before them. Srikkanth hooked Roberts for four, pulled him for six and then square drove a pitched-up express to the Tavern boundary.

Srikkanth was later lbw to Marshall for 38, while Amarnath hung on grimly for 26, but at least they had shown that the West Indian pacemen could be held at bay for a while. Sandeep Patil injected a little acceleration with 27 from 29 balls, and Kapil Dev included three fours in his eight-ball 15, but otherwise it was hard labour against the best and meanest attack in the world, bravely though the Indian tailenders tried to contribute to at least a defendable score.

At the halfway stage, however, it was barely conceivable that the West Indies would be capable of losing, let alone by as many as 43 runs, and despite the failure of Gordon Greenidge – who was bowled offering no stroke – the game seemed there for the taking when Viv Richards arrived at the crease.

Soon, Richards was imposing his will on the Indians with seven boundaries in a quickfire 33. Then, however, came the turning point: Madan Lal, barely above medium pace, tried a cheeky bouncer and Richards skied his instinctive hook. Kapil Dev, running back towards the mid-wicket boundary, clung onto an awkward catch, and now there was hope. Madan Lal, inspired, followed up with the wickets of Desmond Haynes and Larry Gomes – all three of his wickets coming for just six runs in 19 balls – and the West Indies were in big trouble once Clive Lloyd had driven to mid-off and Faoud Bacchus was caught at the wicket.

From 76–6, it would take a mighty effort from the West Indies' lower order to pull off victory, and for a while it seemed as if Jeffrey Dujon and Marshall were equal to the task. They added 43 before Amarnath's gentle seamers wrapped up the game for India. Amarnath took 3–12 from seven overs and, with Kapil Dev dismissing Roberts, the Indian celebrations could begin.

THE INTERVIEW
Kapil Dev

The seed of the tactics India used to such glorious effect in the 1983 World Cup were sown in one of the most unlikely places in the cricket globe: Berbice, in up-country Guyana. It was there, in March, three months before the start of the tournament, that India found themselves playing against the West Indies in a one-day international. It was a blameless pitch, of no great pace, and India had racked up 282 with the bat – at that time the biggest total that had been made against the West Indians in limited-overs international cricket. More to the point, however, was the way in which India had managed to defend their score and win the match. The medium pace of Balwinder Singh Sandhu and the captain, Kapil Dev, had been most effective in keeping the powerful West Indies batting under control, as long as the bowlers kept to a disciplined line and length.

Kapil says the Indian team remembered that experience when they arrived in England for the World Cup, and found themselves playing their first group game against the West Indies at Old Trafford. Once again, India batted first and this time made 262. And again the West Indian batsmen could not shake off the attentions of India's medium-pacers and were bowled out for 228. 'We had faith in our medium pacers throughout the World Cup,' said Kapil, 'because that faith and self-belief in our approach had been born during those two victories against the great West Indians at Berbice and Old Trafford. To beat the West Indies in their own country, especially, was practically unheard of in those days. Yes, those two results were the key to our success.'

Kapil himself was the quickest of the Indian seam attack and a world-class all-rounder in an era remarkably blessed with others of similar talent like Imran Khan, Ian Botham and Richard Hadlee. But Kapil was nowhere near as quick as those other three great all-rounders, nor as fast as the fastest of his generation: the half-a-dozen or more top West Indians; the Australians Lillee, Thomson, Lawson and Hogg; or the banned South Africans Procter, Rice and Le Roux.

What Kapil had as a bowler was the ability to bend the ball in the air, or seam it off the pitch. He had a cunning and patience that perhaps was matched only by Hadlee, the surgically precise New Zealander.

Moreover, what Kapil saw in India's limited attack was an ability to bowl with collective discipline, to build pressure for mutual benefit – and to use likely conditions in England to their best advantage.

India, for decades, had relied so much upon their great spinners that this was a radical departure from tradition. But, as Kapil quickly realised, the confines of one-day cricket made his plan workable in English conditions. In Test cricket, you need the penetration of pace or spin to bowl people out; in one-day cricket, containment in itself is just as likely to bring wickets.

So, in addition to his deceptively innocuous new ball partner, Sandhu, the Indian captain built a game-plan around the experienced medium-paced all-rounders Madan Lal and Roger Binny and the dobbing swing and seam of Mohinder Amarnath, a class batsman who was also battle-hardened enough mentally to be relied upon to keep his nerve under the pressure of combat. In reserve was the slow left-arm spin of Ravi Shastri, another fully-fledged all-rounder.

'For the World Cup we decided, in normal conditions, to bat first if possible and then to keep the pressure on the opposition with tight line and length bowling,' said Kapil.

Crucially, conditions largely favoured Kapil's tactics, although it is revealing that, on a much quicker and harder pitch at the Oval, midway through the tournament, India were well beaten by the West Indies in their second group fixture.

Kapil's own brilliance got them out of the mire at Tunbridge Wells, against Zimbabwe, however, and Binny, Madal Lal and Sandhu took all ten wickets between them when India made sure of their qualification for the semi-finals by trouncing Australia at Chelmsford.

Then, in the semi-final itself, against England, the slow, low bounce of the Old Trafford pitch again played into India's hands. They were now in the final itself, and even bigger underdogs.

Once more, however, the nature of the pitch turned the match into a low-scoring scrap, with the game turning on one false stroke early in the West Indies reply. Fittingly, the ball was delivered by Madan Lal, who took 17 wickets during the tournament and, with Binny (18 wickets), was at the heart of India's effort in the field. A surprise short ball, it was mishooked by Viv Richards for Kapil, running back towards mid-wicket, to take the catch.

'Getting Richards out then was the key for us,' added Kapil. 'After Greenidge had gone early, Viv batted at his most imperious, as though he thought he was destined to repeat his great century in the final four years earlier. But Madan Lal tempted him to mistime a hook and suddenly it was 50–2 and the tempo had changed.

'Clive Lloyd's injury was another factor. He pulled a muscle and was reduced to hobbling around at the wicket when he batted.

'But above all, our medium-pacers did it for us. They took all ten wickets again in the final, with both Madan Lal and Amarnath taking three.'

THE CHAMPIONS

As sporting miracles go, the World Cup win by India in 1983 is right up there. They survived being drawn in the group alongside West Indies – the champions and overwhelming favourites – and Australia, they survived being 17–5 against Zimbabwe, and they survived a semi-final meeting with hosts England in which they were by some distance the second favourites. And they also cocked a snook at the bookmakers, who had quoted them at 66–1 outsiders before the tournament began – possibly as a result of them being bowled out by the Minor Counties for 135 at Monks Risborough in a warm-up match on 4 June and beaten by 19 runs!

Moreover, of course, they survived the final itself, despite being bowled out by the mighty West Indies for just 183 and then seeing their opponents race to 50–1 in reply with the incomparable Vivian Richards bestriding a Lord's stage he had made his own on many previous appearances there for both his country and Somerset, his county.

What followed, with the West Indies collapsing to 140 all out against India's assortment of little medium-pacers, has been described as a surreal experience by many of those who were on the ground to see the drama unfold. It was a cricketing version of David slaying Goliath.

In a historic sense, too, what makes India's triumph even more remarkable is that it was obtained without a scrap of help from the two areas of the game that has given them, traditionally, their greatest strength: world-class spinners and a succession of world-class batsmen.

The age of Bedi, Chandrasekhar, Prasanna and Venkat had passed, and India, remarkably, had been left with no worthy successors to that great quartet of the late 1960s and 1970s. Only the slow left-armers of Ravi Shastri and the occasional off-breaks of Kirti Azad constituted spin in India's 1983 World Cup campaign; and both Shastri and Azad were played primarily as batsmen.

Moreover, India won the Cup without any major contributions from either Sunil Gavaskar or Dilip Vengsarkar, their only two world-class batsmen. Gundappa Viswanath had just retired, too, leaving much of the run-scoring responsibility – seemingly – on the shoulders of Gavaskar and Vengsarkar.

The great Gavaskar, however, was out of touch for the entire tournament. He was even left out of some games, and his scores were 19, 4, 0, 9, 25 and 2. At least his 25 enabled India to get a solid start as they chased England's semi-final total of 213, but he failed in the final.

Vengsarkar, who had a fine career record in English conditions, missed the remainder of the tournament after being hit in the mouth by a ball from Malcolm Marshall in India's group defeat against the West Indies at the Oval.

So what did India have left? What was it that brought them their (to date) only World Cup success – and especially after they had endured a wretched time of it in the previous two tournaments of 1975 and 1979, in which they had won just one game (versus East Africa) out of six?

For a start, they had in Kapil Dev a captain capable of inspiring deeds with both bat and ball, a charismatic character who would not allow setbacks to diffuse the team's spirit.

India, too, had a team spirit and collective belief that was reinforced by the knowledge that, apart from in Kapil's case, they could not keep relying on the big-name players to pull them through. They had a game plan, based on the accuracy and experience of their battery of medium pacers, and they had the courage and commitment to carry it out. They also had some underrated batsmen like Yashpal Sharma and Amarnath, and some dangerous strokeplayers, such as the dashing opener Kris Srikkanth and the piratically bearded Sandeep Patil, who would later become one of India's most popular film actors. Perhaps most importantly, they were a side packed to the rafters with all-rounders.

It would be perhaps harsh to label them a bits-and-pieces outfit, because they possessed some truly world-class performers in Kapil, Gavaskar and Vengsarkar, but their success (taking out Kapil's breathtaking 175 at Tunbridge Wells) was based almost wholly on the fact that the sum of India's parts was far greater than the individuals concerned.

Players like Amarnath, Sharma, Binny, Madan Lal and Syed Kirmani, the veteran wicket-keeper, were hardened fighters. India in 1983 had just enough flair and more than enough courage. It was, unexpectedly but gloriously, a winning combination.

THE PRIZES

Besides the World Cup trophy and silver-gilt medals for each player, India won prize money of £20,000. The West Indies received £8,000, with both losing semi-finalists being awarded £4,000 each.

World cricket benefited to the tune of more than £1 million, over and above the payments of £53,900 to each of the ICC's seven full-member countries and £32,200 to Zimbabwe.

Prudential Assurance, sponsoring the event for the third and final time, paid £500,000 for the privilege. Gate receipts were £1,195,712 and the total attendance for the 27 matches was 232,081 – including 24,609 for the final at Lord's.

THE QUOTES

'The most painful thing for us was to hear those Indian supporters' drums around our hotel all night [after the final]. Some of the guys broke down. Malcolm Marshall took it particularly badly. He cried.' Viv Richards.

'I was sure we were going to win the World Cup. In fact I was so positive about the outcome that I had even ordered a new BMW car in the misguided belief that I could pay for it out of my winnings. What utter folly! Cricket has nasty habit of punishing those who come to believe in their infallibility and so it was [for us] at Lord's on 25 June 1983.' Malcolm Marshall.

TEAM OF THE TOURNAMENT?

Graeme Fowler (England)
Mohinder Amarnath (India)
Viv Richards (West Indies)
David Gower (England)
Zaheer Abbas (Pakistan)
Duncan Fletcher (Zimbabwe)
Kapil Dev (India, captain)
Guy de Alwis (Sri Lanka, wicket-keeper)
Roger Binny (India)
Madan Lal (India)
Malcolm Marshall (West Indies)

THE ROAD TO 1987...

The increase in the profits generated by the 1983 tournament prompted other countries to bid for the right to stage the fourth World Cup. Tenders were invited by the ICC before the end of the year, and after the matter had been debated it was decided to award the 1987 World Cup jointly to India and Pakistan.

This set World Cup history on a different course, and the years after 1983 brought further strides by countries outside of the major cricketing powers. It was as if India's victory had inspired the underdog, for New Zealand also made significant progress in the mid-1980s, as did Pakistan under Imran Khan and Sri Lanka under Duleep Mendis.

Rebel tours of South Africa continued, making what to do about that benighted nation the big issue in the world game. Meanwhile, the West Indies recovered from their shock World Cup defeat and resumed their mastery of the cricketing globe. Australia lost two Ashes series in 1985 and on home soil in 1986–87...and England seemed to be holding the upper hand in the age-old rivalry with their oldest enemy.

Chapter 7

1987: Aussies Win In Sub-Continent

Despite the almost unqualified success of its three predecessors, the triumphant fourth World Cup was probably the most important there has been in terms of the growth of cricket's global popularity and marketability.

On the field, too, there was significance. Australia, after several years in the doldrums, won a victory that was, in effect, a laying down of a marker. From this moment on, the Australians simply grew and grew in power: the past 15 years have been a golden age for the men in the baggy green caps, and it shows no sign of losing its lustre.

One of the junior members of their Cup-winning team, but also a leading member of it, was a certain Steve Waugh, the only Australian (so far) to be twice an official world champion.

There were those in the game who, in the build-up to the 1987 World Cup, questioned the ability of India and Pakistan to run a tournament which, logistically, presented huge problems of communication, travel and wide organisation.

But, despite the strain it put on competing teams, who spent much of their time between matches packing, sat on buses carrying them to and from airports, sat on aircraft or sat in airports waiting for their delayed flights to be called, the tournament was a spectacular success. It caught the imagination of the vast Asian masses, especially as India and Pakistan – playing in opposite groups – qualified with ease for the semi-finals. The two host countries were, of course, heavy favourites for those games, and it is greatly to the credit of both Australia and England that those two countries made it through to contest the final itself.

Australia's victory, achieved in front of an estimated 70,000 at Calcutta's Eden Gardens stadium, was watched on live television by more people than ever before, and the event – despite its logistical flaws – was undeniably more colourful than those previously staged in England.

Critics had also voiced their displeasure that shorter daylight hours in the sub-continent had enforced a change to the 60-overs-per-side format; as it turned out, however, the reduction to 50 overs per side brought similar totals to previous World Cups simply because of the better batting pitches to be found in India and Pakistan. Early-morning dew, too, did little to disrupt play, as had at first been feared. Even to get the 50-overs-per-side games into one day, play began at 9am, but 19 of the 27 matches were won by the side batting first.

If the playing format of the tournament was the same as in 1983, with two groups of four and the seven Test nations being again joined by Zimbabwe, then the staging format was quite different. Matches were spread out more in terms of time – gone was the media-and-marketing folly of holding four group games on the same day – and geographically they were cast far and wide. This 1987 World Cup, as a result, took 32 days to complete, almost twice as long as in 1983.

The organisers, the Indo-Pakistani Joint Managing Committee, insisted that no fewer than 21 different venues should be used to stage the 27 matches. It was the equivalent of deciding to put on an event not just in France and Belgium, for instance, but to spread it throughout an area as big as Europe itself. Rather than concentrating on the main centres, and thus having a more compact tournament with less strain on the competing teams and the Indian and Pakistani infrastructure, the organisers had the vision of making the World Cup as accessible as possible to the vast Asian audience. And even though they made it all more difficult than it could have been, who is to say they were wrong?

At one stage the Sri Lankan team, for example, endured four successive two-day journeys for matches at Peshawar, in the far north-west of Pakistan, to Kanpur in central India, back to Faisalabad in the north of Pakistan, and then south again to Pune on the western coast of India. But would this tournament have caught the wider imagination of the cricket-loving millions if it had been more constrained within the walls of selected big cities? World Cups, more than any other cricket event, are by definition supposed to be shared experiences, and in this the 1987 tournament succeeded beyond the expectation of the watching globe.

As with its predecessors, the weather was kind and just one game was reduced by rain to 30 overs per side. Another stroke of good fortune for the organisers was that a nonsensical rule preventing an unfinished match from being carried over into the reserve day was never invoked, and therefore never exposed to the widespread criticism that would surely have followed.

In purely cricketing terms, however, the greatest legacy of the fourth World Cup was the way that spin bowling was brought back into the limited-overs international game. Most teams fielded two specialist spinners, in response to pitch conditions that demanded a broader range of skills, and in the group stage it was revealing that seven of the nine most economical bowlers were spinners.

Nevertheless, pace bowling still had its place, with Australia's Craig McDermott, with 18 wickets, and Pakistan captain Imran Khan (17) being the two most successful bowlers in the tournament.

The chief virtue during the fourth World Cup, both on and off the field, was patience and the ability to stay focused and professional as the stakes rose. Pitches, if anything, got slower and lower the longer matches went on, and it's perhaps no surprise that, to win it, Australia – disciplined and well-led by a tough captain – managed to hold their nerve while fielding second in seven of their eight matches.

England, under a similarly nuggety captain in Mike Gatting, were also rewarded for the professional application of much one-day experience. The West Indies badly missed the injured Malcolm Marshall, and New Zealand could not overcome the absence of their own spearhead, Richard Hadlee. Sri Lanka still did not have the bowling strength to support their strokeplayers, while Zimbabwe again won themselves admirers for their spirit and magnificent fielding.

Although they did not end up with the India-Pakistan final that the whole sub-continent craved, the organisers of the first World Cup to be held outside the game's motherland can be justly proud of their achievement.

THE MATCHES
GROUP A
9 October

Madras: Australia 270–6 (50 overs) beat India 269 (49.5 overs) by 1 run. Man Of The Match award: Geoff Marsh

What a start to the tournament, with Steve Waugh bowling last man Maninder Singh from the penultimate ball to give Australia a remarkable victory. India should have won after reaching 207–2 on the back of some wonderful early strokeplay from Kris Srikkanth (70 from 83 balls), Navjot Singh Sidhu (73 from 79 balls with five sixes), Sunil Gavaskar (37 from 32 balls) and Dilip Vengsarkar. Craig McDermott, however, bounced back from a chastening opening spell to wreck the Indian middle order, while Simon

O'Donnell also struck a big blow by removing Kapil Dev. India nevertheless required only 15 from the last four overs, with four wickets in hand, but the run-outs of Roger Binny and Manoj Prabhakar left Maninder to take strike with six still needed from the final over. The number 11 managed a pair of twos but then lost his off stump amid scenes of great excitement. Australia's total had also been based on top-order strength, with Geoff Marsh playing the anchor role with a 141-ball 110, and both David Boon (49) and Dean Jones (39) batting with great freedom.

10 October

Hyderabad (India): New Zealand 242–7 (50 overs) beat Zimbabwe 239 (49.4 overs) by 3 runs. Man Of The Match award: Dave Houghton

Zimbabwe, inspired by an heroic 141 from 138 balls by Dave Houghton, also ended up with six needed from the final over, but their gallant attempt to beat New Zealand – and thus repeat their World Cup opening-day deeds of 1983, when they had beaten Australia – was undone when Iain Butchart was run out for 54 from the fourth ball. Houghton and Butchart, who had come together at 104–7, put on a one-day international record 117 for the eighth wicket, and their great effort stunned the New Zealanders and added to the early drama of the competition. Martin Snedden, promoted unexpectedly to open the Kiwi innings, responded with 64 from 97 balls, while Martin Crowe hit an elegant 72 and Jeff Crowe and Ian Smith struck invaluable late runs.

13 October

Madras: Australia 235–9 (50 overs) beat Zimbabwe 139 (42.4 overs) by 96 runs. Man Of The Match award: Steve Waugh

Australia wobbled initially at 20–2 and then saw Allan Border, on one, survive a caught-and-bowled chance to Malcolm Jarvis, the left-arm seamer. Border (67 off 88 balls) then added 113 for the third wicket with Geoff Marsh (62), and late acceleration was provided by Steve Waugh with 45 from 40 deliveries. The Zimbabwean reply never got going against disciplined Australian bowling, with Simon O'Donnell's fast-medium earning him 4–39 and Waugh's clever medium-paced variations allowing just seven runs from his six overs.

14 October

Bangalore: India 252–7 (50 overs) beat New Zealand 236–8 (50 overs) by 16 runs. Man Of The Match award: Kapil Dev

Put in to bat in initially trying conditions, India were not helped when both openers were run out and Dilip Vengsarkar was dismissed for a duck to leave them 21–3. The pressure was on, especially after that narrow defeat to Australia in their opening match, but Navjot Singh Sidhu led a courageous fightback with 75 from 71 balls (including four sixes), and then Kapil Dev was joined by Kiran More, the wicket-keeper, in an unbeaten stand of 82 from the last 51 balls of the innings that proved decisive. Kapil's 72 not out took only 58 balls, and More ended up on 42. New Zealand, missing virus victim John Wright, needed a big innings from Martin Crowe, but he was stumped for just nine after being beaten in the air by Maninder Singh, one of three specialist spinners fielded by the Indians. Ken Rutherford (75) and Andrew Jones (64) batted bravely, but India always remained in control.

17 October

Bombay: Zimbabwe 135 (44.2 overs) lost to India 136–2 (27.5 overs) by eight wickets. Man Of The Match award: Manoj Prabhakar

Andy Pycroft, with 61 from 102 balls, was the only batsman who looked comfortable against the swing of Manoj Prabhakar, who took advantage of the early-morning conditions to take 4–19 from eight overs with the new ball and wreck the Zimbabwean innings. From 13–4, however, there was little hope left for the tournament's minnows and they were left to reflect on their decision to bat first. Sunil Gavaskar's 43 contained nine boundaries as his first scoring shots, and Dilip Vengsarkar also did much to boost India's scoring rate with a flowing, unbeaten 46.

19 October

Indore: Australia 199–4 (30 overs) beat New Zealand 196–9 (30 overs) by three runs. Man Of The Match award: David Boon

Postponed until the reserve day because of heavy rain, it was decided by both captains to accept the resultant conditions and contest a 30-over match rather than just share the no-result points. New Zealand, in particular, needed to win if they were to challenge for a semi-final place, and they were left kicking themselves for not doing so after starting the final over needing only seven runs with four wickets intact. Moreover, Martin Crowe was on strike after hitting a brilliant 58 from 46 balls, but New Zealand's star batsman then lofted a Steve Waugh delivery to deep cover. Waugh's next ball yorked Ian Smith and the Australian then allowed only three singles and ran out Martin Snedden.

David Boon's run-a-ball 87 laid the foundation for Australia's total, in conjunction with a fine 52 from Dean Jones and a rapid 34 from Allan Border, but an opening stand of 83 in 12 overs between John Wright (47) and Ken Rutherford, which later became 133–2, plus Crowe's half-century, should have set up a Kiwi success.

22 October

New Delhi: India 289–6 (50 overs) beat Australia 233 (49 overs) by 56 runs. Man Of The Match award: Mohammad Azharuddin

India had a great incentive for winning this game: if they had lost, the odds were on them having to play a semi-final against Pakistan, in Pakistan. They produced a convincing victory, on a lovely pitch, with Sunil Gavaskar, Navjot Singh Sidhu, Dilip Vengsarkar and Mohammad Azharuddin all scoring attractive half-centuries against an all-seam Aussie attack. David Boon (62) and Geoff Marsh launched the reply with an opening stand of 88, but the complexion of the game changed when the Indian slow left-arm spinners Maninder Singh and Ravi Shastri began to operate in tandem. Only Steve Waugh, with 42, displayed the necessary technique, and in the end Azharuddin picked up three cheap wickets to add to his unbeaten 54 from 47 balls.

23 October

Calcutta: Zimbabwe 227–5 (50 overs) lost to New Zealand 228–6 (47.4 overs) by six wickets. Man Of The Match award: Jeff Crowe

New Zealand looked to be in some difficulty when Martin Crowe fell to Ali Shah for a run-a-ball 58 to leave them at 125–4, but his elder brother, Jeff Crowe, the captain, responded with an unbeaten 88 of great character to steer his side home. Zimbabwe weren't helped by the fact that Kevin Curran, their leading all-rounder, couldn't bowl more than two overs because of a strain. Earlier, following a sound if stolid second-wicket stand of 81 between Shah (41) and Kevin Arnott (51), the Zimbabwean innings was boosted by some exciting strokeplay from David Houghton, whose 50 came from 58 balls, and Andy Pycroft, who remained 52 not out. Thanks to their efforts, 106 came from the last 15 overs.

26 October

Ahmedabad: Zimbabwe 191–7 (50 overs) lost to India 194–3 (42 overs) by seven wickets. Man Of The Match award: Kapil Dev

A straightforward win for India, with Kapil Dev hitting three sixes in a 25-ball 41 not out after Navjot Singh Sidhu and, especially, Sunil Gavaskar had lingered somewhat over their half-centuries. Kevin Arnott, although scoring 60, took 43 overs over it, and the Zimbabwe innings received more urgency only when Andy Waller was compiling his 39.

27 October

Chandigarh: Australia 251–8 (50 overs) beat New Zealand 234 (48.4 overs) by 17 runs. Man Of The Match award: Geoff Marsh

The Australians were aiming for a total of 260 or more in order to improve their run rate and give themselves the best chance of avoiding Pakistan in the semi-finals. It took them 45 overs to reach 200, however, as the innings fell away alarmingly from 151–1, following a stand of 126 between Geoff Marsh and Dean Jones (56 from 80 balls). At least Marsh remained as the wickets clattered, and he was still there to take advantage of a loose final over from Ewen Chatfield which cost 19. Thanks to this late boost, which took Marsh to 126 not out with three sixes (two of them in that 50th over) and 12 fours, Australia were able to post what proved to be a defendable score. Marsh became only the third player, after Sunil Gavaskar and Glenn Turner, to bat through a World Cup innings. Good fortune was with Australia when Martin Crowe, on only four, was run out by bowler Steve Waugh's deflection of John Wright's straight drive. Wright went on to make 61 and Ken Rutherford hit 44, but Allan Border's occasional left-arm spin claimed two important wickets and the Australians never looked like losing.

30 October

Cuttack: Australia 266–5 (50 overs) beat Zimbabwe 196–6 (50 overs) by 70 runs. Man Of The Match award: David Boon

Despite an untrustworthy pitch, on which Andy Waller was later hit in the face by a ball from Bruce Reid, the in-form Australian top order laid the foundations for another excellent total. Geoff Marsh helped his opening partner, David Boon, to put on 90, and then Boon (93) was joined in a further stand of 58 in ten overs with Dean Jones. While Jones then stayed to the end of the innings to score an unbeaten 58, there was a punchy 43 from number six by Mike Veletta. A slow start left Zimbabwe with much to do, and when off-spinner Tim May sent back Kevin Curran and David Houghton in successive overs, the match was all but won.

31 October

Nagpur: New Zealand 221–9 (50 overs) lost to India 224–1 (32.1 overs) by nine wickets. Man Of The Match award: Sunil Gavaskar and Chetan Sharma (shared)

A ragged New Zealand team were pulverised by the brilliance of Sunil Gavaskar and Kris Srikkanth, the Indian openers, after Chetan Sharma had taken the first hat-trick in World Cup competition by clean-bowling Ken Rutherford, Ian Smith and Ewen Chatfield with the last three balls of the 42nd over. To go ahead of Australia at the top of the group, they knew that, after New Zealand had batted, they needed to get the runs in no more than 42.2 overs. It took them ten overs less, with Gavaskar reaching 103 not out from 85 balls and sharing stands of 136 with Srikkanth (75 off 58 balls with three sixes and nine fours) and an unbroken 88 with Mohammad Azharuddin (41 not out). Gavaskar, rumoured to have been unwell before the match, struck Chatfield for 6, 6, 4, 4 from successive deliveries in the sixth over, and India's 100 came up in the 14th over. It was, remarkably, Gavaskar's first one-day international century, in his 106th one-day international.

GROUP B
8 October

Hyderabad (Pakistan): Pakistan 267–6 (50 overs) beat Sri Lanka 252 (49.2 overs) by 15 runs. Man Of The Match award: Javed Miandad

Ramiz Raja was the anchorman with 76, but it was Javed Miandad's 96-ball 103 that was mainly responsible for propelling Pakistan to a challenging total in their opening fixture. Sri Lanka's clutch of strokemakers made a gallant bid for victory, however, which lasted until the last over, with only the timely dismissals of Roshan Mahanama, for 89, and Aravinda De Silva (42) keeping Pakistan in control.

9 October

Gujranwala: West Indies 243–7 (50 overs) lost to England 246–8 (49.3 overs) by two wickets. Man Of The Match award: Allan Lamb

Allan Lamb, with help chiefly from John Emburey and Phillip DeFreitas, plucked a miraculous victory out of the Punjabi air as England made the 91 that they had still needed from the last ten overs with only four wickets remaining. Lamb's 67 not out from 68 balls, with a six and five fours, included a dramatic assault on Courtney Walsh, whose last two overs cost 31. Perhaps it shouldn't have been such a surprise, though, as the West Indies had themselves plundered 92 from their final ten overs, with Roger Harper taking 22 from the 49th over, bowled by Derek Pringle. When England's required runs came down to 35 from three overs, Walsh was hit for 16 (15 to Lamb). Patrick Patterson then conceded only six from his final over, leaving 13 still wanted. Lamb now struck Walsh for a two and four from the first two balls, and then the shell-shocked bowler sent down four leg-side wides. A no-ball followed, tucked for a single by Lamb, and the eventual legal third ball of the over – a full toss – was carved for the winning boundary by Neil Foster.

13 October

Rawalpindi: Pakistan 239–7 (50 overs) beat England 221 (48.4 overs) by 18 runs. Man Of The Match award: Abdul Qadir

This match took place on the reserve day, due to heavy rain, and England should have won it after producing a disciplined performance in the field. Pakistan then had to make do without their captain, Imran Khan, who had batted but was not now able to field because of food poisoning. Yet England could not take advantage. With six wickets in hand, and with 34 more runs required from four overs, England lost all six for 15 runs in only 16 balls, including Allan Lamb, John Emburey and Paul Downton, who were all dismissed in the space of the 47th over, the last to be bowled by Abdul Qadir. The leg-spinner, who had earlier bowled Graham Gooch, finished with 4–31 and was the difference between the two sides.

13 October

Karachi: West Indies 360–4 (50 overs) beat Sri Lanka 169–4 (50 overs) by 191 runs. Man Of The Match award: Viv Richards

An astonishing fusillade of strokes from Viv Richards came after he had entered the arena with West Indies at 45–2 and Ravi Ratnayake on a hat-trick. Richards savaged six sixes and 16 fours in a 125-ball 181, but was eventually caught as he tried for another six off the suffering Asantha de Mel, whose ten overs ended up costing 97. It was the highest individual score in the World Cup and only eight runs short of his own one-day international record. Desmond Haynes was hardly a slouch, either, as he struck 105 from 109 balls and added 182 for the third wicket with Richards. The West Indies' total was also a one-day international record, and unsurprisingly the Sri Lankans decided to settle for batting practice in reply.

16 October

Lahore: West Indies 216 (49.3 overs) lost to Pakistan 217–9 (50 overs) by one wicket. Man Of The Match award: Salim Yousuf

In a finish which sent the capacity crowd of more than 50,000 into raptures of excitement, Abdul Qadir provided the magic to set the seal on a fightback begun by Salim Yousuf and Imran Khan. Pakistan captain Imran had earlier taken 4–37 to restrict the West Indies total following fine half-centuries by Phil Simmons, on debut, and Viv Richards. Imran was then joined by wicket-keeper Yousuf in a sixth-wicket stand of 73 that rallied his side from a perilous 110–5 in the 35th over. Yousuf was finally caught for an adventurous 56 in the 48th over, off Walsh, and it was the Jamaican who also bowled the final over with 14 runs still needed. Singles were taken by Qadir and last man Salim Jaffer from the first two balls, and then Qadir hit the fast bowler for 2, 6, 2, 2 to clinch an extraordinary win. His straight six was greeted by near hysteria: this World Cup, already chock-full of nail-biting finishes at only a week old, was becoming very big news indeed on the sub-continent.

17 October

Peshawar: England 296–4 (50 overs) beat Sri Lanka 158–8 (45 overs) by 109 runs. Man Of The Match award: Allan Lamb

A rejigged England side, now containing Eddie Hemmings and Bill Athey, hammered the lightweight Sri Lankan attack and then comfortably contained the reply as dark clouds rolled down from the Khyber Pass. As it was, only five overs were lost, but England breathed more easily once their minimum of 25 overs had been bowled, and eventually a revised target of 267 from 45 overs was always well out of Sri Lanka's reach. Graham Gooch (84) and Mike Gatting (58) had tucked into the Sri Lankan bowlers, as did Allan Lamb with a 58-ball 76 that featured two sixes and three fours.

20 October

Karachi: England 244–9 (50 overs) lost to Pakistan 247–3 (49 overs) by seven wickets. Man Of The Match award: Imran Khan

England, at 187–2, were going well, but the loss of Bill Athey for 86 and Mike Gatting for 60 in the space of three balls proved costly. Athey was bowled by Tauseef Ahmed, the off-spinner, attempting a reverse sweep to his 104th ball, while Gatting (65 balls) edged leg-spinner Qadir as he tried to sweep conventionally. Imran Khan now brought himself back into the attack with great success, finishing up with 4–37, and England's final total never looked enough on a fine batting surface. Ramiz Raja, with a measured 113 from 148 balls, and Salim Malik (88 from 92 balls) then produced a sensibly paced and match-winning second-wicket partnership of 167. Pakistan's victory assured them of a place in the semi-finals.

21 October

Kanpur: West Indies 236–8 (50 overs) beat Sri Lanka 211–8 (50 overs) by 25 runs. Man Of The Match award: Phil Simmons

There was no repeat of the West Indian power-play against the Sri Lankans in this second group meeting, but a victory was still achieved due to a mixture of assured batting from Phil Simmons (89) and Gus Logie (65 not out), on a sluggish pitch, and a secure final spell from Patrick Patterson, who had returned with Sri Lanka needing 37 from the last four overs. Arjuna Ranatunga had taken Sri Lanka close with a superb, unbeaten 86 from 92 balls, but in the end he couldn't do it all on his own.

23 October

Faisalabad: Pakistan 297–7 (50 overs) beat Sri Lanka 184–8 (50 overs) by 113 runs. Man Of The Match award: Salim Malik

Another heavy beating for Sri Lanka, whose bowlers were this time taken apart by Salim Malik in his first one-day international 100. Malik's century took him only 85 balls, and the Pakistan innings accelerated so rapidly in the last 15 overs that 154 runs were taken from them. Wasim Akram swung two sixes in his 39, Ijaz Ahmed's 30 took just 18 deliveries and Imran Khan weighed in with 39 from 37 balls. The only scare for Pakistan thereafter was when Imran pulled up in his fourth over to massage his ankle, but it proved to be just bruising.

26 October

Jaipur: England 269–5 (50 overs) beat West Indies 235 (48.1 overs) by 34 runs. Man Of The Match award: Graham Gooch

Discipline, and indiscipline, were the causes of the victory England needed badly in their quest for a semi-final place. The discipline was England's, led by Graham Gooch's beautifully controlled 92 from 137 balls at the head of the order, and this continued in the field when Viv Richards and Richie Richardson threatened to snatch the game away from them.

Eddie Hemmings, the archetypal English old pro, provided the breakthrough when he bowled Richards for a run-a-ball 51 (following a stand of 82) and Richardson was finally out for 93 as the West Indies cracked under pressure after being asked to score 65 from the last ten overs with six wickets in hand. The indiscipline, of course, was the West Indies' – especially in the gifting of 22 runs (and, in effect, almost four extra overs) in wides. That profligacy allowed John Emburey and Phillip DeFreitas the opportunity to add critical quick runs at the end of an innings that might otherwise have under-achieved.

30 October

Pune: Sri Lanka 218–7 (50 overs) lost to England 219–2 (41.2 overs) by eight wickets. Man Of The Match award: Graham Gooch

Despite dropping four catches, including Roy Dias (80 off 105 balls) when he was on one, England comfortably completed the victory they needed to make sure of qualification for the last four. Dias batted well after his escape, hitting three sixes and six fours, and the Sri Lankans managed to score 75 runs from their final ten overs, but England's top order merely strolled to their target. Graham Gooch, making light of having suffered a dislocated finger when he dropped the first of the missed catches, scored 61 from 79 balls and put on 123 in 23.3 overs with opening partner Tim Robinson, whose 55 occupied 75 deliveries. After these two dismissals, both Bill Athey and Mike Gatting enjoyed themselves as they quickly knocked off the remaining runs.

30 October

Karachi: West Indies 258–7 (50 overs) beat Pakistan 230–9 (50 overs) by 28 runs. Man Of The Match award: Richie Richardson

A poor performance from Pakistan, even though they had already qualified, and for West Indies a victory that was tinged with disappointment afterwards when they learned that England had won in Pune to clinch the second qualifying place. Richie Richardson included a straight six off Imran Khan in his 110, off 136 balls, while Viv Richards eased to 67 from 74 balls while helping his fellow Antiguan to add 137 in 23 overs for the third wicket. Pakistan's out-cricket was sloppy, and their reply began far too slowly. Despite Ramiz Raja knocking up a respectable 70, the West Indies remained in total control.

SEMI-FINALS
4 November
Lahore: Australia 267–8 (50 overs) beat Pakistan 249 (49 overs) by 18 runs. Man Of The Match award: Craig McDermott

Pakistan's players and supporters were left shattered by a third successive World Cup semi-final exit. For Australia, who won because of a superior all-round display, there was the joyous realisation that their fast-improving team was back in the big time after several years in the doldrums. A solid batting performance was led by David Boon (65) and Dean Jones (38), followed up by Mike Veletta's 48 from 50 balls and some productive hitting at the end by Steve Waugh (32 not out). Waugh struck poor Salim Jaffer for 18 from the final over, including a six off the first ball...and they proved decisive runs. In contrast, Pakistan lost three wickets in their first 10.1 overs, starting when Ramiz was sent back and run out, and were always struggling to play catch-up. Javed Miandad (70) and Imran Khan (58) worked hard to revive the innings, adding 112 in 26 overs, but a target of 118 from the last 15 overs was a tough proposition. Miandad's dismissal, swinging at Bruce Reid in the 44th over, was virtually a mortal blow, and Craig McDermott returned to wrap up the tail and claim the first five-wicket haul of the tournament.

5 November
Bombay: England 254–6 (50 overs) beat India 219 (45.3 overs) by 35 runs. Man Of The Match award: Graham Gooch

Back in England, people were gearing themselves up for Guy Fawkes' Night as Graham Gooch produced some cricketing fireworks of his own. The result, for the second day running, was the sight of a host nation's hopes and dreams going up in smoke. Gooch's 115, and his premeditated, daring and brilliantly executed plan to sweep India's spinners to distraction, took England into their second World Cup final. It was one of the greatest innings in World Cup history, and when Gooch was finally caught on the mid-wicket boundary in the 43rd over, he had faced 136 balls and hit 11 fours. Mike Gatting, the captain, batted almost as well for his 56 as he and Gooch added 117 in 19 overs, and then Allan Lamb's unbeaten 32 from 27 balls ensured a late flurry and a decent total. India were missing Dilip Vengsarkar, who had a stomach upset, and soon they also suffered the further setback of seeing Sunil Gavaskar's off stump being knocked back by a ball from Phillip DeFreitas. Neil Foster later struck three significant blows at crucial times, while Eddie Hemmings overcame an initial mauling from Mohammad Azharuddin to have the last remaining Indian specialist batsman lbw for 64. Hemmings, in fact, was now in the middle of a 34-ball spell in which he took 4–21 as the home side panicked and were bowled out with 4.3 overs left unused.

THE 1987 WORLD CUP FINAL
8 November
Calcutta: Australia 253–5 (50 overs) beat England 246–8 (50 overs) by seven runs. Man Of The Match award: David Boon

Australia's triumph will always be associated with a moment of madness from Mike Gatting, the England captain. On 41 from 44 balls, and with his side cruising along in reasonable comfort at 135–2 after 31 overs, Gatting chose to aim a reverse sweep at the first ball bowled by his opposite number, Allan Border. Although he was introducing his own occasional slow left-armers to fill in a few overs, Border suddenly found himself hitting the jackpot. Gatting top-edged the ball – which was on the line of his leg stump – onto his shoulder, and from there it ricocheted up into the air to give Greg Dyer, the wicket-keeper, a simple catch. Bill Athey and new batsman Allan Lamb tried to bounce back from Gatting's soft dismissal by adding a further 35 in eight overs, but then Athey was run out for 58, going for a third run, and the England asking rate suddenly went up as the Australians tightened their grip. A target of 75 from ten overs became 44 from five, and Steve Waugh delivered a huge blow to England's chances by bowling Lamb for 45 (off 55 balls) in the 47th over. Phillip DeFreitas hit out bravely in the fading cause, taking 4, 6, 4 from successive Craig McDermott deliveries in the 48th over, but he was caught in a 49th over from Waugh that cost only two runs – and that left 17 needed from the last, from McDermott. Australia, who had earlier built another good total through a rock-solid top order in which David Boon's 75 was the anchor, added to late acceleration in which Mike Veletta's 31-ball 45 not out was a vital contribution, once again proved that winning teams are the ones that can hold their nerve when the pressure is on.

THE INTERVIEW
Allan Border
It's a wonderful party night in Madras, as much as the World Cup triumph itself in steamy Calcutta, that Allan Border remembers with most fondness

when he recalls the epic Australian win of 1987. That memory is indicative of the magnificent team spirit that took the emerging Australian team all the way to ultimate victory, and the night in question came after Border's team had beaten co-hosts India in the opening game of the tournament.

Becoming the first Australian to lift the World Cup was the furthest thing from Border's mind when he led his team into the competition. The Australians, and Border, had endured long years of decline, and now this win – by just one run – was just the sort of tonic that a new-look team needed at the start of such a big event.

It would be no exaggeration to say that Australia went into the 1987 tournament hoping for the best, but came out of it believing that they could *be* the best.

'My main memory of that whole World Cup has to be the party we had after the opening victory over India,' said Border. 'It was in our hotel in Madras, and after a magnificent game we partied like we had won the whole tournament. It went on through the night, and it was one of the most magnificent celebrations I've ever been involved in. There were quite a number of Australian tourists there, plus friends of the team, and it definitely lifted our spirits for the remainder of the tournament.'

Border, then 32, had made his Test debut in 1978, when the Australian team had been riven asunder by the Packer Affair. He immediately proved himself a fighter in the middle order and was an important member of the national side by the time some of the Packer players were recalled.

The players central to the great Australian side of the 1970s were in decline by the early 1980s, however, and it was a losing side that he was asked to take charge of during the series against the West Indies in 1984–85.

Border had already taken part in two miserable World Cup campaigns, in 1979 and 1983, and by the time of the 1987 tournament he had also been twice a losing Ashes captain – in 1985 and 1986–87. When he arrived in the sub-continent, therefore, he knew that it was time for his rebuilt team to restore some pride to Australian cricket. Perhaps, as he sunk several beers on that Madras night, Border's happiness was prompted by the deep-down knowledge that, at last, he had players around him who were capable of scaling the heights.

Whatever, the spirit in the side certainly held fast during the following weeks. Australia were involved in a stream of closely fought matches and tight finishes, and they survived them all.

By the time they faced England for the greatest prize, Border's team had visibly grown in stature. It was confident in its collective ability and had become a battle-tough, hard-nosed outfit in the image of the skipper himself.

As he looks back now, what pleases Border most of all is that his World Cup victory was not just a personal triumph after years of struggle. More importantly still, it was the day that a new era of Australian cricket domination was born. It helped, in time, to create a whole culture of excellence which sees Australia, these days, as way out in front of the rest of the world in terms of playing ability, tactical awareness, team preparation and mental strength.

'That 1987 victory will always have a special place in my heart because of where Australia went after it,' says Border. 'It was very important for the well-being of the game in Australia, and it had a knock-on effect in the years that followed. It helped to make us into a very good cricketing side because it cultivated self-belief and the habit of winning, and winning regularly.

'What made our win at Calcutta extra special for me was because it came right out of the blue. Between 1984 and 1987, especially, we had gone through a really tough run in international cricket, but winning the World Cup turned us around. From then until the mid-1990s, the only team we couldn't beat was the West Indies, and now we're number one in the world.

'But the time leading up to the 1987 World Cup was a great one for us. We unearthed players like Steve Waugh, Dean Jones, Simon O'Donnell, Geoff Marsh and Bruce Reid, who all blossomed over the next few years.'

Border still loves to recall how he felt when everything began to come together for him, and Australia. From the party night in Madras to the further celebrations that were sparked off by the Cup win itself in Calcutta, it was a magical journey of fulfilment: 'Yes, we did have another great party after winning it!' he affirms. 'But what I remember best about that night was the surreal feeling that we just couldn't believe what we'd done. There was this element of astonishment about it...but it was a moment that we all cherish.'

THE CHAMPIONS

It's fitting that, in the 1987 Australian side, there is one tangible link to the even greater Aussie teams that conquered the world in the 1990s: Steve Waugh. Then 22, Waugh was still making his way as a talented all-rounder who, in a limited-overs sense, was even more valuable with the ball than he was with the bat.

Waugh's slower ball was, in that tournament, years ahead of its time in terms of one-day cricket history, and the success that both he and, to a lesser extent, Simon O'Donnell had with it went a considerable way to masking Australia's deficiency in the spin department.

Most teams in the 1987 World Cup used two specialist spinners as the basis for their mid-innings tactics in the field, but Tim May's off-breaks were largely ineffective and Australian captain Allan Border was often forced to use his own part-time, quickish left-arm spinners (who didn't turn too sharply, however!) in an effort to make up the fifth bowler's quota.

In Craig McDermott and Bruce Reid, moreover, there was also an excellent new ball attack for Border to employ. McDermott was quick and big-hearted, and the tall, gangling left-armer Reid was also a distinct handful. With better fortune from injury, Reid might have ended his career as one of the very best.

Besides their teamwork and spirit, though, Australia's real strength lay in a dependable and tough batting line-up. Greg Dyer, the wicket-keeper who usually came in at number eight, only got to the crease four times in Australia's eight matches, and one of those was right at the end of an innings.

Just look at the scores made by Australia's top three – Geoff Marsh, David Boon and Dean Jones – during the tournament. Marsh: 110, 62, 5, 33, 126 not out, 37, 31, 24; Boon: 49, 2, 87, 62, 14, 93, 65, 75; Jones: 39, 2, 52, 36, 56, 58 not out, 38, 33.

Such outstanding consistency at the head of the order meant that the Australians were always competitive. Border and Waugh also made important runs and, in the last three matches, Mike Veletta came into the middle order to produce innings of 43 (39 balls), 48 (50 balls) and 45 not out (31 balls) at just the right time.

Even greater days, and greater cricketers like Warne and McGrath, Mark Waugh and Mark Taylor, lay ahead of the Australia of 1987. But Border's happy band were indeed the trailblazers, and the touchstone, for a long and golden era.

THE QUOTES

'That day [in Bombay], Gooch played, in terms of planning, execution and pressure of occasion, the greatest one-day innings I have ever seen – and remember, I was one of those who bowled at Viv Richards when he scored his unbeaten 189 at Old Trafford in 1984.' Derek Pringle, on Gooch's 115 in the semi-final against India.

'Legend has it that the 1987 World Cup came to India because the president of the Indian Cricket Board in 1983, Mr NKP Salve, was given only two complimentary tickets for the final of the 1983 World Cup. So incensed was Mr Salve [the legend further goes] that he vowed to have the next World Cup in India, if India won the event.' Sunil Gavaskar, the former India captain and opening batsman.

'The 1987 World Cup proved to be a real turning point in the life of the Australian cricket team. We now knew we could beat the world, albeit only in the limited-overs game at this point, but it was the start. I truly believe that the Ashes successes of 1989 and 1993, and even the victory over the West Indies in 1995, can be traced back to the confidence we acquired in 1987.' Australia's opening batsman David Boon.

TEAM OF THE TOURNAMENT?
Graham Gooch (England)
Geoff Marsh (Australia)
David Boon (Australia)
Viv Richards (West Indies)
Allan Border (Australia, captain)
David Houghton (Zimbabwe, wicket-keeper)
Steve Waugh (Australia)
Imran Khan (Pakistan)
Phillip DeFreitas (England)
Abdul Qadir (Pakistan)
Craig McDermott (Australia)

THE ROAD TO 1992...
Australia, boosted by their World Cup triumph, went on to regain the Ashes in England in 1989, when they were still under the command of Border. English cricket, however, suffered a further setback during that Ashes summer when it was announced that Mike Gatting, who had been stripped of the captaincy the previous year, was to lead an unofficial side to South Africa in early 1990. Several other leading players were involved, and were subsequently banned for three years, but under Graham Gooch the England team seemed to improve its standing and, in early 1990, came close to beating the West Indies on home soil.

The South Africa question, indeed, came to a head during Gatting's tour. Mass protests at the presence of the English cricketers, and the general political situation surrounding the release of Nelson Mandela, led to the cancellation of the second planned tour in 1990–91 and the shortening of the original visit following peace talks with the protesters.

Less than 18 months later, in July 1991, South Africa was invited back into the international cricket fold – after a 20-year absence because of the apartheid policies of successive former governments – and in early 1992 became a late addition to the list of contestants for the fifth World Cup tournament.

Chapter 8

1992: Imran And Pakistan – The Masters

If the 1987 World Cup was a colourful affair because of its Asian vibrancy, then the 1992 tournament was colourful in a more literal sense. With the introduction of floodlit matches, coloured clothing, white balls and black sightscreens, it's the fifth World Cup that stands out as the first truly modern cricketing event.

It was fitting that Australia, who shared the staging of it with New Zealand, should be the focus of the first World Cup to embrace all the trappings of the floodlit cricket experience.

Moreover, although the cricket establishment would not like to hear it, the increased spectacle of the 1992 tournament was final testimony to the clear-sightedness and marketing nous of Kerry Packer, who was responsible for the introduction of cricket under lights. At Melbourne, on 14 December 1977, an Australian XI played a World XI in a match where, after 6:30pm, floodlights were switched on and a white ball and black sightscreens were used.

On 27 November 1979, soon after Packer had made his peace with the Australian Cricket Board, the first official floodlit one-day international took place, at the Sydney Cricket Ground. Australia, its team reunited for the first time following the World Series Cricket split, played the West Indies, and Australia the country has never lost its appetite for night cricket that was originally whetted by Packer's groundbreaking prototype.

The largest such event until 1999, the fifth World Cup, was made up of 39 matches: 25 staged in Australia and the remaining 14 in New Zealand. No fewer than ten of the Australian matches were day-night contests.

Despite its length – 12 more games than in 1987 – the tournament was completed in 33 days, just one day more than its immediate predecessor. Such a tight schedule, however, given the travelling time also needed to fly teams considerable distances, meant that no reserve days were allowed.

Inevitably, of course, this ended up by exposing the one glaring fault in an otherwise excellent and eminently fair structure in which all nine teams (the eight ICC full members plus Zimbabwe, who were again the ICC Trophy winners) played each other once to determine a league table, from which the top four teams contested the semi-finals.

South Africa, last-minute additions following their re-admittance to the ICC, were the fall guys as the 'rain rule' produced a quite farcical semi-final against England at Sydney.

In short, the organisers had decided to use a method whereby the reduction in the target, after a weather interruption, would be proportionate to the lowest scoring overs of the side batting first. This method was intended to overcome the unfairness of a straight run-rate calculation, which always worked against the side who had batted first.

The theory was good, but unfortunately it didn't look quite so clever in practice. England had already almost fallen foul of it themselves – ironically, in their group game against the South Africans – when an interruption of nine overs led to their target being reduced by a mere 11 runs. A brilliant 75 not out from Neil Fairbrother, however, plus the fact that they still had a reasonable number of overs left when the recalculation was made, enabled England to win that game against the odds.

In the semi-final, however, a 12-minute downpour interrupted South Africa when they had required 22 more runs to win from 13 balls. At first, as the players re-emerged from the pavilion once the storm had passed, the target was shown as 22 from seven balls. Then, once the game was actually ready to restart, the South Africans learned from the scoreboard that their requirement had become 21 from just one ball!

Even though there was a reserve day set aside for the semi-finals and final, the all-powerful demands of television meant that the match had to be completed, according to the rules, on that day. Yes, television had at last become a leading player in World Cup cricket – and not just for the good of the game.

England were happy at being gifted a place in the final but highly embarrassed at how. South Africa, dreaming of a fairytale return to the big time, were angry and distraught – though they did somehow manage to perform a dignified farewell lap of honour after their defeat. Cricket fans around the globe were appalled at the inflexibility of the rules, and spectators in the stadium felt cheated of what had promised to be a classic finish.

Whichever way you looked at it, the 1992 World Cup lost much of its sheen at that moment.

THE MATCHES
22 February

Auckland: New Zealand 248–6 (50 overs) beat Australia 211 (48.1 overs) by 37 runs. Man Of The Match award: Martin Crowe

Perth: England 236–9 (50 overs) beat India 227 (49.2 overs) by nine runs. Man Of The Match award: Ian Botham

In the first match, the holders and favourites, Australia, were unnerved and beaten by the radical tactics employed by Martin Crowe, the New Zealand captain. To the sheer delight of the home crowd, Crowe's brilliant 100 not out (and fine support from Ken Rutherford's 57) ensured a commanding total, and then the Australian challenge disintegrated when their last five wickets fell for 12 runs in 17 balls. Crowe successfully used Dipak Patel's off-breaks in the early overs against the conservative Geoff Marsh and David Boon, and thereafter switched around his battery of dobbing medium-pacers to great effect. Boon ploughed on to 100, but the required run rate kept rising.

Meanwhile, in the first day-night match in World Cup history, Ian Botham's penchant for the big occasion inspired England to a narrow victory at the WACA. Botham's ten overs had brought him outstanding figures of 2–27, but India's batsmen had still managed to whittle their target down to 11 from the final over. Then, however, Botham swooped to run out last man Javagal Srinath off the second ball, and it was all over. Robin Smith's 108-ball 91 was by far the best innings of the game.

23 February

New Plymouth: Zimbabwe 312–4 (50 overs) lost to Sri Lanka 313–7 (49.2 overs) by three wickets. Man Of The Match award: Andy Flower

Melbourne: Pakistan 220–2 (50 overs) lost to West Indies 221–0 (46.5 overs) by ten wickets. Man Of The Match award: Brian Lara

Andy Flower scored an unbeaten 115 on his international debut, Andy Waller struck a remarkable 83 not out from a mere 45 balls (with three sixes and nine fours) – and Zimbabwe still lost. Only John Traicos, the 44-year-old off-spinner, emerged from the carnage with respectable figures as first Rosham Mahanama and Maitipage Samarasekera put on 128 for the opening wicket and then Arjuna Ranatunga swept Sri Lanka home with a superbly judged 88 not out from just 61 balls.

By the time Brian Lara was struck on the foot by a Wasim Akram yorker and had to hobble off, the West Indies were 175 without loss and cruising to victory. Lara had hit 11 fours in his 101-ball 88 and Desmond Haynes remained 93 not out at the end. Earlier, Pakistan paid the penalty for a sluggish start, although Ramiz Raja went on to complete an unbeaten 102 and add 81 in the final ten overs with Javed Miandad, whose livewire 57 took just 61 deliveries.

25 February

Hamilton: Sri Lanka 206–9 (50 overs) lost to New Zealand 210–4 (48.2 overs) by six wickets. Man Of The Match award: Ken Rutherford

Dropped by Arjuna Ranatunga at slip before he had scored, Ken Rutherford went on to guide the Kiwis to victory with an unbeaten 65. The New Zealanders produced another tight display in the field, with only Roshan Mahanama (80) causing them undue alarm. John Wright made 57, despite a shoulder injury suffered when fielding, but it was the stand of 81 between Rutherford and Andrew Jones (49) which settled the match.

26 February

Sydney: Australia 170–9 (49 overs) lost to South Africa 171–1 (46.5 overs) by nine wickets. Man Of The Match award: Kepler Wessels

Another shock for Australia as South Africa joyously won their first World Cup match with considerable ease. Allan Donald led a seam attack which proved too potent for the holders, and no Australian reached 30. In contrast, South Africa were led home by their captain, the South African-born and -bred former Australian Test player Kepler Wessels, who scored 81 not out and was joined in an unbeaten partnership of 97 by Peter Kirsten. President FW De Klerk and Nelson Mandela, the ANC leader, both sent messages of congratulation to the South Africa dressing room.

27 February

Hobart: Pakistan 254–4 (50 overs) beat Zimbabwe 201–7 (50 overs) by 53 runs. Man Of The Match award: Aamir Sohail

Melbourne: West Indies 157 (49.2 overs) lost to England 160–4 (39.5 overs) by six wickets. Man Of The Match award: Chris Lewis

A first one-day international hundred from the left-handed Aamir Sohail, whose 114 took 136 balls and contained 12 fours, plus a typically inventive 94-ball 89 by Javed Miandad, enabled Pakistan to outbat Zimbabwe. The Pakistanis also managed 158 runs from their last 20 overs, and when Zimbabwe collapsed to 33–3 in the 20th over, a rout looked possible. Some sturdy middle-

1992: Imran and Pakistan – The Masters

order batting, however, with David Houghton and Andy Waller prominent, brought a little consolation.

England totally outplayed the West Indies to win a day-night contest at the MCG with more than ten overs to spare. Graham Gooch's decision to bowl first was vindicated by his seamers, who got the ball to move around startlingly. Chris Lewis struck two vital early blows with the wickets of Brian Lara (second ball) and Richie Richardson. Phillip DeFreitas then sent back the two West Indian top scorers, opener Desmond Haynes (38) and Keith Arthurton (54). Gooch (65) set off towards the modest target with complete confidence, and Graeme Hick's 55-ball 54 included a six over cover off Roger Harper.

28 February

Mackay: India 1–0 (0.2 overs) v Sri Lanka. Match abandoned.

Months of preparation for the local organisers sadly came to nothing (well, two balls) as the northern Queensland town of Mackay's attempt to stage its first one-day international fell foul of storms blowing in off the Great Barrier Reef. Play was initially delayed for five hours before a break in the weather allowed plans for a 20-overs-per-side match. However, more torrential rain meant that the single taken by Kris Srikkanth was the only action possible.

29 February

Auckland: South Africa 190–7 (50 overs) lost to New Zealand 191–3 (34.3 overs) by seven wickets. Man Of The Match award: Mark Greatbatch

Brisbane: West Indies 264–8 (50 overs) beat Zimbabwe 189–7 (50 overs) by 75 runs. Man Of The Match award: Brian Lara

Back in Auckland after a gap of nearly 28 years, South Africa found themselves unable to handle a slow, low pitch and a New Zealand team beginning to emerge as a real force with its carefully-thought-out game-plan. Again, the Kiwis gave the new ball to Dipak Patel, the off-spinner, who bowled Andrew Hudson in another effective spell. The medium-pacers were also difficult to get away, and South Africa were grateful for the vast experience of Peter Kirsten (90). In reply, however, the burly duo of Mark Greatbatch and Rod Latham opened up with a bludgeoning stand of 103 in the first 15 overs, when the number of fielders in the outfield was restricted. Greatbatch hit three sixes in his 60-ball 68, while Latham made 60.

Brian Lara (72), Richie Richardson (56) and Carl Hooper (63) all packed far too much firepower for Zimbabwe, who later lost opener Kevin Arnott with a broken finger and could only offer a brave innings of 55 by broken-toe victim Dave Houghton and a solid all-round performance by Ali Shah, who added an unbeaten 60 to a tidy ten-over spell of medium pace.

1 March

Brisbane: Australia 237–9 (50 overs) beat India 234 (47 overs) by one run (revised target). Man Of The Match award: Dean Jones

Adelaide: Pakistan 74 (40.2 overs) v England 24–1 (eight overs) – match abandoned.

An exciting finish at the Gabba also exposed, for the first time in the competition, the ridiculous rain rule. When a sharp shower cut 15 minutes and three overs from India's innings (they were 45–1 from 16.2 overs at the time of the interruption), they found, to their chagrin, that only two runs had been deducted from the target. Nevertheless, India made a gallant attempt, led by Mohammad Azharuddin's stylish 93 from 103 balls and a hard-hit 47 off 42 balls by Sanjay Manjrekar. With 13 needed from the final over, bowled by Tom Moody, Kiran More swung the first two balls to the fine leg boundary but then had his middle stump uprooted. Manoj Prabhakar took a single, but was then sent back and run out from the fifth ball of the over. That left Javagal Srinath wanting a four from the last delivery, and although Steve Waugh dropped his lofted hit just inside the boundary, the fielder's return to stand-in wicket-keeper David Boon prevented non-striker Venkatapathy Raju from completing the third run and levelling the scores.

The destiny of the 1992 World Cup turned on the rain, which ultimately prevented England from beating Pakistan and, in all probability, ejecting them from the tournament itself. Again, it was the absence of a reserve day which helped Pakistan to escape. Before the fateful weather interruption, England's five seamers had torn into the Pakistan batting on a pitch which had been covered from more heavy rain on the previous day. The contributions of Wasim Haider and Mushtaq Ahmed, the numbers nine and ten, also turned out to be vital after Pakistan had tumbled to 47–8 against the seaming and swinging ball. Without their resistance, the game might have been all over by lunch, when England were 17–1 from six overs. Rain allowed just two more overs, although in the end the farcical rain rules meant that, because of the delays, England themselves were facing a win target that had come down to 64 from 16 overs, which might not have been easy in the conditions. All in all, then, a real mess that Pakistan (at least) were relieved to emerge from relatively unscathed.

2 March

Wellington: South Africa 195 (50 overs) lost to Sri Lanka 198–7 (49.5 overs) by three wickets. Man Of The Match award: Arjuna Ranatunga

After enduring a 15-hour journey from northern Queensland to the southern tip of New Zealand's North Island, Sri Lanka produced a gutsy performance to beat the South Africans and move themselves into third place in the group-stage table. Kepler Wessels was becalmed at the start of the South Africa innings, and only Peter Kirsten (47) succeeded in upping the scoring rate. Sri Lanka bowled and fielded well and then recovered grittily with the bat after Allan Donald reduced them to 35–3. Roshan Mahanama (68) led the rally, and Arjuna Ranatunga saw his team home, with one ball to spare, with a calculated 64 not out. Omar Henry, the slow left-armer, became the first coloured player to represent South Africa.

3 March

Napier: New Zealand 162–3 (20.5 overs) beat Zimbabwe 105–7 (18 overs) by 48 runs (revised target). Man Of The Match award: Martin Crowe

After a delayed and then twice-interrupted New Zealand innings, Zimbabwe's target became 154 from 18 overs, thanks to the rain rule. Heavy drizzle had made conditions almost farcical during the final 9.3-over session of the Kiwi innings, in which 110 runs were plundered, the Zimbabwe bowlers slipped in their run-ups and fielding became hazardous. Martin Crowe thumped an unbeaten 74 from just 44 balls, including eight fours and two sixes, while Andrew Jones scored 57 from 58 balls. More drizzle fell during the latter part of the Zimbabwe reply, but the umpires allowed the match to reach its conclusion. At least 15 overs had to be bowled by New Zealand for a result to be reached, and at one stage this had looked debatable.

4 March

Sydney: India 216–7 (49 overs) beat Pakistan 173 (48.1 overs) by 43 runs. Man Of The Match award: Sachin Tendulkar

A confrontation between Kiran More, the India wicket-keeper, and Pakistan batsman Javed Miandad soured a contest between fierce rivals that was comfortably won by India. More had appealed, 'over-optimistically' in the words of *Wisden*, for a leg-side catch against Miandad, and harsh words were exchanged. Miandad later leapt up and down, apparently in mocking imitation of More, and both team managers were asked by the match referee to sort matters out behind closed doors. Miandad, more to the point, laboured 34 overs for his 40, even though helping Aamir Sohail (62) add 88 for the third wicket, and Pakistan's middle order were left with far too much to do. The outstanding innings of the match came from Sachin Tendulkar, who scored 54 not out from 62 balls and added 60 in eight overs with Kapil Dev.

5 March

Christchurch: South Africa 200–8 (50 overs) beat West Indies 136 (38.4 overs) by 64 runs. Man Of The Match award: Meyrick Pringle

Sydney: Australia 171 (49 overs) lost to England 173–2 (40.5 overs) by eight wickets. Man Of The Match award: Ian Botham

A superb burst from the fast bowler Meyrick Pringle, who took four wickets in 11 balls, propelled South Africa to a comfortable victory in their historic first meeting with the West Indies. Pringle removed Lara, Richardson, Hooper and Arthurton, and only a counter-attacking 61 from Gus Logie, supported by a brave 30 from finger-injury victim Desmond Haynes, kept the West Indies in the hunt at all. Nevertheless, they were finally dismissed for their lowest World Cup score. South Africa's batting was solid, if uninspired, with Peter Kirsten's 56 the highlight.

Meanwhile, Ian Botham rolled back the years to provide Australia with a stunning final reminder of his love of putting one across England's oldest enemy. First he helped to wreck the Australian innings by taking four wickets for no runs in seven balls, and then – under the Sydney lights – he hit six fours in a classy 53 (his first World Cup 50) while putting on 107 with Graham Gooch in an opening stand that left Australia doomed. Botham's 4–31 was also his best one-day international bowling figure.

7 March

Hamilton: India 203–7 (32 overs) beat Zimbabwe 104–1 (19.1 overs) by 55 runs (Zimbabwe set revised target). Man Of The Match award: Sachin Tendulkar

Adelaide: Sri Lanka 189–9 (50 overs) lost to Australia 190–3 (44 overs) by seven wickets. Man Of The Match award: Tom Moody

Three hours lost to morning rain initially reduced this to a 32-over-per-side contest. Zimbabwe, however, after making good progress towards their target, were upset when more rain arrived and they were told they had been well beaten. Once again, the rain ruling proved itself inadequate, with India's total being revised to 158 (the runs accrued from their 19 highest scoring overs) and

Zimbabwe's to 103. Sachin Tendulkar's 81 came off just 77 balls, but Andy Flower was replying fluently with 43 not out when the weather had the final, unsatisfactory say.

Only Aravinda de Silva, the captain, made much of an impact as Sri Lanka failed to set Australia a challenging target. To the relief of the Australians, their openers Tom Moody (57) and Geoff Marsh (60) put on 120, and it was plain sailing thereafter.

8 March

Auckland: West Indies 203–7 (50 overs) lost to New Zealand 206–5 (48.3 overs) by five wickets. Man Of The Match award: Martin Crowe

Brisbane: South Africa 211–7 (50 overs) beat Pakistan 173–8 (36 overs) by 20 runs (revised target). Man Of The Match award: Andrew Hudson

Martin Crowe's third match award from five games came as a result of his stylish and calm 81 not out to see off the West Indies, but it was an initial assault from Mark Greatbatch which set up this impressive victory. Greatbatch hit Ambrose, Marshall and Anderson Cummins for sixes and also struck seven fours in his thrilling 63. Earlier, the Kiwi ploy of opening the bowling with off-spinner Dipak Patel succeeded again, and it took Brian Lara's 52 and some late hitting from Keith Arthurton and David Williams to lift the West Indian total above 200. In the context of World Cup history, this was another important staging post: in 13 previous one-day international meetings with the West Indies, there had been just one solitary victory for New Zealand.

A real low point of the tournament for Pakistan saw Aqib Javed join an injury list already containing Javed Miandad, Ramiz Raja and Wasim Haider when the fast bowler was struck on the forehead by a ball thrown by his own wicket-keeper, Moin Khan. They also fell foul of the rain rule after Imran Khan had chosen to risk bowling first despite the dodgy forecast. Andrew Hudson completed a maiden one-day international 50 and Hansie Cronje and Brian McMillan then added 71 in 12 overs. Replying, Pakistan had reached 74–2 in the 22nd over when rain intervened and caused a revision of the target to 194 from 36 overs. In effect, this reduced Pakistan's target by only 18 runs while reducing their overs by 14, increasing the scoring rate required from around five to over eight. On the resumption, Inzamam-ul-Haq and Imran Khan thrashed 61 from nine overs, but Inzamam was then run out by the flying figure of Jonty Rhodes in a moment immortalised by photographers and television stills. A total of 58 from the final five overs proved too much for those who followed.

9 March

Ballarat: England 280–6 (50 overs) beat Sri Lanka 174 (44 overs) by 106 runs. Man Of The Match award: Chris Lewis

Half-centuries from Neil Fairbrother and Alec Stewart highlighted a magnificent batting display by England, for whom Botham and Graeme Hick also starred. Stewart's 59 took just 36 balls, while Chris Lewis then struck an unbeaten 20 from only six balls as a remarkable 73 were plundered from the final five overs. Lewis then made sure that England would win easily by ripping out four wickets in four overs.

10 March

Wellington: India 197 (49.4 overs) lost to West Indies 195–5 (40.2 overs) by five wickets (target revised). Man Of The Match award: Anderson Cummins
Canberra: Zimbabwe 163 (48.3 overs) lost to South Africa 164–3 (45.1 overs) by seven wickets. Man Of The Match award: Peter Kirsten

A rain break of 20 minutes almost cost West Indies this match. The interruption came at 81–1 from just 11 overs, but Brian Lara was out almost immediately after the restart and three more wickets quickly followed. In the end, as they chased a revised target of 195 from 46 overs, the West Indies were indebted to an unbroken stand of 83 from Keith Athurton and Carl Hooper. India's innings had been progressing smoothly until Mohammad Azharuddin (61) became the first of four wickets for Anderson Cummins, the fast bowler from Barbados.

The veteran Peter Kirsten defied a calf strain to be the all-round hero of South Africa's win. He took three middle-order wickets with his occasional off-breaks and then struck an unbeaten 62, then helping to add 112 for the second wicket with Kepler Wessels (70).

11 March

Perth: Pakistan 220–9 (50 overs) beat Australia 172 (45.2 overs) by 48 runs. Man Of The Match award: Aamir Sohail

Nothing continued to go right for the holders as Australia, fielding seven of the side who had won the Cup itself in 1987, slid to a despairing defeat under the WACA lights. Aamir Sohail, caught behind off a no-ball before scoring, went on to make 76 and feature in stands of 78 and 77 with Ramiz Raja and Javed Miandad. Australia reached 116–2, but then, against disciplined bowling, lost their last eight wickets for just 56 runs.

12 March

Dunedin: India 230–6 (50 overs) lost to New Zealand 231–6 (47.1 overs) by four wickets. Man Of The Match award: Mark Greatbatch

Melbourne: South Africa 236–4 (50 overs) lost to England 226–7 (40.5 overs) by three wickets (revised target). Man Of The Match award: Alec Stewart

Memorable strokeplay by Sachin Tendulkar (84), Mohammed Azharuddin (55) and Kapil Dev took India to what looked like being a defendable total – until Mark Greatbatch again cut loose. The big left-hander struck 73 from 77 balls to put New Zealand ahead of the rate, and an unbeaten 67 from Andrew Jones guided them home despite the brilliant run-out of Martin Crowe by Kiran More.

England underlined the potency of their World Cup challenge by beating South Africa in a floodlit thriller in which they overcame several handicaps. The first was the loss of their captain, Graham Gooch, to injury, but Alec Stewart deputised admirably at the head of the order, and the team, with a sparkling 77. Neil Fairbrother was the other batting hero, finishing on 75 not out to steer England past a target revised, stiffly, to 226 from 41 overs after rain had intervened with England 62 without loss after just 12 overs. The key was a stand of 50 in just six overs between Fairbrother and Chris Lewis (33), and when Derek Pringle was caught with the scores level it was left to Phillip DeFreitas to emerge and hit the winning run with one ball to spare. Earlier, Lewis had been unable to bowl because of a side strain, Dermot Reeve fell and bruised his back so badly he could complete his third over, and DeFreitas struggled to finish his ten-over stint due to a leg injury. It was, however, England's 12th successive one-day international victory.

13 March

Berri: West Indies 268–8 (50 overs) beat Sri Lanka 177–9 (50 overs) by 91 runs. Man Of The Match award: Phil Simmons

A century from Phil Simmons, whose 110 came off 125 balls with two sixes and nine fours, spearheaded a win which raised West Indian hopes of a semi-final place. Curtly Ambrose and Carl Hooper both turned in impressive ten-over spells as Sri Lanka failed to build on a quickfire 40 from opener Samarasekera.

14 March

Hobart: Australia 265–6 (46 overs) beat Zimbabwe 137 (41.4 overs) by 128 runs. Man Of The Match award: Steve Waugh

The Waugh twins dominated this straightforward victory for Australia. Mark finished unbeaten on 66, from 39 balls, and with Steve (55) added a violent 113 off 69 deliveries. A rainshower, arriving when Australia were 72–1 from 15 overs, shortened the match to 46 overs per side. Steve Waugh then took two top-order Zimbabwean wickets and Mark Waugh snaffled two catches.

15 March

Wellington: England 200–8 (50 overs) lost to New Zealand 201–3 by seven wickets. Man Of The Match award: Andrew Jones

Adelaide: India 180–6 (30 overs) lost to South Africa 181–4 (29.1 overs) by six wickets. Man Of The Match award: Peter Kirsten

Perth: Sri Lanka 212–6 (50 overs) lost to Pakistan 216–6 (49.1 overs) by four wickets. Man Of The Match award: Javed Miandad

The contest between the two form teams of the tournament to date was marred by England's lengthy injury list: Gooch and Fairbrother were unfit, Lewis was unable to bowl and DeFreitas and Reeve were carrying injuries. In addition, Pringle broke down in his seventh over with damaged ribs. Alec Stewart (41) and Graeme Hick (56) put on 70 for England's second wicket, but the rest of the order struggled. Mark Greatbatch carved 35 from 37 balls, and New Zealand made sure that they would head the qualifying table ahead of England through a third wicket stand of 108 in 23 overs between Andrew Jones (78) and Martin Crowe (73 not out). It was a World Cup record seventh successive win by New Zealand.

A confident chase for victory, in a match reduced by heavy rain to 30 overs per side, saw South Africa confirm their place in the semi-finals – unless, said their Board president Geoff Dakin, the imminent all-white referendum rejected constitutional reform. Other World Cup nations, led by Pakistan and West Indies, urged the South Africans to remain in the competition. Subsequently, the decisive vote for reform settled everything and was another huge boost to South Africa's cricketers. Mohammed Azharuddin (79) and Kapil Dev (42 from 29 balls) led India's charge, but Peter Kirsten's wonderful 84 and another half-century by the equally in-form Andrew Hudson launched the successful reply.

Pakistan overcame a nervy start with both bat and ball to continue their late climb up the qualification table. No balls and wides littered the start of the Sri Lankan innings, which reached 99–2 in quick time. But Pakistan regained control, and with a stand of 101 in 21 overs for the fourth wicket, Javed Miandad (57) and Salim Malik (51) played decisive innings.

18 March

Christchurch: New Zealand 166 (48.2 overs) lost to Pakistan 167–3 (44.4 overs) by seven wickets. Man Of The Match award: Mushtaq Ahmed

Albury: Zimbabwe 134 (46.1 overs) beat England 125 (49.1 overs) by nine runs. Man Of The Match award: Eddo Brandes

Melbourne: Australia 216–6 (50 overs) beat West Indies 159 (42.4 overs) by 57 runs. Man Of The Match award: David Boon

Pakistan confirmed their last-ditch emergence as a World Cup force by defeating previously unbeaten New Zealand on the strength of a magnificent bowling display and an unbeaten 119 from Ramiz Raja, the opener. Australia were eliminated as a result, but Pakistan knew they had only made it into the semi-finals, by the skin of their teeth, when West Indies failed to beat the Australians in Melbourne on the same evening. Mushtaq Ahmed, the leg-spinner, won the match award for not conceding a boundary and taking two important wickets in his skilful ten-over stint, but the award could easily have gone instead to either Ramiz (155 balls and 16 fours) or Wasim Akram, whose own four wickets included the scalps of Andrew Jones and Martin Crowe.

Evidence that injury problems and general tiredness were beginning to catch up with England came at the cricketing outpost of Albury when Zimbabwe won themselves a famous and uplifting victory on a pitch favouring the bowlers. This was a day that also belonged to the chicken farmer Eddo Brandes. The burly pace bowler, who had a full-time job running the family poultry farm, plucked out four prime English wickets in one ten-over spell, including, for nought, Graeme Hick, who as a 17-year-old had been a member of Zimbabwe's 1983 World Cup squad. It was in 1983, against Australia at Trent Bridge in their debut match, that Zimbabwe had last won a World Cup game. Brandes' heroic burst (which began with the wicket of Graham Gooch to the first ball of the innings) spearheaded a fine display in the field by the Zimbabweans, who were defending a small total of their own. Not even a stand of 52 in 24 overs between Alec Stewart and Neil Fairbrother, who came together at 43-5, could pull England around.

Australia, and then the West Indies, had their hopes of a semi-final place dashed on a night of drama in Melbourne. First, 45 minutes into Australia's innings, came news from Christchurch that Pakistan's win had put them out of the Cup. Then, after David Boon's 100 had ensured a reasonable total, the West Indies saw their own chance of reaching the last four disappear as Mike Whitney's four-wicket spell shattered their middle order. Brian Lara alone kept West Indian ambitions alive, but when he was sent back and run out for 70, to leave the total at 137–8, there was no escape.

SEMI-FINALS
21 March
Auckland: New Zealand 262–7 (50 overs) lost to Pakistan 264–6 (49 overs) by four wickets. Man Of The Match award: Inzamam-ul-Haq

The Kiwi nation was left shattered by this second defeat to Pakistan within four days. What made the loss even harder to bear was that they had finished five points ahead of Pakistan in the qualifying table and, up to this point, were unquestionably the team of the tournament. Moreover, after their fine batting display, in which Martin Crowe scored a classy 91 despite a pulled hamstring which later prevented him from leading his side in the field, New Zealand had seemed in control when Pakistan needed to score at more than eight runs per over for the last 15 to win. Yet, for all their careful planning, the New Zealanders had not accounted for a display of extraordinary power from Inzamam-ul-Haq, then just turned 22 and the baby of the Pakistani squad. Championed before the tournament by Imran Khan, who said he had the ability to become one of the world's best batsmen, Inzamam repaid his captain's faith at the moment he needed it most. With a six and seven fours, he scored 60 from 37 balls and transformed the match. He dominated a partnership of 87 in ten overs with Javed Miandad, the senior partner, and when he was eventually run out the target had come down to 36 from five overs. Miandad finished 57 not out as the match was won at a canter in the end with an over to spare. Fierce blows from Wasim Akram and Moin Khan, whose unbeaten 20 took him just 11 deliveries, completed the job in style.

22 March
Sydney: England 252–6 (45 overs) beat South Africa 232–6 (43 overs) by 19 runs (revised target). Man Of The Match award: Graeme Hick

The second semi-final saw a potentially classic game of cricket spoiled by the tournament's inflexible and plain-stupid rain ruling, and the accompanying controversy. Neutrals argued that a sort of justice was done, especially as South Africa had chosen to field first and had then bowled their overs so slowly that

England were denied five overs' worth of late acceleration (for which Kepler Wessels' team was later fined). Yet the match ended with even the victors embarrassed by the way their passage into the final had been clinched: a 12-minute stoppage for heavy rain resulting in South Africa's requirement changing from an exciting 22 runs off 13 balls to a barely credible 22 from seven, and then still further to a farcical 21 off one. Brian McMillan took a single off Chris Lewis, the players shook hands and their heads in equal measure – and the 35,000 crowd, plus millions watching on television around the world, wondered why the match couldn't have just been completed under the blazing floodlights of the SCG. Or why not use the reserve day, now available where in the group stage it had not existed? Whichever way you looked at it, one of the greatest occasions in the sport had been ruined, and the only reason for applause at the end was the dignified way in which the South Africans reacted to having the chance of glory snatched away so cruelly. Graeme Hick, too, deserved more recognition than he received for an increasingly commanding 83 off 90 balls.

THE 1992 WORLD CUP FINAL
25 March
Melbourne: Pakistan 249–6 (50 overs) beat England 227 (49.2 overs) by 22 runs. Man Of The Match award: Wasim Akram

Pakistan's gathering momentum made them an irresistible force in front of a captivated audience of 87,182 at the vast Melbourne Cricket Ground. The drama was heightened by the floodlit atmosphere, as cricket's World Cup at last became a spectacle worthy of the technological age. This really was a stage, with the spotlight of the world's attention illuminating 22 fine cricketers as they strained every sinew in search of the game's greatest prize.

It also became Imran Khan's greatest moment, a crowning glory indeed for the impossibly handsome, outrageously gifted 39-year-old Pakistan captain. He had virtually hand-picked the team, he had overcome his own injury problems earlier in the tournament, he had inspired his team to fight back from a position of near-hopelessness at the group stage, and now he had top-scored for his side with 72 and, if that wasn't enough, snatched the last, match-clinching wicket himself.

While Graham Gooch's England had looked more drained as the tournament had progressed – a legacy, said some embittered senior players, of too much training and not enough rest during their previous two months on the road – Imran's erratic outfit had simply grown stronger.

Victory in the final, which gave them their first World Cup triumph, was Pakistan's fifth win on the trot; England, in contrast, lost three of their last four games.

Imran immediately described Pakistan's win as 'the most fulfilling and satisfying cricket moment of my life', and said the proceeds of his success would be donated to the Lahore cancer hospital he was building in his late mother's memory. He added that victory had been a triumph of his young side's talent over England's wider experience, and could not resist a jibe about Gooch's 'stereotyped' medium-paced all-rounders when comparison was made to the extra aggression and penetration of his balanced, specialist bowling attack.

Famously, Khan had instructed his team to play 'like cornered tigers' when they had faced up to the possibility (or probability) of elimination during the initial group stage. At 24–2, after nine overs, following Imran's decision to bat first, Pakistan were facing another crisis. This time, though, it was the only two veteran survivors of the first World Cup in 1975 – Imran himself and his deputy, Javed Miandad – who fought tigerishly to keep their country in the game.

Seeing off the new ball, and then accelerating smoothly, Imran and Javed (58) added 139 in 31 overs for the third wicket before giving way to the big-hitting prowess of Inzamam and Wasim Akram.

Inzamam's 35-ball 42 and Wasim's 33 from just 18 balls enabled Pakistan to plunder 153 in all from their last 20 overs. England, in reply, were soon up against it at 21–2 themselves, with Ian Botham astonished at being given out caught at the wicket and Alec Stewart out in the same way to the accurate Aqib Javed.

Mushtaq Ahmed's googly then accounted for Graeme Hick, and the leg-spinner also bagged the prized wicket of Gooch. Allan Lamb tried his best to repair the damage in a 14-over stand worth 72 with Neil Fairbrother, but England's flickering fire was doused when Wasim returned to deliver two devastating blows. A late away-swinger castled Lamb and, next ball, a wicked off-cutter was too good for Chris Lewis.

Bravely, and despite needing a runner, Fairbrother fought on to 62 and the tail also wagged defiantly. Fittingly, Imran grabbed the ball for the final over and, after his second ball, raised his arms aloft in joy and triumph as Richard Illingworth, England's last man, skied a catch.

THE INTERVIEW
Imran Khan

Looking back on his crowning glory as one of the game's greatest all-round players, Imran Khan believes the major factors in Pakistan's 1992 World Cup victory were his team's sky-high self-confidence and his own good fortune in winning the toss: 'For that game at Melbourne my biggest job as captain was to make sure my team did not freeze under the pressure. I remember, as the tournament reached its climax, that the players were being offered all sorts of advice whenever they met Pakistani supporters. This only increased their tension.

'As a result, I advised the players to relax in each others' company and not to mingle with friends and supporters on the evening before the final against England. In addition, I also advised them to take a mild sleeping pill, because before a big match it is extremely important to have a good night's sleep.

'Most players, however, found there was too much adrenalin in their systems to get much sleep!

'In fact, my job as captain had been made a lot easier because our team had come through a torrid time in the early matches. Midway through the World Cup, we were second from bottom in the qualifying table for the semi-finals, and only got there in the end because Australia beat the West Indies.

'Yet, by playing under so much pressure for so long in the run-up to the final, we were far better equipped to handle it than England, who had cruised into the last four.

'In 1992, my Pakistan team peaked at the right time; its confidence level was at its greatest. We were also fortunate that we won the toss and batted, because chasing runs in a World Cup final becomes a tougher and tougher proposition with the fall of every wicket.

'Arguably, the 1983 West Indies team was the greatest national XI in cricket history. Yet, in the World Cup final of that year, it could not chase a modest Indian total of 183, despite having a batting order that boasted Viv Richards, Gordon Greenidge, Desmond Haynes and Clive Lloyd.

'The Indian bowling attack, too, was positively friendly compared to the awesome West Indian pace quartet of Andy Roberts, Joel Garner, Malcolm Marshall and Michael Holding. But the pressure told on the West Indies as wickets fell.

'Winning the World Cup was really something special. It gave so much happiness to so many people. Just seeing the joy on the faces of the masses as we landed at Lahore Airport, on our return from the World Cup, made my whole cricket career worthwhile.

'There is no occasion in cricket like the World Cup final. Anyone who has played in one can never forget it. And above all, for the players, it is a test of nerve – even more than a test of skill.'

THE CHAMPIONS

How typical that Pakistan, the most unpredictable nation in world cricket, should pluck glory out of an air of despair a fortnight earlier. And, moreover, that they should perform the miracle without their most devastating bowler, Waqar Younis.

The fearsome Waqar would surely have blazed across the World Cup firmament like a fire-breathing comet. His pace and accuracy, allied to his ability to deliver the most toe-crunchingly lethal yorkers ever seen, was too much for England's batting in the Test series between the two countries later in 1992. In the 1991 English county season, he had taken 113 wickets at an average of 14.65 for Surrey, with 13 five-wicket hauls. Aged 20, he was at his most lethal, already a Test-match winner.

But just before he was due to leave for the World Cup, Waqar had been diagnosed with a stress fracture of the back. Pakistan, at the start of their campaign, looked lacklustre and devoid of sparkle.

Furthermore, Imran Khan was struggling with a shoulder injury and missed two of the three early defeats. Even the inspirational captain seemed out of sorts, and in the group match against England only the weather prevented a likely heavy defeat.

Was it Imran's exhortation to fight like 'cornered tigers' that pulled them around in the nick of time? Or was it their innate ability finally winning through, coupled with a fierce pride and natural competitiveness?

What is certain is that the Pakistan team that won the 1992 World Cup was, in the end, a potent mix of wise old heads and fearless youth. The batting and bowling was varied in style, with an inherent aggression that finally managed to mask the absence of the mighty Waqar.

And yes, Pakistan's 1992 triumph was all about Imran Khan, too, his charisma and his ability to weld together a team of brilliant but often wayward individuals.

It also underlined, following India's 1983 success, that power within the cricketing community was now being spread beyond the traditional boundaries.

Indeed, had the 1987 semi-finals of five years earlier progressed according to the scripts widely predicted for them, Asia would have ruled the World Cup for consecutive tournaments.

THE PRIZES

Pakistan's tangible reward came in the shape of a £7,500 Waterford crystal trophy, presented to Imran Khan by Sir Colin Cowdrey, the ICC chairman, upon a dais that had been wheeled out onto the MCG outfield.

Profit for the organisers was assured by the time that an Australian one-day record crowd watched the final and generated receipts of £880,000 (AUS$2 million).

It was later announced that the event had made a gross profit of AUS $5 million.

THE QUOTES

'It's not the end of the world, but it is close to it.' Beaten captain Graham Gooch after the World Cup final.

'From a personal point of view, our World Cup win created such euphoria in Pakistan that we found that we were able to collect significant funds for our new cancer hospital in Lahore. People gave so generously.' Imran Khan.

'I was thankful to the Almighty that I was able to leave cricket with dignity. It is a blessing that has been denied to greater cricketers than myself.' Imran again.

TEAM OF THE TOURNAMENT?

Aamir Sohail (Pakistan)
Ramiz Raja (Pakistan)
Peter Kirsten (South Africa)
Martin Crowe (New Zealand)
Javed Miandad (Pakistan)
Alec Stewart (England, wicket-keeper)
Imran Khan (Pakistan, captain)
Wasim Akram (Pakistan)
Derek Pringle (England)
Dipak Patel (New Zealand)
Mushtaq Ahmed (Pakistan)

THE ROAD TO 1996...

Their blip of failure at the 1992 World Cup served only to inspire Australia towards greater efforts in their bid to become the best all-round cricket country in the world. They also soon unearthed perhaps the greatest leg-spinner ever to enchant the cricket watcher: Shane Warne.

Two more Ashes wins confirmed their growing superiority over England, for whom the retirements of Ian Botham and David Gower – followed, in early 1995, by those of Graham Gooch and Mike Gatting – signalled the end of an era.

The West Indies continued to decline, despite the excellence of Curtly Ambrose and Courtney Walsh with the ball, and Pakistan built on their World Cup success to become a dangerous and stronger team, although one still with an infuriating inconsistency.

India and Sri Lanka gained strength from their wristy, world-class batsmen like Tendulkar and De Silva, and there also emerged from Sri Lanka a magical new spinner called Muttiah Muralitharan.

Spin, indeed, was fast becoming the new must-have accessory for any aspiring cricket nation: in addition to Warne there were now other world-class 'leggies' in Mushtaq Ahmed and India's Anil Kumble, while the rebirth of the new-look off-spinner began with Muralitharan and continued with the appearance, just before the 1996 World Cup, of another super-talented Pakistani: Saqlain Mushtaq.

Off the field, meanwhile, the road to the sixth World Cup was more rocky than it had been for any of its predecessors. A meeting of the ICC on 2 February 1993 was described in *Wisden* as 'almost certainly the most acrimonious and shambolic in the history of the ICC [and which] broke up amid signs of lasting anguish'.

The cause of this acrimony was the debate on the venue of the 1996 World Cup, which a previous ICC meeting had decided should be awarded to England. Now, a fresh argument had broken out, amid strong feelings from all sides, and the result – after an unscheduled evening and second morning of heated debate – was that it should be staged, jointly, by India, Pakistan and Sri Lanka.

Representatives of the Asian countries, led by India, legally challenged the voting procedures of the ICC, and in the end England backed down with the assurance that it would host the seventh World Cup tournament instead.

Alan Smith, the normally uncontroversial chief executive of England's governing body, the Test and County Cricket Board, said, 'We have acted in the best and wider interests of the world game. We have endured a fractious and unpleasant meeting beset by procedural wrangling. There was no talk of anything like cricket. It was, by a long way, the worst meeting I have ever attended.'

Unpleasant it may have been, but this was incontrovertible evidence – if further evidence was by now needed – that the balance of power in world cricket had changed. The battle to stage as commercially attractive a product as the World Cup had become one of the catalysts of that change.

Chapter 9

1996: Super Sri Lankans Surprise The World

If the 1992 event was flawed in its rain rule, the 1996 World Cup was far more seriously blemished in conception, structure, and organisation.

Hijacked, in effect, by the Asian bloc, it was run by Pilcom, an independent World Cup committee which clearly had its own agenda outside wider cricket responsibilities.

That the ICC should have handed over the World Cup to Pilcom, in the first place, speaks volumes for the lack of authority the game's ruling body possessed at the time.

Pilcom's primary objective was commercial, and yet when the official accounts of the event were presented, they showed a negligible profit. Something, somewhere, had gone wrong.

Money-making, or the ideal of it, also got in the way of the logistic realities of running a tournament as important as the World Cup. Ridiculous travel schedules, criss-crossing the sub-continent, illogical playing itineraries and substandard practice facilities exposed a general disregard for the welfare of those actually taking part in the matches.

It was all well and good to expand the World Cup from nine teams to twelve, especially as that dovetailed with the ICC's express wish to broaden cricket's base as a global sport, but what followed was a seemingly interminable, largely pointless, month-long group stage which was only ever going to eliminate the three associate member countries (Holland, Kenya and the United Arab Emirates) and the weakest of the Test-playing nations, Zimbabwe.

Then, equally ridiculously, half the elite field found themselves being culled in the commercially disastrous quarter-finals, and the exciting knockout stage of the competition was done and dusted in little more than a week.

The event was badly affected, too, by the latest trend in the sub-continent (especially India) to glamorise the leading players to quite irresponsible lengths. To the teeming masses, as a consequence, players such as Sachin Tendulkar and Wasim Akram became living gods quite incapable of suffering defeat.

When defeat for their teams did occur, most notably when India lost to Sri Lanka in the semi-final at Eden Gardens, Calcutta, the predictable outcome was mass disorder. That match, shamefully, became the first in World Cup history to be abandoned because of rioting, bottle-throwing and fire-lighting on the huge terraces.

All this was not the sum of the problems afflicting the sixth World Cup, however. Far from it.

A bomb blast in Colombo a fortnight earlier had led to both Australia and West Indies refusing to play their group matches against Sri Lanka in the city. The Australians, moreover, had just played an acrimonious Test series in Sri Lanka and were also nervous about any possible retribution that might befall them from fanatics upset by their recent bribery allegations against Salim Malik, the Pakistan batsman.

These Colombo matches were subsequently forfeited by Australia and West Indies, gifting Sri Lanka four qualifying points but, because of the laughable format, hardly inconveniencing the progress into the quarter-finals of Australia or West Indies either.

The opening ceremony was also a joke. More than 100,000 spectators attended what had been publicised as an event featuring the very latest in technological wizardry. Instead, the lasers malfunctioned, the compère was an embarrassment and the supposed grand launch was a total flop. As a result, there were calls at government level in Calcutta for the arrest of Jagmohan Dalmiya, the head of Pilcom, on a charge of wasting huge amounts of public money.

At 4am the next morning, too, four competing teams who had been staying at the city's Oberoi Hotel stumbled into the lobby to be transported to their 6am flights to the destinations of their opening matches. It was silly, unnecessary, unprofessional and, sadly, all too representative of the travel burdens placed upon each player in the following weeks.

Equally amateurish was the decision to open the tournament with the low-key match between England and New Zealand in the sprawling, grubby, backwater (in Indian cricket terms) city of Ahmedabad, and to have all 17 of the Indian matches staged at different venues.

However laudable it was that the organisers wanted the cricket to reach out across the vastness of India, the reality of the scheduling merely worsened still further the travel problems inherent in that part of the world. It was not just the teams who were caught up in the maelstrom; television crews, media and travelling supporters all had to endure it.

To the catalogue of misfortunes to bedevil this tournament can now be added the shadow of cricket's match-fixing crisis which, some time later, cast doubts on the validity of the shock victory won by Kenya over the West Indies in Pune.

In the end, it was perhaps only the identity of the winner itself that prevented this World Cup from being remembered solely for its political, social and logistical shortcomings. Sri Lanka's triumph was widely acclaimed and, due to the increased profile – achieved largely on the back of television coverage, which was by far the best the World Cup had known – widely seen.

THE MATCHES
GROUP A
16 February

Hyderabad: Zimbabwe 151–9 (50 overs) lost to West Indies 155–4 (29.3 overs) by six wickets. Man Of The Match award: Curtly Ambrose

Only Paul Strang's leg-spin troubled the West Indians in a day-night affair otherwise dominated by the fast bowling of Curtly Ambrose and the strokeplay of the returning Brian Lara.

17 February

Colombo: Sri Lanka were awarded the match by default when Australia refused to turn up at the Premadasa Stadium.

18 February

Cuttack: Kenya 199–6 (50 overs) lost to India 203–3 (41.5 overs) by seven wickets. Man Of The Match award: Sachin Tendulkar

Kenya's senior one-day international bow was a creditable effort, before they were forced to bend the knee to the great Sachin Tendulkar. The little master hit an unbeaten 127 from 134 balls, with 15 fours and a six, but Steve Tikolo had produced some memorable strokemaking of his own during his earlier innings of 65.

21 February

Colombo (SSC): Zimbabwe 228–6 (50 overs) lost to Sri Lanka 229–4 (37 overs) by six wickets. Man Of The Match award: Aravinda de Silva

Gwalior: West Indies 173 (50 overs) lost to India 174–5 (39.4 overs) by five wickets. Man Of The Match award: Sachin Tendulkar

A good innings by Alistair Campbell and some beefy hitting by Craig Evans brought Zimbabwe a decent enough total, but it was easily overhauled by the dashing Sri Lankans, for whom Aravinda de Silva hit 91 from 86 balls and Asanka Gurusinha six sixes in a crashing 87. That feat equalled the World Cup record shared by Viv Richards and Kapil Dev.

Sachin Tendulkar earned his second successive match award for an innings of 70 from 91 balls as India cruised past West Indies in a day-night fixture which ended with a joyous crowd of around 30,000 celebrating with flaming torches and firecrackers.

23 February

Vishakhapatnam: Australia 304–7 (50 overs) beat Kenya 207–7 (50 overs) by 97 runs. Man Of The Match award: Mark Waugh

Kenya were well beaten but not disgraced after Steve and Mark Waugh had added 207 for the third wicket (the first double-century stand in World Cup history) in 32 overs. Mark's 130 took just 128 balls and Steve's 82 came off 88 deliveries, but Australia's daunting total was chased spiritedly by the Kenyans, who were ahead on runs per over at the halfway mark of their innings, thanks to a stand of 102 between Kennedy Otieno (85) and Maurice Odumbe, the captain, who scored 50 from 63 balls. Victory came at a price for the Aussies, though, with Craig McDermott suffering a recurrence of a calf injury and later flying home.

25 February

Patna: Zimbabwe 45–3 (15.5 overs) v Kenya – match abandoned.

26 February

Colombo (Premadasa Stadium): Sri Lanka beat the West Indies by default after the latter failed to appear

Patna: Kenya 134 (49.4 overs) lost to Zimbabwe 137–5 (42.2 overs) by five wickets. Man Of The Match award: Paul Strang

Crowds of 30,000 watched the initial game washed out, and then a completely new game on the reserve day being decided by the excellent leg-spin of Paul Strang, who recorded Zimbabwe's best one-day international bowling figures of 5–21 after exploiting the turn and bounce in the pitch.

27 February

Bombay: Australia 258 (50 overs) beat India 242 (48 overs) by 12 runs. Man Of The Match award: Mark Waugh

Thrilling batting from Mark Waugh, Mark Taylor and Sachin Tendulkar shone out from the first floodlit one-day international at Bombay. Taylor was the initial aggressor as he made 59, while his opening partner, Waugh, went on to reach 126 from 135 balls (three sixes and eight fours) and become the first to score consecutive World Cup centuries. Early wickets, plus the loss of Azharuddin at 70, left much responsibility on Tendulkar and Sanjay Manjrekar. Tendulkar had made 90 from 84 balls, with 14 fours and a six, when he was stumped off a wide, and Manjrekar (62) then fought out an uneven struggle as more wickets continued to fall.

29 February

Pune: Kenya 166 (49.3 overs) beat the West Indies 93 (35.2 overs) by 73 runs. Man Of The Match award: Maurice Odumbe

A surreal atmosphere surrounded this shock win for Kenya, who failed to reach a substantial total after being put in to bat and yet then dismissed the West Indians with apparent ease. The efforts of Hitesh Modi and 17-year-old Thomas Odoyo were central to Kenya extending their innings into the final over, and Maurice Odumbe then took cheap wickets with his off-breaks after Rajab Ali and Martin Suji had plucked out the top three in the West Indies order with the new ball. At the end, the Kenyans went on an exuberant lap of honour and received a great reception from the local cricket fans.

1 March

Nagpur: Zimbabwe 154 (45.3 overs) lost to Australia 158–2 (36 overs) by eight wickets. Man Of The Match award: Shane Warne

Few spectators were in attendance at a ground which, three months earlier, had witnessed the tragic deaths of nine people when a wall collapsed. On show, however, was a one-sided affair with only Andy Waller (67) taking the game to the Australians with the bat. Shane Warne took four wickets and the in-form Mark Waugh was 76 not out at the finish.

2 March

Delhi: India 271–3 (50 overs) lost to Sri Lanka 272–4 (48.4 overs) by six wickets. Man Of The Match award: Sanath Jayasuriya

The scores at 15 overs reveal both the reason why Sri Lanka won this match at a canter and the dramatic unveiling of their power-hitting strategy at the top of the order. After 15 overs, India were 47–1, compared to Sri Lanka's 117–1. Not even Sachin Tendulkar's run-a-ball 137, with five sixes and eight fours, and an unbeaten 72 from Mohammad Azharuddin, could save India after their sluggish start. Sanath Jayasuriya and Romesh Kaluwitharana, the openers, had 42 on the board by the end of the third over, and the carnage continued even when Kalu fell for 26. Jayasuriya was eventually dismissed for 79 during a mini collapse in the middle-order, but Arjuna Ranatunga (46 not out) was then joined by Hashan Tillekeratne (70 not out) in an unbroken partnership of 131 which gave Sri Lanka a six-wicket victory. Their impressive win assured Sri Lanka first place in the group table.

4 March

Jaipur: Australia 229–6 (50 overs) lost to West Indies 232–6 (48.5 overs) by four wickets. Man Of The Match award: Richie Richardson

An emotional day for Richie Richardson, the universally popular West Indies captain, who scored a superb unbeaten 93 to clinch a victory over the strongly fancied Australians four days after he and his team had been humbled by Kenya. Richardson, however, then announced that he would be retiring from international cricket after the World Cup. It was a stand of 87 between Richardson and Brian Lara, whose 60 came from 70 balls, which inspired the West Indians after Ricky Ponting's 102 had rallied Australia following a slow start against the new ball excellence of Curtly Ambrose and Courtney Walsh. This win assured West Indies of a quarter-final place.

6 March

Kanpur: India 247–5 (50 overs) beat Zimbabwe 207 (49.4 overs) by 40 runs. Man Of The Match award: Ajay Jadeja

Kandy: Sri Lanka 398–5 (50 overs) beat Kenya 254–7 (50 overs) by 144 runs. Man Of The Match award: Aravinda de Silva

India were 32–3, after being put in by Zimbabwe, before Vinod Kambli (106) and Navjot Singh Sidhu (80) added 142 in 29 overs. Ajay Jadeja's unbeaten 44, which included taking 19 from the final over, provided India with a timely late boost, and he also took two prime wickets when Zimbabwe made a spirited effort to get the required runs. The Indian spinners Venkat Raju and Anil Kumble also played a significant role, as no Zimbabwe batsman could play the major innings that might have been decisive.

Kenya's fate, after their glorious win over the West Indies, was to score the third-highest total by a non-Test-playing side in World Cup competition – and still get beaten heavily. Sri Lanka's batting effort was astonishing: Jayasuriya and Kaluwitharana raced to 83 from the first 40 balls of the innings, and then Gurusinha (84) added 184 in 182 balls for the third wicket with Aravinda de Silva. De Silva's magnificent 145 occupied just 115 balls, with 14 fours and five sixes, while Arjuna Ranatunga finished on 75 not out from 40 deliveries. Ranatunga's 50 was reached in a World Cup record 29 balls and the total was, unsurprisingly, a world one-day international record. Steve Tikolo, Kenya's star batsman, shone in a gutsy reply with four sixes and eight fours of his own in a 95-ball 96, and the Kenyan's effort ensured that the match aggregate of runs was also a World Cup record.

GROUP B
14 February
Ahmedabad: New Zealand 239–6 (50 overs) beat England 228–9 (50 overs) by 11 runs. Man Of The Match award: Nathan Astle

Dropped on one by Graham Thorpe at slip, Nathan Astle went on to score 101 from 132 balls and hit two sixes and eight fours. England missed four catches in all, but they might still have won if Mike Atherton – running for hamstring injury victim Graeme Hick – hadn't got involved in a mix-up. The result was Hick being run out for 85, through no fault of his own, and England's effort petering out.

15-16 February
Rawalpindi: South Africa 321–2 (50 overs) beat United Arab Emirates 152–8 (50 overs) by 169 runs. Man Of The Match award: Gary Kirsten

A match played on the reserve day, after an initial washout, became a slaughter as the Emirates team was completely outclassed on their World Cup debut. Gary Kirsten, the left-handed opener, helped himself to a competition record 188 not out from 159 balls, and perhaps the most optimistic, courageous, defiant or just plain stupid act of the tournament (depending on your point of view) came when Sultan Zarawani, the Emirates captain, marched out to bat at number eight sporting a floppy white hat and not a helmet. He was out for an eight-ball duck, and later needed a hospital check-up after being struck on the head by the first ball he faced, from Allan Donald!

17 February

Baroda: New Zealand 307–8 (50 overs) beat Holland 188–7 (50 overs) by 119 runs. Man Of The Match award: Craig Spearman

The Dutch were also overpowered on their World Cup debut but fought with determination and enthusiasm. Craig Spearman (68 from 59 balls) got New Zealand going with a second-wicket stand worth 116 in 19 overs with Stephen Fleming (66). Holland were not disgraced with the bat but had no realistic chance of getting close to the Kiwi total.

18 February

Peshawar: United Arab Emirates 136 (48.3 overs) lost to England 140–2 (35 overs) by eight wickets. Man Of The Match award: Neil Smith

Zarawani again batted without a helmet, this time coming in at number nine and avoiding being hit as he scored two. Not so fortunate were Craig White, the England all-rounder, who pulled an intercostal muscle and put himself out of the tournament, or Neil Smith. The Warwickshire off-spinning all-rounder took three wickets and hit 27 from 31 balls when promoted to open, but then had to leave the field after being violently sick.

20 February

Faisalabad: New Zealand 177–9 (50 overs) lost to South Africa 178–5 (37.3 overs) by five wickets. Man Of The Match award: Hansie Cronje

Wonderful fielding was at the heart of this impressive South African victory, establishing Hansie Cronje's side as the early-form team of the tournament. Cronje himself struck a masterful 78 from only 64 balls, with three sixes and 11 fours, after New Zealand had been restricted to an inadequate total on a blameless pitch.

22 February

Peshawar: England 279–4 (50 overs) beat Holland 230–6 (50 overs) by 49 runs. Man Of The Match award: Graeme Hick

Fine knocks by Graeme Hick (104 not out) and Graham Thorpe (89 from 82 balls) ensured that England would not be beaten, but the Holland batsmen confirmed the good impression they'd made against New Zealand and came out of this match with much credit. Tim de Leede scored a solid 41, while Klaus van Noortwijk (64) and 18-year-old Bas Zuiderent (54) also gave Dutch cricket a massive boost with their stand of 114 in 27 overs.

24 February

Gujranwala: United Arab Emirates 109–9 (33 overs) lost to Pakistan 112–1 (18 overs) by nine wickets. Man Of The Match award: Mushtaq Ahmed

Because of the festival of Ramadan, the Pakistan team began their defence of the World Cup a little later than they might have. They certainly didn't hang about against a game but limited Emirates side after overnight rain had turned their opening match into a 33-overs-per-side affair. Javed Miandad, creating history by becoming the only player to compete in the first six World Cups, was not required to bat as Saeed Anwar and Ijaz Ahmed knocked off a mediocre total. Saleem Raza, the Emirates opener, did swing Wasim Akram over square leg for six in his 20-ball 22, but there was little other defiance from the minnows.

25 February

Rawalpindi: South Africa 230 (50 overs) beat England 152 (44.3 overs) by 78 runs. Man Of The Match award: Jonty Rhodes

A thoroughly professional performance by South Africa was too much for England, for whom both Alec Stewart and Phillip DeFreitas were run out as they failed to ground their bats. Mike Atherton, the captain, was out to the fourth ball of the England innings, and on a pitch that made fluent strokeplay difficult only Graham Thorpe held up the confident South Africans for long, with the match's top score of 46.

26 February

Lahore: Holland 145–7 (50 overs) lost to Pakistan 151–2 (30.4 overs) by eight wickets. Man Of The Match award: Waqar Younis

An easy win for Pakistan, for whom Waqar Younis found some promising pace and swing to take four wickets, while Saeed Anwar scored an unbeaten 83 from 75 balls. Anwar's third six finished the match.

27 February

Faisalabad: New Zealand 276–8 (47 overs) beat United Arab Emirates 167–9 (47 overs) by 109 runs. Man Of The Match award: Roger Twose

Early-morning fog delayed the start and turned this match into a 47-overs-per-side contest, but it was a hopelessly one-sided one. Craig Spearman scored a run-a-ball 78 and Roger Twose (92) helped him to add 120 in 21 overs for the third wicket. Shane Thomson, taking three middle-order Emirates wickets with his off-breaks, was the pick of the New Zealand bowlers.

29 February

Pakistan 242–6 (50 overs) lost to South Africa 243–5 (44.2 overs) by five wickets. Man Of The Match award: Hansie Cronje

South Africa underlined the power of their World Cup challenge with a convincing victory over a Pakistan side seemingly unsure about how best to balance their line-up between specialist batsmen and front-line bowlers. Aamir Sohail's 111 anchored the Pakistan innings, but the South Africans paced their response magnificently. They took 105 from the first 15 overs, and that assault set up a comparative stroll to their target. Daryll Cullinan (65) provided high class in the middle order, while Hansie Cronje guided his team home by adding an unbeaten 45 to his earlier two wickets. The win guaranteed that South Africa would top Group B.

1 March

Lahore: Holland 216–9 (50 overs) lost to United Arab Emirates 220–3 (44.2 overs) by seven wickets. Man Of The Match award (shared): S Dukanwala and Saleem Raza

The tournament's only meeting of ICC associate members resulted in a satisfyingly resounding win for the Emirates team. Holland, in fact, were the favourites for the match, but they struggled to get on top of accurate and varied bowling. Off-spinner Dukanwala captured four wickets in 11 balls on his way to figures of 5–29, while opening batsman Saleem Raza was the star of a thrilling Emirates batting display. Saleem, returning to his native city, equalled the World Cup record by including six sixes (and seven fours) in a stunning 68-ball 84. Mohammad Ishaq also impressed with his 51 not out.

3 March

Karachi: England 249–9 (50 overs) lost to Pakistan 250–3 (47.4 overs) by seven wickets. Man Of The Match award: Aamir Sohail

England's misfortunes continued, even after Robin Smith (75) and Mike Atherton (66) had put on 147 in 28 overs for the first wicket. Only Graham Thorpe, with an unbeaten 52, made any significant contribution thereafter, and Pakistan, led by openers Aamir Sohail and Saeed Anwar in a quickfire stand of 81, cantered to their target. Anwar scored 71 and Ijaz Ahmed 70, while Inzamam-ul-Haq also lumbered out to hit 53 not out and the Karachi crowd reserved a huge reception for Javed Miandad, who made an unbeaten 11 in what was expected to be his last big game on his home turf.

5 March

Rawalpindi: South Africa 328–3 (50 overs) beat Holland 168–8 (50 overs) by 160 runs. Man Of The Match award: Andrew Hudson

South Africa duly made sure of maximum points from the group programme by predictably thumping the Dutch. Andrew Hudson's 161 came from just 132 balls, with four sixes and 13 fours, and he was joined in a World Cup first-wicket record partnership of 186 by Gary Kirsten (83).

6 March

Lahore: Pakistan 281–5 (50 overs) beat New Zealand 235 (47.3 overs) by 46 runs. Man Of The Match award: Salim Malik

It wasn't so much the result of this match that had significance as the matters surrounding it. Firstly, victory for Pakistan meant that they would travel to Bangalore for a titanic quarter-final tie with India, while New Zealand's defeat condemned them to a meeting with their arch-rivals, Australia. Additionally, the staging of the game in Lahore brought into sharp relief the fact that the floodlights needed for the World Cup final itself were still not ready. This match, like the Holland v Emirates fixture five days earlier, was designed to act as a day-night dress rehearsal for the tournament's most important game, but again it had to be played in daylight as workmen continued their race against time to get the ground fully operational. Injuries to Wasim Akram (who strained his side batting) and Danny Morrison (groin) also impacted on the fortunes of both sides. As for the game itself, half-centuries from the in-form Pakistan openers and an unbeaten 55 from Salim Malik left just too much for the New Zealanders to do, given that none of their solid middle order could go on to play a big innings.

QUARTER-FINALS
9 March

Faisalabad: England 235–8 (50 overs) lost to Sri Lanka 236–5 (40.4 overs) by five wickets. Man Of The Match award: Sanath Jayasuriya

Bangalore: India 287–8 (50 overs) beat Pakistan 248–9 (49 overs) by 39 runs. Man Of The Match award: Navjot Singh Sidhu

For the first time in a World Cup tournament, England failed to reach the semi-finals. It was a brutal culling, too, with Sanath Jayasuriya thumping 82 from only 44 balls before departing with the total 113–1 in the 13th over. After that, England's total was made to look pathetically inadequate as the Sri Lankans sauntered into the last four. Phillip DeFreitas, promoted to number five as England belatedly attempted something unorthodox, hit 67 from 64 balls, but none of their specialist batsmen flourished and it was left to Dermot Reeve and Darren Gough to provide a late boost. It proved insignificant as Jayasuriya thrashed three sixes and 13 fours.

Even more dramatic than Jayasuriya's onslaught, however, was the Indian victory over Pakistan in a day-night spectacular in Bangalore. A tense, often thrilling contest had tragic and disturbing consequences when one Pakistan fan, watching at home, reportedly shot first his television set and then himself and various effigies of Wasim Akram were burned in Pakistani streets. Wasim himself, the Pakistan captain, didn't play in the match due to an injured side, a withdrawal which in itself caused an outcry and allegations that he had deliberately pulled out. Wasim denied the charge. Pakistan sorely missed him, however, despite his deputy Ata-ur-Rehman bowling with control. Navjot Singh Sidhu provided the anchor role for India with a determined 93, but the Indian total did not achieve challenging proportions until Ajay Jadeja inspired the tail to heroic deeds. Waqar Younis was plundered for 40 runs from his last two overs as 51 were taken from the final three of the innings. Jadeja's 45 required only 25 balls. Pakistan, though, hit back strongly with Saeed Anwar and Aamir Sohail, the acting captain, bursting from the blocks with an 84-run opening stand. But in the 15th over (the last of the fielding restrictions), and with Pakistan already in a fine position at 113–1, Sohail allowed himself to get involved in some verbals with Venkatesh Prasad, the bowler, and immediately threw away his wicket for 55 with a wild slog. Wickets then fell with regularity as Pakistan tried to regain control and the run-out of Javed Miandad for 38 signalled the end of their reign as World Cup champions.

11 March

Karachi: West Indies 264–8 (50 overs) beat South Africa 245 (49.3 overs) by 19 runs. Man Of The Match award: Brian Lara

Madras: New Zealand 286–9 (50 overs) lost to Australia 289–4 (47.5 overs) by six wickets. Man Of The Match award: Mark Waugh

A brilliant 111 from Brian Lara was the catalyst for a shock result at the National Stadium. In an attempt to outfox the West Indians, who had acquired a reputation for not being the most confident players of slow bowling, South Africa contentiously decided to omit fast bowler Allan Donald and include Pat Symcox and Paul Adams, both specialist spinners. Lara, however, seized on the spinners with relish as he dominated a second wicket stand of 138 with Shivnarine Chanderpaul (56). South Africa still might have won the game, following a second-wicket stand worth 97 between Daryll Cullinan (69) and Andrew Hudson (54), had it not been, ironically, for the West Indies spinners. Roger Harper took 4–47 and the occasional slow left arm of Jimmy Adams and Keith Arthurton accounted for another four South African scalps.

Heroic innings by Lee Germon, the captain, and Chris Harris could not prevent New Zealand from falling to Mark Waugh-inspired Australia. Germon, with 89 from 96 balls, justified both his own promotion to number three and the recall of Harris, whose magnificent 130 off just 124 balls was a maiden one-day international century. Harris struck four sixes and 13 fours and he and Germon added a World Cup and Kiwi fourth-wicket record of 168 at a rate of more than six runs an over. Mark Waugh, however, was more than equal to the task, hitting 110 from 112 balls and setting up his twin brother, Steve, to supervise the later chase. Steve Waugh (59 not out) was helped by Stuart Law (42 not out) in an unbroken stand of 76. The result meant that all four Group A sides had reached the semi-finals; all four beaten Group B qualifiers had, uncannily, been the 1992 World Cup semi-finalists.

SEMI-FINALS
13 March
Calcutta: Sri Lanka 251–8 (50 overs) beat India 120–8 (34.1 overs) by default (crowd riot). Man Of The Match award: Aravinda de Silva

An astonishing match in the teeming powder keg of Eden Gardens ended with many in the 100,000 crowd so dismayed by India's loss of seven wickets for 22 runs that they rioted. Clive Lloyd, the match referee, took the players off the field for 15 minutes and then attempted a restart. When that proved impossible, with bottle-throwing and fire-raising still going on, he awarded the match to Sri Lanka by default. It was, of course, the right decision and the right result, but it was a shame that the rioting should cast a stain on the tournament and on Indian cricket. Bizarrely, once the game had been abandoned, the unrest quietened down and the traditional post-match presentations and interviews were staged as normal! How different the atmosphere in this huge stadium had been, though, soon after the start, when Sri Lanka – put in by Mohammad Azharuddin – lost both openers in the first over to catches at third man. Asanka Gurusinha also went early, but Aravinda de Silva reacted to the crisis with a breathtakingly daring 66 from 47 balls (out of 85), which stayed true to the Sri Lankan tactic of making hay in the first 15 overs, whatever the early cost. Roshan Mahanama, pushed up to number five to help De Silva rally the innings, succeeded by then staying to construct a responsible 58, while both Arjuna Ranatunga and Hashan Tillekeratne aided the later acceleration.

India's reply began well, with Sachin Tendulkar taking charge and Sanjay Manjrekar keeping him company in a second-wicket partnership of 90. Then, however, a quick piece of thinking by Romesh Kaluwitharana, the wicket-keeper, resulted in Tendulkar being stumped after a leg-side delivery from Sanath Jayasuriya had bounced down off his pads. After that, all hell let loose, literally.

14 March
Mohali: Australia 207–8 (50 overs) beat West Indies 202 (49.3 overs) by five runs. Man Of The Match award: Shane Warne

Somehow, the West Indies contrived to lose a match that, on several occasions, it seemed easier to win. Australia, to their credit, hung in doggedly even when they had been reduced to 15–4 after electing to bat, and then when the West Indies had reached 165–2 to leave themselves needing just 43 from the last nine overs. Stuart Law (72) and Michael Bevan (69) had fashioned the first Aussie recovery, adding 138 in 32 overs for the fifth wicket after Curtly Ambrose and Ian Bishop had ripped out the top four. Brian Lara's run-a-ball 45 had then given the West Indies innings early impetus and all seemed set fair when Richie Richardson joined opener Shivnarine Chanderpaul in a third-wicket stand of 72. Chanderpaul, however, was suffering from cramp and, on 80, he rather unnecessarily hit out at Glenn McGrath and was caught. The West Indies then made their most serious errors, promoting both Roger Harper and Ottis Gibson in an effort to bring victory rushing upon them. McGrath, though, almost immediately had Harper lbw, and when Shane Warne had Gibson caught behind for one, panic set in. The remaining two specialist batsmen, Jimmy Adams and Keith Arthurton, were out of form and thus exposed now to added pressure. Both fell cheaply, as Richardson looked on helplessly at the other end, and suddenly the Australians had regained control. Warne then sent back Bishop, too, and his three-over spell had brought the leg-spinner 3–6 and an overall figure of 4–36. Richardson, nevertheless, soon found himself on strike to face the final over, with ten runs wanted and Curtly Ambrose doing well as his latest partner. Damien Fleming was bowling it, and his first delivery was swung away by Richardson for four. Now, perhaps, it was West Indies who were favourites again. Their soaring hopes, however, were soon to be dashed. Fatally, Richardson called Ambrose for a quick single from the next ball – and the giant fast bowler, agonisingly, was given run-out after a television replay. That exposed Courtney Walsh, the last man, and Fleming immediately defeated his desperate swish. The Australians were triumphant, and no West Indian was more dejected than skipper Richardson, stranded on 49 not out.

THE 1996 WORLD CUP FINAL
17 March

Lahore: Australia 241–7 (50 overs) lost to Sri Lanka 245–3 (46.2 overs) by seven wickets. Man Of The Match award: Aravinda de Silva

The pre-tournament 66–1 outsiders thoroughly deserved their triumph in front of a packed and beautifully revamped Gaddafi Stadium. Sri Lanka also became the first side batting second to win a World Cup final, while batting hero Aravinda de Silva joined the illustrious company of Clive Lloyd and Viv Richards as century-makers on the greatest limited-overs stage of all.

Pakistan's first day-night international took place in cool conditions, and the evening dew became a factor for the Australian spinners, who couldn't grip the ball as they would have liked. Nevertheless, Sri Lanka's captain, Arjuna Ranatunga, outsmarted his opponents at every turn – especially in the way he used his own slow bowlers to regain control and then tighten their grip on the Australian batsmen after Mark Taylor (74) and Ricky Ponting (45) had taken the total to 137–1 by the 27th over, following a successful initial assault on the seamers.

Australia, however, did give themselves a fighting chance by battling on to a good-looking total and then striking two early blows with the new ball to leave Sri Lanka wobbling on 23–2.

De Silva was more than up to the challenge. Determined to play the match-winning innings, De Silva was at first content to support the aggressive Asanka Gurusinha, who flat-batted deliveries from Shane Warne back over his head for a four and then an extraordinary six to long-off. When Gurusinha was bowled for a fine 65, De Silva reined himself in again while Ranatunga, his captain, settled. Finally, 51 from the last ten overs became just ten from five as De Silva and Ranatunga accelerated effortlessly. De Silva's century was acclaimed by the crowd, and his eventual 107 not out took him 124 balls and included 13 boundaries.

Ranatunga, the little general, finished on 47 not out before proudly accepting the World Cup trophy itself from Benazir Bhutto, the prime minister of Pakistan.

THE INTERVIEW
Arjuna Ranatunga (and Michael de Zoysa, of the Sinhalese Sports Club)

The portly figure of Sri Lanka's World Cup-winning captain disguised one of the most naturally gifted batsmen of his generation. Arjuna Ranatunga, first and foremost, was a highly accomplished cricketer.

His legacy, however, is a reputation as a tough, uncompromising, clever and often confrontational leader. He believed Sri Lanka could rule the world, and he was determined to show that the former Test minnows were now big fish – with sharp teeth – in the cricketing ocean.

If he caused controversy, he didn't mind. If he had to make hard decisions, he didn't shirk them. He taught Sri Lankan players not to fear their opponents, nor to be overawed by them. He was the architect, in essence, of a modern Sri Lanka, because cricket, as the island's passion, defines the nation's standing in the world.

On the morning of the World Cup final, Ranatunga showed that he had the courage to think for himself, and then act accordingly, by putting Australia in to bat against all accumulated wisdom. Five times in previous finals, the side batting second had lost. Ranatunga, however, was determined – in a wider sense, too – to shed the burden of history. 'I am not a person who takes much notice of history,' he said revealingly when he looked back on Sri Lanka's triumph. 'We knew we could win that game by batting second. When I won the toss, I knew that we would have a very good chance of winning if we could keep the Australians down to 250 or 260.'

Back in Sri Lanka, one of millions glued to his television set was Michael de Zoysa, a man who had known Ranatunga since he was a 13-year-old schoolboy.

That was the age when Ranatunga was invited by de Zoysa and former Test batsman Sunil Wettimuny to join the Sinhalese Sports Club, of which both men were officials.

'I was so tense when I watched Arjuna walk out to toss up with Mark Taylor, the Australian captain,' said de Zoysa. 'I had known Arjuna for many years, and he, plus many of the other players, had become personal friends. 'But those of us crowded around our TV set were concerned about the toss because we knew that Lahore, like Colombo, has a heavy evening dew at that time of year, which can make the outfield pretty wet and slippery for the side fielding second.

'There had also been rain for the previous couple of evenings in Lahore, and, as we knew that the Sri Lankan team was better at chasing a total, we were praying for Arjuna to win the toss. He did!

'I can remember Arjuna causing quite a stir when he first came to the SSC nets, especially because he used to hit almost everything in the air and also vast distances! But I can still recall clearly when Sir Garry Sobers visited the club and watched a 16-year-old Arjuna bat. I told Sir Garry, "Here is Sri Lanka's Neil Harvey," and he saw him make about 20 and said he thought he had tremendous potential.

'Back around the TV, we were happy when Australia were kept to 241-7, but you could have heard a pin drop amongst our crowd when both Jayasuriya and Kalu were out cheaply. Slowly and surely, though, the noise level picked up again as de Silva and Gurusinha, who was another product of the SSC club, put on 125.

'Gurusinha's dismissal momentarily quietened us, but now arriving in the middle was the man himself, Arjuna Ranatunga, and it was not long before victory was in sight. Aravinda batted beautifully and Arjuna also showed just the right amount of aggression; one innings was for the connoisseur and the other, as ever, was about crafty placement, a keen temperament and technique.

'We had won the World Cup! The jubilation in Colombo was amazing to behold. People hugged and kissed those they would not normally have gone near. Everyone seemed to be out in the streets, and car horns were blowing incessantly. Bars that usually closed at 10:30pm were open into the night. We stood on tables, we sang and we danced. Scenes on Galle Face Green in Colombo resembled those of New Year's Eve, only more joyful, with crackers and fireworks. We relived every moment of the game, every ball played.

'It was the most unforgettable day for every Sri Lankan cricket fan, especially those of us heavily involved in our game.'

Ranatunga, too, acknowledged the true meaning of victory for his countrymen in the aftermath of the triumph in Lahore. 'This is a victory for the entire country,' he said. 'My dream was to get to the final and contest it. Now that we have won, and I myself have contributed, makes me very happy. But this honour should go to many a person, and not just me and the team.

'Past presidents of the Sri Lankan Cricket Board, past players and past coaches, they all deserve to be given part of this honour.'

THE CHAMPIONS

Sri Lanka had a plan to win the 1996 World Cup, and the reason they pulled it off was that they also had the courage to stick to the plan, whatever the situation.

Expertly marshalled in the field by Arjuna Ranatunga, whose tactical abilities were revealed for the whole world to see when Australia were pegged back by his skilful field placings in the final, Sri Lanka had assessed the conditions they were likely to play in and had plotted their campaign with precision.

Much has been made of how they caught the rest of the competing countries napping with their decision to launch an all-out attack in the first 15 overs when only two fielders were allowed outside of the 30-metre circle. Yes, that is true, up to a point, but other teams also made hay in the early overs, and in the final itself Australia scored 82–1 from their first 15 overs, as opposed to Sri Lanka's 71–2.

What Sri Lanka also got right was the balance of their side, with seven specialist batsmen giving them a depth that was unmatched. Roshan Mahanama, an experienced Test match opener, was scheduled to come in at number seven, but in fact only batted twice, and then once at number five, when he scored an important 58 to steady the ship in the semi-final win over India.

Ranatunga reasoned that the top order had licence to hit out, simply because the team had such strength in its batting depth and could easily recover from the loss of early wickets.

This is indeed what happened in the semi-final, in the final and in the opening group match against Zimbabwe, but to have the self-belief to carry out in practice what sounds such a good idea in theory set Sri Lanka apart.

Their spinners, too, played a vital role, and again Ranatunga correctly foresaw that it was the slower bowlers who would be best equipped in sub-continental conditions to keep batsmen in check once the opening 15 overs had been delivered. In Aravinda de Silva, the Sri Lankans also had a world-class batsman at the very peak of his powers, and in Sanath Jayasuriya they had a genuine limited-overs all-rounder who, despite not being one of the recognised world stars at the start of hostilities, was deservedly named the most valued player of the tournament.

THE PRIZES

Total official prize money of £200,000 was distributed, with winners Sri Lanka earning themselves £30,000 and runners-up Australia £20,000.

There were cheques too for the semi-final and quarter-final losers, plus £2,000 for each group victory. Aravinda de Silva won £5,000 for being Man Of The Match in the final, and other sums were awarded to each man of the match throughout the tournament. Sanath Jayasuriya, as the most valued player of the tournament, won £5,000 and an Audi car.

Sri Lanka's players, however, also received a bonus of US$100,000 from Pilcom, the tournament organisers, and a similar amount was also gifted to them by one of the event sponsors. The Sri Lankan Cricket Board was later given substantial compensation by Pilcom for the loss of their home group matches against Australia and West Indies.

Pilcom had seemed certain to make a sizeable profit after attracting US$12 million from title sponsors Wills, the Indian tobacco giant, a further US$4 million from co-sponsors Coca-Cola and a sum of US$10 million from WorldTel, who bought the television rights.

THE QUOTES

'One of the things that people didn't seem to notice (before the tournament) was that Sri Lanka were probably the most experienced team in the competition, especially in the batting, both in terms of years and in terms of one-day experience. And when it came down to the last two matches, they were absolutely at their best; they took the pressure really well and rose to the occasion.' Imran Khan, captain of 1992 World Cup winners, Pakistan.

'The refusal of Australia and the West Indies to visit Sri Lanka for their preliminary matches was in my view an over-reaction, lacking in understanding and foresight.' Former England captain Tony Greig.

'When I started playing cricket in 1970, my friends and I used to improvise with maize cobs, using sticks as bats. We then graduated to tennis balls and our own carved wooden bats.' Kenyan hero Steve Tikolo.

'Sri Lanka's triumph must rank as one of the greatest achievements in modern cricket.' Ravi Shastri, former Indian all-rounder.

TEAM OF THE TOURNAMENT?

Sanath Jayasuriya (Sri Lanka)
Saeed Anwar (Pakistan)
Sachin Tendulkar (India)
Mark Waugh (Australia)
Aravinda de Silva (Sri Lanka)

Arjuna Ranatunga (Sri Lanka, captain)
Romesh Kaluwitharana (Sri Lanka, wicket-keeper)
Anil Kumble (India)
Shane Warne (Australia)
Damien Fleming (Australia)
Curtly Ambrose (West Indies)

THE ROAD TO 1999...

Sri Lanka's great triumph shook up the accepted order in world cricket for a while, but as the seventh World Cup approached it became apparent that the Big Three of Australia, South Africa and Pakistan were the teams to beat.

In Test cricket, Australia had no peers, although on the one-day stage there were many who felt that South Africa, well blessed with the all-rounders that the Aussies lacked, were the number-one nation. Indeed, when the 1999 tournament grew near, it was the South Africans who were installed as narrow favourites.

And then there was Pakistan. Led once again by the inspirational Wasim Akram, they were everybody's outside bet. In fact, it was not uncommon in the late 1990s to read the words 'Pakistan' and 'bet' in the same sentence. Match-fixing had raised its ugly head, and the 1999 tournament was about to be the subject of further rumours.

Chapter 10

1999: Gritty Aussies Battle Through

'Nothing you do in your career can prepare you for a moment like that.
I had let down my batting partner, my team and my country.'

– Allan Donald

It started with a risible opening ceremony, ended with an anticlimactic final and had a muddled middle thanks to an idea called (optimistically) the Super Six. Yet the 1999 World Cup was most definitely not all bad.

A chilly mid-May beginning soon gave way to a warmer June, and the cricket likewise went up in temperature…until the deflation of a final in which Australia had blown away a wretchedly under-performing Pakistan by 4:35pm in the afternoon.

Then again, perhaps it was asking too much for the last match in the competition to rival the drama provided by, possibly, the greatest World Cup match of them all, the Edgbaston semi-final, with Australia going through on a technicality after a heart-stopping tie with South Africa.

The seventh World Cup was promoted as a 'Carnival of Cricket' by the host nation, England. Its aim was to establish (and re-establish) cricket in the hearts and minds of the majority of Britain's cosmopolitan and football-obsessed population. That, however, was not helped when England were dumped out of the tournament before its halfway stage, and before the Super Six stage that they had seemed certain to reach until a cruel fate decreed that they should lose to India and, far more surprisingly, Zimbabwe should beat South Africa.

Nevertheless, with 21 days still remaining after England's painful exit, the show did manage to go on. The event did develop a cosmopolitan, party feel, if largely because of the fanaticism (and sound and sight) of the Indian, Pakistani and Bangladeshi communities.

The supposed mismatch between Pakistan and Bangladesh at Northampton was a sell-out, and should have been staged at a Test ground in order to accommodate all those who wanted to see it. India's opening match with South Africa, one of the most attractive fixtures anyway, was far too big an event to be handed to Hove, which could have been literally overrun.

Old Trafford did well on its biggest day, too, but there isn't a cricket stadium in England big enough to cope with the demand of an India v Pakistan confrontation.

In terms of the people it attracted, then, and in the spread of the tournament venues from all around England to Wales, to Scotland and to Ireland and Holland, the event was successful.

So now let's turn our attention to the most obvious flaw. No, not the opening ceremony, which should have featured at least a parade of all the teams against the timeless backdrop of the Lord's pavilion instead of the few cheap-looking fireworks that were let off. Nor the damp squib of a finale. The major problem, in fact, was the Super Six.

It was reasoned by the organisers, quite rightly, that the stupidity of the 1996 quarter-finals should not be repeated. Commercialism, however, demanded a second tier of matches before the knockout format of the last four – the semi-final stage being something which has survived all the different competition structures used in seven World Cups.

Terry Blake, the England and Wales Cricket Board's marketing director, therefore came up with the Super Six. In theory, it would enable the strongest qualifying teams to contest an exciting middle section of the event – and, of course, increase revenues and also (hopefully) prolong England's involvement.

The 12 competing countries – the nine Test-playing nations and three qualifiers from the ICC Trophy – would be split initially into two groups of six. They would play each other once, and then the top three in each group would progress into the Super Six. Furthermore, each Super Six entrant would carry forward with them the points (if any) accrued from the two matches they had already played against their fellow group qualifiers. All clear so far?

Each of the Group A qualifiers would then play each of the Group B qualifiers in the Super Six series, producing a final all-played-all league table from which the top four would go into the semi-finals.

In theory, once it had been explained a few times, it sounded fair enough. In practice, of course, it was revealed as yet another example of a World Cup rule causing more damage than it was worth, a factor which has bedevilled too many World Cups. Australia deliberately and controversially batting as slowly as possible against the West Indies in the match towards the end of the group stage was, unfortunately, the result of flawed rules.

The regulation stating that teams tied on points would be separated by the result of the game between them was, again, fine in theory. Unfortunately, when there were three-way ties in both qualifying groups, and when Zimbabwe and New Zealand finished tied for fourth and fifth places in the Super Six, it was 'net run rate' that carried the day.

To general dismay, it was also the net-run-rate technicality which, even more unfortunately, became a literal tie-breaker when Australia and South Africa tied their epic semi-final. The Australians were awarded the match because, at the Super Six stage, their net run rate had been higher than South Africa's.

Another flaw in the Super Six format was that Zimbabwe almost sailed on through into the semi-finals themselves on the strength of the four points they had carried through for initial group wins against India and South Africa. The fact that they had lost two more matches, to two teams that had been knocked out, didn't count against them in the Super Six; in fact, they began the second stage a potentially decisive two points ahead of South Africa, who had won four matches compared to Zimbabwe's three in the qualifying group.

The exits of both England and the West Indies were also on run rate, although neither team warranted much sympathy as they didn't play well enough when it mattered nor, clearly, did they study the regulations keenly enough. Both the West Indies, against Bangladesh, and England, against Zimbabwe, made little effort to increase their net run rate in games they were winning easily.

There's no doubt that England's early departure badly affected the general perception of the event in the host country, but in some ways the organisers didn't help themselves. Besides the poor choice of venues for certain games, the decision was made not to seek a sole sponsor for the tournament but to offer opportunities for eight equal corporate partners. In the end, after much bad publicity and obviously a shortfall in revenue, only four companies came on board. The planned amount of subsidiary sponsorship was also not forthcoming.

Then there was the song. In a spectacular piece of bungling the official World Cup anthem, 'All Over The World' by Dave Stewart of The Eurythmics wasn't released until the day after England had been knocked out! Even more strangely, the song didn't refer even once to cricket, and it sold hardly a copy.

That the tournament, overall, emerged in credit was due to the quality of much of the cricket, the good crowds and the predominantly fine weather.

Compared to 1996, too, a better balance of power between bat and ball existed in the English conditions.

14 May was a riskily early start, given the likelihood of cool temperatures and rain at that time of the year in Britain, but only one of the 42 matches couldn't be finished and just one other spilled over into the reserve day. The Duckworth-Lewis system, little understood but by now universally recognised and accepted as the best method ever devised to settle rain-ruined contests, was never required.

THE MATCHES
GROUP A
14 May

Lord's: Sri Lanka 204 (48.4 overs) lost to England 207–2 (46.5 overs) by eight wickets. Man Of The Match award: Alec Stewart

A highly efficient start by the hosts, and the beginning of a hugely disappointing defence by the holders. Alan Mullally led a steady seam bowling display, with four wickets, and Alec Stewart, the captain, took England to the verge of victory with a perky 88 and a fine stand of 125 for the second wicket with Graeme Hick (73 not out).

15 May

Hove: India 253–5 (50 overs) lost to South Africa 254–6 (47.2 overs) by four wickets. Man Of The Match award: Jacques Kallis

Taunton: Kenya 229–7 (50 overs) lost to Zimbabwe 231–5 (41 overs) by five wickets. Man Of The Match award: Neil Johnson

A great atmosphere and fine match at Hove was overshadowed a little by South African coach Bob Woolmer's rather bizarre attempt to communicate with his players out on the field via a one-way radio system. Hansie Cronje, the captain, and Allan Donald, the senior bowler, took the field wearing ear pieces and could pick up Woolmer's instructions. Predictably, the ICC referee, Pakistan's Talat Ali, ordered them to be removed during the first drinks break, and the organisers later ruled them out for the remainder of the World Cup. Even without Woolmer's constant advice, though, South Africa won impressively after responding to excellent batting by India's Sourav Ganguly and Rahul Dravid with some fine strokeplay of their own. Jacques Kallis classily led the chase with 96 while Lance Klusener marched in at the death to strike his first three balls for four.

Zimbabwe gained some early confidence with a competent win over Kenya, whose batting and fielding looked considerably stronger than their bowling. Neil Johnson was the all-round star for the Zimbabweans, following up four wickets which included the prized scalp of Steve Tikolo with a lively 59.

18 May

Canterbury: Kenya 203 (49.4 overs) lost to England 204–1 (39 overs) by nine wickets. Man Of The Match award: Steve Tikolo

A muted first one-day international fixture for Canterbury, enlivened only when Steve Tikolo and Tom Odoyo hit out powerfully for Kenya, and then when Nasser Hussain and Graeme Hick finally hurried to the target in light drizzle.

19 May

Leicester: Zimbabwe 252–9 (50 overs) beat India 249 (45 overs) by three runs. Man Of The Match award: Grant Flower

Northampton: South Africa 199–9 (50 overs) beat Sri Lanka 110 (35.2 overs) by 89 runs. Man Of The Match award: Lance Klusener

A disastrous result for India, watched by an overflowing and largely Indian crowd at Grace Road. Despite being docked four overs for their slow over rate earlier, the Indians required just nine runs from two overs when, on a hunch, Zimbabwean captain Alistair Campbell recalled the previously wayward Henry Olonga. The dreadlocked fast bowler responded to the moment with an heroic three wickets in an over: Robin Singh caught at cover from his second ball, Javagal Srinath yorked by his fifth and Venkatesh Prasad lbw to his last.

The South Africans were struggling first at 69–5 and later at 122–8, thanks in part to contentious third umpire decisions by Ken Palmer which confirmed the dismissals of Shaun Pollock and Daryll Cullinan, for 49. But Lance Klusener then hit an unbeaten 52 from 45 balls, including 22 from the final over bowled by Chaminda Vaas, and the fired-up South African pace attack proved far too strong for the struggling Sri Lankan batsmen.

22 May

The Oval: South Africa 225–7 (50 overs) beat England 103 (41 overs) by 122 runs. Man Of The Match award: Lance Klusener

Worcester: Zimbabwe 197–9 (50 overs) lost to Sri Lanka 198–6 (46 overs) by four wickets. Man Of The Match award: Marvan Atapattu

The quality of England's challenge was called into question after this humiliation. Herschelle Gibbs (60) and Gary Kirsten launched the South African innings with a brisk opening stand of 111 and, although the English seamers fought back, Lance Klusener's clubbing 48 not out from 40 deliveries gave his side something to defend. England's feeble batting got nowhere near the target as South Africa's formidable pace attack, led by Allan Donald's 4–17, again showed its teeth.

At last some joy for the World Cup holders as a ragged Zimbabwe performance was punished by a Sri Lankan batting display that had just enough solidity in it through the contributions of Marvan Atapattu (54), Roshan Mahanama and Mahela Jayawardene.

May 23

Bristol: India 329–2 (50 overs) beat Kenya 235–7 (50 overs) by 94 runs. Man Of The Match award: Sachin Tendulkar

A majestic 140 not out by Sachin Tendulkar was dedicated, afterwards, to his late father. The Indian maestro had just returned to England the day before, after leaving the tournament to attend his father's funeral in Bombay, and his innings began in determined fashion and finished in a blaze of glory. He reached 50 in 54 balls, 100 in 84 and his final score from just 101 deliveries. There were 16 fours and three sixes, including one from the final ball of the innings, and Rahul Dravid's beautifully-fashioned 104 not out was quite forgotten – although his stand of 237 in just 27 overs with Tendulkar was a World Cup record (briefly) for any wicket. Steve Tikolo, Kennedy Otieno and Tom Odoyo all batted attractively later, but the day belonged to Tendulkar's tribute.

25 May

Trent Bridge: Zimbabwe 167–8 (50 overs) lost to England 168–3 (38.3 overs) by seven wickets. Man Of The Match award: Alan Mullally

England's seamers destroyed Zimbabwe's challenge in helpfully cool conditions, with Alan Mullally again the pick of the attack, before a third-wicket partnership of 123 in 22 overs between Nasser Hussain (57 not out) and Graham Thorpe (62) made sure of the game.

26 May

Taunton: India 373–6 (50 overs) beat Sri Lanka 216 (42.3 overs) by 157 runs. Man Of The Match award: Sourav Ganguly

Amstelveen: Kenya 152 (44.3 overs) lost to South Africa 153–3 (41 overs) by seven wickets. Man Of The Match award: Lance Klusener

A string of records were set at Taunton after Arjuna Ranatunga put India in and then saw any hope Sri Lanka had left of defending their title blown away. Sourav Ganguly's 183 from 158 balls included an awesome acceleration after he had completed his century from 119 deliveries. The Indian captain struck seven sixes and 17 fours, while Rahul Dravid's 145 was more evenly paced and took him 129 balls. Their stand of 318 in 45 overs was the highest for any wicket in one-day international history, and India's total was the highest against Test opposition in a limited-overs match. The last ten overs cost Sri Lanka an astonishing 129 runs, and for them the game was up in more ways than one.

The VRA ground in Amstelveen, a suburb of Amsterdam, became the 131st one-day international venue as South Africa, led by Lance Klusener's 5–21, overpowered Kenya, despite the underdogs enjoying a fine start through Ravindru Shah (50) and Kennedy Otieno. A crowd of 4,260 relished seeing World Cup action come to Holland, and the new grass pitch played well.

29 May

Chelmsford: Zimbabwe 233–6 (50 overs) beat South Africa 185 (47.2 overs) by 48 runs. Man Of The Match award: Neil Johnson

A rainstorm during the lunch interval seemed to freshen up the pitch conditions and Neil Johnson's opening ball to Gary Kirsten climbed off a length at the South African to have him caught. Herschelle Gibbs was run out by Adam Huckle and then Johnson and Heath Streak shared another four wickets as South Africa, sensationally, collapsed to 40–6. Half-centuries from Shaun Pollock and Lance Klusener, who came in ridiculously low at number nine, only served to hold up the Zimbabweans' celebrations at their first win over their neighbours. Earlier Johnson had scored 76 and Zimbabwe's reward for their unexpected victory was to start the Super Six stage as joint leaders with Pakistan.

29-30 May

Edgbaston: India 232–8 (50 overs) beat England 169 (45.2 overs) by 63 runs. Man Of The Match award: Sourav Ganguly

England's batting fell apart miserably under pressure as the match went into the reserve day because of a late-afternoon thunderstorm. The news of

Zimbabwe's win at Chelmsford had merely added to the tension before England resumed, already three wickets down, on the second morning. Graham Thorpe, who top-scored with 36, looked unlucky to be given out lbw by Javed Akhtar, the umpire, but otherwise England had no excuses as they slipped ignominiously out of the tournament. Sourav Ganguly added three cheap wickets to his earlier innings of 40 to become Man Of The Match.

30 May

Southampton: Sri Lanka 275–8 (50 overs) beat Kenya 230–6 (50 overs) by 45 runs. Man Of The Match award: Maurice Odumbe

A sixth-wicket one-day international record stand of 161 between Maurice Odumbe and Alpesh Vadher earned Kenya a dignified end to their World Cup campaign. A win for Sri Lanka, however, was later not enough to save Arjuna Ranatunga from being sacked as captain four years after he had led his country to the 1996 World Cup title. Ranatunga bowed out with a defiant 50 and Marvan Atapattu scored 52, but a grey day found its most vivid colour when Odumbe (82) and Vadher (73 not out) came together and raised the Kenyan total past the 200 mark from the depths of 52–5.

GROUP B
16 May

Worcester: Scotland 181–7 (50 overs) lost to Australia 182–4 (44.5 overs) by six wickets. Man Of The Match award: Mark Waugh

Bristol: Pakistan 229–8 (50 overs) beat West Indies 202 (48.5 overs) by 27 runs. Man Of The Match award: Azhar Mahmood

Scotland's World Cup debut began with Bruce Patterson, an Ayr estate agent, cover-driving the first ball of the match, from Damien Fleming, for four. With Australia looking below par, the Scots were able to give a good account of themselves, although they never threatened an upset. A crowd of more than 5,000 seemed intent on enjoying the occasion and the beer flowed.

Pakistan set out their stall with a win which owed much to their enviable depth in batting and a full hand of excellent bowlers, three of whom were genuine all-rounders. West Indies made early in-roads but depended too much on their three frontline fast bowlers. The weakness of the support bowlers was revealed when the Pakistani lower middle order plundered 80 from the last eight overs. The great pace of Shoaib Akhtar was also unveiled as a World Cup threat when, from his very first ball, an intended pull by Sherwin Campbell resulted in a top-edged six over the slips. But Shoaib fired another express clean through Campbell's defences in his second over and also later removed West Indies top-scorer Shivnarine Chanderpaul for 77. The steady seamers of Azhar Mahmood and Abdur Razzaq, however, and the subtlety of Saqlain Mushtaq's off-breaks, complemented Shoaib's explosiveness: Pakistan had made a good early impression.

17 May

Chelmsford: Bangladesh 116 (37.4 overs) lost to New Zealand 117–4 (33 overs) by six wickets. Man Of The Match award: Gavin Larsen

Bangladesh's World Cup bow brought a disappointing showing with the bat but a decent performance with the ball as they made New Zealand fight all the way to their modest target. The other feature of the day was the fanatical Bangladeshi support on the boundary edge, irrespective of the state of the game.

20 May

Cardiff: Australia 213–8 (50 overs) lost to New Zealand 214–5 (45.2 overs) by five wickets. Man Of The Match award: Roger Twose

Chester-le-Street: Pakistan 261–6 (50 overs) beat Scotland 167 (38.5 overs) by 94 runs. Man Of The Match award: Yousuf Youhana

The first one-day international staged at Sophia Gardens produced the first upset of the competition, with New Zealand eventually romping home with 28 balls to spare following a tense tussle. Geoff Allott and Gavin Larsen were the pick of the Kiwi bowlers, with Darren Lehmann (76) and Ricky Ponting (47) the only Australian batsmen to flourish in conditions which encouraged swing and seam. New Zealand themselves were initially up against it at 49–4, but by now the sun had come out and a superb stand of 148 in 28 overs between Roger Twose (80 not out) and Chris Cairns (60) swung the game.

There was a first international at the Riverside, too, and the new ball did damage to both teams on a pitch that had been covered all the previous day and helped the seamers considerably. Pakistan recovered from 92–5 thanks to Yousuf Youhana's skilful 81 not out, plus some intelligent (and belligerent) contributions from Moin Khan and Wasim Akram. Scotland, who had given away 48 runs in wides and no balls in a one-day-international record number of 59 extras, were soon 19–5 against the pace and movement of Shoaib Akhtar and Wasim. In the end, they owed damage limitation to Gavin Hamilton, the Yorkshire all-rounder, who played excellently for his 76.

21 May

Dublin: Bangladesh 182 (49.2 overs) lost to West Indies 183–3 (46.3 overs) by seven wickets. Man Of The Match award: Courtney Walsh

The abiding memory of the first one-day international on Irish soil was that of Clive Lloyd, the West Indies manager and twice a World Cup winning captain, sat swathed in blankets as he watched the game unfold in bitterly cold conditions. A chill wind and several rain showers made it a miserable day even for the hardy locals, although the Castle Avenue ground did its best to enter into the spirit of the occasion. Courtney Walsh stood head and shoulders above the rest of a West Indian attack badly missing shoulder-injury victim Curtly Ambrose, and at least the top order had some fun while knocking off the runs in leisurely fashion. Mehrab Hossain (64) and Naimur Rahman (45) earlier won plaudits for their gritty stand of 85.

23 May

Headingley: Pakistan 275–8 (50 overs) beat Australia 265 (49.5 overs) by ten runs. Man Of The Match award: Inzamam-ul-Haq

Fading light on a murky day, as much as the speed and skill of Pakistan's fast attack, played an important part in this thrilling ten-run defeat of Australia. Shoaib Akhtar's rapid inswinger, to bowl Steve Waugh for 49, ended a gutsy fifth-wicket stand of 113 between the Aussie captain and Michael Bevan, who went on to 61. In fact, it took two wickets for Wasim Akram in the final over to finish off Australia. The Pakistan innings earlier had featured a slow start, a couple of farcical run-out moments involving the lumbering Inzamam-ul-Haq and a frantic last ten overs which cost the Aussies 108 runs. Inzamam, however, played wonderfully well for his 81, repairing the innings from 46–3 with a 118-run stand with Abdur Razzaq (60). Moin Khan's remarkable 12-ball 31 not out contributed to the late mayhem and to the entertainment.

24 May

Southampton: New Zealand 156 (48.1 overs) lost to West Indies 158–3 (44.2 overs) by seven wickets. Man Of The Match award: Ridley Jacobs

New Zealand were brought down to earth following their triumph over Australia, with the West Indies fast bowlers proving far too good for them on a pitch giving bounce, pace and movement. Craig McMillan was the only Kiwi specialist batsman to have any idea of how to cope, but in reply Ridley Jacobs and Brian Lara relished the conditions.

24 May

Edinburgh: Bangladesh 185–9 (50 overs) beat Scotland 163 (46.2 overs) by 22 runs. Man Of The Match award: Minhazul Abedin

Home supporters at Raeburn Place were left disappointed after Gavin Hamilton was narrowly and cruelly run out for 63 and the rest of the Scottish team couldn't rise to the challenge of beating their fellow minnows in conditions that were alien to the Bangladeshis. The visitors, indeed, showed considerable spirit in rallying from 26–5, largely through the efforts of Minhazul Abedin, who remained 68 not out. Scotland were also in trouble early on, but Hamilton lifted their spirits as wicket-keeper Alec Davies helped him to add 55 for the seventh wicket. Davies, however, then saw Hamilton just fail to ground his bat when Manjural Islam, the bowler, deflected a straight drive into the stumps.

May 27

Chester-le-Street: Bangladesh 178–7 (50 overs) lost to Australia 181–3 (19.5 overs) by seven wickets. Man Of The Match award: Tom Moody

Although they didn't know it at the time, Australia began to turn around their fortunes while disposing of a worthy Bangladeshi side on a fine pitch at the Riverside. The decision to bring in the experience and all-round talents of Tom Moody began to pay dividends, while Glenn McGrath was also happier at being given the new ball again. Bangladesh battled hard to set some sort of target, mainly through Mehrab Hossain (42) and Minhazul Abedin (53 not out), but Australia simply flew to it inside 20 overs. Unlike other, less switched-on sides, they realised that net run rate might prove important if they were to recover from a shaky start to the tournament and squeeze into the later stages.

27 May

Leicester: Scotland 68 (31.3 overs) lost to West Indies 70–2 (10.1 overs) by eight wickets. Man Of The Match award: Courtney Walsh

George Salmond, the Scottish captain, was unrepentant afterwards about his decision to bat first against an attack containing Courtney Walsh and Curtly Ambrose and in conditions that aided seam, swing and bounce. It was nevertheless an optimistic move (to be kind to him), and only Gavin Hamilton possessed anything like the technique to survive. The match was quickly over in three hours, with the West Indies having 239 balls to spare: both were limited-overs international records.

28 May

Derby: Pakistan 269–8 (50 overs) beat New Zealand 207–8 (50 overs) by 62 runs. Man Of The Match award: Inzamam-ul-Haq

Pakistan simply had too much strength for the New Zealanders, who were content long before the end to nurture their net run rate instead. An initial assault, followed by sensible batting from Ijaz Ahmed and Abdur Razzaq, was then built upon by Inzamam-ul-Haq's 61-ball unbeaten 73. Shoaib Akhtar lopped off the Kiwi openers for negligible cost and, as Pakistan's seamers closed in for the kill, New Zealand were floundering at 70–6 before Stephen Fleming (69) and Chris Harris (42) at last put up some resistance.

30 May

Old Trafford: West Indies 110 (46.4 overs) lost to Australia 111–4 (40.4 overs) by six wickets. Man Of The Match award: Glenn McGrath

In the end, controversy clouded what was a fine and uplifting victory for the Australians. Seizing on an obvious flaw in the regulations, Australia deliberately slowed down their advance to the finishing line after skittling the West Indians for a woefully inadequate total. They knew what their net run rate needed to be to get into the Super Six stage, but they also wanted the West Indies to pip New Zealand for the third qualifying place. If West Indies graduated, you see, the Australians would carry through their two points for this win, as they admitted, quite understandably, later. But if New Zealand went through alongside themselves and Pakistan, the Aussies would carry forward nothing, as they'd already lost to New Zealand and Pakistan. There were boos and slow hand-clapping from the 21,238 crowd as Steve Waugh and Michael Bevan slowed to a crawl with victory in sight, but ire should instead have been directed at the organisers. Earlier, Glenn McGrath had ripped the West Indies batting apart with 5–14. The only resistance of note came from opener Ridley Jacobs, who became the first man to carry his bat through a World Cup innings and finished on 49 not out.

31 May

Northampton: Bangladesh 223–9 (50 overs) beat Pakistan 161 (44.3 overs) by 62 runs. Man Of The Match award: Khaled Mahmud

Edinburgh: Scotland 121 (42.1 overs) lost to New Zealand 123–4 (17.5 overs) by six wickets. Man Of The Match award: Geoff Allott

Dances of delight from the many Bangladeshi fans in the 7,203 crowd greeted the fall of the last Pakistan wicket, and both captains spoke afterwards about the need for Bangladesh to be granted Test status. Scenes of jubilation all over Bangladesh, following widespread TV coverage of the tournament's biggest shock result, reinforced the fact that here was a cricket-mad country ripe for further encouragement from the ICC. It took less than 18 months, indeed, for Bangladesh to make their Test debut, in November 2000, but the fall-out from this result will take a lot longer to settle. News that British bookmakers had been offering odds of 33–1 against Bangladesh winning the match inevitably led to allegations that the game had been fixed; Pakistan, of course, were already through to the Super Six stage, irrespective of what happened here, and the defeat wouldn't affect the points they carried forward. Gordon Greenidge, sacked as Bangladesh coach just before the start, left the ground around lunchtime. Khaled Mahmud followed his 27 from 34 balls with three prime Pakistani wickets.

Winning the toss gave Stephen Fleming, the New Zealand captain, total control of events at Raeburn Place. The Kiwis knew they had to win the match at the same time as boosting their net run rate up above that of the West Indies. After bowling out the Scots for a modest total, with Geoff Allott providing the spearhead and Chris Harris polishing off the tail, they were left needing 122 from 21.2 overs or less. Despite losing some early wickets, the task was achieved comfortably with Roger Twose leading the way with an unbeaten 54, the target being reached with 3.3 overs to spare.

THE SUPER SIX
4 June
The Oval: Australia 282–6 (50 overs) beat India 205 (48.2 overs) by 77 runs. Man Of The Match award: Glenn McGrath

A magnificent new-ball burst from Glenn McGrath provided the decisive moments of a meeting between the two bottom sides in the Super Six starting table. Defeat for India meant, in all likelihood, elimination. Mark Waugh's 83 was the highlight of a rock-solid, efficient Australian batting performance, and then McGrath struck. Moving the ball off the seam, and maintaining enviable accuracy, the tall fast bowler sent back Sachin Tendulkar, Rahul Dravid and Mohammed Azharuddin in his first four overs. With Damien Fleming bowling Sourav Ganguly, the Indians were suddenly 17–4 and not even a brave fifth-wicket stand of 141 between Ajay Jadeja (100 not out) and Robin Singh (75) could then save them.

5 June

Trent Bridge: Pakistan 220–7 (50 overs) lost to South Africa 221–7 (49 overs) by three wickets. Man Of The Match award: Lance Klusener

A pulsating contest between the two heavyweight group winners was turned, late on, when Lance Klusener took on Shoaib Akhtar's terrifying pace and, with a little good fortune, triumphed. South Africa still needed 41 from 27 balls when Shoaib unwisely slipped in a bouncer which Klusener edged for four. The next ball was swung off a good length for six and the following delivery disappeared for four leg byes. Klusener finished on 46 not out and received good late support from Mark Boucher, but the South Africans were also indebted to a fine stand of 77 between Jacques Kallis (54) and Shaun Pollock after they had declined to 58–5. Pakistan's innings owed much to the late acceleration of Moin Khan, with 63.

6-7 June

Headingley: Zimbabwe 175 (49.3 overs); New Zealand 70–3 (15 overs). No result.

A washed-out reserve day prevented a result after rain had forced off New Zealand the previous afternoon. The Kiwis had needed to face at least 25 overs for a result to be possible.

8 June

Old Trafford: India 227–6 (50 overs) beat Pakistan 180 (45.3 overs) by 47 runs. Man Of The Match award: Venkatesh Prasad

A passionate, flag-waving, drum-beating, chanting crowd of 21,953 made this a thrilling World Cup occasion on English soil. Thankfully, too, with the political backdrop of yet more trouble between the two countries in Kashmir, there was little for the massive security operation to worry about. Here were two sets of rival fans intent on living the cricket event unfolding before them, and the thrilling strokeplay of Sachin Tendulkar early on certainly caught their attention. When he departed for 45, there was also high-class batsmanship from Rahul Dravid (61) and Mohammad Azharuddin (59) and testing bowling from the Pakistanis. Saeed Anwar and Moin Khan, however, were the only Pakistan batsmen to attack successfully, and neither of them managed to sustain their assault long enough. Inzamam-ul-Haq uncharacteristically laboured 30 overs for his 41 before becoming one of five victims for the accuracy of Venkatesh Prasad.

9 June

Lord's: Australia 303–4 (50 overs) beat Zimbabwe 259–6 (50 overs) by 44 runs. Man Of The Match award: Neil Johnson

At 153–1, after 28 overs, there seemed just a chance that Zimbabwe could pull off another sensational World Cup victory against Australia...on the 16th anniversary of their famous win during the 1983 tournament. But then Murray Goodwin was caught for 47, Andy Flower quickly followed and five wickets fell in all for just 47 runs. After that, the heroic Neil Johnson was content merely to improve his side's net run rate in the company of Heath Streak. Opener Johnson finished 132 not out, from 144 balls and with two sixes and 14 fours, and he gave the Australians a fright. Earlier, Mark Waugh had become the first player to score four World Cup 100s while his brother Steve walloped 62 from 61 balls despite being struck a nasty blow on the side of his helmet by a riflecrack straight drive from Mark!

10 June

Edgbaston: South Africa 287–5 (50 overs) beat New Zealand 213–8 (50 overs) by 74 runs. Man Of The Match award: Jacques Kallis

The Kiwis were outclassed by a South African side underlining their credentials as World Cup favourites. Herschelle Gibbs (91) and Gary Kirsten (82) set them on their way with 176 for the first wicket, and Jacques Kallis struck 53 from just 36 balls. There was, however, a first dismissal in ten one-day internationals for Lance Klusener, promoted to number three and bowled for only four. Klusener did, however, take his unbeaten run tally to 400, thus beating Javed Miandad's previous mark of 398 from seven innings in 1982–83. He also now had a tournament average of 214!

11 June

The Oval: Pakistan 271–9 (50 overs) beat Zimbabwe 123 (40.3 overs) by 148 runs. Man Of The Match award: Saeed Anwar

A brutally administered end to the brave Zimbabwe challenge was sealed by Saqlain Mushtaq's hat-trick, the second in World Cups, following Chetan Sharma's effort against New Zealand in 1987. Saeed Anwar was the first to illustrate Pakistani dominance, hitting 11 fours in 103, while Shahid Afridi included two remarkable sixes in his 37. Zimbabwe were nursing a catalogue of minor injuries, one of which prevented Neil Johnson (who again batted well for 54) from bowling.

First winners, the West Indies team of 1975 acknowledges the cheers of the Lord's crowd

A rare attacking shot from Sunil Gavaskar during his 60-over 36 not out for India against England at Edgbaston on the World Cup's opening day in 1975

Big Bird flies in: West Indies giant Joel Garner, the wrecker of England's innings at the 1979 World Cup final

Ian Botham during the 1979 World Cup: England's greatest all-rounder, but destined never to be a World Cup winner

Clive Lloyd in 1979: About to become the only man to lift up the World Cup twice

Kapil Dev: India's inspirational captain at the 1983 World Cup

Effortless and elegant: David Gower offers a dash of English flair at the 1983 World Cup

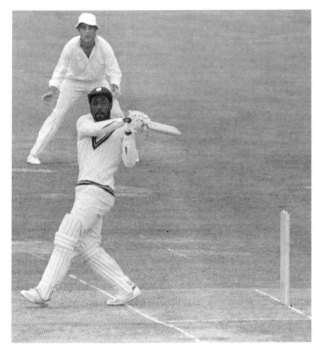

He never needed a helmet: Viv (now Sir Vivian) Richards dismisses another delivery from his presence at the 1979 World Cup

Malcolm Marshall was just one quarter of the awesome West Indies fast-bowling strength at the 1983 World Cup

Richard (later Sir Richard) Hadlee was one of New Zealand's main hopes at the 1983 World Cup

The 1987 World Cup: The Reliance Trophy

India's stylish batsman Dilip Vengsarkar is pictured during the 1987 World Cup

Pakistan's Javed Miandad in action during the 1987 World Cup, two-thirds of the way to becoming the only player to appear in the first six tournaments

Mike Gatting, who came agonisingly close to leading England to the 1987 World Cup

A young Steve Waugh celebrates Australia's World Cup triumph in 1987

Australia's anchor, David Boon, brought his reliable form into the 1987 World Cup final against England

Dean Jones, Australia's number three, in typically aggressive mood during the 1987 World Cup final

Allan Border lifts the 1987 World Cup aloft following Australia's win over England at Calcutta

Colour by numbers: The 1992 World Cup teams

Imran Khan, Pakistan's captain, celebrates his moment of triumph at the 1992 World Cup final

Graham Gooch, England's captain and opening batsman, falls during the 1992 World Cup final

Wasim Akram, one of the architects of Pakistan's 1992 World Cup victory

The great Shane Warne, ultimately thwarted at the 1996 World Cup, but a world champion three years later. Will his shoulder be recovered suffciently to lead the Australian attack once more in 2003?

Sachin Tendulkar hits out during his 90 against Australia on his home ground at Bombay during the 1996 World Cup

Graham Thorpe scored 89 but England only beat minnows Holland by 49 runs at Peshawar during the 1996 World Cup

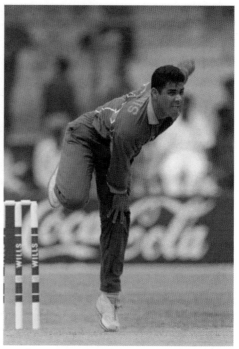

Sri Lanka's thrilling 1996 World Cup win owed much to the classy strokeplay of Aravinda de Silva

Pakistan's Waqar Younis missed out on 1992 World Cup glory because of injury, and was scarcely any more fortunate at the 1996 tournament

Mark Waugh, one of the main reasons Australia made it through to the final of the 1996 World Cup

Sourav Ganguly bowls during India's shock 1999 World Cup defeat to Zimbabwe at Leicester

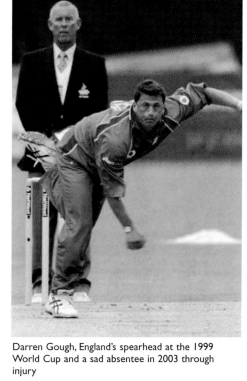

Darren Gough, England's spearhead at the 1999 World Cup and a sad absentee in 2003 through injury

The sledgehammer batting of South Africa's Lance Klusener, the 1999 World Cup's player of the tournament

Inzamam-ul-Haq pulls Glenn McGrath during his innings of 81 in Pakistan's 1999 World Cup group win over Australia at Headingley

Brian Lara, the West Indies captain at the 1999 World Cup

Steve Waugh lifts the trophy after Australia's bowling deadly duo of Warne and McGrath punished slack Pakistan batting in the final to win easily by eight wickets

12 June

Trent Bridge: India 251–6 (50 overs) lost to New Zealand 253–5 (48.2 overs) by five wickets. Man Of The Match award: Roger Twose

Despite most of their top order self-destructing, with the exception of Ajay Jadeja (76), India posted a decent total. New Zealand, anchored by Matthew Horne's 74, were then shepherded into the semi-finals by Roger Twose, who remained 60 not out and was aided superbly in a tense finish by Adam Parore's nerveless strokeplay. Geoff Allott, the left-arm paceman, earlier bowled Sourav Ganguly to become the first player to gain 20 wickets in a World Cup tournament (the previous record was 18).

13 June

Headingley: South Africa 271–7 (50 overs) lost to Australia 272–5 (49.4 overs) by five wickets. Man Of The Match award: Steve Waugh

It would be unfair, and technically inaccurate, to say that Herschelle Gibbs dropped the catch which (so Steve Waugh reportedly told him at the time) ultimately cost South Africa the World Cup. But Gibbs, who put down the simplest of chances at mid-wicket when Waugh was 56, did cost South Africa the opportunity of knocking out the Australians from the competition. That they then lost again to them in an epic semi-final simply twisted the knife agonisingly in Gibbs's wounds. In hindsight, however, the absence of the in-form Jacques Kallis with an abdominal strain was also a hugely significant factor in Australia's great escape: the ten overs that South Africa thus had to fiddle with second-string bowlers Hansie Cronje and Nicky Boje cost 79 runs. Gibbs, who made his error when seemingly in the act of throwing up the ball in premature celebration, had earlier batted with great flair and application to score 101, while Lance Klusener provided much of the late flourish in typically robust fashion. At 48–3 in reply, Australia were in deep trouble, but Waugh joined Ricky Ponting (69) in a stand worth 126 and full of calculated aggression. Then, reprieved, Waugh was supported by Michael Bevan and Tom Moody as he swept on to 120 not out from 110 balls. It was a match-winning, tournament-saving *tour de force* and unforgettable, especially for Herschelle Gibbs.

SEMI-FINALS
16 June

Old Trafford: New Zealand 241–7 (50 overs) lost to Pakistan 242–1 (47.3 overs) by nine wickets. Man Of The Match award: Shoaib Akhtar

New Zealand's total was boosted to reasonable proportions by the 47 assorted extras donated by the brilliant but undisciplined Pakistanis, but it would have been more but for the express deliveries of Shoaib Akhtar which shattered the stumps of Nathan Astle, Stephen Fleming and Chris Harris. In a further display of power, however, which sent an ecstatic and mainly Pakistani crowd of 22,000 into delirium, Saeed Anwar (113 not out) and Wajahatullah Wasti (84) put on 194 for the first wicket to decide the match. There were two pitch invasions at the end, however, one coming when there were only six runs required for victory, and these soured the otherwise joyful spectacle.

17 June

Edgbaston: Australia 213 (49.2 overs) tied with South Africa 213 (49.4 overs).
Man Of The Match award: Shane Warne

The greatest World Cup match of all? Well, the 1975 final certainly had riches beyond what most spectators could have expected to see, but this epic confrontation threw up performances and situations that were gloriously beyond the imagination. The only sadness, at the end of such a day, was that, because of the net-run-rate rule, a match that had finished as a pure tie (with both sides all out) should be remembered as an Australian triumph and a South African foul-up. Yes, Lance Klusener and Allan Donald did lose their heads in a tumultuous final over, but Klusener had pummelled the Australians onto the ropes by crashing the first two balls of it to the extra cover boundary. His 31 not out had taken just 14 balls, and only the extraordinary tension of the moment then prevented him from making the single run he needed from the last four balls of the contest. Steve Waugh, quite rightly, brought all his fielders in to prevent the quick single. Klusener mishit the third delivery and Donald, backing up and sent back, would have been run out if Darren Lehmann's throw had hit the bowlers' stumps. It was a warning that South Africa didn't heed; rather than wait to get a big lofted hit on at least one of the remaining three balls, a suddenly vulnerable-looking Klusener swiped the fourth ball back past Fleming and set off for a suicidal single. Donald, ball-watching, was then transfixed with shock at Klusener's mad charge, dropped his bat and, finally, set off batless for the other end. He was far too late. Mark Waugh, swooping on the ball at mid-on, had flicked the ball back to Fleming, who in turn had rolled it carefully down the pitch to Adam Gilchrist, the wicket-keeper. Gilchrist shattered the stumps, Donald was stranded mid-pitch and South Africa's hearts were also broken.

Looking back, however, has any one-day international ever featured such a glut of wonderful, high-class individual performances as well as such a gut-wrenchingly tight and dramatic finish? There was fast and incisive bowling from Shaun Pollock (5–36) and Donald (4–32) and gritty middle-order batting from Steve Waugh, Michael Bevan and Jonty Rhodes, besides a superb all-round display from Jacques Kallis and power-hitting from Klusener that was ultimately in vain. Over and above all this, though, there was magical leg-spin bowling from the genius that is Shane Warne, who bowled Herschelle Gibbs with a delivery to match the brilliance of the one which castled Mike Gatting at the start of the 1993 Ashes series, and his 4–29 was solely responsible for dragging Australia back into the match and setting up the spectacular conclusion to, yes, the greatest of World Cup matches.

THE 1999 WORLD CUP FINAL
20 June
Lord's: Pakistan 132 (39 overs) lost to Australia 133–2 (20.1 overs) by eight wickets. Man Of The Match award: Shane Warne

Australia, their confidence sky-high after their adventurous journey to the final, blew Pakistan away to make the seventh World Cup final the most disappointing of its genre. With thousands of dedicated Pakistan fans denied tickets due to the organisers' policy of selling them as part of advance packages, the four-and-a-half-hour final was – in every sense – a huge let-down.

Not that Steve Waugh's side cared. Losing the toss, and thus first use of a good pitch, they concentrated instead on asserting their authority over the notoriously temperamental Pakistan batting line-up. Indeed, five of Pakistan's top seven got starts, but none could go on to play a sizeable innings and only Inzamam-ul-Haq – understandably aggrieved at being given out caught behind off his pad – can point to bad luck.

As in the semi-final, Shane Warne was at the heart of Australia's great effort in the field. Coming on at 69–3, after 21 overs, he soon produced yet another of his most unplayable deliveries, a fizzing leg-break which pitched just outside the line of right hander Ijaz Ahmed's pads and hit the top of his off stump.

Moin Khan, Azhar Mahmood and Wasim Akram also fell to Warne, whose 4–33 earned him a second successive Man Of The Match award and a share in Geoff Allott's recently established World Cup tournament record of 20 wickets. Pakistan's miserable 132 was the lowest total in any World Cup final.

Adam Gilchrist (54) reached his half-century in 33 balls as the Australians powered joyously to their modest target. Mark Waugh remained 37 not out, content in his anchor role, but when the match was all over at 4:32pm, more than four hours earlier than the 1975 final, there was no disguising the fact that the 200th World Cup match had been perhaps the most disappointing of the event's very own double century.

THE INTERVIEW
Steve Waugh

To the Australian captain, it was 'inner strength' that carried his team all the way to World Cup glory at Lord's. To the rest of the watching world, it was the extraordinary will to win of Steve Waugh himself.

There's no doubt that a captain leads by example, especially in as complex a game as cricket. He must perform himself, of course, but he must also command respect by the way he holds himself, by the way he deals with his team, by the general example he sets.

Australia won the 1999 World Cup, in the end, by virtue of an awesomely efficient cup-final performance. They got there by dint of the net-run-rate ruling, after just about holding on against South Africa in an epic semi-final.

That they remained in contention for the title at all, at that stage, was down to one man. Waugh's gritty 56 in the semi-final was, in its way, just as important an innings as his magnificent counter-attacking and match-winning 120 not out in the final Super Six fixture, when South Africa blew their chance of knocking the Aussies out of the competition. His leadership, pulling his team around after a poor start, was also faultless.

Waugh, the only Australian to win the World Cup twice, following his appearance as a junior member of Allan Border's 1987 side, said, 'There was enormous pressure on us throughout the run of seven victories which brought us the Cup.

'At several stages in this tournament we were virtually down and out. We went into matches knowing that if we lost we would be out of the competition and going home. But we hung on to every moment we could, and I would put a lot of it down to inner strength. We couldn't believe we got out alive from the South Africa semi-final. Perhaps there was someone looking over us.

'We were pretty relentless in the final itself, though. We just strangled Pakistan. Whenever one of their guys played a false shot, they paid the price.

We were in Pakistan's face all the time, always throwing the ball back to the keeper to underline our intent. They are a flamboyant side and we used discipline to put pressure on them. We knew that pressure would tell.

'There were a lot of young players in their team, and so there was not a lot of experience. We had also done our homework and noticed that, apart from the openers, none of their batsmen had passed 50 in their past five games.'

THE CHAMPIONS

It was to their intense satisfaction that Australia could now refer to themselves as world champions. Beaten in the 1996 final, they had spent the intervening years underlining their dominance of the cricket world, yet their mastery of Test cricket could not be marked by any tangible reward or trophy while South Africa had strongly contested the debate of who should be considered one-day kings.

Now there was no doubt. Steve Waugh's team returned to Melbourne to a ticker-tape welcome and huge country-wide plaudits. Almost a third of Australia's population had watched on television as Pakistan were crushed in the final, and Aussies everywhere revelled, too, in the official recognition that their cricketers were indeed number one.

Perhaps Shoaib Akhtar, the wild-haired and wild-eyed Pakistan tearaway, had proved the most riveting sight of the tournament. The Speedster (the machine, not the man), which for some reason was only introduced after the group stage, recorded one Shoaib thunderbolt at 96 miles per hour. There was also another at 95, two more at 94 and yet another at 92.

The big-hitting South African Lance Klusener was named Player Of The Tournament for his 281 runs (from 230 balls) and 17 wickets, but it was Australia who had most of the classiest acts.

Skipper Waugh himself, his twin brother Mark, fast bowler Glenn McGrath and leg-spinner Shane Warne all produced match-winning performances under pressure. McGrath, once he had been given the new ball, consistently got the best players out, as his dismissals of Brian Lara and Sachin Tendulkar for ducks amply demonstrated. Warne, out of sorts early in the tournament after being dropped from the Test team in the Caribbean, bounced back when it mattered most to bowl decisive spells in both the semi-final and final, when in both cases he was Man Of The Match.

It was the switch in the balance of the team, too, which contributed to the turnabout in Australian fortunes. Tom Moody, the experienced Western

Australian all-rounder, was brought into the side to fulfil the role of fifth specialist bowler and floating hitter capable of batting anywhere in the order.

Moody responded with 117 runs in five innings, at a strike rate of 130 runs per 100 balls (the highest in the tournament among those scoring more than 100 runs), and took seven wickets at an average of 31 and an economy rate of 4.3.

Ricky Ponting and Michael Bevan were extremely consistent in the middle order, with 354 and 264 runs respectively, while Adam Gilchrist finally came good in the final and both Damien Fleming and Paul Reiffel proved dependable frontline seamers.

This was a fine team, indeed, with the added and, in the end, critical advantage of being led by the finest captain.

THE PRIZES

A total prize fund of US$1 million was divided as follows: the winners received US$300,000, the runners-up US$150,000, the losing semi-finalists US$100,000 each, the fifth placed in Super Six US$52,500, the sixth placed in Super Six US$27,500, all group match winners US$6,000 each, and all group match losers US$3,000 each.

THE QUOTES

'Mate, you've just dropped the World Cup.' Steve Waugh (allegedly) to Herschelle Gibbs at Headingley.

'There is no doubt in my mind that the two best sides played in our semi-final; that was the real "final". That one run we failed to get at Edgbaston will haunt me for the rest of my life.' Bob Woolmer, whose term as South Africa coach ended with the World Cup.

'Cricket means so much to Aussie people. More than anything else, they love winners.' Shane Warne.

'I would love to bowl at 100 miles per hour. I like to see fear in a batsman.' Shoaib Akhtar.

'There is, of course, no doubt that the departure of England at such an early stage was disappointing. No one, however, can question the global success of the tournament. The 1999 World Cup will leave a lasting legacy.' Tim Lamb, chief executive of the England and Wales Cricket Board.

'They called me Napoleon when we won the last World Cup. I'm probably Hitler now.' Arjuna Ranatunga, when he was soon to be axed as Sri Lanka captain.

TEAM OF THE TOURNAMENT?

Mark Waugh (Australia)

Neil Johnson (Zimbabwe)

Rahul Dravid (India)

Sourav Ganguly (India)

Steve Waugh (Australia, captain)

Jacques Kallis (South Africa)

Moin Khan (Pakistan, wicket-keeper)

Lance Klusener (South Africa)

Shane Warne (Australia)

Shoaib Akhtar (Pakistan)

Glenn McGrath (Australia)

Chapter 11

An Expanding Future

Each of the seven World Cups to date has had a flavour and a character all of its own. The same, no doubt, will be the case in however many more World Cups the future holds.

After South Africa 2003, the story is due to continue when the West Indies host the event – for the first time – in 2007. This promises to be an important landmark for the future development of cricket in the Caribbean, while the ICC is still considering the option of scheduling at least some of the matches in other North American countries such as Canada, the USA or Bermuda.

The North American mainland, the Far East and the Arab Emirates remain areas of potentially huge growth for cricket, and it's not beyond probability to imagine the 2043 World Cup (for instance) being staged somewhere like Malaysia, New York or Dubai.

And what would World Cups of the future look like? How would they be different?

They could, for a start, be played more often. Matthew Engel, then editor of *Wisden*, argued in the 2000 edition of cricket's bible for a World Cup to be held every two years. It's a persuasive argument, too, which the ICC would do well to consider as a method of rebranding the presentation of the one-day international game in the same constructive way which they are attempting with the fledgling (though still flawed) Test Championship.

Engel also pointed to the ever-growing pulling power and stature of the World Cup and wrote, 'You can sense the tournament gaining strength as an institution and taking its place among the planet's great sporting events.

'Yet [following the 1999 tournament] England could stage an Olympics and a football World Cup before the cricket version returns. It probably will not be back until 2019; it will not even be staged in Asia until 2011 or 2015. Why on Earth not? There is no good reason why cricket remains committed to the self-denying ordinance of holding a World Cup only every four years. It should be every two years.

'Cricket is bedevilled by wrong-headed analogies with football. A football World Cup actually *lasts* two years because almost everyone has to qualify. For the major teams, the cricket World Cup lasts only a few weeks.

'And the game's unique spread – global but scattered – means that all the World Cups outside one's own home country are very distant and quite likely to be played through the night.

'A change would not overwhelm public demand, and it would help to justify the investment in stadia that is going to be vital, especially before the West Indies tournament of 2007.

'The alternative is a continuation and expansion of all the other one-day tournaments that have little meaning and are tainted by the suspicion of betting-related corruption. The World Cup is cricket's most glittering showcase. It needs to be on display.'

Currently, and for the foreseeable future, cricket's five major market-places are Australasia, Asia, southern Africa, northwest Europe and the Caribbean/Americas. What Engel is effectively promoting is an eight-year cycle which takes in all those five centres, most sensibly on a strict rota.

There is, by the way, a case for giving Asia two bites in a cycle expanded to ten years, given the fact that four of the current ten Test-playing countries are from an area of world which, in terms of population, mass interest and commercial potential is now indubitably cricket's powerhouse.

As ever, one suspects that money will drive the engines of progress. The huge estimated profits set to be generated by both the 2003 and 2007 World Cups must surely reinforce the argument for a more regular festival gathering of cricket's far-flung family. Perhaps there will be a move, initially, to once every three years. What does the cricket world think?

Meanwhile, what is more confidently predictable is that, in not too far distant a future, rain interruptions will become a thing of the past as far as World Cup cricket (and possibly Test cricket, too) is concerned. Well before the end of this young century, all major stadiums of the world will surely have the facility to activate a transparent roof covering. Advances in technology will allow such a sliding roof to be opened or closed at the press of a button and, allied to improved and more natural lighting techniques, will guarantee play in the scheduled hours. 'Rain stops play' and 'the Duckworth-Lewis system' are dreaded phrases that will become mere relics from World Cup history.

One-day cricket, moreover, is a far better and more balanced contest when the playing field is a level one. The vagaries caused by the toss and changing weather conditions are important aspects of the richness of Test and first-class cricket, but in the one-day arena it is uniformity of pitch and atmospheric conditions which best ensures an exciting, evenly-fought match in which every ball can be the delivery which tilts the contest.

High-quality roofing and lighting added to advances in pitch preparation would, in turn, ensure better quality limited-overs play. It would also take out of the equation the twilit overs of current day-night matches, which often impact on the result.

Technology, of course, will also bring with it superior facilities for crowds: more comfortable seating, for sure, and what about individual mini-televisions attached to the back of the seat in front on which replays and highlights packages can be viewed at any time? Drinks, refreshments and programmes or information packs might be orderable from your seat, too, when you attend the World Cups of the future.

On-field, there will also be evidence of the march of the technological age. Umpires, both those standing out in the middle and those sat at their monitors in the pavilion, will be in control of mechanical aids which, in time, will help them to make every possible decision.

And was South Africa coach Bob Woolmer, for example, so very far ahead of his time when, in his team's opening match of the 1999 World Cup, he attempted to communicate with his on-field captain and senior professional by radio? In the future, every batsman and every fielder might be allowed to be in constant touch with each other and their management.

Rugby union's revolutionary RefLink facility, which lets each spectator listen via a one-way radio earpiece to the referee's on-field decision-making, might also lead to similar initiatives in cricket, with umpires coming on air to explain decisions, or coaches or expert summarisers giving instant reactions to big moments in the game.

Spectators at a live game may soon, in short, be offered just the kind of information and insight service that cricket's armchair viewers now enjoy from an increasingly spectacular television coverage.

The evolution of the limited-overs game itself, meanwhile, has already meant that the demands on the players of today are far different from those of 27 years ago. It's a safe bet, therefore, that in 27 years' time there will be yet different skills again on view.

Switch-hitting, for a start, could be the next big idea in one-day cricket:

Why shouldn't a top-class right-handed batsman, for instance – especially having practised for long hours – be almost as good a left-handed player? Brian Close, a former England captain of the 1960s, was ambidextrous enough to be a single-figure handicap golfer both ways around. Many cricketers already bat left-handed and bowl or throw right-handed, or indeed vice versa.

When facing a leg-spinner like Shane Warne, for example, would it not make more sense – particularly when scoring runs and not preserving the wicket is the prerogative – for a naturally right-handed batsman to inform the umpire and bowler that he is to play left-handed?

The wide acceptance of the value of the reverse sweep, indeed, is already an indication that cross-over batting is a natural by-product of the flexible and radical thinking increasingly required in one-day cricket. Yet it was only 15 years ago, in the 1987 World Cup final, that England captain Mike Gatting was widely condemned for even attempting it in such a high-profile match.

If the batsmen of the future learn to switch-hit, as a means of dealing with certain types of bowling, or just as a way of disrupting a bowler's line, then what about switch-bowling?

There have been many right-arm bowlers, to give this as an example, who have been able to deliver some serviceable left-arm spinners. Many net sessions or light-hearted club games have ended with someone bowling the other way around, just for the laughs. But could it not be a deadly serious ploy? Again, if it's practised as being an acceptable art for those blessed with ambidextrous ability, could not bowlers emerge who could bowl not just in two different styles – seam or spin – but who were multi-dimensional in terms of what arm they bowled with? As with batsmen who switch-hit, it could be the particular ability or style of the opponent at the other end of the pitch which would determine in which fashion, and with which arm, a bowler would bowl.

Fielding, too, comes into this category of increased flexibility, and perhaps it will become a new feature of limited-overs cricket even less far into the future. In fact, there would be great sense in schoolboy cricketers of today practising from an early age their throwing skills – certainly underarm – with both hands. The added capability to effect run-outs, and save runs, due to a majority of players being able to pick up and throw with either hand (especially from inside the 30-metre fielding circle), would considerably strengthen the armoury of any side in the field.

Writing during the last World Cup, in 1999, the former South African batsman Barry Richards – now a perceptive media analyst and commentator – called for the game's administrators to review all existing one-day rules in order 'to ensure progress'. Since then, indeed, a one-bouncer-per-over regulation in limited-overs internationals has been confirmed by the ICC in the interests of allowing faster bowlers to maintain a certain element of surprise and to prevent batsmen from simply swinging through the line with impunity.

However, Richards, who was himself one of the most innovative of cricketers in his approach to playing the limited-overs game, also predicted switch-hitters, switch-bowlers and completely ambidextrous fielders.

His article, too, neatly summed up the heady acceleration in the profile, popularity and playing techniques produced by the rapid growth of one-day international cricket. He wrote, 'The 1970s was a decade of learning for the players. Batting became more inventive as traditional methods were supplemented by the need to score off a much higher proportion of deliveries. Hitting over the top, and backing away to leg, were just two new methods used to increase the run rate.

'Bowling, as a result, became more defensive and the need to take wickets was less important during the 1970s and 1980s. That balance is now being redressed, with captains realising more and more that wicket-taking does indeed slow down the scoring rate.

'Bowlers, however, were also helped in the 1970s by what we now call leg-side wides only being called if the delivery was well wide of leg stump.

'Fielding positions were also under review as captains realised they had to cover a lot of new angles. The "sweeper" was an early invention, as teams tried to restrict the number of boundaries, but there were still no fielding restrictions (ie staying within a 30-metre circle) until Mike Brearley, England's astute captain, ensured one particular victory by placing all his fielders, including the wicket-keeper, back on the boundary edge. That tactic caused a furore at the time, but administrators soon responded with the inner-circle restriction, much to the relief of those batting in the closing overs.

'During the 1980s, captains had to become more thoughtful and inventive in order to get an edge over the opposition, and the so-called modern (mid-'90s) phenomenon of pinch-hitting was in fact a thing of the past. As far back as 1982, Chris Wilkins, a superb striker of a cricket ball, was used by Natal to give an innings momentum in the early overs.

'At this time, too, swing bowlers rather than the fastest bowlers were given the new ball and were often asked to bowl their ten overs straight through. Sides began to leave their quickest bowlers to either attack or defend in the middle overs – and the slower ball also began to be a potent weapon, with Australian pair Simon O'Donnell and the young Steve Waugh being early masters of it.

'Tactics were becoming far less predictable and indeed less traditional. Spinners, who had become all but extinct towards the end of the 1970s unless they bowled flat and leg-side, made a comeback as captains realised that "taking the pace" off the ball was an often effective method of restricting scoring. Commercially, by now, one-day cricket was also proving itself the medium which sustained all other forms of the game.

'The 1990s will be remembered as both the decade of reverse swing – with Darren Gough and Shoaib Akhtar two particular exponents of the art – and of fielding. One man, Jonty Rhodes, was the leader in this department in one-day cricket. People came just to watch him field. Fielding was now truly one-third of the game, and Rhodes gave new meaning to the term "all-rounder".

'Flexibility will be the key to future one-day-international success. One-dimensional approaches will not work. The "floating" batting order, still a relatively new concept, is perhaps something which will increase in tactical popularity.

'What other innovations may be just around the corner? The one thing, perhaps, that has not changed in the history of one-day international cricket is the accumulation process that normally dominates the "middle overs" of an innings, sometimes leading to the absence of boundaries for many overs and a lack of explosive entertainment.

'Overs 15–40 are thus often seen as a "problem" area, and so further fielding restrictions in the "middle overs" may well be the answer.'

There are many other ways, of course, in which one-day cricket can (and will) change as a skill and as a spectacle. Free hits, specialist substitutes, tactical innovations, improvements to clothing and equipment…the list could well prove endless.

Is it really too fanciful a flight of imagination which might foresee the possibility of the 2075 World Cup final being won off the last ball when a fiendish Bangladeshi lob bowler, having single-handedly revived a dead art in a manner recalling what Warne did with leg-spin towards the end of the previous century, bamboozles an heroic Malaysian century-maker's attempt to swing a match-winning six in front of 180,000 spectators inside the vast Melbourne Cricket Dome?

The stumping would be confirmed within a second by the third umpire speaking to every spectator and player by one-way radio, and the replays would be flashed up on both the big screens and the individual mini-screens in front of every seat. Within minutes, too, words from batsmen, bowlers, captains and coaches would be broadcast around the stadium and to the watching millions on television.

After the presentations of the World Cup trophy, and individual medals, the roof of the giant stadium would be soundlessly peeled back to reveal a night sky soon to be lit up by a massive farewell firework display and a written message – produced by lasers – proclaiming, 'See you in Los Angeles…for the 2077 Cricket World Cup!'

1975 WORLD CUP

Prudential World Cup, 1975, 1st Match
England v India, Group A
Lord's, London
7 June 1975 (60-over match)

Result: England won by 202 runs
Points: England 4, India 0
Toss: England
Umpires: DJ Constant and JG Langridge
ODI Debuts: M Amarnath, AD Gaekwad, KD Ghavri (Ind)
Man Of The Match: DL Amiss

England innings (60 overs maximum)			R	B	4	6
JA Jameson	c Venkataraghavan	b Amarnath	21	42	2	0
DL Amiss	b Madan Lal		137	147	18	0
KWR Fletcher	b Abid Ali		68	07	4	1
AW Greig	lbw	b Abid Ali	4	8	0	0
MH Denness*	not out		37	31	2	1
CM Old	not out		51	30	4	2
Extras (lb 12, w 2, nb 2): **16**						
Total (4 wickets, 60 overs) **334**						

DNB: B Wood, +APE Knott, JA Snow, P Lever, GG Arnold.
FoW: 1-54 (Jameson), 2-230 (Fletcher), 3-237 (Greig), 4-245 (Amiss).

Bowling	O	M	R	W
Madan Lal	12	1	64	1
Amarnath	12	2	60	1
Abid Ali	12	0	58	2
Ghavri	11	1	83	0
Venkataraghavan	12	0	41	0
Solkar	1	0	12	0

India innings (target: 335 runs from 60 overs)			R	B	4	6
SM Gavaskar	not out	36 174	1	0		
ED Solkar	c Lever	b Arnold	8	34	0	0
AD Gaekwad	c Knott	b Lever	22	46	2	0
GR Viswanath	c Fletcher	b Old	37	59	5	0
BP Patel	not out	16	57	0	0	
Extras (lb 3, w 1, nb 9): **13**						
Total (3 wickets, 60 overs): **132**						

DNB: M Amarnath, +FM Engineer, S Abid Ali, S Madan Lal, *S Venkataraghavan, KD Ghavri.
FoW: 1-21 (Solkar), 2-50 (Gaekwad), 3-108 (Viswanath).

Bowling	O	M	R	W
Snow	12	2	24	0
Arnold	10	2	20	1
Old	12	4	26	1
Greig	9	1	26	0
Wood	5	2	4	0
Lever	10	0	16	1
Jameson	2	1	3	0

Prudential World Cup, 1975, 2nd Match
East Africa v New Zealand, Group A
Edgbaston, Birmingham
7 June 1975 (60-over match)

Result: New Zealand won by 181 runs
Points: New Zealand 4, East Africa 0
Toss: New Zealand
Umpires: HD Bird and AE Fagg
ODI Debuts: BJ McKechnie (NZ); Frasat Ali, Harilal Shah, Jawahir Shah, H McLeod, Mehmood Quaraishy, J Nagenda, PG Nana, RK Sethi, S Sumar, S Walusimbi, Zulfiqar Ali (EA)
Man Of The Match: GM Turner

New Zealand innings (60 overs maximum)			R	M	B	4	6
*GM Turner	not out		171	190	201	16	2
JFM Morrison	c & b Nana		14	44	37	0	0
GP Howarth	b Mehmood Quaraishy		20	45	40	2	0
JM Parker	c Zulfiqar Ali	b Sethi	66	74	68	7	0
BF Hastings	c Sethi	b Zulfiqar Ali	8	8	7	1	0
+KJ Wadsworth	b Nagenda		10	7	7	0	1
RJ Hadlee	not out		6	6	4	0	0
Extras (b 1, lb 8, w 5): **14**							
Total (5 wickets, 60 overs): **309**							

DNB: BJ McKechnie, DR Hadlee, HJ Howarth, RO Collinge.
FoW: 1-51 (Morrison), 2-103 (GP Howarth), 3-252 (Parker), 4-278 (Hastings), 5-292 (Wadsworth).

Bowling	O	M	R	W
Nagenda	9	1	50	1
Frasat Ali	9	0	50	0
Nana	12	2	34	1
Sethi	10	1	51	1
Zulfiqar Ali	12	0	71	1
Mehmood Quaraishy	8	0	39	1

East Africa innings (target: 310 runs from 60 overs)			R	M	B	4	6
Frasat Ali	st Wadsworth	b HJ Howarth	45	134	123	1	1
S Walusimbi	b DR Hadlee		15	50	46	1	0
RK Sethi	run out		1	3	3	0	0
S Sumar	b DR Hadlee		4	9	11	0	0
Jawahir Shah	c & b HJ Howarth		5	29	17	0	0
*Harilal Shah	lbw	b HJ Howarth	0	1	1	0	0
Mehmood Quaraishy	not out		16	103	88	0	0
Zulfiqar Ali	b DR Hadlee		30	48	49	4	0
+H McLeod	b Collinge		5	8	8	0	0
PG Nana	not out		1	12	15	0	0
Extras (lb 5, nb 1): **6**							
Total (8 wickets, 60 overs): **128**							

DNB: J Nagenda.
FoW: 1-30 (Walusimbi), 2-32 (Sethi), 3-36 (Sumar), 4-59 (Jawahir Shah), 5-59 (Harilal Shah), 6-84 (Frasat Ali), 7-121 (Zulfiqar Ali), 8-126 (McLeod).

Bowling	O	M	R	W
Collinge	12	5	23	1
RJ Hadlee	12	6	10	0
McKechnie	12	2	39	0
DR Hadlee	12	1	21	3
HJ Howarth	12	3	29	3

Prudential World Cup, 1975, 3rd Match
Australia v Pakistan, Group B
Headingley, Leeds
7 June 1975 (60-over match)

Result: Australia won by 73 runs
Points: Australia 4, Pakistan 0
Toss: Australia
Umpires: WE Alley and TW Spencer
ODI Debuts: RB McCosker, A Turner (Aus); Naseer Malik (Pak)
Man Of The Match: DK Lillee

Australia innings (60 overs maximum)

			R	B	4	6
A Turner	c Mushtaq Mohammad b Asif Iqbal		46	54	4	0
RB McCosker	c Wasim Bari	b Naseer Malik	25	76	2	0
*IM Chappell	c Wasim Raja	b Sarfraz Nawaz	28	30	5	0
GS Chappell	c Asif Iqbal	b Imran Khan	45	56	5	0
KD Walters	c Sarfraz Nawaz	b Naseer Malik	2	13	0	0
R Edwards	not out		80	94	6	0
+RW Marsh	c Wasim Bari	b Imran Khan	1	5	0	0
MHN Walker	b Asif Masood		18	28	2	0
JR Thomson	not out		20	14	2	1
Extras (lb 7, nb 6): **13**						
Total (7 wickets, 60 overs): **278**						

DNB: AA Mallett, DK Lillee.
FoW: 1-63 (Turner), 2-99 (IM Chappell), 3-110 (McCosker), 4-124 (Walters), 5-184 (GS Chappell), 6-195 (Marsh), 7-243 (Walker).

Bowling

	O	M	R	W
Naseer Malik	12	2	37	2
Asif Masood	12	0	50	1
Sarfraz Nawaz	12	0	63	1
Asif Iqbal	12	0	58	1
Imran Khan	10	0	44	2
Wasim Raja	2	0	13	0

Pakistan innings (target: 279 runs from 60 overs)

			R	B	4	6
Sadiq Mohammad	b Lillee		4	12	0	0
Majid Khan	c Marsh	b Mallett	65	76	11	0
Zaheer Abbas	c Turner	b Thomson	8	10	2	0
Mushtaq Mohammad	c GS Chappell	b Walters	8	32	0	0
*Asif Iqbal	b Lillee		53	95	8	0
Wasim Raja	c Thomson	b Walker	31	57	4	0
Imran Khan	c Turner	b Walker	9	19	1	0
Sarfraz Nawaz	c Marsh	b Lillee	0	2	0	0
+Wasim Bari	c Marsh	b Lillee	2	18	0	0
Asif Masood	c Walker	b Lillee	6	7	1	0
Naseer Malik	not out		0	13	0	0
Extras (lb 4, w 3, nb 12): **19**						
Total (all out, 53 overs): **205**						

FoW: 1-15 (Sadiq Mohammad), 2-27 (Zaheer Abbas), 3-68 (Mushtaq Mohammad), 4-104 (Majid Khan), 5-181 (Asif Iqbal), 6-189 (Wasim Raja), 7-189 (Sarfraz Nawaz), 8-195 (Imran Khan), 9-203 (Asif Masood), 10-205 (Wasim Bari).

Bowling

	O	M	R	W
Lillee	12	2	34	5
Thomson	8	2	25	1
Walker	12	3	32	2
Mallett	12	1	49	1
Walters	6	0	29	1
GS Chappell	3	0	17	0

Prudential World Cup, 1975, 4th Match
Sri Lanka v West Indies, Group B
Old Trafford, Manchester
7 June 1975 (60-over match)

Result: West Indies won by 9 wickets
Points: West Indies 4, Sri Lanka 0
Toss: West Indies
Umpires: WL Budd and A Jepson
ODI Debuts: IVA Richards, AME Roberts (WI); DS de Silva, ER Fernando, PD Heyn, LWS
    Kaluperuma, LRD Mendis, ARM Opatha, HSM Pieris, AN Ranasinghe, APB Tennekoon,
    MH Tissera, B Warnapura (SL)
Man Of The Match: BD Julien

Sri Lanka innings (60 overs maximum)			R	M	B	4	6
+ER Fernando	c Murray	b Julien	4	11	6	0	0
B Warnapura	c Murray	b Boyce	8	62	54	1	0
*APB Tennekoon	c Murray	b Julien	0	2	4	0	0
PD Heyn	c Lloyd	b Roberts	2	27	12	0	0
MH Tissera	c Kallicharran	b Julien	14	38	35	1	0
LRD Mendis	c Murray	b Boyce	8	20	13	1	0
AN Ranasinghe	b Boyce		0	5	2	0	0
HSM Pieris	c Lloyd	b Julien	3	13	12	0	0
ARM Opatha	b Roberts		11	26	18	1	0
DS de Silva	c Lloyd	b Holder	21	47	54	2	0
LWS Kaluperuma	not out		6	31	19	0	0
Extras (b 3, lb 3, nb 3): **9**							
Total (all out, 37.2 overs): **86**							

FoW: 1-5 (Fernando), 2-5 (Tennekoon), 3-16 (Heyn), 4-21 (Warnapura), 5-41 (Tissera), 6-41 (Mendis), 7-42 (Ranasinghe), 8-48 (Pieris), 9-58 (Opatha), 10-86 (de Silva).

Bowling	O	M	R	W
Roberts	12	5	16	2
Julien	12	3	20	4
Boyce	8	1	22	3
Gibbs	4	0	17	0
Holder	1.2	0	2	1

West Indies innings (target: 87 runs from 60 overs)			R	M	B	4	6
RC Fredericks	c Warnapura	b de Silva	33	42	38	4	0
+DL Murray	not out		30	69	50	2	1
AI Kallicharran	not out		19	25	37	2	0
Extras (b 2, lb 1, w 1, nb 1): **5**							
Total (1 wicket, 20.4 overs): **87**							

DNB: RB Kanhai, *CH Lloyd, IVA Richards, BD Julien, KD Boyce, VA Holder, AME Roberts, LR Gibbs.
FoW: 1-52 (Fredericks).

Bowling	O	M	R	W
Opatha	4	0	19	0
Pieris	2	0	13	0
de Silva	8	1	33	1
Kaluperuma	6.4	1	17	0

Prudential World Cup, 1975, 5th Match
England v New Zealand, Group A
Trent Bridge, Nottingham
11 June 1975 (60-over match)

Result: England won by 80 runs
Points: England 4, New Zealand 0
Toss: New Zealand
Umpires: WE Alley and TW Spencer
Man Of The Match: KWR Fletcher

England innings (60 overs maximum)			R	B	4	6
DL Amiss	b Collinge		16	18	3	0
JA Jameson	c Wadsworth	b Collinge	11	31	0	0
KWR Fletcher	run out		131	147	13	0
FC Hayes	lbw	b RJ Hadlee	34	80	5	0
*MH Denness	c Morrison	b DR Hadlee	37	52	1	1
AW Greig	b DR Hadlee		9	19	0	0
CM Old	not out		20	16	0	1
Extras (lb 6, w 1, nb 1): **8**						
Total (6 wickets, 60 overs): **266**						

DNB: +APE Knott, DL Underwood, GG Arnold, P Lever.
FoW: 1-27 (Amiss), 2-28 (Jameson), 3-111 (Hayes), 4-177 (Denness), 5-200 (Greig), 6-266 (Fletcher).

Bowling	O	M	R	W
Collinge	12	2	43	2
RJ Hadlee	12	2	66	1
DR Hadlee	12	1	55	2
McKechnie	12	2	38	0
Howarth	12	2	56	0

New Zealand innings (target: 267 runs from 60 overs)			R	B	4	6
JFM Morrison	c Old	b Underwood	55	85	6	1
*GM Turner	b Lever		12	34	1	0
BG Hadlee	b Greig		19	77	1	0
JM Parker	b Greig		1	8	0	0
BF Hastings	c Underwood	b Old	10	26	1	0
+KJ Wadsworth	b Arnold		25	24	3	0
RJ Hadlee	b Old		0	6	0	0
BJ McKechnie	c Underwood	b Greig	27	50	4	0
DR Hadlee	c Arnold	b Greig	20	42	2	0
HJ Howarth	not out		1	7	0	0
RO Collinge	b Underwood		6	6	0	1
Extras (b 1, lb 4, w 1, nb 4): **10**						
Total (all out, 60 overs): **186**						

FoW: 1-30 (Turner), 2-83 (Morrison), 3-91 (Parker), 4-95 (BG Hadlee), 5-129 (Wadsworth), 6-129 (Hastings), 7-129 (RJ Hadlee), 8-177 (DR Hadlee), 9-180 (McKechnie), 10-186 (Collinge).

Bowling	O	M	R	W
Arnold	12	3	35	1
Lever	12	0	37	1
Old	12	2	29	2
Greig	12	0	45	4
Underwood	12	2	30	2

Prudential World Cup, 1975, 6th Match
East Africa v India, Group A
Headingley, Leeds
11 June 1975 (60-over match)

Result: India won by 10 wickets
Points: India 4, East Africa 0
Toss: East Africa
Umpires: HD Bird and A Jepson
ODI Debuts: PS Mehta, DJ Pringle, Yunus Badat (EA)
Man Of The Match: FM Engineer

East Africa innings (60 overs maximum)			R	M	B	4	6
Frasat Ali	b Abid Ali		12	38	36	1	0
S Walusimbi	lbw	b Abid Ali	16	65	50	1	0
+PS Mehta	run out		12	71	41	0	0
Yunus Badat	b Bedi		1	13	4	0	0
Jawahir Shah	b Amarnath		37	60	84	5	0
*Harilal Shah	c Engineer	b Amarnath	0	1	2	0	0
RK Sethi	c Gaekwad	b Madan Lal	23	45	80	2	0
Mehmood Quaraishy	run out		6	19	25	0	0
Zulfiqar Ali	not out		2	8	5	0	0
PG Nana	lbw	b Madan Lal	0	1	2	0	0
DJ Pringle	b Madan Lal		2	4	3	0	0
Extras (lb 8, nb 1): **9**							
Total (all out, 55.3 overs): **120**							

FoW: 1-26 (Frasat Ali), 2-36 (Walusimbi), 3-37 (Yunus Badat), 4-56 (Mehta), 5-56 (Harilal Shah), 6-98 (Jawahir Shah), 7-116 (Sethi), 8-116 (Mehmood Quaraishy), 9-116 (Nana), 10-120 (Pringle).

Bowling	O	M	R	W
Abid Ali	12	5	22	2
Madan Lal	9.3	2	15	3
Bedi	12	8	6	1
Venkataraghavan	12	4	29	0
Amarnath	10	0	39	2

India innings (target: 121 runs from 60 overs)		R	M	B	4	6
SM Gavaskar	not out	65	85	86	9	0
+FM Engineer	not out	54	85	93	7	0
Extras (b 4): **4**						
Total (0 wickets, 29.5 overs): **123**						

DNB: AD Gaekwad, GR Viswanath, BP Patel, ED Solkar, S Abid Ali, S Madan Lal, M Amarnath, *S Venkataraghavan, BS Bedi.

Bowling	O	M	R	W
Frasat Ali	6	1	17	0
Pringle	3	0	14	0
Zulfiqar Ali	11	3	32	0
Nana	4.5	0	36	0
Sethi	5	0	20	0

Prudential World Cup, 1975, 7th Match
Australia v Sri Lanka, Group B
Kennington Oval, London
11 June 1975 (60-over match)

Result: Australia won by 52 runs
Points: Australia 4, Sri Lanka 0
Toss: Sri Lanka
Umpires: WL Budd and AE Fagg
ODI Debuts: SRD Wettimuny (SL)
Man Of The Match: A Turner

Australia innings (60 overs maximum)

			R	B	4	6
RB McCosker	b de Silva		73	111	2	0
A Turner	c Mendis	b de Silva	101	113	9	1
*IM Chappell	b Kaluperuma		4	7	1	0
GS Chappell	c Opatha	b Pieris	50	50	5	1
KD Walters	c Tennekoon	b Pieris	59	66	5	0
JR Thomson	not out		9	7	0	0
+RW Marsh	not out		9	7	0	0
Extras (b 1, lb 20, w 1, nb 1): **23**						
Total (5 wickets, 60 overs): **328**						

DNB: R Edwards, MHN Walker, DK Lillee, AA Mallett.
FoW: 1-182 (Turner), 2-187 (McCosker), 3-191 (IM Chappell), 4-308 (Walters), 5-308 (GS Chappell).

Bowling	O	M	R	W
Opatha	9	0	32	0
Pieris	11	0	68	2
Warnapura	9	0	40	0
Ranasinghe	7	0	55	0
de Silva	12	3	60	2
Kaluperuma	12	0	50	1

Sri Lanka innings (target: 329 runs from 60 overs)

			R	B	4	6
SRD Wettimuny	retired hurt		53	102	7	0
+ER Fernando	b Thomson		22	18	4	0
B Warnapura	st Marsh	b Mallett	31	39	5	0
LRD Mendis	retired hurt		32	45	5	0
*APB Tennekoon	b IM Chappell		48	71	6	0
MH Tissera	c Turner	b IM Chappell	52	72	7	0
AN Ranasinghe	not out		14	18	3	0
HSM Pieris	not out		0	3	0	0
Extras (b 6, lb 8, w 8, nb 2): **24**						
Total (4 wickets, 60 overs): **276**						

DNB: ARM Opatha, DS de Silva, LWS Kaluperuma.
FoW: 1-30 (Fernando), 2-84 (Warnapura), 3-246 (Tennekoon), 4-268 (Tissera).

Bowling	O	M	R	W
Lillee	10	0	42	0
Thomson	12	5	22	1
Mallett	12	0	72	1
Walters	6	1	33	0
Walker	12	1	44	0
GS Chappell	4	0	25	0
IM Chappell	4	0	14	2

Prudential World Cup, 1975, 8th Match
Pakistan v West Indies, Group B
Edgbaston, Birmingham
11 June 1975 (60-over match)

Result: West Indies won by 1 wicket
Points: West Indies 4, Pakistan 0
Toss: Pakistan
Umpires: DJ Constant and JG Langridge
ODI Debuts: CG Greenidge (WI); Javed Miandad, Pervez Mir (Pak)
Man Of The Match: Sarfraz Nawaz

Pakistan innings (60 overs maximum)			R	M	B	4	6
*Majid Khan	c Murray	b Lloyd	60	141	108	6	0
Sadiq Mohammad	c Kanhai	b Julien	7	29	23	1	0
Zaheer Abbas	lbw	b Richards	31	64	56	4	0
Mushtaq Mohammad	b Boyce		55	104	84	3	0
Wasim Raja	b Roberts		58	82	57	6	0
Javed Miandad	run out		24	36	32	2	0
Pervez Mir	run out		4	9	9	0	0
+Wasim Bari	not out		1	1	1	0	0
Sarfraz Nawaz	not out		0	1	0	0	0
Extras (b 1, lb 15, w 4, nb 6): **26**							
Total (7 wickets, 60 overs): **266**							

DNB: Asif Masood, Naseer Malik.
FoW: 1-21 (Sadiq Mohammad), 2-83 (Zaheer Abbas), 3-140 (Majid Khan), 4-202 (Mushtaq Mohammad), 5-249 (Wasim Raja), 6-263 (Pervez Mir), 7-265 (Javed Miandad).

Bowling	O	M	R	W
Roberts	12	1	47	1
Boyce	12	2	44	1
Julien	12	1	41	1
Holder	12	3	56	0
Richards	4	0	21	1
Lloyd	8	1	31	1

West Indies innings (target: 267 runs from 60 overs)			R	M	B	4	6
RC Fredericks	lbw	b Sarfraz Nawaz	12	24	11	2	0
CG Greenidge	c Wasim Bari	b Sarfraz Nawaz	4	6	6	1	0
AI Kallicharran	c Wasim Bari	b Sarfraz Nawaz	16	28	25	1	0
RB Kanhai	b Naseer Malik		24	52	42	3	0
*CH Lloyd	c Wasim Bari	b Javed Miandad	53	105	58	8	0
IVA Richards	c Zaheer Abbas	b Pervez Mir	13	16	23	2	0
BD Julien	c Javed Miandad	b Asif Masood	18	40	40	2	0
+DL Murray	not out		61	106	76	6	0
KD Boyce	b Naseer Malik		7	8	6	0	0
VA Holder	c Pervez Mir	b Sarfraz Nawaz	16	35	28	1	0
AME Roberts	not out		24	55	48	3	0
Extras (lb 10, w 1, nb 8): **19**							
Total: (9 wickets, 59.4 overs): **267**							

FoW: 1-6 (Greenidge), 2-31 (Fredericks), 3-36 (Kallicharran), 4-84 (Kanhai), 5-99 (Richards), 6-145 (Julien), 7-151 (Lloyd), 8-166 (Boyce), 9-203 (Holder).

Bowling	O	M	R	W
Asif Masood	12	1	64	1
Sarfraz Nawaz	12	1	44	4
Naseer Malik	12	2	42	2
Pervez Mir	9	1	42	1
Javed Miandad	12	0	46	1
Mushtaq Mohammad	2	0	7	0
Wasim Raja	0.4	0	3	0

Prudential World Cup, 1975, 9th Match
England v East Africa, Group A
Edgbaston, Birmingham
14 June 1975 (60-over match)

Result: England won by 196 runs
Points: England 4, East Africa 0
Toss: East Africa
Umpires: WE Alley and JG Langridge
Man Of The Match: JA Snow

England innings (60 overs maximum)			R	M	B	4	6
B Wood	b Mehmood Quaraishy		77	144	138	6	0
DL Amiss	c Nana	b Zulfiqar Ali	88	118	116	7	0
FC Hayes	b Zulfiqar Ali		52	50	50	6	2
AW Greig	lbw	b Zulfiqar Ali	9	16	17	0	0
+APE Knott	not out		18	28	19	0	0
CM Old	b Mehmood Quaraishy		18	16	16	3	0
*MH Denness	not out		12	4	6	1	0

Extras (b 7, lb 7, w 1, nb 1): **16**
Total (5 wickets, 60 overs): **290**

DNB: KWR Fletcher, JA Snow, P Lever, DL Underwood.
FoW: 1-158 (Amiss), 2-192 (Wood), 3-234 (Greig), 4-244 (Hayes), 5-277 (Old).

Bowling	O	M	R	W
Frasat Ali	9	0	40	0
Pringle	12	0	41	0
Nana	12	2	46	0
Sethi	5	0	29	0
Zulfiqar Ali	12	0	63	3
Mehmood Quaraishy	10	0	55	2

East Africa innings (target: 291 runs from 60 overs)			R	M	B	4	6
Frasat Ali	b Snow		0	18	17	0	0
S Walusimbi	lbw	b Snow	7	46	30	0	0
Yunus Badat	b Snow		0	1	3	0	0
Jawahir Shah	lbw	b Snow	4	14	13	0	0
RK Sethi	b Lever		30	103	102	3	0
*Harilal Shah	b Greig		6	52	53	0	0
Mehmood Quaraishy	c Amiss	b Greig	19	43	41	2	0
Zulfiqar Ali	b Lever		7	27	22	0	0
+H McLeod	b Lever		0	3	2	0	0
PG Nana	not out		8	33	28	0	0
DJ Pringle	b Old		3	13	12	0	0

Extras (lb 6, w 1, nb 3): **10**
Total (all out, 52.3 overs): **94**

FoW: 1-7 (Frasat Ali), 2-7 (Yunus Badat), 3-15 (Walusimbi), 4-21 (Jawahir Shah), 5-42 (Harilal Shah), 6-72 (Mehmood Quaraishy), 7-76 (Sethi), 8-79 (McLeod), 9-88 (Zulfiqar Ali), 10-94 (Pringle).

Bowling	O	M	R	W
Snow	12	6	11	4
Lever	12	3	32	3
Underwood	10	5	11	0
Wood	7	3	10	0
Greig	10	1	18	2
Old	1.3	0	2	1

Prudential World Cup, 1975, 10th Match
India v New Zealand, Group A
Old Trafford, Manchester
14 June 1975 (60-over match)

Result: New Zealand won by 4 wickets
Points: New Zealand 4, India 0
Toss: India
Umpires: WL Budd and AE Fagg
Man Of The Match: GM Turner

India innings (60 overs maximum)

			R	M	B	4	6
SM Gavaskar	c RJ Hadlee	b DR Hadlee	12	15	14	2	0
+FM Engineer	lbw	b RJ Hadlee	24	15	36	3	0
AD Gaekwad	c Hastings	b RJ Hadlee	37	73	51	3	0
GR Viswanath	lbw	b McKechnie	2	49	9	0	0
BP Patel	c Wadsworth	b HJ Howarth	9	42	32	1	0
ED Solkar	c Wadsworth	b HJ Howarth	13	9	10	2	0
S Abid Ali	c HJ Howarth	b McKechnie	70	107	98	5	1
S Madan Lal	c & b McKechnie		20	52	44	4	0
M Amarnath	c Morrison	b DR Hadlee	1	4	3	0	0
*S Venkataraghavan	not out		26	48	58	3	0
BS Bedi	run out		6	8	10	0	0
Extras (b 5, w 1, nb 4) **10**							
Total (all out, 60 overs): **230**							

FoW: 1-17 (Gavaskar), 2-48 (Engineer), 3-59 (Viswanath), 4-81 (Gaekwad), 5-94 (Solkar), 6-101 (Patel), 7-156 (Madan Lal), 8-157 (Amarnath), 9-217 (Abid Ali), 10-230 (Bedi).

Bowling

	O	M	R	W
Collinge	12	2	43	0
RJ Hadlee	12	2	48	2
DR Hadlee	12	3	32	2
McKechnie	12	1	49	3
HJ Howarth	12	0	48	2

New Zealand innings (target: 231 from 60 overs)

			R	M	B	4	6
*GM Turner	not out		114	180	177	13	0
JFM Morrison	c Engineer	b Bedi	17	35	34	2	0
GP Howarth	run out		9	13	13	2	0
JM Parker	lbw	b Abid Ali	1	15	6	0	0
BF Hastings	c Solkar	b Amarnath	34	47	49	3	0
+KJ Wadsworth	lbw	b Madan Lal	22	28	38	3	0
RJ Hadlee	b Abid Ali		15	27	30	2	0
DR Hadlee	not out		8	3	7	0	0
Extras (b 8, lb 5): **13**							
Total (6 wickets, 58.5 overs): **233**							

DNB: BJ McKechnie, HJ Howarth, RO Collinge.
FoW: 1-45 (Morrison), 2-62 (GP Howarth), 3-70 (Parker), 4-135 (Hastings), 5-185 (Wadsworth), 6-224 (RJ Hadlee).

Bowling

	O	M	R	W
Madan Lal	11.5	1	62	1
Amarnath	8	1	40	1
Bedi	12	6	28	1
Abid Ali	12	2	35	2
Venkataraghavan	12	0	39	0
Solkar	3	0	16	0

Prudential World Cup, 1975, 11th Match
Australia v West Indies, Group B
Kennington Oval, London
14 June 1975 (60-over match)

Result: West Indies won by 7 wickets
Points: West Indies 4, Australia 0
Toss: West Indies
Umpires: HD Bird and DJ Constant
Man Of The Match: AI Kallicharran

Australia innings (60 overs maximum)			R	M	B	4	6
RB McCosker	c Fredericks	b Julien	0	2	3	0	0
A Turner	lbw	b Roberts	7	39	18	0	0
*IM Chappell	c Murray	b Boyce	25	87	63	0	0
GS Chappell	c Murray	b Boyce	15	45	33	0	0
KD Walters	run out		7	22	18	0	0
R Edwards	b Richards		58	94	74	6	0
+RW Marsh	not out		52	127	84	4	0
MHN Walker	lbw	b Holder	8	18	22	1	0
JR Thomson	c Holder	b Richards	1	2	3	0	0
DK Lillee	b Roberts		3	20	12	0	0
AA Mallett	c Murray	b Roberts	0	1	1	0	0

Extras (lb 9, w 1, nb 6): **16**
Total (all out, 53.4 overs): **192**

FoW: 1-0 (McCosker), 2-21 (Turner), 3-49 (GS Chappell), 4-56 (IM Chappell), 5-61 (Walters), 6-160 (Edwards), 7-173 (Walker), 8-174 (Thomson), 9-192 (Lillee), 10-192 (Mallett).

Bowling	O	M	R	W
Julien	12	2	31	1
Roberts	10.4	1	39	3
Boyce	11	0	38	2
Holder	10	0	31	1
Lloyd	4	1	19	0
Richards	6	0	18	2

West Indies innings (target: 193 from 60 overs)			R	M	B	4	6
RC Fredericks	c Marsh	b Mallett	58	150	105	5	0
CG Greenidge	lbw	b Walker	16	23	18	2	0
AI Kallicharran	c Mallett	b Lillee	78	106	83	14	1
IVA Richards	not out		15	44	38	2	0
RB Kanhai	not out		18	27	33	1	0

Extras (b 4, lb 2, w 3, nb 1): **10**
Total (3 wickets, 46 overs): **195**

DNB: *CH Lloyd, BD Julien, +DL Murray, KD Boyce, VA Holder, AME Roberts.
FoW: 1-29 (Greenidge), 2-153 (Kallicharran), 3-159 (Fredericks).

Bowling	O	M	R	W
Lillee	10	0	66	1
Thomson	6	1	21	0
Walker	12	2	41	1
GS Chappell	4	0	13	0
Mallett	11	2	35	1
IM Chappell	3	1	9	0

Prudential World Cup, 1975, 12th Match
Pakistan v Sri Lanka, Group B
Trent Bridge, Nottingham
14 June 1975 (60-over match)

Result: Pakistan won by 192 runs
Points: Pakistan 4, Sri Lanka 0
Toss: Sri Lanka
Umpires: A Jepson and TW Spencer
ODI Debuts: GRA de Silva (SL)
Man Of The Match: Zaheer Abbas

Pakistan innings (60 overs maximum)

			R	B	4	6
Sadiq Mohammad	c Opatha	b Warnapura	74	88	12	1
*Majid Khan	c Tennekoon	b DS de Silva	84	93	9	1
Zaheer Abbas	b Opatha		97	89	10	1
Mushtaq Mohammad	c Heyn	b Warnapura	26	48	2	0
Wasim Raja	c Opatha	b Warnapura	2	6	0	0
Javed Miandad	not out		28	35	1	0
Imran Khan	b Opatha		0	2	0	0
Pervez Mir	not out		4	7	0	0
Extras (b 4, lb 4, w 2, nb 5): **15**						
Total (6 wickets, 60 overs): **330**						

DNB: +Wasim Bari, Asif Masood, Naseer Malik.
FoW: 1-159 (Sadiq Mohammad), 2-168 (Majid Khan), 3-256 (Mushtaq Mohammad), 4-268 (Wasim Raja), 5-318 (Zaheer Abbas), 6-318 (Imran Khan).

Bowling	O	M	R	W
Opatha	12	0	67	2
Pieris	9	0	54	0
GRA de Silva	7	1	46	0
DS de Silva	12	1	61	1
Kaluperuma	9	1	35	0
Warnapura	8	0	42	3
Ranasinghe	3	0	10	0

Sri Lanka innings (target: 331 runs from 60 overs)

			R	B	4	6
+ER Fernando	c & b Javed Miandad		21	42	3	0
B Warnapura	b Imran Khan		2	15	0	0
*APB Tennekoon	lbw	b Naseer Malik	30	36	4	0
MH Tissera	c Wasim Bari	b Sadiq Mohammad	12	40	2	0
PD Heyn	c Zaheer Abbas	b Javed Miandad	1	8	0	0
AN Ranasinghe	b Wasim Raja		9	23	0	0
HSM Pieris	lbw	b Pervez Mir	16	44	2	0
ARM Opatha	c Zaheer Abbas	b Sadiq Mohammad	0	10	0	0
DS de Silva	b Imran Khan		26	59	4	0
LWS Kaluperuma	not out		13	27	1	0
GRA de Silva	c Wasim Raja	b Imran Khan	0	12	0	0
Extras (lb 1, w 3, nb 4): **8**						
Total (all out, 50.1 overs): **138**						

FoW: 1-5 (Warnapura), 2-44 (Fernando), 3-60 (Tissera), 4-61 (Heyn), 5-75 (Tennekoon), 6-79 (Ranasinghe), 7-90 (Opatha), 8-113 (Pieris), 9-135 (DS de Silva), 10-138 (GRA de Silva).

Bowling	O	M	R	W
Asif Masood	6	2	14	0
Imran Khan	7.1	3	15	3
Javed Miandad	7	2	22	2
Naseer Malik	6	1	19	1
Sadiq Mohammad	6	1	20	2
Wasim Raja	7	4	7	1
Mushtaq Mohammad	5	0	16	0
Pervez Mir	6	1	17	1

Prudential World Cup, 1975, 1st Semi-Final
England v Australia
Headingley, Leeds
18 June 1975 (60-over match)

Result: Australia won by 4 wickets
Australia advances to the final
Toss: Australia
Umpires: WE Alley and DJ Constant
Man Of The Match: GJ Gilmour

England innings (60 overs maximum)			R	M	B	4	6
DL Amiss	lbw	b Gilmour	2	11	7	0	0
B Wood	b Gilmour		6	29	19	1	0
KWR Fletcher	lbw	b Gilmour	8	59	45	0	0
AW Greig	c Marsh	b Gilmour	7	24	25	1	0
FC Hayes	lbw	b Gilmour	4	9	6	1	0
*MH Denness	b Walker		27	70	60	1	0
+APE Knott	lbw	b Gilmour	0	3	5	0	0
CM Old	c GS Chappell	b Walker	0	4	3	0	0
JA Snow	c Marsh	b Lillee	2	22	14	0	0
GG Arnold	not out		18	47	30	2	0
P Lever	lbw	b Walker	5	15	13	0	0

Extras (lb 5, w 7, nb 2): **14**
Total (all out, 36.2 overs): **93**

FoW: 1-2 (Amiss), 2-11 (Wood), 3-26 (Greig), 4-33 (Hayes), 5-35 (Fletcher), 6-36 (Knott), 7-37 (Old), 8-52 (Snow), 9-73 (Denness), 10-93 (Lever).

Bowling	O	M	R	W
Lillee	9	3	26	1
Gilmour	12	6	14	6
Walker	9.2	3	22	3
Thomson	6	0	17	0

Australia innings (target: 94 runs from 60 overs)			R	M	B	4	6
A Turner	lbw	b Arnold	7	32	20	0	0
RB McCosker	b Old		15	65	50	0	0
*IM Chappell	lbw	b Snow	2	18	19	0	0
GS Chappell	lbw	b Snow	4	8	9	1	0
KD Walters	not out		20	60	43	2	0
R Edwards	b Old		0	2	3	0	0
+RW Marsh	b Old		5	7	8	0	0
GJ Gilmour	not out		28	44	28	5	0

Extras (b 1, lb 6, nb 6): **13**
Total (6 wickets, 28.4 overs): **94**

DNB: MHN Walker, DK Lillee, JR Thomson.
FoW: 1-17 (Turner), 2-24 (IM Chappell), 3-32 (GS Chappell), 4-32 (McCosker), 5-32 (Edwards), 6-39 (Marsh).

Bowling	O	M	R	W
Arnold	7.4	2	15	1
Snow	12	0	30	2
Old	7	2	29	3
Lever	2	0	7	0

Prudential World Cup, 1975, 2nd Semi-Final
New Zealand v West Indies
Kennington Oval, London
18 June 1975 (60-over match)

Result: West Indies won by 5 wickets
West Indies advances to the final
Toss: West Indies
Umpires: WL Budd and AE Fagg
Man Of The Match: Al Kallicharran

New Zealand innings (60 overs maximum)

			R	B	4	6
*GM Turner	c Kanhai	b Roberts	36	74	3	0
JFM Morrison	lbw	b Julien	5	26	0	0
GP Howarth	c Murray	b Roberts	51	93	3	0
JM Parker	b Lloyd		3	12	0	0
BF Hastings	not out		24	57	4	0
+KJ Wadsworth	c Lloyd	b Julien	11	21	1	0
BJ McKechnie	lbw	b Julien	1	9	0	0
DR Hadlee	c Holder	b Julien	0	10	0	0
BL Cairns	b Holder		10	14	1	0
HJ Howarth	b Holder		0	1	0	0
RO Collinge	b Holder		2	4	0	0

Extras (b 1, lb 5, w 2, nb 7): **15**
Total (all out, 52.2 overs): **158**

FoW: 1-8 (Morrison), 2-98 (Turner), 3-105 (GP Howarth), 4-106 (Parker), 5-125 (Wadsworth), 6-133 (McKechnie), 7-139 (Hadlee), 8-155 (Cairns), 9-155 (HJ Howarth), 10-158 (Collinge).

Bowling	O	M	R	W
Julien	12	5	27	4
Roberts	11	3	18	2
Holder	8.2	0	30	3
Boyce	9	0	31	0
Lloyd	12	1	37	1

West Indies innings (target: 159 runs from 60 overs)

			R	B	4	6
RC Fredericks	c Hastings	b Hadlee	6	14	0	0
CG Greenidge	lbw	b Collinge	55	95	9	1
Al Kallicharran	c & b Collinge		72	92	7	1
IVA Richards	lbw	b Collinge	5	10	1	0
RB Kanhai	not out		12	18	2	0
*CH Lloyd	c Hastings	b McKechnie	3	8	0	0
BD Julien	not out		4	5	1	0

Extras (lb 1, nb 1): **2**
Total (5 wickets, 40.1 overs): **159**

DNB: +DL Murray, KD Boyce, VA Holder, AME Roberts.
FoW: 1-8 (Fredericks), 2-133 (Kallicharran), 3-139 (Richards), 4-142 (Greenidge), 5-151 (Lloyd).

Bowling	O	M	R	W
Collinge	12	4	28	3
Hadlee	10	0	54	1
Cairns	6.1	2	23	0
McKechnie	8	0	37	1
HJ Howarth	4	0	15	0

Prudential World Cup, 1975, Final
Australia v West Indies
Lord's, London
21 June 1975 (60-over match)

Result: West Indies won by 17 runs
West Indies wins the 1975 Prudential World Cup
Toss: Australia
Umpires: HD Bird and TW Spencer
Man Of The Match: CH Lloyd

West Indies innings (60 overs maximum)			R	M	B	4	6
RC Fredericks	hit wicket	b Lillee	7	14	13	0	0
CG Greenidge	c Marsh	b Thomson	13	80	61	1	0
AI Kallicharran	c Marsh	b Gilmour	12	26	18	2	0
RB Kanhai	b Gilmour		55	156	105	8	0
*CH Lloyd	c Marsh	b Gilmour	102	108	85	12	2
IVA Richards	b Gilmour		5	12	11	1	0
KD Boyce	c GS Chappell	b Thomson	34	43	37	3	0
BD Julien	not out		26	54	37	1	0
+DL Murray	c & b Gilmour		14	11	10	1	1
VA Holder	not out		6	1	2	1	0

Extras (lb 6, nb 11): **17**
Total (8 wickets, 60 overs): **291**

DNB: AME Roberts.
FoW: 1-12 (Fredericks), 2-27 (Kallicharran), 3-50 (Greenidge), 4-199 (Lloyd), 5-206 (Kanhai), 6-209 (Richards), 7-261 (Boyce), 8-285 (Murray).

Bowling	O	M	R	W
Lillee	12	1	55	1
Gilmour	12	2	48	5
Thomson	12	1	44	2
Walker	12	1	71	0
GS Chappell	7	0	33	0
Walters	5	0	23	0

Australia innings (target: 292 runs from 60 overs)			R	M	B	4	6
A Turner	run out (Richards)		40		54	4	0
RB McCosker	c Kallicharran	b Boyce	7		24	1	0
*IM Chappell	run out (Richards/Lloyd)		62	125	93	6	0
GS Chappell	run out (Richards)		15	24	23	2	0
KD Walters	b Lloyd		35	52	51	5	0
+RW Marsh	b Boyce		11	34	24	0	0
R Edwards	c Fredericks	b Boyce	28	51	37	2	0
GJ Gilmour	c Kanhai	b Boyce	14	16	11	2	0
MHN Walker	run out (Kallicharran/Holder)		7	10	9	1	0
JR Thomson	run out (Kallicharran/Murray)		21	32	21	2	0
DK Lillee	not out		16	29	19	1	0

Extras (b 2, lb 9, nb 7): **18**
Total (all out, 58.4 overs): **274**

FoW: 1-25 (McCosker), 2-81 (Turner), 3-115 (GS Chappell), 4-162 (IM Chappell), 5-170 (Walters), 6-195 (Marsh), 7-221 (Gilmour), 8-231 (Edwards), 9-233 (Walker), 10-274 (Thomson).

Bowling	O	M	R	W
Julien	12	0	58	0
Roberts	11	1	45	0
Boyce	12	0	50	4
Holder	11.4	1	65	0
Lloyd	12	1	38	1

1979 WORLD CUP

Prudential World Cup, 1979, 1st Match
India v West Indies, Group B
Edgbaston, Birmingham
9 June 1979 (60-over match)

Result: West Indies won by 9 wickets
Points: West Indies 4, India 0
Toss: West Indies
Umpires: DGL Evans and JG Langridge
ODI Debuts: SC Khanna (Ind)
Man Of The Match: CG Greenidge

India innings (60 overs maximum)			R	M	B	4	6
SM Gavaskar	c Holding	b Roberts	8	11	7	1	0
AD Gaekwad	c King	b Holding	11	32	30	2	0
DB Vengsarkar	c Kallicharran	b Holding	7	13	7	1	0
GR Viswanath	b Holding		75	158	134	7	0
BP Patel	run out		15	34	33	2	0
M Amarnath	c Murray	b Croft	8	15	15	1	0
N Kapil Dev	b King		12	19	12	1	0
+SC Khanna	c Haynes	b Holding	0	17	12	0	0
KD Ghavri	c Murray	b Garner	12	40	26	2	0
*S Venkataraghavan	not out		13	42	30	0	0
BS Bedi	c Lloyd	b Roberts	13	29	23	1	0
Extras (b 6, lb 3, w 3, nb 4): **16**							
Total (all out, 53.1 overs): **190**							

FoW: 1-10 (Gavaskar), 2-24 (Vengsarkar), 3-29 (Gaekwad), 4-56 (Patel), 5-77 (Amarnath), 6-112 (Kapil Dev), 7-119 (Khanna), 8-155 (Ghavri), 9-163 (Viswanath), 10-190 (Bedi).

Bowling	O	M	R	W
Roberts	9.1	0	32	2
Holding	12	2	33	4
Garner	12	1	42	1
Croft	10	1	31	1
King	10	1	36	1

West Indies innings (target: 191 from 60 overs)			R	M	B	4	6
CG Greenidge	not out		106	181	173	9	1
DL Haynes	lbw	b Kapil Dev	47	120	99	2	1
IVA Richards	not out		28	60	44	1	1
Extras (lb 6, nb 7): **13**							
Total (1 wicket, 51.3 overs): **194**							

DNB: AI Kallicharran, *CH Lloyd, CL King, +DL Murray, AME Roberts, J Garner, MA Holding, CEH Croft.
FoW: 1-138 (Haynes).

Bowling	O	M	R	W
Kapil Dev	10	1	46	1
Ghavri	10	2	25	0
Venkataraghavan	12	3	30	0
Bedi	12	0	45	0
Amarnath	7.3	0	35	0

Prudential World Cup, 1979, 2nd Match
New Zealand v Sri Lanka, Group B
Trent Bridge, Nottingham
9 June 1979 (60-over match)

Result: New Zealand won by 9 wickets
Points: New Zealand 4, Sri Lanka 0
Toss: New Zealand
Umpires: WL Budd and KE Palmer
    ODI Debuts: JV Coney, WK Lees, LW Stott (NZ); DLS de Silva, RL Dias, SA Jayasinghe, SP Pasqual (SL)
Man Of The Match: GP Howarth

Sri Lanka innings (60 overs maximum)			R	B	4	6
B Warnapura	c & b McKechnie		20	58	2	0
SRD Wettimuny	b Cairns		16	20	1	0
*APB Tennekoon	b Stott		59	96	6	0
RL Dias	c & b Stott		25	46	2	0
LRD Mendis	c Turner	b Troup	14	27	2	0
DS de Silva	c Burgess	b Stott	6	24	0	0
+SA Jayasinghe	run out		1	3	0	0
SP Pasqual	b Hadlee		1	2	0	0
ARM Opatha	b McKechnie		18	27	2	0
DLS de Silva	c Wright	b McKechnie	10	35	0	0
GRA de Silva	not out		2	11	0	0
Extras (lb 13, w 2, nb 2): **17**						
Total (all out, 56.5 overs): **189**						

FoW: 1-26 (Wettimuny), 2-57 (Warnapura), 3-107 (Dias), 4-137 (Mendis), 5-149 (DS de Silva), 6-150 (Jayasinghe), 7-150 (Tennekoon), 8-154 (Pasqual), 9-178 (DLS de Silva), 10-189 (Opatha).

Bowling	O	M	R	W
Hadlee	12	3	24	1
Troup	10	0	30	1
Cairns	12	1	45	1
McKechnie	10.5	2	25	3
Stott	12	1	48	3

New Zealand innings (target: 190 runs from 60 overs)			R	B	4	6
GM Turner	not out		83	143	4	0
JG Wright	c Tennekoon	b GRA de Silva	34	69	6	0
GP Howarth	not out		63	75	8	1
Extras (lb 7, w 2, nb 1): **10**						
Total (1 wicket, 47.4 overs): **190**						

DNB: JV Coney, *MG Burgess, +WK Lees, BJ McKechnie, BL Cairns, RJ Hadlee, LW Stott, GB Troup.
FoW: 1-64 (Wright).

Bowling	O	M	R	W
Opatha	7	1	31	0
DLS de Silva	8	2	18	0
Warnapura	7	0	30	0
DS de Silva	9	0	42	0
GRA de Silva	12	1	39	1
Pasqual	4.4	0	20	0

Prudential World Cup, 1979, 3rd Match
England v Australia, Group A
Lord's, London
9 June 1979 (60-over match)

Result: England won by 6 wickets
Points: England 4, Australia 0
Toss: England
Umpires: DJ Constant and BJ Meyer
Man Of The Match: GA Gooch

Australia innings (60 overs maximum)

			R	M	B	4	6
AMJ Hilditch	b Boycott		47	136	108	2	0
WM Darling	lbw	b Willis	25	82	61	3	0
AR Border	c Taylor	b Edmonds	34	87	74	4	0
*KJ Hughes	c Hendrick	b Boycott	6	13	13	1	0
GN Yallop	run out		10	23	20	1	0
GJ Cosier	run out		6	19	20	0	0
TJ Laughlin	run out		8	40	22	0	0
+KJ Wright	lbw	b Old	6	20	15	0	0
RM Hogg	run out		0	24	5	0	0
AG Hurst	not out		3	4	10	0	0
G Dymock	not out		4	13	12	0	0
Extras (b 4, lb 5, w 1): **10**							
Total (9 wickets, 60 overs): **159**							

FoW: 1-56 (Darling), 2-97 (Hilditch), 3-111 (Hughes), 4-131 (Border), 5-132 (Yallop), 6-137 (Cosier), 7-150 (Wright), 8-153 (Laughlin), 9-153 (Hogg).

Bowling

	O	M	R	W
Willis	11	2	20	1
Hendrick	12	2	24	0
Old	12	2	33	1
Botham	8	0	32	0
Edmonds	11	1	25	1
Boycott	6	0	15	2

England innings (target: 160 runs from 60 overs)

			R	M	B	4	6
*JM Brearley	c Wright	b Laughlin	44	169	147	2	0
G Boycott	lbw	b Hogg	1	11	5	0	0
DW Randall	c Wright	b Hurst	1	5	3	0	0
GA Gooch	lbw	b Laughlin	53	164	96	6	0
DI Gower	not out		22	44	30	2	0
IT Botham	not out		18	31	14	2	0
Extras (lb 10, nb 11): **21**							
Total (4 wickets, 47.1 overs): **160**							

DNB: PH Edmonds, +RW Taylor, CM Old, M Hendrick, RGD Willis.
FoW: 1-4 (Boycott), 2-5 (Randall), 3-113 (Gooch), 4-124 (Brearley).

Bowling

	O	M	R	W
Hogg	9	1	25	1
Hurst	10	3	33	1
Dymock	11	2	19	0
Cosier	8	1	24	0
Laughlin	9.1	0	38	2

Prudential World Cup, 1979, 4th Match
Canada v Pakistan, Group A
Headingley, Leeds
9 June 1979 (60-over match)

Result: Pakistan won by 8 wickets
Points: Pakistan 4, Canada 0
Toss: Canada
Umpires: HD Bird and AGT Whitehead
ODI Debuts: CJD Chappell, FA Dennis, CC Henry, CA Marshall, BM Mauricette, JM Patel,
  GR Sealy, MP Stead, Tariq Javed, JN Valentine, JCB Vaughan (Can)
Man Of The Match: Sadiq Mohammad

Canada innings (60 overs maximum)

			R	M	B	4	6
CJD Chappell	c & b Sikander Bakht		14	73	70	0	0
GR Sealy	c & b Asif Iqbal		45	122	110	5	0
FA Dennis	c Wasim Bari	b Sarfraz Nawaz	25	71	64	2	0
MP Stead	c Zaheer Abbas	b Asif Iqbal	10	42	33	1	0
CA Marshall	b Imran Khan		8	51	34	0	0
JCB Vaughan	c & b Asif Iqbal		0	1	2	0	0
*+BM Mauricette	c Zaheer Abbas	b Sarfraz Nawaz	15	49	38	0	1
Tariq Javed	st Wasim Bari	b Majid Khan	3	5	7	0	0
JM Patel	b Sarfraz Nawaz		0	9	5	0	0
CC Henry	not out		1	3	3	0	0

Extras (lb 10, w 5, nb 3): **18**
Total (9 wickets, 60 overs): **139**

DNB: JN Valentine.
FoW: 1-54 (Chappell), 2-85 (Sealy), 3-103 (Dennis), 4-110 (Stead), 5-110 (Vaughan), 6-129 (Marshall), 7-134 (Tariq Javed), 8-138 (Patel), 9-139 (Mauricette).

Bowling

	O	M	R	W
Imran Khan	11	1	27	1
Sarfraz Nawaz	10	1	26	3
Mudassar Nazar	4	1	11	0
Sikander Bakht	12	5	18	1
Majid Khan	11	4	11	1
Asif Iqbal	12	2	28	3

Pakistan innings (target: 140 runs from 60 overs)

		R	M	B	4	6
Majid Khan	b Valentine	1	11	3	0	0
Sadiq Mohammad	not out	57	138	122	4	0
Zaheer Abbas	run out	36	51	51	4	1
Haroon Rashid	not out	37	74	69	1	0

Extras (b 1, lb 3, w 1, nb 4): **9**
Total (2 wickets, 40.1 overs): **140**

DNB: Javed Miandad, *Asif Iqbal, Mudassar Nazar, Imran Khan, +Wasim Bari, Sarfraz Nawaz, Sikander Bakht.
FoW: 1-4 (Majid Khan), 2-61 (Zaheer Abbas).

Bowling

	O	M	R	W
Valentine	9	3	18	1
Vaughan	5	1	21	0
Henry	5	0	26	0
Patel	11.1	0	27	0
Sealy	6	0	21	0
Stead	4	0	18	0

Prudential World Cup, 1979, 5th Match
West Indies v Sri Lanka
Kennington Oval, London
13,14,15 June 1979

Result: Match abandoned without a ball bowled
Points: West Indies 2, Sri Lanka 2
Toss: No toss
Umpires:

Close Of Play:
Day 1: No play
Day 2: No play

Prudential World Cup, 1979, 6th Match
India v New Zealand, Group B
Headingley, Leeds
13 June 1979 (60-over match)

Result: New Zealand won by 8 wickets
Points: New Zealand 4, India 0
Toss: New Zealand
Umpires: WL Budd and AGT Whitehead
Man Of The Match: BA Edgar

India innings (60 overs maximum)			R	M	B	4	6
SM Gavaskar	c Lees	b Hadlee	55	170	144	5	0
AD Gaekwad	b Hadlee		10	35	31	1	0
DB Vengsarkar	c Lees	b McKechnie	1	16	2	0	0
GR Viswanath	c Turner	b Cairns	9	24	17	0	0
BP Patel	b Troup		38	44	60	5	0
M Amarnath	b Troup		1	9	5	0	0
N Kapil Dev	c & b Cairns		25	30	24	3	0
KD Ghavri	c Coney	b McKechnie	20	32	22	2	0
+SC Khanna	c Morrison	b McKechnie	7	23	16	0	0
*S Venkataraghavan	c Lees	b Cairns	1	7	2	0	0
BS Bedi	not out		1	5	12	0	0
Extras (lb 8, w 5, nb 1): **14**							
Total (all out, 55.5 overs): **182**							

FoW: 1-27 (Gaekwad), 2-38 (Vengsarkar), 3-53 (Viswanath), 4-104 (Patel), 5-107 (Amarnath), 6-147 (Kapil Dev), 7-153 (Gavaskar), 8-180 (Khanna), 9-181 (Ghavri), 10-182 (Venkataraghavan).

Bowling	O	M	R	W
Hadlee	10	2	20	2
Troup	10	2	36	2
Cairns	11.5	0	36	3
McKechnie	12	1	24	3
Coney	7	0	33	0
Morrison	5	0	19	0

New Zealand innings (target: 183 from 60 overs)		R	M	B	4	6
JG Wright	c & b Amarnath	48	131	94	1	0
BA Edgar	not out	84	199	167	8	0
BL Cairns	run out	2	9	4	0	0
GM Turner	not out	43	57	76	6	0
Extras (lb 3, nb 3): **6**						
Total (2 wickets, 57 overs): **183**						

DNB: JV Coney, *MG Burgess, JFM Morrison, BJ McKechnie, +WK Lees, RJ Hadlee, GB Troup.
FoW: 1-100 (Wright), 2-103 (Cairns).

Bowling	O	M	R	W
Amarnath	12	1	39	1
Bedi	12	1	32	0
Venkataraghavan	12	0	34	0
Ghavri	10	1	34	0
Kapil Dev	11	3	38	0

Prudential World Cup, 1979, 7th Match
Australia v Pakistan, Group A
Trent Bridge, Nottingham
13,14 June 1979 (60-over match)

Result: Pakistan won by 89 runs
Points: Pakistan 4, Australia 0
Toss: Australia
Umpires: HD Bird and KE Palmer
ODI Debuts: JK Moss, GD Porter (Aus)
Man Of The Match: Asif Iqbal

Close Of Play:
Day 1: Pakistan 286/7, Australia 17/0 (Darling 10*, Hilditch 6*, 5 overs)

Pakistan innings (60 overs maximum)			R	M	B	4	6
Sadiq Mohammad	c Moss	b Porter	27	110	73	2	0
Majid Khan	b Dymock		61	107	100	7	1
Zaheer Abbas	c & b Cosier		16	45	32	1	0
Haroon Rashid	c Wright	b Cosier	16	51	42	2	0
Javed Miandad	c Border	b Cosier	46	67	46	4	0
*Asif Iqbal	c sub (DF Whatmore)	b Hurst	61	75	57	7	0
Wasim Raja	c Moss	b Border	18	23	12	2	1
Imran Khan	not out		15	10	9	0	0
Mudassar Nazar	not out		1	3	1	0	0
Extras (b 6, lb 4, w 5, nb 10): **25**							
Total (7 wickets, 60 overs): **286**							

DNB: +Wasim Bari, Sikander Bakht.
FoW: 1-99 (Sadiq Mohammad), 2-99 (Majid Khan), 3-133 (Zaheer Abbas), 4-152 (Haroon Rashid), 5-239 (Javed Miandad), 6-268 (Asif Iqbal), 7-274 (Wasim Raja).

Bowling	O	M	R	W
Porter	12	3	20	1
Dymock	12	3	28	1
Cosier	12	1	54	3
Hurst	12	0	65	1
Yallop	8	0	56	0
Border	4	0	38	1

Australia innings (target: 287 runs from 60 overs)			R	M	B	4	6
WM Darling	c Wasim Bari	b Imran Khan	13	26	25	1	0
AMJ Hilditch	c Sadiq Mohammad	b Mudassar Nazar	72	185	129	4	0
AR Border	b Sikander Bakht		0	5	5	0	0
*KJ Hughes	lbw	b Sikander Bakht	15	32	37	2	0
GN Yallop	b Majid Khan		37	64	64	2	0
JK Moss	run out		7	20	16	0	0
GJ Cosier	c & b Majid Khan		0	1	1	0	0
+KJ Wright	c Wasim Bari	b Imran Khan	23	57	37	0	0
GD Porter	c Sadiq Mohammad	b Majid Khan	3	4	9	0	0
G Dymock	lbw	b Sikander Bakht	10	15	18	0	0
AG Hurst	not out		3	4	2	0	0
Extras (b 1, lb 5, w 8): **14**							
Total (all out, 57.1 overs): **197**							

FoW: 1-22 (Darling), 2-24 (Border), 3-46 (Hughes), 4-117 (Hilditch), 5-136 (Moss), 6-137 (Cosier), 7-172 (Yallop), 8-175 (Porter), 9-193 (Dymock), 10-197 (Wright).

Bowling	O	M	R	W
Asif Iqbal	12	0	36	0
Majid Khan	12	0	53	3
Mudassar Nazar	12	0	31	1
Imran Khan	10.1	2	29	2
Sikander Bakht	11	1	34	3

Prudential World Cup, 1979, 8th Match
England v Canada, Group A
Old Trafford, Manchester
13/14 June 1979 (60-over match)

Result: England won by 8 wickets
Points: England 4, Canada 0
Toss: Canada
Umpires: JG Langridge and BJ Meyer
ODI Debuts: RG Callender (Can)
Man Of The Match: CM Old

Close Of Play:

Day 1: No play

Canada innings (60 overs maximum)			R	M	B	4	6
CJD Chappell	lbw	b Botham	5	36	31	0	0
GR Sealy	c Botham	b Hendrick	3	13	9	0	0
FA Dennis	hit wicket	b Willis	21	116	99	2	0
Tariq Javed	lbw	b Old	4	46	40	0	0
JCB Vaughan	b Old		1	9	10	0	0
CA Marshall	b Old		2	11	7	0	0
*+BM Mauricette	b Willis		0	10	8	0	0
MP Stead	b Old		0	14	12	0	0
JM Patel	b Willis		1	23	14	0	0
RG Callender	b Willis		0	2	3	0	0
JN Valentine	not out		3	14	11	0	0
Extras (lb 4, nb 1): **5**							
Total (all out, 40.3 overs): **45**							

FoW: 1-5 (Sealy), 2-13 (Chappell), 3-25 (Tariq Javed), 4-29 (Vaughan), 5-37 (Marshall), 6-38 (Mauricette), 7-41 (Stead), 8-41 (Dennis), 9-42 (Callender), 10-45 (Patel).

Bowling	O	M	R	W
Willis	10.3	3	11	4
Hendrick	8	4	5	1
Botham	9	5	12	1
Miller	2	1	1	0
Boycott	1	0	3	0
Old	10	5	8	4

England innings (target: 46 runs from 60 overs)			R	M	B	4	6
*JM Brearley	lbw	b Valentine	0	10	10	0	0
G Boycott	not out		14	58	36	0	0
DW Randall	b Callender		5	17	11	1	0
GA Gooch	not out		21	27	31	2	1
Extras (w 3, nb 3): **6**							
Total (2 wickets, 13.5 overs): **46**							

DNB: DI Gower, IT Botham, G Miller, +RW Taylor, CM Old, RGD Willis, M Hendrick.
FoW: 1-3 (Brearley), 2-11 (Randall).

Bowling	O	M	R	W
Valentine	7	2	20	1
Callender	6	1	14	1
Stead	0.5	0	6	0

Prudential World Cup, 1979, 9th Match
India v Sri Lanka, Group B
Old Trafford, Manchester
16/18 June 1979 (60-over match)

Result: Sri Lanka won by 47 runs
Points: Sri Lanka 4, India 0
Toss: India
Umpires: KE Palmer and AGT Whitehead
ODI Debuts: FRMD Gunatilleke, RS Madugalle (SL)
Man Of The Match: LRD Mendis

Close Of Play:
Day 1: Sri Lanka 238/5 (60 overs)

Sri Lanka innings (60 overs maximum)			R	M	B	4	6
*B Warnapura	c Gaekwad	b Amarnath	18	56	51	2	0
SRD Wettimuny	c Vengsarkar	b Kapil Dev	67	132	120	8	0
RL Dias	c & b Amarnath		50	92	88	2	0
LRD Mendis	run out		64	72	57	1	3
RS Madugalle	c Khanna	b Amarnath	4	80	16	0	0
SP Pasqual	not out		23	43	26	1	0
DS de Silva	not out		1	8	4	0	0
Extras (lb 8, w 2, nb 1): **11**							
Total (5 wickets, 60 overs): **238**							

DNB: +SA Jayasinghe, ARM Opatha, DLS de Silva, FRMD Gunatilleke.
FoW: 1-31 (Warnapura), 2-127 (Wettimuny), 3-147 (Dias), 4-175 (Madugalle), 5-227 (Mendis).

Bowling	O	M	R	W
Kapil Dev	12	2	53	1
Ghavri	12	0	53	0
Amarnath	12	3	40	3
Bedi	12	2	37	0
Venkataraghavan	12	0	44	0

India innings (target: 239 runs from 60 overs)			R	M	B	4	6
SM Gavaskar	c Dias	b Warnapura	26	71	54	2	0
AD Gaekwad	c sub (GRA de Silva)	b DLS de Silva	33	149	52	2	0
DB Vengsarkar	c DLS de Silva	b DS de Silva	36	21	57	3	0
GR Viswanath	run out		22	75	55	0	0
BP Patel	b DS de Silva		10	12	13	1	0
N Kapil Dev	c Warnapura	b DLS de Silva	16	29	19	2	0
M Amarnath	b DS de Silva		7	18	15	0	0
KD Ghavri	c Warnapura	b Opatha	3	15	8	0	0
+SC Khanna	c Dias	b Opatha	10	20	17	1	0
*S Venkataraghavan	not out		9	16	9	0	0
BS Bedi	c Jayasinghe	b Opatha	5	6	8	0	0
Extras (lb 10, w 3, nb 1): **14**							
Total (all out, 54.1 overs): **191**							

FoW: 1-60 (Gavaskar), 2-76 (Gaekwad), 3-119 (Viswanath), 4-132 (Patel), 5-147 (Vengsarkar), 6-160 (Kapil Dev), 7-162 (Amarnath), 8-170 (Ghavri), 9-185 (Khanna), 10-191 (Bedi).

Bowling	O	M	R	W
Opatha	10.1	0	31	3
Gunatilleke	9	1	34	0
Warnapura	12	0	47	1
DLS de Silva	12	0	36	2
DS de Silva	11	1	29	3

Prudential World Cup, 1979, 10th Match
New Zealand v West Indies, Group B
Trent Bridge, Nottingham
16 June 1979 (60-over match)

Result: West Indies won by 32 runs
Points: West Indies 4, New Zealand 0
Toss: New Zealand
Umpires: HD Bird and BJ Meyer
ODI Debuts: EJ Chatfield (NZ)
Man Of The Match: CH Lloyd

West Indies innings (60 overs maximum)			R	M	B	4	6
CG Greenidge	c Edgar	b Coney	65	115	95	3	1
DL Haynes	lbw	b Hadlee	12		20		
IVA Richards	c Burgess	b Coney	9		30		
AI Kallicharran	b McKechnie		39	68	2	0	
*CH Lloyd	not out		73	80	4	0	
CL King	lbw	b Cairns	12		18		
+DL Murray	c Coney	b Chatfield	12		21		
AME Roberts	c Lees	b Cairns	1	3	0	0	
J Garner	not out		9		25		
Extras (b 5, lb 7): **12**							
Total (7 wickets, 60 overs): **244**							

DNB: MA Holding, CEH Croft.
FoW: 1-23 (Haynes), 2-61 (Richards), 3-117 (Greenidge), 4-152 (Kallicharran), 5-175 (King), 6-202 (Murray), 7-204 (Roberts).

Bowling	O	M	R	W
Hadlee	11	2	41	1
Chatfield	11	0	45	1
Cairns	12	1	48	2
Coney	12	0	40	2
McKechnie	11	0	46	1
Morrison	3	0	12	0

New Zealand innings (target: 245 from 60 overs)			R	M	B	4	6
BA Edgar	run out		12		23		
JG Wright	c Lloyd	b Garner	15		32		
JV Coney	c Garner	b King	36	96	54	3	0
GM Turner	c Lloyd	b Roberts	20		44		
JFM Morrison	c Murray	b Garner	11		41		
*MG Burgess	c Richards	b Roberts	35	79	49	3	0
+WK Lees	b Croft		5		5		0
RJ Hadlee	b Roberts		42	46	48	4	0
BJ McKechnie	not out		13		44		
BL Cairns	b Holding		1	3	0	0	
EJ Chatfield	not out		3	9	0	0	
Extras (lb 14, w 4, nb 1): **19**							
Total (9 wickets, 60 overs): **212**							

FoW: 1-27 (Edgar), 2-38 (Wright), 3-90 (Turner), 4-91 (Coney), 5-138 (Morrison), 6-143 (Lees), 7-160 (Burgess), 8-199 (Hadlee), 9-202 (Cairns).

Bowling	O	M	R	W
Roberts	12	2	43	3
Holding	12	1	29	1
Croft	12	1	38	1
Garner	12	0	45	2
King	12	1	38	1

Prudential World Cup, 1979, 11th Match
Australia v Canada, Group A
Edgbaston, Birmingham
16 June 1979 (60-over match)

Result: Australia won by 7 wickets
Points: Australia 4, Canada 0
Toss: Australia
Umpires: DJ Constant and JG Langridge
ODI Debuts: S Baksh (Can)
Man Of The Match: AG Hurst

Canada innings (60 overs maximum)			R	M	B	4	6
GR Sealy	c Porter	b Dymock	25	25	30	4	0
CJD Chappell	lbw	b Hurst	19	54	42	2	0
FA Dennis	lbw	b Hurst	1	8	8	0	0
Tariq Javed	c Wright	b Porter	8	38	30	1	0
S Baksh	b Hurst		0	7	6	0	0
JCB Vaughan	b Porter		29	48	43	4	0
*+BM Mauricette	c Hilditch	b Cosier	5	25	22	0	0
JM Patel	b Cosier		2	23	4	0	0
RG Callender	c Wright	b Hurst	0	3	2	0	0
CC Henry	c Hughes	b Hurst	5	8	11	1	0
JN Valentine	not out		0	5	6	0	0
Extras (b 4, lb 5, w 1, nb 1): **11**							
Total (all out, 33.2 overs): **105**							

FoW: 1-44 (Sealy), 2-50 (Dennis), 3-51 (Chappell), 4-51 (Baksh), 5-78 (Tariq Javed), 6-97 (Vaughan), 7-97 (Mauricette), 8-98 (Callender), 9-104 (Henry), 10-105 (Patel).

Bowling	O	M	R	W
Hogg	2	0	26	0
Hurst	10	3	21	5
Dymock	8	2	17	1
Porter	6	2	13	2
Cosier	7.2	2	17	2

Australia innings (target: 106 runs from 60 overs)			R	M	B	4	6
AMJ Hilditch	c Valentine	b Henry	24	49	30	3	0
WM Darling	lbw	b Valentine	13	17	16	2	0
AR Border	b Henry		25	53	53	4	0
*KJ Hughes	not out		27	48	40	2	0
GN Yallop	not out		13	26	20	0	0
Extras (lb 1, nb 3): **4**							
Total (3 wickets, 26 overs): **106**							

DNB: GJ Cosier, +KJ Wright, GD Porter, RM Hogg, G Dymock, AG Hurst.
FoW: 1-23 (Darling), 2-53 (Hilditch), 3-72 (Border).

Bowling	O	M	R	W
Valentine	3	0	28	1
Callender	3	0	12	0
Henry	10	0	27	2
Vaughan	6	0	15	0
Patel	4	0	20	0

Prudential World Cup, 1979, 12th Match
England v Pakistan, Group A
Headingley, Leeds
16 June 1979 (60-over match)

Result: England won by 14 runs
Points: England 4, Pakistan 0
Toss: Pakistan
Umpires: WL Budd and DGL Evans
Man Of The Match: M Hendrick

England innings (60 overs maximum)

			R	M	B	4	6
*JM Brearley	c Wasim Bari	b Imran Khan	0	1	2	0	0
G Boycott	lbw	b Majid Khan	18	85	54	2	0
DW Randall	c Wasim Bari	b Sikander Bakht	1	6	5	0	0
GA Gooch	c Sadiq Mohammad	b Sikander Bakht	33	97	90	5	0
DI Gower	b Majid Khan		27	51	40	3	0
IT Botham	b Majid Khan		22	58	48	1	1
PH Edmonds	c Wasim Raja	b Asif Iqbal	2	25	23	0	0
+RW Taylor	not out		20	61	59	1	0
CM Old	c & b Asif Iqbal		2	4	7	0	0
RGD Willis	b Sikander Bakht		24	50	37	3	0
M Hendrick	not out		1	1	1	0	0

Extras (lb 3, w 7, nb 5): **15**
Total (9 wickets, 60 overs): **165**

FoW: 1-0 (Brearley), 2-4 (Randall), 3-51 (Boycott), 4-70 (Gooch), 5-99 (Gower), 6-115 (Botham), 7-115 (Edmonds), 8-118 (Old), 9-161 (Willis).

Bowling

	O	M	R	W
Imran Khan	12	3	24	1
Sikander Bakht	12	3	32	3
Mudassar Nazar	12	4	30	0
Asif Iqbal	12	3	37	2
Majid Khan	12	2	27	3

Pakistan innings (target: 166 runs from 60 overs)

			R	M	B	4	6
Majid Khan	c Botham	b Hendrick	7	29	20	1	0
Sadiq Mohammad	b Hendrick		18	38	27	4	0
Mudassar Nazar	lbw	b Hendrick	0	1	2	0	0
Zaheer Abbas	c Taylor	b Botham	3	23	19	0	0
Haroon Rashid	c Brearley	b Hendrick	1	2	2	0	0
Javed Miandad	lbw	b Botham	0	5	4	0	0
*Asif Iqbal	c Brearley	b Willis	51	109	104	5	0
Wasim Raja	lbw	b Old	21	51	25	4	0
Imran Khan	not out		21	113	82	1	0
+Wasim Bari	c Taylor	b Boycott	17	37	33	2	0
Sikander Bakht	c Hendrick	b Boycott	2	23	19	0	0

Extras (lb 8, w 1, nb 1): **10**
Total (all out, 56 overs): **151**

FoW: 1-27 (Majid Khan), 2-27 (Mudassar Nazar), 3-28 (Sadiq Mohammad), 4-30 (Zaheer Abbas), 5-31 (Javed Miandad), 6-34 (Haroon Rashid), 7-86 (Wasim Raja), 8-115 (Asif Iqbal), 9-145 (Wasim Bari), 10-151 (Sikander Bakht).

Bowling

	O	M	R	W
Willis	11	2	37	1
Hendrick	12	6	15	4
Botham	12	3	38	2
Old	12	2	28	1
Edmonds	3	0	8	0
Boycott	5	0	14	2
Gooch	1	0	1	0

Prudential World Cup, 1979, 1st Semi-Final
England v New Zealand
Old Trafford, Manchester
20 June 1979 (60-over match)

Result: England won by 9 runs
England advances to the final
Toss: New Zealand
Umpires: JG Langridge and KE Palmer
ODI Debuts: W Larkins (Eng)
Man Of The Match: GA Gooch

England innings (60 overs maximum)

			R	M	B	4	6
*JM Brearley	c Lees	b Coney	53	114	115	3	0
G Boycott	c Howarth	b Hadlee	2	30	14	0	0
W Larkins	c Coney	b McKechnie	7	40	37	0	0
GA Gooch	b McKechnie		71	105	84	1	3
DI Gower	run out		1	2	1	0	0
IT Botham	lbw	b Cairns	21	31	30	2	0
DW Randall	not out		42	66	50	1	1
CM Old	c Lees	b Troup	0	2	2	0	0
+RW Taylor	run out		12	30	25	1	0
RGD Willis	not out		1	1	2	0	0

Extras (lb 8, w 3): **11**
Total (8 wickets, 60 overs): **221**

DNB: M Hendrick.
FoW: 1-13 (Boycott), 2-38 (Larkins), 3-96 (Brearley), 4-98 (Gower), 5-145 (Botham), 6-177 (Gooch), 7-178 (Old), 8-219 (Taylor).

Bowling

	O	M	R	W
Hadlee	12	4	32	1
Troup	12	1	38	1
Cairns	12	2	47	1
Coney	12	0	47	1
McKechnie	12	1	46	2

New Zealand innings (target: 222 from 60 overs)

			R	M	B	4	6
JG Wright	run out		69	142	137	9	0
BA Edgar	lbw	b Old	17	58	38	1	0
GP Howarth	lbw	b Boycott	7	13	12	1	0
JV Coney	lbw	b Hendrick	11	56	39	0	0
GM Turner	lbw	b Willis	30	67	51	2	0
*MG Burgess	run out		10	28	13	0	0
RJ Hadlee	b Botham		15	44	32	0	0
+WK Lees	b Hendrick		23	33	20	0	1
BL Cairns	c Brearley	b Hendrick	14	5	6	1	1
BJ McKechnie	not out		4	13	9	0	0
GB Troup	not out		3	2	3	0	0

Extras (b 5, w 4): **9**
Total (9 wickets, 60 overs): **212**

FoW: 1-47 (Edgar), 2-58 (Howarth), 3-104 (Coney), 4-112 (Wright), 5-132 (Burgess), 6-162 (Turner), 7-180 (Hadlee), 8-195 (Cairns), 9-208 (Lees)

Bowling

	O	M	R	W
Botham	12	3	42	1
Hendrick	12	0	55	3
Old	12	1	33	1
Boycott	9	1	24	1
Gooch	3	1	8	0
Willis	12	1	41	1

Prudential World Cup, 1979, 2nd Semi-Final
Pakistan v West Indies
Kennington Oval, London
20 June 1979 (60-over match)

Result: West Indies won by 43 runs
West Indies advances to the final
Toss: Pakistan
Umpires: WL Budd and DJ Constant
Man Of The Match: CG Greenidge

West Indies innings (60 overs maximum)

			R	M	B	4	6
CG Greenidge	c Wasim Bari	b Asif Iqbal	73	122	107	5	1
DL Haynes	c & b Asif Iqbal		65	155	115	4	0
IVA Richards	b Asif Iqbal		42	91	62	1	0
*CH Lloyd	c Mudassar Nazar	b Asif Iqbal	37	53	38	3	0
CL King	c sub	b Sarfraz Nawaz	34	37	25	3	0
AI Kallicharran	b Imran Khan		11	31	14	0	0
AME Roberts	not out		7	6	4	0	0
J Garner	not out		1	4	1	0	0

Extras (b 1, lb 17, w 1, nb 4): 23
Total (6 wickets, 60 overs): 293

DNB: +DL Murray, MA Holding, CEH Croft.
FoW: 1-132 (Greenidge), 2-165 (Haynes), 3-233 (Richards), 4-236 (Lloyd), 5-285 (Kallicharran), 6-285 (King).

Bowling	O	M	R	W
Imran Khan	9	1	43	1
Sarfraz Nawaz	12	1	71	1
Sikander Bakht	6	1	24	0
Mudassar Nazar	10	0	50	0
Majid Khan	12	2	26	0
Asif Iqbal	11	0	56	4

Pakistan innings (target: 294 runs from 60 overs)

			R	M	B	4	6
Majid Khan	c Kallicharran	b Croft	81	175	124	7	0
Sadiq Mohammad	c Murray	b Holding	2	15	7	0	0
Zaheer Abbas	c Murray	b Croft	93	143	122	8	1
Haroon Rashid	run out		15	40	22	1	0
Javed Miandad	lbw	b Croft	0	1	1	0	0
*Asif Iqbal	c Holding	b Richards	17	15	20	1	0
Mudassar Nazar	c Kallicharran	b Richards	2	10	9	0	0
Imran Khan	c & b Richards		6	9	4	1	0
Sarfraz Nawaz	c Haynes	b Roberts	12	16	15	0	0
+Wasim Bari	c Murray	b Roberts	9	13	12	0	0
Sikander Bakht	not out		1	3	4	0	0

Extras (lb 9, w 2, nb 1): 12
Total (all out, 56.2 overs): 250

FoW: 1-10 (Sadiq Mohammad), 2-176 (Zaheer Abbas), 3-187 (Majid Khan), 4-187 (Javed Miandad), 5-208 (Haroon Rashid), 6-220 (Mudassar Nazar), 7-221 (Asif Iqbal), 8-228 (Imran Khan), 9-246 (Wasim Bari), 10-250 (Sarfraz Nawaz).

Bowling	O	M	R	W
Roberts	9.2	2	41	2
Holding	9	1	28	1
Croft	11	0	29	3
Garner	12	1	47	0
King	7	0	41	0
Richards	8	0	52	3

Prudential World Cup, 1979, Final
England v West Indies
Lord's, London
23 June 1979 (60-over match)

Result: West Indies won by 92 runs
West Indies wins the 1979 Prudential World Cup
Toss: England
Umpires: HD Bird and BJ Meyer
Man Of The Match: IVA Richards

West Indies innings (60 overs maximum)			R	M	B	4	6
CG Greenidge	run out (Randall)		9	31	31	0	0
DL Haynes	c Hendrick	b Old	20	49	27	3	0
IVA Richards	not out		138	207	157	11	3
AI Kallicharran	b Hendrick		4	19	17	0	0
*CH Lloyd	c & b Old		13	42	33	2	0
CL King	c Randall	b Edmonds	86	77	66	10	3
+DL Murray	c Gower	b Edmonds	5	12	9	1	0
AME Roberts	c Brearley	b Hendrick	0	8	7	0	0
J Garner	c Taylor	b Botham	0	4	5	0	0
MA Holding	b Botham		0	7	6	0	0
CEH Croft	not out		0	6	2	0	0

Extras (b 1, lb 10): **11**
Total (9 wickets, 60 overs): **286**

FoW: 1-22 (Greenidge), 2-36 (Haynes), 3-55 (Kallicharran), 4-99 (Lloyd), 5-238 (King), 6-252 (Murray), 7-258 (Roberts), 8-260 (Garner), 9-272 (Holding).

Bowling	O	M	R	W
Botham	12	2	44	2
Hendrick	12	2	50	2
Old	12	0	55	2
Boycott	6	0	38	0
Edmonds	12	2	40	2
Gooch	4	0	27	0
Larkins	2	0	21	0

England innings (target: 287 runs from 60 overs)			R	M	B	4	6
*JM Brearley	c King	b Holding	64	130	130	7	0
G Boycott	c Kallicharran	b Holding	57	137	105	3	0
DW Randall	b Croft		15	36	22	0	0
GA Gooch	b Garner		32	31	28	4	0
DI Gower	b Garner		0	6	4	0	0
IT Botham	c Richards	b Croft	4	7	3	0	0
W Larkins	b Garner		0	1	1	0	0
PH Edmonds	not out		5	14	8	0	0
CM Old	b Garner		0	4	2	0	0
+RW Taylor	c Murray	b Garner	0	1	1	0	0
M Hendrick	b Croft		0	4	5	0	0

Extras (lb 12, w 2, nb 3): **17**
Total (all out, 51 overs): **194**

FoW: 1-129 (Brearley), 2-135 (Boycott), 3-183 (Gooch), 4-183 (Gower), 5-186 (Randall), 6-186 (Larkins), 7-192 (Botham), 8-192 (Old), 9-194 (Taylor), 10-194 (Hendrick).

Bowling	O	M	R	W
Roberts	9	2	33	0
Holding	8	1	16	2
Croft	10	1	42	3
Garner	11	0	38	5
Richards	10	0	35	0
King	3	0	13	0

1983 WORLD CUP

Group A

Prudential World Cup, 1983, 1st Match
England v New Zealand, Group A
Kennington Oval, London
9 June 1983 (60-over match)

Result: England won by 106 runs
Points: England 4, New Zealand 0
Toss: England
Umpires: BJ Meyer and DO Oslear
Man Of The Match: AJ Lamb

England innings (60 overs maximum)			R	B	4	6
G Fowler	c Coney	b Cairns	8	19	1	0
CJ Tavare	c Edgar	b Chatfield	45	91	4	0
DI Gower	c Edgar	b Coney	39	62	6	0
AJ Lamb	b Snedden		102	105	12	2
MW Gatting	b Snedden		43	47	3	0
IT Botham	c Lees	b Hadlee	22	16	0	1
+IJ Gould	not out		14	12	1	0
GR Dilley	not out		31	14	4	0
Extras (lb 12, w 1, nb 5): **18**						
Total (6 wickets, 60 overs): **322**						

DNB: VJ Marks, PJW Allott, *RGD Willis.
FoW: 1-13 (Fowler), 2-79 (Gower), 3-117 (Tavare), 4-232 (Gatting), 5-271 (Botham), 6-278 (Lamb).

Bowling	O	M	R	W
Hadlee	12	4	26	1
Cairns	12	4	57	1
Snedden	12	1	105	2
Chatfield	12	1	45	1
Coney	6	1	20	1
Crowe	6	0	51	0

New Zealand innings (target: 323 runs from 60 overs)			R	B	4	6
GM Turner	lbw	b Willis	14	28	2	0
BA Edgar	c Gould	b Willis	3	6	0	0
JG Wright	c Botham	b Dilley	10	17	1	0
*GP Howarth	c Lamb	b Marks	18	44	1	0
JV Coney	run out		23	52	2	0
MD Crowe	run out		97	118	8	0
+WK Lees	b Botham		8	23	0	0
RJ Hadlee	c Lamb	b Marks	1	9	0	0
BL Cairns	lbw	b Botham	1	2	0	0
MC Snedden	c Gould	b Gatting	21	34	1	0
EJ Chatfield	not out		9	24	1	0
Extras (b 2, lb 4, w 4, nb 1): **11**						
Total (all out, 59 overs): **216**						

FoW: 1-3 (Edgar), 2-28 (Wright), 3-31 (Turner), 4-62 (Howarth), 5-85 (Coney), 6-123 (Lees), 7-136 (Hadlee), 8-138 (Cairns), 9-190 (Snedden), 10-216 (Crowe).

Bowling	O	M	R	W
Willis	7	2	9	2
Dilley	8	0	33	1
Botham	12	0	42	2
Allott	12	1	47	0
Marks	12	1	39	2
Gatting	8	1	35	1

Prudential World Cup, 1983, 2nd Match
Pakistan v Sri Lanka, Group A
St Helen's, Swansea
9 June 1983 (60-over match)

Result: Pakistan won by 50 runs
Points: Pakistan 4, Sri Lanka 0
Toss: Sri Lanka
Umpires: KE Palmer and DR Shepherd
ODI Debuts: MAR Samarasekera (SL)
Man Of The Match: Mohsin Khan

Pakistan innings (60 overs maximum)

			R	B	4	6
Mudassar Nazar	c de Silva	b Ratnayake	36	72	2	0
Mohsin Khan	b John		82	121	5	1
Zaheer Abbas	c Kuruppu	b de Mel	82	81	10	0
Javed Miandad	lbw	b de Mel	72	52	4	3
*Imran Khan	not out		56	33	6	2
Ijaz Faqih	run out		2	3	0	0
Tahir Naqqash	not out		0	0	0	0
Extras (b 4, lb 4): **8**						
Total (5 wickets, 60 overs): **338**						

DNB: +Wasim Bari, Rashid Khan, Shahid Mahboob, Sarfraz Nawaz.
FoW: 1-88 (Mudassar Nazar), 2-156 (Mohsin Khan), 3-229 (Zaheer Abbas), 4-325 (Javed Miandad), 5-332 (Ijaz Faqih).

Bowling

	O	M	R	W
de Mel	12	2	69	2
John	12	2	58	1
Ratnayake	12	0	65	1
Ranatunga	9	0	53	0
de Silva	10	0	52	0
Samarasekera	5	0	33	0

Sri Lanka innings (target: 339 runs from 60 overs)

			R	B	4	6
S Wettimuny	c Rashid Khan	b Sarfraz Nawaz	12	26	1	0
DSBP Kuruppu	run out		72	101	7	2
RL Dias	b Rashid Khan		5	21	0	0
*LRD Mendis	b Tahir Naqqash		16	17	3	0
A Ranatunga	c & b Mudassar Nazar		31	42	5	0
MAR Samarasekera	run out		0	2	0	0
DS de Silva	c Wasim Bari	b Sarfraz Nawaz	35	51	1	0
ALF de Mel	c Tahir Naqqash	b Shahid Mahboob	11	22	0	0
+RG de Alwis	not out		59	56	5	1
RJ Ratnayake	c Mudassar Nazar	b Sarfraz Nawaz	13	13	0	1
VB John	not out		12	11	2	0
Extras (lb 8, w 10, nb 4): **22**						
Total (9 wickets, 60 overs): **288**						

FoW: 1-34 (Wettimuny), 2-58 (Dias), 3-85 (Mendis), 4-142 (Ranatunga), 5-143 (Samarasekera), 6-157 (Kuruppu), 7-180 (de Mel), 8-234 (de Silva), 9-262 (Ratnayake).

Bowling

	O	M	R	W
Sarfraz Nawaz	12	1	40	3
Shahid Mahboob	11	0	48	1
Tahir Naqqash	8	0	49	1
Rashid Khan	12	1	55	1
Ijaz Faqih	12	1	52	0
Mudassar Nazar	4	0	18	1
Zaheer Abbas	1	0	4	0

Prudential World Cup, 1983, 5th Match
England v Sri Lanka, Group A
County Ground, Taunton
11 June 1983 (60-over match)

Result: England won by 47 runs
Points: England 4, Sri Lanka 0
Toss: England
Umpires: MJ Kitchen and KE Palmer
Man Of The Match: DI Gower

England innings (60 overs maximum)			R	B	4	6
G Fowler	b John		22	59	1	0
CJ Tavare	c de Alwis	b Ranatunga	32	61	4	0
DI Gower	b de Mel		130	120	12	5
AJ Lamb	b Ratnayake		53	51	4	2
MW Gatting	run out		7	8	0	0
IT Botham	run out		0	1	0	0
+IJ Gould	c Ranatunga	b Ratnayake	35	40	2	0
GR Dilley	b de Mel		29	16	5	0
VJ Marks	run out		5	5	0	0
PJW Allott	not out		0	0	0	0
Extras (lb 11, w 9): **20**						
Total (9 wickets, 60 overs): **333**						

DNB: *RGD Willis.
FoW: 1-49 (Fowler), 2-78 (Tavare), 3-174 (Lamb), 4-193 (Gatting), 5-194 (Botham), 6-292 (Gould), 7-298 (Gower), 8-333 (Dilley), 9-333 (Marks).

Bowling	O	M	R	W
de Mel	12	3	62	2
John	12	0	55	1
Ratnayake	12	0	66	2
Ranatunga	12	0	65	1
de Silva	12	0	65	0

Sri Lanka innings (target: 334 runs from 60 overs)			R	B	4	6
S Wettimuny	lbw	b Marks	33	66	3	1
DSBP Kuruppu	c Gatting	b Dilley	4	3	1	0
RL Dias	c Botham	b Dilley	2	15	0	0
*LRD Mendis	c Willis	b Marks	56	64	5	1
RS Madugalle	c Tavare	b Marks	12	26	1	0
A Ranatunga	c Lamb	b Marks	34	45	4	0
DS de Silva	st Gould	b Marks	28	37	2	0
+RG de Alwis	not out		58	51	6	1
ALF de Mel	c Dilley	b Allott	27	26	2	0
RJ Ratnayake	c Lamb	b Dilley	15	18	1	0
VB John	b Dilley		0	1	0	0
Extras (lb 12, w 2, nb 3): **17**						
Total (all out, 58 overs): **286**						

FoW: 1-11 (Kuruppu), 2-17 (Dias), 3-92 (Wettimuny), 4-108 (Madugalle), 5-117 (Mendis), 6-168 (Ranatunga), 7-192 (de Silva), 8-246 (de Mel), 9-281 (Ratnayake), 10-286 (John).

Bowling	O	M	R	W
Willis	11	3	43	0
Dilley	11	0	45	4
Allott	12	1	82	1
Botham	12	0	60	0
Marks	12	3	39	5

Prudential World Cup, 1983, 6th Match
New Zealand v Pakistan, Group A
Edgbaston, Birmingham
11/12 June 1983 (60-over match)

Result: New Zealand won by 52 runs
Points: New Zealand 4, Pakistan 0
Toss: Pakistan
Umpires: HD Bird and B Leadbeater
ODI Debuts: JG Bracewell (NZ); Abdul Qadir (Pak)
Man Of The Match: Abdul Qadir

Close Of Play:
Day 1: New Zealand 211/8 (Crowe 30*, Lees 15*, 56 overs)

New Zealand innings (60 overs maximum)

			R	B	4	6
GM Turner	c Wasim Bari	b Rashid Khan	27	37	5	0
BA Edgar	c Imran Khan	b Abdul Qadir	44	107	3	0
JG Wright	c Wasim Bari	b Abdul Qadir	9	14	2	0
BL Cairns	b Abdul Qadir		4	6	1	0
*GP Howarth	st Wasim Bari	b Abdul Qadir	16	35	1	0
JV Coney	c Ijaz Faqih	b Shahid Mahboob	33	65	3	0
MD Crowe	c Mohsin Khan	b Rashid Khan	34	53	2	0
RJ Hadlee	c Wasim Bari	b Sarfraz Nawaz	13	11	1	0
JG Bracewell	lbw	b Rashid Khan	3	6	0	0
+WK Lees	not out		24	21	2	0
EJ Chatfield	not out		6	8	0	0
Extras (lb 20, w 4, nb 1): 25						
Total (9 wickets, 60 overs): 238						

FoW: 1-57 (Turner), 2-68 (Wright), 3-80 (Cairns), 4-109 (Edgar), 5-120 (Howarth), 6-166 (Coney), 7-197 (Hadlee), 8-202 (Bracewell), 9-223 (Crowe).

Bowling	O	M	R	W
Sarfraz Nawaz	11	1	49	1
Shahid Mahboob	10	2	38	1
Rashid Khan	11	0	47	3
Mudassar Nazar	12	1	40	0
Abdul Qadir	12	4	21	4
Ijaz Faqih	1	0	6	0
Zaheer Abbas	3	0	12	0

Pakistan innings (target: 239 runs from 60 overs)

			R	B	4	6
Mohsin Khan	lbw	b Hadlee	0	3	0	0
Mudassar Nazar	c Lees	b Cairns	0	2	0	0
Zaheer Abbas	b Hadlee		0	3	0	0
Javed Miandad	lbw	b Chatfield	35	61	3	0
*Imran Khan	c Chatfield	b Hadlee	9	26	1	0
Ijaz Faqih	c Edgar	b Coney	12	37	1	0
Shahid Mahboob	c Wright	b Coney	17	31	2	0
+Wasim Bari	c Edgar	b Coney	34	71	2	0
Abdul Qadir	not out		41	68	2	1
Sarfraz Nawaz	c Crowe	b Chatfield	13	14	2	0
Rashid Khan	c & b Cairns		9	21	0	0
Extras (b 5, lb 6, w 3, nb 2): 16						
Total (all out, 55.2 overs): 186						

FoW: 1-0 (Mohsin Khan), 2-0 (Zaheer Abbas), 3-0 (Mudassar Nazar), 4-22 (Imran Khan), 5-54 (Ijaz Faqih), 6-60 (Javed Miandad), 7-102 (Shahid Mahboob), 8-131 (Wasim Bari), 9-158 (Sarfraz Nawaz), 10-186 (Rashid Khan).

Bowling	O	M	R	W
Hadlee	9	2	20	3
Cairns	9.2	3	21	2
Chatfield	12	0	50	2
Crowe	2	0	12	0
Coney	12	3	28	3
Bracewell	11	2	39	0

Prudential World Cup, 1983, 9th Match
England v Pakistan, Group A
Lord's, London
13 June 1983 (60-over match)

Result: England won by 8 wickets
Points: England 4, Pakistan 0
Toss: Pakistan
Umpires: BJ Meyer and AGT Whitehead
Man Of The Match: Zaheer Abbas

Pakistan innings (60 overs maximum)			R	B	4	6
Mohsin Khan	c Tavare	b Willis	3	29	0	0
Mudassar Nazar	c Gould	b Allott	26	98	2	0
Mansoor Akhtar	c Gould	b Willis	3	15	0	0
Javed Miandad	c Gould	b Botham	14	26	2	0
Zaheer Abbas	not out		83	104	7	1
*Imran Khan	run out		7	35	1	0
Wasim Raja	c Botham	b Marks	9	19	2	0
Abdul Qadir	run out		0	2	0	0
Sarfraz Nawaz	c & b Botham		11	15	2	0
+Wasim Bari	not out		18	21	1	0
*Extras (b 5, lb 8, w 3, nb 3): **19***						
*Total (8 wickets, 60 overs): **193***						

DNB: Rashid Khan.
FoW: 1-29 (Mohsin Khan), 2-33 (Mansoor Akhtar), 3-49 (Javed Miandad), 4-67 (Mudassar Nazar), 5-96 (Imran Khan), 6-112 (Wasim Raja), 7-118 (Abdul Qadir), 8-154 (Sarfraz Nawaz).

Bowling	O	M	R	W
Willis	12	4	24	2
Dilley	12	1	33	0
Allott	12	2	48	1
Botham	12	3	36	2
Marks	12	1	33	1

England innings (target: 194 runs from 60 overs)			R	B	4	6
G Fowler	not out		78	151	5	0
CJ Tavare	lbw	b Rashid Khan	8	21	0	0
DI Gower	c Sarfraz Nawaz	b Mansoor Akhtar	48	72	6	0
AJ Lamb	not out		48	62	5	1
*Extras (b 1, lb 12, w 2, nb 2): **17***						
*Total (2 wickets, 50.4 overs): **199***						

DNB: MW Gatting, IT Botham, +IJ Gould, VJ Marks, GR Dilley, PJW Allott, *RGD Willis.
FoW: 1-15 (Tavare), 2-93 (Gower).

Bowling	O	M	R	W
Rashid Khan	7	2	19	1
Sarfraz Nawaz	11	5	22	0
Wasim Raja	3	0	14	0
Mudassar Nazar	8	0	30	0
Abdul Qadir	9.4	0	53	0
Mansoor Akhtar	12	2	44	1

Prudential World Cup, 1983, 10th Match
New Zealand v Sri Lanka, Group A
Phoenix County Ground, Bristol
13 June 1983 (60-over match)

Result: New Zealand won by 5 wickets
Points: New Zealand 4, Sri Lanka 0
Toss: New Zealand
Umpires: HD Bird and DR Shepherd
Man Of The Match: RJ Hadlee

Sri Lanka innings (60 overs maximum)			R	B	4	6
S Wettimuny	lbw	b Hadlee	7	19	1	0
DSBP Kuruppu	c Hadlee	b Chatfield	26	60	5	0
RL Dias	b Chatfield		25	43	4	0
*LRD Mendis	b Hadlee		43	70	2	0
RS Madugalle	c Snedden	b Coney	60	87	3	1
A Ranatunga	lbw	b Hadlee	0	3	0	0
DS de Silva	b Coney		13	20	0	0
+RG de Alwis	c Howarth	b Snedden	16	17	2	0
ALF de Mel	c & b Hadlee		1	6	0	0
RJ Ratnayake	b Hadlee		5	9	0	0
VB John	not out		2	5	0	0
Extras (lb 6, w 1, nb 1): **8**						
Total (all out, 56.1 overs): **206**						

FoW: 1-16 (Wettimuny), 2-56 (Kuruppu), 3-73 (Dias), 4-144 (Mendis), 5-144 (Ranatunga), 6-171 (de Silva), 7-196 (Madugalle), 8-199 (de Alwis), 9-199 (de Mel), 10-206 (Ratnayake).

Bowling	O	M	R	W
Hadlee	10.1	4	25	5
Snedden	10	1	38	1
Chatfield	12	4	24	2
Cairns	7	0	35	0
Coney	12	0	44	2
MD Crowe	5	0	32	0

New Zealand innings (target: 207 runs from 60 overs)			R	B	4	6
GM Turner	c Mendis	b de Silva	50	60	8	0
JG Wright	lbw	b de Mel	45	52	8	0
*GP Howarth	c Madugalle	b Ratnayake	76	79	14	0
MD Crowe	c de Alwis	b de Mel	0	11	0	0
JJ Crowe	lbw	b John	23	26	4	0
JV Coney	not out		2	10	0	0
+IDS Smith	not out		4	1	1	0
Extras (lb 6, w 3): **9**						
Total (5 wickets, 39.2 overs): **209**						

DNB: RJ Hadlee, BL Cairns, MC Snedden, EJ Chatfield.
FoW: 1-89 (Wright), 2-99 (Turner), 3-110 (MD Crowe), 4-176 (JJ Crowe), 5-205 (Howarth).

Bowling	O	M	R	W
de Mel	8	2	30	2
John	8.2	0	49	1
Ratnayake	12	0	60	1
de Silva	9	0	39	1
Ranatunga	2	0	22	0

Prudential World Cup, 1983, 13th Match
England v New Zealand, Group A
Edgbaston, Birmingham
15 June 1983 (60-over match)

Result: New Zealand won by 2 wickets
Points: New Zealand 4, England 0
Toss: England
Umpires: J Birkenshaw and KE Palmer
Man Of The Match: JV Coney

England innings (60 overs maximum)			R	M	B	4	6
G Fowler	c JJ Crowe	b Chatfield	69	98	112	9	0
CJ Tavare	c Cairns	b Coney	18	55	44	1	0
IT Botham	c & b Bracewell		12	13	9	1	1
DI Gower	not out		92	123	96	6	4
AJ Lamb	c JJ Crowe	b Cairns	8	16	14	1	0
MW Gatting	b Cairns		1	9	5	0	0
+IJ Gould	lbw	b Cairns	4	13	14	0	0
VJ Marks	b Hadlee		5	23	15	0	0
GR Dilley	b Hadlee		10	24	19	0	0
PJW Allott	c Smith	b Hadlee	0	1	1	0	0
*RGD Willis	lbw	b Chatfield	0	2	3	0	0

Extras (b 4, lb 10, w 1): **15**
Total (all out, 55.2 overs): **234**

FoW: 1-63 (Tavare), 2-77 (Botham), 3-117 (Fowler), 4-143 (Lamb), 5-154 (Gatting), 6-162 (Gould), 7-203 (Marks), 8-233 (Dilley), 9-233 (Allott), 10-234 (Willis).

Bowling	O	M	R	W
Hadlee	10	3	32	3
Cairns	11	0	44	3
Coney	12	2	27	1
Bracewell	12	0	66	1
Chatfield	10.2	0	50	2

New Zealand innings (target: 235 from 60 overs)			R	M	B	4	6
GM Turner	lbw	b Willis	2	4	5	0	0
BA Edgar	c Gould	b Willis	1	13	6	0	0
*GP Howarth	run out		60	160	104	5	1
JJ Crowe	b Allott		17	57	46	1	0
MD Crowe	b Marks		20	36	40	2	0
JV Coney	not out		66	144	97	9	0
+IDS Smith	b Botham		4	6	6	1	0
RJ Hadlee	b Willis		31	58	45	3	0
BL Cairns	lbw	b Willis	5	11	6	0	0
JG Bracewell	not out		4	9	7	1	0

Extras (b 2, lb 22, w 1, nb 3): **28**
Total (8 wickets, 59.5 overs): **238**

DNB: EJ Chatfield.
FoW: 1-2 (Turner), 2-3 (Edgar), 3-47 (JJ Crowe), 4-75 (MD Crowe), 5-146 (Howarth), 6-151 (Smith), 7-221 (Hadlee), 8-231 (Cairns).

Bowling	O	M	R	W
Willis	12	1	42	4
Dilley	12	1	43	0
Botham	12	1	47	1
Allott	11.5	2	44	1
Marks	12	1	34	1

Prudential World Cup, 1983, 15th Match
Pakistan v Sri Lanka, Group A
Headingley, Leeds
16 June 1983 (60-over match)

Result: Pakistan won by 11 runs
Points: Pakistan 4, Sri Lanka 0
Toss: Sri Lanka
Umpires: DO Oslear and AGT Whitehead
Man Of The Match: Abdul Qadir

Pakistan innings (60 overs maximum)			R	B	4	6
Mohsin Khan	c Ranatunga	b de Mel	3	14	0	0
Mansoor Akhtar	c de Alwis	b de Mel	6	32	0	0
Zaheer Abbas	c Dias	b de Mel	15	28	2	0
Javed Miandad	lbw	b Ratnayake	7	14	1	0
*Imran Khan	not out		102	133	11	0
Ijaz Faqih	lbw	b Ratnayake	0	1	0	0
Shahid Mahboob	c de Silva	b de Mel	77	126	6	0
Sarfraz Nawaz	c Madugalle	b de Mel	9	10	1	0
Abdul Qadir	not out		5	7	0	0
Extras (b 1, lb 4, w 4, nb 2): **11**						
Total (7 wickets, 60 overs): **235**						

DNB: +Wasim Bari, Rashid Khan.
FoW: 1-6 (Mohsin Khan), 2-25 (Mansoor Akhtar), 3-30 (Zaheer Abbas), 4-43 (Javed Miandad), 5-43 (Ijaz Faqih), 6-187 (Shahid Mahboob), 7-204 (Sarfraz Nawaz).

Bowling	O	M	R	W
de Mel	12	1	39	5
John	12	1	48	0
Ratnayake	12	2	42	2
Ranatunga	11	0	49	0
de Silva	12	1	42	0
Wettimuny	1	0	4	0

Sri Lanka innings (target: 236 runs from 60 overs)			R	B	4	6
S Wettimuny	c Shahid Mahboob	b Rashid Khan	50	127	4	0
DSBP Kuruppu	b Rashid Khan		12	36	1	0
RL Dias	st Wasim Bari	b Abdul Qadir	47	73	7	0
*LRD Mendis	c Wasim Bari	b Abdul Qadir	33	49	5	0
RJ Ratnayake	st Wasim Bari	b Abdul Qadir	1	6	0	0
RS Madugalle	c Abdul Qadir	b Shahid Mahboob	26	20	1	1
A Ranatunga	c Zaheer Abbas	b Abdul Qadir	0	1	0	0
DS de Silva	run out		1	3	0	0
+RG de Alwis	c Javed Miandad	b Abdul Qadir	4	5	1	0
ALF de Mel	c Imran Khan	b Sarfraz Nawaz	17	19	1	0
VB John	not out		6	15	0	0
Extras (lb 8, w 17, nb 2): **27**						
Total (all out, 58.3 overs): **224**						

FoW: 1-22 (Kuruppu), 2-101 (Dias), 3-162 (Wettimuny), 4-162 (Mendis), 5-166 (Ratnayake), 6-166 (Ranatunga), 7-171 (de Silva), 8-193 (de Alwis), 9-199 (Madugalle), 10-224 (de Mel).

Bowling	O	M	R	W
Rashid Khan	12	4	31	2
Sarfraz Nawaz	11.3	2	25	1
Shahid Mahboob	10	1	62	1
Mansoor Akhtar	1	0	8	0
Ijaz Faqih	12	0	27	0
Abdul Qadir	12	1	44	5

Prudential World Cup, 1983, 17th Match
England v Pakistan, Group A
Old Trafford, Manchester
18 June 1983 (60-over match)

Result: England won by 7 wickets
Points: England 4, Pakistan 0
Toss: Pakistan
Umpires: HD Bird and DO Oslear
Man Of The Match: G Fowler

Pakistan innings (60 overs maximum)			R	B	4	6
Mohsin Khan	c Marks	b Allott	32	98	3	0
Mudassar Nazar	c Gould	b Dilley	18	23	2	0
Zaheer Abbas	c Gould	b Dilley	0	8	0	0
Javed Miandad	run out		67	100	6	0
*Imran Khan	c Willis	b Marks	13	28	2	0
Wasim Raja	c Willis	b Marks	15	24	3	0
Ijaz Faqih	not out		42	52	5	0
Sarfraz Nawaz	b Willis		17	20	1	1
Abdul Qadir	run out		6	7	0	0
+Wasim Bari	not out		2	3	0	0
Extras (b 3, lb 14, w 2, nb 1): **20**						
Total (8 wickets, 60 overs): **232**						

DNB: Rashid Khan.
FoW: 1-33 (Mudassar Nazar), 2-34 (Zaheer Abbas), 3-87 (Mohsin Khan), 4-116 (Imran Khan), 5-144 (Wasim Raja), 6-169 (Javed Miandad), 7-204 (Sarfraz Nawaz), 8-221 (Abdul Qadir).

Bowling	O	M	R	W
Willis	12	3	37	1
Dilley	12	2	46	2
Allott	12	1	33	1
Botham	12	1	51	0
Marks	12	0	45	2

England innings (target: 233 runs from 60 overs)			R	B	4	6
G Fowler	c Javed Miandad	b Mudassar Nazar	69	96	7	0
CJ Tavare	c Wasim Raja	b Zaheer Abbas	58	116	5	0
DI Gower	c Zaheer Abbas	b Mudassar Nazar	31	48	3	0
AJ Lamb	not out		38	57	4	0
MW Gatting	not out		14	27	1	0
Extras (b 1, lb 15, w 7): **23**						
Total (3 wickets, 57.2 overs): **233**						

DNB: IT Botham, +IJ Gould, VJ Marks, GR Dilley, PJW Allott, *RGD Willis.
FoW: 1-115 (Fowler), 2-165 (Tavare), 3-181 (Gower).

Bowling	O	M	R	W
Rashid Khan	11	1	58	0
Sarfraz Nawaz	10.2	2	22	0
Abdul Qadir	11	0	51	0
Ijaz Faqih	6	0	19	0
Mudassar Nazar	12	2	34	2
Zaheer Abbas	7	0	26	1

Prudential World Cup, 1983, 18th Match
New Zealand v Sri Lanka, Group A
County Ground, Derby
18 June 1983 (60-over match)

Result: Sri Lanka won by 3 wickets
Points: Sri Lanka 4, New Zealand 0
Toss: Sri Lanka
Umpires: DJ Constant and B Leadbeater
Man Of The Match: ALF de Mel

New Zealand innings (60 overs maximum)

			R	B	4	6
GM Turner	c Dias	b de Mel	6	10	1	0
JG Wright	c de Alwis	b de Mel	0	7	0	0
*GP Howarth	b Ratnayake		15	23	2	0
MD Crowe	lbw	b Ratnayake	8	32	0	0
BA Edgar	c Samarasekera	b de Silva	27	77	3	0
JV Coney	c sub	b de Silva	22	50	2	0
RJ Hadlee	c Madugalle	b de Mel	15	39	3	0
+WK Lees	c Ranatunga	b de Mel	2	16	0	0
BL Cairns	c Dias	b de Mel	6	7	1	0
MC Snedden	run out		40	55	5	0
EJ Chatfield	not out		19	48	2	0
Extras (b 4, lb 5, w 11, nb 1): **21**						
Total (all out, 58.2 overs): **181**						

FoW: 1-8 (Turner), 2-8 (Wright), 3-32 (Howarth), 4-47 (Crowe), 5-88 (Coney), 6-91 (Edgar), 7-105 (Lees), 8-115 (Cairns), 9-116 (Hadlee), 10-181 (Snedden).

Bowling

	O	M	R	W
de Mel	12	4	32	5
Ratnayake	11	4	18	2
Ranatunga	10	2	50	0
de Silva	12	5	11	2
Samarasekera	11.2	2	38	0
Wettimuny	2	0	11	0

Sri Lanka innings (target: 182 runs from 60 overs)

			R	B	4	6
S Wettimuny	b Cairns		4	30	0	0
DSBP Kuruppu	c & b Snedden		62	120	10	0
A Ranatunga	b Crowe		15	22	2	0
RL Dias	not out		64	101	9	0
*LRD Mendis	lbw	b Chatfield	0	2	0	0
RS Madugalle	c Lees	b Snedden	6	18	0	0
MAR Samarasekera	c Lees	b Hadlee	5	11	0	0
DS de Silva	run out		2	10	0	0
+RG de Alwis	not out		11	10	1	0
Extras (b 1, lb 4, w 10): **15**						
Total (7 wickets, 52.5 overs): **184**						

DNB: ALF de Mel, RJ Ratnayake.
FoW: 1-15 (Wettimuny), 2-49 (Ranatunga), 3-129 (Kuruppu), 4-130 (Mendis), 5-139 (Madugalle), 6-151 (Samarasekera), 7-161 (de Silva).

Bowling

	O	M	R	W
Hadlee	12	3	16	1
Cairns	10	2	35	1
Snedden	10.5	1	58	2
Chatfield	12	3	23	1
Crowe	4	2	15	1
Coney	4	1	22	0

Prudential World Cup, 1983, 21st Match
England v Sri Lanka, Group A
Headingley, Leeds
20 June 1983 (60-over match)

Result: England won by 9 wickets
Points: England 4, Sri Lanka 0
Toss: England
Umpires: B Leadbeater and R Palmer
Man Of The Match: RGD Willis

Sri Lanka innings (60 overs maximum)

			R	B	4	6
S Wettimuny	lbw	b Botham	22	49	3	0
DSBP Kuruppu	c Gatting	b Willis	6	36	1	0
A Ranatunga	c Lamb	b Botham	0	6	0	0
RL Dias	c Gould	b Cowans	7	24	1	0
*LRD Mendis	b Allott		10	38	0	0
RS Madugalle	c Gould	b Allott	0	16	0	0
DS de Silva	c Gower	b Marks	15	36	1	0
+RG de Alwis	c Marks	b Cowans	19	20	2	1
ALF de Mel	c Lamb	b Marks	10	23	2	0
RJ Ratnayake	not out		20	32	1	1
VB John	c Cowans	b Allott	15	27	1	0
Extras (b 5, lb 2, w 3, nb 2): **12**						
Total (all out, 50.4 overs): **136**						

FoW: 1-25 (Kuruppu), 2-30 (Ranatunga), 3-32 (Wettimuny), 4-40 (Dias), 5-43 (Madugalle), 6-54 (Mendis), 7-81 (de Silva), 8-97 (de Alwis), 9-103 (de Mel), 10-136 (John).

Bowling	O	M	R	W
Willis	9	4	9	1
Cowans	12	3	31	2
Botham	9	4	12	2
Allott	10.4	0	41	3
Gatting	4	2	13	0
Marks	6	2	18	2

England innings (target: 137 runs from 60 overs)

			R	B	4	6
G Fowler	not out		81	77	11	0
CJ Tavare	c de Alwis	b de Mel	19	48	1	1
DI Gower	not out		27	24	3	0
Extras (b 1, lb 3, w 3, nb 3): **10**						
Total (1 wicket, 24.1 overs): **137**						

DNB: AJ Lamb, MW Gatting, IT Botham, +IJ Gould, VJ Marks, PJW Allott, *RGD Willis, NG Cowans.
FoW: 1-68 (Tavare).

Bowling	O	M	R	W
de Mel	10	1	33	1
Ratnayake	5	0	23	0
John	6	0	41	0
de Silva	3	0	29	0
Ranatunga	0.1	0	1	0

Prudential World Cup, 1983, 22nd Match
New Zealand v Pakistan, Group A
Trent Bridge, Nottingham
20 June 1983 (60-over match)

Result: Pakistan won by 11 runs
Points: Pakistan 4, New Zealand 0
Toss: Pakistan
Umpires: DGL Evans and MJ Kitchen
Man Of The Match: Imran Khan

Pakistan innings (60 overs maximum)			R	B	4	6
Mohsin Khan	c Cairns	b Coney	33	64	3	0
Mudassar Nazar	b Coney		15	60	0	0
Javed Miandad	b Hadlee		25	45	1	0
Zaheer Abbas	not out		103	121	6	0
*Imran Khan	not out		79	74	7	1
Extras (b 1, lb 2, w 2, nb 1): **6**						
Total (3 wickets, 60 overs): **261**						

DNB: Ijaz Faqih, Shahid Mahboob, Sarfraz Nawaz, Abdul Qadir, +Wasim Bari, Rashid Khan.
FoW: 1-48 (Mohsin Khan), 2-54 (Mudassar Nazar), 3-114 (Javed Miandad).

Bowling	O	M	R	W
Hadlee	12	1	61	1
Cairns	12	1	45	0
Chatfield	12	0	57	0
Coney	12	0	42	2
Bracewell	12	0	50	0

New Zealand innings (target: 262 runs from 60 overs)			R	B	4	6
GM Turner	c Wasim Bari	b Sarfraz Nawaz	4	16	0	0
JG Wright	c Imran Khan	b Abdul Qadir	19	57	1	0
*GP Howarth	c Javed Miandad	b Zaheer Abbas	39	51	3	0
MD Crowe	b Mudassar Nazar		43	62	4	0
BA Edgar	lbw	b Shahid Mahboob	6	22	0	0
JV Coney	run out		51	78	3	0
RJ Hadlee	c Mohsin Khan	b Mudassar Nazar	11	20	1	0
BL Cairns	c Imran Khan	b Abdul Qadir	0	3	0	0
+WK Lees	c sub (Mansoor Akhtar) b Mudassar Nazar		26	25	4	0
JG Bracewell	c Mohsin Khan	b Sarfraz Nawaz	34	24	7	0
EJ Chatfield	not out		3	6	0	0
Extras (lb 8, w 5, nb 1): **14**						
Total (all out, 59.1 overs): **250**						

FoW: 1-13 (Turner), 2-44 (Wright), 3-85 (Howarth), 4-102 (Edgar), 5-130 (Crowe), 6-150 (Hadlee), 7-152 (Cairns), 8-187 (Lees), 9-246 (Bracewell), 10-250 (Coney).

Bowling	O	M	R	W
Rashid Khan	6	1	24	0
Sarfraz Nawaz	9.1	1	50	2
Abdul Qadir	12	0	53	2
Ijaz Faqih	6	1	21	0
Shahid Mahboob	10	0	37	1
Mudassar Nazar	12	0	43	3
Zaheer Abbas	4	1	8	1

1983 WORLD CUP

Group B

Prudential World Cup, 1983, 3rd Match
Australia v Zimbabwe, Group B
Trent Bridge, Nottingham
9 June 1983 (60-over match)

Result: Zimbabwe won by 13 runs
Points: Zimbabwe 4, Australia 0
Toss: Australia
Umpires: DJ Constant and MJ Kitchen
ODI Debuts: IP Butchart, KM Curran, DAG Fletcher, JG Heron, VR Hogg, DL Houghton, AH
   Omarshah, GA Paterson, AJ Pycroft, PWE Rawson, AJ Traicos (Zim)
Man Of The Match: DAG Fletcher

Zimbabwe innings (60 overs maximum)			R	M	B	4	6
AH Omarshah	c Marsh	b Lillee	16	80	57	0	0
GA Paterson	c Hookes	b Lillee	27	78	59	2	0
JG Heron	c Marsh	b Yallop	14	38	40	1	0
AJ Pycroft	b Border		21	53	41	1	0
+DL Houghton	c Marsh	b Yallop	0	1	1	0	0
*DAG Fletcher	not out		69	139	84	5	0
KM Curran	c Hookes	b Hogg	27	59	46	2	0
IP Butchart	not out		34	55	38	2	0
Extras (lb 18, w 7, nb 6): **31**							
Total (6 wickets, 60 overs): **239**							

DNB: PWE Rawson, AJ Traicos, VR Hogg.
FoW: 1-55 (Paterson), 2-55 (Omarshah), 3-86 (Heron), 4-86 (Houghton), 5-94 (Pycroft), 6-164 (Curran).

Bowling	O	M	R	W
Lawson	11	2	33	0
Hogg	12	3	43	1
Lillee	12	1	47	2
Thomson	11	1	46	0
Yallop	9	0	28	2
Border	5	0	11	1

Australia innings (target: 240 runs from 60 overs)			R	M	B	4	6
GM Wood	c Houghton	b Fletcher	31	69	60	3	0
KC Wessels	run out		76	147	130	5	0
*KJ Hughes	c Omarshah	b Fletcher	0	7	4	0	0
DW Hookes	c Traicos	b Fletcher	20	45	48	1	0
GN Yallop	c Pycroft	b Fletcher	2	15	17	0	0
AR Border	c Pycroft	b Curran	17	34	33	0	0
+RW Marsh	not out		50	63	42	3	2
GF Lawson	b Butchart		0	4	4	0	0
RM Hogg	not out		19	29	22	1	0
Extras (b 2, lb 7, w 2): **11**							
Total (7 wickets, 60 overs): **226**							

DNB: DK Lillee, JR Thomson.
FoW: 1-61 (Wood), 2-63 (Hughes), 3-114 (Hookes), 4-133 (Yallop), 5-138 (Wessels), 6-168 (Border), 7-176 (Lawson).

Bowling	O	M	R	W
Hogg	6	2	15	0
Rawson	12	1	54	0
Butchart	10	0	39	1
Fletcher	11	1	42	4
Traicos	12	2	27	0
Curran	9	0	38	1

Prudential World Cup, 1983, 4th Match
India v West Indies, Group B
Old Trafford, Manchester
9/10 June 1983 (60-over match)

Result: India won by 34 runs
Points: India 4, West Indies 0
Toss: West Indies
Umpires: B Leadbeater and AGT Whitehead
Man Of The Match: Yashpal Sharma

Close Of Play:
Day 1: India 262/8, West Indies 67/2 (Richards 12*, Bacchus 3*, 22 overs)

India innings (60 overs maximum)			R	M	B	4	6
SM Gavaskar	c Dujon	b Marshall	19		44		
K Srikkanth	c Dujon	b Holding	14		17		
M Amarnath	c Dujon	b Garner	21		60		
SM Patil	b Gomes		36		52		
Yashpal Sharma	b Holding		89	133	120	9	0
*N Kapil Dev	c Richards	b Gomes	6		13		
RMH Binny	lbw	b Marshall	27		38		
S Madan Lal	not out		21		22		
+SMH Kirmani	run out		1		2	0	0
RJ Shastri	not out		5		3		0
Extras (b 4, lb 10, w 1, nb 8): **23**							
Total (8 wickets, 60 overs): **262**							

DNB: BS Sandhu.
FoW: 1-21 (Srikkanth), 2-46 (Gavaskar), 3-76 (Amarnath), 4-125 (Patil), 5-141 (Kapil Dev), 6-214 (Binny), 7-243 (Yashpal Sharma), 8-246 (Kirmani).

Bowling	O	M	R	W
Holding	12	3	32	2
Roberts	12	1	51	0
Marshall	12	1	48	2
Garner	12	1	49	1
Richards	2	0	13	0
Gomes	10	0	46	2

West Indies innings (target: 263 runs from 60 overs)			R	B	4	6
CG Greenidge	b Sandhu		24	55		
DL Haynes	run out		24	29		
IVA Richards	c Kirmani	b Binny	17	36		
SFAF Bacchus	b Madan Lal		14	24		
*CH Lloyd	b Binny		25	38		
+PJL Dujon	c Sandhu	b Binny	7	12		
HA Gomes	run out		8	16		
MD Marshall	st Kirmani	b Shastri	2	5	0	0
AME Roberts	not out		37	58		
MA Holding	b Shastri		8	11		
J Garner	st Kirmani	b Shastri	37	29	0	1
Extras (b 4, lb 17, w 4): **25**						
Total (all out, 54.1 overs): **228**						

FoW: 1-49 (Haynes), 2-56 (Greenidge), 3-76 (Richards), 4-96 (Bacchus), 5-107 (Dujon), 6-124 (Gomes), 7-126 (Marshall), 8-130 (Lloyd), 9-157 (Holding), 10-228 (Garner).

Bowling	O	M	R	W
Kapil Dev	10	0	34	0
Sandhu	12	1	36	1
Madan Lal	12	1	34	1
Binny	12	1	48	3
Shastri	5.1	0	26	3
Patil	3	0	25	0

Prudential World Cup, 1983, 7th Match
Australia v West Indies, Group B
Headingley, Leeds
11/12 June 1983 (60-over match)

Result: West Indies won by 101 runs
Points: West Indies 4, Australia 0
Toss: Australia
Umpires: DJ Constant and DGL Evans
Man Of The Match: WW Davis

Close Of Play
Day 1: West Indies 160/5 (Gomes 60*, Dujon 3*, 42 overs)

West Indies innings (60 overs maximum)			R	B	4	6
CG Greenidge	c Wood	b Hogg	4	8	1	0
DL Haynes	c Marsh	b Lawson	13	29	1	0
IVA Richards	b Lawson		7	16	1	0
HA Gomes	c Marsh	b Lillee	78	153	4	0
*CH Lloyd	lbw	b MacLeay	19	42	1	1
SFAF Bacchus	c Wessels	b Yallop	47	59	5	0
+PJL Dujon	lbw	b Lawson	12	34	0	0
AME Roberts	c Marsh	b Lillee	5	14	0	0
MA Holding	run out		20	13	2	0
WW Daniel	not out		16	12	2	0
Extras (b 1, lb 9, w 10, nb 11) 31						
Total (9 wickets, 60 overs): 252						

DNB: WW Davis.
FoW: 1-7 (Greenidge), 2-25 (Richards), 3-32 (Haynes), 4-78 (Lloyd), 5-154 (Bacchus), 6-192 (Dujon), 7-208 (Roberts), 8-211 (Gomes), 9-252 (Holding).

Bowling	O	M	R	W
Lawson	12	3	29	3
Hogg	12	1	49	1
MacLeay	12	1	31	1
Lillee	12	0	55	2
Yallop	5	0	26	1
Border	7	0	31	0

Australia innings (target: 253 runs from 60 overs)			R	B	4	6
GM Wood	retired hurt		2	19	0	0
KC Wessels	b Roberts		11	27	2	0
*KJ Hughes	c Lloyd	b Davis	18	16	0	2
DW Hookes	c Dujon	b Davis	45	45	5	0
GN Yallop	c Holding	b Davis	29	26	4	0
AR Border	c Lloyd	b Davis	17	22	2	0
KH MacLeay	c Haynes	b Davis	1	8	0	0
+RW Marsh	c Haynes	b Holding	8	15	1	0
GF Lawson	c Dujon	b Davis	2	8	0	0
RM Hogg	not out		0	2	0	0
DK Lillee	b Davis		0	2	0	0
Extras (b 1, lb 4, w 5, nb 8): 18						
Total (all out, 30.3 overs): 151						

FoW: 1-18 (Wessels), 2-55 (Hughes), 3-114 (Yallop), 4-116 (Hookes), 5-126 (MacLeay), 6-137 (Marsh), 7-141 (Lawson), 8-150 (Border), 9-151 (Lillee).

Bowling	O	M	R	W
Roberts	7	0	14	1
Holding	8	2	23	1
Davis	10.3	0	51	7
Daniel	3	0	35	0
Gomes	2	0	10	0

Prudential World Cup, 1983, 8th Match
India v Zimbabwe, Group B
Grace Road, Leicester
11 June 1983 (60-over match)

Result: India won by 5 wickets
Points: India 4, Zimbabwe 0
Toss: India
Umpires: J Birkenshaw and R Palmer
ODI Debuts: RD Brown (Zim)
Man Of The Match: S Madan Lal

Zimbabwe innings (60 overs maximum)			R	B	4	6
AH Omarshah	c Kirmani	b Sandhu	8	32	1	0
GA Paterson	lbw	b Madan Lal	22	51	2	0
JG Heron	c Kirmani	b Madan Lal	18	30	2	0
AJ Pycroft	c Shastri	b Binny	14	21	1	0
+DL Houghton	c Kirmani	b Madan Lal	21	47	1	0
*DAG Fletcher	b Kapil Dev		13	32	0	0
KM Curran	run out		8	16	0	0
IP Butchart	not out		22	35	2	0
RD Brown	c Kirmani	b Shastri	6	27	0	0
PWE Rawson	c Kirmani	b Binny	3	6	0	0
AJ Traicos	run out		2	13	0	0
Extras (lb 9, w 9): **18**						
Total (all out, 51.4 overs): **155**						

FoW: 1-13 (Omarshah), 2-55 (Heron), 3-56 (Paterson), 4-71 (Pycroft), 5-106 (Fletcher), 6-114 (Houghton), 7-115 (Curran), 8-139 (Brown), 9-148 (Rawson), 10-155 (Traicos).

Bowling	O	M	R	W
Kapil Dev	9	3	18	1
Sandhu	9	1	29	1
Madan Lal	10.4	0	27	3
Binny	11	2	25	2
Shastri	12	1	38	1

India innings (target: 156 runs from 60 overs)			R	B	4	6
K Srikkanth	c Butchart	b Rawson	20	27	0	0
SM Gavaskar	c Heron	b Rawson	4	11	0	0
M Amarnath	c sub	b Traicos	44	79	4	0
SM Patil	b Fletcher		50	54	7	1
RJ Shastri	c Brown	b Omarshah	17	27	1	0
Yashpal Sharma	not out		18	19	2	0
*N Kapil Dev	not out		2	8	0	0
Extras (w 2): **2**						
Total (5 wickets, 37.3 overs): **157**						

DNB: RMH Binny, S Madan Lal, +SMH Kirmani, BS Sandhu.
FoW: 1-13 (Gavaskar), 2-32 (Srikkanth), 3-101 (Amarnath), 4-128 (Patil), 5-148 (Shastri).

Bowling	O	M	R	W
Rawson	5.1	1	11	2
Curran	6.5	1	33	0
Butchart	5	1	21	0
Traicos	11	1	41	1
Fletcher	6	1	32	1
Omarshah	3.3	0	17	1

Prudential World Cup, 1983, 11th Match
Australia v India, Group B
Trent Bridge, Nottingham
13 June 1983 (60-over match)

Result: Australia won by 162 runs
Points: Australia 4, India 0
Toss: Australia
Umpires: DO Oslear and R Palmer
Man Of The Match: TM Chappell

Australia innings (60 overs maximum)

			R	B	4	6
KC Wessels	b Kapil Dev		5	11	1	0
TM Chappell	c Srikkanth	b Amarnath	110	131	11	0
*KJ Hughes	b Madan Lal		52	86	3	0
DW Hookes	c Kapil Dev	b Madan Lal	1	4	0	0
GN Yallop	not out		66	73	5	0
AR Border	c Yashpal Sharma	b Binny	26	23	1	0
+RW Marsh	c Sandhu	b Kapil Dev	12	15	1	0
KH MacLeay	c & b Kapil Dev		4	5	0	0
TG Hogan	b Kapil Dev		11	9	0	1
GF Lawson	c Srikkanth	b Kapil Dev	6	3	1	0
RM Hogg	not out		2	2	0	0

*Extras (b 1, lb 14, w 8, nb 2): **25***
*Total (9 wickets, 60 overs): **320***

FoW: 1-11 (Wessels), 2-155 (Hughes), 3-159 (Hookes), 4-206 (Chappell), 5-254 (Border), 6-277 (Marsh), 7-289 (MacLeay), 8-301 (Hogan), 9-307 (Lawson).

Bowling

	O	M	R	W
Kapil Dev	12	2	43	5
Sandhu	12	1	52	0
Binny	12	0	52	1
Shastri	2	0	16	0
Madan Lal	12	0	69	2
Patil	6	0	36	0
Amarnath	4	0	27	1

India innings (target: 321 runs from 60 overs)

			R	B	4	6
RJ Shastri	lbw	b Lawson	11	18	1	0
K Srikkanth	c Border	b Hogan	39	63	6	0
M Amarnath	run out		2	17	0	0
DB Vengsarkar	lbw	b MacLeay	5	14	1	0
SM Patil	b MacLeay		0	7	0	0
Yashpal Sharma	c & b MacLeay		3	11	0	0
*N Kapil Dev	b Hogan		40	27	2	1
S Madan Lal	c Hogan	b MacLeay	27	39	2	0
RMH Binny	lbw	b MacLeay	0	6	0	0
+SMH Kirmani	b MacLeay		12	23	2	0
BS Sandhu	not out		9	12	0	1

*Extras (b 1, lb 4, w 3, nb 2): **10***
*Total (all out, 37.5 overs): **158***

FoW: 1-38 (Shastri), 2-43 (Amarnath), 3-57 (Vengsarkar), 4-57 (Patil), 5-64 (Yashpal Sharma), 6-66 (Srikkanth), 7-124 (Madan Lal), 8-126 (Binny), 9-136 (Kapil Dev), 10-158 (Kirmani).

Bowling

	O	M	R	W
Lawson	5	1	25	1
Hogg	7	2	23	0
Hogan	12	1	48	2
MacLeay	11.5	3	39	6
Border	2	0	13	0

Prudential World Cup, 1983, 12th Match
West Indies v Zimbabwe, Group B
County Ground, New Road, Worcester
13 June 1983 (60-over match)

Result: West Indies won by 8 wickets
Points: West Indies 4, Zimbabwe 0
Toss: West Indies
Umpires: J Birkenshaw and DGL Evans
ODI Debuts: GE Peckover (Zim)
Man Of The Match: CG Greenidge

Zimbabwe innings (60 overs maximum)			R	B	4	6
AH Omarshah	b Roberts		2	20	0	0
GA Paterson	c Dujon	b Holding	4	20	0	0
JG Heron	st Dujon	b Gomes	12	73	0	0
AJ Pycroft	run out		13	35	1	0
+DL Houghton	c Dujon	b Roberts	54	92	5	1
*DAG Fletcher	not out		71	88	7	0
KM Curran	b Roberts		7	15	1	0
IP Butchart	lbw	b Holding	0	3	0	0
GE Peckover	not out		16	21	3	0
Extras (b 1, lb 23, w 7, nb 7): ***38***						
Total (7 wickets, 60 overs): ***217***						

DNB: PWE Rawson, AJ Traicos.
FoW: 1-7 (Omarshah), 2-7 (Paterson), 3-35 (Pycroft), 4-65 (Heron), 5-157 (Houghton), 6-181 (Curran), 7-183 (Butchart).

Bowling	O	M	R	W
Roberts	12	4	36	3
Holding	12	2	33	2
Daniel	12	4	21	0
Davis	12	2	34	0
Gomes	8	0	42	1
Richards	4	1	13	0

West Indies innings (target: 218 runs from 60 overs)			R	B	4	6
CG Greenidge	not out		105	147	5	1
DL Haynes	c Houghton	b Rawson	2	5	0	0
IVA Richards	lbw	b Rawson	16	13	2	0
HA Gomes	not out		75	128	5	0
Extras (b 1, lb 8, w 9, nb 2): ***20***						
Total (2 wickets, 48.3 overs): ***218***						

DNB: SFAF Bacchus, *CH Lloyd, +PJL Dujon, AME Roberts, MA Holding, WW Daniel, WW Davis.
FoW: 1-3 (Haynes), 2-23 (Richards).

Bowling	O	M	R	W
Rawson	12	1	39	2
Curran	10.3	1	37	0
Butchart	9	1	40	0
Fletcher	4	0	22	0
Traicos	9	0	37	0
Omarshah	4	0	23	0

Prudential World Cup, 1983, 14th Match
India v West Indies, Group B
Kennington Oval, London
15 June 1983 (60-over match)

Result: West Indies won by 66 runs
Points: West Indies 4, India 0
Toss: West Indies
Umpires: BJ Meyer and DR Shepherd
Man Of The Match: IVA Richards

West Indies innings (60 overs maximum)

			R	B	4	6
CG Greenidge	c Vengsarkar	b Kapil Dev	9	13		
DL Haynes	c Kapil Dev	b Amarnath	38	93		
IVA Richards	c Kirmani	b Sandhu	119	146	6	1
*CH Lloyd	run out		41	42		
SFAF Bacchus	b Binny		8	8		
+PJL Dujon	c Shastri	b Binny	9	13		
HA Gomes	not out		27	22		
AME Roberts	c Patil	b Binny	7	9		
MD Marshall	run out		4	7	0	
MA Holding	c sub	b Madan Lal	2	5	0	0
WW Davis	not out		0	2	0	0

Extras (lb 13, w 5): 18
Total (9 wickets, 60 overs): 282

FoW: 1-17 (Greenidge), 2-118 (Haynes), 3-198 (Lloyd), 4-213 (Bacchus), 5-239 (Dujon), 6-240 (Richards), 7-257 (Roberts), 8-270 (Marshall), 9-280 (Holding).

Bowling	O	M	R	W
Kapil Dev	12	0	46	1
Sandhu	12	2	42	1
Binny	12	0	71	3
Amarnath	12	0	58	1
Madan Lal	12	0	47	1

India innings (target: 283 runs from 60 overs)

			R	B	4	6
K Srikkanth	c Dujon	b Roberts	2	9	0	0
RJ Shastri	c Dujon	b Roberts	6	15		
M Amarnath	c Lloyd	b Holding	80	139		
DB Vengsarkar	retired hurt		32	59		
SM Patil	c & b Gomes		21	31		
Yashpal Sharma	run out		9	10		
*N Kapil Dev	c Haynes	b Holding	36	46		
RMH Binny	lbw	b Holding	1	4	0	0
S Madan Lal	not out		8	15		
+SMH Kirmani	b Marshall		0	2	0	0
BS Sandhu	run out		0	2	0	0

Extras (b 3, lb 13, nb 5): 21
Total (all out, 53.1 overs): 216

FoW: 1-2 (Srikkanth), 2-21 (Shastri), 3-130 (Patil), 4-143 (Yashpal Sharma), 5-193 (Amarnath), 6-195 (Binny), 7-212 (Kapil Dev), 8-214 (Kirmani), 9-216 (Sandhu).

Bowling	O	M	R	W
Roberts	9	1	29	2
Holding	9.1	0	40	3
Marshall	11	3	20	1
Davis	12	2	51	0
Gomes	12	1	55	1

Prudential World Cup, 1983, 16th Match
Australia v Zimbabwe, Group B
County Ground, Southampton
16 June 1983 (60-over match)

Result: Australia won by 32 runs
Points: Australia 4, Zimbabwe 0
Toss: Australia
Umpires: DGL Evans and R Palmer
Man Of The Match: DL Houghton

Australia innings (60 overs maximum)

			R	B	4	6
GM Wood	c Rawson	b Traicos	73	121	5	0
TM Chappell	c Traicos	b Rawson	22	29	4	0
*KJ Hughes	b Traicos		31	59	2	0
DW Hookes	c Brown	b Fletcher	10	21	0	0
GN Yallop	c Houghton	b Curran	20	42	3	0
AR Border	b Butchart		43	47	2	0
+RW Marsh	not out		35	28	2	1
KH MacLeay	c Rawson	b Butchart	9	9	0	1
TG Hogan	not out		5	10	0	0

Extras (lb 16, w 2, nb 6): **24**
Total (7 wickets, 60 overs): **272**

DNB: DK Lillee, RM Hogg.
FoW: 1-46 (Chappell), 2-124 (Hughes), 3-150 (Wood), 4-150 (Hookes), 5-219 (Yallop), 6-231 (Border), 7-249 (MacLeay).

Bowling

	O	M	R	W
Hogg	9	2	34	0
Rawson	9	0	50	1
Fletcher	9	1	27	1
Butchart	10	0	52	2
Traicos	12	1	28	2
Curran	11	0	57	1

Zimbabwe innings (target: 273 runs from 60 overs)

			R	B	4	6
RD Brown	c Marsh	b Hogan	38	80	4	0
GA Paterson	lbw	b Hogg	17	41	1	0
JG Heron	run out		3	11	0	0
AJ Pycroft	run out		13	24	1	0
+DL Houghton	c Hughes	b Chappell	84	108	9	1
*DAG Fletcher	b Hogan		2	11	0	0
KM Curran	lbw	b Chappell	35	53	2	0
IP Butchart	lbw	b Hogg	0	1	0	0
PWE Rawson	lbw	b Hogg	0	1	0	0
AJ Traicos	b Chappell		19	21	1	0
VR Hogg	not out		7	19	0	0

Extras (b 1, lb 10, w 1, nb 10): **22**
Total (all out, 59.5 overs): **240**

FoW: 1-48 (Paterson), 2-53 (Heron), 3-79 (Pycroft), 4-97 (Brown), 5-109 (Fletcher), 6-212 (Curran), 7-213 (Butchart), 8-213 (Rawson), 9-213 (Houghton), 10-240 (Traicos).

Bowling

	O	M	R	W
Hogg	12	0	40	3
Lillee	9	1	23	0
Hogan	12	0	33	2
MacLeay	9	0	45	0
Border	9	1	30	0
Chappell	8.5	0	47	3

Prudential World Cup, 1983, 19th Match
Australia v West Indies, Group B
Lord's, London
18 June 1983 (60-over match)

Result: West Indies won by 7 wickets
Points: West Indies 4, Australia 0
Toss: Australia
Umpires: KE Palmer and AGT Whitehead
Man Of The Match: IVA Richards

Australia innings (60 overs maximum)			R	B	4	6
GM Wood	b Marshall		17	24	0	0
TM Chappell	c Dujon	b Marshall	5	14	1	0
*KJ Hughes	b Gomes		69	124	8	0
DW Hookes	c Greenidge	b Davis	56	74	4	2
GN Yallop	not out		52	74	3	0
AR Border	c & b Gomes		11	24	1	0
+RW Marsh	c Haynes	b Holding	37	26	4	2
TG Hogan	not out		0	1	0	0
Extras (b 1, lb 18, w 6, nb 1): **26**						
Total (6 wickets, 60 overs): **273**						

DNB: JR Thomson, DK Lillee, RM Hogg.
FoW: 1-10 (Chappell), 2-37 (Wood), 3-138 (Hookes), 4-176 (Hughes), 5-202 (Border), 6-266 (Marsh).

Bowling	O	M	R	W
Roberts	12	0	51	0
Marshall	12	0	36	2
Davis	12	0	57	1
Holding	12	1	56	1
Gomes	12	0	47	2

West Indies innings (target: 274 runs from 60 overs)			R	B	4	6
CG Greenidge	c Hughes	b Hogg	90	140	8	0
DL Haynes	b Hogan		33	46	3	0
IVA Richards	not out		95	117	9	3
HA Gomes	b Chappell		15	26	1	0
*CH Lloyd	not out		19	22	3	0
Extras (b 3, lb 18, w 1, nb 2): **24**						
Total (3 wickets, 57.5 overs): **276**						

DNB: SFAF Bacchus, +PJL Dujon, MD Marshall, AME Roberts, MA Holding, WW Davis.
FoW: 1-79 (Haynes), 2-203 (Greenidge), 3-228 (Gomes).

Bowling	O	M	R	W
Hogg	12	0	25	1
Thomson	11	0	64	0
Hogan	12	0	60	1
Lillee	12	0	52	0
Chappell	10.5	0	51	1

Prudential World Cup, 1983, 20th Match
India v Zimbabwe, Group B
Nevill Ground, Tunbridge Wells
18 June 1983 (60-over match)

Result: India won by 31 runs
Points: India 4, Zimbabwe 0
Toss: India
Umpires: MJ Kitchen and BJ Meyer
Man Of The Match: N Kapil Dev

India innings (60 overs maximum)

			R	B	4	6
SM Gavaskar	lbw	b Rawson	0	2	0	0
K Srikkanth	c Butchart	b Curran	0	13	0	0
M Amarnath	c Houghton	b Rawson	5	20	1	0
SM Patil	c Houghton	b Curran	1	10	0	0
Yashpal Sharma	c Houghton	b Rawson	9	28	1	0
*N Kapil Dev	not out		175	138	16	6
RMH Binny	lbw	b Traicos	22	48	2	0
RJ Shastri	c Pycroft	b Fletcher	1	6	0	0
S Madan Lal	c Houghton	b Curran	17	39	1	0
+SMH Kirmani	not out		24	56	2	0
Extras (lb 9, w 3): **12**						
Total (8 wickets, 60 overs): **266**						

DNB: BS Sandhu.
FoW: 1-0 (Gavaskar), 2-6 (Srikkanth), 3-6 (Amarnath), 4-9 (Patil), 5-17 (Yashpal Sharma), 6-77 (Binny), 7-78 (Shastri), 8-140 (Madan Lal).

Bowling	O	M	R	W
Rawson	12	4	47	3
Curran	12	1	65	3
Butchart	12	2	38	0
Fletcher	12	2	59	1
Traicos	12	0	45	1

Zimbabwe innings (target: 267 runs from 60 overs)

			R	B	4	6
RD Brown	run out		35	66	2	0
GA Paterson	lbw	b Binny	23	35	4	0
JG Heron	run out		3	8	0	0
AJ Pycroft	c Kirmani	b Sandhu	6	15	0	0
+DL Houghton	lbw	b Madan Lal	17	35	2	0
*DAG Fletcher	c Kapil Dev	b Amarnath	13	23	0	0
KM Curran	c Shastri	b Madan Lal	73	93	8	0
IP Butchart	b Binny		18	43	1	0
GE Peckover	c Yashpal Sharma	b Madan Lal	14	18	0	0
PWE Rawson	not out		2	6	0	0
AJ Traicos	c & b Kapil Dev		3	7	0	0
Extras (lb 17, w 7, nb 4): **28**						
Total (all out, 57 overs): **235**						

FoW: 1-44 (Paterson), 2-48 (Heron), 3-61 (Pycroft), 4-86 (Brown), 5-103 (Houghton), 6-113 (Fletcher), 7-168 (Butchart), 8-189 (Peckover), 9-230 (Curran), 10-235 (Traicos).

Bowling	O	M	R	W
Kapil Dev	11	1	32	1
Sandhu	11	2	44	1
Binny	11	2	45	2
Madan Lal	11	2	42	3
Amarnath	12	1	37	1
Shastri	1	0	7	0

Prudential World Cup, 1983, 23rd Match
Australia v India, Group B
County Ground, Chelmsford
20 June 1983 (60-over match)

Result: India won by 118 runs
Points: India 4, Australia 0
Toss: India
Umpires: J Birkenshaw and DR Shepherd
Man Of The Match: RMH Binny

India innings (60 overs maximum)			R	B	4	6
SM Gavaskar	c Chappell	b Hogg	9	10	1	0
K Srikkanth	c Border	b Thomson	24	22	3	0
M Amarnath	c Marsh	b Thomson	13	20	2	0
Yashpal Sharma	c Hogg	b Hogan	40	40	1	0
SM Patil	c Hogan	b MacLeay	30	25	4	0
*N Kapil Dev	c Hookes	b Hogg	28	32	3	0
KBJ Azad	c Border	b Lawson	15	18	1	0
RMH Binny	run out		21	32	2	0
S Madan Lal	not out		12	15	0	0
+SMH Kirmani	lbw	b Hogg	10	20	1	0
BS Sandhu	b Thomson		8	18	1	0
Extras (lb 13, w 9, nb 15): **37**						
Total (all out, 55.5 overs): **247**						

FoW: 1-27 (Gavaskar), 2-54 (Srikkanth), 3-65 (Amarnath), 4-118 (Patil), 5-157 (Yashpal Sharma), 6-174 (Kapil Dev), 7-207 (Azad), 8-215 (Binny), 9-232 (Kirmani), 10-247 (Sandhu).

Bowling	O	M	R	W
Lawson	10	1	40	1
Hogg	12	2	40	3
Hogan	11	1	31	1
Thomson	10.5	0	51	3
MacLeay	12	2	48	1

Australia innings (target: 248 runs from 60 overs)			R	B	4	6
TM Chappell	c Madan Lal	b Sandhu	2	5	0	0
GM Wood	c Kirmani	b Binny	21	32	2	0
GN Yallop	c & b Binny		18	30	2	0
*DW Hookes	b Binny		1	2	0	0
AR Border	b Madan Lal		36	49	5	0
+RW Marsh	lbw	b Madan Lal	0	2	0	0
KH MacLeay	c Gavaskar	b Madan Lal	5	6	1	0
TG Hogan	c Srikkanth	b Binny	8	10	2	0
GF Lawson	b Sandhu		16	20	1	0
RM Hogg	not out		8	12	1	0
JR Thomson	b Madan Lal		0	5	0	0
Extras (lb 5, w 5, nb 4): **14**						
Total (all out, 38.2 overs): **129**						

FoW: 1-3 (Chappell), 2-46 (Wood), 3-48 (Hookes), 4-52 (Yallop), 5-52 (Marsh), 6-69 (MacLeay), 7-78 (Hogan), 8-115 (Lawson), 9-129 (Border), 10-129 (Thomson).

Bowling	O	M	R	W
Kapil Dev	8	2	16	0
Sandhu	10	1	26	2
Madan Lal	8.2	3	20	4
Binny	8	2	29	4
Amarnath	2	0	17	0
Azad	2	0	7	0

Prudential World Cup, 1983, 24th Match
West Indies v Zimbabwe, Group B
Edgbaston, Birmingham
20 June 1983 (60-over match)

Result: West Indies won by 10 wickets
Points: West Indies 4, Zimbabwe 0
Toss: Zimbabwe
Umpires: HD Bird and DJ Constant
Man Of The Match: SFAF Bacchus

Zimbabwe innings (60 overs maximum)

			R	B	4	6
RD Brown	c Lloyd	b Marshall	14	69	0	0
GA Paterson	c Richards	b Garner	6	28	1	0
JG Heron	c Dujon	b Garner	0	1	0	0
AJ Pycroft	c Dujon	b Marshall	4	39	0	0
+DL Houghton	c Lloyd	b Daniel	0	3	0	0
*DAG Fletcher	b Richards		23	51	2	0
KM Curran	b Daniel		62	92	4	1
IP Butchart	c Haynes	b Richards	8	27	0	0
GE Peckover	c & b Richards		3	15	0	0
PWE Rawson	b Daniel		19	40	1	0
AJ Traicos	not out		1	2	0	0
*Extras (b 4, lb 13, w 7, nb 7): **31***						
*Total (all out, 60 overs): **171***						

FoW: 1-17 (Paterson), 2-17 (Heron), 3-41 (Pycroft), 4-42 (Houghton), 5-42 (Brown), 6-79 (Fletcher), 7-104 (Butchart), 8-115 (Peckover), 9-170 (Curran), 10-171 (Rawson).

Bowling

	O	M	R	W
Marshall	12	3	19	2
Garner	7	4	13	2
Davis	8	2	13	0
Daniel	9	2	28	3
Gomes	12	2	26	0
Richards	12	1	41	3

West Indies innings (target: 172 runs from 60 overs)

		R	B	4	6
DL Haynes	not out	88	136	9	0
SFAF Bacchus	not out	80	135	8	0
*Extras (lb 1, w 3): **4***					
*Total (0 wickets, 45.1 overs): **172***					

DNB: AL Logie, IVA Richards, HA Gomes, *CH Lloyd, +PJL Dujon, MD Marshall, J Garner, WW Daniel, WW Davis.

Bowling

	O	M	R	W
Rawson	12	3	38	0
Butchart	4	0	23	0
Traicos	12	2	24	0
Curran	9	0	44	0
Fletcher	8.1	0	39	0

1983 WORLD CUP

Finals

Prudential World Cup, 1983, 1st Semi-Final
England v India
Old Trafford, Manchester
22 June 1983 (60-over match)

Result: India won by 6 wickets
India advances to the final
Toss: England
Umpires: DGL Evans and DO Oslear
Man Of The Match: M Amarnath

England innings (60 overs maximum)			R	B	4	6
G Fowler	b Binny		33	59	3	0
CJ Tavare	c Kirmani	b Binny	32	51	4	0
DI Gower	c Kirmani	b Amarnath	17	30	1	0
AJ Lamb	run out		29	58	1	0
MW Gatting	b Amarnath		18	46	1	0
IT Botham	b Azad		6	26	0	0
+IJ Gould	run out		13	36	0	0
VJ Marks	b Kapil Dev		8	18	0	0
GR Dilley	not out		20	26	2	0
PJW Allott	c Patil	b Kapil Dev	8	14	0	0
*RGD Willis	b Kapil Dev		0	2	0	0

Extras (b 1, lb 17, w 7, nb 4): **29**
Total (all out, 60 overs): **213**

FoW: 1-69 (Tavare), 2-84 (Fowler), 3-107 (Gower), 4-141 (Lamb), 5-150 (Gatting), 6-160 (Botham), 7-175 (Gould), 8-177 (Marks), 9-202 (Allott), 10-213 (Willis).

Bowling	O	M	R	W
Kapil Dev	11	1	35	3
Sandhu	8	1	36	0
Binny	12	1	43	2
Madan Lal	5	0	15	0
Azad	12	1	28	1
Amarnath	12	1	27	2

India innings (target: 214 runs from 60 overs)			R	B	4	6
SM Gavaskar	c Gould	b Allott	25	41	3	0
K Srikkanth	c Willis	b Botham	19	44	3	0
M Amarnath	run out		46	92	4	1
Yashpal Sharma	c Allott	b Willis	61	115	3	2
SM Patil	not out		51	32	8	0
*N Kapil Dev	not out		1	6	0	0

Extras (b 5, lb 6, w 1, nb 2): **14**
Total (4 wickets, 54.4 overs): **217**

DNB: KBJ Azad, RMH Binny, S Madan Lal, +SMH Kirmani, BS Sandhu.
FoW: 1-46 (Srikkanth), 2-50 (Gavaskar), 3-142 (Amarnath), 4-205 (Yashpal Sharma).

Bowling	O	M	R	W
Willis	10.4	2	42	1
Dilley	11	0	43	0
Allott	10	3	40	1
Botham	11	4	40	1
Marks	12	1	38	0

Prudential World Cup, 1983, 2nd Semi-Final
Pakistan v West Indies
Kennington Oval, London
22 June 1983 (60-over match)

Result: West Indies won by 8 wickets
West Indies advances to the final
Toss: West Indies
Umpires: DJ Constant and AGT Whitehead
Man Of The Match: IVA Richards

Pakistan innings (60 overs maximum)			R	B	4	6
Mohsin Khan	b Roberts		70	176	1	0
Mudassar Nazar	c & b Garner		11	39	0	0
Ijaz Faqih	c Dujon	b Holding	5	19	0	0
Zaheer Abbas	b Gomes		30	38	1	0
*Imran Khan	c Dujon	b Marshall	17	41	0	0
Wasim Raja	lbw	b Marshall	0	3	0	0
Shahid Mahboob	c Richards	b Marshall	6	10	0	0
Sarfraz Nawaz	c Holding	b Roberts	3	12	0	0
Abdul Qadir	not out		10	21	0	0
+Wasim Bari	not out		4	7	0	0
Extras (b 6, lb 13, w 4, nb 5): **28**						
Total (8 wickets, 60 overs): **184**						

DNB: Rashid Khan.

FoW: 1-23 (Mudassar Nazar), 2-34 (Ijaz Faqih), 3-88 (Zaheer Abbas), 4-139 (Imran Khan), 5-139 (Wasim Raja), 6-159 (Shahid Mahboob), 7-164 (Sarfraz Nawaz), 8-171 (Mohsin Khan).

Bowling	O	M	R	W
Roberts	12	3	25	2
Garner	12	1	31	1
Marshall	12	2	28	3
Holding	12	1	25	1
Gomes	7	0	29	1
Richards	5	0	18	0

West Indies innings (target: 185 runs from 60 overs)			R	B	4	6
CG Greenidge	lbw	b Rashid Khan	17	38		
DL Haynes	b Abdul Qadir		29	58		
IVA Richards	not out		80	96	11	1
HA Gomes	not out		50	100	3	0
Extras (b 2, lb 6, w 4): **12**						
Total (2 wickets, 48.4 overs): **188**						

DNB: *CH Lloyd, SFAF Bacchus, +PJL Dujon, MD Marshall, AME Roberts, J Garner, MA Holding.
FoW: 1-34 (Greenidge), 2-56 (Haynes).

Bowling	O	M	R	W
Rashid Khan	12	2	32	1
Sarfraz Nawaz	8	0	23	0
Abdul Qadir	11	1	42	1
Shahid Mahboob	11	1	43	0
Wasim Raja	1	0	9	0
Zaheer Abbas	4.4	1	24	0
Mohsin Khan	1	0	3	0

Prudential World Cup, 1983, Final
India v West Indies
Lord's, London
25 June 1983 (60-over match)

Result: India won by 43 runs
India wins the 1983 Prudential World Cup
Toss: West Indies
Umpires: HD Bird and BJ Meyer
Man Of The Match: M Amarnath

India innings (60 overs maximum)			R	M	B	4	6
SM Gavaskar	c Dujon	b Roberts	2	14	12	0	0
K Srikkanth	lbw	b Marshall	38	82	57	7	1
M Amarnath	b Holding		26	108	80	3	0
Yashpal Sharma	c sub (AL Logie)	b Gomes	11	45	32	1	0
SM Patil	c Gomes	b Garner	27	48	29	0	1
*N Kapil Dev	c Holding	b Gomes	15	10	8	3	0
KBJ Azad	c Garner	b Roberts	0	3	3	0	0
RMH Binny	c Garner	b Roberts	2	9	8	0	0
S Madan Lal	b Marshall		17	31	27	0	1
+SMH Kirmani	b Holding		14	55	43	0	0
BS Sandhu	not out		11	42	30	1	0

Extras (b 5, lb 5, w 9, nb 1): **20**
Total (all out, 54.4 overs): **183**

FoW: 1-2 (Gavaskar), 2-59 (Srikkanth), 3-90 (Amarnath), 4-92 (Yashpal Sharma), 5-110 (Kapil Dev), 6-111 (Azad), 7-130 (Binny), 8-153 (Patil), 9-161 (Madan Lal), 10-183 (Kirmani).

Bowling	O	M	R	W
Roberts	10	3	32	3
Garner	12	4	24	1
Marshall	11	1	24	2
Holding	9.4	2	26	2
Gomes	11	1	49	2
Richards	1	0	8	0

West Indies innings (target: 184 from 60 overs)			R	M	B	4	6
CG Greenidge	b Sandhu		1	11	12	0	0
DL Haynes	c Binny	b Madan Lal	13	45	33	2	0
IVA Richards	c Kapil Dev	b Madan Lal	33	42	28	7	0
*CH Lloyd	c Kapil Dev	b Binny	8	32	17	1	0
HA Gomes	c Gavaskar	b Madan Lal	5	18	16	0	0
SFAF Bacchus	c Kirmani	b Sandhu	8	37	25	0	0
+PJL Dujon	b Amarnath		25	94	73	0	1
MD Marshall	c Gavaskar	b Amarnath	18	73	51	0	0
AME Roberts	lbw	b Kapil Dev	4	16	14	0	0
J Garner	not out		5	34	19	0	0
MA Holding	lbw	b Amarnath	6	28	24	0	0

Extras (lb 4, w 10): **14**
Total (all out, 52 overs): **140**

FoW: 1-5 (Greenidge), 2-50 (Haynes), 3-57 (Richards), 4-66 (Gomes), 5-66 (Lloyd), 6-76 (Bacchus), 7-119 (Dujon), 8-124 (Marshall), 9-126 (Roberts), 10-140 (Holding).

Bowling	O	M	R	W
Kapil Dev	11	4	21	1
Sandhu	9	1	32	2
Madan Lal	12	2	31	3
Binny	10	1	23	1
Amarnath	7	0	12	3
Azad	3	0	7	0

1987 WORLD CUP

Group A

Reliance World Cup, 1987/88, 3rd Match
India v Australia, Group A
MA Chidambaram Stadium, Chepauk, Madras
9 October 1987 (50-over match)

Result: Australia won by 1 run
Points: Australia 4, India 0
Toss: India
Umpires: DM Archer (WI) and HD Bird (Eng)
ODI Debuts: TM Moody (Aus); NS Sidhu (Ind)
Man Of The Match: GR Marsh

Australia innings (50 overs maximum)			R	B	4	6
DC Boon	lbw	b Shastri	49	68	5	0
GR Marsh	c Azharuddin	b Prabhakar	110	141	7	1
DM Jones	c Sidhu	b Maninder Singh	39	35	2	2
*AR Border	b Binny		16	22	0	0
TM Moody	c Kapil Dev	b Prabhakar	8	13	1	0
SR Waugh	not out		19	17	0	0
SP O'Donnell	run out		7	10	0	0
Extras (lb 18, w 2, nb 2): **22**						
Total (6 wickets, 50 overs): **270**						

DNB: +GC Dyer, PL Taylor, CJ McDermott, BA Reid.
FoW: 1-110 (Boon), 2-174 (Jones), 3-228 (Border), 4-237 (Marsh), 5-251 (Moody), 6-270 (O'Donnell).

Bowling	O	M	R	W
Kapil Dev	10	0	41	0
Prabhakar	10	0	47	2
Binny	7	0	46	1
Maninder Singh	10	0	48	1
Shastri	10	0	50	1
Azharuddin	3	0	20	0

India innings (target: 271 runs from 50 overs)			R	B	4	6
SM Gavaskar	c Reid	b Taylor	37	32	6	1
K Srikkanth	lbw	b Waugh	70	83	7	0
NS Sidhu	b McDermott		73	79	4	5
DB Vengsarkar	c Jones	b McDermott	29	45	2	0
M Azharuddin	b McDermott		10	14	1	0
*N Kapil Dev	c Boon	b O'Donnell	6	10	0	0
RJ Shastri	c & b McDermott		12	11	1	0
+KS More	not out		12	14	2	0
RMH Binny	run out		0	3	0	0
M Prabhakar	run out		5	7	0	0
Maninder Singh	b Waugh		4	5	0	0
Extras (b 2, lb 7, w 2): **11**						
Total (all out, 49.5 overs): **269**						

FoW: 1-69 (Gavaskar), 2-131 (Srikkanth), 3-207 (Sidhu), 4-229 (Azharuddin), 5-232 (Vengsarkar), 6-246 (Shastri), 7-256 (Kapil Dev), 8-256 (Binny), 9-265 (Prabhakar), 10-269 (Maninder Singh).

Bowling	O	M	R	W
McDermott	10	0	56	4
Reid	10	2	35	0
O'Donnell	9	1	32	1
Taylor	5	0	46	1
Waugh	9.5	0	52	2
Border	6	0	39	0

Reliance World Cup, 1987/88, 4th Match
New Zealand v Zimbabwe, Group A
Lal Bahadur Shastri Stadium, Hyderabad, Deccan
10 October 1987 (50-over match)

Result: New Zealand won by 3 runs
Points: New Zealand 4, Zimbabwe 0
Toss: Zimbabwe
Umpires: Mahboob Shah (Pak) and PW Vidanagamage (SL)
ODI Debuts: AH Jones (NZ); EA Brandes, AC Waller (Zim)
Man Of The Match: DL Houghton

New Zealand innings (50 overs maximum)			R	M	B	4	6
MC Snedden	c Waller	b Rawson	64	130	96	3	0
JG Wright	c Houghton	b Traicos	18	54	40	1	0
MD Crowe	c & b Rawson		72	93	88	5	1
AH Jones	c Brandes	b Omarshah	0	4	6	0	0
*JJ Crowe	c Brown	b Curran	31	38	35	2	0
DN Patel	lbw	b Omarshah	0	3	2	0	0
JG Bracewell	not out		13	38	20	0	0
+IDS Smith	c Brown	b Curran	29	14	20	2	1
SL Boock	not out		0	1	0	0	0
Extras (b 4, lb 4, w 4, nb 3): **15**							
Total (7 wickets, 50 overs): **242**							

DNB: EJ Chatfield, W Watson.
FoW: 1-59 (Wright), 2-143 (Snedden), 3-145 (Jones), 4-166 (MD Crowe), 5-169 (Patel), 6-205 (JJ Crowe), 7-240 (Smith).

Bowling	O	M	R	W
Curran	10	0	51	2
Rawson	10	0	62	2
Brandes	7	2	24	0
Traicos	10	2	28	1
Butchart	4	0	27	0
Omarshah	9	0	42	2

Zimbabwe innings (target: 243 runs from 50 overs)			R	M	B	4	6
RD Brown	c JJ Crowe	b Chatfield	1	10	10	0	0
AH Omarshah	lbw	b Snedden	5	11	13	0	0
+DL Houghton	c MD Crowe	b Snedden	142	178	137	13	6
AJ Pycroft	run out		12	37	22	2	0
KM Curran	c Boock	b Watson	4	6	8	0	0
AC Waller	c Smith	b Watson	5	17	14	0	0
GA Paterson	c Smith	b Boock	2	10	11	0	0
PWE Rawson	lbw	b Boock	1	10	10	0	0
IP Butchart	run out		54	98	70	2	1
EA Brandes	run out		0	1	0	0	0
*AJ Traicos	not out		4	13	6	0	0
Extras (lb 7, w 1, nb 1): **9**							
Total (all out, 49.4 overs): **239**							

FoW: 1-8 (Brown), 2-10 (Omarshah), 3-61 (Pycroft), 4-67 (Curran), 5-86 (Waller), 6-94 (Paterson), 7-104 (Rawson), 8-221 (Houghton), 9-221 (Brandes), 10-239 (Butchart).

Bowling	O	M	R	W
Chatfield	10	2	26	1
Snedden	9	0	53	2
Watson	10	2	36	2
Bracewell	7	0	48	0
Patel	5	0	27	0
Boock	8.4	0	42	2

Reliance World Cup, 1987/88, 6th Match
Australia v Zimbabwe, Group A
MA Chidambaram Stadium, Chepauk, Madras
13 October 1987 (50-over match)

Result: Australia won by 96 runs
Points: Australia 4, Zimbabwe 0
Toss: Zimbabwe
Umpires: Khizer Hayat (Pak) and DR Shepherd (Eng)
ODI Debuts: TBA May (Aus); MP Jarvis (Zim)
Man Of The Match: SR Waugh

Australia innings (50 overs maximum)			R	M	B	4	6
GR Marsh	c Curran	b Omarshah	62	146	101	8	0
DC Boon	c Houghton	b Curran	2	19	15	0	0
DM Jones	run out		2	17	12	0	0
*AR Border	c Omarshah	b Butchart	67	91	88	8	0
SR Waugh	run out		45	48	41	3	2
SP O'Donnell	run out		3	10	11	0	0
+GC Dyer	c Paterson	b Butchart	27	35	20	1	2
PL Taylor	not out		17	22	13	1	0
CJ McDermott	c Brown	b Curran	1	3	3	0	0
TBA May	run out		1	3	1	0	0
Extras (w 8): **8**							
Total (9 wickets, 50 overs): **235**							

DNB: BA Reid.
FoW: 1-10 (Boon), 2-20 (Jones), 3-133 (Border), 4-143 (Marsh), 5-155 (O'Donnell), 6-202 (Dyer), 7-228 (Waugh), 8-230 (McDermott), 9-235 (May).

Bowling	O	M	R	W
Curran	8	0	29	2
Jarvis	10	0	40	0
Rawson	6	0	39	0
Butchart	10	1	59	2
Traicos	10	0	36	0
Omarshah	6	0	32	1

Zimbabwe innings (target: 236 runs from 50 overs)			R	M	B	4	6
RD Brown	b O'Donnell		3	35	30	0	0
GA Paterson	run out		16	51	53	1	0
+DL Houghton	c O'Donnell	b May	11	46	22	1	0
AJ Pycroft	run out		9	30	29	1	0
KM Curran	b O'Donnell		30	53	38	1	3
AC Waller	c & b May		19	23	22	1	1
AH Omarshah	b McDermott		2	16	9	0	0
PWE Rawson	b Reid		15	27	14	2	0
IP Butchart	c Jones	b O'Donnell	18	39	32	2	0
*AJ Traicos	c & b O'Donnell		6	11	5	1	0
MP Jarvis	not out		1	2	1	0	0
Extras (b 2, lb 3, w 3, nb 1): **9**							
Total (all out, 42.4 overs): **139**							

FoW: 1-13 (Brown), 2-27 (Paterson), 3-41 (Pycroft), 4-44 (Houghton), 5-79 (Waller), 6-97 (Omarshah), 7-97 (Curran), 8-124 (Rawson), 9-137 (Traicos), 10-139 (Butchart).

Bowling	O	M	R	W
McDermott	7	1	13	1
Reid	7	1	21	1
O'Donnell	9.4	1	39	4
Waugh	6	3	7	0
May	8	0	29	2
Taylor	5	0	25	0

Reliance World Cup, 1987/88, 8th Match
India v New Zealand, Group A
M.Chinnaswamy Stadium, Bangalore
14 October 1987 (50-over match)

Result: India won by 16 runs
Points: India 4, New Zealand 0
Toss: New Zealand
Umpires: DM Archer (WI) and HD Bird (Eng)
Man Of The Match: N Kapil Dev

India innings (50 overs maximum)			R	M	B	4	6
K Srikkanth	run out		9	29	19	1	0
SM Gavaskar	run out		2	19	14	0	0
NS Sidhu	c Jones	b Patel	75	101	71	4	4
DB Vengsarkar	c & b Watson		0	9	8	0	0
M Azharuddin	c Boock	b Patel	21	60	57	1	0
RJ Shastri	c & b Patel		22	61	44	0	1
*N Kapil Dev	not out		72	88	58	4	1
M Prabhakar	c & b Chatfield		3	4	5	0	0
+KS More	not out		42	47	26	5	0
Extras (lb 4, w 2): **6**							
Total (7 wickets, 50 overs): **252**							

DNB: L Sivaramakrishnan, Maninder Singh.
FoW: 1-11 (Gavaskar), 2-16 (Srikkanth), 3-21 (Vengsarkar), 4-86 (Azharuddin), 5-114 (Sidhu), 6-165 (Shastri), 7-170 (Prabhakar).

Bowling	O	M	R	W
Chatfield	10	1	39	1
Snedden	10	1	56	0
Watson	9	0	59	1
Boock	4	0	26	0
Bracewell	7	0	32	0
Patel	10	0	36	3

New Zealand innings (target: 253 from 50 overs)			R	M	B	4	6
MC Snedden	c Shastri	b Azharuddin	33	63	63	2	0
KR Rutherford	c Srikkanth	b Shastri	75	121	95	6	2
MD Crowe	st More	b Maninder Singh	9	15	12	1	0
AH Jones	run out		64	95	86	2	0
*JJ Crowe	c Vengsarkar	b Maninder Singh	7	17	11	0	0
DN Patel	run out		1	5	3	0	0
JG Bracewell	c Maninder Singh	b Shastri	8	17	14	0	0
+IDS Smith	b Prabhakar		10	9	5	0	0
SL Boock	not out		7	11	8	0	0
W Watson	not out		2	2	3	0	0
Extras (b 5, lb 9, w 5, nb 1): **20**							
Total (8 wickets, 50 overs): **236**							

DNB: EJ Chatfield.
FoW: 1-67 (Snedden), 2-86 (MD Crowe), 3-146 (Rutherford), 4-168 (JJ Crowe), 5-170 (Patel), 6-189 (Bracewell), 7-206 (Smith), 8-225 (Jones).

Bowling	O	M	R	W
Kapil Dev	10	1	54	0
Prabhakar	8	0	38	1
Azharuddin	4	0	11	1
Sivaramakrishnan	8	0	34	0
Maninder Singh	10	0	40	2
Shastri	10	0	45	2

Reliance World Cup, 1987/88, 11th Match
India v Zimbabwe, Group A
Wankhede Stadium, Bombay
17 October 1987 (50-over match)

Result: India won by 8 wickets
Points: India 4, Zimbabwe 0
Toss: Zimbabwe
Umpires: Mahboob Shah (Pak) and DR Shepherd (Eng)
ODI Debuts: KJ Arnott, MA Meman (Zim)
Man Of The Match: M Prabhakar

Zimbabwe innings (50 overs maximum)			R	B	4	6
GA Paterson	b Prabhakar		6	21	0	0
KJ Arnott	lbw	b Prabhakar	1	6	0	0
+DL Houghton	b Prabhakar		0	12	0	0
AJ Pycroft	st More	b Shastri	61	102	2	0
KM Curran	c More	b Prabhakar	0	1	0	0
AC Waller	st More	b Maninder Singh	16	42	1	0
IP Butchart	c Sivaramakrishnan	b Maninder Singh	10	23	1	0
AH Omarshah	c More	b Maninder Singh	0	1	0	0
MA Meman	run out		19	22	2	0
*AJ Traicos	c Gavaskar	b Sivaramakrishnan	0	1	0	0
MP Jarvis	not out		8	35	0	0
Extras (b 2, lb 6, w 6): **14**						
Total (all out, 44.2 overs): **135**						

FoW: 1-3 (Arnott), 2-12 (Houghton), 3-13 (Paterson), 4-13 (Curran), 5-47 (Waller), 6-67 (Butchart), 7-67 (Omarshah), 8-98 (Meman), 9-99 (Traicos), 10-135 (Pycroft).

Bowling	O	M	R	W
Kapil Dev	8	1	17	0
Prabhakar	8	1	19	4
Maninder Singh	10	0	21	3
Azharuddin	1	0	6	0
Sivaramakrishnan	9	0	36	1
Shastri	8.2	0	28	1

India innings (target: 136 runs from 50 overs)			R	B	4	6
K Srikkanth	c Paterson	b Traicos	31	38	4	0
SM Gavaskar	st Houghton	b Traicos	43	52	9	0
M Prabhakar	not out		11	41	1	0
DB Vengsarkar	not out		46	37	4	3
Extras (lb 1, w 4): **5**						
Total (2 wickets, 27.5 overs): **136**						

DNB: NS Sidhu, M Azharuddin, *N Kapil Dev, RJ Shastri, +KS More, L Sivaramakrishnan, Maninder Singh.
FoW: 1-76 (Srikkanth), 2-80 (Gavaskar).

Bowling	O	M	R	W
Curran	6	0	32	0
Jarvis	4	0	22	0
Butchart	3	0	20	0
Traicos	8	0	27	2
Meman	6.5	0	34	0

Reliance World Cup, 1987/88, 12th Match
Australia v New Zealand, Group A
Nehru Stadium, Indore
18/19 October 1987 (50-over match)

Result: Australia won by 3 runs
Points: Australia 4, New Zealand 0
Toss: New Zealand
Umpires: DM Archer (WI) and Khizer Hayat (Pak)
Man Of The Match: DC Boon

Close Of Play:
Day 1: No play

Australia innings (30 overs maximum)			R	M	B	4	6
DC Boon	c Wright	b Snedden	87	110	96	5	2
GR Marsh	c JJ Crowe	b Snedden	5	16	9	0	0
DM Jones	c Rutherford	b Patel	52	69	48	1	3
*AR Border	c MD Crowe	b Chatfield	34	34	28	3	0
SR Waugh	not out		13	14	8	1	1
TM Moody	not out		0	3	3	0	0
Extras (b 1, lb 5, w 2): **8**							
Total (4 wickets, 30 overs): **199**							

DNB: SP O'Donnell, +GC Dyer, TBA May, CJ McDermott, BA Reid.
FoW: 1-17 (Marsh), 2-134 (Jones), 3-171 (Boon), 4-196 (Border).

Bowling	O	M	R	W
Snedden	6	0	36	2
Chatfield	6	0	27	1
Watson	6	0	34	0
Patel	6	0	45	1
Bracewell	6	0	51	0

New Zealand innings (target: 200 from 30 overs)			R	M	B	4	6
KR Rutherford	b O'Donnell		37	60	38	2	2
JG Wright	c Dyer	b O'Donnell	47	52	44	1	2
MD Crowe	c Marsh	b Waugh	58	71	48	5	0
AH Jones	c Marsh	b McDermott	15	28	23	0	0
*JJ Crowe	c & b Reid		3	8	10	0	0
DN Patel	run out		13	11	9	1	0
JG Bracewell	c & b Reid		6	5	4	1	0
+IDS Smith	b Waugh		1	8	2	0	0
MC Snedden	run out		1	5	1	0	0
FJ Chatfield	not out		0	6	0	0	0
W Watson	not out		2	1	3	0	0
Extras (b 4, lb 5, w 4): **13**							
Total (9 wickets, 30 overs): **196**							

FoW: 1-83 (Wright), 2-94 (Rutherford), 3-133 (Jones), 4-140 (JJ Crowe), 5-165 (Patel), 6-183 (Bracewell), 7-193 (MD Crowe), 8-193 (Smith), 9-194 (Snedden).

Bowling	O	M	R	W
McDermott	6	0	30	1
Reid	6	0	38	2
May	6	0	39	0
O'Donnell	6	0	44	2
Waugh	6	0	36	2

Reliance World Cup, 1987/88, 15th Match
India v Australia, Group A
Feroz Shah Kotla, Delhi
22 October 1987 (50-over match)

Result: India won by 56 runs
Points: India 4, Australia 0
Toss: Australia
Umpires: Khalid Aziz (Pak) and DR Shepherd (Eng)
ODI Debuts: AK Zesers (Aus)
Man Of The Match: M Azharuddin

India innings (50 overs maximum)			R	M	B	4	6
K Srikkanth	c Dyer	b McDermott	26	41	37	3	0
SM Gavaskar	b O'Donnell		61	99	72	7	0
NS Sidhu	c Moody	b McDermott	51	88	70	2	0
DB Vengsarkar	c O'Donnell	b Reid	63	84	60	3	2
*N Kapil Dev	c Dyer	b McDermott	3	9	5	0	0
M Azharuddin	not out		54	45	5	1	
RJ Shastri	c & b Waugh		8	10	7	1	0
+KS More	not out		5	4	0	0	
Extras (b 1, lb 6, w 11): **18**							
Total (6 wickets, 50 overs): **289**							

DNB: M Prabhakar, C Sharma, Maninder Singh.
FoW: 1-50 (Srikkanth), 2-125 (Gavaskar), 3-167 (Sidhu), 4-178 (Kapil Dev), 5-243 (Vengsarkar), 6-274 (Shastri).

Bowling	O	M	R	W
O'Donnell	9	1	45	1
Reid	10	0	65	1
Waugh	10	0	59	1
McDermott	10	0	61	3
Moody	2	0	15	0
Zesers	9	1	37	0

Australia innings (target: 290 runs from 50 overs)			R	M	B	4	6
GR Marsh	st More	b Maninder Singh	33	72	56	2	0
DC Boon	c More	b Shastri	62	85	59	7	0
DM Jones	c Kapil Dev	b Maninder Singh	36	64	55	0	0
*AR Border	c Prabhakar	b Maninder Singh	12	22	24	0	0
SR Waugh	c Sidhu	b Kapil Dev	42	73	52	3	0
TM Moody	run out		2	4	6	0	0
SP O'Donnell	b Azharuddin		5	14	10	0	0
+GC Dyer	c Kapil Dev	b Prabhakar	15	13	12	0	1
CJ McDermott	c & b Azharuddin		4	15	5	0	0
AK Zesers	not out		2	11	0	0	
BA Reid	c Sidhu	b Azharuddin	1	6	0	0	
Extras (lb 11, w 8): **19**							
Total (all out, 49 overs): **233**							

FoW: 1-88 (Marsh), 2-104 (Boon), 3-135 (Border), 4-164 (Jones), 5-167 (Moody), 6-182 (O'Donnell), 7-214 (Dyer), 8-227 (McDermott), 9-231 (Waugh), 10-233 (Reid).

Bowling	O	M	R	W
Kapil Dev	8	1	41	1
Prabhakar	10	0	56	1
Maninder Singh	10	0	34	3
Shastri	10	0	35	1
Sharma	7.1	0	37	0
Azharuddin	3.5	0	19	3

Reliance World Cup, 1987/88, 16th Match
New Zealand v Zimbabwe, Group A
Eden Gardens, Calcutta
23 October 1987 (50-over match)

Result: New Zealand won by 4 wickets
Points: New Zealand 4, Zimbabwe 0
Toss: New Zealand
Umpires: Khizer Hayat (Pak) and PW Vidanagamage (SL)
Man Of The Match: JJ Crowe

Zimbabwe innings (50 overs maximum)			R	B	4	6
GA Paterson	run out		0	8	0	0
AH Omarshah	c MD Crowe	b Watson	41	90	2	0
KJ Arnott	run out		51	83	5	0
+DL Houghton	c MD Crowe	b Boock	50	57	5	0
AJ Pycroft	not out		52	46	2	1
KM Curran	b Boock		12	11	1	0
AC Waller	not out		8	5	1	0
Extras (lb 7, w 6): **13**						
Total (5 wickets, 50 overs): **227**						

DNB: IP Butchart, EA Brandes, *AJ Traicos, MP Jarvis.
FoW: 1-1 (Paterson), 2-82 (Arnott), 3-121 (Omarshah), 4-180 (Houghton), 5-216 (Curran).

Bowling	O	M	R	W
Snedden	10	2	32	0
Chatfield	10	2	47	0
Patel	10	1	53	0
Watson	10	1	45	1
Boock	10	1	43	2

New Zealand innings (target: 228 runs from 50 overs)			R	B	4	6
KR Rutherford	b Brandes		22	32	2	0
JG Wright	b Omarshah		12	32	1	0
MD Crowe	c Butchart	b Omarshah	58	58	8	0
DN Patel	c Arnott	b Brandes	1	4	0	0
*JJ Crowe	not out		88	105	8	0
AH Jones	c Jarvis	b Traicos	15	35	1	0
MC Snedden	b Jarvis		4	13	0	0
+IDS Smith	not out		17	10	2	0
Extras (b 1, lb 5, w 4, nb 1): **11**						
Total (6 wickets, 47.4 overs): **228**						

DNB: SL Boock, EJ Chatfield, W Watson.
FoW: 1-37 (Wright), 2-53 (Rutherford), 3-56 (Patel), 4-125 (MD Crowe), 5-158 (Jones), 6-182 (Snedden).

Bowling	O	M	R	W
Curran	2	0	12	0
Jarvis	7.4	0	39	1
Brandes	10	1	44	2
Omarshah	10	0	34	2
Butchart	8	0	50	0
Traicos	10	0	43	1

Reliance World Cup, 1987/88, 19th Match
India v Zimbabwe, Group A
Gujarat Stadium, Motera, Ahmedabad
26 October 1987 (50-over match)

Result: India won by 7 wickets
Points: India 4, Zimbabwe 0
Toss: India
Umpires: DM Archer (WI) and HD Bird (Eng)
Man Of The Match: N Kapil Dev

Zimbabwe innings (50 overs maximum)			R	B	4	6
RD Brown	c More	b Sharma	13	52	2	0
AH Omarshah	run out		0	3	0	0
KJ Arnott	b Kapil Dev		60	126	1	0
AJ Pycroft	c More	b Sharma	2	9	0	0
+DL Houghton	c Kapil Dev	b Shastri	22	35	0	0
AC Waller	c Shastri	b Maninder Singh	39	44	4	1
IP Butchart	b Kapil Dev		13	14	1	0
PWE Rawson	not out		16	17	0	0
EA Brandes	not out		3	4	0	0
Extras (b 1, lb 12, w 9, nb 1): **23**						
Total (7 wickets, 50 overs): **191**						

DNB: MP Jarvis, *AJ Traicos.
FoW: 1-4 (Omarshah), 2-36 (Brown), 3-40 (Pycroft), 4-83 (Houghton), 5-150 (Arnott), 6-155 (Waller), 7-184 (Butchart).

Bowling	O	M	R	W
Kapil Dev	10	2	44	2
Prabhakar	7	2	12	0
Sharma	10	0	41	2
Maninder Singh	10	1	32	1
Shastri	10	0	35	1
Azharuddin	3	0	14	0

India innings (target: 192 runs from 50 overs)			R	B	4	6
K Srikkanth	lbw	b Jarvis	6	9	1	0
SM Gavaskar	c Butchart	b Rawson	50	114	3	0
NS Sidhu	c Brandes	b Rawson	55	61	5	1
DB Vengsarkar	not out		33	43	1	0
*N Kapil Dev	not out		41	25	2	3
Extras (lb 6, w 3): **9**						
Total (3 wickets, 42 overs): **194**						

DNB: M Azharuddin, RJ Shastri, +KS More, M Prabhakar, C Sharma, Maninder Singh.
FoW: 1-11 (Srikkanth), 2-105 (Sidhu), 3-132 (Gavaskar).

Bowling	O	M	R	W
Brandes	6	0	28	0
Jarvis	8	1	21	1
Omarshah	8	0	40	0
Traicos	10	0	39	0
Rawson	8	0	46	2
Butchart	2	0	14	0

Reliance World Cup, 1987/88, 20th Match
Australia v New Zealand, Group A
Sector 16 Stadium, Chandigarh
27 October 1987 (50-over match)

Result: Australia won by 17 runs
Points: Australia 4, New Zealand 0
Toss: Australia
Umpires: Khizer Hayat (Pak) and DR Shepherd (Eng)
Man Of The Match: GR Marsh

Australia innings (50 overs maximum)			R	M	B	4	6
GR Marsh	not out		126	206	149	12	3
DC Boon	run out		14	40	28	1	0
DM Jones	c Smith	b Watson	56	90	80	1	2
*AR Border	b Snedden		1	6	4	0	0
MRJ Veletta	run out		0	3	1	0	0
SR Waugh	b Watson		1	10	7	0	0
+GC Dyer	b Chatfield		8	16	10	0	0
CJ McDermott	lbw	b Chatfield	5	8	7	0	0
TBA May	run out		15	13	10	1	0
AK Zesers	not out		8	4	3	1	0
Extras (lb 10, w 7): **17**							
Total (8 wickets, 50 overs): **251**							

DNB: BA Reid.
FoW: 1-25 (Boon), 2-151 (Jones), 3-158 (Border), 4-158 (Veletta), 5-175 (Waugh), 6-193 (Dyer), 7-201 (McDermott), 8-228 (May).

Bowling	O	M	R	W
Snedden	10	0	48	1
Chatfield	10	2	52	2
Boock	10	1	45	0
Bracewell	4	0	24	0
Patel	8	0	26	0
Watson	8	0	46	2

New Zealand innings (target: 252 from 50 overs)			R	M	B	4	6
MC Snedden	b Waugh		32	67	56	3	0
JG Wright	c & b Zesers		61	115	82	4	0
MD Crowe	run out		4	11	5	0	0
KR Rutherford	c Jones	b McDermott	44	69	57	4	0
*JJ Crowe	c & b Border		27	23	28	3	0
DN Patel	st Dyer	b Border	3	18	10	0	0
JG Bracewell	run out		12	26	20	0	0
+IDS Smith	c Boon	b Waugh	12	18	15	0	0
SL Boock	run out		12	6	8	1	0
W Watson	run out		8	17	8	0	1
EJ Chatfield	not out		5	7	6	0	0
Extras (b 1, lb 7, w 4, nb 2): **14**							
Total (all out, 48.4 overs): **234**							

FoW: 1-72 (Snedden), 2-82 (MD Crowe), 3-127 (Wright), 4-173 (JJ Crowe), 5-179 (Rutherford), 6-186 (Patel), 7-206 (Bracewell), 8-208 (Smith), 9-221 (Boock), 10-234 (Watson).

Bowling	O	M	R	W
McDermott	10	1	43	1
Reid	6	0	30	0
Waugh	9.4	0	37	2
Zesers	6	0	37	1
May	10	0	52	0
Border	7	0	27	2

Reliance World Cup, 1987/88, 21st Match
Australia v Zimbabwe, Group A
Barabati Stadium, Cuttack
30 October 1987 (50-over match)

Result: Australia won by 70 runs
Points: Australia 4, Zimbabwe 0
Toss: Zimbabwe
Umpires: Mahboob Shah (Pak) and PW Vidanagamage (SL)
Man Of The Match: DC Boon

Australia innings (50 overs maximum)			R	M	B	4	6
DC Boon	c Houghton	b Butchart	93	125	101	9	1
GR Marsh	run out		37	86	65	1	0
DM Jones	not out		58	115	72	1	1
CJ McDermott	c Rawson	b Traicos	9	5	10	0	1
*AR Border	st Houghton	b Traicos	4	9	6	0	0
MRJ Veletta	run out		43	49	39	3	0
SR Waugh	not out		10	10	14	1	0

Extras (b 3, lb 3, w 6): **12**
Total (5 wickets, 50 overs): **266**

DNB: SP O'Donnell, +GC Dyer, TBA May, BA Reid.
FoW: 1-90 (Marsh), 2-148 (Boon), 3-159 (McDermott), 4-170 (Border), 5-248 (Veletta).

Bowling	O	M	R	W
Rawson	9	0	41	0
Jarvis	6	0	33	0
Omarshah	7	0	31	0
Brandes	10	1	58	0
Traicos	10	0	45	2
Butchart	8	0	52	1

Zimbabwe innings (target: 267 runs from 50 overs)			R	M	B	4	6
AH Omarshah	b Waugh		32	67	90	4	0
AC Waller	c Waugh	b McDermott	38	60	83	2	0
KM Curran	c Waugh	b May	29	79	57	2	0
AJ Pycroft	c Dyer	b McDermott	38	89	46	2	0
+DL Houghton	lbw	b May	1	6	11	0	0
IP Butchart	st Dyer	b Border	3	13	5	0	0
PWE Rawson	not out		24	37	29	2	1
EA Brandes	not out		18	19	11	1	2

Extras (lb 5, w 6, nb 2): **13**
Total (6 wickets, 50 overs): **196**

DNB: KJ Arnott, MP Jarvis, *AJ Traicos.
FoW: 1-55 (Omarshah), 2-89 (Curran), 3-92 (Houghton), 4-97 (Butchart), 5-139 (Pycroft), 6-156 (Waller).

Bowling	O	M	R	W
McDermott	10	0	43	2
Reid	9	2	30	0
Waugh	4	0	9	1
O'Donnell	7	1	21	0
May	10	1	30	2
Border	8	0	36	1
Jones	1	0	5	0
Boon	1	0	17	0

Reliance World Cup, 1987/88, 24th Match
India v New Zealand, Group A
Vidarbha C.A. Ground, Nagpur
31 October 1987 (50-over match)

Result: India won by 9 wickets
Points: India 4, New Zealand 0
Toss: New Zealand
Umpires: HD Bird (Eng) and DR Shepherd (Eng)
ODI Debuts: DK Morrison (NZ)
Men Of The Match: SM Gavaskar and C Sharma

New Zealand innings (50 overs maximum)			R	M	B	4	6
JG Wright	run out		35	90	59	4	0
PA Horne	b Prabhakar		18	49	35	1	0
MD Crowe	c Pandit	b Azharuddin	21	35	24	2	0
*JJ Crowe	b Maninder Singh		24	79	24	3	0
DN Patel	c Kapil Dev	b Shastri	40	22	51	3	0
KR Rutherford	b Sharma		26	45	54	1	0
MC Snedden	run out		23	42	28	2	0
+IDS Smith	b Sharma		0	1	1	0	0
EJ Chatfield	b Sharma		0	1	1	0	0
W Watson	not out		12	31	25	1	0
Extras (lb 14, w 7, nb 1): **22**							
Total (9 wickets, 50 overs): **221**							

DNB: DK Morrison.
FoW: 1-46 (Horne), 2-84 (MD Crowe), 3-90 (Wright), 4-122 (JJ Crowe), 5-181 (Patel), 6-182 (Rutherford), 7-182 (Smith), 8-182 (Chatfield), 9-221 (Snedden).

Bowling	O	M	R	W
Kapil Dev	6	0	24	0
Prabhakar	7	0	23	1
Sharma	10	2	51	3
Azharuddin	7	0	26	1
Maninder Singh	10	0	51	1
Shastri	10	1	32	1

India innings (target: 222 runs from 50 overs)			R	M	B	4	6
K Srikkanth	c Rutherford	b Watson	75	80	58	9	3
SM Gavaskar	not out		103	149	88	10	3
M Azharuddin	not out		41	68	51	5	0
Extras (lb 1, w 2, nb 2): **5**							
Total (1 wicket, 32.1 overs): **224**							

DNB: NS Sidhu, DB Vengsarkar, *N Kapil Dev, RJ Shastri, +CS Pandit, M Prabhakar, C Sharma, Maninder Singh.
FoW: 1-136 (Srikkanth).

Bowling	O	M	R	W
Morrison	10	0	69	0
Chatfield	4.1	1	39	0
Snedden	4	0	29	0
Watson	10	0	50	1
Patel	4	0	36	0

1987 WORLD CUP

Group B

Reliance World Cup, 1987/88, 1st Match
Pakistan v Sri Lanka, Group B
Niaz Stadium, Hyderabad, Sind
8 October 1987 (50-over match)

Result: Pakistan won by 15 runs
Points: Pakistan 4, Sri Lanka 0
Toss: Pakistan
Umpires: VK Ramaswamy (Ind) and SJ Woodward (NZ)
Man Of The Match: Javed Miandad

Pakistan innings (50 overs maximum)			R	B	4	6
Rameez Raja	c Ratnayake	b Anurasiri	76	115	3	0
Ijaz Ahmed	c Kuruppu	b Ratnayake	16	34	2	0
Mansoor Akhtar	c Ratnayake	b Ratnayeke	12	23	0	0
Javed Miandad	b Ratnayeke		103	100	6	0
Wasim Akram	run out		14	14	0	0
Saleem Malik	not out		18	12	1	0
*Imran Khan	b Ratnayake		2	4	0	0
+Saleem Yousuf	not out		1	1	0	0
Extras (lb 15, w 9, nb 1): **25**						
Total (6 wickets, 50 overs): **267**						

DNB: Mudassar Nazar, Abdul Qadir, Tauseef Ahmed.
FoW: 1-48 (Ijaz Ahmed), 2-67 (Mansoor Akhtar), 3-180 (Rameez Raja), 4-226 (Wasim Akram), 5-259 (Javed Miandad), 6-266 (Imran Khan).

Bowling	O	M	R	W
John	10	2	37	0
Ratnayake	10	0	64	2
Ratnayeke	9	0	47	2
de Silva	10	0	44	0
Anurasiri	10	0	52	1
Gurusinha	1	0	8	0

Sri Lanka innings (target: 268 runs from 50 overs)			R	B	4	6
+DSBP Kuruppu	c Saleem Yousuf	b Imran Khan	9	24	1	0
RS Mahanama	c Javed Miandad	b Mansoor Akhtar	89	117	7	1
RL Dias	b Abdul Qadir		5	21	0	0
A Ranatunga	b Tauseef Ahmed		24	29	3	0
*LRD Mendis	run out		1	6	0	0
AP Gurusinha	b Abdul Qadir		37	39	2	1
PA de Silva	b Imran Khan		42	32	3	1
JR Ratnayeke	c Saleem Yousuf	b Wasim Akram	7	13	0	0
RJ Ratnayake	c Mudassar Nazar	b Wasim Akram	8	9	0	0
VB John	not out		1	4	0	0
SD Anurasiri	run out		0	3	0	0
Extras (b 7, lb 14, w 7, nb 1): **29**						
Total (all out, 49.2 overs): **252**						

FoW: 1-29 (Kuruppu), 2-57 (Dias), 3-100 (Ranatunga), 4-103 (Mendis), 5-182 (Mahanama), 6-190 (Gurusinha), 7-209 (Ratnayeke), 8-223 (Ratnayake), 9-251 (de Silva), 10-252 (Anurasiri).

Bowling	O	M	R	W
Imran Khan	10	2	42	2
Wasim Akram	9.2	1	41	2
Mudassar Nazar	9	0	63	0
Abdul Qadir	10	1	30	2
Tauseef Ahmed	10	0	48	1
Mansoor Akhtar	1	0	7	1

Reliance World Cup, 1987/88, 2nd Match
England v West Indies, Group B
Municipal Stadium, Gujranwala
9 October 1987 (50-over match)

Result: England won by 2 wickets
Points: England 4, West Indies 0
Toss: England
Umpires: AR Crafter (Aus) and RB Gupta (Ind)
Man Of The Match: AJ Lamb

West Indies innings (50 overs maximum)		R	B	4	6
DL Haynes	run out	19	45	1	0
CA Best	b DeFreitas	5	15	0	0
RB Richardson	b Foster	53	80	8	0
*IVA Richards	b Foster	27	36	3	0
+PJL Dujon	run out	46	76	3	0
AL Logie	b Foster	49	41	3	1
RA Harper	b Small	24	10	3	1
CL Hooper	not out	1	2	0	0
WKM Benjamin	not out	7	2	1	0
Extras (lb 9, nb 3): **12**					
Total (7 wickets, 50 overs): **243**					

DNB: CA Walsh, BP Patterson.
FoW: 1-8 (Best), 2-53 (Haynes), 3-105 (Richards), 4-122 (Richardson), 5-205 (Dujon), 6-235 (Logie), 7-235 (Harper).

Bowling	O	M	R	W
DeFreitas	10	2	31	1
Foster	10	0	53	3
Emburey	10	1	22	0
Small	10	0	45	1
Pringle	10	0	83	0

England innings (target: 244 runs from 50 overs)			R	B	4	6
GA Gooch	c Dujon	b Hooper	47	93	3	0
BC Broad	c Dujon	b Walsh	3	12	0	0
RT Robinson	run out		12	35	1	0
*MW Gatting	b Hooper		25	23	3	0
AJ Lamb	not out		67	68	5	1
DR Pringle	c Best	b Hooper	12	23	0	0
+PR Downton	run out		3	4	0	0
JE Emburey	b Patterson		22	15	2	1
PAJ DeFreitas	b Patterson		23	21	2	0
NA Foster	not out		9	6	1	0
Extras (lb 14, w 6, nb 3): **23**						
Total (8 wickets, 49.3 overs): **246**						

DNB: GC Small.
FoW: 1-14 (Broad), 2-40 (Robinson), 3-98 (Gatting), 4-99 (Gooch), 5-123 (Pringle), 6-131 (Downton), 7-162 (Emburey), 8-209 (DeFreitas).

Bowling	O	M	R	W
Patterson	10	0	49	2
Walsh	9.3	0	65	1
Harper	10	0	44	0
Benjamin	10	2	32	0
Hooper	10	0	42	3

Reliance World Cup, 1987/88, 5th Match
Pakistan v England, Group B
Pindi Club Ground, Rawalpindi
12/13 October 1987 (50-over match)

Result: Pakistan won by 18 runs
Points: Pakistan 4, England 0
Toss: England
Umpires: AR Crafter (Aus) and RB Gupta (Ind)
Man Of The Match: Abdul Qadir

Close Of Play

Day 1: No play

Pakistan innings (50 overs maximum)			R	B	4	6
Mansoor Akhtar	c Downton	b Foster	6	24	1	0
Rameez Raja	run out		15	40	1	0
Saleem Malik	c Downton	b DeFreitas	65	80	8	0
Javed Miandad	lbw	b DeFreitas	23	50	3	0
Ijaz Ahmed	c Robinson	b Small	59	59	4	1
*Imran Khan	b Small		22	32	2	0
Wasim Akram	b DeFreitas		5	3	1	0
+Saleem Yousuf	not out		16	10	0	0
Abdul Qadir	not out		12	7	1	1
Extras (lb 10, w 3, nb 3): **16**						
Total (7 wickets, 50 overs): **239**						

DNB: Tauseef Ahmed, Saleem Jaffar.
FoW: 1-13 (Mansoor Akhtar), 2-51 (Rameez Raja), 3-112 (Javed Miandad), 4-123 (Saleem Malik), 5-202 (Imran Khan), 6-210 (Wasim Akram), 7-210 (Ijaz Ahmed).

Bowling	O	M	R	W
DeFreitas	10	1	42	3
Foster	10	1	35	1
Small	10	1	47	2
Pringle	10	0	54	0
Emburey	10	0	51	0

England innings (target: 240 runs from 50 overs)			R	B	4	6
GA Gooch	b Abdul Qadir		21	41	3	0
BC Broad	b Tauseef Ahmed		36	78	2	0
RT Robinson	b Abdul Qadir		33	62	1	0
*MW Gatting	b Saleem Jaffar		43	47	4	0
AJ Lamb	lbw	b Abdul Qadir	30	38	3	0
DR Pringle	run out		8	14	0	0
JE Emburey	run out		1	1	0	0
+PR Downton	c Saleem Yousuf	b Abdul Qadir	0	2	0	0
PAJ DeFreitas	not out		3	3	0	0
NA Foster	run out		6	5	0	0
GC Small	lbw	b Saleem Jaffar	0	1	0	0
Extras (b 6, lb 26, w 8): **40**						
Total (all out, 48.4 overs): **221**						

FoW: 1-52 (Gooch), 2-92 (Broad), 3-141 (Robinson), 4-186 (Gatting), 5-206 (Lamb), 6-207 (Emburey), 7-207 (Downton), 8-213 (Pringle), 9-221 (Foster), 10-221 (Small).

Bowling	O	M	R	W
Wasim Akram	9	0	32	0
Saleem Jaffar	9.4	0	42	2
Tauseef Ahmed	10	0	39	1
Abdul Qadir	10	0	31	4
Saleem Malik	7	0	29	0
Mansoor Akhtar	3	0	16	0

Reliance World Cup, 1987/88, 7th Match
Sri Lanka v West Indies, Group B
National Stadium, Karachi
13 October 1987 (50-over match)

Result: West Indies won by 191 runs
Points: West Indies 4, Sri Lanka 0
Toss: Sri Lanka
Umpires: VK Ramaswamy (Ind) and SJ Woodward (NZ)
Man Of The Match: IVA Richards

West Indies innings (50 overs maximum)			R	B	4	6
DL Haynes	b Gurusinha		105	124	10	1
CA Best	b Ratnayeke		18	30	1	0
RB Richardson	c Kuruppu	b Ratnayeke	0	1	0	0
*IVA Richards	c Mahanama	b de Mel	181	125	16	7
AL Logie	not out		31	25	0	0
RA Harper	not out		5	2	0	0
Extras (b 4, lb 8, w 4, nb 4): **20**						
Total (4 wickets, 50 overs): **360**						

DNB: CL Hooper, +PJL Dujon, WKM Benjamin, CA Walsh, BP Patterson.
FoW: 1-45 (Best), 2-45 (Richardson), 3-227 (Haynes), 4-343 (Richards).

Bowling	O	M	R	W
John	10	1	48	0
Ratnayeke	8	0	68	2
Anurasiri	10	0	39	0
de Mel	10	0	97	1
de Silva	6	0	35	0
Ranatunga	2	0	18	0
Gurusinha	4	0	43	1

Sri Lanka innings (target: 361 runs from 50 overs)			R	B	4	6
RS Mahanama	c Dujon	b Walsh	12	4	3	0
+DSBP Kuruppu	lbw	b Patterson	14	14	0	0
AP Gurusinha	b Hooper		36	108	1	1
PA de Silva	c Dujon	b Hooper	9	27	0	0
A Ranatunga	not out		52	93	5	0
*LRD Mendis	not out		37	45	5	0
Extras (b 1, lb 2, w 6): **9**						
Total (4 wickets, 50 overs): **169**						

DNB: RS Madugalle, JR Ratnayeke, ALF de Mel, VB John, SD Anurasiri.
FoW: 1-24 (Mahanama), 2-31 (Kuruppu), 3-57 (de Silva), 4-112 (Gurusinha).

Bowling	O	M	R	W
Patterson	7	0	32	1
Walsh	7	2	23	1
Harper	10	2	15	0
Benjamin	4	0	11	0
Hooper	10	0	39	2
Richards	8	0	22	0
Richardson	4	0	24	0

Reliance World Cup, 1987/88, 9th Match
Pakistan v West Indies, Group B
Gaddafi Stadium, Lahore
16 October 1987 (50-over match)

Result: Pakistan won by 1 wicket
Points: Pakistan 4, West Indies 0
Toss: West Indies
Umpires: AR Crafter (Aus) and SJ Woodward (NZ)
ODI Debuts: PV Simmons (WI)
Man Of The Match: Saleem Yousuf

West Indies innings (50 overs maximum)

			R	B	4	6
DL Haynes	b Saleem Jaffar		37	81	3	0
PV Simmons	c & b Tauseef Ahmed		50	57	8	0
RB Richardson	c Ijaz Ahmed	b Saleem Jaffar	11	22	1	0
*IVA Richards	c Saleem Malik	b Imran Khan	51	52	4	1
AL Logie	c Mansoor Akhtar	b Saleem Jaffar	2	4	0	0
CL Hooper	lbw	b Wasim Akram	22	37	2	0
+PJL Dujon	lbw	b Wasim Akram	5	12	0	0
RA Harper	c Mansoor Akhtar	b Imran Khan	0	1	0	0
EAE Baptiste	b Imran Khan		14	20	1	0
CA Walsh	lbw	b Imran Khan	7	6	1	0
BP Patterson	not out		0	4	0	0
Extras (b 1, lb 14, w 2): **17**						
Total (all out, 49.3 overs): **216**						

FoW: 1-91 (Haynes), 2-97 (Simmons), 3-118 (Richardson), 4-121 (Logie), 5-169 (Hooper), 6-184 (Richards), 7-184 (Harper), 8-196 (Dujon), 9-207 (Baptiste), 10-216 (Walsh).

Bowling

	O	M	R	W
Imran Khan	8.3	2	37	4
Wasim Akram	10	0	45	2
Abdul Qadir	8	0	42	0
Tauseef Ahmed	10	2	35	1
Saleem Jaffar	10	0	30	3
Saleem Malik	3	0	12	0

Pakistan innings (target: 217 runs from 50 overs)

			R	B	4	6
Rameez Raja	c Richards	b Harper	42	87	1	0
Mansoor Akhtar	b Patterson		10	24	2	0
Saleem Malik	c Baptiste	b Walsh	4	7	1	0
Javed Miandad	c & b Hooper		33	72	1	0
Ijaz Ahmed	b Walsh		6	14	0	0
*Imran Khan	c Logie	b Walsh	18	26	0	0
+Saleem Yousuf	c Hooper	b Walsh	56	49	7	0
Wasim Akram	c Richardson	b Patterson	7	8	0	0
Abdul Qadir	not out		16	9	0	1
Tauseef Ahmed	run out		0	1	0	0
Saleem Jaffar	not out		1	3	0	0
Extras (b 5, lb 12, w 7): **24**						
Total (9 wickets, 50 overs): **217**						

FoW: 1-23 (Mansoor Akhtar), 2-28 (Saleem Malik), 3-92 (Rameez Raja), 4-104 (Ijaz Ahmed), 5-110 (Javed Miandad), 6-183 (Imran Khan), 7-200 (Wasim Akram), 8-202 (Saleem Yousuf), 9-203 (Tauseef Ahmed).

Bowling

	O	M	R	W
Patterson	10	1	51	2
Walsh	10	1	40	4
Baptiste	8	1	33	0
Harper	10	0	28	1
Hooper	10	0	38	1
Richards	2	0	10	0

Reliance World Cup, 1987/88, 10th Match
England v Sri Lanka, Group B
Arbab Niaz Stadium, Peshawar
17 October 1987 (50-over match)

Result: England won by 109 runs (revised target)
Points: England 4, Sri Lanka 0
Toss: England
Umpires: RB Gupta (Ind) and VK Ramaswamy (Ind)
Man Of The Match: AJ Lamb

England innings (50 overs maximum)			R	B	4	6
GA Gooch	c & b Anurasiri		84	100	8	0
BC Broad	c de Silva	b Ratnayeke	28	60	1	0
*MW Gatting	b Ratnayake		58	63	3	0
AJ Lamb	c de Silva	b Ratnayeke	76	58	3	2
JE Emburey	not out		30	19	3	1
CWJ Athey	not out		2	2	0	0
Extras (lb 13, w 5): **18**						
Total (4 wickets, 50 overs): **296**						

DNB: +PR Downton, PAJ DeFreitas, DR Pringle, EE Hemmings, GC Small.
FoW: 1-89 (Broad), 2-142 (Gooch), 3-218 (Gatting), 4-287 (Lamb).

Bowling	O	M	R	W
Ratnayeke	9	0	62	2
John	10	0	44	0
de Silva	7	0	33	0
Ratnayake	10	0	60	1
Anurasiri	8	0	44	1
Ranatunga	6	0	40	0

Sri Lanka innings (target: 267 runs from 45 overs)			R	B	4	6
RS Mahanama	c Gooch	b Pringle	11	39	2	0
+DSBP Kuruppu	c Hemmings	b Emburey	13	26	1	0
AP Gurusinha	run out		1	12	0	0
RS Madugalle	b Hemmings		30	49	3	0
A Ranatunga	lbw	b DeFreitas	40	67	4	0
*LRD Mendis	run out		14	33	1	0
PA de Silva	c Emburey	b Hemmings	6	14	0	0
JR Ratnayeke	c Broad	b Emburey	1	5	0	0
RJ Ratnayake	not out		14	22	1	0
VB John	not out		8	7	1	0
Extras (b 2, lb 9, w 6, nb 3): **20**						
Total (8 wickets, 45 overs): **158**						

DNB: SD Anurasiri.
FoW: 1-31 (Mahanama), 2-32 (Gurusinha), 3-37 (Kuruppu), 4-99 (Madugalle), 5-105 (Ranatunga), 6-113 (de Silva), 7-119 (Ratnayeke), 8-137 (Mendis).

Bowling	O	M	R	W
DeFreitas	9	2	24	1
Small	7	0	27	0
Pringle	4	0	11	1
Emburey	10	1	26	2
Hemmings	10	1	31	2
Gooch	2	0	9	0
Athey	1	0	10	0
Broad	1	0	6	0
Lamb	1	0	3	0

Reliance World Cup, 1987/88, 13th Match
Pakistan v England, Group B
National Stadium, Karachi
20 October 1987 (50-over match)

Result: Pakistan won by 7 wickets
Points: Pakistan 4, England 0
Toss: Pakistan
Umpires: AR Crafter (Aus) and VK Ramaswamy (Ind)
Man Of The Match: Imran Khan

England innings (50 overs maximum)			R	B	4	6
GA Gooch	c Wasim Akram	b Imran Khan	16	27	2	0
RT Robinson	b Abdul Qadir		16	26	1	0
CWJ Athey	b Tauseef Ahmed		86	104	6	2
*MW Gatting	c Saleem Yousuf	b Abdul Qadir	60	65	3	1
AJ Lamb	b Imran Khan		9	15	0	0
JE Emburey	lbw	b Abdul Qadir	3	11	0	0
+PR Downton	c Saleem Yousuf	b Imran Khan	6	13	0	0
PAJ DeFreitas	c Saleem Yousuf	b Imran Khan	13	15	1	0
NA Foster	not out		20	20	2	0
GC Small	run out		0	1	0	0
EE Hemmings	not out		4	3	0	0
Extras (lb 7, w 4): **11**						
Total (9 wickets, 50 overs): **244**						

FoW: 1-26 (Gooch), 2-52 (Robinson), 3-187 (Athey), 4-187 (Gatting), 5-192 (Emburey), 6-203 (Lamb), 7-206 (Downton), 8-230 (DeFreitas), 9-230 (Small).

Bowling	O	M	R	W
Imran Khan	9	0	37	4
Wasim Akram	8	0	44	0
Tauseef Ahmed	10	0	46	1
Abdul Qadir	10	0	31	3
Saleem Jaffar	8	0	44	0
Saleem Malik	5	0	35	0

Pakistan innings (target: 245 runs from 50 overs)			R	B	4	6
Rameez Raja	c Gooch	b DeFreitas	113	148	5	0
Mansoor Akhtar	run out		29	49	3	0
Saleem Malik	c Athey	b Emburey	88	92	7	0
Javed Miandad	not out		6	3	1	0
Ijaz Ahmed	not out		4	2	1	0
Extras (lb 6, w 1): **7**						
Total (3 wickets, 49 overs): **247**						

DNB: *Imran Khan, +Saleem Yousuf, Wasim Akram, Abdul Qadir, Tauseef Ahmed, Saleem Jaffar.
FoW: 1-61 (Mansoor Akhtar), 2-228 (Saleem Malik), 3-243 (Rameez Raja).

Bowling	O	M	R	W
DeFreitas	8	2	41	1
Foster	10	0	51	0
Hemmings	10	1	40	0
Emburey	10	0	34	1
Small	9	0	63	0
Gooch	2	0	12	0

Reliance World Cup, 1987/88, 14th Match
Sri Lanka v West Indies, Group B
Green Park, Kanpur
21 October 1987 (50-over match)

Result: West Indies won by 25 runs
Points: West Indies 4, Sri Lanka 0
Toss: Sri Lanka
Umpires: Amanullah Khan (Pak) and Mahboob Shah (Pak)
Man Of The Match: PV Simmons

West Indies innings (50 overs maximum)

			R	B	4	6
DL Haynes	b Anurasiri		24	36	3	0
PV Simmons	c Madugalle	b Ratnayeke	89	126	11	0
RB Richardson	c Mahanama	b Jeganathan	4	12	0	0
*IVA Richards	c Ratnayake	b de Silva	14	25	0	0
AL Logie	not out		65	66	7	0
CL Hooper	st Kuruppu	b de Silva	6	8	1	0
+PJL Dujon	c Kuruppu	b Ratnayeke	6	14	0	0
RA Harper	b Ratnayeke		3	6	0	0
WKM Benjamin	b Ratnayake		0	3	0	0
CA Walsh	not out		9	8	1	0
Extras (b 2, lb 7, w 7): **16**						
Total (8 wickets, 50 overs): **236**						

DNB: BP Patterson.
FoW: 1-62 (Haynes), 2-80 (Richardson), 3-115 (Richards), 4-155 (Simmons), 5-168 (Hooper), 6-199 (Dujon), 7-213 (Harper), 8-214 (Benjamin).

Bowling	O	M	R	W
Ratnayeke	10	1	41	3
John	5	1	25	0
Ratnayake	5	0	39	1
Jeganathan	10	1	33	1
Anurasiri	10	1	46	1
de Silva	10	0	43	2

Sri Lanka innings (target: 237 runs from 50 overs)

			R	B	4	6
RS Mahanama	b Patterson		0	3	0	0
+DSBP Kuruppu	c & b Hooper		33	82	1	0
JR Ratnayeke	lbw	b Benjamin	15	22	1	0
RS Madugalle	c Haynes	b Harper	18	42	0	0
A Ranatunga	not out		86	100	7	2
*LRD Mendis	b Walsh		19	34	1	0
PA de Silva	b Patterson		8	9	0	0
RJ Ratnayake	c Walsh	b Patterson	5	7	0	0
S Jeganathan	run out		3	9	0	0
VB John	not out		1	3	0	0
Extras (b 2, lb 11, nb 10): **23**						
Total (8 wickets, 50 overs): **211**						

DNB: SD Anurasiri.
FoW: 1-2 (Mahanama), 2-28 (Ratnayeke), 3-66 (Madugalle), 4-86 (Kuruppu), 5-156 (Mendis), 6-184 (de Silva), 7-200 (Ratnayake), 8-209 (Jeganathan).

Bowling	O	M	R	W
Patterson	10	0	31	3
Walsh	9	2	43	1
Benjamin	10	0	43	1
Harper	10	1	29	1
Hooper	8	0	35	1
Richards	3	0	17	0

Reliance World Cup, 1987/88, 17th Match
Pakistan v Sri Lanka, Group B
Iqbal Stadium, Faisalabad
25 October 1987 (50-over match)

Result: Pakistan won by 113 runs
Points: Pakistan 4, Sri Lanka 0
Toss: Pakistan
Umpires: RB Gupta (Ind) and SJ Woodward (NZ)
Man Of The Match: Saleem Malik

Pakistan innings (50 overs maximum)			R	B	4	6
Rameez Raja	c & b Anurasiri		32	49	2	0
Mansoor Akhtar	b Jeganathan		33	61	2	0
Saleem Malik	b Ratnayeke		100	95	10	0
Javed Miandad	run out		1	8	0	0
Wasim Akram	c Ranatunga	b de Silva	39	40	2	2
Ijaz Ahmed	c & b John		30	18	5	0
*Imran Khan	run out		39	20	5	1
Manzoor Elahi	not out		4	6	0	0
+Saleem Yousuf	not out		11	6	0	1
Extras (lb 6, w 2): **8**						
Total (7 wickets, 50 overs): **297**						

DNB: Abdul Qadir, Tauseef Ahmed.
FoW: 1-64 (Rameez Raja), 2-72 (Mansoor Akhtar), 3-77 (Javed Miandad), 4-137 (Wasim Akram), 5-197 (Ijaz Ahmed), 6-264 (Imran Khan), 7-285 (Saleem Malik).

Bowling	O	M	R	W
Ratnayeke	10	0	58	1
John	8	1	53	1
de Mel	10	0	53	0
Jeganathan	9	1	45	1
Anurasiri	7	0	45	1
de Silva	6	0	37	1

Sri Lanka innings (target: 298 runs from 50 overs)			R	B	4	6
RS Mahanama	run out		8	13	1	0
+DSBP Kuruppu	c Saleem Yousuf	b Imran Khan	0	1	0	0
JR Ratnayeke	run out		22	60	2	0
RS Madugalle	c Saleem Yousuf	b Manzoor Elahi	15	38	2	0
A Ranatunga	c & b Abdul Qadir		50	66	4	0
*LRD Mendis	b Abdul Qadir		58	65	6	0
PA de Silva	not out		13	35	0	0
ALF de Mel	b Abdul Qadir		0	3	0	0
S Jeganathan	c Saleem Yousuf	b Javed Miandad	1	11	0	0
VB John	not out		1	12	0	0
Extras (b 4, lb 4, w 6, nb 2): **16**						
Total (8 wickets, 50 overs): **184**						

DNB: SD Anurasiri.
FoW: 1-4 (Kuruppu), 2-11 (Mahanama), 3-41 (Madugalle), 4-70 (Ratnayeke), 5-150 (Ranatunga), 6-173 (Mendis), 7-173 (de Mel), 8-179 (Jeganathan).

Bowling	O	M	R	W
Imran Khan	3.2	1	13	1
Wasim Akram	7	0	34	0
Manzoor Elahi	9.4	0	32	1
Tauseef Ahmed	10	1	23	0
Abdul Qadir	10	0	40	3
Saleem Malik	7	1	29	0
Javed Miandad	3	0	5	1

Reliance World Cup, 1987/88, 18th Match
England v West Indies, Group B
Sawai Mansingh Stadium, Jaipur
26 October 1987 (50-over match)

Result: England won by 34 runs
Points: England 4, West Indies 0
Toss: West Indies
Umpires: Mahboob Shah (Pak) and PW Vidanagamage (SL)
Man Of The Match: GA Gooch

England innings (50 overs maximum)			R	B	4	6
GA Gooch	c Harper	b Patterson	92	137	7	0
RT Robinson	b Patterson		13	19	2	0
CWJ Athey	c Patterson	b Harper	21	44	3	0
*MW Gatting	lbw	b Richards	25	24	1	0
AJ Lamb	c Richardson	b Patterson	40	52	3	0
JE Emburey	not out		24	16	4	0
PAJ DeFreitas	not out		16	9	3	0
Extras (b 5, lb 10, w 22, nb 1): **38**						
Total (5 wickets, 50 overs): **269**						

DNB: +PR Downton, NA Foster, GC Small, EE Hemmings.
FoW: 1-35 (Robinson), 2-90 (Athey), 3-154 (Gatting), 4-209 (Gooch), 5-250 (Lamb).

Bowling	O	M	R	W
Patterson	9	0	56	3
Walsh	10	0	24	0
Benjamin	10	0	63	0
Harper	10	1	52	1
Hooper	3	0	27	0
Richards	8	0	32	1

West Indies innings (target: 270 runs from 50 overs)			R	B	4	6
DL Haynes	c Athey	b DeFreitas	9	14	2	0
PV Simmons	b Emburey		25	28	5	0
RB Richardson	c Downton	b Small	93	130	8	1
*IVA Richards	b Hemmings		51	51	4	3
AL Logie	c Hemmings	b Emburey	22	21	3	0
CL Hooper	c Downton	b DeFreitas	8	11	1	0
+PJL Dujon	c Downton	b Foster	1	4	0	0
RA Harper	run out		3	4	0	0
WKM Benjamin	c Foster	b DeFreitas	8	16	0	0
CA Walsh	b Hemmings		2	3	0	0
BP Patterson	not out		4	8	0	0
Extras (lb 7, w 1, nb 1): **9**						
Total (all out, 48.1 overs): **235**						

FoW: 1-18 (Haynes), 2-65 (Simmons), 3-147 (Richards), 4-182 (Logie), 5-208 (Hooper), 6-211 (Dujon), 7-219 (Harper), 8-221 (Richardson), 9-224 (Walsh), 10-235 (Benjamin).

Bowling	O	M	R	W
DeFreitas	9.1	2	28	3
Foster	10	0	52	1
Emburey	9	0	41	2
Small	10	0	61	1
Hemmings	10	0	46	2

Reliance World Cup, 1987/88, 22nd Match
England v Sri Lanka, Group B
Nehru Stadium, Pune
30 October 1987 (50-over match)

Result: England won by 8 wickets
Points: England 4, Sri Lanka 0
Toss: Sri Lanka
Umpires: DM Archer (WI) and Khizer Hayat (Pak)
Man Of The Match: GA Gooch

Sri Lanka innings (50 overs maximum)			R	B	4	6
RS Mahanama	c Emburey	b DeFreitas	14	28	1	0
JR Ratnayeke	lbw	b Small	7	11	1	0
+AP Gurusinha	run out		34	63	3	0
RL Dias	st Downton	b Hemmings	80	105	6	3
*LRD Mendis	b DeFreitas		7	26	0	0
RS Madugalle	c sub (PW Jarvis)	b Hemmings	22	38	0	1
PA de Silva	not out		23	18	2	0
ALF de Mel	c Lamb	b Hemmings	0	2	0	0
S Jeganathan	not out		20	15	2	1
Extras (lb 3, w 3, nb 5): **11**						
Total (7 wickets, 50 overs): **218**						

DNB: VB John, SD Anurasiri.
FoW: 1-23 (Ratnayeke), 2-25 (Mahanama), 3-113 (Gurusinha), 4-125 (Mendis), 5-170 (Dias), 6-177 (Madugalle), 7-180 (de Mel).

Bowling	O	M	R	W
DeFreitas	10	2	46	2
Small	10	1	33	1
Foster	10	0	37	0
Emburey	10	1	42	0
Hemmings	10	0	57	3

England innings (target: 219 runs from 50 overs)		R	B	4	6
GA Gooch	c & b Jeganathan	61	79	7	0
RT Robinson	b Jeganathan	55	75	7	0
CWJ Athey	not out	40	55	0	0
*MW Gatting	not out	46	40	4	0
Extras (b 1, lb 13, w 3): **17**					
Total (2 wickets, 41.2 overs): **219**					

DNB: AJ Lamb, +PR Downton, JE Emburey, PAJ DeFreitas, NA Foster, GC Small, EE Hemmings.
FoW: 1-123 (Robinson), 2-132 (Gooch).

Bowling	O	M	R	W
Ratnayeke	8	1	37	0
John	6	2	19	0
de Mel	4.2	0	34	0
Jeganathan	10	0	45	2
Anurasiri	10	0	45	0
de Silva	3	0	25	0

Reliance World Cup, 1987/88, 23rd Match
Pakistan v West Indies, Group B
National Stadium, Karachi
30 October 1987 (50-over match)

Result: West Indies won by 28 runs
Points: West Indies 4, Pakistan 0
Toss: West Indies
Umpires: RB Gupta (Ind) and VK Ramaswamy (Ind)
Man Of The Match: RB Richardson

West Indies innings (50 overs maximum)			R	B	4	6
DL Haynes	c Imran Khan	b Mudassar Nazar	25	52	1	0
PV Simmons	b Wasim Akram		6	9	1	0
RB Richardson	c Abdul Qadir	b Imran Khan	110	135	8	2
*IVA Richards	b Wasim Akram		67	75	2	2
AL Logie	c Mudassar Nazar	b Imran Khan	12	17	0	0
RA Harper	b Wasim Akram		2	7	0	0
CL Hooper	not out		5	7	0	0
WKM Benjamin	c Mudassar Nazar	b Imran Khan	0	1	0	0
+PJL Dujon	not out		1	1	0	0
Extras (b 3, lb 10, w 16, nb 1): **30**						
Total (7 wickets, 50 overs): **258**						

DNB: CA Walsh, BP Patterson.
FoW: 1-19 (Simmons), 2-84 (Haynes), 3-221 (Richards), 4-242 (Logie), 5-248 (Harper), 6-255 (Richardson), 7-255 (Benjamin).

Bowling	O	M	R	W
Imran Khan	9	0	57	3
Wasim Akram	10	0	45	3
Abdul Qadir	10	1	29	0
Mudassar Nazar	10	0	47	1
Saleem Jaffar	6	0	37	0
Saleem Malik	5	0	30	0

Pakistan innings (target: 259 runs from 50 overs)			R	B	4	6
Mudassar Nazar	b Harper		40	55	3	0
Rameez Raja	c Hooper	b Patterson	70	111	3	0
Saleem Malik	c Richards	b Walsh	23	37	0	0
Javed Miandad	b Benjamin		38	38	3	0
Ijaz Ahmed	b Benjamin		6	10	0	0
*Imran Khan	c Harper	b Walsh	8	11	0	0
+Saleem Yousuf	b Patterson		7	10	0	0
Wasim Akram	lbw	b Patterson	0	2	0	0
Abdul Qadir	not out		8	11	0	0
Shoaib Mohammad	b Benjamin		0	1	0	0
Saleem Jaffar	not out		8	16	0	0
Extras (b 4, lb 6, w 10, nb 2): **22**						
Total (9 wickets, 50 overs): **230**						

FoW: 1-78 (Mudassar Nazar), 2-128 (Saleem Malik), 3-147 (Rameez Raja), 4-167 (Ijaz Ahmed), 5-186 (Imran Khan), 6-202 (Saleem Yousuf), 7-202 (Wasim Akram), 8-208 (Javed Miandad), 9-208 (Shoaib Mohammad).

Bowling	O	M	R	W
Patterson	10	1	34	3
Walsh	10	1	34	2
Harper	10	0	38	1
Benjamin	10	0	69	3
Richards	10	0	45	0

1987 WORLD CUP

Finals

Reliance World Cup, 1987/88, 1st Semi-Final
Pakistan v Australia
Gaddafi Stadium, Lahore
4 November 1987 (50-over match)

Result: Australia won by 18 runs
Australia advances to the final
Toss: Australia
Umpires: HD Bird (Eng) and DR Shepherd (Eng)
Man Of The Match: CJ McDermott

Australia innings (50 overs maximum)			R	M	B	4	6
GR Marsh	run out		31	78	57	2	0
DC Boon	st +Javed Miandad	b Saleem Malik	65	133	91	4	0
DM Jones	b Tauseef Ahmed		38	58	45	3	0
*AR Border	run out		18	43	22	2	0
MRJ Veletta	b Imran Khan		48	57	50	2	0
SR Waugh	not out		32	38	28	4	1
SP O'Donnell	run out		0	1	2	0	0
+GC Dyer	b Imran Khan		0	2	1	0	0
CJ McDermott	b Imran Khan		1	6	3	0	0
TBA May	not out		0	8	2	0	0
Extras (b 1, lb 19, w 13, nb 1): **34**							
Total (8 wickets, 50 overs): **267**							

DNB: BA Reid.
FoW: 1-73 (Marsh), 2-155 (Boon), 3-155 (Jones), 4-215 (Border), 5-236 (Veletta), 6-236 (O'Donnell), 7-241 (Dyer), 8-249 (McDermott).

Bowling	O	M	R	W
Imran Khan	10	1	36	3
Saleem Jaffar	6	0	57	0
Wasim Akram	10	0	54	0
Abdul Qadir	10	0	39	0
Tauseef Ahmed	10	1	39	1
Saleem Malik	4	0	22	1

Pakistan innings (target: 268 runs from 50 overs)			R	M	B	4	6
Rameez Raja	run out		1	2	1	0	0
Mansoor Akhtar	b McDermott		9	36	19	0	0
Saleem Malik	c McDermott	b Waugh	25	43	31	3	0
Javed Miandad	b Reid		70	149	103	4	0
*Imran Khan	c Dyer	b Border	58	98	84	4	0
Wasim Akram	b McDermott		20	16	13	0	2
Ijaz Ahmed	c Jones	b Reid	8	11	7	1	0
+Saleem Yousuf	c Dyer	b McDermott	21	23	15	2	0
Abdul Qadir	not out		20	23	16	2	0
Saleem Jaffar	c Dyer	b McDermott	0	7	2	0	0
Tauseef Ahmed	c Dyer	b McDermott	1	3	3	0	0
Extras (lb 6, w 10): **16**							
Total (all out, 49 overs): **249**							

FoW: 1-2 (Rameez Raja), 2-37 (Mansoor Akhtar), 3-38 (Saleem Malik), 4-150 (Imran Khan), 5-177 (Wasim Akram), 6-192 (Ijaz Ahmed), 7-212 (Javed Miandad), 8-236 (Saleem Yousuf), 9-247 (Saleem Jaffar), 10-249 (Tauseef Ahmed).

Bowling	O	M	R	W
McDermott	10	0	44	5
Reid	10	2	41	2
Waugh	9	1	51	1
O'Donnell	10	1	45	0
May	6	0	36	0
Border	4	0	26	1

Reliance World Cup, 1987/88, 2nd Semi-Final
India v England
Wankhede Stadium, Bombay
5 November 1987 (50-over match)

Result: England won by 35 runs
England advances to the final
Toss: India
Umpires: AR Crafter (Aus) and SJ Woodward (NZ)
Man Of The Match: GA Gooch

England innings (50 overs maximum)			R	B	4	6
GA Gooch	c Srikkanth	b Maninder Singh	115	136	11	0
RT Robinson	st More	b Maninder Singh	13	36	2	0
CWJ Athey	c More	b Sharma	4	17	0	0
*MW Gatting	b Maninder Singh		56	62	5	0
AJ Lamb	not out		32	29	2	0
JE Emburey	lbw	b Kapil Dev	6	10	0	0
PAJ DeFreitas	b Kapil Dev		7	8	1	0
+PR Downton	not out		1	5	0	0
Extras (b 1, lb 18, w 1): **20**						
Total (6 wickets, 50 overs): **254**						

DNB: NA Foster, GC Small, EE Hemmings.
FoW: 1-40 (Robinson), 2-79 (Athey), 3-196 (Gatting), 4-203 (Gooch), 5-219 (Emburey), 6-231 (DeFreitas).

Bowling	O	M	R	W
Kapil Dev	10	1	38	2
Prabhakar	9	1	40	0
Maninder Singh	10	0	54	3
Sharma	9	0	41	1
Shastri	10	0	49	0
Azharuddin	2	0	13	0

India innings (target: 255 runs from 50 overs)			R	B	4	6
K Srikkanth	b Foster		31	55	4	0
SM Gavaskar	b DeFreitas		4	7	1	0
NS Sidhu	c Athey	b Foster	22	40	0	0
M Azharuddin	lbw	b Hemmings	64	74	7	0
CS Pandit	lbw	b Foster	24	30	3	0
*N Kapil Dev	c Gatting	b Hemmings	30	22	3	0
RJ Shastri	c Downton	b Hemmings	21	32	2	0
+KS More	c & b Emburey		0	5	0	0
M Prabhakar	c Downton	b Small	4	11	0	0
C Sharma	c Lamb	b Hemmings	0	1	0	0
Maninder Singh	not out		0	0	0	0
Extras (b 1, lb 9, w 6, nb 3): **19**						
Total (all out, 45.3 overs): **219**						

FoW: 1-7 (Gavaskar), 2-58 (Srikkanth), 3-73 (Sidhu), 4-121 (Pandit), 5-168 (Kapil Dev), 6-204 (Azharuddin), 7-205 (More), 8-218 (Prabhakar), 9-219 (Sharma), 10-219 (Shastri).

Bowling	O	M	R	W
DeFreitas	7	0	37	1
Small	6	0	22	1
Emburey	10	1	35	1
Foster	10	0	47	3
Hemmings	9.3	1	52	4
Gooch	3	0	16	0

Reliance World Cup, 1987/88, Final
Australia v England
Eden Gardens, Calcutta
8 November 1987 (50-over match)

Result: Australia won by 7 runs
Australia wins the 1987/88 Reliance World Cup
Toss: Australia
Umpires: RB Gupta and Mahboob Shah (Pak)
Man Of The Match: DC Boon

Australia innings (50 overs maximum)			R	M	B	4	6
DC Boon	c Downton	b Hemmings	75	159	125	7	0
GR Marsh	b Foster		24	71	49	3	0
DM Jones	c Athey	b Hemmings	33	75	57	1	1
CJ McDermott	b Gooch		14	6	8	2	0
*AR Border	run out (Robinson/Downton)		31	48	31	3	0
MRJ Veletta	not out		45	50	31	6	0
SR Waugh	not out		5	5	4	0	0
Extras (b 1, lb 13, w 5, nb 7): **26**							
Total (5 wickets, 50 overs): **253**							

DNB: SP O'Donnell, +GC Dyer, TBA May, BA Reid.
FoW: 1-75 (Marsh), 2-151 (Jones), 3-166 (McDermott), 4-168 (Boon), 5-241 (Border).

Bowling	O	M	R	W
DeFreitas	6	1	34	0
Small	6	0	33	0
Foster	10	0	38	1
Hemmings	10	1	48	2
Emburey	10	0	44	0
Gooch	8	1	42	1

England innings (target: 254 runs from 50 overs)			R	M	B	4	6
GA Gooch	lbw	b O'Donnell	35	74	57	4	0
RT Robinson	lbw	b McDermott	0	2	1	0	0
CWJ Athey	run out (Waugh/Reid)		58	126	103	2	0
*MW Gatting	c Dyer	b Border	41	55	45	3	1
AJ Lamb	b Waugh		45	56	45	4	0
+PR Downton	c O'Donnell	b Border	9	13	8	1	0
JE Emburey	run out (Boon/McDermott)		10	27	16	0	0
PAJ DeFreitas	c Reid	b Waugh	17	10	10	2	1
NA Foster	not out		7	12	6	0	0
GC Small	not out		3	6	3	0	0
Extras (b 1, lb 14, w 2, nb 4): **21**							
Total (8 wickets, 50 overs): **246**							

DNB: EE Hemmings.
FoW: 1-1 (Robinson), 2-66 (Gooch), 3-135 (Gatting), 4-170 (Athey), 5-188 (Downton), 6-218 (Lamb), 7-220 (Emburey), 8-235 (DeFreitas).

Bowling	O	M	R	W
McDermott	10	1	51	1
Reid	10	0	43	0
Waugh	9	0	37	2
O'Donnell	10	1	35	1
May	4	0	27	0
Border	7	0	38	2

1992 WORLD CUP

Benson & Hedges World Cup, 1991/92, 1st Match
New Zealand v Australia
Eden Park, Auckland
22 February 1992 (50-over match)

Result: New Zealand won by 37 runs
Points: New Zealand 2, Australia 0
Toss: New Zealand
Umpires: Khizer Hayat (Pak) and DR Shepherd (Eng)
World Cup Referee: PD McDermott
Man Of The Match: MD Crowe

New Zealand innings (50 overs maximum)			R	M	B	4	6
JG Wright	b McDermott		0	3	1	0	0
RT Latham	c Healy	b Moody	26	65	44	4	0
AH Jones	lbw	b Reid	4	16	14	1	0
*MD Crowe	not out		100	180	134	11	0
KR Rutherford	run out		57	88	71	6	0
CZ Harris	run out		14	14	15	2	0
+IDS Smith	c Healy	b McDermott	14	15	14	1	0
CL Cairns	not out		16	15	11	2	0
Extras (lb 6, w 7, nb 4): **17**							
Total (6 wickets, 50 overs): **248**							

DNB: DN Patel, GR Larsen, W Watson.
FoW: 1-2 (Wright), 2-13 (Jones), 3-53 (Latham), 4-171 (Rutherford), 5-191 (Harris), 6-215 (Smith).

Bowling	O	M	R	W
McDermott	10	1	43	2 (2w)
Reid	10	0	39	1 (4nb 2w)
Moody	9	1	37	1
SR Waugh	10	0	60	0 (2w)
Taylor	7	0	36	0
ME Waugh	4	0	27	0 (1w)

Australia innings (target: 249 runs from 50 overs)			R	M	B	4	6
DC Boon	run out		100	176	131	11	0
GR Marsh	c Latham	b Larsen	19	60	56	2	0
DM Jones	run out		21	28	27	3	0
*AR Border	c Cairns	b Patel	3	13	11	0	0
TM Moody	c & b Latham		7	10	11	0	0
ME Waugh	lbw	b Larsen	2	9	5	0	0
SR Waugh	c & b Larsen		38	48	34	3	1
+IA Healy	not out		7	16	9	0	0
CJ McDermott	run out		1	4	1	0	0
PL Taylor	c Rutherford	b Watson	1	3	2	0	0
BA Reid	c Jones	b Harris	3	4	4	0	0
Extras (lb 6, w 2, nb 1): **9**							
Total (all out, 48.1 overs): **211**							

FoW: 1-62 (Marsh), 2-92 (Jones), 3-104 Border), 4-120 (Moody), 5-125 (ME Waugh), 6-199 (SR Waugh), 7-200 (Boon), 8-205 (McDermott), 9-206 (Taylor), 10-211 (Reid).

Bowling	O	M	R	W
Cairns	4	0	30	0 (1nb 1w)
Patel	10	1	36	1 (1w)
Watson	9	1	39	1
Larsen	10	1	30	3
Harris	7.1	0	35	1
Latham	8	0	35	1

Benson & Hedges World Cup, 1991/92, 2nd Match
England v India
W.A.C.A. Ground, Perth (day/night)
22 February 1992 (50-over match)

Result: England won by 9 runs
Points: England 2, India 0
Toss: England
Umpires: JD Buultjens (SL) and PJ McConnell
World Cup Referee: Tony Mann
Man Of The Match: IT Botham

England innings (50 overs maximum)			R	M	B	4	6
*GA Gooch	c Tendulkar	b Shastri	51	121	89	1	0
IT Botham	c More	b Kapil Dev	9	33	21	1	0
RA Smith	c Azharuddin	b Prabhakar	91	145	108	8	2
GA Hick	c More	b Banerjee	5	5	6	1	0
NH Fairbrother	c Srikkanth	b Srinath	24	47	34	1	0
+AJ Stewart	b Prabhakar		13	22	15	1	0
CC Lewis	c Banerjee	b Kapil Dev	10	10	6	1	0
DR Pringle	c Srikkanth	b Srinath	1	4	3	0	0
DA Reeve	not out		8	14	8	0	0
PAJ DeFreitas	run out		1	2	5	0	0
PCR Tufnell	not out		3	7	5	0	0
Extras (b 1, lb 6, w 13): **20**							
Total (9 wickets, 50 overs): **236**							

FoW: 1-21 (Botham), 2-131 (Gooch), 3-137 (Hick), 4-197 (Fairbrother), 5-198 (Smith), 6-214 Lewis), 7-222 (Pringle), 8-223 (Stewart), 9-224 DeFreitas).

Bowling	O	M	R	W	
Kapil Dev	10	0	38	2 (6w)	
Prabhakar	10	3	34	2	
Srinath	9	1	47	2 (5w)	
Banerjee	7	0	45	1	
Tendulkar	10	0	37	0 (1w)	
Shastri	4	0	28	1 (1w)	

India innings (target: 237 runs from 50 overs)			R	M	B	4	6
RJ Shastri	run out		57	151	112	2	0
K Srikkanth	c Botham	b DeFreitas	39	63	50	7	0
*M Azharuddin	c Stewart	b Reeve	0	2	1	0	0
SR Tendulkar	c Stewart	b Botham	35	51	44	5	0
VG Kambli	c Hick	b Botham	3	16	11	0	0
PK Amre	run out		22	44	31	0	0
N Kapil Dev	c DeFreitas	b Reeve	17	24	18	2	0
ST Banerjee	not out		25	28	16	1	1
+KS More	run out		1	6	4	0	0
M Prabhakar	b Reeve		0	1	2	0	0
J Srinath	run out		11	10	8	0	0
Extras (lb 9, w 7, nb 1): **17**							
Total (all out, 49.2 overs): **227**							

FoW: 1-63 (Srikkanth), 2-63 (Azharuddin), 3-126 (Tendulkar), 4-140 (Kambli), 5-149 (Shastri), 6-187 (Kapil Dev), 7-194 Amre), 8-200 (More), 9-201 (Prabhakar), 10-227 (Srinath).

Bowling	O	M	R	W	
Pringle	10	0	53	0 (1w)	
Lewis	9.2	0	36	0 (1nb 5w)	
DeFreitas	10	0	39	1	
Reeve	6	0	38	3 (1w)	
Botham	10	0	27	2	
Tufnell	4	0	25	0	

Benson & Hedges World Cup, 1991/92, 3rd Match
Sri Lanka v Zimbabwe
Pukekura Park, New Plymouth
23 February 1992 (50-over match)

Result: Sri Lanka won by 3 wickets
Points: Sri Lanka 2, Zimbabwe 0
Toss: Sri Lanka
Umpires: PD Reporter (Ind) and SJ Woodward
World Cup Referee: PW Moody
ODI Debuts: KG Duers, A Flower, WR James (Zim)
Man Of The Match: A Flower

Zimbabwe innings (50 overs maximum)

			R	M	B	4	6
+A Flower	not out		115	215	152	8	1
WR James	c Tillakaratne	b Wickramasinghe	17	31	21	3	0
AJ Pycroft	c Ramanayake	b Gurusinha	5	31	22	0	0
*DL Houghton	c Tillakaratne	b Gurusinha	10	23	19	1	0
KJ Arnott	c Tillakaratne	b Wickramasinghe	52	66	56	4	1
AC Waller	not out		83	57	45	9	3
Extras (b 2, lb 6, w 13, nb 9): **30**							
Total (4 wickets, 50 overs): **312**							

DNB: IP Butchart, EA Brandes, KG Duers, MP Jarvis, AJ Traicos.
FoW: 1-30 (James), 2-57 (Pycroft), 3-82 (Houghton), 4-167 (Arnott).

Bowling	O	M	R	W
Ramanayake	10	0	59	0 (1nb 3w)
Wijegunawardene	7	0	54	0 (6nb 3w)
Wickramasinghe	10	1	50	2 (2nb 1w)
Gurusinha	10	0	72	2 (6w)
Kalpage	10	0	51	0
Jayasuriya	3	0	18	0

Sri Lanka innings (target: 313 runs from 50 overs)

			R	M	B	4	6
RS Mahanama	c Arnott	b Brandes	59	100	89	4	0
MAR Samarasekera	c Duers	b Traicos	75	81	61	11	1
*PA de Silva	c Houghton	b Brandes	14	40	28	1	0
AP Gurusinha	run out		5	9	6	0	0
A Ranatunga	not out		88	117	61	9	1
ST Jayasuriya	c Flower	b Houghton	32	24	23	2	2
+HP Tillakaratne	b Jarvis		18	25	12	1	1
RS Kalpage	c Houghton	b Brandes	11	19	14	1	0
CPH Ramanayake	not out		1	2	1	0	0
Extras (lb 5, w 5): **10**							
Total (7 wickets, 49.2 overs): **313**							

DNB: KIW Wijegunawardene, GP Wickramasinghe.
FoW: 1-128 (Samarasekera), 2-144 (Mahanama), 3-155 (Gurusinha), 4-167 (de Silva), 5-212 (Jayasuriya), 6-273 (Tillakaratne), 7-309 (Kalpage).

Bowling	O	M	R	W
Jarvis	9.2	0	51	1 (1w)
Brandes	10	0	70	3
Duers	10	0	72	0
Butchart	8	0	63	0 (3w)
Traicos	10	1	33	1 (1w)
Houghton	2	0	19	1

Benson & Hedges World Cup, 1991/92, 4th Match
Pakistan v West Indies
Melbourne Cricket Ground
23 February 1992 (50-over match)

Result: West Indies won by 10 wickets
Points: West Indies 2, Pakistan 0
Toss: West Indies
Umpires: SG Randell and ID Robinson (Zim)
World Cup Referee: Jack Edwards
ODI Debuts: Iqbal Sikander, Wasim Haider (Pak)
Man Of The Match: BC Lara

Pakistan innings (50 overs maximum)			R	M	B	4	6
Rameez Raja	not out		102	181	158	4	0
Aamer Sohail	c Logie	b Benjamin	23	53	44	3	0
Inzamam-ul-Haq	c Hooper	b Harper	27	46	39	0	0
*Javed Miandad	not out		57	80	61	5	0
Extras (b 1, lb 3, w 5, nb 2): **11**							
Total (2 wickets, 50 overs): **220**							

DNB: Saleem Malik, Ijaz Ahmed, Wasim Akram, Iqbal Sikander, Wasim Haider, +Moin Khan, Aaqib Javed.
FoW: 1-45 (Aamer Sohail), 2-97 (Inzamam-ul-Haq).

Bowling	O	M	R	W	
Marshall	10	1	53	0	(3w)
Ambrose	10	0	40	0	(2nb 1w)
Benjamin	10	0	49	1	(1w)
Hooper	10	0	41	0	
Harper	10	0	33	1	

West Indies innings (target: 221 runs from 50 overs)		R	M	B	4	6
DL Haynes	not out	93	192	144	7	0
BC Lara	retired hurt	88	150	101	11	0
*RB Richardson	not out	20	41	40	1	0
Extras (b 2, lb 8, w 7, nb 3): **20**						
Total (0 wickets, 46.5 overs): **221**						

DNB: CL Hooper, AL Logie, KLT Arthurton, RA Harper, MD Marshall, WKM Benjamin, +D Williams, CEL Ambrose.

Bowling	O	M	R	W	
Wasim Akram	10	0	37	0	(7w)
Aaqib Javed	8.5	0	42	0	(2nb)
Wasim Haider	8	0	42	0	(1nb)
Ijaz Ahmed	6	1	29	0	
Iqbal Sikander	8	1	26	0	
Aamer Sohail	6	0	35	0	

Benson & Hedges World Cup, 1991/92, 5th Match
New Zealand v Sri Lanka
Trust Bank Park, Hamilton
25 February 1992 (50-over match)

Result: New Zealand won by 6 wickets
Points: New Zealand 2, Sri Lanka 0
Toss: New Zealand
Umpires: PD Reporter (Ind) and DR Shepherd (Eng)
World Cup Referee: BJ Paterson
Man Of The Match: KR Rutherford

Sri Lanka innings (50 overs maximum)

			R	M	B	4	6
RS Mahanama	c & b Harris		80	175	131	6	0
MAR Samarasekera	c Wright	b Watson	9	25	20	1	0
AP Gurusinha	c Smith	b Harris	9	41	33	0	0
*PA de Silva	run out		31	61	45	2	0
A Ranatunga	c Rutherford	b Harris	20	40	26	2	0
ST Jayasuriya	run out		5	10	7	0	0
+HP Tillakaratne	c Crowe	b Watson	8	21	19	0	0
RS Kalpage	c Larsen	b Watson	11	20	17	0	0
CPH Ramanayake	run out		2	2	1	0	0
SD Anurasiri	not out		3	7	2	0	0
GP Wickramasinghe	not out		3	2	4	0	0

Extras (b 1, lb 15, w 4, nb 5): **25**
Total (9 wickets, 50 overs): **206**

FoW: 1-18 (Samarasekera), 2-50 (Gurusinha), 3-120 (de Silva), 4-172 (Ranatunga), 5-172 (Mahanama), 6-181 (Jayasuriya), 7-195 (Tillakaratne), 8-199 (Ramanayake), 9-202 (Kalpage).

Bowling	O	M	R	W	
Morrison	8	0	36	0	(2nb 1w)
Watson	10	0	37	3	(2nb 1w)
Larsen	10	1	29	0	(1w)
Harris	10	0	43	3	(1nb 1w)
Latham	3	0	13	0	
Patel	9	0	32	0	

New Zealand innings (target: 207 from 50 overs)

			R	M	B	4	6
JG Wright	c & b Kalpage		57	89	76	9	0
RT Latham	b Kalpage		20	72	41	3	0
AH Jones	c Jayasuriya	b Gurusinha	49	106	77	4	0
*MD Crowe	c Ramanayake	b Wickramasinghe	5	25	23	0	0
KR Rutherford	not out		65	79	71	6	1
CZ Harris	not out		5	13	5	0	0

Extras (lb 3, w 3, nb 3): **9**
Total (4 wickets, 48.2 overs): **210**

DNB: +IDS Smith, DN Patel, DK Morrison, GR Larsen, W Watson.
FoW: 1-77 (Latham), 2-91 (Wright), 3-105 (Crowe), 4-186 (Jones).

Bowling	O	M	R	W	
Ramanayake	9.2	0	46	0	(2nb 2w)
Wickramasinghe	8	1	40	1	(1w)
Anurasiri	10	1	27	0	
Kalpage	10	0	33	2	
Gurusinha	4	0	19	1	
Ranatunga	4	0	22	0	
Jayasuriya	2	0	14	0	
de Silva	1	0	6	0	(1w)

Benson & Hedges World Cup, 1991/92, 6th Match
Australia v South Africa
Sydney Cricket Ground (day/night)
26 February 1992 (50-over match)

Result: South Africa won by 9 wickets
Points: South Africa 2, Australia 0
Toss: Australia
Umpires: BL Aldridge (NZ) and SA Bucknor (WI)
World Cup Referee: Ted Wykes
ODI Debuts: WJ Cronje, MW Pringle, JN Rhodes (SA)
Man Of The Match: KC Wessels

Australia innings (49 overs maximum)

			R	M	B	4	6
GR Marsh	c Richardson	b Kuiper	25	89	72	1	0
DC Boon	run out (Snell/Cronje)		27	31	32	4	0
DM Jones	c Richardson	b McMillan	24	79	51	1	0
*AR Border	b Kuiper		0	1	1	0	0
TM Moody	lbw	b Donald	10	47	33	0	0
SR Waugh	c Cronje	b McMillan	27	58	51	1	0
+IA Healy	c McMillan	b Donald	16	34	24	2	0
PL Taylor	b Donald		4	18	9	0	0
CJ McDermott	run out (Rhodes/Snell)		6	20	12	0	0
MR Whitney	not out		9	19	15	1	0
BA Reid	not out		5	13	10	0	0

Extras (lb 2, w 11, nb 4): **17**
Total (9 wickets, 49 overs, 215 mins): **170**

FoW: 1-42 (Boon), 2-76 (Marsh), 3-76 (Border), 4-97 (Jones), 5-108 (Moody), 6-143 (Healy), 7-146 (Waugh), 8-156 (Taylor), 9-161 (McDermott).

Bowling	O	M	R	W	
Donald	10	0	34	3 (5w)	
Pringle	10	0	52	0 (1w, 2nb)	
Snell	9	1	15	0	
McMillan	10	0	35	2 (3w, 2nb)	
Kuiper	5	0	15	2 (1w)	
Cronje	5	1	17	0 (1w)	

South Africa innings (target: 171 from 49 overs)

		R	M	B	4	6
*KC Wessels	not out	81	173	148	9	0
AC Hudson	b Taylor	28	81	52	3	0
PN Kirsten	not out	49	91	88	1	0

Extras (lb 5, w 6, nb 2): **13**
Total (1 wicket, 46.5 overs, 173 mins): **171**

DNB: WJ Cronje, AP Kuiper, JN Rhodes, BM McMillan, +DJ Richardson, RP Snell, MW Pringle, AA Donald.
FoW: 1-74 (Hudson).

Bowling	O	M	R	W	
McDermott	10	1	23	0 (2nb)	
Reid	8.5	0	41	0 (4w)	
Whitney	6	0	26	0	
Waugh	4	1	16	0 (1w)	
Taylor	10	1	32	1 (1w)	
Border	4	0	13	0	
Moody	4	0	15	0	

Note: Wides count as 'balls faced' in the batsmen's analyses

Benson & Hedges World Cup, 1991/92, 7th Match
Pakistan v Zimbabwe
Bellerive Oval, Hobart
27 February 1992 (50-over match)

Result: Pakistan won by 53 runs
Points: Pakistan 2, Zimbabwe 0
Toss: Zimbabwe
Umpires: JD Buultjens (SL) and SG Randell
World Cup Referee: Denis Rogers
Man Of The Match: Aamer Sohail

Pakistan innings (50 overs maximum)			R	M	B	4	6
Rameez Raja	c Flower	b Jarvis	9	25	16	1	0
Aamer Sohail	c Pycroft	b Butchart	114	178	136	12	0
Inzamam-ul-Haq	c Brandes	b Butchart	14	49	43	0	0
Javed Miandad	lbw	b Butchart	89	125	94	5	0
Saleem Malik	not out		14	24	12	0	0
Wasim Akram	not out		1	1	1	0	0
Extras (lb 9, nb 4): **13**							
Total (4 wickets, 50 overs): **254**							

DNB: *Imran Khan, Mushtaq Ahmed, Iqbal Sikander, +Moin Khan, Aaqib Javed.
FoW: 1-29 (Rameez Raja), 2-63 (Inzamam-ul-Haq), 3-208 (Aamer Sohail), 4-253 (Javed Miandad).

Bowling	O	M	R	W
Brandes	10	1	49	0 (4nb)
Jarvis	10	1	52	1
Omarshah	10	1	24	0
Butchart	10	0	57	3
Traicos	10	0	63	0

Zimbabwe innings (target: 255 runs from 50 overs)			R	M	B	4	6
KJ Arnott	c Wasim Akram	b Iqbal Sikander	7	69	61	0	0
+A Flower	c Inzamam-ul-Haq	b Wasim Akram	6	34	21	0	0
AJ Pycroft	b Wasim Akram		0	3	4	0	0
*DL Houghton	c Rameez Raja	b Aamer Sohail	44	92	82	3	0
AH Omarshah	b Aamer Sohail		33	55	58	2	0
AC Waller	b Wasim Akram		44	53	36	3	1
IP Butchart	c Javed Miandad	b Aaqib Javed	33	42	27	4	0
EA Brandes	not out		2	12	3	0	0
AJ Traicos	not out		8	7	7	0	0
Extras (b 3, lb 15, w 6): **24**							
Total (7 wickets, 50 overs): **201**							

DNB: WR James, MP Jarvis.
FoW: 1-14 Flower), 2-14 (Pycroft), 3-33 (Arnott), 4-103 (Omarshah), 5-108 (Houghton), 6-187 (Butchart), 7-190 (Waller).

Bowling	O	M	R	W
Wasim Akram	10	2	21	3 (3w)
Aaqib Javed	10	1	49	1 (1w)
Iqbal Sikander	10	1	35	1 (1w)
Mushtaq Ahmed	10	1	34	0
Aamer Sohail	6	1	26	2
Saleem Malik	4	0	18	0 (1w)

Benson & Hedges World Cup, 1991/92, 8th Match
England v West Indies
Melbourne Cricket Ground (day/night)
27 February 1992 (50-over match)

Result: England won by 6 wickets
Points: England 2, West Indies 0
Toss: England
Umpires: KE Liebenberg (SA) and SJ Woodward (NZ)
World Cup Referee: Jim Mann
Man Of The Match: CC Lewis

West Indies innings (50 overs maximum)			R	M	B	4	6
DL Haynes	c Fairbrother	b DeFreitas	38	85	68	5	0
BC Lara	c Stewart	b Lewis	0	6	2	0	0
*RB Richardson	c Botham	b Lewis	5	27	17	1	0
CL Hooper	c Reeve	b Botham	5	26	20	0	0
KLT Arthurton	c Fairbrother	b DeFreitas	54	130	101	2	2
AL Logie	run out		20	42	27	0	1
RA Harper	c Hick	b Reeve	3	20	14	0	0
MD Marshall	run out		3	13	8	0	0
+D Williams	c Pringle	b DeFreitas	6	19	19	0	0
CEL Ambrose	c DeFreitas	b Lewis	4	23	6	0	0
WKM Benjamin	not out		11	14	15	1	0

Extras (lb 4, w 3, nb 1): 8
Total (all out, 49.2 overs): 157

FoW: 1-0 (Lara), 2-22 (Richardson), 3-36 (Hooper), 4-55 (Haynes), 5-91 (Logie), 6-102 (Harper), 7-116 (Marshall), 8-131 (Williams), 9-145 (Arthurton), 10-157 (Ambrose).

Bowling	O	M	R	W
Pringle	7	3	16	0
Lewis	8.2	1	30	3 (1nb)
DeFreitas	9	2	34	3 (2w)
Botham	10	0	30	1
Reeve	10	1	23	1 (1w)
Tufnell	5	0	20	0

England innings (target: 158 runs from 50 overs)			R	M	B	4	6
*GA Gooch	st Williams	b Hooper	65	130	101	7	0
IT Botham	c Williams	b Benjamin	8	56	28	0	0
RA Smith	c Logie	b Benjamin	8	29	28	1	0
GA Hick	c & b Harper		54	73	55	3	1
NH Fairbrother	not out		13	33	28	1	0
+AJ Stewart	not out		0	3	1	0	0

Extras (lb 7, w 4, nb 1): 12
Total (4 wickets, 39.5 overs): 160

DNB: DA Reeve, CC Lewis, DR Pringle, PAJ DeFreitas, PCR Tufnell.
FoW: 1-50 (Botham), 2-71 (Smith), 3-126 (Gooch), 4-156 (Hick).

Bowling	O	M	R	W
Ambrose	8	1	26	0
Marshall	8	0	37	0 (2w)
Benjamin	9.5	2	22	2 (1nb 2w)
Hooper	10	1	38	1
Harper	4	0	30	1

Benson & Hedges World Cup, 1991/92, 9th Match
India v Sri Lanka
Harrup Park, Mackay
28 February 1992 (50-over match)

Result: No result
Points: India 1, Sri Lanka 1
Toss: Sri Lanka
Umpires: ID Robinson (Zim) and DR Shepherd (Eng)
World Cup Referee: A Pettigrew
ODI Debuts: A Jadeja (Ind)

India innings (20 overs maximum)		R	M	B	4	6
K Srikkanth	not out	1	2	2	0	0
N Kapil Dev	not out	0	2	0	0	0
Extras: *0*						
Total (0 wickets, 0.2 overs): *1*						

DNB: *M Azharuddin, SR Tendulkar, VG Kambli, PK Amre, A Jadeja, SLV Raju, M Prabhakar, +KS More, J Srinath.

Bowling	O	M	R	W
Ramanayake	0.2	0	1	0

Sri Lanka team: RS Mahanama, UC Hathurusingha, AP Gurusinha, *PA de Silva, A Ranatunga, ST Jayasuriya, +HP Tillakaratne, RS Kalpage, CPH Ramanayake, KIW Wijegunawardene, GP Wickramasinghe.

The match was initially reduced to 20 overs a side due to rain. A helicopter was used to dry the pitch, but as play began rain fell again, washing out the game.

Benson & Hedges World Cup, 1991/92, 10th Match
New Zealand v South Africa
Eden Park, Auckland
29 February 1992 (50-over match)

Result: New Zealand won by 7 wickets
Points: New Zealand 2, South Africa 0
Toss: South Africa
Umpires: Khizer Hayat (Pak) and PD Reporter (Ind)
World Cup Referee: PD McDermott
ODI Debuts: T Bosch (SA)
Man Of The Match: MJ Greatbatch

South Africa innings (50 overs maximum)

			R	M	B	4	6
*KC Wessels	c Smith	b Watson	3	22	18	0	0
AC Hudson	b Patel		1	18	16	0	0
PN Kirsten	c Cairns	b Watson	90	156	129	10	0
WJ Cronje	c Smith	b Harris	7	30	22	0	0
+DJ Richardson	c Larsen	b Cairns	28	69	53	1	0
AP Kuiper	run out		2	2	2	0	0
JN Rhodes	c Crowe	b Cairns	6	17	13	0	0
BM McMillan	not out		33	44	40	1	0
RP Snell	not out		11	13	8	1	0
Extras (lb 8, nb 1): **9**							
Total (7 wickets, 50 overs): **190**							

DNB: AA Donald, T Bosch.
FoW: 1-8 (Hudson), 2-10 (Wessels), 3-29 (Cronje), 4-108 (Richardson), 5-111 (Kuiper), 6-121 (Rhodes), 7-162 (Kirsten).

Bowling	O	M	R	W
Watson	10	2	30	2
Patel	10	1	28	1
Larsen	10	1	29	0
Harris	10	2	33	1
Latham	2	0	19	0
Cairns	8	0	43	2 (1nb)

New Zealand innings (target: 191 from 50 overs)

			R	M	B	4	6
MJ Greatbatch	b Kirsten		68	80	60	9	2
RT Latham	c Wessels	b Snell	60	117	69	7	0
AH Jones	not out		34	64	63	4	0
+IDS Smith	c Kirsten	b Donald	19	9	8	4	0
*MD Crowe	not out		3	17	9	0	0
Extras (b 1, w 5, nb 1): **7**							
Total (3 wickets, 34.3 overs): **191**							

DNB: KR Rutherford, CZ Harris, CL Cairns, DN Patel, GR Larsen, W Watson.
FoW: 1-114 Greatbatch), 2-155 (Latham), 3-179 (Smith).

Bowling	O	M	R	W
Donald	10	0	38	1 (1nb 1w)
McMillan	5	1	23	0 (3w)
Snell	7	0	56	1
Bosch	2.3	0	19	0
Cronje	2	0	14	0 (1w)
Kuiper	1	0	18	0
Kirsten	7	1	22	1

Benson & Hedges World Cup, 1991/92, 11th Match
West Indies v Zimbabwe
Brisbane Cricket Ground, Woolloongabba, Brisbane
29 February 1992 (50-over match)

Result: West Indies won by 75 runs
Points: West Indies 2, Zimbabwe 0
Toss: Zimbabwe
Umpires: KE Liebenberg (SA) and SJ Woodward (NZ)
World Cup Referee: MW Johnson
ODI Debuts: ADR Campbell (Zim)
Man Of The Match: BC Lara

West Indies innings (50 overs maximum)			R	M	B	4	6
PV Simmons	b Brandes		21	60	45	3	0
BC Lara	c Houghton	b Omarshah	72	86	71	12	0
*RB Richardson	c Brandes	b Jarvis	56	102	76	2	2
CL Hooper	c Pycroft	b Traicos	63	72	67	5	1
KLT Arthurton	b Duers		26	28	18	2	2
AL Logie	run out		5	7	6	0	0
MD Marshall	c Houghton	b Brandes	2	11	10	0	0
+D Williams	not out		8	10	6	1	0
WKM Benjamin	b Brandes		1	5	4	0	0
Extras (b 1, lb 6, w 2, nb 1): **10**							
Total (8 wickets, 50 overs): **264**							

DNB: AC Cummins, BP Patterson.
FoW: 1-78 (Simmons), 2-103 (Lara), 3-220 (Hooper), 4-221 (Richardson), 5-239 (Logie), 6-254 (Marshall), 7-255 (Arthurton), 8-264 Benjamin).

Bowling	O	M	R	W
Brandes	10	1	45	3 (1nb 2w)
Jarvis	10	1	71	1
Duers	10	0	52	1
Omarshah	10	2	39	1
Traicos	10	0	50	1

Zimbabwe innings (target: 265 runs from 50 overs)			R	M	B	4	6
KJ Arnott	retired hurt		16	55	36	1	0
+A Flower	b Patterson		6	23	20	0	0
AJ Pycroft	c Williams	b Benjamin	10	26	24	0	0
*DL Houghton	c Patterson	b Hooper	55	94	88	3	0
AC Waller	c Simmons	b Benjamin	0	13	9	0	0
ADR Campbell	c Richardson	b Hooper	1	27	18	0	0
AH Omarshah	not out		60	93	87	4	0
EA Brandes	c & b Benjamin		6	16	9	0	0
AJ Traicos	run out		8	21	19	0	0
MP Jarvis	not out		5	6	4	1	0
Extras (lb 9, w 5, nb 8): **22**							
Total (7 wickets, 50 overs): **189**							

DNB: KG Duers.
FoW: 1-21 (Flower), 2-43 (Pycroft), 3-48 (Waller), 4-63 (Campbell), 5-132 (Houghton), 6-161 (Brandes), 7-181 (Traicos).

Bowling	O	M	R	W
Patterson	10	0	25	1 (1w)
Marshall	6	0	23	0 (2nb)
Benjamin	10	2	27	3 (3nb 3w)
Cummins	10	0	33	0 (3nb 1w)
Hooper	10	0	47	2
Arthurton	4	0	25	0

Benson & Hedges World Cup, 1991/92, 12th Match
Australia v India
Brisbane Cricket Ground, Woolloongabba, Brisbane
1 March 1992 (50-over match)

Result: Australia won by 1 run (revised target)
Points: Australia 2, India 0
Toss: Australia
Umpires: BL Aldridge (NZ) and ID Robinson (Zim)
World Cup Referee: MW Johnson
Man Of The Match: DM Jones

Australia innings (50 overs maximum)			R	M	B	4	6
MA Taylor	c More	b Kapil Dev	13	18	18	0	0
GR Marsh	b Kapil Dev		8	41	28	1	0
+DC Boon	c Shastri	b Raju	43	76	60	4	0
DM Jones	c & b Prabhakar		90	145	108	6	2
SR Waugh	b Srinath		29	48	48	1	0
TM Moody	b Prabhakar		25	28	23	3	0
*AR Border	c Jadeja	b Kapil Dev	10	17	10	0	0
CJ McDermott	c Jadeja	b Prabhakar	2	6	5	0	0
PL Taylor	run out		1	6	1	0	0
MG Hughes	not out		0	3	4	0	0
Extras (lb 7, w 5, nb 4): **16**							
Total (9 wickets, 50 overs): **237**							

DNB: MR Whitney.
FoW: 1-18 (MA Taylor), 2-31 (Marsh), 3-102 (Boon), 4-156 (Waugh), 5-198 (Moody), 6-230 (Jones), 7-235 (Border), 8-236 (McDermott), 9-237 (PL Taylor).

Bowling	O	M	R	W	
Kapil Dev	10	2	41	3	(1nb 1w)
Prabhakar	10	0	41	3	(1nb 2w)
Srinath	8	0	48	1	(2nb 1w)
Tendulkar	5	0	29	0	(1w)
Raju	10	0	37	1	
Jadeja	7	0	34	0	

India innings (target: 236 runs from 47 overs)			R	M	B	4	6
RJ Shastri	c Waugh	b Moody	25	75	67	1	0
K Srikkanth	b McDermott		0	13	10	0	0
*M Azharuddin	run out		93	147	103	10	0
SR Tendulkar	c Waugh	b Moody	11	19	19	1	0
N Kapil Dev	lbw	b Waugh	21	26	21	3	0
SV Manjrekar	run out		47	50	42	3	1
A Jadeja	b Hughes		1	5	4	0	0
+KS More	b Moody		14	13	8	2	0
J Srinath	not out		8	11	8	0	0
M Prabhakar	run out		1	1	1	0	0
SLV Raju	run out		0	1	0	0	0
Extras (lb 8, w 5): **13**							
Total (all out, 47 overs): **234**							

FoW: 1-6 (Srikkanth), 2-53 (Shastri), 3-86 (Tendulkar), 4-128 (Kapil Dev), 5-194 Azharuddin), 6-199 (Jadeja), 7-216 (Manjrekar), 8-231 (More), 9-232 (Prabhakar), 10-234 Raju).

Bowling	O	M	R	W
McDermott	9	1	35	1
Whitney	10	2	36	0
Hughes	9	1	49	1
Moody	9	0	56	3
Waugh	10	0	50	1

Rain interrupted play after 16.2 overs in the Indian innings (45/1). India's target recalculated to 236 off 47 overs.

Benson & Hedges World Cup, 1991/92, 13th Match
England v Pakistan
Adelaide Oval
1 March 1992 (50-over match)

Result: No result
Points: England 1, Pakistan 1
Toss: England
Umpires: SA Bucknor (WI) and PJ McConnell
World Cup Referee: Barry Gibbs
Man Of The Match: No award

Pakistan innings (50 overs maximum)			R	M	B	4	6
Rameez Raja	c Reeve	b DeFreitas	1	13	10	0	0
Aamer Sohail	c & b Pringle		9	52	39	0	0
Inzamam-ul-Haq	c Stewart	b DeFreitas	0	1	1	0	0
*Javed Miandad	b Pringle		3	29	22	0	0
Saleem Malik	c Reeve	b Botham	17	45	20	3	0
Ijaz Ahmed	c Stewart	b Small	0	16	15	0	0
Wasim Akram	b Botham		1	12	13	0	0
+Moin Khan	c Hick	b Small	2	25	14	0	0
Wasim Haider	c Stewart	b Reeve	13	46	46	1	0
Mushtaq Ahmed	c Reeve	b Pringle	17	54	42	1	0
Aaqib Javed	not out		1	24	21	0	0
Extras (lb 1, w 8, nb 1): **10**							
Total (all out, 40.2 overs): **74**							

FoW: 1-5 (Rameez Raja), 2-5 (Inzamam-ul-Haq), 3-14 Javed Miandad), 4-20 (Aamer Sohail), 5-32 (Ijaz Ahmed), 6-35 (Wasim Akram), 7-42 (Saleem Malik), 8-47 (Moin Khan), 9-62 (Wasim Haider), 10-74 (Mushtaq Ahmed).

Bowling	O	M	R	W
Pringle	8.2	5	8	3 (1nb)
DeFreitas	7	1	22	2 (7w)
Small	10	1	29	2 (1w)
Botham	10	4	12	2
Reeve	5	3	2	1

England innings (target: 64 runs from 16 overs)			R	M	B	4	6
*GA Gooch	c Moin Khan	b Wasim Akram	3	24	14	0	0
IT Botham	not out		6	42	22	0	0
RA Smith	not out		5	17	13	1	0
Extras (b 1, lb 3, w 5, nb 1): **10**							
Total (1 wicket, 8 overs): **24**							

DNB: GA Hick, NH Fairbrother, +AJ Stewart, CC Lewis, DA Reeve, DR Pringle, PAJ DeFreitas, GC Small.
FoW: 1-14 Gooch).

Bowling	O	M	R	W
Wasim Akram	3	0	7	1 (1nb 3w)
Aaqib Javed	3	1	7	0 (2w)
Wasim Haider	1	0	1	0
Ijaz Ahmed	1	0	5	0

Benson & Hedges World Cup, 1991/92, 14th Match
South Africa v Sri Lanka
Basin Reserve, Wellington
2 March 1992 (50-over match)

Result: Sri Lanka won by 3 wickets
Points: Sri Lanka 2, South Africa 0
Toss: Sri Lanka
Umpires: Khizer Hayat (Pak) and SJ Woodward
World Cup Referee: AR Isaac
ODI Debuts: O Henry, MW Rushmere (SA)
Man Of The Match: A Ranatunga

South Africa innings (50 overs maximum)

			R	M	B	4	6
*KC Wessels	c & b Ranatunga		40	130	94	0	0
AP Kuiper	b Anurasiri		18	53	44	3	0
PN Kirsten	c Hathurusingha	b Kalpage	47	74	81	5	1
JN Rhodes	c Jayasuriya	b Wickramasinghe	28	27	21	2	0
MW Rushmere	c Jayasuriya	b Ranatunga	4	7	9	0	0
WJ Cronje	st Tillakaratne	b Anurasiri	3	10	6	0	0
RP Snell	b Anurasiri		9	10	5	2	0
BM McMillan	not out		18	35	22	0	0
+DJ Richardson	run out		0	1	0	0	0
O Henry	c Kalpage	b Ramanayake	11	17	13	1	0
AA Donald	run out		3	9	6	0	0

Extras (lb 9, w 4, nb 1): **14**
Total (all out, 50 overs): **195**

FoW: 1-27 (Kuiper), 2-114 Kirsten), 3-114 Wessels), 4-128 (Rushmere), 5-149 (Cronje), 6-153 (Rhodes), 7-165 (Snell), 8-165 (Richardson), 9-186 (Henry), 10-195 (Donald).

Bowling

	O	M	R	W
Ramanayake	9	2	19	1
Wickramasinghe	7	0	32	1
Anurasiri	10	1	41	3
Kalpage	10	0	38	1
Gurusinha	8	0	30	0
Ranatunga	6	0	26	2

Sri Lanka innings (target: 196 runs from 50 overs)

			R	M	B	4	6
RS Mahanama	c Richardson	b McMillan	68	181	121	6	0
UC Hathurusingha	c Wessels	b Donald	5	10	9	1	0
AP Gurusinha	lbw	b Donald	0	7	4	0	0
*PA de Silva	b Donald		7	27	16	1	0
+HP Tillakaratne	c Rushmere	b Henry	17	75	63	0	0
A Ranatunga	not out		64	96	73	6	0
ST Jayasuriya	st Richardson	b Kirsten	3	11	7	0	0
RS Kalpage	run out		5	21	11	0	0
CPH Ramanayake	not out		4	3	2	1	0

Extras (b 1, lb 7, w 13, nb 4): **25**
Total (7 wickets, 49.5 overs): **198**

DNB: SD Anurasiri, GP Wickramasinghe.
FoW: 1-11 (Hathurusingha), 2-12 (Gurusinha), 3-35 (de Silva), 4-87 (Tillakaratne), 5-154 Mahanama), 6-168 (Jayasuriya), 7-189 (Kalpage).

Bowling

	O	M	R	W
McMillan	10	2	34	1 (3nb)
Donald	9.5	0	42	3 (9w)
Snell	10	1	33	0 (2w)
Henry	10	0	31	1 (1nb 2w)
Kuiper	5	0	25	0
Kirsten	5	0	25	1

Benson & Hedges World Cup, 1991/92, 15th Match
New Zealand v Zimbabwe
McLean Park, Napier
3 March 1992 (50-over match)

Result: New Zealand won by 48 runs (revised target)
Points: New Zealand 2, Zimbabwe 0
Toss: Zimbabwe
Umpires: JD Buultjens (SL) and KE Liebenberg (SA)
World Cup Referee: PW Moody
ODI Debuts: MG Burmester (Zim)
Man Of The Match: MD Crowe

New Zealand innings (20.5 overs maximum)			R	M	B	4	6
MJ Greatbatch	b Duers		15	27	16	2	0
RT Latham	b Brandes		2	10	6	0	0
AH Jones	c Waller	b Butchart	57	76	58	9	0
*MD Crowe	not out		74	64	44	8	2
CL Cairns	not out		1	4	2	0	0
Extras (b 6, lb 7): **13**							
Total (3 wickets, 20.5 overs): **162**							

DNB: KR Rutherford, CZ Harris, +IDS Smith, DN Patel, DK Morrison, GR Larsen.
FoW: 1-9 (Latham), 2-25 (Greatbatch), 3-154 Jones).

Bowling	O	M	R	W
Brandes	5	1	28	1
Duers	6	0	17	1
Omarshah	4	0	34	0
Butchart	4	0	53	1
Burmester	1.5	0	17	0

Zimbabwe innings (target: 154 runs from 18 overs)			R	M	B	4	6
+A Flower	b Larsen		30	45	27	5	0
AC Waller	b Morrison		11	14	11	1	1
*DL Houghton	b Larsen		10	19	14	2	0
IP Butchart	c Cairns	b Larsen	3	9	7	0	0
EA Brandes	b Harris		6	9	8	0	0
AJ Pycroft	not out		13	25	20	0	0
ADR Campbell	c Crowe	b Harris	8	6	9	1	0
AH Omarshah	b Harris		7	5	8	1	0
MG Burmester	not out		4	3	8	0	0
Extras (lb 9, w 3, nb 1): **13**							
Total (7 wickets, 18 overs): **105**							

DNB: AJ Traicos, KG Duers.
FoW: 1-21 (Waller), 2-41 (Houghton), 3-63 (Flower), 4-63 (Butchart), 5-75 (Brandes), 6-86 (Campbell), 7-97 (Omarshah).

Bowling	O	M	R	W	
Morrison	4	0	14	1	(1nb 2w)
Cairns	2	0	27	0	
Larsen	4	0	16	3	
Harris	4	0	15	3	(1w)
Latham	3	0	18	0	
Crowe	1	0	6	0	

Rain stopped play during the NZ innings three times and, in accordance with the rules, Zimbabwe was set a target of 154 within 18 overs.

Benson & Hedges World Cup, 1991/92, 16th Match
India v Pakistan
Sydney Cricket Ground (day/night)
4 March 1992 (50-over match)

Result: India won by 43 runs
Points: India 2, Pakistan 0
Toss: India
Umpires: PJ McConnell and DR Shepherd (Eng)
World Cup Referee: Ted Wykes
Man Of The Match: SR Tendulkar

India innings (49 overs maximum)			R	M	B	4	6
A Jadeja	c Zahid Fazal	b Wasim Haider	46	118	81	2	0
K Srikkanth	c Moin Khan	b Aaqib Javed	5	41	40	0	0
*M Azharuddin	c Moin Khan	b Mushtaq Ahmed	32	61	51	4	0
VG Kambli	c Inzamam-ul-Haq	b Mushtaq Ahmed	24	60	42	0	0
SR Tendulkar	not out		54	91	62	3	0
SV Manjrekar	b Mushtaq Ahmed		0	2	1	0	0
N Kapil Dev	c Imran Khan	b Aaqib Javed	35	34	26	2	1
+KS More	run out		4	3	4	0	0
M Prabhakar	not out		2	2	1	0	0
Extras (lb 3, w 9, nb 2): **14**							
Total (7 wickets, 49 overs): **216**							

DNB: J Srinath, SLV Raju.
FoW: 1-25 (Srikkanth), 2-86 (Azharuddin), 3-101 (Jadeja), 4-147 (Kambli), 5-148 (Manjrekar), 6-208 (Kapil Dev), 7-213 (More).

Bowling	O	M	R	W
Wasim Akram	10	0	45	0
Aaqib Javed	8	2	28	2
Imran Khan	8	0	25	0
Wasim Haider	10	1	36	1
Mushtaq Ahmed	10	0	59	3
Aamer Sohail	3	0	20	0

Pakistan innings (target: 217 runs from 49 overs)			R	M	B	4	6
Aamer Sohail	c Srikkanth	b Tendulkar	62	118	103	6	0
Inzamam-ul-Haq	lbw	b Kapil Dev	2	9	7	0	0
Zahid Fazal	c More	b Prabhakar	2	14	10	0	0
Javed Miandad	b Srinath		40	132	113	2	0
Saleem Malik	c More	b Prabhakar	12	12	9	2	0
*Imran Khan	run out		0	12	5	0	0
Wasim Akram	st More	b Raju	4	9	8	0	0
Wasim Haider	b Srinath		13	41	25	0	0
+Moin Khan	c Manjrekar	b Kapil Dev	12	16	12	1	0
Mushtaq Ahmed	run out		3	5	4	0	0
Aaqib Javed	not out		1	15	12	0	0
Extras (lb 6, w 15, nb 1): **22**							
Total (all out, 48.1 overs): **173**							

FoW: 1-8 (Inzamam-ul-Haq), 2-17 (Zahid Fazal), 3-105 (Aamer Sohail), 4-127 (Saleem Malik), 5-130 (Imran Khan), 6-141 (Wasim Akram), 7-141 (Javed Miandad), 8-161 (Moin Khan), 9-166 (Mushtaq Ahmed), 10-173 (Wasim Haider).

Bowling	O	M	R	W
Kapil Dev	10	0	30	2
Prabhakar	10	1	22	2
Srinath	8.1	0	37	2
Tendulkar	10	0	37	1
Raju	10	1	41	1

India and Pakistan's first meeting in a World Cup

Benson & Hedges World Cup, 1991/92, 17th Match
South Africa v West Indies
Lancaster Park, Christchurch
5 March 1992 (50-over match)

Result: South Africa won by 64 runs
Points: South Africa 2, West Indies 0
Toss: West Indies
Umpires: BL Aldridge and SG Randell (Aus)
World Cup Referee: CL Bull
Man Of The Match: MW Pringle

South Africa innings (50 overs maximum)			R	M	B	4	6
AC Hudson	c Lara	b Cummins	22	67	60	3	0
*KC Wessels	c Haynes	b Marshall	1	11	9	0	0
PN Kirsten	c Williams	b Marshall	56	124	91	2	0
MW Rushmere	st Williams	b Hooper	10	24	24	0	0
AP Kuiper	b Ambrose		23	31	29	0	1
JN Rhodes	c Williams	b Cummins	22	33	27	0	0
BM McMillan	c Lara	b Benjamin	20	44	29	2	0
+DJ Richardson	not out		20	41	26	1	0
RP Snell	c Haynes	b Ambrose	3	5	6	0	0
MW Pringle	not out		5	12	6	0	0
Extras (lb 8, w 3, nb 7): **18**							
Total (8 wickets, 50 overs): **200**							

DNB: AA Donald.
FoW: 1-8 (Wessels), 2-52 (Hudson), 3-73 (Rushmere), 4-118 (Kuiper), 5-127 (Kirsten), 6-159 (Rhodes), 7-181 (McMillan), 8-187 (Snell).

Bowling	O	M	R	W
Ambrose	10	1	34	2 (3nb)
Marshall	10	1	26	2
Hooper	10	0	45	1 (2w)
Cummins	10	0	40	2 (4nb)
Benjamin	10	0	47	1 (1w)

West Indies innings (target: 201 from 50 overs)			R	M	B	4	6
DL Haynes	c Richardson	b Kuiper	30	113	83	3	0
BC Lara	c Rhodes	b Pringle	9	14	13	2	0
*RB Richardson	lbw	b Pringle	1	7	3	0	0
CL Hooper	c Wessels	b Pringle	0	3	4	0	0
KLT Arthurton	c Wessels	b Pringle	0	6	4	0	0
AL Logie	c Pringle	b Kuiper	61	102	69	9	1
MD Marshall	c Rhodes	b Snell	6	14	10	1	0
+D Williams	c Richardson	b Snell	0	2	3	0	0
CEL Ambrose	run out		12	24	15	2	0
AC Cummins	c McMillan	b Donald	6	30	24	0	0
WKM Benjamin	not out		1	9	4	0	0
Extras (lb 9, w 1): **10**							
Total (all out, 38.4 overs): **136**							

FoW: 1-10 (Lara), 2-19 (Richardson), 3-19 (Hooper), 4-19 (Arthurton), 5-70 (Marshall), 6-70 (Williams), 7-116 (Haynes), 8-117 (Logie), 9-132 (Ambrose), 10-136 (Cummins).

Bowling	O	M	R	W
Donald	6.4	2	13	1 (1w)
Pringle	8	4	11	4
Snell	7	2	16	2
McMillan	8	2	36	0
Kuiper	9	0	51	2

DL Haynes retired hurt on 13* from 50/4 to 70/6.

Benson & Hedges World Cup, 1991/92, 18th Match
Australia v England
Sydney Cricket Ground (day/night)
5 March 1992 (50-over match)

Result: England won by 8 wickets
Points: England 2, Australia 0
Toss: Australia
Umpires: SA Bucknor (WI) and Khizer Hayat (Pak)
World Cup Referee: Ted Wykes
Man Of The Match: IT Botham

Australia innings (50 overs maximum)			R	M	B	4	6
TM Moody	b Tufnell		51	131	88	3	0
MA Taylor	lbw	b Pringle	0	11	11	0	0
DC Boon	run out		18	29	27	2	0
DM Jones	c Lewis	b DeFreitas	22	78	49	2	0
SR Waugh	run out		27	65	43	2	0
*AR Border	b Botham		16	30	22	1	0
+IA Healy	c Fairbrother	b Botham	9	6	7	0	1
PL Taylor	lbw	b Botham	0	2	2	0	0
CJ McDermott	c DeFreitas	b Botham	0	1	2	0	0
MR Whitney	not out		8	33	27	1	0
BA Reid	b Reeve		1	21	21	0	0

Extras (b 2, lb 8, w 5, nb 4): **19**
Total (all out, 49 overs): **171**

FoW: 1-5 (MA Taylor), 2-35 (Boon), 3-106 (Jones), 4-114 Moody), 5-145 (Border), 6-155 (Healy), 7-155 (PL Taylor), 8-155 (McDermott), 9-164 Waugh), 10-171 (Reid).

Bowling	O	M	R	W
Pringle	9	1	24	1 (3nb 1w)
Lewis	10	2	28	0 (2w)
DeFreitas	10	3	23	1 (1w)
Botham	10	1	31	4 1w)
Tufnell	9	0	52	1 (1nb)
Reeve	1	0	3	1

England innings (target: 172 runs from 50 overs)			R	M	B	4	6
*GA Gooch	b Waugh		58	157	112	7	0
IT Botham	c Healy	b Whitney	53	103	77	6	0
RA Smith	not out		30	66	58	5	0
GA Hick	not out		7	13	5	1	0

Extras (lb 13, w 8, nb 4): **25**
Total (2 wickets, 40.5 overs): **173**

DNB: NH Fairbrother, +AJ Stewart, CC Lewis, DA Reeve, DR Pringle, PAJ DeFreitas, PCR Tufnell.
FoW: 1-107 (Botham), 2-153 (Gooch).

Bowling	O	M	R	W
McDermott	10	1	29	0 (1nb 3w)
Reid	7.5	0	49	0 (5nb 2w)
Whitney	10	2	28	1 (1w)
Waugh	6	0	29	1 (2w)
PL Taylor	3	0	7	0
Moody	4	0	18	0

Benson & Hedges World Cup, 1991/92, 19th Match
India v Zimbabwe
Trust Bank Park, Hamilton
7 March 1992 (50-over match)

Result: India won by 55 runs (revised target)
Points: India 2, Zimbabwe 0
Toss: India
Umpires: JD Buultjens (SL) and SG Randell (Aus)
World Cup Referee: BJ Paterson
Man Of The Match: SR Tendulkar

India innings (32 overs maximum)			R	M	B	4	6
K Srikkanth	b Burmester		32	50	32	5	0
N Kapil Dev	lbw	b Brandes	10	19	14	0	1
*M Azharuddin	c Flower	b Burmester	12	14	15	2	0
SR Tendulkar	c Campbell	b Burmester	81	88	77	8	1
SV Manjrekar	c Duers	b Traicos	34	57	34	2	0
VG Kambli	b Traicos		1	2	2	0	0
A Jadeja	c Omarshah	b Traicos	6	8	6	0	0
+KS More	not out		15	9	8	0	1
J Srinath	not out		6	6	4	1	0
Extras (lb 3, w 3): **6**							
Total (7 wickets, 32 overs): **203**							

DNB: M Prabhakar, SLV Raju.
FoW: 1-23 (Kapil Dev), 2-43 (Azharuddin), 3-69 (Srikkanth), 4-168 (Manjrekar), 5-170 (Kambli), 6-182 (Jadeja), 7-184 Tendulkar).

Bowling	O	M	R	W	
Brandes	7	0	43	1	
Duers	7	0	48	0	
Burmester	6	0	36	3 (3w)	
Omarshah	6	1	38	0	
Traicos	6	0	35	3	

Zimbabwe innings (target: 159 runs from 19 overs)		R	M	B	4	6
AH Omarshah	b Tendulkar	31	55	51	3	0
+A Flower	not out	43	66	56	3	0
AC Waller	not out	13	10	7	2	0
Extras (b 1, lb 11, w 5): **17**						
Total (1 wicket, 19.1 overs): **104**						

DNB: AJ Pycroft, *DL Houghton, ADR Campbell, IP Butchart, EA Brandes, MG Burmester, AJ Traicos, KG Duers.
FoW: 1-79 (Omarshah).

Bowling	O	M	R	W	
Kapil Dev	4	0	6	0 (2w)	
Prabhakar	3	0	14	0 (1w)	
Srinath	4	0	20	0 (1w)	
Tendulkar	6	0	35	1 (1w)	
Raju	2.1	0	17	0	

After rain forced the early close of the Zimbabwe innings, the target was recalculated to 159 runs in the 19 overs. After 19 overs, Zimbabwe were 103.

Benson & Hedges World Cup, 1991/92, 20th Match
Australia v Sri Lanka
Adelaide Oval
7 March 1992 (50-over match)

Result: Australia won by 7 wickets
Points: Australia 2, Sri Lanka 0
Toss: Australia
Umpires: PD Reporter (Ind) and ID Robinson (Zim)
World Cup Referee: Barry Gibbs
Man Of The Match: TM Moody

Sri Lanka innings (50 overs maximum)			R	M	B	4	6
RS Mahanama	run out		7	9	10	1	0
MAR Samarasekera	c Healy	b Taylor	34	87	63	3	0
AP Gurusinha	lbw	b Whitney	5	30	23	1	0
*PA de Silva	c Moody	b McDermott	62	133	83	2	0
A Ranatunga	c Jones	b Taylor	23	48	52	0	0
ST Jayasuriya	lbw	b Border	15	25	29	1	0
+HP Tillakaratne	run out		5	17	13	0	0
RS Kalpage	run out		14	25	15	1	0
CPH Ramanayake	run out		5	12	10	0	0
SD Anurasiri	not out		4	6	4	0	0

Extras (b 3, lb 6, w 5, nb 1): **15**
Total (9 wickets, 50 overs): **189**

DNB: GP Wickramasinghe.
FoW: 1-8 (Mahanama), 2-28 (Gurusinha), 3-72 (Samarasekera), 4-123 (Ranatunga), 5-151 (Jayasuriya), 6-163 (de Silva), 7-166 (Tillakaratne), 8-182 (Ramanayake), 9-189 (Kalpage).

Bowling	O	M	R	W
McDermott	10	0	28	1 (1w)
SR Waugh	7	0	34	0 (1nb 4w)
Whitney	10	3	26	1
Moody	3	0	18	0
Taylor	10	0	34	2
Border	10	0	40	1

Australia innings (target: 190 runs from 50 overs)			R	M	B	4	6
TM Moody	c Mahanama	b Wickramasinghe	57	115	86	4	0
GR Marsh	c Anurasiri	b Kalpage	60	127	113	3	1
ME Waugh	c Mahanama	b Wickramasinghe	26	39	37	1	0
DC Boon	not out		27	44	26	0	2
DM Jones	not out		12	16	8	0	1

Extras (lb 2, w 3, nb 3): **8**
Total (3 wickets, 44 overs): **190**

DNB: SR Waugh, *AR Border, +IA Healy, PL Taylor, CJ McDermott, MR Whitney.
FoW: 1-120 (Moody), 2-130 (Marsh), 3-165 (ME Waugh).

Bowling	O	M	R	W
Wickramasinghe	10	3	29	2 (1nb 1w)
Ramanayake	9	1	44	0 (2nb 2w)
Anurasiri	10	0	43	0
Gurusinha	6	0	20	0
Kalpage	8	0	41	1
Ranatunga	1	0	11	0

Benson & Hedges World Cup, 1991/92, 21st Match
New Zealand v West Indies
Eden Park, Auckland
8 March 1992 (50-over match)

Result: New Zealand won by 5 wickets
Points: New Zealand 2, West Indies 0
Toss: New Zealand
Umpires: KE Liebenberg (SA) and PJ McConnell (Aus)
World Cup Referee: PD McDermott
Man Of The Match: MD Crowe

West Indies innings (50 overs maximum)			R	M	B	4	6
DL Haynes	c & b Harris		22	74	61	0	1
BC Lara	c Rutherford	b Larsen	52	104	81	0	0
*RB Richardson	c Smith	b Watson	29	68	54	1	0
CL Hooper	c Greatbatch	b Patel	2	10	9	0	0
KLT Arthurton	b Morrison		40	77	54	3	0
AL Logie	b Harris		3	4	4	0	0
MD Marshall	b Larsen		5	19	14	0	0
+D Williams	not out		32	26	24	5	0
WKM Benjamin	not out		2	1	1	0	0
Extras (lb 8, w 7, nb 1): **16**							
Total (7 wickets, 50 overs): **203**							

DNB: CEL Ambrose, AC Cummins.
FoW: 1-65 (Haynes), 2-95 (Lara), 3-100 (Hooper), 4-136 (Richardson), 5-142 (Logie), 6-156 (Marshall), 7-201 (Arthurton).

Bowling	O	M	R	W	
Morrison	9	1	33	1	(1nb 2w)
Patel	10	2	19	1	(1w)
Watson	10	2	56	1	
Larsen	10	0	41	2	
Harris	10	2	32	2	
Latham	1	0	14	0	(4w)

New Zealand innings (target: 204 from 50 overs)			R	M	B	4	6
MJ Greatbatch	c Haynes	b Benjamin	63	102	77	7	3
RT Latham	c Williams	b Cummins	14	51	27	1	0
AH Jones	c Williams	b Benjamin	10	42	35	0	0
*MD Crowe	not out		81	105	81	12	0
KR Rutherford	c Williams	b Ambrose	8	32	32	1	0
CZ Harris	c Williams	b Cummins	7	36	23	0	0
DN Patel	not out		10	27	18	0	0
Extras (lb 7, w 5, nb 1): **13**							
Total (5 wickets, 48.3 overs): **206**							

DNB: +IDS Smith, DK Morrison, GR Larsen, W Watson.
FoW: 1-67 (Latham), 2-97 (Jones), 3-100 (Greatbatch), 4-135 (Rutherford), 5-174 (Harris).

Bowling	O	M	R	W	
Ambrose	10	1	41	1	(3w)
Marshall	9	1	35	0	(1nb 1w)
Cummins	10	0	53	2	(1w)
Benjamin	9.3	3	34	2	
Hooper	10	0	36	0	

Benson & Hedges World Cup, 1991/92, 22nd Match
Pakistan v South Africa
Brisbane Cricket Ground, Woolloongabba, Brisbane
8 March 1992 (50-over match)

Result: South Africa won by 20 runs (revised target)
Points: South Africa 2, Pakistan 0
Toss: Pakistan
Umpires: BL Aldridge (NZ) and SA Bucknor (WI)
World Cup Referee: MW Johnson
Man Of The Match: AC Hudson

South Africa innings (50 overs maximum)			R	M	B	4	6
AC Hudson	c Ijaz Ahmed	b Imran Khan	54	97	81	8	0
*KC Wessels	c Moin Khan	b Aaqib Javed	7	32	26	0	0
MW Rushmere	c Aamer Sohail	b Mushtaq Ahmed	35	86	70	2	0
AP Kuiper	c Moin Khan	b Imran Khan	5	13	12	0	0
JN Rhodes	lbw	b Iqbal Sikander	5	25	17	0	0
WJ Cronje	not out		47	78	53	4	0
BM McMillan	b Wasim Akram		33	47	44	1	0
+DJ Richardson	b Wasim Akram		5	9	10	0	0
RP Snell	not out		1	2	1	0	0

*Extras (lb 8, w 9, nb 2): **19***
*Total (7 wickets, 50 overs): **211***

DNB: MW Pringle, AA Donald.
FoW: 1-31 (Wessels), 2-98 (Hudson), 3-110 (Kuiper), 4-111 (Rushmere), 5-127 (Rhodes), 6-198 (McMillan), 7-207 (Richardson).

Bowling	O	M	R	W	
Wasim Akram	10	0	42	2	(2nb 7w)
Aaqib Javed	7	1	36	1	(2w)
Imran Khan	10	0	34	2	
Iqbal Sikander	8	0	30	1	
Ijaz Ahmed	7	0	26	0	
Mushtaq Ahmed	8	1	35	1	

Pakistan innings (target: 194 runs from 36 overs)			R	M	B	4	6
Aamer Sohail	b Snell		23	61	53	2	0
Zahid Fazal	c Richardson	b McMillan	11	63	46	1	0
Inzamam-ul-Haq	run out		48	70	45	5	0
*Imran Khan	c Richardson	b McMillan	34	70	53	5	0
Saleem Malik	c Donald	b Kuiper	12	15	11	0	0
Wasim Akram	c Snell	b Kuiper	9	15	8	1	0
Ijaz Ahmed	c Rhodes	b Kuiper	6	4	3	1	0
+Moin Khan	not out		5	11	5	0	0
Mushtaq Ahmed	run out		4	5	4	0	0
Iqbal Sikander	not out		1	2	3	0	0

*Extras (lb 2, w 17, nb 1): **20***
*Total (8 wickets, 36 overs): **173***

DNB: Aaqib Javed.
FoW: 1-50 (Aamer Sohail), 2-50 (Zahid Fazal), 3-135 (Inzamam-ul-Haq), 4-136 (Imran Khan), 5-156 (Saleem Malik), 6-157 (Wasim Akram), 7-163 (Ijaz Ahmed), 8-171 (Mushtaq Ahmed).

Bowling	O	M	R	W	
Donald	7	1	31	0	(7w)
Pringle	7	0	31	0	(1nb 3w)
Snell	8	2	26	1	(1w)
McMillan	7	0	34	2	(4w)
Kuiper	6	0	40	3	(2w)
Cronje	1	0	9	0	

When Pakistan was 74/2 in the 22nd over, rain halted the play and the target was revised to 194 in 36 overs.

Benson & Hedges World Cup, 1991/92, 23rd Match
England v Sri Lanka
Eastern Oval, Ballarat
9 March 1992 (50-over match)

Result: England won by 106 runs
Points: England 2, Sri Lanka 0
Toss: England
Umpires: Khizer Hayat (Pak) and PD Reporter (Ind)
World Cup Referee: Bob Merriman
Man Of The Match: CC Lewis

England innings (50 overs maximum)			R	M	B	4	6
*GA Gooch	b Labrooy		8	40	28	1	0
IT Botham	b Anurasiri		47	106	63	5	2
RA Smith	run out		19	46	39	2	0
GA Hick	b Ramanayake		41	73	62	3	0
NH Fairbrother	c Ramanayake	b Gurusinha	63	96	70	3	2
+AJ Stewart	c Jayasuriya	b Gurusinha	59	48	36	7	1
CC Lewis	not out		20	9	6	1	2
DR Pringle	not out		0	2	0	0	0
Extras (b 1, lb 9, w 9, nb 4): **23**							
Total (6 wickets, 50 overs): **280**							

DNB: DA Reeve, PAJ DeFreitas, RK Illingworth.
FoW: 1-44 Gooch), 2-80 (Smith), 3-105 (Botham), 4-164 Hick), 5-244 Fairbrother), 6-268 (Stewart).

Bowling	O	M	R	W
Wickramasinghe	9	0	54	0 (3w)
Ramanayake	10	1	42	1 (4nb 3w)
Labrooy	10	1	68	1 (2w)
Anurasiri	10	1	27	1
Gurusinha	10	0	67	2 (1w)
Jayasuriya	1	0	12	0

Sri Lanka innings (target: 281 runs from 50 overs)			R	M	B	4	6
RS Mahanama	c Botham	b Lewis	9	31	19	1	0
MAR Samarasekera	c Illingworth	b Lewis	23	42	29	4	0
AP Gurusinha	c & b Lewis		7	31	9	0	0
*PA de Silva	c Fairbrother	b Lewis	7	10	10	1	0
A Ranatunga	c Stewart	b Botham	36	67	51	6	0
+HP Tillakaratne	run out		4	40	30	0	0
ST Jayasuriya	c DeFreitas	b Illingworth	19	20	16	2	0
GF Labrooy	c Smith	b Illingworth	19	42	34	1	0
CPH Ramanayake	c & b Reeve		12	35	38	0	0
SD Anurasiri	lbw	b Reeve	11	17	19	0	0
GP Wickramasinghe	not out		6	14	16	0	0
Extras (lb 7, w 8, nb 6): **21**							
Total (all out, 44 overs): **174**							

FoW: 1-33 (Mahanama), 2-46 (Samarasekera), 3-56 (de Silva), 4-60 (Gurusinha), 5-91 (Tillakaratne), 6-119 (Ranatunga), 7-123 (Jayasuriya), 8-156 (Ramanayake), 9-158 (Labrooy), 10-174 Anurasiri).

Bowling	O	M	R	W
Pringle	7	1	27	0 (3nb 1w)
Lewis	8	0	30	4 2nb 2w)
DeFreitas	5	1	31	0 (1nb 3w)
Botham	10	0	33	1 (1w)
Illingworth	10	0	32	2
Reeve	4	0	14	2 (1w)

Benson & Hedges World Cup, 1991/92, 24th Match
India v West Indies
Basin Reserve, Wellington
10 March 1992 (50-over match)

Result: West Indies won by 5 wickets (revised target)
Points: West Indies 2, India 0
Toss: India
Umpires: SG Randell (Aus) and SJ Woodward
World Cup Referee: AR Isaac
Man Of The Match: AC Cummins

India innings (50 overs maximum)

			R	M	B	4	6
A Jadeja	c Benjamin	b Simmons	27	64	61	2	0
K Srikkanth	c Logie	b Hooper	40	101	70	2	0
*M Azharuddin	c Ambrose	b Cummins	61	89	84	4	0
SR Tendulkar	c Williams	b Ambrose	4	11	11	0	0
SV Manjrekar	run out		27	53	40	0	0
N Kapil Dev	c Haynes	b Cummins	3	9	4	0	0
PK Amre	c Hooper	b Ambrose	4	14	8	0	0
+KS More	c Hooper	b Cummins	5	5	5	1	0
M Prabhakar	c Richardson	b Cummins	8	10	10	1	0
J Srinath	not out		5	7	5	0	0
SLV Raju	run out		1	2	1	0	0
Extras (lb 6, w 5, nb 1): **12**							
Total (all out, 49.4 overs): **197**							

FoW: 1-56 (Jadeja), 2-102 (Srikkanth), 3-115 (Tendulkar), 4-166 (Azharuddin), 5-171 (Kapil Dev), 6-173 (Manjrekar), 7-180 (More), 8-186 (Amre), 9-193 (Prabhakar), 10-197 (Raju).

Bowling	O	M	R	W
Ambrose	10	1	24	2
Benjamin	9.4	0	35	0 (4w)
Cummins	10	0	33	4
Simmons	9	0	48	1 (1nb 1w)
Hooper	10	0	46	1
Arthurton	1	0	5	0

West Indies innings (target: 195 from 46 overs)

			R	M	B	4	6
DL Haynes	c Manjrekar	b Kapil Dev	16	28	16	3	0
BC Lara	c Manjrekar	b Srinath	41	51	37	6	1
PV Simmons	c Tendulkar	b Prabhakar	22	27	20	2	1
*RB Richardson	c Srikkanth	b Srinath	3	19	8	0	0
KLT Arthurton	not out		58	101	99	3	0
AL Logie	c More	b Raju	7	15	10	1	0
CL Hooper	not out		34	70	57	3	0
Extras (lb 8, w 2, nb 4): **14**							
Total (5 wickets, 40.2 overs): **195**							

DNB: +D Williams, WKM Benjamin, CEL Ambrose, AC Cummins.
FoW: 1-57 (Haynes), 2-81 (Lara), 3-88 (Simmons), 4-98 (Richardson), 5-112 (Logie).

Bowling	O	M	R	W
Kapil Dev	8	0	45	1
Prabhakar	9	0	55	1 (1nb 1w)
Raju	10	2	32	1 (1w)
Srinath	9	2	23	2 (3nb)
Tendulkar	3	0	20	0
Srikkanth	1	0	7	0
Jadeja	0.2	0	5	0

Benson & Hedges World Cup, 1991/92, 25th Match
South Africa v Zimbabwe
Manuka Oval, Canberra
10 March 1992 (50-over match)

Result: South Africa won by 7 wickets
Points: South Africa 2, Zimbabwe 0
Toss: South Africa
Umpires: SA Bucknor (WI) and DR Shepherd (Eng)
World Cup Referee: Roger Webb
Man Of The Match: PN Kirsten

Zimbabwe innings (50 overs maximum)			R	M	B	4	6
WR James	lbw	b Pringle	5	12	12	0	0
+A Flower	c Richardson	b Cronje	19	71	44	0	0
AJ Pycroft	c Wessels	b McMillan	19	63	47	0	0
*DL Houghton	c Cronje	b Kirsten	15	75	53	0	0
AC Waller	c Cronje	b Kirsten	15	28	28	1	0
AH Omarshah	c Wessels	b Kirsten	3	10	4	0	0
EA Brandes	c Richardson	b McMillan	20	49	28	1	1
MG Burmester	c Kuiper	b Cronje	1	8	10	0	0
AJ Traicos	not out		16	49	40	1	0
MP Jarvis	c & b McMillan		17	28	21	1	1
KG Duers	b Donald		5	9	10	0	0
Extras (lb 11, w 13, nb 4): **28**							
Total (all out, 48.3 overs): **163**							

FoW: 1-7 (James), 2-51 (Pycroft), 3-72 (Waller), 4-80 (Houghton), 5-80 (Omarshah), 6-115 (Flower), 7-117 (Burmester), 8-123 (Brandes), 9-151 (Jarvis), 10-163 (Duers).

Bowling	O	M	R	W
Donald	9.3	1	25	1 (2nb 1w)
Pringle	9	0	25	1 (3nb 6w)
Snell	10	3	24	0
McMillan	10	1	30	3 (6w)
Cronje	5	0	17	2
Kirsten	5	0	31	3

South Africa innings (target: 164 from 50 overs)			R	M	B	4	6
*KC Wessels	b Omarshah		70	148	137	6	0
AC Hudson	b Jarvis		13	26	22	1	0
PN Kirsten	not out		62	138	103	3	0
AP Kuiper	c Burmester	b Brandes	7	9	9	0	0
JN Rhodes	not out		3	6	3	0	0
Extras (lb 4, w 2, nb 3): **9**							
Total (3 wickets, 45.1 overs): **164**							

DNB: WJ Cronje, BM McMillan, +DJ Richardson, RP Snell, MW Pringle, AA Donald.
FoW: 1-27 (Hudson), 2-139 (Wessels), 3-152 (Kuiper).

Bowling	O	M	R	W
Brandes	9.1	0	40	1 (1nb 1w)
Jarvis	9	2	23	1 (2nb)
Burmester	5	0	20	0 (1w)
Omarshah	8	2	32	1
Duers	8	1	19	0
Traicos	6	0	26	0

A Flower retired hurt on 6* from 26/1 to 80/5

Benson & Hedges World Cup, 1991/92, 26th Match
Australia v Pakistan
W.A.C.A. Ground, Perth (day/night)
11 March 1992 (50-over match)

Result: Pakistan won by 48 runs
Points: Pakistan 2, Australia 0
Toss: Pakistan
Umpires: KE Liebenberg (SA) and PD Reporter (Ind)
World Cup Referee: Tony Mann
Man Of The Match: Aamer Sohail

Pakistan innings (50 overs maximum)			R	M	B	4	6
Aamer Sohail	c Healy	b Moody	76	150	106	8	0
Rameez Raja	c Border	b Whitney	34	82	61	4	0
Saleem Malik	b Moody		0	4	6	0	0
Javed Miandad	c Healy	b SR Waugh	46	90	75	3	0
*Imran Khan	c Moody	b SR Waugh	13	31	22	0	1
Inzamam-ul-Haq	run out		16	20	16	0	0
Ijaz Ahmed	run out		0	8	2	0	0
Wasim Akram	c ME Waugh	b SR Waugh	0	1	1	0	0
+Moin Khan	c Healy	b McDermott	5	13	8	0	0
Mushtaq Ahmed	not out		3	6	5	0	0
Extras (lb 9, w 16, nb 2): 27							
Total (9 wickets, 50 overs): 220							

DNB: Aaqib Javed.
FoW: 1-78 (Rameez Raja), 2-80 (Saleem Malik), 3-157 (Aamer Sohail), 4-193 (Javed Miandad), 5-194 Imran Khan), 6-205 (Ijaz Ahmed), 7-205 (Wasim Akram), 8-214 Inzamam-ul-Haq), 9-220 (Moin Khan).

Bowling	O	M	R	W	
McDermott	10	0	33	1	(3w)
Reid	9	0	37	0	(2nb 4w)
SR Waugh	10	0	36	3	(6w)
Whitney	10	1	50	1	(2w)
Moody	10	0	42	2	(1w)
ME Waugh	1	0	13	0	(1nb)

Australia innings (target: 221 runs from 50 overs)			R	M	B	4	6
TM Moody	c Saleem Malik	b Aaqib Javed	4	22	18	0	0
GR Marsh	c Moin Khan	b Imran Khan	39	139	91	1	0
DC Boon	c Mushtaq Ahmed	b Aaqib Javed	5	22	15	1	0
DM Jones	c Aaqib Javed	b Mushtaq Ahmed	47	82	79	2	0
ME Waugh	c Ijaz Ahmed	b Mushtaq Ahmed	30	51	42	2	0
*AR Border	c Ijaz Ahmed	b Mushtaq Ahmed	1	4	4	0	0
SR Waugh	c Moin Khan	b Imran Khan	5	4	6	1	0
+IA Healy	c Ijaz Ahmed	b Aaqib Javed	8	19	15	0	0
CJ McDermott	lbw	b Wasim Akram	0	5	2	0	0
MR Whitney	b Wasim Akram		5	8	9	0	0
BA Reid	not out		0	4	0	0	0
Extras (lb 7, w 14, nb 7): 28							
Total (all out, 45.2 overs): 172							

FoW: 1-13 (Moody), 2-31 (Boon), 3-116 (Jones), 4-122 (Marsh), 5-123 (Border), 6-130 (SR Waugh), 7-156 (Healy), 8-162 (McDermott), 9-167 (ME Waugh), 10-172 (Whitney).

Bowling	O	M	R	W	
Wasim Akram	7.2	0	28	2	(5nb 4w)
Aaqib Javed	8	1	21	3	(1nb 5w)
Imran Khan	10	1	32	2	
Ijaz Ahmed	10	0	43	0	(3nb 4w)
Mushtaq Ahmed	10	0	41	3	

Benson & Hedges World Cup, 1991/92, 27th Match
New Zealand v India
Carisbrook, Dunedin
12 March 1992 (50-over match)

Result: New Zealand won by 4 wickets
Points: New Zealand 2, India 0
Toss: New Zealand
Umpires: PJ McConnell (Aus) and ID Robinson (Zim)
World Cup Referee: WJ Henderson
Man Of The Match: MJ Greatbatch

India innings (50 overs maximum)

			R	M	B	4	6
A Jadeja	retired hurt		13	28	32	1	0
K Srikkanth	c Latham	b Patel	0	5	3	0	0
*M Azharuddin	c Greatbatch	b Patel	55	127	98	3	1
SR Tendulkar	c Smith	b Harris	84	122	107	6	0
SV Manjrekar	c & b Harris		18	37	25	0	0
N Kapil Dev	c Larsen	b Harris	33	27	16	5	0
ST Banerjee	c Greatbatch	b Watson	11	11	9	1	0
+KS More	not out		2	5	8	0	0
J Srinath	not out		4	3	3	0	0
Extras (b 1, lb 4, w 4, nb 1): **10**							
Total (6 wickets, 50 overs): **230**							

DNB: M Prabhakar, SLV Raju.
FoW: 1-4 Srikkanth), 2-149 (Azharuddin), 3-166 (Tendulkar), 4-201 (Manjrekar), 5-222 (Kapil Dev), 6-223 (Banerjee).

Bowling

	O	M	R	W	
Cairns	8	1	40	0	(1nb)
Patel	10	0	29	2	
Watson	10	1	34	1	
Larsen	9	0	43	0	
Harris	9	0	55	3	(2w)
Latham	4	0	24	0	(2w)

New Zealand innings (target: 231 from 50 overs)

			R	M	B	4	6
MJ Greatbatch	c Banerjee	b Raju	73	99	77	5	4
RT Latham	b Prabhakar		8	32	22	1	0
AH Jones	not out		67	160	107	8	0
*MD Crowe	run out		26	27	28	3	1
+IDS Smith	c sub (PK Amre)	b Prabhakar	9	11	8	1	0
KR Rutherford	lbw	b Raju	21	25	22	3	1
CZ Harris	b Prabhakar		4	20	17	0	0
CL Cairns	not out		4	6	5	1	0
Extras (b 4, lb 3, w 4, nb 8): **19**							
Total (6 wickets, 47.1 overs): **231**							

DNB: DN Patel, GR Larsen, W Watson.
FoW: 1-36 (Latham), 2-118 (Greatbatch), 3-162 (Crowe), 4-172 (Smith), 5-206 (Rutherford), 6-225 (Harris).

Bowling

	O	M	R	W	
Kapil Dev	10	0	55	0	(1nb 1w)
Prabhakar	10	0	46	3	(2w)
Banerjee	6	1	40	0	(1nb)
Srinath	9	0	35	0	(3nb 2w)
Raju	10	0	38	2	
Tendulkar	1	0	2	0	
Srikkanth	1.1	0	8	0	(1nb)

A Jadeja retired hurt at 22/1

Benson & Hedges World Cup, 1991/92, 28th Match
England v South Africa
Melbourne Cricket Ground (day/night)
12 March 1992 (50-over match)

Result: England won by 3 wickets (revised target)
Points: England 2, South Africa 0
Toss: England
Umpires: BL Aldridge (NZ) and JD Buultjens (SL)
World Cup Referee: Jack Edwards
Man Of The Match: AJ Stewart

South Africa innings (50 overs maximum)			R	M	B	4	6
*KC Wessels	c Smith	b Hick	85	170	126	6	0
AC Hudson	c & b Hick		79	132	115	7	0
PN Kirsten	c Smith	b DeFreitas	11	14	12	0	1
JN Rhodes	run out		18	25	23	0	0
AP Kuiper	not out		15	17	12	1	0
WJ Cronje	not out		13	14	15	0	0
Extras (b 4, lb 4, w 4, nb 3): **15**							
Total (4 wickets, 50 overs): **236**							

DNB: BM McMillan, +DJ Richardson, RP Snell, MW Pringle, AA Donald.
FoW: 1-151 (Hudson), 2-170 (Kirsten), 3-201 (Wessels), 4-205 (Rhodes).

Bowling	O	M	R	W
Pringle	9	2	34	0 (3nb 2w)
DeFreitas	10	1	41	1 (1w)
Botham	8	0	37	0
Small	2	0	14	0 (1w)
Illingworth	10	0	43	0
Reeve	2.4	0	15	0
Hick	8.2	0	44	2

England innings (target: 226 runs from 41 overs)			R	M	B	4	6
*+AJ Stewart	run out		77	122	88	7	0
IT Botham	b McMillan		22	54	30	1	0
RA Smith	c Richardson	b McMillan	0	2	2	0	0
GA Hick	c Richardson	b Snell	1	4	4	0	0
NH Fairbrother	not out		75	133	83	6	0
DA Reeve	c McMillan	b Snell	10	29	15	0	0
CC Lewis	run out		33	29	22	4	0
DR Pringle	c Kuiper	b Snell	1	11	3	0	0
PAJ DeFreitas	not out		1	2	1	0	0
Extras (lb 3, w 1, nb 2): **6**							
Total (7 wickets, 40.5 overs): **226**							

DNB: RK Illingworth, GC Small.
FoW: 1-63 (Botham), 2-63 (Smith), 3-64 (Hick), 4-132 (Stewart), 5-166 (Reeve), 6-216 (Lewis), 7-225 (Pringle).

Bowling	O	M	R	W
Donald	9	1	43	0 (1nb)
Pringle	8	0	44	0 (1nb 1w)
Snell	7.5	0	42	3
McMillan	8	1	39	2
Kuiper	4	0	32	0
Cronje	3	0	14	0
Kirsten	1	0	9	0

Rain disrupted play in England's innings when they were 62-0 at the end of 12 overs. The target was revised to 226 in 41 overs.

Benson & Hedges World Cup, 1991/92, 29th Match
Sri Lanka v West Indies
Berri Oval
13 March 1992 (50-over match)

Result: West Indies won by 91 runs
Points: West Indies 2, Sri Lanka 0
Toss: Sri Lanka
Umpires: DR Shepherd (Eng) and SJ Woodward (NZ)
World Cup Referee: Bruce Martin
Man Of The Match: PV Simmons

West Indies innings (50 overs maximum)			R	M	B	4	6
DL Haynes	c Tillakaratne	b Ranatunga	38	78	47	3	1
BC Lara	c & b Ramanayake		1	8	6	0	0
PV Simmons	c Wickramasinghe	b Hathurusingha	110	153	125	8	2
*RB Richardson	run out		8	25	23	0	0
KLT Arthurton	c Tillakaratne	b Hathurusingha	40	84	54	1	0
AL Logie	b Anurasiri		0	3	2	0	0
CL Hooper	c Gurusinha	b Hathurusingha	12	12	12	1	0
+D Williams	c Tillakaratne	b Hathurusingha	2	3	3	0	0
CEL Ambrose	not out		15	24	14	0	1
WKM Benjamin	not out		24	18	20	1	0
Extras (lb 9, w 3, nb 6): **18**							
Total (8 wickets, 50 overs): **268**							

DNB: AC Cummins.
FoW: 1-6 (Lara), 2-72 (Haynes), 3-103 (Richardson), 4-197 (Simmons), 5-199 (Logie), 6-219 (Hooper), 7-223 (Williams), 8-228 (Arthurton).

Bowling	O	M	R	W	
Wickramasinghe	7	0	30	0 (1nb 2w)	
Ramanayake	7	1	17	1 (1nb 1w)	
Anurasiri	10	0	46	1	
Gurusinha	1	0	10	0	
Ranatunga	7	0	35	1	
Kalpage	10	0	64	0	
Hathurusingha	8	0	57	4 (4nb)	

Sri Lanka innings (target: 269 runs from 50 overs)			R	M	B	4	6
RS Mahanama	c Arthurton	b Cummins	11	77	50	0	0
MAR Samarasekera	lbw	b Hooper	40	48	41	4	1
UC Hathurusingha	run out		16	35	25	0	0
*PA de Silva	c & b Hooper		11	26	19	0	0
A Ranatunga	c Benjamin	b Arthurton	24	60	40	0	1
AP Gurusinha	c Richardson	b Ambrose	10	28	30	0	0
+HP Tillakaratne	b Ambrose		3	4	9	0	0
RS Kalpage	not out		13	51	40	0	0
CPH Ramanayake	b Arthurton		1	8	13	0	0
SD Anurasiri	b Benjamin		3	12	11	0	0
GP Wickramasinghe	not out		21	22	21	1	0
Extras (lb 8, w 14, nb 2): **24**							
Total (9 wickets, 50 overs): **177**							

FoW: 1-56 (Samarasekera), 2-80 (Hathurusingha), 3-86 (Mahanama), 4-99 (de Silva), 5-130 (Gurusinha), 6-135 (Tillakaratne), 7-137 (Ranatunga), 8-139 (Ramanayake), 9-149 (Anurasiri).

Bowling	O	M	R	W	
Ambrose	10	2	24	2 (6w)	
Benjamin	10	0	34	1 (5w)	
Cummins	9	0	49	1 (1nb 3w)	
Hooper	10	1	19	2	
Arthurton	10	0	40	2 (1nb)	
Simmons	1	0	3	0	

Benson & Hedges World Cup, 1991/92, 30th Match
Australia v Zimbabwe
Bellerive Oval, Hobart
14 March 1992 (50-over match)

Result: Australia won by 128 runs
Points: Australia 2, Zimbabwe 0
Toss: Australia
Umpires: BL Aldridge (NZ) and SA Bucknor (WI)
World Cup Referee: Brent Palfreyman
Man Of The Match: ME Waugh

Australia innings (46 overs maximum)

			R	M	B	4	6
TM Moody	run out		6	4	8	0	0
DC Boon	b Omarshah		48	92	84	4	0
DM Jones	b Burmester		54	123	71	4	0
*AR Border	st Flower	b Traicos	22	24	29	2	0
ME Waugh	not out		66	68	39	5	2
SR Waugh	b Brandes		55	48	43	4	0
+IA Healy	lbw	b Duers	0	3	2	0	0
PL Taylor	not out		1	3	1	0	0
Extras (b 2, lb 8, w 2, nb 1): **13**							
Total (6 wickets, 46 overs): **265**							

DNB: CJ McDermott, MR Whitney, BA Reid.
FoW: 1-8 (Moody), 2-102 (Boon), 3-134 (Border), 4-144 (Jones), 5-257 (SR Waugh), 6-258 (Healy).

Bowling

	O	M	R	W
Brandes	9	0	59	1 (1nb)
Duers	9	1	48	1 (1w)
Burmester	9	0	65	1 (1w)
Omarshah	9	0	53	1
Traicos	10	0	30	1

Zimbabwe innings (target: 266 runs from 46 overs)

			R	M	B	4	6
AH Omarshah	run out		23	57	47	2	0
+A Flower	c Border	b SR Waugh	20	73	49	1	0
ADR Campbell	c ME Waugh	b Whitney	4	24	20	1	0
AJ Pycroft	c ME Waugh	b SR Waugh	0	1	1	0	0
*DL Houghton	b McDermott		2	26	10	0	0
AC Waller	c Taylor	b Moody	18	37	39	2	0
KJ Arnott	b Whitney		8	27	15	0	0
EA Brandes	c McDermott	b Taylor	23	53	28	3	0
MG Burmester	c Border	b Reid	12	21	24	0	0
AJ Traicos	c Border	b Taylor	3	12	9	0	0
KG Duers	not out		2	6	10	0	0
Extras (lb 12, w 8, nb 2): **22**							
Total (all out, 41.4 overs): **137**							

FoW: 1-47 (Omarshah), 2-51 (Flower), 3-51 (Pycroft), 4-57 (Campbell), 5-69 (Houghton), 6-88 (Waller), 7-97 (Arnott), 8-117 (Burmester), 9-132 (Traicos), 10-137 (Brandes).

Bowling

	O	M	R	W
McDermott	8	0	26	1 (1nb 3w)
Reid	9	2	17	1 (1nb)
SR Waugh	7	0	28	2 (4w)
Whitney	10	3	15	2
Moody	4	0	25	1 (1w)
Taylor	3.4	0	14	2

Benson & Hedges World Cup, 1991/92, 31st Match
New Zealand v England
Basin Reserve, Wellington
15 March 1992 (50-over match)

Result: New Zealand won by 7 wickets
Points: New Zealand 2, England 0
Toss: New Zealand
Umpires: SG Randell (Aus) and ID Robinson (Zim)
World Cup Referee: BJ Paterson
Man Of The Match: AH Jones

England innings (50 overs maximum)			R	M	B	4	6
*+AJ Stewart	c Harris	b Patel	41	77	59	7	0
IT Botham	b Patel		8	21	25	1	0
GA Hick	c Greatbatch	b Harris	56	94	70	6	1
RA Smith	c Patel	b Jones	38	67	72	3	0
AJ Lamb	c Cairns	b Watson	12	39	29	0	0
CC Lewis	c & b Watson		0	1	1	0	0
DA Reeve	not out		21	37	27	1	0
DR Pringle	c sub (RT Latham)	b Jones	10	20	16	0	0
PAJ DeFreitas	c Cairns	b Harris	0	3	1	0	0
RK Illingworth	not out		2	3	2	0	0
Extras (b 1, lb 7, w 4): **12**							
Total (8 wickets, 50 overs): **200**							

DNB: GC Small.
FoW: 1-25 (Botham), 2-95 (Stewart), 3-135 (Hick), 4-162 (Smith), 5-162 (Lewis), 6-169 (Lamb), 7-189 (Pringle), 8-195 (DeFreitas).

Bowling	O	M	R	W	
Patel	10	1	26	2	
Harris	8	0	39	2 (1w)	
Watson	10	0	40	2 (1w)	
Cairns	3	0	21	0 (1w)	
Larsen	10	3	24	0 (1w)	
Jones	9	0	42	2	

New Zealand innings (target: 201 from 50 overs)			R	M	B	4	6
MJ Greatbatch	c DeFreitas	b Botham	35	51	37	4	1
JG Wright	b DeFreitas		1	5	5	0	0
AH Jones	run out		78	123	113	13	0
*MD Crowe	not out		73	105	81	4	0
KR Rutherford	not out		3	27	12	0	0
Extras (b 1, lb 8, w 1, nb 1): **11**							
Total (3 wickets, 40.5 overs): **201**							

DNB: CZ Harris, CL Cairns, +IDS Smith, DN Patel, GR Larsen, W Watson.
FoW: 1-5 (Wright), 2-64 Greatbatch), 3-172 (Jones).

Bowling	O	M	R	W	
Pringle	6.2	1	34	0 (1nb 1w)	
DeFreitas	8.3	1	45	1	
Botham	4	0	19	1	
Illingworth	9	1	46	0	
Hick	6	0	26	0	
Reeve	3	0	9	0	
Small	4	0	13	0	

Benson & Hedges World Cup, 1991/92, 32nd Match
India v South Africa
Adelaide Oval
15 March 1992 (50-over match)

Result: South Africa won by 6 wickets
Points: South Africa 2, India 0
Toss: South Africa
Umpires: JD Buultjens (SL) and Khizer Hayat (Pak)
World Cup Referee: Barry Gibbs
Man Of The Match: PN Kirsten

India innings (30 overs maximum)			R	M	B	4	6
K Srikkanth	c Kirsten	b Donald	0	5	5	0	0
SV Manjrekar	b Kuiper		28	72	53	0	0
*M Azharuddin	c Kuiper	b Pringle	79	125	77	6	0
SR Tendulkar	c Wessels	b Kuiper	14	14	14	1	0
N Kapil Dev	b Donald		42	33	29	3	1
VG Kambli	run out		1	4	3	0	0
PK Amre	not out		1	3	1	0	0
J Srinath	not out		0	1	0	0	0
Extras (lb 7, w 6, nb 2): **15**							
Total (6 wickets, 30 overs): **180**							

DNB: +KS More, M Prabhakar, SLV Raju.
FoW: 1-1 (Srikkanth), 2-79 (Manjrekar), 3-103 (Tendulkar), 4-174 Kapil Dev), 5-177 (Kambli), 6-179 (Azharuddin).

Bowling	O	M	R	W
Donald	6	0	34	2 (3w)
Pringle	6	0	37	1 (2nb 2w)
Snell	6	1	46	0
McMillan	6	0	28	0
Kuiper	6	0	28	2 (1w)

South Africa innings (target: 181 from 30 overs)			R	M	B	4	6
AC Hudson	b Srinath		53	85	73	4	0
PN Kirsten	b Kapil Dev		84	104	86	7	0
AP Kuiper	run out		7	13	6	0	0
JN Rhodes	c Raju	b Prabhakar	7	8	3	0	1
*KC Wessels	not out		9	13	6	1	0
WJ Cronje	not out		8	9	6	1	0
Extras (lb 10, nb 3): **13**							
Total (4 wickets, 29.1 overs): **181**							

DNB: BM McMillan, +DJ Richardson, RP Snell, MW Pringle, AA Donald.
FoW: 1-128 (Hudson), 2-149 (Kuiper), 3-157 (Kirsten), 4-163 (Rhodes).

Bowling	O	M	R	W
Kapil Dev	6	0	36	1
Prabhakar	5.1	1	33	1
Tendulkar	6	0	20	0
Srinath	6	0	39	1 (3nb)
Raju	6	0	43	0

Rain reduced the match to 30 overs per side

Benson & Hedges World Cup, 1991/92, 33rd Match
Pakistan v Sri Lanka
W.A.C.A. Ground, Perth
15 March 1992 (50-over match)

Result: Pakistan won by 4 wickets
Points: Pakistan 2, Sri Lanka 0
Toss: Sri Lanka
Umpires: KE Liebenberg (SA) and PJ McConnell
World Cup Referee: Tony Mann
Man Of The Match: Javed Miandad

Sri Lanka innings (50 overs maximum)			R	M	B	4	6
RS Mahanama	b Wasim Akram		12	35	36	1	0
MAR Samarasekera	st Moin Khan	b Mushtaq Ahmed	38	106	59	1	0
UC Hathurusingha	b Mushtaq Ahmed		5	32	29	0	0
*PA de Silva	c Aamer Sohail	b Ijaz Ahmed	43	64	56	2	0
AP Gurusinha	c Saleem Malik	b Imran Khan	37	77	54	2	0
A Ranatunga	c sub (Zahid Fazal)	b Aamer Sohail	7	18	19	0	0
+HP Tillakaratne	not out		25	44	34	3	0
RS Kalpage	not out		13	16	14	0	0
Extras (lb 15, w 11, nb 6): **32**							
Total (6 wickets, 50 overs): **212**							

DNB: CPH Ramanayake, KIW Wijegunawardene, GP Wickramasinghe.
FoW: 1-29 (Mahanama), 2-48 (Hathurusingha), 3-99 (Samarasekera), 4-132 (de Silva), 5-158 (Ranatunga), 6-187 (Gurusinha).

Bowling	O	M	R	W	
Wasim Akram	10	0	37	1	(4nb 2w)
Aaqib Javed	10	0	39	0	(2nb 3w)
Imran Khan	8	1	36	1	
Mushtaq Ahmed	10	0	43	2	(2w)
Ijaz Ahmed	8	0	28	1	(3w)
Aamer Sohail	4	0	14	1	(1w)

Pakistan innings (target: 213 runs from 50 overs)			R	M	B	4	6
Aamer Sohail	c Mahanama	b Ramanayake	1	11	10	0	0
Rameez Raja	c Gurusinha	b Wickramasinghe	32	92	56	3	0
*Imran Khan	c de Silva	b Hathurusingha	22	98	69	2	0
Javed Miandad	c Wickramasinghe	b Gurusinha	57	99	84	3	0
Saleem Malik	c Kalpage	b Ramanayake	51	98	66	2	0
Inzamam-ul-Haq	run out		11	15	11	0	0
Ijaz Ahmed	not out		8	11	6	1	0
Wasim Akram	not out		5	7	5	1	0
Extras (lb 12, w 9, nb 8): **29**							
Total (6 wickets, 49.1 overs): **216**							

DNB: +Moin Khan, Mushtaq Ahmed, Aaqib Javed.
FoW: 1-7 (Aamer Sohail), 2-68 (Rameez Raja), 3-84 Imran Khan), 4-185 (Javed Miandad), 5-201 (Saleem Malik), 6-205 (Inzamam-ul-Haq).

Bowling	O	M	R	W	
Wijegunawardene	10	1	34	0	(7nb)
Ramanayake	10	1	37	2	(4w)
Wickramasinghe	9.1	0	41	1	(1w)
Gurusinha	9	0	38	1	(1w)
Hathurusingha	9	0	40	1	(1nb 2w)
Kalpage	2	0	14	0	(1w)

Benson & Hedges World Cup, 1991/92, 34th Match
New Zealand v Pakistan
Lancaster Park, Christchurch
18 March 1992 (50-over match)

Result: Pakistan won by 7 wickets
Points: Pakistan 2, New Zealand 0
Toss: Pakistan
Umpires: SA Bucknor (WI) and SG Randell (Aus)
World Cup Referee: CL Bull
Man Of The Match: Mushtaq Ahmed

New Zealand innings (50 overs maximum)			R	M	B	4	6
MJ Greatbatch	c Saleem Malik	b Mushtaq Ahmed	42	106	67	5	1
RT Latham	c Inzamam-ul-Haq	b Aaqib Javed	6	18	9	1	0
AH Jones	lbw	b Wasim Akram	2	5	3	0	0
*MD Crowe	c Aamer Sohail	b Wasim Akram	3	23	20	0	0
KR Rutherford	run out		8	41	35	0	0
CZ Harris	st Moin Khan	b Mushtaq Ahmed	1	6	6	0	0
DN Patel	c Mushtaq Ahmed	b Aamer Sohail	7	27	13	0	0
+IDS Smith	b Imran Khan		1	5	4	0	0
GR Larsen	b Wasim Akram		37	86	80	3	0
DK Morrison	c Inzamam-ul-Haq	b Wasim Akram	12	55	45	1	0
W Watson	not out		5	17	13	0	0

Extras (b 3, lb 23, w 12, nb 4): **42**
Total (all out, 48.2 overs): **166**

FoW: 1-23 (Latham), 2-26 (Jones), 3-39 (Crowe), 4-85 (Rutherford), 5-88 (Harris), 6-93 (Greatbatch), 7-96 (Smith), 8-106 (Patel), 9-150 (Morrison), 10-166 (Larsen).

Bowling	O	M	R	W
Wasim Akram	9.2	0	32	4
Aaqib Javed	10	1	34	1
Mushtaq Ahmed	10	0	18	2
Imran Khan	8	0	22	1
Aamer Sohail	10	1	29	1
Ijaz Ahmed	1	0	5	0

Pakistan innings (target: 167 runs from 50 overs)			R	M	B	4	6
Aamer Sohail	c Patel	b Morrison	0	1	1	0	0
Rameez Raja	not out		119	173	155	16	0
Inzamam-ul-Haq	b Morrison		5	12	8	1	0
Javed Miandad	lbw	b Morrison	30	123	85	1	0
Saleem Malik	not out		9	34	23	1	0

Extras (lb 1, w 1, nb 2): **4**
Total (3 wickets, 44.4 overs): **167**

DNB: *Imran Khan, Wasim Akram, Ijaz Ahmed, +Moin Khan, Mushtaq Ahmed, Aaqib Javed.
FoW: 1-0 (Aamer Sohail), 2-9 (Inzamam-ul-Haq), 3-124 Javed Miandad).

Bowling	O	M	R	W
Morrison	10	0	42	3
Patel	10	2	25	0
Watson	10	3	26	0
Harris	4	0	18	0
Larsen	3	0	16	0
Jones	3	0	10	0
Latham	2	0	13	0
Rutherford	1.4	0	11	0
Greatbatch	1	0	5	0

Benson & Hedges World Cup, 1991/92, 35th Match
England v Zimbabwe
Lavington Sports Oval, Albury
18 March 1992 (50-over match)

Result: Zimbabwe won by 9 runs
Points: Zimbabwe 2, England 0
Toss: England
Umpires: BL Aldridge (NZ) and Khizer Hayat (Pak)
World Cup Referee: Bruce Stanton
Man Of The Match: EA Brandes

Zimbabwe innings (50 overs maximum)			R	M	B	4	6
WR James	c & b Illingworth		13	55	46	1	0
+A Flower	b DeFreitas		7	17	16	1	0
AJ Pycroft	c Gooch	b Botham	3	24	13	0	0
KJ Arnott	lbw	b Botham	11	43	33	0	0
*DL Houghton	c Fairbrother	b Small	29	90	74	2	0
AC Waller	b Tufnell		8	15	16	1	0
AH Omarshah	c Lamb	b Tufnell	3	21	16	0	0
IP Butchart	c Fairbrother	b Botham	24	42	36	2	0
EA Brandes	st Stewart	b Illingworth	14	25	24	1	0
AJ Traicos	not out		0	12	6	0	0
MP Jarvis	lbw	b Illingworth	6	9	6	0	0

*Extras (lb 8, w 8): **16***
*Total (all out, 46.1 overs): **134***

FoW: 1-12 (Flower), 2-19 (Pycroft), 3-30 (James), 4-52 (Arnott), 5-65 (Waller), 6-77 (Omarshah), 7-96 (Houghton), 8-127 (Butchart), 9-127 (Brandes), 10-134 Jarvis).

Bowling	O	M	R	W
DeFreitas	8	1	14	1
Small	9	1	20	1
Botham	10	2	23	3
Illingworth	9.1	0	33	3
Tufnell	10	2	36	2

England innings (target: 135 runs from 50 overs)			R	M	B	4	6
*GA Gooch	lbw	b Brandes	0	1	1	0	0
IT Botham	c Flower	b Omarshah	18	45	34	4	0
AJ Lamb	c James	b Brandes	17	29	26	2	0
RA Smith	b Brandes		2	15	13	0	0
GA Hick	b Brandes		0	12	6	0	0
NH Fairbrother	c Flower	b Butchart	20	132	77	0	0
+AJ Stewart	c Waller	b Omarshah	29	94	96	3	0
PAJ DeFreitas	c Flower	b Butchart	4	14	17	0	0
RK Illingworth	run out		11	28	20	0	0
GC Small	c Pycroft	b Jarvis	5	20	18	0	0
PCR Tufnell	not out		0	3	0	0	0

*Extras (b 4, lb 3, w 11, nb 1): **19***
*Total (all out, 49.1 overs): **125***

FoW: 1-0 (Gooch), 2-32 (Lamb), 3-42 (Botham), 4-42 (Smith), 5-43 (Hick), 6-95 (Stewart), 7-101 (DeFreitas), 8-108 (Fairbrother), 9-124 Illingworth), 10-125 (Small).

Bowling	O	M	R	W
Brandes	10	4	21	4
Jarvis	9.1	0	32	1
Omarshah	10	3	17	2
Traicos	10	4	16	0
Butchart	10	1	32	2

Benson & Hedges World Cup, 1991/92, 36th Match
Australia v West Indies
Melbourne Cricket Ground (day/night)
18 March 1992 (50-over match)

Result: Australia won by 57 runs
Points: Australia 2, West Indies 0
Toss: Australia
Umpires: PD Reporter (Ind) and DR Shepherd (Eng)
World Cup Referee: Jim Mann
Man Of The Match: DC Boon

Australia innings (50 overs maximum)			R	M	B	4	6
TM Moody	c Benjamin	b Simmons	42	95	70	3	0
DC Boon	c Williams	b Cummins	100	173	147	8	0
DM Jones	c Williams	b Cummins	6	19	14	0	0
*AR Border	lbw	b Simmons	8	12	10	1	0
ME Waugh	st Williams	b Hooper	21	38	31	0	0
SR Waugh	b Cummins		6	18	14	0	0
+IA Healy	not out		11	22	11	0	0
PL Taylor	not out		10	9	6	1	0
Extras (lb 3, w 3, nb 6): **12**							
Total (6 wickets, 50 overs): **216**							

DNB: CJ McDermott, MR Whitney, BA Reid.
FoW: 1-107 (Moody), 2-128 (Jones), 3-141 (Border), 4-185 (ME Waugh), 5-189 (Boon), 6-200 (SR Waugh).

Bowling	O	M	R	W
Ambrose	10	0	46	0
Benjamin	10	1	49	0
Cummins	10	1	38	3
Hooper	10	0	40	1
Simmons	10	1	40	2

West Indies innings (target: 217 from 50 overs)			R	M	B	4	6
DL Haynes	c Jones	b McDermott	14	27	24	2	0
BC Lara	run out		70	180	97	3	0
PV Simmons	lbw	b McDermott	0	1	1	0	0
*RB Richardson	c Healy	b Whitney	10	50	44	0	0
KLT Arthurton	c McDermott	b Whitney	15	16	21	1	0
AL Logie	c Healy	b Whitney	5	14	15	0	0
CL Hooper	c ME Waugh	b Whitney	4	16	11	0	0
+D Williams	c Border	b Reid	4	17	15	0	0
WKM Benjamin	lbw	b SR Waugh	15	34	15	2	0
CEL Ambrose	run out		2	12	7	0	0
AC Cummins	not out		5	8	10	0	0
Extras (b 3, lb 5, w 3, nb 4): **15**							
Total (all out, 42.4 overs): **159**							

FoW: 1-27 (Haynes), 2-27 (Simmons), 3-59 (Richardson), 4-83 (Arthurton), 5-99 (Logie), 6-117 (Hooper), 7-128 (Williams), 8-137 (Lara), 9-150 (Ambrose), 10-159 (Benjamin).

Bowling	O	M	R	W
McDermott	6	1	29	2
Reid	10	1	26	1
Whitney	10	1	34	4
SR Waugh	6.4	0	24	1
Taylor	4	0	24	0
Moody	6	1	14	0

Benson & Hedges World Cup, 1991/92, 1st Semi-Final
New Zealand v Pakistan
Eden Park, Auckland
21 March 1992 (50-over match)

Result: Pakistan won by 4 wickets
Pakistan advances to the final
Toss: New Zealand
Umpires: SA Bucknor (WI) and DR Shepherd (Eng)
Match Referee: PJP Burge (Aus)
Man Of The Match: Inzamam-ul-Haq

New Zealand innings (50 overs maximum)			R	M	B	4	6
MJ Greatbatch	b Aaqib Javed		17	41	22	0	2
JG Wright	c Rameez Raja	b Mushtaq Ahmed	13	57	44	1	0
AH Jones	lbw	b Mushtaq Ahmed	21	60	53	2	0
*MD Crowe	run out		91	132	83	7	3
KR Rutherford	c Moin Khan	b Wasim Akram	50	68	68	5	1
CZ Harris	st Moin Khan	b Iqbal Sikander	13	15	12	1	0
+IDS Smith	not out		18	21	10	3	0
DN Patel	lbw	b Wasim Akram	8	10	6	1	0
GR Larsen	not out		8	7	6	1	0
Extras (lb 11, w 8, nb 4): **23**							
Total (7 wickets, 50 overs): **262**							

DNB: DK Morrison, W Watson.
FoW: 1-35 (Greatbatch), 2-39 (Wright), 3-87 (Jones), 4-194 Rutherford), 5-214 Harris), 6-221 (Crowe), 7-244 Patel).

Bowling	O	M	R	W	
Wasim Akram	10	1	40	2	(4nb 2w)
Aaqib Javed	10	2	45	1	(2w)
Mushtaq Ahmed	10	0	40	2	
Imran Khan	10	0	59	0	(3w)
Iqbal Sikander	9	0	56	1	(1w)
Aamer Sohail	1	0	11	0	

Pakistan innings (target: 263 runs from 50 overs)			R	M	B	4	6
Aamer Sohail	c Jones	b Patel	14	26	20	1	0
Rameez Raja	c Morrison	b Watson	44	81	55	6	0
*Imran Khan	c Larsen	b Harris	44	98	93	1	2
Javed Miandad	not out		57	125	69	4	0
Saleem Malik	c sub	b Larsen	1	4	2	0	0
Inzamam-ul-Haq	run out		60	48	37	7	1
Wasim Akram	b Watson		9	12	8	1	0
+Moin Khan	not out		20	15	11	2	1
Extras (b 4, lb 10, w 1): **15**							
Total (6 wickets, 49 overs): **264**							

DNB: Mushtaq Ahmed, Iqbal Sikander, Aaqib Javed.
FoW: 1-30, 2-84, 3-134, 4-140, 5-227, 6-238.

Bowling	O	M	R	W	
Patel	10	1	50	1	
Morrison	9	0	55	0	(1w)
Watson	10	2	39	2	(1nb)
Larsen	10	1	34	1	
Harris	10	0	72	1	

Benson & Hedges World Cup, 1991/92, 2nd Semi-Final
England v South Africa
Sydney Cricket Ground (day/night)
22 March 1992 (50-over match)

Result: England won by 19 runs (revised target)
England advances to the final
Toss: South Africa
Umpires: BL Aldridge (NZ) and SG Randell
Match Referee: FJ Cameron (NZ)
Man Of The Match: GA Hick

England innings (45 overs maximum)			R	M	B	4	6
*GA Gooch	c Richardson	b Donald	2	15	9	0	0
IT Botham	b Pringle		21	38	23	3	0
+AJ Stewart	c Richardson	b McMillan	33	87	54	4	0
GA Hick	c Rhodes	b Snell	83	133	90	9	0
NH Fairbrother	b Pringle		28	64	50	1	0
AJ Lamb	c Richardson	b Donald	19	27	22	1	0
CC Lewis	not out		18	37	16	2	0
DA Reeve	not out		25	13	14	4	0
Extras (b 1, lb 7, w 9, nb 6): 23							
Total (6 wickets, 45 overs): 252							

DNB: PAJ DeFreitas, GC Small, RK Illingworth.
FoW: 1-20 (Gooch), 2-39 (Botham), 3-110 (Stewart), 4-183 (Fairbrother), 5-187 (Hick), 6-221 (Lamb).

Bowling	O	M	R	W	
Donald	10	0	69	2 (2nb 5w)	
Pringle	9	2	36	2 (4nb 1w)	
Snell	8	0	52	1 (2w)	
McMillan	9	0	47	1	
Kuiper	5	0	26	0	
Cronje	4	0	14	0	

South Africa innings (target: 252 from 43 overs)			R	M	B	4	6
*KC Wessels	c Lewis	b Botham	17	17	21	1	0
AC Hudson	lbw	b Illingworth	46	78	52	6	0
PN Kirsten	b DeFreitas		11	30	26	0	0
AP Kuiper	b Illingworth		36	62	44	5	0
WJ Cronje	c Hick	b Small	24	72	45	1	0
JN Rhodes	c Lewis	b Small	43	61	38	3	0
BM McMillan	not out		21	41	21	0	0
+DJ Richardson	not out		13	19	10	1	0
Extras (lb 17, w 4): 21							
Total (6 wickets, 43 overs): 232							

DNB: RP Snell, MW Pringle, AA Donald.
FoW: 1-26 (Wessels), 2-61 (Kirsten), 3-90 (Hudson), 4-131 (Kuiper), 5-176 (Cronje), 6-206 (Rhodes).

Bowling	O	M	R	W	
Botham	10	0	52	1 (3w)	
Lewis	5	0	38	0	
DeFreitas	8	1	28	1 (1w)	
Illingworth	10	1	46	2	
Small	10	1	51	2	

Play was delayed by ten minutes due to early rain, and ten minutes were removed from the lunch interval – no reduction in the number of overs. The innings were shortened when the overs weren't completed by the time for the innings to end. Rain interrupted play after five balls of the 42nd over. Two overs were lost but the target remained unchanged – 22 were needed from the one ball that remained.

Benson & Hedges World Cup, 1991/92, Final
England v Pakistan
Melbourne Cricket Ground (day/night)
25 March 1992 (50-over match)

Result: Pakistan won by 22 runs
Series: Pakistan wins the 1991/92 Benson & Hedges World Cup
Toss: Pakistan
Umpires: BL Aldridge (NZ) and SA Bucknor (WI)
Match Referee: PJP Burge
Man Of The Match: Wasim Akram
Man Of The Series: MD Crowe (NZ)

Pakistan innings (50 overs maximum)

			R	M	B	4	6
Aamer Sohail	c Stewart	b Pringle	4	20	19	0	0
Rameez Raja	lbw	b Pringle	8	36	26	1	0
*Imran Khan	c Illingworth	b Botham	72	159	110	5	1
Javed Miandad	c Botham	b Illingworth	58	125	98	4	0
Inzamam-ul-Haq	b Pringle		42	46	35	4	0
Wasim Akram	run out		33	21	19	4	0
Saleem Malik	not out		0	2	1	0	0
Extras (lb 19, w 6, nb 7): ***32***							
Total (6 wickets, 50 overs): ***249***							

DNB: Ijaz Ahmed, +Moin Khan, Mushtaq Ahmed, Aaqib Javed.
FoW: 1-20 (Aamer Sohail), 2-24 (Rameez Raja), 3-163 (Javed Miandad), 4-197 (Imran Khan), 5-249 (Inzamam-ul-Haq), 6-249 (Wasim Akram).

Bowling

	O	M	R	W	
Pringle	10	2	22	3	(5nb 3w)
Lewis	10	2	52	0	(2nb 1w)
Botham	7	0	42	1	
DeFreitas	10	1	42	0	(1w)
Illingworth	10	0	50	1	
Reeve	3	0	22	0	(1w)

England innings (target: 250 runs from 50 overs)

			R	M	B	4	6
*GA Gooch	c Aaqib Javed	b Mushtaq Ahmed	29	93	66	1	0
IT Botham	c Moin Khan	b Wasim Akram	0	12	6	0	0
+AJ Stewart	c Moin Khan	b Aaqib Javed	7	22	16	1	0
GA Hick	lbw	b Mushtaq Ahmed	17	49	36	1	0
NH Fairbrother	c Moin Khan	b Aaqib Javed	62	97	70	3	0
AJ Lamb	b Wasim Akram		31	54	41	2	0
CC Lewis	b Wasim Akram		0	1	6	0	0
DA Reeve	c Rameez Raja	b Mushtaq Ahmed	15	38	32	0	0
DR Pringle	not out		18	29	16	1	0
PAJ DeFreitas	run out		10	13	8	0	0
RK Illingworth	c Rameez Raja	b Imran Khan	14	9	11	2	0
Extras (lb 5, w 13, nb 6): ***24***							
Total (all out, 49.2 overs): ***227***							

FoW: 1-6 (Botham), 2-21 (Stewart), 3-59 (Hick), 4-69 (Gooch), 5-141 (Lamb), 6-141 (Lewis), 7-180 (Fairbrother), 8-183 (Reeve), 9-208 (DeFreitas), 10-227 (Illingworth).

Bowling

	O	M	R	W	
Wasim Akram	10	0	49	3	(4nb 6w)
Aaqib Javed	10	2	27	2	(1nb 3w)
Mushtaq Ahmed	10	1	41	3	(1w)
Ijaz Ahmed	3	0	13	0	(2w)
Imran Khan	6.2	0	43	1	(1nb)
Aamer Sohail	10	0	49	0	(1w)

1996 WORLD CUP

Group A

Wills World Cup, 1995/96, 3rd Match
West Indies v Zimbabwe, Group A
Lal Bahadur Shastri Stadium, Hyderabad, Deccan (day/night)
16 February 1996 (50-over match)

Result: West Indies won by 6 wickets
Points: West Indies 2, Zimbabwe 0
Toss: Zimbabwe
Umpires: RS Dunne (NZ) and S Venkataraghavan
TV Umpire: Mian Mohammad Aslam (Pak)
Match Referee: R Subba Row (Eng)
Man Of The Match: CEL Ambrose

Zimbabwe innings (50 overs maximum)			R	M	B	4	6
*+A Flower	c Browne	b Ambrose	3	9	4	0	0
GW Flower	c & b Gibson		31	70	54	6	0
GJ Whittall	run out		14	79	62	0	0
ADR Campbell	run out (Lara)		0	10	8	0	0
AC Waller	st Browne	b Harper	21	62	44	2	0
CN Evans	c Browne	b Ambrose	21	34	31	2	0
SG Davies	run out (Bishop)		9	41	35	0	0
HH Streak	lbw	b Walsh	7	29	18	0	0
PA Strang	not out		22	34	28	2	0
EA Brandes	c Chanderpaul	b Ambrose	7	17	13	1	0
ACI Lock	not out		1	7	5	0	0

Extras (lb 10, w 4, nb 1): **15**
Total (9 wickets, 50 overs): **151**

FoW: 1-11 (A Flower), 2-53 (GW Flower), 3-56 (Campbell), 4-59 (Whittall), 5-91 (Evans), 6-103 (Waller), 7-115 (Davies), 8-125 (Streak), 9-142 (Brandes).

Bowling	O	M	R	W
Ambrose	10	2	28	3 (4w)
Walsh	10	3	27	1
Gibson	9	1	27	1
Bishop	10	3	18	0 (1nb)
Harper	10	1	30	1
Arthurton	1	0	11	0

West Indies innings (target: 152 runs from 50 overs)			R	M	B	4	6
SL Campbell	b Strang		47	106	88	5	0
*RB Richardson	c Campbell	b Strang	32	83	47	3	0
BC Lara	not out		43	44	31	5	2
S Chanderpaul	b Strang		8	2	4	2	0
KLT Arthurton	c Campbell	b Strang	1	7	3	0	0
RA Harper	not out		5	9	6	1	0

Extras (b 5, lb 3, w 10, nb 1): **19**
Total (4 wickets, 29.3 overs): **155**

DNB: +CO Browne, OD Gibson, IR Bishop, CEL Ambrose, CA Walsh.
FoW: 1-78 (Richardson), 2-115 (Campbell), 3-123 (Chanderpaul), 4-136 (Arthurton).

Bowling	O	M	R	W
Streak	7	0	34	0 (5w, 1nb)
Lock	6	0	23	0 (4w)
Brandes	7	0	42	0 (1w)
Whittall	2	0	8	0
Strang	7.3	1	40	4

Wills World Cup, 1995/96, 5th Match
Sri Lanka v Australia
R Premadasa (Khettarama) Stadium, Colombo.
17 February 1996 (50-over match)

Result: Sri Lanka won by walkover without a ball bowled
Points: Sri Lanka 2, Australia 0
Toss: None
Umpires: CJ Mitchley (SA) and Mehboob Shah (Pak)
TV Umpire: Farid Malik (UAE)
Match Referee: Nasim-ul-Ghani (Pak)
Man Of The Match: No award

Sri Lanka team (from): MS Atapattu, UDU Chandana, PA de Silva, HDPK Dharmasena
AP Gurusinha, ST Jayasuriya, RS Kaluwitharana, RS Mahanama
M Muralitharan, KR Pushpakumara, A Ranatunga, HP Tillakaratne WPUCJ Vaas,
GP Wickramasinghe.

Wills World Cup, 1995/96, 6th Match
India v Kenya, Group A
Barabati Stadium, Cuttack
18 February 1996 (50-over match)

Result: India won by 7 wickets
Points: India 2, Kenya 0
Toss: India
Umpires: KT Francis (SL) and DR Shepherd (Eng)
TV Umpire: S Toohey (NL)
Match Referee: CH Lloyd (WI)
ODI Debuts: RW Ali, DN Chudasama, AY Karim, HS Modi, TM Odoyo, EO Odumbe, MO
  Odumbe, KO Otieno, MA Suji, LO Tikolo, SO Tikolo (Kenya)
Man Of The Match: SR Tendulkar

Kenya innings (50 overs maximum)

			R	M	B	4	6
DN Chudasama	c Mongia	b Prasad	29	54	51	5	0
+KO Otieno	c Mongia	b Raju	27	90	58	3	0
SO Tikolo	c Kumble	b Raju	65	110	83	4	1
*MO Odumbe	st Mongia	b Kumble	26	70	57	0	0
HS Modi	c Jadeja	b Kumble	2	12	3	0	0
TM Odoyo	c Prabhakar	b Kumble	8	12	18	0	0
EO Odumbe	not out		15	28	21	0	0
AY Karim	not out		6	11	11	0	0

Extras (b 2, lb 11, w 7, nb 1): **21**
Total (6 wickets, 50 overs): **199**

DNB: LO Tikolo, MA Suji, RW Ali.
FoW: 1-41 (Chudasama), 2-65 (Otieno), 3-161 (MO Odumbe), 4-161 (SO Tikolo), 5-165 (Modi), 6-184 (Odoyo).

Bowling

	O	M	R	W
Prabhakar	5	1	19	0
Srinath	10	0	38	0 (5w)
Prasad	10	0	41	1 (2w)
Kumble	10	0	28	3
Raju	10	2	34	2
Tendulkar	5	0	26	0

India innings (target: 200 runs from 50 overs)

			R	M	B	4	6
A Jadeja	c Ali	b Karim	53	134	85	4	1
SR Tendulkar	not out		127	175	138	15	1
NS Sidhu	c Suji	b SO Tikolo	1	19	11	0	0
VG Kambli	c LO Tikolo	b MO Odumbe	2	11	11	0	0
+NR Mongia	not out		8	10	7	1	0

Extras (lb 5, w 6, nb 1): **12**
Total (3 wickets, 41.5 overs): **203**

DNB: *M Azharuddin, M Prabhakar, J Srinath, A Kumble, BKV Prasad, SLV Raju.
FoW: 1-163 (Jadeja), 2-167 (Sidhu), 3-182 (Kambli).

Bowling

	O	M	R	W
Ali	5	0	25	0
EO Odumbe	3	0	18	0 (3w)
Suji	5	0	20	0
Odoyo	3	0	22	0 (1nb)
Karim	10	1	27	1
LO Tikolo	3	0	21	0 (3w)
MO Odumbe	9.5	1	39	1
SO Tikolo	3	0	26	1

Wills World Cup, 1995/96, 9th Match
Sri Lanka v Zimbabwe, Group A
Sinhalese Sports Club Ground, Colombo
21 February 1996 (50-over match)

Result: Sri Lanka won by 6 wickets
Points: Sri Lanka 2, Zimbabwe 0
Toss: Zimbabwe
Umpires: RS Dunne (NZ) and Mahboob Shah (Pak)
TV Umpire: Farid Malik (UAE)
Match Referee: Nasim-ul-Ghani (Pak)
Man Of The Match: PA de Silva

Zimbabwe innings (50 overs maximum)			R	M	B	4	6
*+A Flower	run out (Vaas)		8	27	18	1	0
GW Flower	run out (Jayasuriya)		15	58	32	0	0
GJ Whittall	c Jayasuriya	b Muralitharan	35	74	64	5	0
ADR Campbell	c Muralitharan	b Vaas	75	125	102	8	0
AC Waller	b Jayasuriya		19	55	36	1	0
CN Evans	not out		39	45	34	5	0
HH Streak	c de Silva	b Vaas	15	17	13	0	0
PA Strang	not out		0	2	1	0	0
Extras (b 1, lb 16, w 4, nb 1): **22**							
Total (6 wickets, 50 overs): **228**							

DNB: ACI Lock, EA Brandes, SG Peall.
FoW: 1-19 (A Flower), 2-51 (GW Flower), 3-92 (Whittall), 4-160 (Waller), 5-194 (Campbell), 6-227 (Streak).

Bowling	O	M	R	W
Vaas	10	0	30	2
Wickramasinghe	8	0	36	0
Ranatunga	2	0	14	0
Dharmasena	10	1	50	0
Muralitharan	10	0	37	1
Jayasuriya	10	0	44	1

Sri Lanka innings (target: 229 runs from 50 overs)			R	M	B	4	6
ST Jayasuriya	b Streak		6	25	11	1	0
+RS Kaluwitharana	c Peall	b Streak	0	5	1	0	0
AP Gurusinha	run out		87	144	100	5	6
PA de Silva	lbw	b Streak	91	137	86	10	2
*A Ranatunga	not out		13	29	11	1	0
HP Tillakaratne	not out		7	16	16	1	0
Extras (lb 5, w 17, nb 3): **25**							
Total (4 wickets, 37 overs): **229**							

DNB: RS Mahanama, WPUJC Vaas, HDPK Dharmasena, GP Wickramasinghe, M Muralitharan.
FoW: 1-5 (Kaluwitharana), 2-23 (Jayasuriya), 3-195 (Gurusinha), 4-209 (de Silva).

Bowling	O	M	R	W	
Streak	10	0	60	3	(12w, 2nb)
Lock	4	0	17	0	(4w)
Brandes	8	0	35	0	(1w, 1nb)
Peall	3	0	23	0	
Strang	5	0	43	0	
Whittall	2	0	20	0	
GW Flower	5	1	26	0	

Wills World Cup, 1995/96, 10th Match
India v West Indies, Group A
Captain Roop Singh Stadium, Gwalior (day/night)
21 February 1996 (50-over match)

Result: India won by 5 wickets
Points: India 2, West Indies 0
Toss: West Indies
Umpires: Khizer Hayat (Pak) and ID Robinson (Zim)
TV Umpire: S Toohey (NL)
Match Referee: R Subba Row (Eng)
Man Of The Match: SR Tendulkar

West Indies innings (50 overs maximum)			R	M	B	4	6
SL Campbell	b Srinath		5	17	14	1	0
*RB Richardson	c Kambli	b Prabhakar	47	111	70	4	0
BC Lara	c Mongia	b Srinath	2	8	5	0	0
S Chanderpaul	c Azharuddin	b Kapoor	38	94	66	6	0
RIC Holder	b Kumble		0	7	3	0	0
RA Harper	b Kumble		23	52	40	1	1
+CO Browne	b Prabhakar		18	52	45	0	0
OD Gibson	b Kumble		6	5	5	1	0
IR Bishop	run out		9	38	28	0	0
CEL Ambrose	c Kumble	b Prabhakar	8	19	15	1	0
CA Walsh	not out		9	12	11	2	0

Extras (lb 2, w 5, nb 1): **8**
Total (all out, 50 overs): **173**

FoW: 1-16 (Campbell), 2-24 (Lara), 3-91 (Richardson), 4-99 (Holder), 5-99 (Chanderpaul), 6-141 (Harper), 7-141 (Browne), 8-149 (Gibson), 9-162 (Ambrose), 10-173 (Bishop). ·

Bowling	O	M	R	W
Prabhakar	10	0	39	3 (1nb)
Srinath	10	0	22	2
Kumble	10	0	35	3 (5w)
Prasad	10	0	34	0
Kapoor	10	2	41	1

India innings (target: 174 runs from 50 overs)			R	M	B	4	6
A Jadeja	b Ambrose		1	3	3	0	0
SR Tendulkar	run out		70	137	91	8	0
NS Sidhu	b Ambrose		1	14	5	0	0
*M Azharuddin	c Walsh	b Harper	32	83	59	4	0
VG Kambli	not out		33	83	48	4	1
M Prabhakar	c & b Harper		1	9	12	0	0
+NR Mongia	not out		24	48	33	3	0

Extras (lb 3, w 1, nb 8): **12**
Total (5 wickets, 39.4 overs): **174**

DNB: AR Kapoor, A Kumble, J Srinath, BKV Prasad.
FoW: 1-2 (Jadeja), 2-15 (Sidhu), 3-94 (Azharuddin), 4-125 (Tendulkar), 5-127 (Prabhakar).

Bowling	O	M	R	W
Ambrose	8	1	41	2 (2nb, 1w)
Walsh	9	3	18	0 (2nb)
Bishop	5	0	28	0 (3nb)
Gibson	8.4	0	50	0 (1nb)
Harper	9	1	34	2

Wills World Cup, 1995/96, 12th Match
Australia v Kenya, Group A
Indira Priyadarshini Stadium, Visakhapatnam
23 February 1996 (50-over match)

Result: Australia won by 97 runs
Points: Australia 2, Kenya 0
Toss: Kenya
Umpires: CJ Mitchley (SA) and DR Shepherd (Eng)
TV Umpire: Shakeel Khan (Pak)
Match Referee: CH Lloyd (WI)
Man Of The Match: ME Waugh

Australia innings (50 overs maximum)

			R	M	B	4	6
*MA Taylor	c Modi	b Suji	6	19	20	0	0
ME Waugh	c Suji	b Ali	130	167	128	14	1
RT Ponting	c Otieno	b Ali	6	15	12	1	0
SR Waugh	c & b Suji		82	136	88	5	1
SG Law	run out (MO Odumbe)	35	43	30	3	0	
MG Bevan	b Ali		12	14	12	0	0
+IA Healy	c EO Odumbe	b Karim	17	21	11	2	0
PR Reiffel	not out		3	4	2	0	0
SK Warne	not out		0	2	2	0	0

Extras (b 1, w 10, nb 2): **13**
Total (7 wickets, 50 overs): **304**

DNB: CJ McDermott, GD McGrath.
FoW: 1-10 (Taylor), 2-26 (Ponting), 3-233 (ME Waugh), 4-237 (SR Waugh), 5-261 (Bevan), 6-301 (Law), 7-301 (Healy).

Bowling	O	M	R	W
Suji	10	1	55	2 (1w, 1nb)
Ali	10	0	45	3 (4w)
Odoyo	8	0	58	0 (1w, 1nb)
EO Odumbe	4	0	21	0 (2w)
Karim	10	1	54	1
MO Odumbe	4	0	35	0 (1w)
LO Tikolo	3	0	21	0
SO Tikolo	1	0	14	0 (1w)

Kenya innings (target: 305 runs from 50 overs)

			R	M	B	4	6
+KO Otieno	b McGrath		85	164	137	8	1
DN Chudasama	c Healy	b McDermott	5	10	7	1	0
SO Tikolo	c Ponting	b Reiffel	6	33	8	1	0
*MO Odumbe	c Reiffel	b Bevan	50	72	53	7	0
HS Modi	b Bevan		10	31	20	1	0
EO Odumbe	c Bevan	b Reiffel	14	33	33	0	0
LO Tikolo	not out		11	57	35	0	0
TM Odoyo	st Healy	b Warne	10	5	6	2	0
MA Suji	not out		1	1	4	0	0

Extras (lb 7, w 6, nb 2): **15**
Total (7 wickets, 50 overs): **207**

DNB: AY Karim, RW Ali.
FoW: 1-12 (Chudasama), 2-30 (SO Tikolo), 3-132 (MO Odumbe), 4-167 (Modi), 5-188 (EO Odumbe), 6-195 (Otieno), 7-206 (Odoyo).

Bowling	O	M	R	W
McDermott	3	0	12	1 (1w)
Reiffel	7	1	18	2 (1w, 1nb)
McGrath	10	0	44	1 (1w)
SR Waugh	7	0	43	0 (1nb)
Warne	10	0	25	1
Bevan	8	0	35	2 (2w)
ME Waugh	5	0	23	0 (1w)

Wills World Cup, 1995/96, 14th Match
Sri Lanka v West Indies, Group A
R Premadasa (Khettarama) Stadium, Colombo
25 February 1996 (50-over match)

Result: Sri Lanka won by walkover without a ball bowled
Points: Sri Lanka 2, West Indies 0
Toss: None
Umpires: Mehboob Shah (Pak) and VK Ramaswamy (Ind)
TV Umpire: M Aslam
Match Referee: Nasim-ul-Ghani (Pak)
Man Of The Match: No award

Sri Lanka team (from): MS Atapattu, UDU Chandana, PA de Silva, HDPK Dharmasena AP Gurusinha, ST Jayasuriya, RS Kaluwitharana, RS Mahanama, M Muralitharan, KR Pushpakumara, A Ranatunga, HP Tillakaratne, WPUCJ Vaas, GP Wickramasinghe.

West Indies forfeited the match due to safety concerns.

Wills World Cup, 1995/96, 16th Match
Kenya v Zimbabwe, Group A
Moin-ul-Haq Stadium, Patna
27 February 1996 (50-over match)

Result: Zimbabwe won by 5 wickets
Points: Zimbabwe 2, Kenya 0
Toss: Zimbabwe
Umpires: Khizer Hayat (Pak) and CJ Mitchley (SA)
TV Umpire: Farid Malik (UAE)
Match Referee: MAK Pataudi
Man Of The Match: PA Strang

Kenya innings (50 overs maximum)			R	M	B	4	6
DN Chudasama	run out		34	98	66	5	0
+IT Iqbal	b Lock		1	20	20	0	0
KO Otieno	b Peall		19	64	51	0	0
SO Tikolo	st A Flower	b BC Strang	0	4	6	0	0
*MO Odumbe	c BC Strang	b PA Strang	30	92	64	1	0
HS Modi	b BC Strang		3	7	10	0	0
EO Odumbe	c Campbell	b PA Strang	20	51	55	0	0
TM Odoyo	c GW Flower	b PA Strang	0	1	2	0	0
AY Karim	lbw	b PA Strang	0	1	1	0	0
MA Suji	c GW Flower	b PA Strang	15	21	23	1	0
RW Ali	not out		0	1	0	0	0

Extras (lb 3, w 8, nb 1): **12**
Total (all out, 49.4 overs): **134**

FoW: 1-7 (Iqbal), 2-60 (Otieno), 3-61 (Tikolo), 4-63 (Chudasama), 5-67 (Modi), 6-109 (MO Odumbe), 7-109 (Odoyo), 8-109 (Karim), 9-134 (Suji), 10-134 (EO Odumbe).

Bowling	O	M	R	W
Streak	7	2	23	0 (4w)
Lock	8	2	19	1
Whittall	5	0	21	0 (3w, 1nb)
Peall	10	1	23	1 (1w)
BC Strang	10	0	24	2
PA Strang	9.4	1	21	5

Zimbabwe innings (target: 135 runs from 50 overs)			R	M	B	4	6
AC Waller	c Tikolo	b MO Odumbe	30	57	32	3	0
GW Flower	b Ali		45	134	112	4	0
ADR Campbell	c Tikolo	b MO Odumbe	6	43	26	1	0
GJ Whittall	c EO Odumbe	b Ali	6	43	36	0	0
*+A Flower	lbw	b Ali	5	16	8	1	0
CN Evans	not out		8	39	18	1	0
HH Streak	not out		15	31	27	1	0

Extras (b 3, lb 4, w 12, nb 3): **22**
Total (5 wickets, 42.2 overs): **137**

DNB: PA Strang, SG Peall, BC Strang, ACI Lock.
FoW: 1-59, 2-79, 3-104, 4-108, 5-113.

Bowling	O	M	R	W
Suji	9.2	0	37	0
Ali	8	1	22	3
EO Odumbe	2	0	14	0
Odoyo	2	0	7	0
Karim	10	1	21	0
MO Odumbe	10	2	24	2
Tikolo	1	0	5	0

Wills World Cup, 1995/96, 19th Match
India v Australia, Group A
Wankhede Stadium, Mumbai (day/night)
27 February 1996 (50-over match)

Result: Australia won by 16 runs
Points: Australia 2, India 0
Toss: Australia
Umpires: RS Dunne (NZ) and DR Shepherd (Eng)
TV Umpire: TM Samarasinghe (SL)
Match Referee: CH Lloyd (WI)
Man Of The Match: ME Waugh

Australia innings (50 overs maximum)			R	M	B	4	6
ME Waugh	run out (Prasad)		126	195	135	8	3
*MA Taylor	c Srinath	b Raju	59	95	73	8	1
RT Ponting	c Manjrekar	b Raju	12	31	21	0	0
SR Waugh	run out (Raju)		7	21	15	0	0
SG Law	c & b Kumble		21	49	31	1	0
MG Bevan	run out (Jadeja)		6	8	5	0	0
S Lee	run out (Mongia)		9	14	10	0	0
+IA Healy	c Kumble	b Prasad	6	13	10	0	0
SK Warne	c Azharuddin	b Prasad	0	1	1	0	0
DW Fleming	run out (Mongia/Prasad)		0	3	1	0	0
GD McGrath	not out		0	1	0	0	0
Extras (lb 8, w 2, nb 2): **12**							
Total (all out, 50 overs): **258**							

FoW: 1-103 (Taylor), 2-140 (Ponting), 3-157 (SR Waugh), 4-232 (ME Waugh), 5-237 (Law), 6-244 (Bevan), 7-258 (Lee), 8-258 (Warne), 9-258 (Healy), 10-258 (Fleming).

Bowling	O	M	R	W
Prabhakar	10	0	55	0
Srinath	10	1	51	0
Prasad	10	0	49	2 (2nb, 2w)
Kumble	10	1	47	1
Raju	10	0	48	2

India innings (target: 259 runs from 50 overs)			R	M	B	4	6
A Jadeja	lbw	b Fleming	1	16	17	0	0
SR Tendulkar	st Healy	b ME Waugh	90	124	84	14	1
VG Kambli	b Fleming		0	6	2	0	0
*M Azharuddin	b Fleming		10	40	17	1	0
SV Manjrekar	c Healy	b SR Waugh	62	103	91	7	0
M Prabhakar	run out (Ponting)		3	4	6	0	0
+NR Mongia	c Taylor	b Warne	27	35	32	3	0
A Kumble	b Fleming		17	32	22	3	0
J Srinath	c Lee	b Fleming	7	16	12	1	0
BKV Prasad	c Bevan	b SR Waugh	0	5	2	0	0
SLV Raju	not out		3	6	4	0	0
Extras (b 5, lb 8, w 8, nb 1): **22**							
Total (all out, 48 overs): **242**							

FoW: 1-7 (Jadeja), 2-7 (Kambli), 3-70 (Azharuddin), 4-143 (Tendulkar), 5-147 (Prabhakar), 6-201 (Mongia), 7-205 (Manjrekar), 8-224 (Srinath), 9-231 (Prasad), 10-242 (Kumble).

Bowling	O	M	R	W
McGrath	8	3	48	0 (1nb)
Fleming	9	0	36	5 (2w)
Warne	10	1	28	1 (2w)
Lee	3	0	23	0 (2w)
ME Waugh	10	0	44	1 (1w)
Bevan	5	0	28	0
SR Waugh	3	0	22	2 (1w)

Wills World Cup, 1995/96, 20th Match
Kenya v West Indies, Group A
Nehru Stadium, Poona
29 February 1996 (50-over match)

Result: Kenya won by 73 runs
Points: Kenya 2, West Indies 0
Toss: West Indies
Umpires: Khizer Hayat (Pak) and VK Ramaswamy
TV Umpire: SK Bansal
Match Referee: MAK Pataudi
Man Of The Match: MO Odumbe

Kenya innings (50 overs maximum)			R	M	B	4	6
DN Chudasama	c Lara	b Walsh	8	8	7	2	0
+IT Iqbal	c Cuffy	b Walsh	16	44	32	2	0
KO Otieno	c Adams	b Walsh	2	7	5	0	0
SO Tikolo	c Adams	b Harper	29	85	50	3	1
*MO Odumbe	hit wicket	b Bishop	6	48	30	0	0
HS Modi	c Adams	b Ambrose	26	111	74	1	0
MA Suji	c Lara	b Harper	0	8	4	0	0
TM Odoyo	st Adams	b Harper	24	61	59	3	0
EO Odumbe	b Cuffy		1	2	4	0	0
AY Karim	c Adams	b Ambrose	11	43	27	1	0
RW Ali	not out		6	16	19	0	0
Extras (lb 10, w 14, nb 13): **37**							
Total (all out, 49.3 overs): **166**							

FoW: 1-15 (Chudasama), 2-19 (Otieno), 3-45 (Iqbal), 4-72 (MO Odumbe), 5-77 (Tikolo), 6-81 (Suji), 7-125 (Odoyo), 8-126 (EO Odumbe), 9-155 (Modi), 10-166 (Karim).

Bowling	O	M	R	W	
Ambrose	8.3	1	21	2 (5w)	
Walsh	9	0	46	3 (6nb, 3w)	
Bishop	10	2	30	1 (2nb, 1w)	
Cuffy	8	0	31	1 (7nb, 5w)	
Harper	10	4	15	3	
Arthurton	4	0	13	0	

West Indies innings (target: 167 from 50 overs)			R	M	B	4	6
SL Campbell	b Suji		4	19	12	1	0
*RB Richardson	b Ali		5	15	11	1	0
BC Lara	c Iqbal	b Ali	8	19	11	1	0
S Chanderpaul	c Tikolo	b MO Odumbe	19	72	48	3	0
KLT Arthurton	run out		0	8	6	0	0
+JC Adams	c Modi	b MO Odumbe	9	57	37	1	0
RA Harper	c Iqbal	b MO Odumbe	17	26	18	3	0
IR Bishop	not out		6	55	42	0	0
CEL Ambrose	run out		3	13	13	0	0
CA Walsh	c Chudasama	b Karim	4	15	8	1	0
CE Cuffy	b Ali		1	8	8	0	0
Extras (b 5, lb 6, w 4, nb 2): **17**							
Total (all out, 35.2 overs): **93**							

FoW: 1-18 (Richardson), 2-22 (Campbell), 3-33 (Lara), 4-35 (Arthurton), 5-55 (Chanderpaul), 6-65 (Adams), 7-78 (Harper), 8-81 (Ambrose), 9-89 (Walsh), 10-93 (Cuffy).

Bowling	O	M	R	W
Suji	7	2	16	1
Ali	7.2	2	17	3
Karim	8	1	19	1
MO Odumbe	10	3	15	3
Odoyo	3	0	15	0

Wills World Cup, 1995/96, 22nd Match
Australia v Zimbabwe, Group A
Vidarbha CA Ground, Nagpur
1 March 1996 (50-over match)

Result: Australia won by 8 wickets
Points: Australia 2, Zimbabwe 0
Toss: Zimbabwe
Umpires: RS Dunne (NZ) and DR Shepherd (Eng)
TV Umpire: TM Samarasinghe (SL)
Match Referee: CH Lloyd (WI)
Man Of The Match: SK Warne

Zimbabwe innings (50 overs maximum)

			R	M	B	4	6
AC Waller	run out		67	137	101	10	0
GW Flower	b McGrath		4	24	16	0	0
GJ Whittall	c & b SR Waugh		6	24	22	1	0
ADR Campbell	c ME Waugh	b SR Waugh	5	18	10	1	0
*+A Flower	st Healy	b Warne	7	14	15	1	0
CN Evans	c Healy	b Warne	18	29	24	2	1
HH Streak	c SR Waugh	b Fleming	13	43	41	0	0
PA Strang	not out		16	42	29	1	0
BC Strang	b Fleming		0	2	2	0	0
SG Peall	c Healy	b Warne	0	5	4	0	0
ACI Lock	b Warne		5	13	11	1	0

Extras (lb 8, w 3, nb 2): **13**
Total (all out, 45.3 overs): **154**

FoW: 1-21 (GW Flower), 2-41 (Whittall), 3-55 (Campbell), 4-68 (A Flower), 5-106 (Evans), 6-126 (Waller), 7-140 (Streak), 8-140 (BC Strang), 9-145 (Peall), 10-154 (Lock).

Bowling	O	M	R	W	
McGrath	8	2	12	1	
Fleming	9	1	30	2	(1nb)
Lee	4	2	8	0	(1nb)
SR Waugh	7	2	22	2	
Warne	9.3	1	34	4	(3w)
ME Waugh	5	0	30	0	
Law	3	0	10	0	

Australia innings (target: 155 runs from 50 overs)

			R	M	B	4	6
*MA Taylor	c BC Strang	b PA Strang	34	72	50	5	0
ME Waugh	not out		76	129	109	10	0
RT Ponting	c & b PA Strang		33	47	51	4	0
SR Waugh	not out		5	8	7	1	0

Extras (b 6, lb 2, w 1, nb 1): **10**
Total (2 wickets, 36 overs): **158**

DNB: SG Law, MG Bevan, S Lee, +IA Healy, SK Warne, DW Fleming, GD McGrath.
FoW: 1-92 (Taylor), 2-150 (Ponting).

Bowling	O	M	R	W	
Streak	10	3	29	0	(1nb, 1w)
Lock	4	0	25	0	
BC Strang	3	0	20	0	
Whittall	2	0	11	0	
PA Strang	10	2	33	2	
Peall	4	0	20	0	
GW Flower	3	0	12	0	

Wills World Cup, 1995/96, 24th Match
India v Sri Lanka, Group A
Feroz Shah Kotla, Delhi
2 March 1996 (50-over match)

Result: Sri Lanka won by 6 wickets
Points: Sri Lanka 2, India 0
Toss: Sri Lanka
Umpires: CJ Mitchley (SA) and ID Robinson (Zim)
TV Umpire: Ikram Rabbani (Pak)
Match Referee: JR Reid (NZ)
Man Of The Match: ST Jayasuriya

India innings (50 overs maximum)			R	M	B	4	6
M Prabhakar	c Gurusinha	b Pushpakumara	7	41	36	1	0
SR Tendulkar	run out		137	198	137	8	5
SV Manjrekar	c Kaluwitharana	b Dharmasena	32	56	46	2	1
*M Azharuddin	not out		72	101	80	4	0
VG Kambli	not out		1	2	1	0	0
Extras (b 4, lb 7, w 11): **22**							
Total (3 wickets, 50 overs): **271**							

DNB: A Jadeja, +NR Mongia, J Srinath, A Kumble, SA Ankola, BKV Prasad.
FoW: 1-27 (Prabhakar), 2-93 (Manjrekar), 3-268 (Tendulkar).

Bowling	O	M	R	W
Vaas	9	3	37	0 (2w)
Pushpakumara	8	0	53	1 (7w)
Muralitharan	10	1	42	0 (1w)
Dharmasena	9	0	53	1 (1w)
Jayasuriya	10	0	52	0
Ranatunga	4	0	23	0

Sri Lanka innings (target: 272 runs from 50 overs)			R	M	B	4	6
ST Jayasuriya	c Prabhakar	b Kumble	79	93	76	9	2
+RS Kaluwitharana	c Kumble	b Prasad	26	22	16	6	0
AP Gurusinha	run out		25	61	27	2	1
PA de Silva	st Mongia	b Kumble	8	14	14	1	0
*A Ranatunga	not out		46	118	63	2	0
HP Tillakaratne	not out		70	110	98	6	0
Extras (b 4, lb 9, w 3, nb 2): **18**							
Total (4 wickets, 48.4 overs): **272**							

DNB: RS Mahanama, HDPK Dharmasena, WPUJC Vaas, KR Pushpakumara, M Muralitharan.
FoW: 1-53 (Kaluwitharana), 2-129 (Gurusinha), 3-137 (Jayasuriya), 4-141 (de Silva).

Bowling	O	M	R	W
Prabhakar	4	0	47	0
Srinath	9.4	0	51	0
Prasad	10	1	53	1 (1w, 2nb)
Ankola	5	0	28	0
Kumble	10	1	39	2
Tendulkar	10	0	41	0 (2w)

Wills World Cup, 1995/96, 26th Match
Australia v West Indies, Group A
Sawai Mansingh Stadium, Jaipur
4 March 1996 (50-over match)

Result: West Indies won by 4 wickets
Points: West Indies 2, Australia 0
Toss: Australia
Umpires: Mahboob Shah (Pak) and DR Shepherd (Eng)
TV Umpire: Shakeel Khan (Pak)
Match Referee: R Subba Row (Eng)
Man Of The Match: RB Richardson

Australia innings (50 overs maximum)			R	M	B	4	6
ME Waugh	st Browne	b Harper	30	102	62	1	0
*MA Taylor	c Browne	b Walsh	9	49	38	0	0
RT Ponting	run out		102	143	112	5	1
SR Waugh	b Walsh		57	74	64	3	1
MG Bevan	run out		2	6	3	0	0
SG Law	not out		12	22	12	0	0
+IA Healy	run out		3	6	4	0	0
PR Reiffel	not out		4	6	6	0	0
Extras (lb 3, w 6, nb 1): **10**							
Total (6 wickets, 50 overs): **229**							

DNB: SK Warne, DW Fleming, GD McGrath.
FoW: 1-22 (Taylor), 2-84 (ME Waugh), 3-194 (SR Waugh), 4-200 (Bevan), 5-216 (Ponting), 6-224 (Healy).

Bowling	O	M	R	W	
Ambrose	10	4	25	0 (1w)	
Walsh	9	2	35	2	
Bishop	9	0	52	0 (1nb, 4w)	
Harper	10	0	46	1	
Arthurton	9	0	53	0	
Adams	3	0	15	0 (1w)	

West Indies innings (target: 230 from 50 overs)			R	M	B	4	6
SL Campbell	c Healy	b Fleming	1	7	5	0	0
+CO Browne	run out		10	33	18	2	0
BC Lara	c McGrath	b ME Waugh	60	102	70	7	0
*RB Richardson	not out		93	178	133	10	1
S Chanderpaul	b ME Waugh		10	28	17	0	0
RA Harper	lbw	b Reiffel	22	38	27	2	0
KLT Arthurton	lbw	b ME Waugh	0	5	3	0	0
JC Adams	not out		17	27	22	3	0
Extras (lb 12, w 5, nb 2): **19**							
Total (6 wickets, 48.5 overs): **232**							

DNB: IR Bishop, CEL Ambrose, CA Walsh.
FoW: 1-1 (Campbell), 2-26 (Browne), 3-113 (Lara), 4-146 (Chanderpaul), 5-194 (Harper), 6-196 (Arthurton).

Bowling	O	M	R	W	
Reiffel	10	2	45	1 (2nb, 1w)	
Fleming	7.5	1	44	1 (1w)	
McGrath	9	0	46	0 (1w)	
Warne	10	1	30	0 (1w)	
ME Waugh	10	1	38	3 (1w)	
Bevan	2	0	17	0	

Wills World Cup, 1995/96, 28th Match
Sri Lanka v Kenya, Group A
Asgiriya Stadium, Kandy
6 March 1996 (50-over match)

Result: Sri Lanka won by 144 runs
Points: Sri Lanka 2, Kenya 0
Toss: Kenya
Umpires: RS Dunne (NZ) and VK Ramaswamy (Ind)
TV Umpire: Ikram Rabbani (Pak)
Match Referee: MAK Pataudi (Ind)
ODI Debuts: LN Onyango (Kenya)
Man Of The Match: PA de Silva

Sri Lanka innings (50 overs maximum)

			R	M	B	4	6
ST Jayasuriya	c LO Tikolo	b EO Odumbe	44	43	27	5	3
+RS Kaluwitharana	b EO Odumbe		33	51	18	4	2
AP Gurusinha	c Onyango	b Karim	84	120	103	7	3
PA de Silva	c Modi	b Suji	145	153	115	14	5
*A Ranatunga	not out		75	49	40	13	1
HP Tillakaratne	run out		0	4	1	0	0
RS Mahanama	not out		0	3	0	0	0
Extras (b 1, lb 5, w 11): **17**							
Total (5 wickets, 50 overs): **398**							

DNB: WPUJC Vaas, HDPK Dharmasena, KR Pushpakumara, M Muralitharan.
FoW: 1-83 (Jayasuriya), 2-88 (Kaluwitharana), 3-271 (Gurusinha), 4-377 (de Silva), 5-383 (Tillakaratne).

Bowling

	O	M	R	W	
Suji	9	0	85	1	.
Ali	6	0	67	0	
Onyango	4	0	31	0	
EO Odumbe	5	0	34	2	
Karim	10	0	50	1	
LO Tikolo	2	0	13	0	
MO Odumbe	9	0	74	0	
SO Tikolo	5	0	38	0	

Kenya innings (target: 399 runs from 50 overs)

			R	M	B	4	6
DN Chudasama	b Muralitharan		27	40	23	5	0
+KO Otieno	b Vaas		14	34	28	1	1
SO Tikolo	b Dharmasena		96	122	95	8	4
*MO Odumbe	st Kaluwitharana	b Muralitharan	0	2	2	0	0
HS Modi	run out (Muralitharan)		41	111	82	2	0
LO Tikolo	not out		25	45	40	2	1
EO Odumbe	c Muralitharan	b Ranatunga	4	15	17	0	0
LN Onyango	c sub (MS Atapattu)	b Ranatunga	23	22	18	2	1
MA Suji	not out		2	4	4	0	0
Extras (b 1, lb 9, w 7, nb 5): **22**							
Total (7 wickets, 50 overs): **254**							

DNB: AY Karim, RW Ali.
FoW: 1-47 (Chudasama), 2-51 (Otieno), 3-51 (MO Odumbe), 4-188 (SO Tikolo), 5-196 (Modi), 6-215 (EO Odumbe), 7-246 (Onyango).

Bowling

	O	M	R	W
Vaas	10	0	44	1
Muralitharan	10	1	40	2
Pushpakumara	7	0	46	0
Ranatunga	5	0	31	2
Dharmasena	10	0	45	1
Jayasuriya	7	0	34	0
Tillakaratne	1	0	4	0

Wills World Cup, 1995/96, 29th Match
India v Zimbabwe, Group A
Green Park, Kanpur
6 March 1996 (50-over match)

Result: India won by 40 runs
Points: India 2, Zimbabwe 0
Toss: Zimbabwe
Umpires: SA Bucknor (WI) and CJ Mitchley (SA)
TV Umpire: TM Samarasinghe (SL)
Match Referee: JR Reid (NZ)
Man Of The Match: A Jadeja

India innings (50 overs maximum)			R	M	B	4	6
SR Tendulkar	b Streak		3	10	12	0	0
NS Sidhu	c Streak	b PA Strang	80	166	116	5	0
SV Manjrekar	c Campbell	b Lock	2	27	18	0	0
*M Azharuddin	c Campbell	b BC Strang	2	14	10	0	0
VG Kambli	c GW Flower	b Lock	106	137	110	11	0
A Jadeja	not out		44	39	27	3	2
+NR Mongia	not out		6	13	9	0	0
Extras (lb 1, w 3): **4**							
Total (5 wickets, 50 overs): **247**							

DNB: A Kumble, J Srinath, BKV Prasad, SLV Raju.
FoW: 1-5 (Tendulkar), 2-25 (Manjrekar), 3-32 (Azharuddin), 4-174 (Sidhu), 5-219 (Kambli).

Bowling	O	M	R	W
Streak	10	3	29	1 (1nb)
Lock	10	1	57	2 (2w)
BC Strang	5	1	22	1
PA Strang	10	0	55	1
Peall	6	0	35	0 (1w)
Whittall	3	0	19	0
GW Flower	3	0	16	0
Campbell	3	0	13	0

Zimbabwe innings (target: 248 runs from 50 overs)			R	M	B	4	6
AC Waller	c Tendulkar	b Kumble	22	62	36	1	0
GW Flower	c Azharuddin	b Raju	30	58	42	1	0
GJ Whittall	run out		10	58	29	0	0
ADR Campbell	c & b Jadeja		28	48	55	4	0
*+A Flower	b Raju		28	65	40	1	0
CN Evans	c Srinath	b Jadeja	6	5	5	1	0
HH Streak	lbw	b Raju	30	45	39	3	0
PA Strang	b Srinath		14	25	21	1	0
BC Strang	lbw	b Srinath	3	21	13	0	0
SG Peall	c Raju	b Kumble	9	12	14	2	0
ACI Lock	not out		2	8	4	0	0
Extras (b 4, lb 9, w 11, nb 1): **25**							
Total (all out, 49.4 overs): **207**							

FoW: 1-59 (GW Flower), 2-59 (Waller), 3-96 (Campbell), 4-99 (Whittall), 5-106 (Evans), 6-168 (Streak), 7-173 (A Flower), 8-193 (PA Strang), 9-195 (BC Strang), 10-207 (Peall).

Bowling	O	M	R	W
Srinath	10	1	36	2 (1w)
Prasad	7	0	40	0 (4w)
Kumble	9.4	1	33	2 (1w)
Raju	10	2	30	3
Tendulkar	6	0	23	0
Jadeja	7	0	32	2 (1w)

1996 WORLD CUP

Group B

Wills World Cup, 1995/96, 1st Match
England v New Zealand, Group B
Gujarat Stadium, Motera, Ahmedabad
14 February 1996 (50-over match)

Result: New Zealand won by 11 runs
Points: New Zealand 2, England 0
Toss: England
Umpires: BC Cooray (SL) and SG Randell (Aus)
TV Umpire: S Toohey (NL)
Match Referee: MAK Pataudi
Man Of The Match: NJ Astle

New Zealand innings (50 overs maximum)			R	M	B	4	6
CM Spearman	c & b Cork		5	22	16	0	0
NJ Astle	c Hick	b Martin	101	172	132	8	2
SP Fleming	c Thorpe	b Hick	28	73	47	3	0
RG Twose	c Thorpe	b Hick	17	26	26	1	0
CL Cairns	c Cork	b Illingworth	36	36	30	4	1
CZ Harris	run out		10	22	16	1	0
SA Thomson	not out		17	22	23	1	0
*+LK Germon	not out		13	16	12	0	0

Extras (b 4, lb 2, w 4, nb 2): **12**
Total (6 wickets, 50 overs): **239**

DNB: GR Larsen, DJ Nash, DK Morrison.
FoW: 1-12 (Spearman), 2-108 (Fleming), 3-141 (Twose), 4-196 (Cairns), 5-204 (Astle), 6-212 (Harris).

Bowling	O	M	R	W	
Cork	10	1	36	1 (1nb, 1w)	
Martin	6	0	37	1	
Gough	10	0	63	0	
Illingworth	10	1	31	1	
Hick	9	0	45	2 (3w)	
White	5	0	21	0 (1nb)	

England innings (target: 240 runs from 50 overs)			R	M	B	4	6
*MA Atherton	b Nash		1	5	3	0	0
AJ Stewart	c & b Harris		34	96	71	3	0
GA Hick	run out		85	134	102	9	0
GP Thorpe	b Larsen		9	22	21	0	0
NH Fairbrother	b Morrison		36	47	46	1	0
+RC Russell	c Morrison	b Larsen	2	12	9	0	0
C White	c Cairns	b Thomson	13	18	12	0	1
DG Cork	c Germon	b Nash	19	21	11	2	1
D Gough	not out		15	32	17	0	0
PJ Martin	c Cairns	b Nash	3	9	7	0	0
RK Illingworth	not out		3	6	4	0	0

Extras (b 1, lb 4, w 1, nb 2): **8**
Total (9 wickets, 50 overs): **228**

FoW: 1-1 (Atherton), 2-100 (Stewart), 3-123 (Thorpe), 4-144 (Hick), 5-151 (Russell), 6-180 (White), 7-185 (Fairbrother), 8-210 (Cork), 9-222 (Martin).

Bowling	O	M	R	W	
Morrison	8	0	38	1 (1nb, 1w)	
Nash	7	1	26	3 (1w)	
Cairns	4	0	24	0	
Larsen	10	1	33	2	
Thomson	10	0	51	1	
Harris	9	0	45	1	
Astle	2	0	6	0	

Wills World Cup, 1995/96, 2nd Match
South Africa v United Arab Emirates, Group B
Rawalpindi Cricket Stadium
16 February 1996 (50-over match)

Result: South Africa won by 169 runs
Points: South Africa 2, United Arab Emirates 0
Toss: United Arab Emirates
Umpires: SA Bucknor (WI) and VK Ramaswamy (Ind)
TV Umpire: A Sarkar (Ken)
Match Referee: RS Madugalle (SL)
ODI Debuts: SF Dukanwala, Mohammad Aslam, G Mylvaganam, Shehzad Altaf (UAE)
Man Of The Match: G Kirsten

South Africa innings (50 overs maximum)

			R	M	B	4	6
AC Hudson	b Samarasekera		27	51	33	5	0
G Kirsten	not out		188	210	159	13	4
*WJ Cronje	st Imtiaz Abbasi	b Zarawani	57	77	62	1	1
DJ Cullinan	not out		41	80	50	2	0
Extras (b 1, lb 1, w 3, nb 3): **8**							
Total (2 wickets, 50 overs): **321**							

DNB: JH Kallis, JN Rhodes, BM McMillan, SM Pollock, +SJ Palframan, CR Matthews, AA Donald.
FoW: 1-60 (Hudson), 2-176 (Cronje).

Bowling	O	M	R	W	
Samarasekera	9	2	39	1	(2w, 2nb)
Shehzad Altaf	3	0	22	0	(1w)
Arshad Laeeq	6	0	52	0	
Dukanwala	10	0	64	0	
Azhar Saeed	7	0	41	0	
Zarawani	10	0	69	1	
Mazhar Hussain	5	0	32	0	(1nb)

UAE innings (target: 322 runs from 50 overs)

			R	M	B	4	6
Azhar Saeed	c McMillan	b Pollock	11	25	24	2	0
G Mylvaganam	c Palframan	b Donald	23	49	36	3	0
Mazhar Hussain	b Donald		14	56	42	0	0
V Mehra	run out (McMillan)		2	13	12	0	0
Mohammad Aslam	b McMillan		9	18	5	1	0
Arshad Laeeq	not out		43	122	79	4	0
JA Samarasekera	c Hudson	b Donald	4	15	12	0	0
*Sultan Zarawani	c Cronje	b McMillan	0	7	7	0	0
+Imtiaz Abbasi	c Palframan	b McMillan	1	7	7	0	0
SF Dukanwala	not out		40	81	78	4	0
Extras (w 3, nb 2): **5**							
Total (8 wickets, 50 overs): **152**							

DNB: Shehzad Altaf.
FoW: 1-24 (Azhar Saeed), 2-42 (Mylvaganam), 3-46 (Mehra), 4-60 (Mohammad Aslam), 5-62 (Mazhar Hussain), 6-68 (Samarasekera), 7-70 (Zarawani), 8-72 (Imtiaz Abbasi).

Bowling	O	M	R	W
Pollock	9	2	28	1
Matthews	10	0	39	0
Donald	10	0	21	3
Cronje	4	0	17	0
McMillan	8	1	11	3
Kallis	6	0	27	0
Kirsten	3	1	9	0

Wills World Cup, 1995/96, 4th Match
Netherlands v New Zealand, Group B
IPCL Sports Complex Ground, Baroda
17 February 1996 (50-over match)

Result: New Zealand won by 119 runs
Points: New Zealand 2, Netherlands 0
Toss: New Zealand
Umpires: Khizer Hayat (Pak) and ID Robinson (Zim)
TV Umpire: Shakeel Khan (Pak)
Match Referee: MAK Pataudi
ODI Debuts: GJAF Aponso, PJ Bakker, PE Cantrell, NE Clarke, TBM de Leede, EL Gouka, RP Lefebvre, SW Lubbers, MMC Schewe, KJJ van Noortwijk, B Zuiderent (NL)
Man Of The Match: CM Spearman

New Zealand innings (50 overs maximum)			R	M	B	4	6
CM Spearman	c Zuiderent	b Lubbers	68	77	59	8	0
NJ Astle	run out		0	5	5	0	0
SP Fleming	c Zuiderent	b Lubbers	66	97	79	4	0
RG Twose	st Schewe	b Lubbers	25	34	32	1	0
CL Cairns	b Cantrell		52	54	37	4	2
AC Parore	c Clarke	b Aponso	55	57	55	0	3
CZ Harris	c Schewe	b Bakker	8	20	12	0	0
*+LK Germon	not out		14	19	11	1	0
DN Patel	c Schewe	b Bakker	11	8	10	1	0
DK Morrison	not out		0	1	0	0	0
Extras (lb 7, w 1): **8**							
Total (8 wickets, 50 overs): **307**							

DNB: RJ Kennedy.
FoW: 1-1 (Astle), 2-117 (Spearman), 3-155 (Fleming), 4-165 (Twose), 5-253 (Cairns), 6-279 (Parore), 7-292 (Harris), 8-306 (Patel).

Bowling	O	M	R	W	
Lefebvre	10	0	48	0	
Bakker	10	0	51	2	
de Leede	7	0	58	0 (1w)	
Aponso	10	0	60	1	
Lubbers	9	0	48	3	
Cantrell	4	0	35	1	

Netherlands innings (target: 308 from 50 overs)			R	M	B	4	6
NE Clarke	b Kennedy		14	23	21	2	0
PE Cantrell	c Astle	b Harris	45	115	86	5	0
GJAF Aponso	c Astle	b Harris	11	40	31	2	0
*SW Lubbers	run out		5	23	19	0	0
RP Lefebvre	b Kennedy		45	76	64	3	0
TBM de Leede	lbw	b Harris	1	10	4	0	0
KJJ van Noortwijk	not out		36	71	54	3	0
+MMC Schewe	st Germon	b Fleming	12	24	16	1	0
B Zuiderent	not out		1	4	6	0	0
Extras (b 3, lb 5, w 8, nb 2): **18**							
Total (7 wickets, 50 overs): **188**							

DNB: EL Gouka, PJ Bakker.
FoW: 1-18 (Clarke), 2-52 (Aponso), 3-66 (Lubbers), 4-100 (Cantrell), 5-102 (de Leede), 6-147 (Lefebvre), 7-181 (Schewe).

Bowling	O	M	R	W	
Morrison	4	1	11	0	
Kennedy	10	2	36	2 (1nb, 4w)	
Cairns	7	1	24	0 (1nb)	
Harris	10	1	24	3	
Patel	10	0	43	0	
Astle	5	0	20	0	
Fleming	2	0	8	1	
Twose	2	0	14	0 (4w)	

Wills World Cup, 1995/96, 7th Match
England v United Arab Emirates, Group B
Arbab Niaz Stadium, Peshawar
18 February 1996 (50-over match)

Result: England won by 8 wickets
Points: England 2, United Arab Emirates 0
Toss: United Arab Emirates
Umpires: BC Cooray (SL) and VK Ramaswamy (Ind)
TV Umpire: RC Sharma (Ind)
Match Referee: JR Reid (NZ)
Man Of The Match: NMK Smith

UAE innings (50 overs maximum)

			R	M	B	4	6
Azhar Saeed	lbw	b DeFreitas	9	47	36	1	0
G Mylvaganam	c Fairbrother	b DeFreitas	0	9	6	0	0
Mazhar Hussain	b Smith		33	89	59	6	0
V Mehra	c Russell	b Smith	1	46	34	0	0
Mohammad Aslam	b Gough		23	40	47	1	0
Arshad Laeeq	b Smith		0	6	6	0	0
Saleem Raza	b Cork		10	45	31	0	0
JA Samarasekera	run out		29	57	39	3	0
*Sultan Zarawani	b Cork		2	10	8	0	0
SF Dukanwala	lbw	b Illingworth	15	25	21	1	0
+Imtiaz Abbasi	not out		1	4	5	0	0

*Extras (b 4, lb 4, w 4, nb 1): **13***
*Total (all out, 48.3 overs): **136***

FoW: 1-3 (Mylvaganam), 2-32 (Azhar Saeed), 3-48 (Mehra), 4-49 (Mazhar Hussain), 5-49 (Arshad Laeeq), 6-80 (Mohammad Aslam), 7-88 (Saleem Raza), 8-100 (Zarawani), 9-135 (Dukanwala), 10-136 (Samarasekera).

Bowling

	O	M	R	W	
Cork	10	1	33	2 (2w)	
DeFreitas	9.3	3	16	2 (2w, 1nb)	
Gough	8	3	23	1	
White	1.3	1	2	0	
Smith	9.3	2	29	3	
Illingworth	10	2	25	1	

England innings (target: 137 runs from 50 overs)

			R	M	B	4	6
AJ Stewart	c Mylvaganam	b Arshad Laeeq	23	56	52	3	0
NMK Smith	retired ill		27	62	31	4	0
GP Thorpe	not out		44	83	66	5	0
*MA Atherton	b Azhar Saeed		20	52	40	1	0
NH Fairbrother	not out		12	24	29	1	0

*Extras (b 4, lb 2, w 2, nb 6): **14***
*Total (2 wickets, 35 overs): **140***

DNB: +RC Russell, C White, DG Cork, PAJ DeFreitas, D Gough, RK Illingworth.
FoW: 1-52 (Stewart), 2-109 (Atherton).

Bowling

	O	M	R	W	
Samarasekera	7	1	35	0 (1w, 3nb)	
Arshad Laeeq	7	0	25	1 (5nb)	
Saleem Raza	5	1	20	0	
Azhar Saeed	10	1	26	1	
Zarawani	6	0	28	0	

Wills World Cup, 1995/96, 8th Match
New Zealand v South Africa, Group B
Iqbal Stadium, Faisalabad
20 February 1996 (50-over match)

Result: South Africa won by 5 wickets
Points: South Africa 2, New Zealand 0
Toss: New Zealand
Umpires: SG Randell (Aus) and S Venkataraghavan (Ind)
TV Umpire: SK Bansal (Ind)
Match Referee: RS Madugalle (SL)
Man Of The Match: WJ Cronje

New Zealand innings (50 overs maximum)			R	M	B	4	6
CM Spearman	c Palframan	b Matthews	14	16	14	3	0
NJ Astle	run out		1	7	4	0	0
SP Fleming	b McMillan		33	99	79	2	0
RG Twose	c McMillan	b Pollock	13	20	17	2	0
CL Cairns	b Donald		9	30	20	2	0
AC Parore	run out		27	78	48	0	0
CZ Harris	run out		8	22	21	0	0
SA Thomson	c Cronje	b Donald	29	56	54	4	0
*+LK Germon	not out		31	52	33	2	0
GR Larsen	c Cullinan	b Donald	1	9	7	0	0
DK Morrison	not out		5	7	6	0	0
Extras (lb 4, nb 2): **6**							
Total (9 wickets, 50 overs): **177**							

FoW: 1-7 (Astle), 2-17 (Spearman), 3-36 (Twose), 4-54 (Cairns), 5-85 (Fleming), 6-103 (Harris), 7-116 (Parore), 8-158 (Thomson), 9-165 (Larsen).

Bowling	O	M	R	W
Pollock	10	1	45	1
Matthews	10	2	30	1 (1nb)
Donald	10	0	34	3
Cronje	3	0	13	0
Symcox	10	1	25	0
McMillan	7	1	26	1 (1nb)

South Africa innings (target: 178 from 50 overs)			R	M	B	4	6
G Kirsten	lbw	b Harris	35	61	46	5	0
+SJ Palframan	b Morrison		16	33	26	3	0
*WJ Cronje	c Fleming	b Astle	78	73	64	11	3
DJ Cullinan	c Thomson	b Astle	27	58	42	2	0
JH Kallis	not out		11	35	25	1	0
JN Rhodes	c & b Larsen		9	10	13	1	0
BM McMillan	not out		2	11	10	0	0
Extras: **0**							
Total (5 wickets, 37.3 overs): **178**							

DNB: SM Pollock, PL Symcox, CR Matthews, AA Donald.
FoW: 1-41 (Palframan), 2-87 (Kirsten), 3-146 (Cronje), 4-159 (Cullinan), 5-170 (Rhodes).

Bowling	O	M	R	W
Morrison	8	0	44	1
Cairns	6	0	24	0
Larsen	8	1	41	1
Harris	4	0	25	1
Thomson	8.3	0	34	0
Astle	3	1	10	2

Wills World Cup, 1995/96, 11th Match
England v Netherlands, Group B
Arbab Niaz Stadium, Peshawar
22 February 1996 (50-over match)

Result: England won by 49 runs
Points: England 2, Netherlands 0
Toss: England
Umpires: SA Bucknor (WI) and KT Francis (SL)
TV Umpire: A Sarkar (Ken)
Match Referee: JR Reid (NZ)
ODI Debuts: F Jansen (NL)
Man Of The Match: GA Hick

England innings (50 overs maximum)

			R	M	B	4	6
AJ Stewart	b Bakker		5	11	13	0	0
NMK Smith	c Clarke	b Jansen	31	39	33	5	0
GA Hick	not out		104	170	133	6	2
GP Thorpe	lbw	b Lefebvre	89	90	82	7	1
*MA Atherton	b Lubbers		10	19	10	0	0
NH Fairbrother	not out		24	31	29	1	0

Extras (lb 12, w 4): **16**
Total (4 wickets, 50 overs): **279**

DNB: +RC Russell, DG Cork, PAJ DeFreitas, D Gough, PJ Martin.
FoW: 1-11 (Stewart), 2-42 (Smith), 3-185 (Thorpe), 4-212 (Atherton).

Bowling

	O	M	R	W
Lefebvre	10	1	40	1
Bakker	8	0	46	1 (4w)
Jansen	7	0	40	1
Aponso	8	0	55	0
Lubbers	10	0	51	1
de Leede	2	0	9	0
Cantrell	5	0	26	0

Netherlands innings (target: 280 from 50 overs)

			R	M	B	4	6
NE Clarke	lbw	b Cork	0	9	8	0	0
PE Cantrell	lbw	b DeFreitas	28	50	44	4	0
TBM de Leede	lbw	b DeFreitas	41	69	42	7	0
*SW Lubbers	c Russell	b DeFreitas	9	17	8	1	0
KJJ van Noortwijk	c Gough	b Martin	64	99	82	3	2
B Zuiderent	c Thorpe	b Martin	54	99	93	2	0
RP Lefebvre	not out		11	24	14	0	0
+MMC Schewe	not out		11	14	12	1	0

Extras (lb 4, w 6, nb 2): **12**
Total (6 wickets, 50 overs): **230**

DNB: GJAF Aponso, F Jansen, PJ Bakker.
FoW: 1-1 (Clarke), 2-46 (Cantrell), 3-70 (Lubbers), 4-81 (de Leede), 5-195 (van Noortwijk), 6-210 (Zuiderent).

Bowling

	O	M	R	W
Cork	8	0	52	1 (4w, 2nb)
DeFreitas	10	3	31	3
Smith	8	0	27	0
Gough	3	0	23	0
Martin	10	1	42	2 (1w)
Hick	5	0	23	0
Thorpe	6	0	28	0 (1w)

Wills World Cup, 1995/96, 13th Match
Pakistan v United Arab Emirates, Group B
Jinnah Stadium, Gujranwala
24 February 1996 (50-over match)

Result: Pakistan won by 9 wickets
Points: Pakistan 2, United Arab Emirates 0
Toss: Pakistan
Umpires: BC Cooray (SL) and S Venkataraghavan (Ind)
TV Umpire: SK Bansal (Ind)
Match Referee: RS Madugalle (SL)
Man Of The Match: Mushtaq Ahmed

United Arab Emirates innings (33 overs maximum)			R	M	B	4	6
G Mylvaganam	b Mushtaq Ahmed		13	66	50	1	0
Saleem Raza	c Javed Miandad	b Aaqib Javed	22	27	20	2	1
Azhar Saeed	run out		1	24	13	0	0
Mazhar Hussain	c Waqar Younis	b Mushtaq Ahmed	7	28	21	0	0
Mohammad Aslam	b Mushtaq Ahmed		5	8	9	1	0
Mohammad Ishaq	b Wasim Akram		12	31	20	1	0
Arshad Laeeq	c Ijaz Ahmed	b Aaqib Javed	9	15	19	2	0
JA Samarasekera	b Waqar Younis		10	30	22	0	0
SF Dukanwala	not out		21	26	19	1	1
*Sultan Zarawani	b Wasim Akram		1	2	3	0	0
+Imtiaz Abbasi	not out		0	2	4	0	0
Extras (lb 1, w 5, nb 2): **8**							
Total (9 wickets, 33 overs): **109**							

FoW: 1-27 (Saleem Raza), 2-40 (Azhar Saeed), 3-47 (Mylvaganam), 4-53 (Mohammad Aslam), 5-54 (Mazhar Hussain), 6-70 (Arshad Laeeq), 7-80 (Mohammad Ishaq), 8-108 (Samarasekera), 9-109 (Zarawani).

Bowling	O	M	R	W
Wasim Akram	7	1	25	2 (2nb, 1w)
Waqar Younis	7	1	33	1 (1w)
Aaqib Javed	6	0	18	2 (2w)
Mushtaq Ahmed	7	0	16	3 (1w)
Aamer Sohail	6	1	16	0

Pakistan innings (target: 110 runs from 33 overs)		R	M	B	4	6
Aamer Sohail	b Samarasekera	5	4	5	1	0
Saeed Anwar	not out	40	84	50	4	0
Ijaz Ahmed	not out	50	79	57	4	1
Extras (lb 1, w 12, nb 4): **17**						
Total (1 wicket, 18 overs): **112**						

DNB: Inzamam-ul-Haq, Javed Miandad, Saleem Malik, *Wasim Akram, +Rashid Latif, Mushtaq Ahmed, Aaqib Javed, Waqar Younis.
FoW: 1-7 (Aamer Sohail).

Bowling	O	M	R	W
Samarasekera	3	0	17	1 (2nb, 6w)
Arshad Laeeq	4	0	24	0 (2nb, 3w)
Dukanwala	3	1	14	0
Saleem Raza	3	0	17	0
Zarawani	3	0	23	0 (3w)
Azhar Saeed	2	0	16	0

Wills World Cup, 1995/96, 14th Match
England v South Africa, Group B
Rawalpindi Cricket Stadium
25 February 1996 (50-over match)

Result: South Africa won by 78 runs
Points: South Africa 2, England 0
Toss: South Africa
Umpires: SG Randell (Aus) and ID Robinson (Zim)
TV Umpire: K Parthasarathy (Ind)
Match Referee: JR Reid (NZ)
Man Of The Match: JN Rhodes

South Africa innings (50 overs maximum)			R	M	B	4	6
G Kirsten	run out		38	86	60	4	0
+SJ Palframan	c Russell	b Martin	28	51	36	3	0
*WJ Cronje	c Russell	b Gough	15	43	31	1	0
DJ Cullinan	b DeFreitas		34	49	42	2	0
JH Kallis	c Russell	b Cork	26	59	42	2	0
JN Rhodes	b Martin		37	37	32	3	0
BM McMillan	b Smith		11	25	17	0	0
SM Pollock	c Fairbrother	b Cork	12	17	13	0	0
PL Symcox	c Thorpe	b Martin	1	4	4	0	0
CR Matthews	not out		9	20	13	0	0
PS de Villiers	c Smith	b Gough	12	13	11	1	0
Extras (lb 1, w 5, nb 1): **7**							
Total (all out, 50 overs): **230**							

FoW: 1-56 (Palframan), 2-85 (Kirsten), 3-88 (Cronje), 4-137 (Cullinan), 5-163 (Kallis), 6-195 (Rhodes), 7-199 (McMillan), 8-202 (Symcox), 9-213 (Pollock), 10-230 (de Villiers).

Bowling	O	M	R	W
Cork	10	0	36	2 (1w)
DeFreitas	10	0	55	1 (1nb, 1w)
Gough	10	0	48	2
Martin	10	0	33	3 (3w)
Smith	8	0	40	1
Thorpe	2	0	17	0

England innings (target: 231 runs from 50 overs)			R	M	B	4	6
*MA Atherton	c Palframan	b Pollock	0	2	4	0	0
NMK Smith	b de Villiers		11	45	24	1	0
GA Hick	c McMillan	b de Villiers	14	24	27	1	0
GP Thorpe	c Palframan	b Symcox	46	101	69	3	0
AJ Stewart	run out		7	41	29	0	0
NH Fairbrother	c Palframan	b Symcox	3	15	10	0	0
+RC Russell	c Rhodes	b Pollock	12	30	32	0	0
DG Cork	b Matthews		17	45	33	1	0
PAJ DeFreitas	run out		22	34	24	1	1
D Gough	b Matthews		11	13	12	2	0
PJ Martin	not out		1	7	3	0	0
Extras (lb 7, w 1): **8**							
Total (all out, 44.3 overs): **152**							

FoW: 1-0 (Atherton), 2-22 (Hick), 3-33 (Smith), 4-52 (Stewart), 5-62 (Fairbrother), 6-97 (Thorpe), 7-97 (Russell), 8-139 (DeFreitas), 9-141 (Cork), 10-152 (Gough).

Bowling	O	M	R	W
Pollock	8	1	16	2
de Villiers	7	1	27	2 (1w)
Matthews	9.3	0	30	2
McMillan	6	0	17	0
Symcox	10	0	38	2
Cronje	4	0	17	0

Wills World Cup, 1995/96, 17th Match
Pakistan v Netherlands, Group B
Gaddafi Stadium, Lahore
26 February 1996 (50-over match)

Result: Pakistan won by 8 wickets
Points: Pakistan 2, Netherlands 0
Toss: Netherlands
Umpires: SA Bucknor (WI) and KT Francis (SL)
TV Umpire: RC Sharma (Ind)
Match Referee: R Subba Row (Eng)
Man Of The Match: Waqar Younis

Netherlands innings (50 overs maximum)

			R	M	B	4	6
NE Clarke	c Rashid Latif	b Aaqib Javed	4	31	26	0	0
PE Cantrell	c Ijaz Ahmed	b Waqar Younis	17	53	32	1	0
TBM de Leede	c Rashid Latif	b Waqar Younis	0	25	19	0	0
KJJ van Noortwijk	c Mushtaq Ahmed	b Aaqib Javed	33	100	89	2	1
GJAF Aponso	b Waqar Younis		58	129	105	3	1
*RP Lefebvre	b Waqar Younis		10	42	26	0	0
B Zuiderent	run out		6	13	6	1	0
EL Gouka	not out		0	2	1	0	0
Extras (lb 7, w 4, nb 6): **17**							
Total (7 wickets, 50 overs): **145**							

DNB: +MMC Schewe, F Jansen, PJ Bakker.
FoW: 1-16 (Clarke), 2-28 (Cantrell), 3-29 (de Leede), 4-102 (van Noortwijk), 5-130 (Lefebvre), 6-143 (Aponso), 7-145 (Zuiderent).

Bowling

	O	M	R	W
Wasim Akram	10	1	30	0 (3nb, 1w)
Waqar Younis	10	0	26	4 (2nb, 1w)
Aaqib Javed	9	2	25	2 (1nb, 1w)
Mushtaq Ahmed	10	2	27	0
Aamer Sohail	9	0	21	0 (1w)
Saleem Malik	2	0	9	0

Pakistan innings (target: 146 runs from 50 overs)

			R	M	B	4	6
Aamer Sohail	c Jansen	b Lefebvre	9	16	24	1	0
Saeed Anwar	not out		83	112	92	9	3
Ijaz Ahmed	c Lefebvre	b Cantrell	39	77	55	2	1
Inzamam-ul-Haq	not out		18	17	13	0	1
Extras (lb 1, w 1): **2**							
Total (2 wickets, 30.4 overs): **151**							

DNB: Javed Miandad, Saleem Malik, *Wasim Akram, +Rashid Latif, Mushtaq Ahmed, Aaqib Javed, Waqar Younis.
FoW: 1-10 (Aamer Sohail), 2-104 (Ijaz Ahmed).

Bowling

	O	M	R	W
Lefebvre	7	1	20	1
Bakker	7	1	13	0
Jansen	2	0	22	0 (1w)
de Leede	4	0	20	0
Aponso	5	0	38	0
Cantrell	4	0	18	1
Gouka	1.4	0	19	0

Wills World Cup, 1995/96, 18th Match
New Zealand v United Arab Emirates, Group B
Iqbal Stadium, Faisalabad
27 February 1996 (50-over match)

Result: New Zealand won by 109 runs
Points: New Zealand 2, United Arab Emirates 0
Toss: United Arab Emirates
Umpires: BC Cooray (SL) and S Venkataraghavan (Ind)
TV Umpire: Ikram Rabbani
Match Referee: RS Madugalle (SL)
Man Of The Match: RG Twose

New Zealand innings (47 overs maximum)			R	M	B	4	6
CM Spearman	b Saleem Raza		78	114	77	10	0
NJ Astle	b Samarasekera		2	11	2	0	0
SP Fleming	c & b Dukanwala		16	17	11	4	0
RG Twose	c Mazhar Hussain	b Azhar Saeed	92	134	112	8	0
CL Cairns	c Imtiaz Abbasi	b Zarawani	6	10	20	0	0
AC Parore	c Azhar Saeed	b Zarawani	15	24	18	0	0
SA Thomson	not out		31	40	35	2	0
*+LK Germon	b Azhar Saeed		3	8	6	0	0
DJ Nash	lbw	b Azhar Saeed	8	14	12	0	0
DK Morrison	not out		10	2	2	1	1
Extras (b 2, lb 12, nb 1): **15**							
Total (8 wickets, 47 overs): **276**							

DNB: RJ Kennedy.
FoW: 1-11 (Astle), 2-42 (Fleming), 3-162 (Spearman), 4-173 (Cairns), 5-210 (Parore), 6-228 (Twose), 7-239 (Germon), 8-266 (Nash).

Bowling	O	M	R	W	
Samarasekera	6	0	30	1	
Arshad Laeeq	2	0	16	0	
Saleem Raza	9	0	48	1	
Dukanwala	10	0	46	1 (1nb)	
Mazhar Hussain	3	0	28	0	
Azhar Saeed	7	0	45	3	
Zarawani	10	0	49	2	

UAE innings (target: 277 runs from 47 overs)			R	M	B	4	6
Azhar Saeed	c Fleming	b Nash	5	25	20	0	0
Saleem Raza	c Kennedy	b Morrison	21	30	17	3	1
Mazhar Hussain	c Cairns	b Thomson	29	63	53	5	0
V Mehra	c Cairns	b Thomson	12	49	21	1	0
Mohammad Ishaq	c Fleming	b Kennedy	8	19	9	0	0
Mohammad Aslam	c Twose	b Thomson	1	22	12	0	0
SF Dukanwala	c & b Cairns		8	21	21	0	0
Arshad Laeeq	run out		14	39	36	3	0
JA Samarasekera	not out		47	65	59	5	0
*Sultan Zarawani	c Thomson	b Nash	13	29	18	1	0
+Imtiaz Abbasi	not out		2	5	6	0	0
Extras (lb 2, w 3, nb 2): **7**							
Total (9 wickets, 47 overs): **167**							

FoW: 1-23 (Azhar Saeed), 2-29 (Saleem Raza), 3-65 (Mehra), 4-70 (Mazhar Hussain), 5-81 (Mohammad Ishaq), 6-88 (Mohammad Aslam), 7-92 (Dukanwala), 8-124 (Arshad Laeeq), 9-162 (Zarawani).

Bowling	O	M	R	W	
Morrison	7	0	37	1 (2nb)	
Nash	9	1	34	2 (2w)	
Cairns	10	2	31	1	
Kennedy	6	0	20	1 (1w)	
Thomson	10	2	20	3	
Astle	5	0	23	0	

Wills World Cup, 1995/96, 21th Match
Pakistan v South Africa, Group B
National Stadium, Karachi
29 February 1996 (50-over match)

Result: South Africa won by 5 wickets
Points: South Africa 2, Pakistan 0
Toss: Pakistan
Umpires: SA Bucknor (WI) and KT Francis (SL)
TV Umpire: K Parthasarathy (Ind)
Match Referee: R Subba Row (Eng)
Man Of The Match: WJ Cronje

Pakistan innings (50 overs maximum)			R	M	B	4	6
Aamer Sohail	c Cronje	b Pollock	111	205	139	8	0
Saeed Anwar	c McMillan	b Cronje	25	47	30	3	0
Ijaz Ahmed	lbw	b Cronje	0	2	2	0	0
Inzamam-ul-Haq	run out		23	54	39	3	0
Saleem Malik	c Palframan	b Adams	40	73	66	3	0
*Wasim Akram	not out		32	35	25	3	0
+Rashid Latif	lbw	b Matthews	0	3	1	0	0
Rameez Raja	not out		2	5	2	0	0
Extras (b 1, lb 2, w 4, nb 2): **9**							
Total (6 wickets, 50 overs): **242**							

DNB: Mushtaq Ahmed, Saqlain Mushtaq, Waqar Younis.
FoW: 1-52 (Saeed Anwar), 2-52 (Ijaz Ahmed), 3-112 (Inzamam-ul-Haq), 4-189 (Saleem Malik), 5-233 (Aamer Sohail), 6-235 (Rashid Latif).

Bowling	O	M	R	W	
Pollock	9	0	49	1 (1nb)	
Matthews	10	0	47	1 (1w)	
Cronje	5	0	20	2	
Donald	8	0	50	0 (1nb, 1w)	
Adams	10	0	42	1 (2w)	
McMillan	8	0	31	0	

South Africa innings (target: 243 from 50 overs)			R	M	B	4	6
AC Hudson	b Waqar Younis		33	36	26	6	0
G Kirsten	b Saqlain Mushtaq		44	89	57	5	0
BM McMillan	lbw	b Waqar Younis	1	7	4	0	0
DJ Cullinan	b Waqar Younis		65	115	76	6	0
JH Kallis	c & b Saqlain Mushtaq		9	11	14	0	0
*WJ Cronje	not out		45	93	73	2	0
SM Pollock	not out		20	34	28	1	0
Extras (b 8, lb 4, w 6, nb 8): **26**							
Total (5 wickets, 44.2 overs): **243**							

DNB: +SJ Palframan, CR Matthews, AA Donald, PR Adams.
FoW: 1-51 (Hudson), 2-53 (McMillan), 3-111 (Kirsten), 4-125 (Kallis), 5-203 (Cullinan).

Bowling	O	M	R	W	
Wasim Akram	9.2	0	49	0 (4nb)	
Waqar Younis	8	0	50	3 (2nb, 3w)	
Mushtaq Ahmed	10	0	54	0	
Aamer Sohail	6	0	35	0 (2nb, 2w)	
Saqlain Mushtaq	10	1	38	2 (1w)	
Saleem Malik	1	0	5	0	

Wills World Cup, 1995/96, 23rd Match
Netherlands v United Arab Emirates, Group B
Gaddafi Stadium, Lahore
1 March 1996 (50-over match)

Result: United Arab Emirates won by 7 wickets
Points: United Arab Emirates 2, Netherlands 0
Toss: United Arab Emirates
Umpires: Mahboob Shah and SG Randell (Aus)
TV Umpire: RC Sharma (Ind)
Match Referee: Nasim-ul-Ghani
ODI Debuts: RF van Oosterom (NL); Saeed-al-Saffar (UAE)
Men Of The Match: SF Dukanwala and Saleem Raza

Netherlands innings (50 overs maximum)			R	M	B	4	6
NE Clarke	c Mehra	b Shehzad Altaf	0	12	11	0	0
PE Cantrell	c Imtiaz Abbasi	b Azhar Saeed	47	160	106	1	0
GJAF Aponso	c & b Dukanwala		45	89	80	6	0
TBM de Leede	c & b Azhar Saeed		36	55	47	3	0
KJJ van Noortwijk	c Zarawani	b Dukanwala	26	29	19	3	0
*SW Lubbers	c Saeed-al-Saffar	b Zarawani	8	10	8	1	0
RP Lefebvre	c Mohammad Ishaq	b Dukanwala	12	17	8	0	1
B Zuiderent	st Imtiaz Abbasi	b Dukanwala	3	10	5	0	0
+MMC Schewe	b Dukanwala		6	11	6	0	0
RF van Oosterom	not out		2	10	4	0	0
PJ Bakker	not out		1	8	4	0	0
Extras (b 4, lb 15, w 11): **30**							
Total (9 wickets, 50 overs): **216**							

FoW: 1-3 (Clarke), 2-77 (Aponso), 3-148 (de Leede), 4-153 (Cantrell), 5-168 (Lubbers), 6-200 (van Noortwijk), 7-200 (Lefebvre), 8-209 (Zuiderent), 9-210 (Schewe).

Bowling	O	M	R	W
Shehzad Altaf	10	3	15	1
Samarasekera	9	1	36	0
Saeed-al-Saffar	3	0	25	0
Dukanwala	10	0	29	5
Zarawani	8	0	40	1
Saleem Raza	5	0	23	0
Azhar Saeed	5	0	29	2

UAE innings (target: 217 runs from 50 overs)			R	M	B	4	6
Azhar Saeed	run out		32	101	82	2	0
Saleem Raza	c Zuiderent	b Lubbers	84	79	68	7	6
Mazhar Hussain	c Clarke	b Lefebvre	16	14	14	3	0
V Mehra	not out		29	69	45	2	0
Mohammad Ishaq	not out		51	62	55	8	0
Extras (lb 7, w 1): **8**							
Total (3 wickets, 44.2 overs): **220**							

DNB: JA Samarasekera, SF Dukanwala, *Sultan Zarawani, Saeed-al-Saffar, +Imtiaz Abbasi, Shehzad Altaf.
FoW: 1-117 (Saleem Raza), 2-135 (Mazhar Hussain), 3-138 (Azhar Saeed).

Bowling	O	M	R	W
Bakker	8	0	41	0
Lefebvre	8	0	24	1 (1w)
Lubbers	9	0	38	1
Cantrell	8	0	30	0
Aponso	7.2	0	47	0
de Leede	4	0	33	0

Wills World Cup, 1995/96, 25th Match
Pakistan v England, Group B
National Stadium, Karachi
3 March 1996 (50-over match)

Result: Pakistan won by 7 wickets
Points: Pakistan 2, England 0
Toss: England
Umpires: BC Cooray (SL) and S Venkataraghavan (Ind)
TV Umpire: K Parthasarathy (Ind)
Match Referee: RS Madugalle (SL)
Man Of The Match: Aamer Sohail

England innings (50 overs maximum)			R	M	B	4	6
RA Smith	c Waqar Younis	b Saleem Malik	75	115	92	8	1
*MA Atherton	b Aamer Sohail		66	127	91	6	0
GA Hick	st Rashid Latif	b Aamer Sohail	1	4	2	0	0
GP Thorpe	not out		52	92	64	3	0
NH Fairbrother	c Wasim Akram	b Mushtaq Ahmed	13	24	21	1	0
+RC Russell	c & b Mushtaq Ahmed		4	10	7	0	0
DA Reeve	b Mushtaq Ahmed		3	9	5	0	0
DG Cork	lbw	b Waqar Younis	0	5	2	0	0
D Gough	b Wasim Akram		14	22	15	1	0
PJ Martin	run out		2	6	4	0	0
RK Illingworth	not out		1	1	1	0	0
Extras (lb 11, w 4, nb 3): **18**							
Total (9 wickets, 50 overs): **249**							

FoW: 1-147 (Smith), 2-151 (Hick), 3-156 (Atherton), 4-194 (Fairbrother), 5-204 (Russell), 6-212 (Reeve), 7-217 (Cork), 8-241 (Gough), 9-247 (Martin).

Bowling	O	M	R	W	
Wasim Akram	7	1	31	1 (3w)	
Waqar Younis	10	1	45	1	
Aaqib Javed	7	0	34	0 (3nb)	
Mushtaq Ahmed	10	0	53	3	
Aamer Sohail	10	0	48	2 (1nb, 1w)	
Saleem Malik	6	1	27	1	

Pakistan innings (target: 250 runs from 50 overs)			R	M	B	4	6
Aamer Sohail	c Thorpe	b Illingworth	42	70	56	6	0
Saeed Anwar	c Russell	b Cork	71	125	72	8	0
Ijaz Ahmed	c Russell	b Cork	70	113	83	6	0
Inzamam-ul-Haq	not out		53	89	54	6	0
Javed Miandad	not out		11	29	21	1	0
Extras (lb 1, w 2): **3**							
Total (3 wickets, 47.4 overs): **250**							

DNB: Saleem Malik, *Wasim Akram, +Rashid Latif, Mushtaq Ahmed, Waqar Younis, Aaqib Javed.
FoW: 1-81 (Aamer Sohail), 2-139 (Saeed Anwar), 3-214 (Ijaz Ahmed).

Bowling	O	M	R	W	
Cork	10	0	59	2 (2w)	
Martin	9	0	45	0	
Gough	10	0	45	0	
Illingworth	10	0	46	1	
Reeve	6.4	0	37	0	
Hick	2	0	17	0	

Wills World Cup, 1995/96, 27th Match
Netherlands v South Africa, Group B
Rawalpindi Cricket Stadium
5 March 1996 (50-over match)

Result: South Africa won by 160 runs
Points: South Africa 2, Netherlands 0
Toss: South Africa
Umpires: Khizer Hayat and SG Randell (Aus)
TV Umpire: Mian Mohammad Aslam
Match Referee: Nasim-ul-Ghani
Man Of The Match: AC Hudson

South Africa innings (50 overs maximum)			R	M	B	4	6
G Kirsten	c Zuiderent	b Aponso	83	118	98	6	0
AC Hudson	c van Oosterom	b Gouka	161	153	132	13	4
*WJ Cronje	c Lubbers	b Cantrell	41	48	39	3	0
DJ Cullinan	not out		19	31	17	1	0
JH Kallis	not out		17	17	16	0	0
Extras (lb 5, w 2): **7**							
Total (3 wickets, 50 overs): **328**							

DNB: BM McMillan, SM Pollock, +SJ Palframan, PL Symcox, CR Matthews, AA Donald.
FoW: 1-186 (Kirsten), 2-274 (Hudson), 3-301 (Cronje).

Bowling	O	M	R	W
Bakker	10	1	64	0 (1w)
Lubbers	8	0	50	0
de Leede	10	0	59	0 (1w)
Aponso	10	0	57	1
Cantrell	10	0	61	1
Gouka	2	0	32	1 (1nb)

Netherlands innings (target: 329 from 50 overs)			R	M	B	4	6
NE Clarke	c Pollock	b Donald	32	64	46	6	1
PE Cantrell	c & b Matthews		23	47	39	3	0
TBM de Leede	b Donald		12	36	26	1	0
KJJ van Noortwijk	c Palframan	b Symcox	9	38	24	1	0
GJAF Aponso	c Kirsten	b Symcox	6	41	31	0	0
B Zuiderent	run out		27	49	50	2	0
+MMC Schewe	b Matthews		20	62	34	1	0
EL Gouka	c Kallis	b Pollock	19	28	35	2	0
RF van Oosterom	not out		5	15	15	0	0
*SW Lubbers	not out		2	8	2	0	0
Extras (lb 7, w 5, nb 1): **13**							
Total (8 wickets, 50 overs): **168**							

DNB: PJ Bakker.
FoW: 1-56 (Cantrell), 2-70 (Clarke), 3-81 (de Leede), 4-86 (van Noortwijk), 5-97 (Aponso), 6-126 (Zuiderent), 7-158 (Gouka), 8-163 (Schewe).

Bowling	O	M	R	W
Pollock	8	0	35	1 (5w)
Matthews	10	0	38	2
Donald	6	0	21	2 (1w)
Cronje	3	1	3	0
Symcox	10	1	22	2
McMillan	4	2	5	0
Kallis	7	1	30	0
Cullinan	2	0	7	0

Wills World Cup, 1995/96, 30th Match
Pakistan v New Zealand, Group B
Gaddafi Stadium, Lahore
6 March 1996 (50-over match)

Result: Pakistan won by 46 runs
Points: Pakistan 2, New Zealand 0
Toss: New Zealand
Umpires: KT Francis (SL) and ID Robinson (Zim)
TV Umpire: RC Sharma (Ind)
Match Referee: CH Lloyd (WI)
Man Of The Match: Saleem Malik

Pakistan innings (50 overs maximum)			R	M	B	4	6
Aamer Sohail	c Thomson	b Kennedy	50	60	62	10	0
Saeed Anwar	run out (Thomson)		62	113	67	0	0
Ijaz Ahmed	c Spearman	b Cairns	26	68	46	0	0
Inzamam-ul-Haq	run out		39	63	41	4	1
Javed Miandad	run out (sub [CZ Harris])		5	27	19	0	0
Saleem Malik	not out		55	62	47	5	0
*Wasim Akram	not out		28	42	26	2	0
*Extras (lb 5, w 5, nb 6): **16**							
*Total (5 wickets, 50 overs): **281**							

DNB: +Rashid Latif, Waqar Younis, Mushtaq Ahmed, Aaqib Javed.
FoW: 1-70 (Aamer Sohail), 2-139 (Saeed Anwar), 3-155 (Ijaz Ahmed), 4-173 (Javed Miandad), 5-201 (Inzamam-ul-Haq).

Bowling	O	M	R	W
Morrison	2	0	17	0
Nash	10	1	49	0
Cairns	10	1	53	1
Kennedy	5	0	32	1
Astle	9	0	50	0
Thomson	6	0	35	0
Twose	8	0	40	0

New Zealand innings (target: 282 from 50 overs)			R	M	B	4	6
CM Spearman	c Rashid Latif	b Aaqib Javed	14	29	13	2	0
NJ Astle	c Rashid Latif	b Waqar Younis	6	23	17	1	0
*+LK Germon	c sub (Ata-ur-Rehman)	b Mushtaq Ahmed	41	110	67	1	0
SP Fleming	st Rashid Latif	b Saleem Malik	42	63	43	7	0
RG Twose	c Saleem Malik	b Mushtaq Ahmed	24	49	38	0	0
CL Cairns	c Rashid Latif	b Aamer Sohail	32	28	34	1	2
AC Parore	c Mushtaq Ahmed	b Saleem Malik	36	41	34	3	0
SA Thomson	c Rashid Latif	b Waqar Younis	13	32	25	0	0
DJ Nash	not out		5	18	12	0	0
RJ Kennedy	b Aaqib Javed		2	7	3	0	0
DK Morrison	absent – hurt		-				
*Extras (b 4, lb 9, w 6, nb 1): **20**							
*Total (all out, 47.3 overs): **235**							

FoW: 1-23 (Astle), 2-23 (Spearman), 3-83 (Fleming), 4-132 (Germon), 5-138 (Twose), 6-182 (Cairns), 7-221 (Parore), 8-228 (Thomson), 9-235 (Kennedy).

Bowling	O	M	R	W
Waqar Younis	9	2	32	2 (1w)
Aaqib Javed	7.3	0	45	2 (2w)
Mushtaq Ahmed	10	0	32	2
Saleem Malik	7	0	41	2 (1w)
Ijaz Ahmed	4	0	21	0 (1nb)
Aamer Sohail	10	0	51	1

1996 WORLD CUP

Finals

Wills World Cup, 1995/96, 1st Quarter-Final
England v Sri Lanka
Iqbal Stadium, Faisalabad
9 March 1996 (50-over match)

Result: Sri Lanka won by 5 wickets
Sri Lanka advances to the semi-finals
Toss: England
Umpires: Mahboob Shah and ID Robinson (Zim)
TV Umpire: VK Ramaswamy (Ind)
Match Referee: Nasim-ul-Ghani
Man Of The Match: ST Jayasuriya

England innings (50 overs maximum)			R	M	B	4	6
RA Smith	run out		25	78	41	3	0
*MA Atherton	c Kaluwitharana	b Vaas	22	32	27	2	0
GA Hick	c Ranatunga	b Muralitharan	8	27	21	0	0
GP Thorpe	b Dharmasena		14	39	31	1	0
PAJ DeFreitas	lbw	b Jayasuriya	67	89	64	5	2
AJ Stewart	b Muralitharan		17	50	38	0	0
+RC Russell	b Dharmasena		9	18	17	0	0
DA Reeve	b Jayasuriya		35	37	34	2	0
D Gough	not out		26	34	26	5	0
PJ Martin	not out		0	1	1	0	0

Extras (lb 8, w 4): **12**
Total (8 wickets, 50 overs): **235**

DNB: RK Illingworth.
FoW: 1-31 (Atherton), 2-58 (Hick), 3-66 (Smith), 4-94 (Thorpe), 5-145 (Stewart), 6-171 (Russell), 7-173 (DeFreitas), 8-235 (Reeve).

Bowling	O	M	R	W
Wickramasinghe	7	0	43	0 (1w)
Vaas	8	1	29	1 (1w)
Muralitharan	10	1	37	2 (1w)
Dharmasena	10	0	30	2
Jayasuriya	9	0	46	2
de Silva	6	0	42	0 (1w)

Sri Lanka innings (target: 236 runs from 50 overs)			R	M	B	4	6
ST Jayasuriya	st Russell	b Reeve	82	67	44	13	3
+RS Kaluwitharana	b Illingworth		8	7	3	2	0
AP Gurusinha	run out		45	124	63	5	0
PA de Silva	c Smith	b Hick	31	38	30	5	0
*A Ranatunga	lbw	b Gough	25	14	17	5	0
HP Tillakaratne	not out		19	65	50	1	0
RS Mahanama	not out		22	55	38	2	0

Extras (lb 1, w 2, nb 1): **4**
Total (5 wickets, 40.4 overs): **236**

DNB: HDPK Dharmasena, WPUJC Vaas, M Muralitharan, GP Wickramasinghe.
FoW: 1-12 (Kaluwitharana), 2-113 (Jayasuriya), 3-165 (de Silva), 4-194 (Ranatunga), 5-198 (Gurusinha).

Bowling	O	M	R	W
Martin	9	1	41	0 (2w)
Illingworth	10	1	72	1
Gough	10	1	36	1
DeFreitas	3.4	0	38	0
Reeve	4	1	14	1 (1nb)
Hick	4	0	34	1

Wills World Cup, 1995/96, 2nd Quarter-Final
India v Pakistan
M Chinnaswamy Stadium, Bangalore (day/night)
9 March 1996 (50-over match)

Result: India won by 39 runs
India advances to the semi-finals
Toss: India
Umpires: SA Bucknor (WI) and DR Shepherd (Eng)
TV Umpire: RS Dunne (NZ)
Match Referee: R Subba Row (Eng)
Man Of The Match: NS Sidhu

India innings (50 overs maximum)			R	M	B	4	6
NS Sidhu	b Mushtaq Ahmed		93	160	115	11	0
SR Tendulkar	b Ata-ur-Rehman		31	103	59	3	0
SV Manjrekar	c Javed Miandad	b Aamer Sohail	20	42	43	0	0
*M Azharuddin	c Rashid Latif	b Waqar Younis	27	27	22	1	1
VG Kambli	b Mushtaq Ahmed		24	41	26	1	0
A Jadeja	c Aamer Sohail	b Waqar Younis	45	41	25	4	2
+NR Mongia	run out		3	6	3	0	0
A Kumble	c Javed Miandad	b Aaqib Javed	10	9	6	2	0
J Srinath	not out		12	8	4	2	0
BKV Prasad	not out		0	2	0	0	0
Extras (lb 3, w 15, nb 4): **22**							
Total (8 wickets, 50 overs): **287**							

DNB: SLV Raju.
FoW: 1-90 (Tendulkar), 2-138 (Manjrekar), 3-168 (Sidhu), 4-200 (Azharuddin), 5-226 (Kambli), 6-236 (Mongia), 7-260 (Kumble), 8-279 (Jadeja).

Bowling	O	M	R	W
Waqar Younis	10	1	67	2 (1w)
Aaqib Javed	10	0	67	1 (1nb, 4w)
Ata-ur-Rehman	10	0	40	1 (3nb, 1w)
Mushtaq Ahmed	10	0	56	2 (3w)
Aamer Sohail	5	0	29	1 (4w)
Saleem Malik	5	0	25	0 (2w)

Pakistan innings (target: 288 runs from 49 overs)			R	M	B	4	6
*Aamer Sohail	b Prasad		55	67	46	9	1
Saeed Anwar	c Kumble	b Srinath	48	32	32	5	2
Ijaz Ahmed	c Srinath	b Prasad	12	24	23	1	0
Inzamam-ul-Haq	c Mongia	b Prasad	12	26	20	1	0
Saleem Malik	lbw	b Kumble	38	58	50	4	0
Javed Miandad	run out		38	88	64	2	0
+Rashid Latif	st Mongia	b Raju	26	28	25	1	2
Mushtaq Ahmed	c & b Kumble		0	3	2	0	0
Waqar Younis	not out		4	24	21	0	0
Ata-ur-Rehman	lbw	b Kumble	0	1	1	0	0
Aaqib Javed	not out		6	13	10	0	0
Extras (b 1, lb 3, w 5): **9**							
Total (9 wickets, 49 overs): **248**							

FoW: 1-84 (Saeed Anwar), 2-113 (Aamer Sohail), 3-122 (Ijaz Ahmed), 4-132 (Inzamam-ul-Haq), 5-184 (Saleem Malik), 6-231 (Rashid Latif), 7-232 (Mushtaq Ahmed), 8-239 (Javed Miandad), 9-239 (Ata-ur-Rehman).

Bowling	O	M	R	W
Srinath	9	0	61	1 (1w)
Prasad	10	0	45	3 (2w)
Kumble	10	0	48	3
Raju	10	0	46	1 (1w)
Tendulkar	5	0	25	0
Jadeja	5	0	19	0 (1w)

Wills World Cup, 1995/96, 3rd Quarter-Final
South Africa v West Indies
National Stadium, Karachi
11 March 1996 (50-over match)

Result: West Indies won by 19 runs
West Indies advances to the semi-finals
Toss: West Indies
Umpires: KT Francis (SL) and SG Randell (Aus)
TV Umpire: BC Cooray (SL)
Match Referee: RS Madugalle (SL)
Man Of The Match: BC Lara

West Indies innings (50 overs maximum)

			R	M	B	4	6
S Chanderpaul	c Cullinan	b McMillan	56	126	93	4	0
+CO Browne	c Cullinan	b Matthews	26	25	18	3	0
BC Lara	c Pollock	b Symcox	111	142	94	16	0
*RB Richardson	c Kirsten	b Symcox	10	32	27	0	0
RA Harper	lbw	b McMillan	9	20	15	1	0
RIC Holder	run out (Adams)		5	18	9	0	0
KLT Arthurton	c Hudson	b Adams	1	4	5	0	0
JC Adams	not out		13	26	17	1	0
IR Bishop	b Adams		17	32	22	1	1
CEL Ambrose	not out		0	3	1	0	0

Extras (b 2, lb 11, w 2, nb 1): *16*
Total (8 wickets, 50 overs): *264*

DNB: CA Walsh.
FoW: 1-42 (Browne), 2-180 (Chanderpaul), 3-210 (Richardson), 4-214 (Lara), 5-227 (Harper), 6-230 (Arthurton), 7-230 (Holder), 8-254 (Bishop).

Bowling	O	M	R	W
Pollock	9	0	46	0 (1w)
Matthews	10	0	42	1
Cronje	3	0	17	0
McMillan	10	1	37	2 (1nb)
Symcox	10	0	64	2
Adams	8	0	45	2 (1w)

South Africa innings (target: 265 from 50 overs)

			R	M	B	4	6
AC Hudson	c Walsh	b Adams	54	110	80	8	0
G Kirsten	hit wicket	b Ambrose	3	24	14	0	0
DJ Cullinan	c Bishop	b Adams	69	104	78	3	3
*WJ Cronje	c Arthurton	b Adams	40	55	47	2	2
JN Rhodes	c Adams	b Harper	13	45	24	0	0
BM McMillan	lbw	b Harper	6	11	7	0	0
SM Pollock	c Adams	b Harper	6	20	7	0	0
+SJ Palframan	c & b Harper		1	3	2	0	0
PL Symcox	c Harper	b Arthurton	24	20	20	1	2
CR Matthews	not out		8	23	12	0	0
PR Adams	b Walsh		10	17	14	0	0

Extras (b 1, lb 4, w 2, nb 4): *11*
Total (all out, 49.3 overs): *245*

FoW: 1-21 (Kirsten), 2-118 (Hudson), 3-140 (Cullinan), 4-186 (Cronje), 5-196 (Rhodes), 6-196 (McMillan), 7-198 (Palframan), 8-227 (Pollock), 9-228 (Symcox), 10-245 (Adams).

Bowling	O	M	R	W
Ambrose	10	0	29	1
Walsh	8.3	0	51	1 (1w, 2nb)
Bishop	5	0	31	0 (3nb)
Harper	10	0	47	4 (1nb)
Adams	10	0	53	3
Arthurton	6	0	29	1

Wills World Cup, 1995/96, 4th Quarter-Final
Australia v New Zealand
MA Chidambaram Stadium, Chepauk, Madras (day/night)
11 March 1996 (50-over match)

Result: Australia won by 6 wickets
Australia advances to the semi-finals
Toss: New Zealand
Umpires: CJ Mitchley (SA) and S Venkataraghavan
TV Umpire: Khizer Hayat (Pak)
Match Referee: MAK Pataudi
Man Of The Match: ME Waugh

New Zealand innings (50 overs maximum)			R	M	B	4	6
CM Spearman	c Healy	b Reiffel	12	16	12	3	0
NJ Astle	c Healy	b Fleming	1	10	6	0	0
*+LK Germon	c Fleming	b McGrath	89	149	96	9	1
SP Fleming	c SR Waugh	b McGrath	8	18	18	0	0
CZ Harris	c Reiffel	b Warne	130	162	124	13	4
RG Twose	b Bevan		4	14	12	0	0
CL Cairns	c Reiffel	b ME Waugh	4	6	9	0	0
AC Parore	lbw	b Warne	11	16	13	0	0
SA Thomson	run out		11	13	10	1	0
DN Patel	not out		3	3	4	0	0
Extras (lb 6, w 3, nb 4): **13**							
Total (9 wickets, 50 overs): **286**							

DNB: DJ Nash.
FoW: 1-15 (Astle), 2-16 (Spearman), 3-44 (Fleming), 4-212 (Germon), 5-227 (Twose), 6-240 (Cairns), 7-259 (Parore), 8-282 (Harris), 9-286 (Thomson).

Bowling	O	M	R	W	
Reiffel	4	0	38	1 (3nb, 1w)	
Fleming	5	1	20	1	
McGrath	9	2	50	2 (1nb)	
ME Waugh	8	0	43	1	
Warne	10	0	52	2 (1w)	
Bevan	10	0	52	1 (1nb, 1w)	
SR Waugh	4	0	25	0	

Australia innings (target: 287 runs from 50 overs)			R	M	B	4	6
*MA Taylor	c Germon	b Patel	10	23	24	1	0
ME Waugh	c Parore	b Nash	110	156	112	6	2
RT Ponting	c sub (RJ Kennedy)	b Thomson	31	32	43	4	0
SK Warne	lbw	b Astle	24	40	14	1	2
SR Waugh	not out		59	99	68	5	0
SG Law	not out		42	47	30	3	1
Extras (b 1, lb 6, w 3, nb 3): **13**							
Total (4 wickets, 47.5 overs): **289**							

DNB: MG Bevan, +IA Healy, PR Reiffel, DW Fleming, GD McGrath.
FoW: 1-19 (Taylor), 2-84 (Ponting), 3-127 (Warne), 4-213 (ME Waugh).

Bowling	O	M	R	W	
Nash	9	1	44	1 (1w)	
Patel	8	0	45	1	
Cairns	6.5	0	51	0 (1nb)	
Harris	10	0	41	0 (2nb, 1w)	
Thomson	8	0	57	1 (1w)	
Astle	3	0	21	1	
Twose	3	0	23	0	

Wills World Cup, 1995/96, 1st Semi-Final
India v Sri Lanka
Eden Gardens, Calcutta (day/night)
13 March 1996 (50-over match)

Result: Sri Lanka won by default
Sri Lanka advances to the final
Toss: India
Umpires: RS Dunne (NZ) and CJ Mitchley (SA)
TV Umpire: Mahboob Shah (Pak)
Match Referee: CH Lloyd (WI)
Man Of The Match: PA de Silva

Sri Lanka innings (50 overs maximum)			R	M	B	4	6
ST Jayasuriya	c Prasad	b Srinath	1	4	3	0	0
+RS Kaluwitharana	c Manjrekar	b Srinath	0	1	1	0	0
AP Gurusinha	c Kumble	b Srinath	1	29	16	0	0
PA de Silva	b Kumble		66	63	47	14	0
RS Mahanama	retired hurt		58	126	101	6	0
*A Ranatunga	lbw	b Tendulkar	35	72	42	4	0
HP Tillakaratne	c Tendulkar	b Prasad	32	51	43	1	0
HDPK Dharmasena	b Tendulkar		9	21	20	0	0
WPUJC Vaas	run out (Azharuddin)		23	19	16	3	0
GP Wickramasinghe	not out		4	10	9	0	0
M Muralitharan	not out		5	4	4	0	0

Extras (b 1, lb 10, w 4, nb 2): **17**
Total (8 wickets, 50 overs): **251**

FoW: 1-1 (Kaluwitharana), 2-1 (Jayasuriya), 3-35 (Gurusinha), 4-85 (de Silva), 5-168 (Ranatunga), 6-206 (Dharmasena), 7-236 (Tillakaratne), 8-244 (Vaas).

Bowling	O	M	R	W
Srinath	7	1	34	3
Kumble	10	0	51	1 (1w)
Prasad	8	0	50	1 (2nb, 2w)
Kapoor	10	0	40	0
Jadeja	5	0	31	0
Tendulkar	10	1	34	2 (1w)

India innings (target: 252 runs from 50 overs)			R	M	B	4	6
SR Tendulkar	st Kaluwitharana	b Jayasuriya	65	96	88	9	0
NS Sidhu	c Jayasuriya	b Vaas	3	7	8	0	0
SV Manjrekar	b Jayasuriya		25	105	48	1	0
*M Azharuddin	c & b Dharmasena		0	3	6	0	0
VG Kambli	not out		10	49	29	0	0
J Srinath	run out		6	8	6	1	0
A Jadeja	b Jayasuriya		0	9	11	0	0
+NR Mongia	c Jayasuriya	b de Silva	1	10	8	0	0
AR Kapoor	c de Silva	b Muralitharan	0	1	1	0	0
A Kumble	not out		0	1	0	0	0

Extras (lb 5, w 5): **10**
Total (8 wickets, 34.1 overs): **120**

DNB: BKV Prasad.
FoW: 1-8 (Sidhu), 2-98 (Tendulkar), 3-99 (Azharuddin), 4-101 (Manjrekar), 5-110 (Srinath), 6-115 (Jadeja), 7-120 (Mongia), 8-120 (Kapoor).

Bowling	O	M	R	W
Wickramasinghe	5	0	24	0 (2w)
Vaas	6	1	23	1
Muralitharan	7.1	0	29	1 (1w)
Dharmasena	7	0	24	1
Jayasuriya	7	1	12	3 (1w)
de Silva	2	0	3	1 (1w)

Wills World Cup, 1995/96, 2nd Semi-Final
Australia v West Indies
Punjab CA Stadium, Mohali, Chandigarh (day/night)
14 March 1996 (50-over match)

Result: Australia won by 5 runs
Australia advances to the final
Toss: Australia
Umpires: BC Cooray (SL) and S Venkataraghavan
TV Umpire: Khizer Hayat (Pak)
Match Referee: JR Reid (NZ)
Man Of The Match: SK Warne

Australia innings (50 overs maximum)			R	M	B	4	6
ME Waugh	lbw	b Ambrose	0	2	2	0	0
*MA Taylor	b Bishop		1	16	11	0	0
RT Ponting	lbw	b Ambrose	0	18	15	0	0
SR Waugh	b Bishop		3	22	18	0	0
SG Law	run out		72	152	105	5	0
MG Bevan	c Richardson	b Harper	69	146	110	4	1
+IA Healy	run out		31	36	28	2	0
PR Reiffel	run out		7	10	11	0	0
SK Warne	not out		6	10	6	0	0
Extras (lb 11, w 5, nb 2): **18**							
Total (8 wickets, 50 overs): **207**							

DNB: DW Fleming, GD McGrath.
FoW: 1-0 (ME Waugh), 2-7 (Taylor), 3-8 (Ponting), 4-15 (SR Waugh), 5-153 (Law), 6-171 (Bevan), 7-186 (Reiffel), 8-207 (Healy).

Bowling	O	M	R	W
Ambrose	10	1	26	2 (3w)
Bishop	10	1	35	2 (3nb, 1w)
Walsh	10	1	33	0 (1nb)
Gibson	2	0	13	0 (1nb)
Harper	9	0	47	1
Adams	9	0	42	0 (1w)

West Indies innings (target: 208 from 50 overs)			R	M	B	4	6
S Chanderpaul	c Fleming	b McGrath	80	172	126	7	0
+CO Browne	c & b Warne		10	26	18	0	0
BC Lara	b SR Waugh		45	69	45	4	0
*RB Richardson	not out		49	123	83	4	0
RA Harper	lbw	b McGrath	2	8	5	0	0
OD Gibson	c Healy	b Warne	1	3	2	0	0
JC Adams	lbw	b Warne	2	10	11	0	0
KLT Arthurton	c Healy	b Fleming	0	5	4	0	0
IR Bishop	lbw	b Warne	3	2	3	0	0
CEL Ambrose	run out		2	4	2	0	0
CA Walsh	b Fleming		0	1	1	0	0
Extras (lb 4, w 2, nb 2): **8**							
Total (all out, 49.3 overs): **202**							

FoW: 1-25 (Browne), 2-93 (Lara), 3-165 (Chanderpaul), 4-173 (Harper), 5-178 (Gibson), 6-183 (Adams), 7-187 (Arthurton), 8-194 (Bishop), 9-202 (Ambrose), 10-202 (Walsh).

Bowling	O	M	R	W
McGrath	10	2	30	2 (1nb)
Fleming	8.3	0	48	2 (1w)
Warne	9	0	36	4 (1w)
ME Waugh	4	0	16	0
SR Waugh	7	0	30	1
Reiffel	5	0	13	0 (2nb)
Bevan	4	1	12	0
Law	2	0	13	0

Wills World Cup, 1995/96, Final
Australia v Sri Lanka
Gaddafi Stadium, Lahore (day/night)
17 March 1996 (50-over match)

Result: Sri Lanka won by 7 wickets
Sri Lanka wins the 1995/96 Wills World Cup
Toss: Sri Lanka
Umpires: SA Bucknor (WI) and DR Shepherd (Eng)
TV Umpire: CJ Mitchley (SA)
Match Referee: CH Lloyd (WI)
Man Of The Match: PA de Silva
Man Of The Series: ST Jayasuriya

Australia innings (50 overs maximum)

			R	M	B	4	6
*MA Taylor	c Jayasuriya	b de Silva	74	109	83	8	1
ME Waugh	c Jayasuriya	b Vaas	12	29	15	1	0
RT Ponting	b de Silva		45	90	73	2	0
SR Waugh	c de Silva	b Dharmasena	13	32	25	0	0
SK Warne	st Kaluwitharana	b Muralitharan	2	4	5	0	0
SG Law	c de Silva	b Jayasuriya	22	43	30	0	1
MG Bevan	not out		36	58	49	2	0
+IA Healy	b de Silva		2	2	3	0	0
PR Reiffel	not out		13	21	18	0	0

Extras (lb 10, w 11, nb 1): **22**
Total (7 wickets, 50 overs): **241**

DNB: DW Fleming, GD McGrath.
FoW: 1-36 (ME Waugh), 2-137 (Taylor), 3-152 (Ponting), 4-156 (Warne), 5-170 (SR Waugh), 6-202 (Law), 7-205 (Healy).

Bowling

	O	M	R	W
Wickramasinghe	7	0	38	0 (2w)
Vaas	6	1	30	1
Muralitharan	10	0	31	1 (1w)
Dharmasena	10	0	47	1 (1nb)
Jayasuriya	8	0	43	1 (5w)
de Silva	9	0	42	3 (3w)

Sri Lanka innings (target: 242 runs from 50 overs)

			R	M	B	4	6
ST Jayasuriya	run out		9	9	7	1	0
+RS Kaluwitharana	c Bevan	b Fleming	6	27	13	0	0
AP Gurusinha	b Reiffel		65	119	99	6	1
PA de Silva	not out		107	176	124	13	0
*A Ranatunga	not out		47	72	37	4	1

Extras (b 1, lb 4, w 5, nb 1): **11**
Total (3 wickets, 46.2 overs): **245**

DNB: HP Tillakaratne, RS Mahanama, HDPK Dharmasena, WPUJC Vaas, GP Wickramasinghe, M Muralitharan.
FoW: 1-12 (Jayasuriya), 2-23 (Kaluwitharana), 3-148 (Gurusinha).

Bowling

	O	M	R	W
McGrath	8.2	1	28	0
Fleming	6	0	43	1 (4w)
Warne	10	0	58	0 (1nb, 1w)
Reiffel	10	0	49	1
ME Waugh	6	0	35	0
SR Waugh	3	0	15	0 (1nb)
Bevan	3	0	12	0

1999 WORLD CUP

Group A

**ICC World Cup, 1999, 1st Match
England v Sri Lanka, Group A
Lord's, London
14 May 1999 (50-over match)**

Result: England won by 8 wickets
Points: England 2, Sri Lanka 0
Toss: England
Umpires: RE Koertzen (SA) and S Venkataraghavan (Ind)
TV Umpire: DL Orchard (SA)
Match Referee: CW Smith (WI)
Man Of The Match: AJ Stewart

Sri Lanka innings (50 overs maximum)			R	M	B	4	6
ST Jayasuriya	c Hick	b Mullally	29	73	52	4	0
RS Mahanama	c Hick	b Mullally	16	47	30	2	0
MS Atapattu	c Thorpe	b Austin	3	9	9	0	0
HP Tillakaratne	c Stewart	b Ealham	0	26	12	0	0
PA de Silva	c Thorpe	b Mullally	0	13	6	0	0
*A Ranatunga	c Hussain	b Ealham	32	71	42	1	1
+RS Kaluwitharana	c Stewart	b Mullally	57	73	66	7	0
WPUJC Vaas	not out		12	59	27	0	0
KEA Upashantha	c Thorpe	b Hollioake	11	25	25	1	0
GP Wickramasinghe	c Stewart	b Austin	11	15	18	1	0
M Muralitharan	b Gough		12	6	8	2	0
Extras (lb 9, w 9, nb 3): **21**							
Total (all out, 48.4 overs): **204**							

FoW: 1-42 (Mahanama, 10.6 ov), 2-50 (Atapattu, 13.2 ov), 3-63 (Jayasuriya, 16.5 ov), 4-63 (Tillakaratne, 17.1 ov), 5-65 (de Silva, 18.5 ov), 6-149 (Ranatunga, 33.6 ov), 7-155 (Kaluwitharana, 36.5 ov), 8-174 (Upashantha, 43.5 ov), 9-190 (Wickramasinghe, 47.2 ov), 10-204 (Muralitharan, 48.4 ov).

Bowling	O	M	R	W	
Gough	8.4	0	50	1	(2nb, 1w)
Austin	9	1	25	2	(5w)
Mullally	10	1	37	4	(1nb, 1w)
Ealham	10	0	31	2	
Flintoff	2	0	12	0	
Hick	3	0	19	0	(1w)
Hollioake	6	0	21	1	

England innings (target: 205 runs from 50 overs)			R	M	B	4	6
N Hussain	st Kaluwitharana	b Muralitharan	14	69	33	1	0
*+AJ Stewart	c Kaluwitharana	b Vaas	88	182	146	6	0
GA Hick	not out		73	135	88	2	2
GP Thorpe	not out		13	23	15	1	0
Extras (lb 6, w 12, nb 1): **19**							
Total (2 wickets, 46.5 overs): **207**							

DNB: NH Fairbrother, A Flintoff, AJ Hollioake, MA Ealham, ID Austin, D Gough, AD Mullally.
FoW: 1-50 (Hussain, 14.5 ov), 2-175 (Stewart, 41.3 ov).

Bowling	O	M	R	W	
Vaas	10	2	27	1	
Wickramasinghe	10	0	41	0	
Upashantha	8	0	38	0	(1nb, 8w)
Muralitharan	10	0	33	1	(2w)
Jayasuriya	7.5	0	55	0	(2w)
de Silva	1	0	7	0	

ICC World Cup, 1999, 2nd Match
India v South Africa, Group A
New County Ground, Hove, Brighton
15 May 1999 (50-over match)

Result: South Africa won by 4 wickets
Points: South Africa 2, India 0
Toss: India
Umpires: SA Bucknor (WI) and DR Shepherd
TV Umpire: ID Robinson (Zim)
Match Referee: Talat Ali (Pak)
Man Of The Match: JH Kallis

India innings (50 overs maximum)			R	M	B	4	6
SC Ganguly	run out (Rhodes/Kallis)		97	187	142	11	1
SR Tendulkar	c Boucher	b Klusener	28	71	46	5	0
R Dravid	b Klusener		54	103	75	5	0
*M Azharuddin	c Boje	b Klusener	24	40	24	2	0
A Jadeja	c Kirsten	b Donald	16	20	14	2	0
RR Singh	not out		4	9	3	0	0
+NR Mongia	not out		5	2	2	1	0
Extras (b 6, lb 2, w 11, nb 6): **25**							
Total (5 wickets, 50 overs): **253**							

DNB: AB Agarkar, J Srinath, A Kumble, BKV Prasad.
FoW: 1-67 (Tendulkar, 15.3 ov), 2-197 (Dravid, 41.4 ov), 3-204 (Ganguly, 43.4 ov), 4-235 (Jadeja, 48.2 ov), 5-247 (Azharuddin, 49.3 ov).

Bowling	O	M	R	W
Pollock	10	0	47	0 (4nb)
Kallis	10	1	43	0 (2w)
Donald	10	0	34	1 (2w)
Klusener	10	0	66	3 (2nb, 2w)
Boje	5	0	31	0 (1w)
Cronje	5	0	24	0

South Africa innings (target: 254 from 50 overs)			R	M	B	4	6
G Kirsten	b Srinath		3	31	22	0	0
HH Gibbs	lbw	b Srinath	7	12	8	1	0
+MV Boucher	b Kumble		34	52	36	4	1
JH Kallis	run out (Prasad/Srinath)		96	178	128	7	0
DJ Cullinan	c Singh	b Ganguly	19	52	35	3	0
*WJ Cronje	c Jadeja	b Agarkar	27	59	30	3	0
JN Rhodes	not out		39	42	31	5	0
L Klusener	not out		12	9	4	3	0
Extras (lb 4, w 3, nb 10): **17**							
Total (6 wickets, 47.2 overs): **254**							

DNB: SM Pollock, N Boje, AA Donald.
FoW: 1-13 (Gibbs, 2.4 ov), 2-22 (Kirsten, 6.5 ov), 3-68 (Boucher, 13.6 ov), 4-116 (Cullinan, 25.4 ov), 5-180 (Cronje, 38.4 ov), 6-227 (Kallis, 45.4 ov).

Bowling	O	M	R	W
Srinath	10	0	69	2 (4nb, 1w)
Prasad	8.2	0	32	0 (1w)
Kumble	10	0	44	1 (1w)
Agarkar	9	0	57	1 (5nb)
Singh	2	0	10	0
Ganguly	4	0	16	1 (1nb)
Tendulkar	4	0	22	0

ICC World Cup, 1999, 3rd Match
Kenya v Zimbabwe, Group A
County Ground, Taunton
15 May 1999 (50-over match)

Result: Zimbabwe won by 5 wickets
Points: Zimbabwe 2, Kenya 0
Toss: Zimbabwe
Umpires: DB Cowie (NZ) and Javed Akhtar (Pak)
TV Umpire: KT Francis (SL)
Match Referee: JR Reid (NZ)
ODI Debut: JK Kamande (Kenya)
Man Of The Match: NC Johnson

Kenya innings (50 overs maximum)

			R	M	B	4	6
+KO Otieno	c GW Flower	b Johnson	16	53	35	2	0
RD Shah	c Strang	b AR Whittall	37	56	43	5	0
SO Tikolo	c A Flower	b Johnson	9	15	17	1	0
MO Odumbe	lbw	b Strang	20	109	57	0	0
HS Modi	b Johnson		7	17	19	1	0
AV Vadher	c AR Whittall	b Strang	54	105	90	5	1
TM Odoyo	b Johnson		28	21	20	2	2
*AY Karim	not out		19	21	19	2	1
AO Suji	not out		3	5	4	0	0

*Extras (b 2, lb 5, w 25, nb 4): **36***
*Total (7 wickets, 50 overs): **229***

DNB: MA Suji, JK Kamande.
FoW: 1-62 (Otieno, 12.5 ov), 2-64 (Shah, 13.1 ov), 3-74 (Tikolo, 16.2 ov), 4-87 (Modi, 20.4 ov), 5-171 (Odumbe, 42.2 ov), 6-181 (Vadher, 44.1 ov), 7-219 (Odoyo, 48.4 ov).

Bowling

	O	M	R	W	
Streak	9	1	50	0 (8w)	
Mbangwa	8	0	37	0 (1nb, 3w)	
Johnson	10	0	42	4 (3nb, 2w)	
AR Whittall	9	0	51	1 (2w)	
GJ Whittall	6	0	20	0 (5w)	
Strang	8	0	22	2	

Zimbabwe innings (target: 230 runs from 50 overs)

			R	M	B	4	6
NC Johnson	c Modi	b Odoyo	59	91	70	7	2
GW Flower	c Shah	b Karim	20	61	33	1	0
PA Strang	c AO Suji	b Odoyo	29	18	21	3	2
MW Goodwin	c Karim	b Odumbe	17	32	22	2	0
+A Flower	c Tikolo	b Odumbe	34	76	46	3	0
*ADR Campbell	not out		33	60	50	5	0
GJ Whittall	not out		11	7	11	1	1

*Extras (lb 5, w 16, nb 7): **28***
*Total (5 wickets, 41 overs): **231***

DNB: SV Carlisle, HH Streak, AR Whittall, M Mbangwa.
FoW: 1-81 (GW Flower, 13.4 ov), 2-119 (Strang, 18.2 ov), 3-123 (Johnson, 20.3 ov), 4-147 (Goodwin, 25.2 ov), 5-213 (A Flower, 38.2 ov).

Bowling

	O	M	R	W	
MA Suji	7	0	47	0 (1nb, 4w)	
AO Suji	6	1	32	0 (1w)	
Odoyo	9	0	40	2 (5nb)	
Kamande	9	0	38	0 (1nb, 3w)	
Karim	3	0	30	1	
Odumbe	7	1	39	2 (3w)	

ICC World Cup, 1999, 7th Match
England v Kenya, Group A
St Lawrence Ground, Canterbury
18 May 1999 (50-over match)

Result: England won by 9 wickets
Points: England 2, Kenya 0
Toss: England
Umpires: KT Francis (SL) and RE Koertzen (SA)
TV Umpire: DB Cowie (NZ)
Match Referee: Talat Ali (Pak)
Man Of The Match: SO Tikolo

Kenya innings (50 overs maximum)			R	M	B	4	6
+KO Otieno	c Thorpe	b Austin	0	13	8	0	0
RD Shah	c Stewart	b Gough	46	102	80	4	0
SO Tikolo	c Gough	b Ealham	71	141	107	8	0
MO Odumbe	b Gough		6	9	13	0	0
HS Modi	run out (Fairbrother)		5	15	11	1	0
AV Vadher	b Croft		6	14	19	1	0
TM Odoyo	not out		34	49	32	3	1
*AY Karim	b Ealham		9	20	17	1	0
AO Suji	b Gough		4	3	5	0	0
M Sheikh	b Gough		7	7	6	1	0
MA Suji	run out (Thorpe)		0	2	3	0	0
Extras (b 1, lb 5, w 6, nb 3): **15**							
Total (all out, 49.4 overs): **203**							

FoW: 1-7 (Otieno, 3.5 ov), 2-107 (Shah, 26.3 ov), 3-115 (Odumbe, 28.6 ov), 4-130 (Modi, 33.1 ov), 5-142 (Vadher, 37.5 ov), 6-150 (Tikolo, 40.1 ov), 7-181 (Karim, 45.4 ov), 8-186 (AO Suji, 46.4 ov), 9-202 (Sheikh, 48.5 ov), 10-203 (MA Suji, 49.4 ov).

Bowling	O	M	R	W	
Gough	10	1	34	4	(1nb, 2w)
Austin	9.4	0	41	1	(2w)
Mullally	10	0	41	0	(2nb, 2w)
Ealham	10	0	49	2	
Croft	10	1	32	1	

England innings (target: 204 runs from 50 overs)		R	M	B	4	6
N Hussain	not out	88	205	127	11	1
*+AJ Stewart	b Odoyo	23	42	26	4	0
GA Hick	not out	61	160	89	9	0
Extras (b 5, lb 6, w 13, nb 8): **32**						
Total (1 wicket, 39 overs): **204**						

DNB: GP Thorpe, NH Fairbrother, A Flintoff, MA Ealham, RDB Croft, ID Austin, D Gough, AD Mullally.
FoW: 1-45 (Stewart, 9.4 ov).

Bowling	O	M	R	W	
MA Suji	9	0	46	0	(4nb, 4w)
AO Suji	3	0	6	0	(2w)
Odoyo	10	0	65	1	(4nb, 2w)
Karim	8	0	39	0	(4w)
Odumbe	6	1	23	0	(1w)
Sheikh	3	0	14	0	

ICC World Cup, 1999, 8th Match
India v Zimbabwe, Group A
Grace Road, Leicester
19 May 1999 (50-over match)

Result: Zimbabwe won by 3 runs
Points: Zimbabwe 2, India 0
Toss: India
Umpires: DL Orchard (SA) and P Willey
TV Umpire: DB Hair (Aus)
Match Referee: CW Smith (WI)
Man Of The Match: GW Flower

Zimbabwe innings (50 overs maximum)			R	M	B	4	6
NC Johnson	c Mongia	b Srinath	7	11	10	1	0
GW Flower	c Mongia	b Jadeja	45	148	89	4	0
PA Strang	b Agarkar		18	32	26	1	0
MW Goodwin	c Singh	b Ganguly	17	51	40	3	0
+A Flower	not out		68	120	85	2	0
*ADR Campbell	st Mongia	b Kumble	24	38	29	3	0
GJ Whittall	b Kumble		4	7	8	0	0
SV Carlisle	b Srinath		1	2	2	0	0
HH Streak	c Mongia	b Prasad	14	14	18	2	0
EA Brandes	c Mongia	b Prasad	2	6	5	0	0
HK Olonga	not out		1	5	4	0	0
Extras (lb 14, w 21, nb 16): **51**							
Total (9 wickets, 50 overs): **252**							

FoW: 1-12 (Johnson, 2.4 ov), 2-45 (Strang, 9.5 ov), 3-87 (Goodwin, 21.2 ov), 4-144 (GW Flower, 31.1 ov), 5-204 (Campbell, 40.3 ov), 6-211 (Whittall, 42.4 ov), 7-214 (Carlisle, 43.2 ov), 8-244 (Streak, 47.6 ov), 9-250 (Brandes, 49.2 ov).

Bowling	O	M	R	W	
Srinath	10	1	35	2 (5nb, 1w)	
Prasad	10	1	37	2 (1nb, 4w)	
Agarkar	9	0	70	1 (5nb, 4w)	
Ganguly	5	0	22	1 (3nb, 1w)	
Singh	2	0	11	0	
Kumble	10	0	41	2 (1nb, 2w)	
Jadeja	4	0	22	1 (3w)	

India innings (target: 253 runs from 46 overs)			R	M	B	4	6
SC Ganguly	c Brandes	b Johnson	9	7	8	2	0
S Ramesh	c Goodwin	b GW Flower	55	134	77	3	1
R Dravid	c GW Flower	b Streak	13	23	14	2	0
*M Azharuddin	c Campbell	b Streak	7	8	11	1	0
A Jadeja	lbw	b Streak	43	108	76	3	0
RR Singh	c Campbell	b Olonga	35	75	47	1	0
AB Agarkar	run out (Goodwin)		1	4	5	0	0
+NR Mongia	b Whittall		28	32	24	2	1
J Srinath	b Olonga		18	21	12	0	2
A Kumble	not out		1	3	1	0	0
BKV Prasad	lbw	b Olonga	0	1	1	0	0
Extras (b 1, lb 4, w 24, nb 10): **39**							
Total (all out, 45 overs): **249**							

FoW: 1-13 (Ganguly, 1.5 ov), 2-44 (Dravid, 6.4 ov), 3-56 (Azharuddin, 8.6 ov), 4-155 (Ramesh, 27.5 ov), 5-174 (Jadeja, 32.2 ov), 6-175 (Agarkar, 33.2 ov), 7-219 (Mongia, 40.5 ov), 8-246 (Singh, 44.2 ov), 9-249 (Srinath, 44.5 ov), 10-249 (Prasad, 44.6 ov).

Bowling	O	M	R	W
Brandes	3	0	27	0 (3w)
Johnson	7	0	51	1 (5nb, 1w)
Streak	9	0	36	3 (1nb, 7w)
Olonga	4	0	22	3 (6w)
Whittall	4	0	26	1 (2w)
Strang	8	0	49	0
GW Flower	10	0	33	1 (1w)

ICC World Cup, 1999, 9th Match
South Africa v Sri Lanka, Group A
County Ground, Northampton
19 May 1999 (50-over match)

Result: South Africa won by 89 runs
Points: South Africa 2, Sri Lanka 0
Toss: Sri Lanka
Umpires: SA Bucknor (WI) and RS Dunne (NZ)
TV Umpire: KE Palmer
Match Referee: JR Reid (NZ)
Man Of The Match: L Klusener

South Africa innings (50 overs maximum)			R	M	B	4	6
G Kirsten	b Vaas		14	17	14	3	0
HH Gibbs	c Kaluwitharana	b Vaas	5	29	15	1	0
+MV Boucher	b Wickramasinghe		1	16	10	0	0
JH Kallis	c Mahanama	b Wickramasinghe	12	42	26	0	0
DJ Cullinan	c Vaas	b Muralitharan	49	117	82	4	0
*WJ Cronje	run out (Jayawardene/Kaluwitharana)		8	27	21	0	0
JN Rhodes	c Jayasuriya	b Muralitharan	17	23	25	2	0
SM Pollock	c & b Muralitharan		2	15	9	0	0
L Klusener	not out		52	69	45	5	2
S Elworthy	c Kaluwitharana	b Vaas	23	40	40	3	0
AA Donald	not out		3	17	16	0	0

Extras (lb 2, w 7, nb 4): **13**
Total (9 wickets, 50 overs): **199**

FoW: 1-22 (Kirsten, 3.3 ov), 2-24 (Gibbs, 5.5 ov), 3-24 (Boucher, 6.3 ov), 4-53 (Kallis, 14.5 ov), 5-69 (Cronje, 20.4 ov), 6-103 (Rhodes, 28.2 ov), 7-115 (Pollock, 32.2 ov), 8-122 (Cullinan, 34.2 ov), 9-166 (Elworthy, 45.3 ov).

Bowling	O	M	R	W	
Wickramasinghe	10	1	45	2 (1nb, 4w)	
Vaas	10	0	46	3 (3nb)	
Jayawardene	10	0	46	0 (1w)	
Muralitharan	10	1	25	3 (1w)	
Chandana	7	0	26	0 (1w)	
Jayasuriya	3	1	9	0	

Sri Lanka innings (target: 200 runs from 50 overs)			R	M	B	4	6
ST Jayasuriya	b Kallis		5	19	14	0	0
+RS Kaluwitharana	c Cullinan	b Kallis	5	16	10	1	0
MS Atapattu	c Boucher	b Kallis	1	10	10	0	0
PA de Silva	lbw	b Pollock	1	13	8	0	0
RS Mahanama	lbw	b Pollock	36	128	71	3	0
*A Ranatunga	c Boucher	b Donald	7	29	19	1	0
DPMD Jayawardene	c Kallis	b Elworthy	22	37	32	4	0
UDU Chandana	c Cullinan	b Klusener	9	23	22	1	0
WPUJC Vaas	c Pollock	b Klusener	1	13	10	0	0
GP Wickramasinghe	b Klusener		6	18	17	0	0
M Muralitharan	not out		0	1	0	0	0

Extras (lb 5, w 10, nb 2): **17**
Total (all out, 35.2 overs): **110**

FoW: 1-12 (Kaluwitharana, 3.3 ov), 2-13 (Jayasuriya, 3.6 ov), 3-14 (Atapattu, 5.5 ov), 4-14 (de Silva, 6.6 ov), 5-31 (Ranatunga, 13.2 ov), 6-66 (Jayawardene, 22.1 ov), 7-87 (Chandana, 27.6 ov), 8-98 (Vaas, 31.1 ov), 9-110 (Mahanama, 34.6 ov), 10-110 (Wickramasinghe, 35.2 ov).

Bowling	O	M	R	W
Pollock	8	3	10	2 (2nb)
Kallis	8	0	26	3 (6w)
Elworthy	8	1	23	1
Donald	6	1	25	1 (3w)
Klusener	5.2	1	21	3

ICC World Cup, 1999, 13th Match
England v South Africa, Group A
Kennington Oval, London
22 May 1999 (50-over match)

Result: South Africa won by 122 runs
Points: South Africa 2, England 0
Toss: England
Umpires: RS Dunne (NZ) and S Venkataraghavan (Ind)
TV Umpire: Javed Akhtar (Pak)
Match Referee: CW Smith (WI)
Man Of The Match: L Klusener

South Africa innings (50 overs maximum)

			R	M	B	4	6
G Kirsten	c Stewart	b Ealham	45	105	62	3	0
HH Gibbs	c Hick	b Ealham	60	99	94	6	1
JH Kallis	b Mullally		0	10	5	0	0
DJ Cullinan	c Fraser	b Mullally	10	23	20	2	0
*WJ Cronje	c Stewart	b Flintoff	16	39	28	0	0
JN Rhodes	c sub (NV Knight)	b Gough	18	38	24	1	0
L Klusener	not out		48	57	40	3	1
SM Pollock	b Gough		0	1	1	0	0
+MV Boucher	not out		16	38	27	0	0

Extras (lb 7, w 5): 12
Total (7 wickets, 50 overs): 225

DNB: S Elworthy, AA Donald.
FoW: 1-111 (Gibbs, 24.6 ov), 2-112 (Kirsten, 26.2 ov), 3-112 (Kallis, 27.2 ov), 4-127 (Cullinan, 31.6 ov), 5-146 (Cronje, 36.5 ov), 6-168 (Rhodes, 40.3 ov), 7-168 (Pollock, 40.4 ov).

Bowling

	O	M	R	W
Gough	10	1	33	2
Fraser	10	0	54	0 (1w)
Mullally	10	1	28	2 (2w)
Croft	2	0	13	0 (1w)
Ealham	10	2	48	2
Flintoff	8	0	42	1 (1w)

England innings (target: 226 runs from 50 overs)

			R	M	B	4	6
N Hussain	c Boucher	b Kallis	2	14	14	0	0
*+AJ Stewart	lbw	b Kallis	0	4	1	0	0
GA Hick	c Gibbs	b Elworthy	21	66	50	2	0
GP Thorpe	lbw	b Donald	14	43	29	1	0
NH Fairbrother	lbw	b Donald	21	107	44	1	0
A Flintoff	c Rhodes	b Donald	0	6	9	0	0
MA Ealham	c Cullinan	b Donald	5	23	17	1	0
RDB Croft	c Rhodes	b Klusener	12	25	25	2	0
D Gough	c Cronje	b Elworthy	10	29	34	1	0
ARC Fraser	c Kirsten	b Pollock	3	22	18	0	0
AD Mullally	not out		1	14	6	0	0

Extras (lb 4, w 9, nb 1): 14
Total (all out, 41 overs): 103

FoW: 1-2 (Stewart, 0.6 ov), 2-6 (Hussain, 2.6 ov), 3-39 (Thorpe, 13.5 ov), 4-44 (Hick, 16.1 ov), 5-45 (Flintoff, 17.5 ov), 6-60 (Ealham, 23.3 ov), 7-78 (Croft, 29.3 ov), 8-97 (Gough, 36.2 ov), 9-99 (Fairbrother, 37.5 ov), 10-103 (Fraser, 40.6 ov).

Bowling

	O	M	R	W
Kallis	8	0	29	2 (6w)
Pollock	9	3	13	1 (1nb)
Elworthy	10	3	24	2 (1w)
Donald	8	1	17	4 (2w)
Klusener	6	0	16	1

ICC World Cup, 1999, 14th Match
Sri Lanka v Zimbabwe, Group A
County Ground, New Road, Worcester
22 May 1999 (50-over match)

Result: Sri Lanka won by 4 wickets
Points: Sri Lanka 2, Zimbabwe 0
Toss: Sri Lanka
Umpires: SA Bucknor (WI) and DR Shepherd
TV Umpire: MJ Kitchen
Match Referee: Talat Ali (Pak)
Man Of The Match: MS Atapattu

Zimbabwe innings (50 overs maximum)			R	M	B	4	6
NC Johnson	c Wickramasinghe	b Upashantha	8	36	17	1	0
GW Flower	c Kaluwitharana	b Wickramasinghe	42	100	69	6	0
PA Strang	b Wickramasinghe		5	12	8	1	0
MW Goodwin	run out (Jayasuriya/Muralitharan)		21	39	29	2	0
+A Flower	c Kaluwitharana	b Jayasuriya	41	80	60	3	0
*ADR Campbell	c Kaluwitharana	b Wickramasinghe	6	7	8	1	0
GJ Whittall	c Ranatunga	b Muralitharan	4	9	11	1	0
SV Carlisle	run out (Vaas/Jayasuriya)		27	52	36	1	1
HH Streak	c Atapattu	b Muralitharan	10	23	23	0	0
EA Brandes	not out		19	35	29	1	1
HK Olonga	not out		5	11	10	1	0
Extras (lb 3, w 6): **9**							
Total (9 wickets, 50 overs): **197**							

FoW: 1-21 (Johnson, 7.3 ov), 2-34 (Strang, 10.5 ov), 3-78 (Goodwin, 19.2 ov), 4-81 (GW Flower, 20.4 ov), 5-89 (Campbell, 22.4 ov), 6-94 (Whittall, 25.5 ov), 7-162 (Carlisle, 39.3 ov), 8-162 (A Flower, 39.4 ov), 9-176 (Streak, 46.6 ov).

Bowling	O	M	R	W
Vaas	10	1	47	0 (1w)
Upashantha	10	1	43	1 (4w)
Wickramasinghe	10	1	30	3
Jayawardene	1	0	8	0
Muralitharan	10	2	29	2 (1w)
Jayasuriya	7	0	28	1
de Silva	2	0	9	0

Sri Lanka innings (target: 198 runs from 50 overs)			R	M	B	4	6
ST Jayasuriya	c Goodwin	b Johnson	6	22	17	0	0
RS Mahanama	b Whittall		31	84	64	3	0
MS Atapattu	c Campbell	b Streak	54	141	90	4	0
PA de Silva	c sub (AR Whittall)	b Whittall	6	25	15	0	0
*A Ranatunga	c & b Whittall		3	18	12	0	0
DPMD Jayawardene	lbw	b Streak	31	40	36	4	0
+RS Kaluwitharana	not out		18	43	30	2	0
WPUJC Vaas	not out		17	32	17	2	0
Extras (lb 6, w 21, nb 5): **32**							
Total (6 wickets, 46 overs): **198**							

DNB: KEA Upashantha, GP Wickramasinghe, M Muralitharan.
FoW: 1-13 (Jayasuriya, 5.4 ov), 2-75 (Mahanama, 19.1 ov), 3-93 (de Silva, 25.2 ov), 4-108 (Ranatunga, 29.2 ov), 5-150 (Atapattu, 36.3 ov), 6-157 (Jayawardene, 38.5 ov).

Bowling	O	M	R	W
Brandes	8	0	28	0 (2w)
Johnson	7	1	29	1 (5w)
Streak	8	1	30	2 (6w)
Whittall	10	1	35	3 (1nb, 2w)
Olonga	9	0	50	0 (4nb, 3w)
GW Flower	2	0	10	0
Strang	2	0	10	0

ICC World Cup, 1999, 15th Match
India v Kenya, Group A
County Ground, Bristol
23 May 1999 (50-over match)

Result: India won by 94 runs
Points: India 2, Kenya 0
Toss: Kenya
Umpires: DB Cowie (NZ) and ID Robinson (Zim)
TV Umpire: JW Holder
Match Referee: PJP Burge (Aus)
Man Of The Match: SR Tendulkar

India innings (50 overs maximum)			R	M	B	4	6
S Ramesh	run out (Tikolo)		44	97	66	7	0
SC Ganguly	lbw	b Suji	13	53	26	3	0
R Dravid	not out		104	158	109	10	0
SR Tendulkar	not out		140	114	101	16	3
Extras (lb 5, w 21, nb 2): **28**							
Total (2 wickets, 50 overs): **329**							

DNB: *M Azharuddin, A Jadeja, +NR Mongia, N Chopra, AB Agarkar, J Srinath, DS Mohanty.
FoW: 1-50 (Ganguly, 10.4 ov), 2-92 (Ramesh, 20.5 ov).

Bowling	O	M	R	W
Suji	10	2	26	1 (3w)
Angara	7	0	66	0 (1nb, 6w)
Odoyo	9	0	59	0 (1nb, 2w)
Tikolo	9	1	62	0 (2w)
Karim	7	0	52	0 (5w)
Odumbe	8	0	59	0

Kenya innings (target: 330 runs from 50 overs)			R	M	B	4	6
+KO Otieno	c Agarkar	b Chopra	56	120	82	5	0
RD Shah	c sub (RR Singh)	b Mohanty	9	49	29	1	0
SK Gupta	lbw	b Mohanty	0	1	1	0	0
SO Tikolo	lbw	b Mohanty	58	88	75	6	1
MO Odumbe	c sub (RR Singh)	b Mohanty	14	47	28	1	0
TM Odoyo	b Agarkar		39	64	55	2	2
*AY Karim	b Srinath		8	17	15	1	0
AV Vadher	not out		6	22	13	1	0
MA Suji	not out		1	2	4	0	0
Extras (lb 10, w 31, nb 3): **44**							
Total (7 wickets, 50 overs): **235**							

DNB: HS Modi, JO Angara.
FoW: 1-29 (Shah, 11.1 ov), 2-29 (Gupta, 11.2 ov), 3-147 (Otieno, 27.6 ov), 4-165 (Tikolo, 32.3 ov), 5-193 (Odumbe, 40.2 ov), 6-209 (Karim, 44.4 ov), 7-233 (Odoyo, 49.1 ov).

Bowling	O	M	R	W
Srinath	10	3	31	1 (4w)
Agarkar	10	0	35	1 (1nb, 7w)
Mohanty	10	0	56	4 (1nb)
Ganguly	9	0	47	0 (1nb, 3w)
Chopra	10	2	33	1 (2w)
Tendulkar	1	0	23	0 (2w)

ICC World Cup, 1999, 19th Match
England v Zimbabwe, Group A
Trent Bridge, Nottingham
25 May 1999 (50-over match)

Result: England won by 7 wickets
Points: England 2, Zimbabwe 0
Toss: England
Umpires: SA Bucknor (WI) and DB Hair (Aus)
TV Umpire: RE Koertzen (SA)
Match Referee: Talat Ali (Pak)
Man Of The Match: AD Mullally

Zimbabwe innings (50 overs maximum)			R	M	B	4	6
NC Johnson	b Gough		6	23	12	0	0
GW Flower	c Thorpe	b Ealham	35	119	90	4	0
PA Strang	c Hick	b Mullally	0	21	17	0	0
MW Goodwin	c Thorpe	b Mullally	4	21	18	0	0
+A Flower	run out (Hussain)		10	36	24	0	0
*ADR Campbell	c Stewart	b Fraser	24	49	35	2	0
GJ Whittall	lbw	b Ealham	28	65	51	3	0
SV Carlisle	c Fraser	b Gough	14	40	38	2	0
HH Streak	not out		11	21	13	1	0
HK Olonga	not out		1	4	3	0	0
Extras (lb 16, w 17, nb 1): **34**							
Total (8 wickets, 50 overs): **167**							

DNB: M Mbangwa.
FoW: 1-21 (Johnson, 6.1 ov), 2-29 (Strang, 11.5 ov), 3-47 (Goodwin, 17.3 ov), 4-79 (A Flower, 26.2 ov), 5-86 (GW Flower, 28.1 ov), 6-124 (Campbell, 38.1 ov), 7-141 (Whittall, 44.3 ov), 8-159 (Carlisle, 48.5 ov).

Bowling	O	M	R	W	
Gough	10	2	24	2 (3w)	
Fraser	10	0	27	1 (1nb, 2w)	
Mullally	10	4	16	2 (4w)	
Ealham	10	1	35	2 (1w)	
Flintoff	3	0	14	0 (5w)	
Hollioake	7	0	35	0 (2w)	

England innings (target: 168 runs from 50 overs)			R	M	B	4	6
N Hussain	not out		57	164	93	7	0
*+AJ Stewart	c Goodwin	b Johnson	12	35	31	1	0
GA Hick	c A Flower	b Mbangwa	4	14	11	0	0
GP Thorpe	c Campbell	b Mbangwa	62	92	80	7	0
NH Fairbrother	not out		7	15	23	0	0
Extras (lb 3, w 16, nb 7): **26**							
Total (3 wickets, 38.3 overs): **168**							

DNB: A Flintoff, AJ Hollioake, MA Ealham, D Gough, ARC Fraser, AD Mullally.
FoW: 1-21 (Stewart, 8.3 ov), 2-36 (Hick, 11.2 ov), 3-159 (Thorpe, 33.3 ov).

Bowling	O	M	R	W	
Johnson	7	2	20	1 (3nb)	
Streak	8	0	37	0 (8w)	
Mbangwa	7	1	28	2 (2w)	
Whittall	4	0	23	0 (2w)	
Olonga	3	0	27	0 (4nb, 4w)	
Strang	9.3	1	30	0	

ICC World Cup, 1999, 20th Match
Kenya v South Africa, Group A
VRA Ground, Amstelveen
26 May 1999 (50-over match)

Result: South Africa won by 7 wickets
Points: South Africa 2, Kenya 0
Toss: South Africa
Umpires: DB Cowie (NZ) and P Willey (Eng)
TV Umpire: DJ Constant (Eng)
Match Referee: R Subba Row (Eng)
Man Of The Match: L Klusener

Kenya innings (50 overs maximum)			R	M	B	4	6
+KO Otieno	lbw	b Elworthy	26	59	42	3	0
RD Shah	c Boucher	b Donald	50	76	64	7	0
SK Gupta	b Elworthy		1	11	7	0	0
SO Tikolo	c Cronje	b Klusener	10	50	35	0	0
MO Odumbe	b Donald		7	16	15	1	0
AV Vadher	c & b Klusener		2	37	24	0	0
TM Odoyo	lbw	b Klusener	0	1	1	0	0
*AY Karim	lbw	b Cronje	22	46	40	2	0
M Sheikh	b Klusener		8	43	26	0	0
MA Suji	not out		6	11	10	1	0
JO Angara	b Klusener		6	7	5	1	0

Extras (lb 5, w 7, nb 2): **14**
Total (all out, 44.3 overs): **152**

FoW: 1-66 (Otieno, 15.2 ov), 2-80 (Gupta, 17.6 ov), 3-82 (Shah, 18.3 ov), 4-91 (Odumbe, 22.5 ov), 5-104 (Tikolo, 30.3 ov), 6-104 (Odoyo, 30.4 ov), 7-107 (Vadher, 32.1 ov), 8-138 (Karim, 41.4 ov), 9-140 (Sheikh, 42.2 ov), 10-152 (Angara, 44.3 ov).

Bowling	O	M	R	W	
Pollock	8	1	22	0	(1nb, 1w)
Kallis	8	0	37	0	(1w)
Donald	8	1	42	2	(1nb, 3w)
Elworthy	10	2	20	2	(1w)
Klusener	8.3	3	21	5	
Cronje	2	0	5	1	(1w)

South Africa innings (target: 153 from 50 overs)			R	M	B	4	6
G Kirsten	b Odumbe		27	88	71	3	0
HH Gibbs	lbw	b Odoyo	38	38	38	4	1
+MV Boucher	c Sheikh	b Angara	3	9	6	0	0
JH Kallis	not out		44	100	81	4	1
DJ Cullinan	not out		35	60	51	3	2

Extras (b 4, w 1, nb 1): **6**
Total (3 wickets, 41 overs): **153**

DNB: JN Rhodes, L Klusener, SM Pollock, *WJ Cronje, S Elworthy, AA Donald.
FoW: 1-55 (Gibbs, 10.6 ov), 2-58 (Boucher, 13.3 ov), 3-86 (Kirsten, 22.5 ov).

Bowling	O	M	R	W	
Suji	6	0	18	0	(1nb)
Karim	7	0	43	0	(1w)
Angara	8	1	34	1	
Odoyo	9	3	18	1	
Sheikh	4	0	21	0	
Odumbe	7	1	15	1	

ICC World Cup, 1999, 21st Match
India v Sri Lanka, Group A
County Ground, Taunton
26 May 1999 (50-over match)

Result: India won by 157 runs
Points: India 2, Sri Lanka 0
Toss: Sri Lanka
Umpires: RS Dunne (NZ) and DR Shepherd
TV Umpire: R Julian
Match Referee: CW Smith (WI)
Man Of The Match: SC Ganguly

India innings (50 overs maximum)		R	M	B	4	6
S Ramesh	b Vaas	5	3	4	1	0
SC Ganguly	c sub (UDU Chandana) b Wickramasinghe	183	230	158	17	7
+R Dravid	run out (Muralitharan)	145	179	129	17	1
SR Tendulkar	b Jayasuriya	2	10	3	0	0
A Jadeja	c & b Wickramasinghe	5	15	4	0	0
RR Singh	c de Silva b Wickramasinghe	0	1	1	0	0
*M Azharuddin	not out	12	8	7	0	1
J Srinath	not out	0	2	0	0	0
Extras (lb 3, w 12, nb 6): **21**						
Total (6 wickets, 50 overs): **373**						

DNB: A Kumble, BKV Prasad, DS Mohanty.
FoW: 1-6 (Ramesh, 0.5 ov), 2-324 (Dravid, 45.4 ov), 3-344 (Tendulkar, 46.5 ov), 4-349 (Jadeja, 47.3 ov), 5-349 (Singh, 47.4 ov), 6-372 (Ganguly, 49.5 ov).

Bowling	O	M	R	W
Vaas	10	0	84	1 (3nb, 1w)
Upashantha	10	0	80	0 (3nb, 3w)
Wickramasinghe	10	0	65	3 (1w)
Muralitharan	10	0	60	0 (2w)
Jayawardene	3	0	21	0
Jayasuriya	3	0	37	1 (2w)
de Silva	4	0	23	0 (1w)

Sri Lanka innings (target: 374 runs from 50 overs)			R	M	B	4	6
ST Jayasuriya	run out (Srinath)		3	10	7	0	0
+RS Kaluwitharana	lbw	b Srinath	7	20	15	1	0
MS Atapattu	lbw	b Mohanty	29	50	29	5	0
PA de Silva	lbw	b Singh	56	105	74	7	0
DPMD Jayawardene	lbw	b Kumble	4	4	5	1	0
*A Ranatunga	b Singh		42	83	57	7	0
RS Mahanama	run out (Tendulkar)		32	56	45	3	0
WPUJC Vaas	c Ramesh	b Singh	1	4	4	0	0
KEA Upashantha	c Azharuddin	b Singh	5	13	17	0	0
GP Wickramasinghe	not out		2	7	6	0	0
M Muralitharan	c Tendulkar	b Singh	4	4	3	1	0
Extras (b 4, lb 12, w 8, nb 7): **31**							
Total (all out, 42.3 overs): **216**							

FoW: 1-5 (Jayasuriya, 2.1 ov), 2-23 (Kaluwitharana, 4.3 ov), 3-74 (Atapattu, 14.2 ov), 4-79 (Jayawardene, 15.3 ov), 5-147 (de Silva, 28.1 ov), 6-181 (Ranatunga, 34.3 ov), 7-187 (Vaas, 36.4 ov), 8-203 (Upashantha, 40.6 ov), 9-204 (Mahanama, 41.3 ov), 10-216 (Muralitharan, 42.3 ov).

Bowling	O	M	R	W
Srinath	7	0	33	1 (1nb, 2w)
Prasad	8	0	41	0
Mohanty	5	0	31	1
Kumble	8	0	27	1 (2w)
Ganguly	5	0	37	0 (2nb, 1w)
Singh	9.3	0	31	5 (4nb, 2w)

ICC World Cup, 1999, 25th Match
England v India, Group A
Edgbaston, Birmingham
29/30 May 1999 (50-over match)

Result: India won by 63 runs
Points: India 2, England 0
Toss: England
Umpires: DB Hair (Aus) and Javed Akhtar (Pak)
TV Umpire: DB Cowie (NZ)
Match Referee: PJP Burge (Aus)
Man Of The Match: SC Ganguly

Close Of Play

Day 1: India 232/8, England 73/3 (Thorpe 31*, Fairbrother 1*; 20.3 ov)

India innings (50 overs maximum)			R	M	B	4	6
SC Ganguly	run out (Ealham)		40	99	59	6	0
S Ramesh	c Hick	b Mullally	20	57	41	2	0
R Dravid	c Ealham	b Flintoff	53	116	82	6	0
SR Tendulkar	c Hick	b Ealham	22	49	40	2	0
*M Azharuddin	c Hussain	b Ealham	26	37	35	3	0
A Jadeja	c Fraser	b Gough	39	39	30	5	0
+NR Mongia	b Mullally		2	11	5	0	0
J Srinath	b Gough		1	2	2	0	0
A Kumble	not out		6	11	8	0	0
BKV Prasad	not out		2	1	3	0	0

Extras (lb 7, w 10, nb 4): 21
Total (8 wickets, 50 overs): 232

DNB: DS Mohanty.
FoW: 1-49 (Ramesh, 12.5 ov), 2-93 (Ganguly, 21.2 ov), 3-139 (Tendulkar, 33.3 ov), 4-174 (Dravid, 39.5 ov), 5-188 (Azharuddin, 43.5 ov), 6-209 (Mongia, 46.4 ov), 7-210 (Srinath, 47.1 ov), 8-228 (Jadeja, 49.1 ov).

Bowling	O	M	R	W	
Gough	10	0	51	2	(2nb, 3w)
Fraser	10	2	30	0	(2w)
Mullally	10	0	54	2	(1nb, 4w)
Ealham	10	2	28	2	(1nb, 1w)
Flintoff	5	0	28	1	
Hollioake	5	0	34	0	

England innings (target: 233 runs from 50 overs)			R	M	B	4	6
N Hussain	b Ganguly		33	89	63	3	0
*+AJ Stewart	c Azharuddin	b Mohanty	2	14	9	0	0
GA Hick	b Mohanty		0	1	1	0	0
GP Thorpe	lbw	b Srinath	36	92	57	7	0
NH Fairbrother	c Mongia	b Ganguly	29	93	62	2	0
A Flintoff	lbw	b Kumble	15	34	21	1	1
AJ Hollioake	lbw	b Kumble	6	15	13	0	0
MA Ealham	c Azharuddin	b Ganguly	0	3	3	0	0
D Gough	c Kumble	b Prasad	19	28	25	1	0
ARC Fraser	not out		15	27	17	3	0
AD Mullally	b Srinath		0	4	2	0	0

Extras (b 4, lb 4, w 5, nb 1): 14
Total (all out, 45.2 overs): 169

FoW: 1-12 (Stewart, 3.1 ov), 2-13 (Hick, 3.2 ov), 3-72 (Hussain, 19.1 ov), 4-81 (Thorpe, 23.4 ov), 5-118 (Flintoff, 31.3 ov), 6-130 (Hollioake, 35.5 ov), 7-131 (Ealham, 36.5 ov), 8-132 (Fairbrother, 38.4 ov), 9-161 (Gough, 44.1 ov), 10-169 (Mullally, 45.2 ov).

Bowling	O	M	R	W
Srinath	8.2	3	25	2
Mohanty	10	0	54	2 (1nb, 5w)
Prasad	9	1	25	1
Ganguly	8	0	27	3
Kumble	10	1	30	2

ICC World Cup, 1999, 26th Match
South Africa v Zimbabwe, Group A
County Ground, Chelmsford
29 May 1999 (50-over match)

Result: Zimbabwe won by 48 runs
Points: Zimbabwe 2, South Africa 0
Toss: Zimbabwe
Umpires: DR Shepherd and S Venkataraghavan (Ind)
TV Umpire: JW Holder
Match Referee: R Subba Row
Man Of The Match: NC Johnson

Zimbabwe innings (50 overs maximum)			R	M	B	4	6
NC Johnson	c Pollock	b Donald	76	159	117	10	0
GW Flower	c Cullinan	b Elworthy	19	55	43	3	0
MW Goodwin	c Kirsten	b Klusener	34	70	45	5	0
+A Flower	run out (Pollock/Boucher)		29	47	35	3	1
*ADR Campbell	lbw	b Donald	0	2	1	0	0
GJ Whittall	c Cullinan	b Donald	20	33	31	0	1
SV Carlisle	not out		18	36	19	1	0
HH Streak	not out		9	15	13	1	0
Extras (b 1, lb 15, w 8, nb 4): **28**							
Total (6 wickets, 50 overs): **233**							

DNB: AR Whittall, AG Huckle, HK Olonga.
FoW: 1-65 (GW Flower, 13.4 ov), 2-131 (Goodwin, 30.4 ov), 3-170 (Johnson, 38.1 ov), 4-175 (Campbell, 38.4 ov), 5-186 (A Flower, 41.3 ov), 6-214 (GJ Whittall, 46.4 ov).

Bowling	O	M	R	W	
Pollock	10	1	39	0	(2nb)
Kallis	6	0	36	0	(1nb, 2w)
Donald	10	1	41	3	(1w)
Elworthy	6	0	32	1	(1w)
Klusener	9	0	36	1	(1nb, 1w)
Cronje	9	0	33	0	(2w)

South Africa innings (target: 234 from 50 overs)			R	M	B	4	6
G Kirsten	c AR Whittall	b Johnson	0	1	1	0	0
HH Gibbs	run out (Huckle/A Flower)		9	31	21	0	0
+MV Boucher	lbw	b Streak	8	34	23	1	0
JH Kallis	c A Flower	b Johnson	0	9	4	0	0
DJ Cullinan	c & b AR Whittall		29	87	67	3	0
*WJ Cronje	b Johnson		4	8	6	1	0
JN Rhodes	lbw	b Streak	5	7	5	1	0
SM Pollock	c Olonga	b AR Whittall	52	114	81	4	0
L Klusener	not out		52	76	58	3	2
S Elworthy	c AR Whittall	b Streak	1	5	6	0	0
AA Donald	c Streak	b Olonga	7	22	18	0	0
Extras (b 2, lb 1, w 8, nb 7): **18**							
Total (all out, 47.2 overs): **185**							

FoW: 1-0 (Kirsten, 0.1 ov), 2-24 (Gibbs, 6.4 ov), 3-25 (Boucher, 7.3 ov), 4-25 (Kallis, 8.2 ov), 5-34 (Cronje, 10.1 ov), 6-40 (Rhodes, 11.4 ov), 7-106 (Cullinan, 29.2 ov), 8-149 (Pollock, 41.2 ov), 9-150 (Elworthy, 42.2 ov), 10-185 (Donald, 47.2 ov).

Bowling	O	M	R	W	
Johnson	8	1	27	3	(3nb, 3w)
Streak	9	1	35	3	(1nb, 4w)
GJ Whittall	4	0	20	0	(1w)
Olonga	4.2	0	17	1	(2nb)
Huckle	10	1	35	0	
AR Whittall	10	0	41	2	
GW Flower	2	0	7	0	

ICC World Cup, 1999, 27th Match
Kenya v Sri Lanka, Group A
County Ground, Southampton
30 May 1999 (50-over match)

Result: Sri Lanka won by 45 runs
Points: Sri Lanka 2, Kenya 0
Toss: Kenya
Umpires: DL Orchard (SA) and P Willey
TV Umpire: B Dudleston
Match Referee: Talat Ali (Pak)
Man Of The Match: MO Odumbe

Sri Lanka innings (50 overs maximum)			R	M	B	4	6
ST Jayasuriya	lbw	b Odoyo	39	68	50	5	1
RS Mahanama	b Odoyo		21	77	45	2	0
MS Atapattu	c Otieno	b Angara	52	105	67	3	0
PA de Silva	c Suji	b Odoyo	10	14	19	2	0
*A Ranatunga	run out (Angara)		50	74	61	4	0
UDU Chandana	c Otieno	b Kamande	0	1	1	0	0
DPMD Jayawardene	c Shah	b Suji	45	43	33	7	0
+RS Kaluwitharana	c Chudasama	b Angara	3	5	5	0	0
WPUJC Vaas	not out		29	31	22	1	2
GP Wickramasinghe	not out		0	1	0	0	0
Extras (lb 7, w 16, nb 3): **26**							
Total (8 wickets, 50 overs): **275**							

DNB: M Muralitharan.
FoW: 1-72 (Jayasuriya, 14.6 ov), 2-74 (Mahanama, 16.2 ov), 3-87 (de Silva, 20.3 ov), 4-191 (Ranatunga, 39.3 ov), 5-191 (Chandana, 39.4 ov), 6-199 (Atapattu, 40.5 ov), 7-209 (Kaluwitharana, 42.2 ov), 8-273 (Jayawardene, 49.5 ov).

Bowling	O	M	R	W	
Suji	9	1	58	1 (2nb, 2w)	
Angara	10	0	50	2 (1nb, 1w)	
Odoyo	10	2	56	3 (2w)	
Karim	10	0	35	0 (1w)	
Kamande	9	0	51	1 (3w)	
Odumbe	2	0	18	0 (1w)	

Kenya innings (target: 276 runs from 50 overs)			R	M	B	4	6
+KO Otieno	lbw	b Vaas	0	1	2	0	0
RD Shah	c Muralitharan	b Jayawardene	12	61	40	1	0
DN Chudasama	b Vaas		3	25	24	0	0
SO Tikolo	lbw	b Wickramasinghe	19	21	17	4	0
*AY Karim	lbw	b Jayawardene	4	26	16	1	0
MO Odumbe	b Jayasuriya		82	111	95	7	0
AV Vadher	not out		73	104	98	6	0
TM Odoyo	not out		16	8	9	2	1
Extras (b 4, lb 8, w 8, nb 1): **21**							
Total (6 wickets, 50 overs): **230**							

DNB: MA Suji, JO Angara, JK Kamande.
FoW: 1-0 (Otieno, 0.2 ov), 2-10 (Chudasama, 6.6 ov), 3-33 (Tikolo, 11.6 ov), 4-36 (Shah, 14.1 ov), 5-52 (Karim, 18.3 ov), 6-213 (Odumbe, 47.4 ov).

Bowling	O	M	R	W	
Vaas	7	1	26	2	
Wickramasinghe	9	1	27	1 (1w)	
Jayawardene	10	0	56	2 (2w)	
Muralitharan	3	0	11	0	
Chandana	1	0	13	0	
Jayasuriya	10	1	39	1 (1nb, 3w)	
de Silva	10	0	46	0	

1999 WORLD CUP

Group B

ICC World Cup, 1999, 4th Match
Australia v Scotland, Group B
County Ground, New Road, Worcester
16 May 1999 (50-over match)

Result: Australia won by 6 wickets
Points: Australia 2, Scotland 0
Toss: Australia
Umpires: RS Dunne (NZ) and P Willey
TV Umpire: G Sharp
Match Referee: RS Madugalle (SL)
ODI Debuts: MJD Allingham, Asim Butt, JAR Blain, JE Brinkley, AG Davies, NR Dyer, GM
  Hamilton, BMW Patterson, IL Philip, G Salmond, MJ Smith (Scot)
Man Of The Match: ME Waugh

Scotland innings (50 overs maximum)			R	M	B	4	6
BMW Patterson	c Gilchrist	b Fleming	10	40	36	2	0
IL Philip	c SR Waugh	b McGrath	17	98	66	0	0
MJD Allingham	st Gilchrist	b Warne	3	34	28	0	0
MJ Smith	c Bevan	b Lee	13	56	32	1	0
*G Salmond	c Gilchrist	b SR Waugh	31	56	54	2	0
GM Hamilton	b Warne		34	62	42	3	0
JE Brinkley	c Dale	b Warne	23	38	32	3	0
+AG Davies	not out		8	12	11	0	0
JAR Blain	not out		3	9	7	0	0

Extras (lb 9, w 22, nb 8): **39**
Total (7 wickets, 50 overs): **181**

DNB: Asim Butt, NR Dyer.
FoW: 1-19 (Patterson, 10.5 ov), 2-37 (Allingham, 17.6 ov), 3-52 (Philip, 22.5 ov), 4-87 (Smith, 32.1 ov), 5-105 (Salmond, 37.1 ov), 6-167 (Brinkley, 46.4 ov), 7-169 (Hamilton, 46.6 ov).

Bowling	O	M	R	W	
Fleming	9	2	19	1	
Dale	10	2	35	0	(3nb, 7w)
McGrath	9	0	32	1	(5nb, 6w)
Warne	10	0	39	3	(2w)
Lee	6	1	25	1	(3w)
SR Waugh	6	0	22	1	(4w)

Australia innings (target: 182 runs from 50 overs)			R	M	B	4	6
+AC Gilchrist	c Philip	b Asim Butt	6	21	16	1	0
ME Waugh	c & b Dyer		67	144	114	5	0
RT Ponting	c Allingham	b Blain	33	87	62	3	0
DS Lehmann	b Dyer		0	1	2	0	0
*SR Waugh	not out		49	68	69	7	0
MG Bevan	not out		11	37	14	1	0

Extras (lb 3, w 4, nb 9): **16**
Total (4 wickets, 44.5 overs): **182**

DNB: S Lee, SK Warne, DW Fleming, AC Dale, GD McGrath.
FoW: 1-17 (Gilchrist, 5.2 ov), 2-101 (Ponting, 26.6 ov), 3-101 (Lehmann, 27.2 ov), 4-141 (ME Waugh, 35.5 ov).

Bowling	O	M	R	W	
Blain	8	0	35	1	(5nb, 1w)
Asim Butt	10	3	21	1	(1nb, 1w)
Brinkley	8	0	43	0	
Hamilton	8.5	0	37	0	(2nb, 2w)
Dyer	10	1	43	2	

ICC World Cup, 1999, 5th Match
Pakistan v West Indies, Group B
County Ground, Bristol
16 May 1999 (50-over match)

Result: Pakistan won by 27 runs
Points: Pakistan 2, West Indies 0
Toss: Pakistan
Umpires: DB Hair (Aus) and DL Orchard (SA)
TV Umpire: KE Palmer
Match Referee: R Subba Row
ODI Debut: RL Powell (WI)
Man Of The Match: Azhar Mahmood

Pakistan innings (50 overs maximum)			R	M	B	4	6
Saeed Anwar	c Lara	b Walsh	10	32	31	2	0
Shahid Afridi	c Jacobs	b Walsh	11	27	19	1	0
Abdur Razzaq	b Dillon		7	35	34	1	0
Ijaz Ahmed	lbw	b Dillon	36	84	70	4	0
Inzamam-ul-Haq	c Jacobs	b Dillon	0	1	1	0	0
Yousuf Youhana	c & b Simmons		34	78	53	2	0
Azhar Mahmood	c sub (NO Perry)	b Ambrose	37	67	51	1	2
*Wasim Akram	b Walsh		43	44	29	4	2
+Moin Khan	not out		11	11	10	0	0
Saqlain Mushtaq	not out		2	4	3	0	0
Extras (b 1, lb 12, w 23, nb 2): **38**							
Total (8 wickets, 50 overs): **229**							

DNB: Shoaib Akhtar.
FoW: 1-22 (Shahid Afridi, 7.6 ov), 2-23 (Saeed Anwar, 9.2 ov), 3-42 (Abdur Razzaq, 18.3 ov), 4-42 (Inzamam-ul-Haq, 18.4 ov), 5-102 (Ijaz Ahmed, 30.1 ov), 6-135 (Yousuf Youhana, 38.3 ov), 7-209 (Azhar Mahmood, 47.3 ov), 8-217 (Wasim Akram, 48.5 ov).

Bowling	O	M	R	W	
Ambrose	10	1	36	1 (1nb)	
Walsh	10	3	28	3 (1nb)	
Dillon	10	1	29	3 (10w)	
Simmons	10	0	40	1 (4w)	
Arthurton	1	0	10	0	
Adams	8	0	57	0 (3w)	
Powell	1	0	16	0 (1w)	

West Indies innings (target: 230 from 50 overs)			R	M	B	4	6
SL Campbell	b Shoaib Akhtar		9	12	14	0	1
+RD Jacobs	c Inzamam-ul-Haq	b Abdur Razzaq	25	103	53	3	1
JC Adams	c Inzamam-ul-Haq	b Azhar Mahmood	23	59	45	4	0
*BC Lara	c sub (M Ahmed)	b Abdur Razzaq	11	8	9	2	0
S Chanderpaul	c Yousuf Youhana	b Shoaib Akhtar	77	147	96	6	0
RL Powell	c Yousuf Youhana	b Saqlain Mushtaq	4	38	18	0	0
PV Simmons	c Moin Khan	b Azhar Mahmood	5	20	16	0	0
CEL Ambrose	c Moin Khan	b Abdur Razzaq	1	5	9	0	0
KLT Arthurton	c Saeed Anwar	b Azhar Mahmood	6	17	14	0	0
M Dillon	run out (Shoaib Akhtar)		6	32	23	0	0
CA Walsh	not out		0	4	1	0	0
Extras (b 1, lb 8, w 20, nb 6): **35**							
Total (all out, 48.5 overs): **202**							

FoW: 1-14 (Campbell, 3.2 ov), 2-72 (Adams, 16.1 ov), 3-84 (Lara, 18.2 ov), 4-101 (Jacobs, 22.2 ov), 5-121 (Powell, 29.4 ov), 6-141 (Simmons, 35.2 ov), 7-142 (Ambrose, 36.6 ov), 8-161 (Arthurton, 41.1 ov), 9-195 (Dillon, 48.1 ov), 10-202 (Chanderpaul, 48.5 ov).

Bowling	O	M	R	W	
Wasim Akram	10	3	37	0 (3nb, 6w)	
Shoaib Akhtar	9.5	1	54	2 (3w)	
Saqlain Mushtaq	9	0	22	1 (1w)	
Azhar Mahmood	10	0	48	3 (5w)	
Abdur Razzaq	10	3	32	3 (3nb, 4w)	

ICC World Cup, 1999, 6th Match
Bangladesh v New Zealand, Group B
County Ground, Chelmsford
17 May 1999 (50-over match)

Result: New Zealand won by 6 wickets
Points: New Zealand 2, Bangladesh 0
Toss: New Zealand
Umpires: ID Robinson (Zim) and S Venkataraghavan (Ind)
TV Umpire: DR Shepherd
Match Referee: PJP Burge (Aus)
Man Of The Match: GR Larsen

Bangladesh innings (50 overs maximum)			R	M	B	4	6
Shahriar Hossain	lbw	b Allott	0	2	3	0	0
Mehrab Hossain	lbw	b Allott	2	10	4	0	0
Akram Khan	c & b Larsen		16	56	33	2	0
*Aminul Islam	b Cairns		15	43	41	2	0
+Khaled Mashud	b Larsen		4	22	15	0	0
Naimur Rahman	lbw	b Larsen	18	72	51	0	0
Khaled Mahmud	c Twose	b Cairns	3	7	7	0	0
Mohammad Rafique	lbw	b Cairns	0	5	1	0	0
Enamul Haque	b Harris		19	60	41	3	0
Hasibul Hossain	c Horne	b Allott	16	34	28	1	1
Manjural Islam	not out		6	17	6	0	0

Extras (lb 4, w 5, nb 8): **17**
Total (all out, 37.4 overs): **116**

FoW: 1-0 (Shahriar Hossain, 0.3 ov), 2-7 (Mehrab Hossain, 2.3 ov), 3-38 (Aminul Islam, 12.4 ov), 4-38 (Akram Khan, 13.3 ov), 5-46 (Khaled Mashud, 17.2 ov), 6-49 (Khaled Mahmud, 18.6 ov), 7-51 (Mohammad Rafique, 20.1 ov), 8-85 (Naimur Rahman, 29.5 ov), 9-96 (Enamul Haque, 33.5 ov), 10-116 (Hasibul Hossain, 37.4 ov).

Bowling	O	M	R	W	
Allott	8.4	0	30	3 (1nb, 3w)	
Nash	10	1	30	0 (1nb)	
Cairns	7	1	19	3 (1nb, 1w)	
Larsen	10	0	19	3 (1nb, 1w)	
Harris	2	0	14	1	

New Zealand innings (target: 117 from 50 overs)			R	M	B	4	6
MJ Horne	lbw	b Naimur Rahman	35	116	86	4	0
NJ Astle	c Aminul Islam	b Manjural Islam	4	8	5	1	0
CD McMillan	c Naimur Rahman	b Hasibul Hossain	20	34	26	4	0
*SP Fleming	c Khaled Mashud	b Mohammad Rafique	16	45	33	2	0
RG Twose	not out		30	35	36	3	1
CL Cairns	not out		7	11	12	0	0

Extras (lb 1, w 4): **5**
Total (4 wickets, 33 overs): **117**

DNB: +AC Parore, CZ Harris, DJ Nash, GR Larsen, GI Allott.
FoW: 1-5 (Astle, 1.5 ov), 2-33 (McMillan, 10.4 ov), 3-78 (Fleming, 23.2 ov), 4-105 (Horne, 29.5 ov).

Bowling	O	M	R	W	
Hasibul Hossain	10	2	33	1 (2w)	
Manjural Islam	8	3	23	1 (2w)	
Khaled Mahmud	7	2	12	0	
Enamul Haque	3	0	21	0	
Mohammad Rafique	3	0	22	1	
Naimur Rahman	2	0	5	1	

ICC World Cup, 1999, 10th Match
Australia v New Zealand, Group B
Sophia Gardens, Cardiff
20 May 1999 (50-over match)

Result: New Zealand won by 5 wickets
Points: New Zealand 2, Australia 0
Toss: Australia
Umpires: Javed Akhtar (Pak) and DR Shepherd
TV Umpire: RE Koertzen (SA)
Match Referee: R Subba Row
Man Of The Match: RG Twose

Australia innings (50 overs maximum)			R	M	B	4	6
ME Waugh	lbw	b Allott	2	9	5	0	0
+AC Gilchrist	c Astle	b Allott	14	38	28	1	0
RT Ponting	c Harris	b Astle	47	120	88	4	0
DS Lehmann	c Astle	b Harris	76	133	94	8	0
*SR Waugh	c Astle	b Harris	7	18	18	0	0
MG Bevan	b Allott		21	47	32	1	0
S Lee	run out (Nash)		2	8	8	0	0
SK Warne	b Allott		15	24	14	2	0
DW Fleming	not out		8	14	11	0	0
AC Dale	not out		3	4	5	0	0
Extras (lb 10, w 5, nb 3): **18**							
Total (8 wickets, 50 overs): **213**							

DNB: GD McGrath.
FoW: 1-7 (ME Waugh, 2.1 ov), 2-32 (Gilchrist, 8.1 ov), 3-126 (Ponting, 30.6 ov), 4-149 (SR Waugh, 35.5 ov), 5-172 (Lehmann, 41.4 ov), 6-175 (Lee, 43.4 ov), 7-192 (Bevan, 46.2 ov), 8-204 (Warne, 48.3 ov).

Bowling	O	M	R	W	
Allott	10	0	37	4 (2nb, 2w)	
Nash	8	1	30	0	
Cairns	7	0	44	0 (1nb, 2w)	
Larsen	10	2	26	0 (1w)	
Harris	10	0	50	2	
Astle	5	0	16	1	

New Zealand innings (target: 214 from 50 overs)			R	M	B	4	6
MJ Horne	c Gilchrist	b Dale	5	5	8	1	0
NJ Astle	c Ponting	b Fleming	4	25	8	0	0
CD McMillan	c Fleming	b Warne	29	59	55	3	0
*SP Fleming	b McGrath		9	34	20	1	0
RG Twose	not out		80	131	99	10	0
CL Cairns	c Dale	b Fleming	60	111	77	5	3
+AC Parore	not out		10	10	9	1	1
Extras (lb 2, w 11, nb 4): **17**							
Total (5 wickets, 45.2 overs): **214**							

DNB: CZ Harris, DJ Nash, GR Larsen, GI Allott.
FoW: 1-5 (Horne, 1.2 ov), 2-21 (Astle, 6.1 ov), 3-47 (Fleming, 14.4 ov), 4-49 (McMillan, 15.3 ov), 5-197 (Cairns, 43.1 ov).

Bowling	O	M	R	W	
Fleming	8.2	1	43	2 (3w)	
Dale	5	1	18	1 (1w)	
McGrath	9	0	43	1 (4nb)	
Lee	6	0	24	0 (1w)	
Warne	10	1	44	1 (4w)	
SR Waugh	4	0	25	0 (1w)	
Bevan	3	0	15	0 (1w)	

ICC World Cup, 1999, 11th Match
Pakistan v Scotland, Group B
Riverside Ground, Chester-le-Street
20 May 1999 (50-over match)

Result: Pakistan won by 94 runs
Points: Pakistan 2, Scotland 0
Toss: Scotland
Umpires: DB Cowie (NZ) and ID Robinson (Zim)
TV Umpire: JH Hampshire
Match Referee: PJP Burge (Aus)
ODI Debut: IM Stanger (Scot)
Man Of The Match: Yousuf Youhana

Pakistan innings (50 overs maximum)

			R	M	B	4	6
Saeed Anwar	c Davies	b Asim Butt	6	38	22	0	0
Shahid Afridi	run out (Stanger)		7	20	9	1	0
Abdur Razzaq	lbw	b Brinkley	12	50	53	0	0
Inzamam-ul-Haq	st Davies	b Dyer	12	82	50	0	0
Saleem Malik	lbw	b Hamilton	0	3	3	0	0
Yousuf Youhana	not out		81	135	119	6	0
+Moin Khan	c Brinkley	b Hamilton	47	68	41	5	0
*Wasim Akram	not out		37	22	19	2	2

Extras (b 5, lb 6, w 33, nb 15): **59**
Total (6 wickets, 50 overs): **261**

DNB: Saqlain Mushtaq, Shoaib Akhtar, Azhar Mahmood.
FoW: 1-21 (Shahid Afridi, 3.6 ov), 2-35 (Saeed Anwar, 7.5 ov), 3-55 (Abdur Razzaq, 15.6 ov), 4-58 (Saleem Malik, 16.6 ov), 5-92 (Inzamam-ul-Haq, 26.4 ov), 6-195 (Moin Khan, 44.4 ov).

Bowling	O	M	R	W	
Blain	7	0	49	0	(6nb, 6w)
Asim Butt	9	1	55	1	(3nb, 8w)
Hamilton	10	1	36	2	(3nb, 8w)
Brinkley	10	0	29	1	(6w)
Dyer	9	0	48	1	
Stanger	5	0	33	0	(3nb, 1w)

Scotland innings (target: 262 runs from 49 overs)

			R	M	B	4	6
BMW Patterson	b Wasim Akram		0	1	5	0	0
IL Philip	lbw	b Shoaib Akhtar	0	17	6	0	0
MJ Smith	b Shoaib Akhtar		3	11	3	0	0
IM Stanger	b Wasim Akram		3	24	24	0	0
*G Salmond	c Moin Khan	b Shoaib Akhtar	5	11	7	0	0
GM Hamilton	b Wasim Akram		76	149	111	3	3
JE Brinkley	c Moin Khan	b Saqlain Mushtaq	22	72	43	3	0
+AG Davies	c sub (W Wasti)	b Abdur Razzaq	19	41	28	1	0
JAR Blain	lbw	b Abdur Razzaq	0	4	5	0	0
Asim Butt	c Moin Khan	b Abdur Razzaq	1	4	5	0	0
NR Dyer	not out		1	5	4	0	0

Extras (b 1, lb 11, w 17, nb 8): **37**
Total (all out, 38.5 overs): **167**

FoW: 1-1 (Patterson, 0.5 ov), 2-5 (Smith, 1.2 ov), 3-9 (Philip, 3.5 ov), 4-16 (Salmond, 7.1 ov), 5-19 (Stanger, 8.4 ov), 6-78 (Brinkley, 24.6 ov), 7-139 (Davies, 33.6 ov), 8-149 (Blain, 35.5 ov), 9-160 (Asim Butt, 37.1 ov), 10-167 (Hamilton, 38.5 ov).

Bowling	O	M	R	W	
Wasim Akram	7.5	0	23	3	(6w)
Shoaib Akhtar	6	2	11	3	(1nb, 2w)
Azhar Mahmood	7	2	21	0	(3w)
Abdur Razzaq	10	0	38	3	(5nb, 1w)
Saqlain Mushtaq	6	0	46	1	(2w)
Shahid Afridi	2	0	16	0	(2nb)

ICC World Cup, 1999, 12th Match
Bangladesh v West Indies, Group B
Castle Avenue, Dublin
21 May 1999 (50-over match)

Result: West Indies won by 7 wickets
Points: West Indies 2, Bangladesh 0
Toss: Bangladesh
Umpires: KT Francis (SL) and DB Hair (Aus)
TV Umpire: G Sharp (Eng)
Match Referee: RS Madugalle (SL)
Man Of The Match: CA Walsh

Bangladesh innings (50 overs maximum)			R	M	B	4	6
Shahriar Hossain	c Campbell	b Walsh	2	10	5	0	0
Mehrab Hossain	c Chanderpaul	b Simmons	64	173	129	4	1
Akram Khan	c Lara	b Dillon	4	35	19	0	0
*Aminul Islam	c Jacobs	b King	2	28	24	0	0
Minhajul Abedin	c Jacobs	b King	5	21	20	0	0
Naimur Rahman	lbw	b Walsh	45	83	72	4	0
Khaled Mahmud	c Bryan	b Walsh	13	25	15	0	0
+Khaled Mashud	b King		4	5	6	0	0
Enamul Haque	c Lara	b Walsh	4	10	7	0	0
Hasibul Hossain	b Bryan		1	4	3	0	0
Manjural Islam	not out		0	2	2	0	0

Extras (lb 8, w 25, nb 5): **38**
Total (all out, 49.2 overs): **182**

FoW: 1-8 (Shahriar Hossain, 2.1 ov), 2-29 (Akram Khan, 9.6 ov), 3-39 (Aminul Islam, 16.3 ov), 4-55 (Minhajul Abedin, 22.2 ov), 5-140 (Mehrab Hossain, 42.3 ov), 6-159 (Naimur Rahman, 44.3 ov), 7-167 (Khaled Mashud, 45.6 ov), 8-180 (Khaled Mahmud, 48.1 ov), 9-182 (Enamul Haque, 48.4 ov), 10-182 (Hasibul Hossain, 49.2 ov).

Bowling	O	M	R	W	
Walsh	10	0	25	4 (4nb, 1w)	
Dillon	10	0	43	1 (6w)	
Bryan	9.2	0	30	1 (11w)	
King	10	1	30	3 (3w)	
Simmons	10	0	46	1 (1nb, 4w)	

West Indies innings (target: 183 runs from 50 overs)			R	M	B	4	6
SL Campbell	c Manjural Islam	b Khaled Mahmud	36	78	70	4	0
+RD Jacobs	run out (Shahriar Hossain/Khaled Mashud)		51	116	82	4	1
JC Adams	not out		53	84	82	6	0
*BC Lara	c Hasibul Hossain	b Minhajul Abedin	25	20	25	4	0
S Chanderpaul	not out		11	22	19	2	0

Extras (lb 2, w 5): **7**
Total (3 wickets, 46.3 overs): **183**

DNB: SC Williams, PV Simmons, HR Bryan, M Dillon, RD King, CA Walsh.
FoW: 1-67 (Campbell, 20.3 ov), 2-115 (Jacobs, 32.2 ov), 3-150 (Lara, 38.6 ov).

Bowling	O	M	R	W	
Hasibul Hossain	7	1	28	0 (3w)	
Manjural Islam	7	1	15	0	
Khaled Mahmud	8	0	36	1	
Enamul Haque	8	1	31	0 (1w)	
Naimur Rahman	9.3	0	43	0 (1w)	
Minhajul Abedin	7	0	28	1	

ICC World Cup, 1999, 16th Match
Australia v Pakistan, Group B
Headingley, Leeds
23 May 1999 (50-over match)

Result: Pakistan won by 10 runs
Points: Pakistan 2, Australia 0
Toss: Australia
Umpires: RE Koertzen (SA) and P Willey
TV Umpire: R Julian
Match Referee: R Subba Row
Man Of The Match: Inzamam-ul-Haq

Pakistan innings (50 overs maximum)			R	M	B	4	6
Wajahatullah Wasti	c SR Waugh	b McGrath	9	47	31	1	0
Saeed Anwar	c Gilchrist	b Reiffel	25	32	23	5	0
Abdur Razzaq	c Fleming	b Warne	60	126	99	3	1
Ijaz Ahmed	lbw	b Fleming	0	6	6	0	0
Inzamam-ul-Haq	run out (Fleming)		81	131	104	6	1
Yousuf Youhana	run out (Warne/Lehmann)		29	17	16	4	1
*Wasim Akram	c Gilchrist	b Fleming	13	22	12	1	0
+Moin Khan	not out		31	20	12	2	3
Azhar Mahmood	run out (Martyn/McGrath)		1	2	1	0	0
Saqlain Mushtaq	not out		0	3	0	0	0
Extras (b 1, lb 5, w 15, nb 5): **26**							
Total (8 wickets, 50 overs): **275**							

DNB: Shoaib Akhtar.
FoW: 1-32 (Saeed Anwar, 7.4 ov), 2-44 (Wajahatullah, 11.1 ov), 3-46 (Ijaz Ahmed, 12.3 ov), 4-164 (Abdur Razzaq, 39.3 ov), 5-216 (Yousuf Youhana, 44.4 ov), 6-230 (Inzamam-ul-Haq, 46.2 ov), 7-262 (Wasim Akram, 48.6 ov), 8-265 (Azhar Mahmood, 49.3 ov).

Bowling	O	M	R	W
Fleming	10	3	37	2 (1nb, 4w)
Reiffel	10	1	49	1 (1nb, 4w)
McGrath	10	1	54	1 (1nb, 4w)
Warne	10	0	50	1 (1w)
SR Waugh	6	0	37	0 (1w)
Martyn	2	0	25	0 (1nb)
Lehmann	2	0	17	0

Australia innings (target: 276 runs from 50 overs)			R	M	B	4	6
+AC Gilchrist	b Wasim Akram		0	2	3	0	0
ME Waugh	c Moin Khan	b Abdur Razzaq	41	74	49	6	0
RT Ponting	c Saeed Anwar	b Saqlain Mushtaq	47	82	60	7	0
DS Lehmann	c Moin Khan	b Saqlain Mushtaq	5	12	9	1	0
*SR Waugh	b Shoaib Akhtar		49	122	65	2	1
MG Bevan	c Ijaz Ahmed	b Wasim Akram	61	102	80	3	1
DR Martyn	b Wasim Akram		18	49	25	0	0
SK Warne	run out (Ijaz Ahmed)		1	11	6	0	0
PR Reiffel	c Wasim Akram	b Saqlain Mushtaq	1	5	4	0	0
DW Fleming	not out		4	15	3	0	0
GD McGrath	b Wasim Akram		0	1	2	0	0
Extras (b 7, lb 10, w 14, nb 7): **38**							
Total (all out, 49.5 overs): **265**							

FoW: 1-0 (Gilchrist, 0.3 ov), 2-91 (ME Waugh, 16.6 ov), 3-100 (Ponting, 19.2 ov), 4-101 (Lehmann, 19.4 ov), 5-214 (Bevan, 41.3 ov), 6-238 (SR Waugh, 44.5 ov), 7-248 (Warne, 46.2 ov), 8-251 (Reiffel, 47.2 ov), 9-265 (Martyn, 49.3 ov), 10-265 (McGrath, 49.5 ov).

Bowling	O	M	R	W
Wasim Akram	9.5	1	40	4 (5nb, 1w)
Shoaib Akhtar	10	0	46	1 (3w)
Azhar Mahmood	10	0	61	0 (3w)
Saqlain Mushtaq	10	1	51	3 (2nb)
Abdur Razzaq	10	0	50	1 (5w)

ICC World Cup, 1999, 17th Match
Scotland v Bangladesh, Group B
Raeburn Place, Edinburgh
24 May 1999 (50-over match)

Result: Bangladesh won by 22 runs
Points: Bangladesh 2, Scotland 0
Toss: Scotland
Umpires: KT Francis (SL) and DL Orchard (SA)
TV Umpire: B Dudleston (Eng)
Match Referee: JR Reid (NZ)
Man Of The Match: Minhajul Abedin

Bangladesh innings (50 overs maximum)			R	M	B	4	6
+Khaled Mashud	c Philip	b Blain	0	11	9	0	0
Mehrab Hossain	c Dyer	b Asim Butt	3	23	20	0	0
Faruk Ahmed	b Blain		7	40	24	1	0
*Aminul Islam	lbw	b Blain	0	2	1	0	0
Akram Khan	c Philip	b Asim Butt	0	16	14	0	0
Minhajul Abedin	not out		68	179	116	6	0
Naimur Rahman	c Stanger	b Brinkley	36	89	58	5	0
Khaled Mahmud	c Salmond	b Dyer	0	4	4	0	0
Enamul Haque	c Philip	b Dyer	19	36	40	1	0
Hasibul Hossain	c & b Blain		6	23	18	0	0
Manjural Islam	not out		2	11	7	0	0

Extras (lb 5, w 28, nb 11): **44**
Total (9 wickets, 50 overs): **185**

FoW: 1-6 (Khaled Mashud, 2.3 ov), 2-12 (Mehrab Hossain, 5.3 ov), 3-13 (Aminul Islam, 6.1 ov), 4-24 (Akram Khan, 9.4 ov), 5-26 (Faruk Ahmed, 10.3 ov), 6-95 (Naimur Rahman, 29.4 ov), 7-96 (Khaled Mahmud, 30.6 ov), 8-133 (Enamul Haque, 40.5 ov), 9-164 (Hasibul Hossain, 46.6 ov).

Bowling	O	M	R	W	
Blain	10	1	37	4	(8nb, 7w)
Asim Butt	9	1	24	2	(1nb, 7w)
Hamilton	10	3	25	0	(2nb, 5w)
Brinkley	10	0	45	1	(4w)
Stanger	4	0	23	0	(1w)
Dyer	7	1	26	2	(2w)

Scotland innings (target: 186 runs from 49 overs)			R	M	B	4	6
BMW Patterson	lbw	b Hasibul Hossain	0	1	2	0	0
IL Philip	lbw	b Manjural Islam	3	26	17	0	0
MJ Smith	c Khaled Mashud	b Hasibul Hossain	1	20	13	0	0
IM Stanger	lbw	b Minhajul Abedin	10	56	35	0	0
*G Salmond	c Faruk Ahmed	b Manjural Islam	19	35	31	3	0
GM Hamilton	run out (Manjural Islam)		63	106	71	4	1
JE Brinkley	c Hasibul Hossain	b Khaled Mahmud	5	31	31	0	0
+AG Davies	c Manjural Islam	b Khaled Mahmud	32	73	65	3	0
JAR Blain	run out (Naimur Rahman)		9	21	16	0	0
Asim Butt	c Aminul Islam	b Enamul Haque	1	5	3	0	0
NR Dyer	not out		0	1	0	0	0

Extras (lb 1, w 13, nb 6): **20**
Total (all out, 46.2 overs): **163**

FoW: 1-0 (Patterson, 0.2 ov), 2-8 (Smith, 4.5 ov), 3-8 (Philip, 5.2 ov), 4-37 (Salmond, 13.6 ov), 5-49 (Stanger, 17.3 ov), 6-83 (Brinkley, 26.3 ov), 7-138 (Hamilton, 41.3 ov), 8-158 (Davies, 45.2 ov), 9-163 (Blain, 46.1 ov), 10-163 (Asim Butt, 46.2 ov).

Bowling	O	M	R	W	
Hasibul Hossain	8	1	26	2	(4nb, 4w)
Manjural Islam	9	0	33	2	(3w)
Khaled Mahmud	9	2	27	2	(2nb, 1w)
Minhajul Abedin	3	0	12	1	(1w)
Naimur Rahman	10	0	41	0	(2w)
Enamul Haque	7.2	0	23	1	

ICC World Cup, 1999, 18th Match
New Zealand v West Indies, Group B
County Ground, Southampton
24 May 1999 (50-over match)

Result: West Indies won by 7 wickets
Points: West Indies 2, New Zealand 0
Toss: West Indies
Umpires: Javed Akhtar (Pak) and S Venkataraghavan (Ind)
TV Umpire: JH Hampshire
Match Referee: RS Madugalle (SL)
Man Of The Match: RD Jacobs

New Zealand innings (50 overs maximum)			R	M	B	4	6
MJ Horne	c Lara	b Walsh	2	20	21	0	0
NJ Astle	c Jacobs	b Ambrose	2	6	6	0	0
CD McMillan	c Jacobs	b Simmons	32	102	78	1	0
*SP Fleming	c Jacobs	b King	0	23	17	0	0
RG Twose	c Williams	b King	0	26	12	0	0
CL Cairns	c Lara	b Dillon	23	58	40	2	0
+AC Parore	c Jacobs	b Dillon	23	63	41	4	0
CZ Harris	c Campbell	b Dillon	30	80	50	2	0
DJ Nash	c Williams	b Dillon	1	12	10	0	0
GR Larsen	c Jacobs	b Simmons	14	20	18	2	0
GI Allott	not out		0	3	2	0	0

Extras (lb 6, w 17, nb 6): **29**
Total (all out, 48.1 overs): **156**

FoW: 1-2 (Astle, 1.6 ov), 2-13 (Horne, 4.5 ov), 3-22 (Fleming, 10.3 ov), 4-31 (Twose, 16.4 ov), 5-59 (McMillan, 25.1 ov), 6-75 (Cairns, 30.5 ov), 7-125 (Parore, 40.3 ov), 8-130 (Nash, 42.5 ov), 9-155 (Larsen, 47.4 ov), 10-156 (Harris, 48.1 ov).

Bowling	O	M	R	W	
Walsh	10	1	23	1 (4nb, 2w)	
Ambrose	10	0	19	1 (2w)	
King	10	1	29	2 (1nb, 5w)	
Simmons	9	2	33	2 (1nb, 4w)	
Dillon	9.1	0	46	4 (3w)	

West Indies innings (target: 157 from 50 overs)			R	M	B	4	6
SL Campbell	lbw	b Nash	8	42	32	0	0
+RD Jacobs	not out		80	185	131	8	1
JC Adams	c Parore	b Allott	3	48	29	0	0
*BC Lara	c Nash	b Harris	36	61	54	3	1
SC Williams	not out		14	31	28	1	0

Extras (lb 4, w 5, nb 8): **17**
Total (3 wickets, 44.2 overs): **158**

DNB: S Chanderpaul, PV Simmons, CEL Ambrose, M Dillon, RD King, CA Walsh.
FoW: 1-29 (Campbell, 9.6 ov), 2-49 (Adams, 20.5 ov), 3-121 (Lara, 35.4 ov).

Bowling	O	M	R	W	
Allott	10	2	39	1 (2nb, 1w)	
Nash	10	2	25	1 (3nb, 3w)	
Cairns	9.2	1	42	0 (3nb, 1w)	
Larsen	7	1	29	0	
Harris	8	2	19	1	

ICC World Cup, 1999, 22nd Match
Australia v Bangladesh, Group B
Riverside Ground, Chester-le-Street
27 May 1999 (50-over match)

Result: Australia won by 7 wickets
Points: Australia 2, Bangladesh 0
Toss: Australia
Umpires: SA Bucknor (WI) and DL Orchard (SA)
TV Umpire: MJ Kitchen
Match Referee: JR Reid (NZ)
Man Of The Match: TM Moody

Bangladesh innings (50 overs maximum)			R	M	B	4	6
Khaled Mahmud	lbw	b McGrath	6	17	19	0	0
Mehrab Hossain	c Ponting	b Moody	42	91	75	7	0
Faruk Ahmed	c Ponting	b McGrath	9	25	16	1	0
Naimur Rahman	c Ponting	b Moody	2	8	5	0	0
*Aminul Islam	b Fleming		13	54	30	1	0
Minhajul Abedin	not out		53	113	99	6	0
Akram Khan	lbw	b Warne	0	15	7	0	0
+Khaled Mashud	lbw	b Moody	17	49	42	1	0
Enamul Haque	not out		17	22	14	2	0
Extras (b 2, w 10, nb 7): **19**							
Total (7 wickets, 50 overs): **178**							

DNB: Hasibul Hossain, Manjural Islam.
FoW: 1-10 (Khaled Mahmud, 4.2 ov), 2-39 (Faruk Ahmed, 10.6 ov), 3-47 (Naimur Rahman, 13.2 ov), 4-72 (Mehrab Hossain, 21.2 ov), 5-91 (Aminul Islam, 26.3 ov), 6-99 (Akram Khan, 31.2 ov), 7-143 (Khaled Mashud, 44.3 ov).

Bowling	O	M	R	W
McGrath	10	0	44	2 (4nb, 2w)
Fleming	10	0	45	1 (4w)
Moody	10	4	25	3 (1w)
Julian	10	1	44	0 (3nb, 1w)
Warne	10	2	18	1 (2w)

Australia innings (target: 179 runs from 50 overs)			R	M	B	4	6
ME Waugh	st Khaled Mashud	b Enamul Haque	33	54	35	3	0
+AC Gilchrist	st Khaled Mashud	b Minhajul Abedin	63	49	39	12	0
BP Julian	b Enamul Haque		9	11	6	2	0
TM Moody	not out		56	33	29	6	2
RT Ponting	not out		18	24	10	1	1
Extras (w 2): **2**							
Total (3 wickets, 19.5 overs): **181**							

DNB: MG Bevan, DS Lehmann, *SR Waugh, SK Warne, DW Fleming, GD McGrath.
FoW: 1-98 (Gilchrist, 11.5 ov), 2-98 (ME Waugh, 12.3 ov), 3-111 (Julian, 14.1 ov).

Bowling	O	M	R	W
Hasibul Hossain	4	0	24	0
Manjural Islam	3	0	23	0
Khaled Mahmud	2.5	0	39	0
Naimur Rahman	2	0	17	0
Enamul Haque	5	0	40	2
Minhajul Abedin	3	0	38	1 (2w)

ICC World Cup, 1999, 23rd Match
Scotland v West Indies, Group B
Grace Road, Leicester
27 May 1999 (50-over match)

Result: West Indies won by 8 wickets
Points: West Indies 2, Scotland 0
Toss: Scotland
Umpires: Javed Akhtar (Pak) and ID Robinson (Zim)
TV Umpire: S Venkataraghavan (Ind)
Match Referee: PJP Burge (Aus)
ODI Debut: JG Williamson (Scot)
Man Of The Match: CA Walsh

Scotland innings (50 overs maximum)			R	M	B	4	6
MJ Smith	c Jacobs	b Simmons	1	18	23	0	0
MJD Allingham	c Jacobs	b Ambrose	6	46	43	0	0
IM Stanger	c Jacobs	b Walsh	7	35	27	0	0
*G Salmond	c Jacobs	b Ambrose	1	10	4	0	0
GM Hamilton	not out		24	82	43	3	0
JG Williamson	c Williams	b Bryan	1	19	11	0	0
JE Brinkley	c Simmons	b Walsh	2	5	6	0	0
+AG Davies	lbw	b Walsh	0	1	2	0	0
JAR Blain	lbw	b Bryan	3	25	21	0	0
Asim Butt	c Williams	b King	11	23	10	0	1
NR Dyer	c Williams	b King	0	1	2	0	0
Extras (w 9, nb 3): **12**							
Total (all out, 31.3 overs): **68**							

FoW: 1-6 (Smith, 5.6 ov), 2-18 (Allingham, 14.2 ov), 3-20 (Stanger, 15.5 ov), 4-20 (Salmond, 16.2 ov), 5-25 (Williamson, 20.3 ov), 6-29 (Brinkley, 21.4 ov), 7-29 (Davies, 21.6 ov), 8-47 (Blain, 28.2 ov), 9-67 (Asim Butt, 31.2 ov), 10-68 (Dyer, 31.3 ov).

Bowling	O	M	R	W	
Ambrose	10	4	8	2 (1nb, 1w)	
Simmons	7	1	15	1 (4w)	
Walsh	7	1	7	3 (1nb, 1w)	
Bryan	6	0	29	2 (3w)	
King	1.3	0	9	2 (1nb)	

West Indies innings (target: 69 from 50 overs)			R	M	B	4	6
PV Simmons	c Stanger	b Blain	7	18	15	1	0
S Chanderpaul	not out		30	46	30	6	0
SC Williams	lbw	b Blain	0	4	1	0	0
*BC Lara	not out		25	13	17	3	1
Extras (lb 2, w 4, nb 2): **8**							
Total (2 wickets, 10.1 overs): **70**							

DNB: JC Adams, +RD Jacobs, SL Campbell, RD King, CEL Ambrose, HR Bryan, CA Walsh.
FoW: 1-21 (Simmons, 4.5 ov), 2-22 (Williams, 6.1 ov).

Bowling	O	M	R	W	
Blain	5.1	0	36	2 (1nb, 2w)	
Asim Butt	4	1	15	0 (1nb, 1w)	
Hamilton	1	0	17	0 (1w)	

ICC World Cup, 1999, 24th Match
New Zealand v Pakistan, Group B
County Ground, Derby
28 May 1999 (50-over match)

Result: Pakistan won by 62 runs
Points: Pakistan 2, New Zealand 0
Toss: New Zealand
Umpires: KT Francis (SL) and RE Koertzen (SA)
TV Umpire: P Willey
Match Referee: RS Madugalle (SL)
Man Of The Match: Inzamam-ul-Haq

Pakistan innings (50 overs maximum)			R	M	B	4	6
Saeed Anwar	b Allott		28	44	25	4	0
Shahid Afridi	c Parore	b Allott	17	25	22	2	1
Abdur Razzaq	run out (Astle)		33	92	82	4	0
Ijaz Ahmed	run out (Harris)		51	107	68	0	0
Inzamam-ul-Haq	not out		73	86	61	7	0
Saleem Malik	b Allott		8	10	9	1	0
+Moin Khan	c McMillan	b Astle	19	20	17	3	0
*Wasim Akram	lbw	b Cairns	1	6	7	0	0
Azhar Mahmood	c Twose	b Allott	14	14	12	2	0
Saqlain Mushtaq	not out		0	3	0	0	0
Extras (b 4, lb 10, w 8, nb 3): **25**							
Total (8 wickets, 50 overs): **269**							

DNB: Shoaib Akhtar.
FoW: 1-40 (Shahid Afridi, 5.3 ov), 2-51 (Saeed Anwar, 9.5 ov), 3-127 (Abdur Razzaq, 28.3 ov), 4-163 (Ijaz Ahmed, 36.2 ov), 5-180 (Saleem Malik, 38.5 ov), 6-221 (Moin Khan, 43.4 ov), 7-226 (Wasim Akram, 45.2 ov), 8-255 (Azhar Mahmood, 48.6 ov).

Bowling	O	M	R	W	
Nash	10	1	36	0 (1nb)	
Allott	10	0	64	4 (2nb, 5w)	
Larsen	10	0	35	0	
Cairns	7	0	46	1 (1w)	
Harris	8	0	47	0 (1w)	
Astle	5	0	27	1 (1w)	

New Zealand innings (target: 270 from 50 overs)			R	M	B	4	6
MJ Horne	c Moin Khan	b Shoaib Akhtar	1	22	20	0	0
NJ Astle	c Moin Khan	b Shoaib Akhtar	0	7	6	0	0
CD McMillan	c Saleem Malik	b Wasim Akram	20	38	25	3	0
*SP Fleming	c Wasim Akram	b Azhar Mahmood	69	143	100	4	0
RG Twose	c Inzamam-ul-Haq	b Saqlain Mushtaq	13	34	25	0	1
CL Cairns	lbw	b Azhar Mahmood	0	3	4	0	0
+AC Parore	lbw	b Azhar Mahmood	0	1	1	0	0
CZ Harris	c Abdur Razzaq	b Saqlain Mushtaq	42	111	96	0	0
DJ Nash	not out		21	41	32	0	0
GR Larsen	not out		3	3	4	0	0
Extras (lb 15, w 13, nb 10): **38**							
Total (8 wickets, 50 overs): **207**							

DNB: GI Allott.
FoW: 1-2 (Astle, 1.5 ov), 2-12 (Horne, 5.1 ov), 3-35 (McMillan, 10.4 ov), 4-70 (Twose, 18.4 ov), 5-71 (Cairns, 19.4 ov), 6-71 (Parore, 19.5 ov), 7-154 (Fleming, 38.5 ov), 8-200 (Harris, 48.6 ov).

Bowling	O	M	R	W	
Wasim Akram	9	0	27	1 (5nb, 2w)	
Shoaib Akhtar	7	1	31	2 (4nb, 1w)	
Azhar Mahmood	10	0	38	3 (2w)	
Saqlain Mushtaq	10	1	34	2 (1nb, 1w)	
Shahid Afridi	6	1	26	0 (2nb, 1w)	
Abdur Razzaq	8	0	36	0 (2w)	

ICC World Cup, 1999, 28th Match
Australia v West Indies, Group B
Old Trafford, Manchester
30 May 1999 (50-over match)

Result: Australia won by 6 wickets
Points: Australia 2, West Indies 0
Toss: Australia
Umpires: RS Dunne (NZ) and KT Francis (SL)
TV Umpire: DJ Constant
Match Referee: JR Reid (NZ)
Man Of The Match: GD McGrath

West Indies innings (50 overs maximum)			R	M	B	4	6
SL Campbell	c ME Waugh	b McGrath	2	19	14	0	0
+RD Jacobs	not out		49	197	142	3	0
JC Adams	lbw	b McGrath	0	1	1	0	0
*BC Lara	b McGrath		9	14	15	1	0
S Chanderpaul	b Warne		16	60	38	0	0
SC Williams	c ME Waugh	b Moody	3	4	6	0	0
PV Simmons	b Fleming		1	6	8	0	0
CEL Ambrose	lbw	b Warne	1	4	7	0	0
M Dillon	lbw	b McGrath	0	11	9	0	0
RD King	lbw	b Warne	1	38	30	0	0
CA Walsh	b McGrath		6	23	11	1	0
Extras (lb 3, w 18, nb 1): **22**							
Total (all out, 46.4 overs): **110**							

FoW: 1-7 (Campbell, 4.2 ov), 2-7 (Adams, 4.3 ov), 3-20 (Lara, 8.2 ov), 4-64 (Chanderpaul, 22.3 ov), 5-67 (Williams, 23.4 ov), 6-69 (Simmons, 25.2 ov), 7-70 (Ambrose, 26.4 ov), 8-71 (Dillon, 29.5 ov), 9-88 (King, 40.5 ov), 10-110 (Walsh, 46.4 ov).

Bowling	O	M	R	W	
McGrath	8.4	3	14	5	
Fleming	7	1	12	1 (2w)	
Moody	7	0	16	1 (1w)	
Julian	7	1	36	0 (1nb, 4w)	
Warne	10	4	11	3 (1w)	
Bevan	7	0	18	0 (5w)	

Australia innings (target: 111 runs from 50 overs)			R	M	B	4	6
+AC Gilchrist	b Ambrose		21	44	36	1	0
ME Waugh	c Jacobs	b Ambrose	3	9	5	0	0
RT Ponting	c Chanderpaul	b King	20	77	56	1	0
DS Lehmann	c Adams	b Ambrose	9	25	13	1	0
*SR Waugh	not out		19	100	73	2	0
MG Bevan	not out		20	85	69	2	0
Extras (lb 4, w 7, nb 8): **19**							
Total (4 wickets, 40.4 overs): **111**							

DNB: TM Moody, BP Julian, SK Warne, DW Fleming, GD McGrath.
FoW: 1-10 (ME Waugh, 2.1 ov), 2-43 (Gilchrist, 10.1 ov), 3-53 (Lehmann, 16.2 ov), 4-62 (Ponting, 19.3 ov).

Bowling	O	M	R	W	
Ambrose	10	0	31	3 (1w)	
Walsh	10	3	25	0 (7nb, 1w)	
Dillon	7.4	1	22	0 (1nb, 2w)	
King	10	2	27	1 (1w)	
Simmons	3	2	2	0 (2w)	

ICC World Cup, 1999, 29th Match
Bangladesh v Pakistan, Group B
County Ground, Northampton
31 May 1999 (50-over match)

Result: Bangladesh won by 62 runs
Points: Bangladesh 2, Pakistan 0
Toss: Pakistan
Umpires: DB Cowie (NZ) and DB Hair (Aus)
TV Umpire: DR Shepherd
Match Referee: RS Madugalle (SL)
Man Of The Match: Khaled Mahmud

Bangladesh innings (50 overs maximum)			R	M	B	4	6
Shahriar Hossain	lbw	b Saqlain Mushtaq	39	102	60	5	0
Mehrab Hossain	st Moin Khan	b Saqlain Mushtaq	9	79	42	0	0
Akram Khan	c Wasim Akram	b Waqar Younis	42	88	66	6	0
*Aminul Islam	b Shahid Afridi		15	44	26	2	0
Naimur Rahman	b Waqar Younis		13	20	20	2	0
Minhajul Abedin	c & b Saqlain Mushtaq		14	27	14	2	0
Khaled Mahmud	st Moin Khan	b Saqlain Mushtaq	27	36	34	3	0
+Khaled Mashud	not out		15	29	21	1	0
Mohammad Rafique	c Shoaib Akhtar	b Saqlain Mushtaq	6	13	19	0	0
Niamur Rashid	lbw	b Wasim Akram	1	1	2	0	0
Shafiuddin Ahmed	not out		2	1	3	0	0

Extras (lb 5, w 28, nb 7): **40**
Total (9 wickets, 50 overs): **223**

FoW: 1-69 (Mehrab Hossain, 15.3 ov), 2-70 (Shahriar Hossain, 17.4 ov), 3-120 (Aminul Islam, 29.1 ov), 4-148 (Akram Khan, 34.3 ov), 5-148 (Naimur Rahman, 34.5 ov), 6-187 (Minhajul Abedin, 41.1 ov), 7-195 (Khaled Mahmud, 43.1 ov), 8-208 (Mohammad Rafique, 47.1 ov), 9-212 (Niamur Rashid, 48.1 ov).

Bowling	O	M	R	W	
Waqar Younis	9	1	36	2 (1w)	
Shoaib Akhtar	8	0	30	0 (2nb, 1w)	
Wasim Akram	10	0	35	1 (4nb, 8w)	
Azhar Mahmood	8	0	56	0 (3w)	
Saqlain Mushtaq	10	1	35	5 (6w)	
Shahid Afridi	5	0	26	1 (1nb, 1w)	

Pakistan innings (target: 224 runs from 49 overs)			R	M	B	4	6
Saeed Anwar	run out (Khaled Mashud)		9	33	20	0	0
Shahid Afridi	c Mehrab Hossain	b Khaled Mahmud	2	5	4	0	0
Ijaz Ahmed	b Shafiuddin Ahmed		0	3	5	0	0
Inzamam-ul-Haq	lbw	b Khaled Mahmud	7	27	16	1	0
Saleem Malik	lbw	b Khaled Mahmud	5	22	17	0	0
Azhar Mahmood	run out (Khaled Mashud)		29	79	61	3	0
*Wasim Akram	c Shahriar Hossain	b Minhajul Abedin	29	66	52	2	1
+Moin Khan	c Mehrab Hossain	b Naimur Rahman	18	28	17	2	0
Saqlain Mushtaq	run out (Khaled Mashud)		21	60	51	2	0
Waqar Younis	b Mohammad Rafique	11	26	20	0	0	0
Shoaib Akhtar	not out		1	7	5	0	0

Extras (b 1, lb 6, w 21, nb 1): **29**
Total (all out, 44.3 overs): **161**

FoW: 1-5 (Shahid Afridi, 0.5 ov), 2-7 (Ijaz Ahmed, 1.6 ov), 3-26 (Saeed Anwar, 7.1 ov), 4-29 (Inzamam-ul-Haq, 8.1 ov), 5-42 (Saleem Malik, 12.3 ov), 6-97 (Azhar Mahmood, 27.5 ov), 7-102 (Wasim Akram, 29.1 ov), 8-124 (Moin Khan, 34.6 ov), 9-160 (Waqar Younis, 43.3 ov), 10-161 (Saqlain Mushtaq, 44.3 ov).

Bowling	O	M	R	W	
Khaled Mahmud	10	2	31	3 (1nb, 7w)	
Shafiuddin Ahmed	8	0	26	1 (6w)	
Niamur Rashid	5	1	20	0	
Mohammad Rafique	8	0	28	1 (1w)	
Minhajul Abedin	7	2	29	1 (1w)	
Naimur Rahman	6.3	2	20	1 (1w)	

ICC World Cup, 1999, 30th Match
Scotland v New Zealand, Group B
Raeburn Place, Edinburgh
31 May 1999 (50-over match)

Result: New Zealand won by 6 wickets
Points: New Zealand 2, Scotland 0
Toss: New Zealand
Umpires: RE Koertzen (SA) and ID Robinson (Zim)
TV Umpire: SA Bucknor (WI)
Match Referee: CW Smith (WI)
Man Of The Match: GI Allott

Scotland innings (50 overs maximum)			R	M	B	4	6
MJ Smith	c Cairns	b Nash	1	14	14	0	0
MJD Allingham	c Fleming	b Allott	2	42	25	0	0
*G Salmond	lbw	b Allott	1	13	13	0	0
GM Hamilton	c Allott	b Astle	20	69	49	2	0
IM Stanger	c Astle	b Cairns	27	68	58	1	0
JE Brinkley	c Parore	b Allott	0	9	6	0	0
JG Williamson	c & b Harris		10	35	24	0	0
+AG Davies	c sub (DL Vettori)	b Harris	24	62	48	3	0
JAR Blain	lbw	b Harris	0	1	1	0	0
Asim Butt	c Twose	b Harris	10	6	10	0	1
NR Dyer	not out		2	20	8	0	0
Extras (b 1, lb 7, w 13, nb 3): **24**							
Total (all out, 42.1 overs): **121**							

FoW: 1-2 (Smith, 3.4 ov), 2-11 (Salmond, 6.6 ov), 3-12 (Allingham, 10.1 ov), 4-66 (Hamilton, 24.4 ov), 5-68 (Brinkley, 26.4 ov), 6-68 (Stanger, 27.2 ov), 7-100 (Williamson, 35.1 ov), 8-100 (Blain, 35.2 ov), 9-110 (Asim Butt, 37.2 ov), 10-121 (Davies, 42.1 ov).

Bowling	O	M	R	W
Allott	10	3	15	3 (1w)
Nash	10	3	16	1 (1nb)
Bulfin	6	0	31	0 (1nb, 2w)
Cairns	8	0	26	1 (1nb, 3w)
Astle	5	1	18	1 (2w)
Harris	3.1	0	7	4 (1w)

New Zealand innings (target: 122 from 50 overs)			R	M	B	4	6
MN Hart	b Blain		0	2	2	0	0
NJ Astle	c Davies	b Blain	11	12	10	1	0
CD McMillan	c & b Hamilton		19	49	27	2	0
RG Twose	not out		54	68	49	5	1
*SP Fleming	b Blain		7	7	7	1	0
CL Cairns	not out		20	20	16	1	1
Extras (b 1, lb 2, w 5, nb 4): **12**							
Total (4 wickets, 17.5 overs): **123**							

DNB: +AC Parore, CZ Harris, CE Bulfin, DJ Nash, GI Allott.
FoW: 1-0 (Hart, 0.2 ov), 2-19 (Astle, 2.3 ov), 3-81 (McMillan, 11.5 ov), 4-92 (Fleming, 12.6 ov).

Bowling	O	M	R	W
Blain	7	0	53	3 (3nb, 2w)
Asim Butt	5	0	33	0 (1nb, 2w)
Hamilton	5.5	0	34	1

1999 WORLD CUP

Super Six

ICC World Cup, 1999, 1st Super Six Match
Australia v India
Kennington Oval, London
4 June 1999 (50-over match)

Result: Australia won by 77 runs
Points: Australia 2, India 0
Toss: India
Umpires: SA Bucknor (WI) and P Willey
TV Umpire: ID Robinson (Zim)
Match Referee: RS Madugalle (SL)
Man Of The Match: GD McGrath

Australia innings (50 overs maximum)			R	M	B	4	6
ME Waugh	c Prasad	b Singh	83	131	99	8	1
+AC Gilchrist	c Mohanty	b Ganguly	31	91	52	1	0
RT Ponting	b Singh		23	43	36	1	1
DS Lehmann	run out (Jadeja)		26	56	33	2	0
*SR Waugh	c Kumble	b Mohanty	36	42	40	3	0
MG Bevan	c Mongia	b Prasad	22	32	27	1	1
TM Moody	not out		26	25	20	3	0
SK Warne	not out		0	2	0	0	0
Extras (lb 14, w 10, nb 11): **35**							
Total (6 wickets, 50 overs): **282**							

DNB: PR Reiffel, DW Fleming, GD McGrath.
FoW: 1-97 (Gilchrist, 20.1 ov), 2-157 (ME Waugh, 30.1 ov), 3-158 (Ponting, 30.4 ov), 4-218 (SR Waugh, 41.5 ov), 5-231 (Lehmann, 43.6 ov), 6-275 (Bevan, 49.3 ov).

Bowling	O	M	R	W	
Srinath	10	2	34	0	(2nb, 4w)
Mohanty	7	0	47	1	(1nb, 1w)
Prasad	10	0	60	1	(1nb, 1w)
Kumble	10	0	49	0	
Ganguly	5	0	31	1	(1nb, 1w)
Singh	7	0	43	2	(2nb, 3w)
Tendulkar	1	0	4	0	

India innings (target: 283 runs from 50 overs)			R	M	B	4	6
SC Ganguly	b Fleming		8	18	12	0	0
SR Tendulkar	c Gilchrist	b McGrath	0	5	4	0	0
R Dravid	c Gilchrist	b McGrath	2	8	6	0	0
A Jadeja	not out		100	188	138	7	2
*M Azharuddin	c SR Waugh	b McGrath	3	11	9	0	0
RR Singh	c Reiffel	b Moody	75	124	94	5	3
+NR Mongia	run out (Bevan)		2	21	9	0	0
J Srinath	c Gilchrist	b SR Waugh	0	2	2	0	0
A Kumble	c Gilchrist	b SR Waugh	3	5	6	0	0
BKV Prasad	lbw	b Fleming	2	13	9	0	0
DS Mohanty	run out (Warne/Gilchrist)		0	3	3	0	0
Extras (lb 3, w 4, nb 3): **10**							
Total (all out, 48.2 overs): **205**							

FoW: 1-1 (Tendulkar, 0.6 ov), 2-10 (Dravid, 2.5 ov), 3-12 (Ganguly, 3.4 ov), 4-17 (Azharuddin, 6.2 ov), 5-158 (Singh, 37.3 ov), 6-181 (Mongia, 42.2 ov), 7-186 (Srinath, 42.6 ov), 8-192 (Kumble, 44.4 ov), 9-204 (Prasad, 47.4 ov), 10-205 (Mohanty, 48.2 ov).

Bowling	O	M	R	W
McGrath	10	1	34	3 (2nb, 1w)
Fleming	9	1	33	2 (1w)
Reiffel	10	1	30	0
Moody	10	0	41	1 (1w)
ME Waugh	1	0	7	0
Warne	6.2	0	49	0 (1w)
SR Waugh	2	0	8	2

ICC World Cup, 1999, 2nd Super Six Match
Pakistan v South Africa
Trent Bridge, Nottingham
5 June 1999 (50-over match)

Result: South Africa won by 3 wickets
Points: South Africa 2, Pakistan 0
Toss: Pakistan
Umpires: DB Hair (Aus) and DR Shepherd
TV Umpire: DB Cowie (NZ)
Match Referee: JR Reid (NZ)
Man Of The Match: L Klusener

Pakistan innings (50 overs maximum)			R	M	B	4	6
Saeed Anwar	c Boucher	b Elworthy	23	55	37	2	0
Wajahatullah Wasti	c Boucher	b Donald	17	81	56	2	0
Abdur Razzaq	c Kirsten	b Elworthy	30	76	60	2	0
Ijaz Ahmed	c Cullinan	b Klusener	23	61	36	1	1
Inzamam-ul-Haq	run out (Rhodes)		4	24	15	0	0
Yousuf Youhana	run out (Klusener)		17	47	27	1	0
+Moin Khan	run out (Cronje/Boucher)		63	62	56	6	2
Azhar Mahmood	not out		15	34	10	1	0
*Wasim Akram	not out		5	6	3	1	0
Extras (b 4, lb 8, w 11): **23**							
Total (7 wickets, 50 overs): **220**							

DNB: Saqlain Mushtaq, Shoaib Akhtar.
FoW: 1-41 (Saeed Anwar, 13.2 ov), 2-58 (Wajahatullah, 18.4 ov), 3-102 (Abdur Razzaq, 29.5 ov), 4-111 (Ijaz Ahmed, 32.3 ov), 5-118 (Inzamam-ul-Haq, 35.1 ov), 6-150 (Yousuf Youhana, 42.6 ov), 7-206 (Moin Khan, 48.5 ov).

Bowling	O	M	R	W	
Pollock	10	1	42	0	
Kallis	10	0	47	0 (7w)	
Donald	10	2	49	1 (2w)	
Elworthy	10	2	23	2 (1w)	
Klusener	9	0	41	1	
Cronje	1	0	6	0 (1w)	

South Africa innings (target: 221 from 50 overs)			R	M	B	4	6
G Kirsten	lbw	b Wasim Akram	19	54	38	3	0
HH Gibbs	c Ijaz Ahmed	b Shoaib Akhtar	0	6	3	0	0
*WJ Cronje	c Saqlain Mushtaq	b Shoaib Akhtar	4	20	15	1	0
DJ Cullinan	c Saeed Anwar	b Azhar Mahmood	18	56	42	2	0
JH Kallis	c Moin Khan	b Saqlain Mushtaq	54	148	98	3	0
JN Rhodes	lbw	b Azhar Mahmood	0	8	6	0	0
SM Pollock	c Inzamam-ul-Haq	b Azhar Mahmood	30	70	45	3	0
L Klusener	not out		46	61	41	3	3
+MV Boucher	not out		12	22	15	0	1
Extras (lb 11, w 14, nb 13): **38**							
Total (7 wickets, 49 overs): **221**							

DNB: S Elworthy, AA Donald.
FoW: 1-7 (Gibbs, 1.3 ov), 2-19 (Cronje, 5.4 ov), 3-39 (Kirsten, 10.6 ov), 4-55 (Cullinan, 17.4 ov), 5-58 (Rhodes, 19.6 ov), 6-135 (Pollock, 36.1 ov), 7-176 (Kallis, 44.2 ov).

Bowling	O	M	R	W	
Wasim Akram	10	0	44	1 (5nb, 2w)	
Shoaib Akhtar	9	1	51	2 (3nb, 1w)	
Azhar Mahmood	10	1	24	3 (3w)	
Abdur Razzaq	10	1	40	0 (1nb, 3w)	
Saqlain Mushtaq	10	0	51	1 (3w)	

ICC World Cup, 1999, 3rd Super Six Match
New Zealand v Zimbabwe
Headingley, Leeds
6/7 June 1999 (50-over match)

Result: No result
Points: New Zealand 1, Zimbabwe 1
Toss: Zimbabwe
Umpires: DL Orchard (SA) and S Venkataraghavan (Ind)
TV Umpire: RE Koertzen (SA)
Match Referee: PJP Burge (Aus)
Man Of The Match: No award

Close Of Play
Day 1: Zimbabwe 175, New Zealand 70/3 (Fleming 9*, Twose 0*, 15 ov)

Zimbabwe innings (50 overs maximum)			R	M	B	4	6
NC Johnson	b Allott		25	37	32	5	0
GW Flower	run out (Horne)		1	12	9	0	0
MW Goodwin	c Parore	b Harris	57	136	90	6	0
+A Flower	c McMillan	b Allott	0	6	2	0	0
*ADR Campbell	c Nash	b Larsen	40	122	101	2	0
GJ Whittall	c Astle	b Allott	21	54	34	1	0
SV Carlisle	c McMillan	b Astle	2	13	11	0	0
HH Streak	b Cairns		4	13	13	0	0
AR Whittall	c Astle	b Cairns	3	12	6	0	0
AG Huckle	c Twose	b Cairns	0	1	1	0	0
HK Olonga	not out		1	1	1	0	0

Extras (b 4, lb 11, w 3, nb 3): **21**
Total (all out, 49.3 overs): **175**

FoW: 1-10 (GW Flower, 2.5 ov), 2-35 (Johnson, 8.5 ov), 3-45 (A Flower, 10.1 ov), 4-136 (Goodwin, 36.3 ov), 5-148 (Campbell, 41.4 ov), 6-154 (Carlisle, 44.5 ov), 7-163 (Streak, 47.2 ov), 8-174 (GJ Whittall, 48.6 ov), 9-174 (Huckle, 49.1 ov), 10-175 (AR Whittall, 49.3 ov).

Bowling	O	M	R	W
Allott	10	1	24	3 (1nb)
Nash	10	2	48	0 (1nb)
Larsen	10	0	27	1
Cairns	6.3	2	24	3 (1nb, 3w)
Harris	4	0	12	1
Astle	9	0	25	1

New Zealand innings (target: 176 from 50 overs)			R	M	B	4	6
MJ Horne	lbw	b GJ Whittall	35	35	35	6	0
NJ Astle	c Streak	b Olonga	20	41	28	4	0
CD McMillan	lbw	b Streak	1	15	9	0	0
*SP Fleming	not out		9	25	17	1	0
RG Twose	not out		0	12	5	0	0

Extras (lb 1, nb 4): **5**
Total (3 wickets, 15 overs): **70**

DNB: CL Cairns, +AC Parore, CZ Harris, GR Larsen, DJ Nash, GI Allott.
FoW: 1-58 (Horne, 8.6 ov), 2-59 (Astle, 9.6 ov), 3-65 (McMillan, 12.3 ov).

Bowling	O	M	R	W
Johnson	3	0	21	0 (1nb)
Streak	5	0	25	1
GJ Whittall	3	0	9	1
Olonga	4	1	14	1 (3nb)

ICC World Cup, 1999, 4th Super Six Match
India v Pakistan
Old Trafford, Manchester
8 June 1999 (50-over match)

Result: India won by 47 runs
Points: India 2, Pakistan 0
Toss: India
Umpires: SA Bucknor (WI) and DR Shepherd
TV Umpire: DB Hair (Aus)
Match Referee: R Subba Row
Man Of The Match: BKV Prasad

India innings (50 overs maximum)

			R	M	B	4	6
SR Tendulkar	c Saqlain Mushtaq	b Azhar Mahmood	45	92	65	5	0
S Ramesh	b Abdur Razzaq		20	48	31	2	0
R Dravid	c Shahid Afridi	b Wasim Akram	61	119	89	4	0
A Jadeja	c Inzamam-ul-Haq	b Azhar Mahmood	6	15	14	0	0
*M Azharuddin	c Ijaz Ahmed	b Wasim Akram	59	97	77	3	1
RR Singh	c Wasim Akram	b Shoaib Akhtar	16	44	21	0	1
+NR Mongia	not out		6	5	4	0	0

Extras (b 1, lb 3, w 8, nb 2): **14**
Total (6 wickets, 50 overs): **227**

DNB: J Srinath, A Kumble, BKV Prasad, DS Mohanty.
FoW: 1-37 (Ramesh, 11.2 ov), 2-95 (Tendulkar, 20.5 ov), 3-107 (Jadeja, 24.3 ov), 4-158 (Dravid, 39.5 ov), 5-218 (Azharuddin, 48.5 ov), 6-227 (Singh, 49.6 ov).

Bowling

	O	M	R	W
Wasim Akram	10	0	27	2 (1nb)
Shoaib Akhtar	10	0	54	1 (2w)
Abdur Razzaq	10	0	40	1 (4w)
Azhar Mahmood	10	0	35	2
Saqlain Mushtaq	10	0	67	0 (2w)

Pakistan innings (target: 228 runs from 50 overs)

			R	M	B	4	6
Saeed Anwar	c Azharuddin	b Prasad	36	79	44	6	0
Shahid Afridi	c Kumble	b Srinath	6	10	5	1	0
Ijaz Ahmed	c Azharuddin	b Srinath	11	29	24	1	0
Saleem Malik	lbw	b Prasad	6	19	19	1	0
Inzamam-ul-Haq	lbw	b Prasad	41	135	93	1	0
Azhar Mahmood	c Mongia	b Kumble	10	27	17	1	0
+Moin Khan	c Tendulkar	b Prasad	34	41	37	2	1
Abdur Razzaq	b Srinath		11	22	12	0	1
*Wasim Akram	c Kumble	b Prasad	12	33	16	1	0
Saqlain Mushtaq	lbw	b Kumble	0	3	4	0	0
Shoaib Akhtar	not out		0	3	3	0	0

Extras (lb 11, w 2): **13**
Total (all out, 45.3 overs): **180**

FoW: 1-19 (Shahid Afridi, 2.3 ov), 2-44 (Ijaz Ahmed, 9.4 ov), 3-52 (Saleem Malik, 13.5 ov), 4-65 (Saeed Anwar, 17.4 ov), 5-78 (Azhar Mahmood, 24.2 ov), 6-124 (Moin Khan, 34.2 ov), 7-146 (Abdur Razzaq, 39.1 ov), 8-175 (Inzamam-ul-Haq, 43.4 ov), 9-176 (Saqlain Mushtaq, 44.3 ov), 10-180 (Wasim Akram, 45.3 ov).

Bowling

	O	M	R	W
Srinath	8	1	37	3
Mohanty	10	2	31	0 (2w)
Prasad	9.3	2	27	5
Kumble	10	0	43	2
Singh	8	1	31	0

ICC World Cup, 1999, 5th Super Six Match
Australia v Zimbabwe
Lord's, London
9 June 1999 (50-over match)

Result: Australia won by 44 runs
Points: Australia 2, Zimbabwe 0
Toss: Zimbabwe
Umpires: DB Cowie (NZ) and RE Koertzen (SA)
TV Umpire: DL Orchard (SA)
Match Referee: Talat Ali (Pak)
Man Of The Match: NC Johnson

Australia innings (50 overs maximum)

			R	M	B	4	6
+AC Gilchrist	lbw	b Johnson	10	26	28	1	0
ME Waugh	c Goodwin	b Johnson	104	181	120	13	0
RT Ponting	b Olonga		36	39	35	4	0
DS Lehmann	retired hurt		6	18	8	0	0
*SR Waugh	b GJ Whittall		62	76	61	5	2
MG Bevan	not out		37	51	35	2	0
TM Moody	not out		20	32	22	0	1
Extras (lb 6, w 13, nb 9): **28**							
Total (4 wickets, 50 overs): **303**							

DNB: SK Warne, DW Fleming, PR Reiffel, GD McGrath.
FoW: 1-18 (Gilchrist, 6.2 ov), 2-74 (Ponting, 14.1 ov), 3-226 (SR Waugh, 38.5 ov), 4-248 (ME Waugh, 42.5 ov).

Bowling

	O	M	R	W	
Johnson	8	0	43	2	(1nb, 3w)
Streak	10	0	50	0	(2nb, 1w)
Olonga	7	0	62	1	(5nb, 1w)
GJ Whittall	4	0	24	1	(2w)
Strang	10	1	47	0	(1w)
AR Whittall	8	1	51	0	(1nb, 1w)
GW Flower	3	0	20	0	

Zimbabwe innings (target: 304 runs from 50 overs)

			R	M	B	4	6
NC Johnson	not out		132	214	144	14	2
GW Flower	lbw	b McGrath	21	41	32	1	0
MW Goodwin	c Moody	b Bevan	47	76	56	7	0
+A Flower	c Gilchrist	b Reiffel	0	4	1	0	0
*ADR Campbell	c Fleming	b Reiffel	17	26	22	2	0
GJ Whittall	c ME Waugh	b Reiffel	0	3	3	0	0
DP Viljoen	st Gilchrist	b Warne	5	12	13	0	0
HH Streak	not out		18	44	29	0	0
Extras (lb 6, w 13): **19**							
Total (6 wickets, 50 overs): **259**							

DNB: PA Strang, AR Whittall, HK Olonga.
FoW: 1-39 (GW Flower, 10.1 ov), 2-153 (Goodwin, 28.2 ov), 3-154 (A Flower, 29.1 ov), 4-188 (Campbell, 35.2 ov), 5-189 (GJ Whittall, 35.5 ov), 6-200 (Viljoen, 38.5 ov).

Bowling

	O	M	R	W	
McGrath	10	1	33	1	(2w)
Fleming	10	0	46	0	(3w)
Warne	9	0	55	1	(1w)
Reiffel	10	0	55	3	(4w)
Moody	6	0	38	0	
Bevan	5	1	26	1	(2w)

ICC World Cup, 1999, 6th Super Six Match
New Zealand v South Africa
Edgbaston, Birmingham
10 June 1999 (50-over match)

Result: South Africa won by 74 runs
Points: South Africa 2, New Zealand 0
Toss: South Africa
Umpires: ID Robinson (Zim) and S Venkataraghavan (Ind)
TV Umpire: P Willey
Match Referee: CW Smith (WI)
Man Of The Match: JH Kallis

South Africa innings (50 overs maximum)			R	M	B	4	6
G Kirsten	c Nash	b Astle	82	139	121	6	1
HH Gibbs	b Allott		91	171	118	6	1
L Klusener	b Larsen		4	6	5	1	0
JH Kallis	not out		53	50	36	1	3
DJ Cullinan	c & b Cairns		0	2	2	0	0
*WJ Cronje	run out (Nash)		39	20	22	2	2
JN Rhodes	not out		0	2	0	0	0
Extras (lb 11, w 3, nb 4): **18**							
Total (5 wickets, 50 overs): **287**							

DNB: SM Pollock, +MV Boucher, S Elworthy, AA Donald.
FoW: 1-176 (Kirsten, 36.3 ov), 2-187 (Klusener, 37.5 ov), 3-228 (Gibbs, 43.6 ov), 4-229 (Cullinan, 44.3 ov), 5-283 (Cronje, 49.4 ov).

Bowling	O	M	R	W	
Allott	10	0	42	1 (1nb, 1w)	
Nash	8	0	44	0 (1w)	
Cairns	7	0	55	1 (3nb)	
Larsen	9	0	47	1	
Harris	10	0	59	0	
Astle	6	0	29	1 (1w)	

New Zealand innings (target: 288 from 50 overs)			R	M	B	4	6
MJ Horne	c Pollock	b Kallis	12	23	20	3	0
NJ Astle	c Cullinan	b Kallis	9	50	32	1	0
CD McMillan	c Gibbs	b Cronje	23	91	54	1	0
*SP Fleming	c Pollock	b Cronje	42	80	64	6	0
RG Twose	c Cronje	b Klusener	35	69	40	3	1
CL Cairns	b Klusener		17	21	16	1	1
+AC Parore	run out (Kirsten/Boucher)		3	5	5	0	0
CZ Harris	not out		27	60	38	1	0
DJ Nash	b Pollock		9	20	22	1	0
GR Larsen	not out		13	13	13	1	0
Extras (lb 9, w 11, nb 3): **23**							
Total (8 wickets, 50 overs): **213**							

DNB: GI Allott.
FoW: 1-20 (Horne, 5.3 ov), 2-34 (Astle, 11.3 ov), 3-93 (McMillan, 25.6 ov), 4-107 (Fleming, 29.4 ov), 5-144 (Cairns, 34.3 ov), 6-148 (Parore, 35.4 ov), 7-171 (Twose, 40.4 ov), 8-194 (Nash, 46.3 ov).

Bowling	O	M	R	W	
Pollock	10	1	29	1	
Kallis	6	2	15	2 (4w)	
Elworthy	8	0	35	0 (1nb, 2w)	
Donald	10	0	42	0 (1nb, 1w)	
Klusener	9	0	46	2 (1nb, 3w)	
Cronje	7	0	37	2 (1w)	

ICC World Cup, 1999, 7th Super Six Match
Pakistan v Zimbabwe
Kennington Oval, London
11 June 1999 (50-over match)

Result: Pakistan won by 148 runs
Points: Pakistan 2, Zimbabwe 0
Toss: Pakistan
Umpires: SA Bucknor (WI) and DL Orchard (SA)
TV Umpire: DB Cowie (NZ)
Match Referee: PJP Burge (Aus)
Man Of The Match: Saeed Anwar

Pakistan innings (50 overs maximum)			R	M	B	4	6
Saeed Anwar	c A Flower	b Olonga	103	167	144	11	0
Wajahatullah Wasti	c Huckle	b Whittall	40	86	42	5	1
Ijaz Ahmed	run out (Goodwin/A Flower)		5	12	5	0	0
Inzamam-ul-Haq	st A Flower	b Strang	21	52	36	0	0
*Wasim Akram	lbw	b Huckle	0	11	2	0	0
+Moin Khan	run out (GW Flower)		13	24	17	0	0
Shahid Afridi	c Johnson	b Olonga	37	41	29	1	2
Azhar Mahmood	c A Flower	b Streak	2	1	3	0	0
Abdur Razzaq	b Streak		0	1	1	0	0
Saqlain Mushtaq	not out		17	19	22	0	0
Shoaib Akhtar	not out		1	4	1	0	0

Extras (b 6, lb 3, w 20, nb 3): 32
Total (9 wickets, 50 overs): 271

FoW: 1-95 (Wajahatullah, 18.5 ov), 2-116 (Ijaz Ahmed, 21.2 ov), 3-183 (Inzamam-ul-Haq, 35.6 ov), 4-194 (Saeed Anwar, 37.6 ov), 5-195 (Wasim Akram, 38.4 ov), 6-228 (Moin Khan, 43.3 ov), 7-231 (Azhar Mahmood, 44.1 ov), 8-231 (Abdur Razzaq, 44.2 ov), 9-260 (Shahid Afridi, 48.3 ov).

Bowling	O	M	R	W	
Streak	10	0	63	2 (1nb, 5w)	
Mbangwa	8	0	28	0 (3w)	
Whittall	8	1	39	1 (3w)	
Olonga	5	0	38	2 (1nb, 5w)	
Huckle	10	0	43	1 (1w)	
GW Flower	2	0	13	0 (2w)	
Strang	7	0	38	1 (1w)	

Zimbabwe innings (target: 272 runs from 49 overs)			R	M	B	4	6
NC Johnson	lbw	b Azhar Mahmood	54	120	94	5	0
GW Flower	b Shoaib Akhtar		2	24	9	0	0
MW Goodwin	c Shahid Afridi	b Abdur Razzaq	4	17	15	0	0
+A Flower	b Abdur Razzaq		4	16	12	0	0
*ADR Campbell	c Wasim Akram	b Abdur Razzaq	3	7	7	0	0
GJ Whittall	c Shahid Afridi	b Azhar Mahmood	16	38	31	2	0
HH Streak	not out		16	62	31	1	0
PA Strang	c Azhar Mahmood	b Shoaib Akhtar	5	21	15	0	0
HK Olonga	st Moin Khan	b Saqlain Mushtaq	5	23	31	0	0
AG Huckle	st Moin Khan	b Saqlain Mushtaq	0	1	1	0	0
M Mbangwa	lbw	b Saqlain Mushtaq	0	1	1	0	0

Extras (lb 3, w 7, nb 4): 14
Total (all out, 40.3 overs): 123

FoW: 1-12 (GW Flower, 5.5 ov), 2-28 (Goodwin, 9.3 ov), 3-46 (A Flower, 13.4 ov), 4-50 (Campbell, 15.2 ov), 5-83 (Whittall, 26.1 ov), 6-95 (Johnson, 28.2 ov), 7-110 (Strang, 33.2 ov), 8-123 (Olonga, 40.1 ov), 9-123 (Huckle, 40.2 ov), 10-123 (Mbangwa, 40.3 ov).

Bowling	O	M	R	W	
Wasim Akram	6	1	23	0 (1nb)	
Shoaib Akhtar	7	1	22	2 (3nb, 1w)	
Abdur Razzaq	9	1	25	3 (1w)	
Saqlain Mushtaq	6.3	1	16	3	
Shahid Afridi	4	0	20	0 (1w)	
Azhar Mahmood	8	1	14	2	

ICC World Cup, 1999, 8th Super Six Match
India v New Zealand
Trent Bridge, Nottingham
12 June 1999 (50-over match)

Result: New Zealand won by 5 wickets
Points: New Zealand 2, India 0
Toss: India
Umpires: DB Hair (Aus) and DR Shepherd
TV Umpire: RE Koertzen (SA)
Match Referee: Talat Ali (Pak)
Man Of The Match: RG Twose

India innings (50 overs maximum)

			R	M	B	4	6
SR Tendulkar	b Nash		16	26	22	2	0
SC Ganguly	b Allott		29	109	62	0	0
R Dravid	c Fleming	b Cairns	29	45	35	5	0
A Jadeja	c Parore	b Cairns	76	134	103	6	2
*M Azharuddin	c Parore	b Larsen	30	67	43	2	0
RR Singh	run out (Fleming/Cairns)		27	33	29	1	1
J Srinath	not out		6	10	7	0	0
+NR Mongia	not out		3	6	6	0	0
Extras (b 4, lb 8, w 13, nb 10): **35**							
Total (6 wickets, 50 overs): **251**							

DNB: A Kumble, BKV Prasad, DS Mohanty.
FoW: 1-26 (Tendulkar, 5.1 ov), 2-71 (Dravid, 14.6 ov), 3-97 (Ganguly, 22.6 ov), 4-187 (Azharuddin, 40.4 ov), 5-241 (Jadeja, 47.3 ov), 6-243 (Singh, 47.6 ov).

Bowling	O	M	R	W	
Allott	10	1	33	1	(2w)
Nash	10	1	57	1	(3nb, 5w)
Cairns	10	0	44	2	(2nb)
Larsen	10	0	40	1	(1nb, 1w)
Astle	7	0	49	0	
Harris	3	0	16	0	

New Zealand innings (target: 252 from 50 overs)

			R	M	B	4	6
MJ Horne	run out (sub [N Chopra])		74	160	116	10	0
NJ Astle	c Dravid	b Mohanty	26	41	27	4	0
CD McMillan	c Dravid	b Srinath	6	16	7	1	0
*SP Fleming	c Mongia	b Mohanty	15	40	23	3	0
RG Twose	not out		60	125	77	5	0
CL Cairns	c Kumble	b Singh	11	45	30	0	0
+AC Parore	not out		26	16	14	5	0
Extras (b 4, lb 11, w 16, nb 4): **35**							
Total (5 wickets, 48.2 overs): **253**							

DNB: CZ Harris, DJ Nash, GR Larsen, GI Allott.
FoW: 1-45 (Astle, 9.3 ov), 2-60 (McMillan, 13.1 ov), 3-90 (Fleming, 21.5 ov), 4-173 (Horne, 34.4 ov), 5-218 (Cairns, 45.1 ov).

Bowling	O	M	R	W	
Srinath	10	1	49	1	(2nb, 1w)
Mohanty	10	0	41	2	(1w)
Prasad	10	0	44	0	(2w)
Singh	4	0	27	1	
Ganguly	2	0	15	0	(2nb)
Kumble	9.2	0	48	0	(2w)
Tendulkar	3	0	14	0	(2w)

ICC World Cup, 1999, 9th Super Six Match
Australia v South Africa
Headingley, Leeds
13 June 1999 (50-over match)

Result: Australia won by 5 wickets
Points: Australia 2, South Africa 0
Toss: South Africa
Umpires: S Venkataraghavan (Ind) and P Willey
TV Umpire: ID Robinson (Zim)
Match Referee: JR Reid (NZ)
Man Of The Match: SR Waugh

South Africa innings (50 overs maximum)			R	M	B	4	6
G Kirsten	c Ponting	b Reiffel	21	54	46	3	0
HH Gibbs	b McGrath		101	185	134	10	1
DJ Cullinan	b Warne		50	79	62	4	1
*WJ Cronje	lbw	b Warne	0	2	3	0	0
JN Rhodes	c ME Waugh	b Fleming	39	65	36	2	2
L Klusener	c Warne	b Fleming	36	25	21	4	1
SM Pollock	b Fleming		3	10	4	0	0
+MV Boucher	not out		0	1	0	0	0
Extras (lb 7, w 8, nb 6): **21**							
Total (7 wickets, 50 overs): **271**							

DNB: N Boje, S Elworthy, AA Donald.
FoW: 1-45 (Kirsten, 12.4 ov), 2-140 (Cullinan, 32.3 ov), 3-141 (Cronje, 32.5 ov), 4-219 (Gibbs, 44.2 ov), 5-250 (Rhodes, 47.5 ov), 6-271 (Klusener, 49.5 ov), 7-271 (Pollock, 49.6 ov).

Bowling	O	M	R	W	
McGrath	10	0	49	1 (4nb, 1w)	
Fleming	10	0	57	3 (3w)	
Reiffel	9	0	47	1 (1w)	
Moody	8	1	56	0 (1w)	
Warne	10	1	33	2 (2nb, 1w)	
Bevan	3	0	22	0 (1w)	

Australia innings (target: 272 runs from 50 overs)			R	M	B	4	6
ME Waugh	run out (Boje/Boucher)		5	23	9	0	0
+AC Gilchrist	b Elworthy		5	6	7	1	0
RT Ponting	c Donald	b Klusener	69	144	110	5	2
DR Martyn	c Boje	b Elworthy	11	25	20	1	0
*SR Waugh	not out		120	176	110	10	2
MG Bevan	c Cullinan	b Cronje	27	49	33	2	0
TM Moody	not out		15	24	16	2	0
Extras (lb 6, w 7, nb 7): **20**							
Total (5 wickets, 49.4 overs): **272**							

DNB: SK Warne, PR Reiffel, DW Fleming, GD McGrath.
FoW: 1-6 (Gilchrist, 1.4 ov), 2-20 (ME Waugh, 5.2 ov), 3-48 (Martyn, 11.3 ov), 4-174 (Ponting, 34.1 ov), 5-247 (Bevan, 45.4 ov).

Bowling	O	M	R	W	
Pollock	9.4	0	45	0 (3nb, 1w)	
Elworthy	10	1	46	2 (2nb)	
Donald	10	0	43	0 (1nb, 2w)	
Klusener	10	0	53	1 (1w)	
Cronje	7	0	50	1 (1w)	
Boje	3	0	29	0 (1nb, 2w)	

1999 WORLD CUP

Finals

ICC World Cup, 1999, 1st Semi-Final
New Zealand v Pakistan
Old Trafford, Manchester
16 June 1999 (50-over match)

Result: Pakistan won by 9 wickets
Pakistan advances to the final
Toss: New Zealand
Umpires: DB Hair (Aus) and P Willey
TV Umpire: DL Orchard (SA)
Match Referee: CW Smith (WI)
Man Of The Match: Shoaib Akhtar

New Zealand innings (50 overs maximum)			R	M	B	4	6
MJ Horne	b Abdur Razzaq		35	67	48	5	0
NJ Astle	b Shoaib Akhtar		3	24	18	0	0
CD McMillan	c Moin Khan	b Wasim Akram	3	22	19	0	0
*SP Fleming	b Shoaib Akhtar		41	93	57	5	0
RG Twose	c Ijaz Ahmed	b Abdur Razzaq	46	101	83	3	0
CL Cairns	not out		44	77	48	3	0
CZ Harris	b Shoaib Akhtar		16	26	21	0	0
+AC Parore	b Wasim Akram		0	5	4	0	0
DJ Nash	not out		6	17	10	1	0
Extras (b 4, lb 14, w 17, nb 12): **47**							
Total (7 wickets, 50 overs): **241**							

DNB: GR Larsen, GI Allott.
FoW: 1-20 (Astle, 5.3 ov), 2-38 (McMillan, 10.3 ov), 3-58 (Horne, 15.1 ov), 4-152 (Fleming, 33.5 ov), 5-176 (Twose, 39.3 ov), 6-209 (Harris, 45.4 ov), 7-211 (Parore, 46.4 ov).

Bowling	O	M	R	W	
Wasim Akram	10	0	45	2 (4nb, 7w)	
Shoaib Akhtar	10	0	55	3 (2nb, 1w)	
Abdur Razzaq	8	0	28	2 (1w)	
Saqlain Mushtaq	8	0	36	0 (1w)	
Azhar Mahmood	9	0	32	0 (3w)	
Shahid Afridi	5	0	27	0 (2nb, 2w)	

Pakistan innings (target: 242 runs from 50 overs)			R	M	B	4	6
Saeed Anwar	not out		113	193	148	9	0
Wajahatullah Wasti	c Fleming	b Cairns	84	166	123	10	1
Ijaz Ahmed	not out		28	25	21	4	1
Extras (lb 3, w 7, nb 7): **17**							
Total (1 wicket, 47.3 overs): **242**							

DNB: Inzamam-ul-Haq, Abdur Razzaq, Shahid Afridi, +Moin Khan, *Wasim Akram, Azhar Mahmood, Saqlain Mushtaq, Shoaib Akhtar.
FoW: 1-194 (Wajahatullah, 40.3 ov).

Bowling	O	M	R	W	
Allott	9	0	41	0 (1nb, 1w)	
Nash	5	0	34	0 (2nb, 2w)	
Larsen	10	0	40	0 (1nb)	
Cairns	8	0	33	1 (3nb)	
Harris	6	0	31	0	
Astle	7.3	0	41	0 (1w)	
McMillan	2	0	19	0 (1w)	

ICC World Cup, 1999, 2nd Semi-Final
Australia v South Africa
Edgbaston, Birmingham
17 June 1999 (50-over match)

Result: Match tied
Series: Australia advances to the final
Toss: South Africa
Umpires: DR Shepherd and S Venkataraghavan (Ind)
TV Umpire: SA Bucknor (WI)
Match Referee: R Subba Row
Man Of The Match: SK Warne

Australia innings (50 overs maximum)			R	M	B	4	6
+AC Gilchrist	c Donald	b Kallis	20	70	39	1	1
ME Waugh	c Boucher	b Pollock	0	3	4	0	0
RT Ponting	c Kirsten	b Donald	37	49	48	3	1
DS Lehmann	c Boucher	b Donald	1	4	4	0	0
*SR Waugh	c Boucher	b Pollock	56	108	76	6	1
MG Bevan	c Boucher	b Pollock	65	151	101	6	0
TM Moody	lbw	b Pollock	0	2	3	0	0
SK Warne	c Cronje	b Pollock	18	36	24	1	0
PR Reiffel	b Donald		0	2	1	0	0
DW Fleming	b Donald		0	2	2	0	0
GD McGrath	not out		0	4	1	0	0

Extras (b 1, lb 6, w 3, nb 6): **16**
Total (all out, 49.2 overs): **213**

FoW: 1-3 (ME Waugh, 0.5 ov), 2-54 (Ponting, 13.1 ov), 3-58 (Lehmann, 13.6 ov), 4-68 (Gilchrist, 16.6 ov), 5-158 (SR Waugh, 39.3 ov), 6-158 (Moody, 39.6 ov), 7-207 (Warne, 47.6 ov), 8-207 (Reiffel, 48.1 ov), 9-207 (Fleming, 48.3 ov), 10-213 (Bevan, 49.2 ov).

Bowling	O	M	R	W	
Pollock	9.2	1	36	5	
Elworthy	10	0	59	0	(2nb, 1w)
Kallis	10	2	27	1	(1nb, 1w)
Donald	10	1	32	4	(1w)
Klusener	9	1	50	0	(3nb)
Cronje	1	0	2	0	

South Africa innings (target: 214 from 50 overs)			R	M	B	4	6
G Kirsten	b Warne		18	59	42	1	0
HH Gibbs	b Warne		30	51	36	6	0
DJ Cullinan	run out (Bevan)		6	39	30	0	0
*WJ Cronje	c ME Waugh	b Warne	0	2	2	0	0
JH Kallis	c SR Waugh	b Warne	53	119	92	3	0
JN Rhodes	c Bevan	b Reiffel	43	70	55	2	1
SM Pollock	b Fleming		20	27	14	1	1
L Klusener	not out		31	32	16	4	1
+MV Boucher	b McGrath		5	13	10	0	0
S Elworthy	run out (Reiffel/McGrath)		1	3	1	0	0
AA Donald	run out (ME Waugh/Fleming/Gilchrist)		0	7	0	0	0

Extras (lb 1, w 5): **6**
Total (all out, 49.4 overs): **213**

FoW: 1-48 (Gibbs, 12.2 ov), 2-53 (Kirsten, 14.1 ov), 3-53 (Cronje, 14.3 ov), 4-61 (Cullinan, 21.2 ov), 5-145 (Rhodes, 40.3 ov), 6-175 (Kallis, 44.5 ov), 7-183 (Pollock, 45.5 ov), 8-196 (Boucher, 48.2 ov), 9-198 (Elworthy, 48.4 ov), 10-213 (Donald, 49.4 ov).

Bowling	O	M	R	W	
McGrath	10	0	51	1	(1w)
Fleming	8.4	1	40	1	(3w)
Reiffel	8	0	28	1	
Warne	10	4	29	4	(1w)
ME Waugh	8	0	37	0	
Moody	5	0	27	0	

ICC World Cup, 1999, Final
Australia v Pakistan
Lord's, London
20 June 1999 (50-over match)

Result: Australia won by 8 wickets
Australia wins the 1999 ICC World Cup
Toss: Pakistan
Umpires: SA Bucknor (WI) and DR Shepherd
TV Umpire: S Venkataraghavan (Ind)
Match Referee: RS Madugalle (SL)
Man Of The Match: SK Warne
Player Of The Tournament: L Klusener (SA)

Pakistan innings (50 overs maximum)			R	M	B	4	6
Saeed Anwar	b Fleming		15	26	17	3	0
Wajahatullah Wasti	c ME Waugh	b McGrath	1	20	14	0	0
Abdur Razzaq	c SR Waugh	b Moody	17	67	51	2	0
Ijaz Ahmed	b Warne		22	79	46	2	0
Inzamam-ul-Haq	c Gilchrist	b Reiffel	15	47	33	0	0
+Moin Khan	c Gilchrist	b Warne	6	16	12	0	0
Shahid Afridi	lbw	b Warne	13	22	16	2	0
Azhar Mahmood	c & b Moody		8	32	17	1	0
*Wasim Akram	c SR Waugh	b Warne	8	23	20	0	1
Saqlain Mushtaq	c Ponting	b McGrath	0	10	4	0	0
Shoaib Akhtar	not out		2	8	6	0	0

Extras (lb 10, w 13, nb 2): **25**
Total (all out, 39 overs): **132**

FoW: 1-21 (Wajahatullah, 4.4 ov), 2-21 (Saeed Anwar, 5.1 ov), 3-68 (Abdur Razzaq, 19.4 ov), 4-77 (Ijaz Ahmed, 23.4 ov), 5-91 (Moin Khan, 27.1 ov), 6-104 (Inzamam-ul-Haq, 30.1 ov), 7-113 (Shahid Afridi, 31.6 ov), 8-129 (Azhar Mahmood, 36.6 ov), 9-129 (Wasim Akram, 37.2 ov), 10-132 (Saqlain Mushtaq, 38.6 ov).

Bowling	O	M	R	W
McGrath	9	3	13	2
Fleming	6	0	30	1 (2nb, 4w)
Reiffel	10	1	29	1 (2w)
Moody	5	0	17	2 (1w)
Warne	9	1	33	4 (2w)

Australia innings (target: 133 runs from 50 overs)			R	M	B	4	6
ME Waugh	not out		37	95	52	4	0
+AC Gilchrist	c Inzamam-ul-Haq	b Saqlain Mushtaq	54	49	36	8	1
RT Ponting	c Moin Khan	b Wasim Akram	24	32	27	3	0
DS Lehmann	not out		13	12	9	2	0

Extras (lb 1, w 1, nb 3): **5**
Total (2 wickets, 20.1 overs): **133**

DNB: *SR Waugh, MG Bevan, TM Moody, SK Warne, PR Reiffel, DW Fleming, GD McGrath.
FoW: 1-75 (Gilchrist, 10.1 ov), 2-112 (Ponting, 17.4 ov).

Bowling	O	M	R	W
Wasim Akram	8	1	41	1 (2nb, 1w)
Shoaib Akhtar	4	0	37	0 (1nb)
Abdur Razzaq	2	0	13	0
Azhar Mahmood	2	0	20	0
Saqlain Mushtaq	4.1	0	21	1

STATISTICAL RECORD

Highest Team Totals
398-5 – Sri Lanka v Kenya (Kandy) 1996
373-6 – India v Sri Lanka (Taunton) 1999
360-4 – West Indies v Sri Lanka (Karachi) 1987
338-5 – Pakistan v Sri Lanka (Swansea) 1983
334-4 – England v India (Lord's) 1975
333-9 – England v Sri Lanka (Taunton) 1983
330-6 – Pakistan v Sri Lanka (Trent Bridge) 1975
329-2 – India v Kenya (Bristol) 1999
328-3 – South Africa v Holland (Rawalpindi) 1996
328-5 – Australia v Sri Lanka (The Oval) 1975

Lowest Team Totals
45 – Canada v England (Old Trafford) 1979
68 – Scotland v West Indies (Leicester) 1999
74 – Pakistan v England (Adelaide) 1992
86 – Sri Lanka v West Indies (Old Trafford) 1975
93 – England v Australia (Headingley) 1975
93 – West Indies v Kenya (Pune) 1996
94 – East Africa v England (Edgbaston) 1975
103 England v South Africa (The Oval) 1999
105 Canada v Australia (Edgbaston) 1979
110 Sri Lanka v South Africa (Northampton) 1999
110 West Indies v Australia (Old Trafford) 1999

Highest Individual Scores
188* – Gary Kirsten South Africa v UAE (Rawalpindi) 1996
183 – Sourav Ganguly India v Sri Lanka (Taunton) 1999
181 – Viv Richards West Indies v Sri Lanka (Karachi) 1987
175* – Kapil Dev India v Zimbabwe (Tunbridge Wells) 1983
171* – Glenn Turner New Zealand v East Africa (Edgbaston) 1975
161 – Andrew Hudson South Africa v Holland (Rawalpindi) 1996
145 – Aravinda de Silva Sri Lanka v Kenya (Kandy) 1996
145 – Rahul Dravid India v Sri Lanka (Taunton) 1999
142 – David Houghton Zimbabwe v New Zealand (Hyderabad) 1987
140* – Sachin Tendulkar India v Kenya (Bristol) 1999

*Not out

Best Individual Bowling Figures
7-51 – Winston Davis West Indies v Australia (Headingley) 1983
6-14 – Gary Gilmour Australia v England (Headingley) 1975
6-39 – Ken MacLeay Australia v India (Trent Bridge) 1983
5-14 – Glenn McGrath Australia v West Indies (Old Trafford) 1999
5-21 – Lance Klusener South Africa v Kenya (Amsterdam) 1999
5-21 – Alan Hurst Australia v Canada (Edgbaston) 1979
5-21 – Paul Strang Zimbabwe v Kenya (Patna) 1996
5-25 – Richard Hadlee New Zealand v Sri Lanka (Bristol) 1983
5-27 – Venkatesh Prasad India v Pakistan (Old Trafford) 1999
5-29 – Shaukat Dukanwala UAE v Holland (Lahore) 1996
5-31 – Robin Singh India v Sri Lanka (Taunton) 1999

Record Partnerships For Each Wicket
1st – 194 Saeed Anwar & Wajahatullah Wasti Pakistan v New Zealand (Old Trafford) 1999
2nd – 318 Sourav Ganguly & Rahul Dravid India v Sri Lanka (Taunton) 1999
3rd – 237* Rahul Dravid & Sachin Tendulkar India v Kenya (Bristol) 1999
4th – 168 Lee Germon & Chris Harris New Zealand v Australia (Madras) 1996
5th – 148 Roger Twose & Chris Cairns New Zealand v Australia (Cardiff) 1999

6th – 161 Maurice Odumbe & Alpesh Vadher Kenya v Sri Lanka (Southampton) 1999
7th – 82 Stephen Fleming & Chris Harris New Zealand v Pakistan (Derby) 1999
8th – 117 David Houghton & Iain Butchart Zimbabwe v New Zealand (Hyderabad) 1987
9th – 126* Kapil Dev & Syed Kirmani India v Zimbabwe (Tunbridge Wells) 1983
10th – 71 Andy Roberts & Joel Garner West Indies v India (Old Trafford) 1983

*Unbroken partnership

Biggest Winning Margins
202 runs – England beat India (Lord's) 1975
196 runs – England beat East Africa (Edgbaston) 1975
192 runs – Pakistan beat Sri Lanka (Trent Bridge) 1975
191 runs – West Indies beat Sri Lanka (Karachi) 1987
181 runs – New Zealand beat East Africa (Edgbaston) 1975
10 wickets – India beat East Africa (Headingley) 1975
10 wickets – West Indies beat Zimbabwe (Edgbaston) 1983
10 wickets – West Indies beat Pakistan (Melbourne) 1992

Leading Batsmen
1083 runs in 33 matches – Javed Miandad (Pakistan)
1059 (22) – Sachin Tendulkar (India)
1013 (23) – Viv Richards (West Indies)
1004 (22) – Mark Waugh (Australia)
978 (33) – Steve Waugh (Australia)
969 (30) – Arjuna Ranatunga (Sri Lanka)
897 (21) – Graham Gooch (England)
880 (21) – Martin Crowe (New Zealand)
854 (25) – Desmond Haynes (West Indies)
826 (30) – Mohammed Azharuddin (India)
815 (16) – David Boon (Australia)
797 (25) – Aravinda de Silva (Sri Lanka)

Leading Bowlers
43 wickets in 32 matches – Wasim Akram (Pakistan)
37 (22) – Allan Donald (South Africa)
34 (26) – Imran Khan (Pakistan)
32 (17) – Shane Warne (Australia)
30 (22) – Ian Botham (England)
30 (22) – Chris Harris (New Zealand)
29 (22) – Phillip DeFreitas (England)
28 (23) – Javagal Srinath (India)
28 (26) – Kapil Dev (India)
27 (17) – Courtney Walsh (West Indies)
27 (17) – Craig McDermott (Australia)
27 (33) – Steve Waugh (Australia)

Most Appearances
33 – Javed Miandad (Pakistan)
33 – Steve Waugh (Australia)
32 – Wasim Akram (Pakistan)
30 – Arjuna Ranatunga (Sri Lanka)
30 – Mohammed Azharuddin (India)

Index